Readers in a Revolution

The mid-nineteenth century brought a revolution in popular and scholarly understandings of old and second-hand books. Manuals introduced new ideas and practices to increasing numbers of collectors, exhibitions offered opportunities previously unheard of, and scholars worked together to transform how the history of printing was understood. These dramatic changes would have profound consequences for bibliographical study and collecting, accompanied as they were by a proliferation in means of access. Many ideas arising during this time would even continue to exert their influence in the digitised arena of today. This book traces this revolution to its roots in commercial and personal ties between key players in England, France and beyond, illuminating how exhibitions, libraries, booksellers, scholars and popular writers all contributed to the modern world of book studies. For students and researchers, it offers an invaluable means of orientation in a field now once again undergoing deep and wide-ranging transformations.

DAVID MCKITTERICK is Emeritus Honorary Professor of Historical Bibliography at the University of Cambridge. He is the editor of *The Cambridge History of the Book in Britain Volume VI: 1830–1914* (Cambridge University Press, 2009). His most recent monograph, based on the Panizzi lectures delivered at the British Library, is *The Invention of Rare Books* (Cambridge University Press, 2018).

Readers in a Revolution

Bibliographical Change in the Nineteenth Century

DAVID MCKITTERICK

University of Cambridge

CAMBRIDGE
UNIVERSITY PRESS

University Printing House, Cambridge CB2 8BS, United Kingdom

One Liberty Plaza, 20th Floor, New York, NY 10006, USA

477 Williamstown Road, Port Melbourne, VIC 3207, Australia

314–321, 3rd Floor, Plot 3, Splendor Forum, Jasola District Centre, New Delhi – 110025, India

103 Penang Road, #05–06/07, Visioncrest Commercial, Singapore 238467

Cambridge University Press is part of the University of Cambridge.

It furthers the University's mission by disseminating knowledge in the pursuit of education, learning, and research at the highest international levels of excellence.

www.cambridge.org
Information on this title: www.cambridge.org/9781009200844
DOI: 10.1017/9781009200882

© David McKitterick 2022

This publication is in copyright. Subject to statutory exception and to the provisions of relevant collective licensing agreements, no reproduction of any part may take place without the written permission of Cambridge University Press.

First published 2022

Printed in the United Kingdom by TJ Books Limited, Padstow Cornwall

A catalogue record for this publication is available from the British Library.

ISBN 978-1-009-20084-4 Hardback

Cambridge University Press has no responsibility for the persistence or accuracy of URLs for external or third-party internet websites referred to in this publication and does not guarantee that any content on such websites is, or will remain, accurate or appropriate.

For Rosamond

Contents

List of Illustrations [*page* ix]
List of Abbreviations [xi]
Prologue [xiii]

1 Introduction [1]

2 Re-Shaping the World [15]

3 Books in Abundance [36]

4 Celebrating Print [47]

LIBRARIES

5 Access: National Collections [71]

6 The British Museum Commission, 1847–1850 [80]

7 Libraries in Confusion [93]

8 Collaboration [108]

TRADING AND COLLECTING

9 The Trade in Second-Hand Books [119]

10 Private Collectors and the Public [139]

BOOKS IN DETAIL

11 Writing in Books [155]

12 Bookbinding [161]

BOOKS ON SHOW

13 Reproduction [187]

14 Exhibitions [194]

ANOTHER GENERATION

15 Changes in Direction   [219]

16 Advice and Guidance   [251]

17 Standing Back   [280]

18 The Next Generation   [289]

CONCLUSION

19 Then and Now   [311]

Notes   [321]
Select Bibliography   [381]
Index   [419]

Illustrations

1   William Blades, *The pentateuch of printing* (1891). Title-page.   [*page* 5]
2   Caxton's reputed house in the Almonry, Westminster. From George Cooke, *Views in London and its vicinity* (1834), after a drawing by Samuel Prout.   [26]
3   Laurens Janszoon Coster. Commemorative medal issued in 1856. From William Blades, *The pentateuch of printing* (1891).   [48]
4   Statue of Gutenberg by David d'Angers, erected at Strasbourg in 1840. From the *Magasin Pittoresque*, July 1840.   [49]
5   Henry Bradshaw, *A classified index of the fifteenth century books in the collection of M.J. De Meyer, which were sold at Ghent in November 1869* (Macmillan, 1870).   [53]
6   Catalogue of the extraordinary collection of manuscripts, chiefly upon vellum ... formed by Guglielmo Libri ... Sotheby's, 28 March 1859 ...   [102]
7   *Bibliotheca Sunderlandiana. Sale catalogue of the library of printed books known as the Sunderland or Blenheim library ... To be sold by auction by Puttick and Simpson*, 1881.   [120]
8   Anatole Claudin, *Archives du Bibliophile*, founded in 1858.   [127]
9   Outside a bookseller's shop. Etching by George Cruikshank, from Charles Dickens, *Oliver Twist* (1838).   [130]
10 The old reading room, British Museum. After a watercolour by Thomas Hosmer Shepherd (1793–1864).   [141]
11 John Power, *A handy-book about books* (1870). Top cover, with a facsimile by F.C. Price of a binding in the British Museum.   [257]
12 The reference collection, Wigan Public Library, *c*.1900. From H.T. Folkard, *Wigan Free Public Library, its rise and progress* (1900).   [271]

Abbreviations

BB	*Bulletin du Bibliophile*
BMC	*Catalogue of books printed in the XVth century now in the British Museum (Library)*. Thirteen parts, some reprinted with annotations (London and 'tGoy-Houten, 1963–2007)
ESTC	*English short-title catalogue*: www.estc.bl.uk
Goff	F.R. Goff, *Incunabula in American libraries; a third census of fifteenth-century books recorded in North American collections, reproduced from the annotated copy maintained by Frederick R. Goff* (Millwood, NY, 1973)
ISTC	*Incunabula short-title catalogue*: www.bl.uk/catalogues/istc
JPHS	*Journal of the Printing Historical Society*
Oates	J.C.T. Oates, *A catalogue of the fifteenth-century printed books in the University Library, Cambridge* (Cambridge, 1954)
ODNB	*Oxford dictionary of national biography*
PBSA	*Papers of the Bibliographical Society of America*
SB	*Studies in Bibliography*
STC	A.W. Pollard and G.R. Redgrave, *A short-title catalogue of books printed in England, Scotland, & Ireland, and of English books printed abroad, 1475–1640*, 2nd ed., revised by William A. Jackson, F.S. Ferguson and Katharine F. Pantzer, with a chronological index by Philip R. Rider. 3 vols (Bibliographical Society, 1975–91)
TCBS	*Transactions of Cambridge Bibliographical Society*
USTC	*Universal short title catalogue*: www.ustc.ac.uk

Prologue

In summer 2020, King's College London issued the following statement about its libraries:

During this time our focus will be on maintaining and enabling access to our online resources. We will not be purchasing print resources for the foreseeable and due off-campus working we will be unable to digitise non-accessible format print materials.[1]

It referred to specific circumstances: the lack of physical access to the library during the Covid-19 pandemic. While clearly no one checked the grammar of the statement, the meaning and the implications were clear enough: that the focus for library provision had fundamentally shifted from paper to screen.

In 2018 – long before the Covid-19 crisis – the University of Stirling library issued the following:

An ebook is an electronic version of a traditional print book. Ebooks are always available and provide quick and convenient access. You can access ebooks at any time from any PC or laptop connected to the University network. We purchase ebooks from a number of different suppliers and there are variations in what you can and cannot do with each ebook.

Not all books are available as ebooks which the library can purchase but where possible we will try to purchase books in ebook format.[2]

It is generally agreed by librarians, publishers and library suppliers alike that the demand for remote access in the exceptional circumstances of 2020–21 forced the pace of change concerning the acquisition of e-resources at the expense of print. Libraries were obliged to re-allocate money and staff, and in the process discovered many circumstance-specific benefits. Readers have also been frustrated by a multitude of unexpected technical and managerial inadequacies. Within a few months, what was formerly a gradual, if frequently confused, development away from an emphasis on paper, and towards a mixed economy, became a precipitate rush.[3] While the emphases have varied among different sectors, in journals and books, in sciences and the humanities, similar trends have applied to libraries across the world. Publishers have responded by drastically altering their priorities. At least for some kinds of works, paper is for the present in retreat. It remains to be seen how, in the longer term, readers will react in their different ways and for their individual needs: how far electronic access is a panacea, how much a stopgap, how much a *pis aller* and how much a last rather than first resort.

Obviously the same does not apply equally to all older material. Whether in libraries or remotely at home, readers continue to face a mixed economy, paper and screen. While the vast majority of older work remains only available on paper, in its original form, some of the first digital applications were to the reproduction and circulation of early printed books, and scholars have relied on this for several years. Yet, as more general habits, use, assumptions and expectations thus shift, it becomes all the more imperative to comprehend what can easily be forgotten: the principles and habits formed over many centuries concerning a medium which has always required management in changing environments. Even at an elementary level, the limitations, advantages and ways of understanding ebooks and other digital resources are not the same as those required or possible for codices. At the same time, as social media play an ever-increasing part in the sharing of ideas and information, and in some fields are already dominant, so there arise new questions of responsibility and access.

Most of this book has been written when libraries were either closed, or severely restricted. In these exceptional circumstances, I am grateful both to the few staff in those that have still been accessible, and to the numerous booksellers who have supplied what libraries could not.

1 | Introduction

This book is concerned with several linked revolutions in the use, study and appreciation of older books that occurred over a little more than half a century, between the 1830s and the early 1890s. Changes in the manufacture and presentation of new books in this period, dominated by mechanisation, have been much discussed elsewhere. What, on the other hand, of earlier books? Jean Viardot, writing in the *Histoire de l'édition française*, and others before him, noted a revolution in taste for rare books in about 1830.[1] What of material questions concerning these? How and where could they be studied? What opportunities were available for a population whose wealth, literacy and education were changing fundamentally? How and when did tastes and values change? How did the book trade and customers accommodate or lead change? The following considers what happened to the study and treatment of early books and some related aspects of manuscript traditions at a critical turning point in the mid-nineteenth century. By the 1880s, interests were being newly defined. Being concerned primarily with older materials, these pages have little to say about the manufacture or trade of contemporary books, though inevitably these impinged at every level of interest, influencing directions of enquiry and of enjoyment.

Over all this hovered larger questions. Who owned the past? What exactly was the past, insofar as it was defined by the surviving printed and written inheritance? How much of it was recoverable? By whom? While this book is concerned mostly with the printed word, many of the questions were as applicable to the study of early or recent manuscripts. They are also concerned as much with amateurs of varying wealth as with professionals. How and why did attitudes change among very disparate bodies of people? By focusing on questions of materiality, of access and of the place of booksellers, publishers, librarians and readers in this transformative period, it becomes possible to understand the foundations of modern assumptions that are only now being challenged in a digital world.

Fifty Years

In June 1887 Queen Victoria celebrated fifty years since her accession. There was a thanksgiving service in Westminster Abbey, to which she was driven in a long procession noted for a prominent group of Indian cavalrymen, past what were said to be ten miles of enthusiastic people lining the streets. A celebratory banquet was attended by guests from across the world including several dozen foreign kings and princes as well as the heads of Britain's colonies and dominions. The same week she visited a gathering of 27,000 London schoolchildren in Hyde Park. Other parts of the country celebrated in their own ways, and an assortment of commemorative ceramics, medals and publications fed a population eager to mark the event. All this – and such large-scale occasions as a jubilee exhibition in the Royal Botanical Gardens at Manchester, besides further celebrations in London – was more than a commemoration of half a century. It all contributed to a self-conscious national mood that presented a new face to the world.

The long list of guests for the June programme, dominated by members of her family, reflected the many connections between Victoria and Germany. France was represented by a small group of the House of Orléans. Other guests came from around the world, but apart from the family the emphasis both in the public pageantry and among those attending was on Britain's overseas possessions. Taking advantage of the opportunity of there being so many appropriate people in London, the first colonial conference took place in late spring, designed to bring peoples and interests closer together.

If France, Britain's closest neighbour, seemed less prominent among all this, there were innumerable other ties that bound the two countries. Relations over the past half-century ranged from strained and near enmity to jealous, suspicious, supportive and cordial. With two very different political traditions, the countries depended commercially and culturally on each other, but they were also in competition with each other. Socially, the roots had been put down even more firmly than previously in the years between 1815 and 1830.[2] By the 1840s the cosmopolitan newspaper trade in Paris included titles in Dutch, German, Italian, Polish, Russian and Spanish, as well as English. Of the last, *Galignani's Messenger* was the best known, and the same printer produced the *London and Paris Observer*. The *Illustrated London News* had an office near the Palais Royal.[3] Politically, and notwithstanding the Chartist agitation of the 1840s, Britain seemed usually stable apart from the stain of starvation and continuing failings in

Ireland. France, on the other hand, had faced major upheavals in the July Revolution of 1830, in 1848, in 1851 and in 1870–1. England was a place of refuge, for Louis-Philippe after he abdicated in 1848 and settled at Claremont in Surrey, and for Napoleon III during his last years at Chislehurst in Kent in 1871–3. Both were buried in England.[4]

No Frenchman was more familiar with the higher ranks of English society than the aged duc d'Aumale, son of Louis-Philippe, exiled in England since 1848 and now settled back in France after the turmoil of 1870–1.[5] Quite apart from his family and political connections, he was a reminder of shared bibliophile concerns, the possessor of one of the finest private libraries to be assembled in Victorian England and of a collection of paintings considered by some to be second only to that in the Louvre itself. By 1887 these collections had been moved from Orleans House in Twickenham back to France, where he was restoring and rebuilding the vast château at Chantilly in order to house them. At the highest social level, Aumale represented common interests, part of a tradition that had survived revolution, war and economic difference. In friendship and in rivalry alike, in manufacture, trading and in scholarship, the two countries repeatedly compared each other and drew from each other's intellectual and material resources. In the one comparatively small area of activity that is the subject of the following pages, the multifarious world of older books, repeated manifestations of this wider collaborative view were unavoidable, and sometimes to be welcomed.

It was impossible not to see that in fifty years the world had been transformed. The last years of Victoria's reign brought biographies, picture books and a stream of other books and articles, published across the English-speaking world, reflecting on innovations, improvements and vicissitudes since the 1830s. In the first years of her reign there was no system of public libraries, the old reading room of the British Museum still served small numbers of readers mostly limited by their social connections, and few other public museums or art galleries of any size existed either in London or the provinces. The great mass of the nation's artistic and bibliographical inherited wealth was privately owned.

Few people used the new-fangled typewriter, invented in 1867. A host of further inventions in paper-making, typesetting, photography, binding and printing affected books' appearances and the ways in which they were produced. All affected the ways that books were sold, collected, cared for and consulted.

A fundamental shift in the availability, management, choice and use of books occurred in the mid-nineteenth century. With this shift there also developed fresh interests in the history of books' manufacture and of their purposes. The study of manuscripts and the study of old printed matter alike were put on a new footing. New questions were asked, sometimes revolutionary methods of investigation were developed; and new, often transformative, conclusions were reached. During these years fresh foundations were laid for the public use of books at national and local levels alike. They remain in place today in an increasingly digital world. In the same period readerships changed, and with this came demands for different kinds of books and other printed matter. For the management of ever greater numbers of publications, both surviving from the past and added to in the present, the ideas, debates and achievements of these years took a turn which is recognisably modern in its priorities. Connoisseurship in book collecting, a pastime long familiar among the wealthier parts of the population, took new directions, both in the preferences of collectors for particular kinds of books and among new generations of people, predominantly of lesser wealth, for whom the activity was a novelty. For the detailed study of older books, the antiquarianism characteristic of earlier learning was replaced by a new discipline, often described today as historical bibliography and focusing on material aspects: partly sometimes now referred to as the archaeology of the book. Authors strove to explain two principal differences encompassed in the word 'bibliography', which developed characteristics ever more divergent, and yet also constantly feeding on each other. They may be partially summarised, albeit inadequately, as on the one hand the listing and management of books, and on the other the study of their physical properties. In sum, the former assumptions of much of the literate world were redeployed.

Roots of Change

In 1961 Stanley Morison identified the printer William Blades (Figure 1) as 'the master printer to whom Europe owes the foundation of the modern English school of scientific bibliography'.[6] This was a bold claim, and certainly Blades's two-volume study of William Caxton published in 1861–3 was instrumental in advancing what he called 'minute typographical research', 'by no means a matter of idle or trivial curiosity'. Blades's analysis in his second volume of the successive typographical equipment employed by Caxton, first in the Low Countries and then in Westminster, was pioneering, and appeared even as J.W. Holtrop of the Royal Library in The Hague was publishing his own account of printing types in the

Figure 1 William Blades, *The pentateuch of printing* (1891). Title-page.

fifteenth-century Low Countries: beginning in 1856, by the end of 1862 fifteen of the final twenty-four fascicles had appeared.[7] The two men were working in parallel: one a printer, the other a librarian and bibliographer. Holtrop's was the more complicated task, involving several dozen printers over a long period, while Blades brought to a single establishment the eye of a professional printer for detail. In Henry Bradshaw, University Librarian at Cambridge, they had a mutual friend, who admitted to Holtrop that without his work, including his analytical catalogue of the incunabula at The Hague (1856), much of his own inspired work on early printing would have been impossible.[8] Bradshaw's copy of Blades's two volumes is dense with additions, observations and corrections.[9] In reality, the foundation of which Morison wrote depended on these three men, working between the 1850s and the 1880s.

While libraries, and the care and use of books, have a history since antiquity, their modern condition has its origins comparatively recently. Several of our principal assumptions in everyday reading experience are creatures of the nineteenth century, developed at that time whether as a direct result of the need to manage unprecedented quantities of print in a population that was growing both in size and in literacy, or developed within this growth as new ways of looking at books and caring for them.

Further, some key features of the wealth of computer applications that now lie at the heart of library management have their roots in ideas and practices that evolved in the mid-nineteenth century. Among the most obvious, it is now assumed, for example, that we can access lists of the holdings of libraries not just within our small local communities but also across the world. The idea of a union catalogue is a much older one, in circulation long before the early fourteenth century, when a group of Franciscans at Oxford compiled a catalogue of works of the Church Fathers held in over 180 monastic and cathedral libraries in England and Scotland.[10] At the beginning of the fifteenth century, the Augustinian monk John Boston of Bury St Edmunds gathered information under the names of authors, and so created what John Bale later described as 'one library out of many'.[11] In 1697 Edward Bernard at Oxford assembled the catalogues of manuscripts in many public and private collections in England and Ireland.[12] In 1739 Bernard de Montfaucon's *Bibliotheca bibliothecarum manuscriptorum nova*, especially useful for French and Italian collections, was published in Paris. In 1830, the Leipzig jurist and legal historian Gustav Haenel issued a more ambitious compilation covering France, Switzerland, the Low Countries, Britain, Spain and Portugal, information gathered in the course of his research on early legal manuscripts.[13] The far larger scale required for printed books was first put into effect only about four generations ago, long after Gutenberg. Further, it is now assumed that digitised images can be shared worldwide, pursuing a way of thinking that emerged during the nineteenth century with the exploitation of photography.

The technologies are different, but the concept of sharing is an old one. For many libraries today, whether or not they contain extensive collections of old books, the future depends on co-operation, the successful implementation and management of consortia in order to minimise effort and expenditure, whether dealing with paper or with computer-based resources. The principles of what have become watchwords for current practice and an aspiration for future development are repeatedly traceable to practices and debates several generations ago.

By the mid-sixteenth century, the need for bibliographical ordering of knowledge was acute, and it became only more so as articles in the new genre of periodicals from the seventeenth century onwards contributed to the disparities and inadequacies that were all too clear among the books arranged on library shelves. While each generation produced new suggestions and recommendations, it was only with the work of Melvil Dewey, and the publication of his decimal classification in 1876, that any kind of widespread agreement was reached.[14] In public and academic libraries alike, readers of all kinds, in countries across the world, became accustomed to commonly held arrangements for the organisation of knowledge. Although much developed since, and now challenged by numerous alternatives, the principle of common approaches was established.

Not everything has been necessarily for the better.[15] In the nineteenth century many learned and skilled, not to say sometimes also opinionated, people considered how books should be catalogued. The printed catalogue of the British Museum library, which begun to be published in 1881, was a triumphant conclusion following often bitter arguments. Based on rules originally formulated for the Museum by Antonio Panizzi and published in 1841, both in its detail and in its arrangement it set a standard.[16] There were other cataloguing codes, notably from the United States (set out in Charles Cutter's work of 1876) or in the so-called Prussian code, worked out by Karl Dziatzko at Breslau in the 1890s. Subsequent generations of librarians have devised new codes, and while each could offer improvements supported by logical arguments, they sometimes also destroyed alternative ways of searching for books. The old form headings that were such a prominent feature of the printed British Museum catalogue, headings such as Ephemerides (including almanacs and calendars), Hymnals, or

Directories, and the gathering of anonymous works under, for example, proper names on the title-page, were easy prey for purist revisionists; but conveniently for many readers they gathered into a single place matter that was not easy to identify. In the great mass of entries under authors, the visual sequence of publications organised title by title, edition by edition, translation by translation, whether in card drawers (as in most libraries) or in manuscript or printed guard books (such as in the British Museum, Cambridge University Library and the Bodleian Library) provided instantly obvious analyses and portraits of bibliographical relationships that have generally been abandoned in large computer files.[17]

Losses of a different kind can occur when libraries share information. The records on cards, composed as a result of major investment by libraries in time and staff, naturally vary from library to library, sometimes in accuracy, sometimes in detail. When in 1968–81 the immense American *NUC pre-'56*, that is, the national union catalogue of pre-1956 imprints,[18] was composed from the thousands of cards submitted to the Library of Congress by hundreds of libraries in the United States and Canada, the world welcomed a bibliographical research tool of unprecedented scale: it ran to 754 large volumes, and it remains one of the fullest such resources available. Few people at first realised that in the process of amalgamating the cards, created in traditions established in the late nineteenth century, seeking common bibliographical denominators and reflecting priorities developed further in the twentieth, an immense amount of further information regarding copies and editions had been cast out. The faults do not lie in the concept of a union catalogue; they lie in execution. In the most basic information, to locate copies, the same tensions between shared information, varied accuracy and the challenges of determining indenticality as distinct from similarity, challenge major computer-based databases, whether the ESTC, USTC or ISTC – none of which seeks to provide systematic copy-specific details.[19]

There is a further fundamental issue especially in the catalogues of individual institutions. As we shall see, in the nineteenth century their purposes were much debated. Distracted by the best of different intentions, one of the key rules of librarianship tends now to be forgotten: to save the time of the reader.[20] Among other things, that means not to overwhelm the reader with irrelevancies. The sheer technical possibilities of computer catalogues, with their sometimes sophisticated – but always limited – search mechanisms, their immense and seductive capacity, and their speed of delivery, encourage proliferation of unwanted detail at the expense of focused concision. The computerised catalogues of some major research libraries, over-burdened with detail and not pretending to any intellectual orderliness or coherence, may actually offer less help, less efficiently, than what was clearly available on card or paper. Computer catalogues offer a great deal; but it cannot be pretended that they reflect contexts in more than the most rudimentary way. In this, they are radically different from many of their paper predecessors, from the ways in which these were conceived and developed over several generations, and where rules for orderly filing as well as for composition of individual entries were paramount.

In 1864 Henry Bradshaw contemplated a key aspect of how bibliographical information was to be presented. For him, the multiple entries to complex matters offered by a printed volume which itself was organised in a rational manner provided a practical means to pursuing understanding. Writing to J.W. Holtrop about his catalogue of incunabula in The Hague, and reflecting also on the more recent account of Caxton by William Blades, he concluded:

It is not until you get a book like his [Blades's] Caxton or your own *Catalogus*, where a large number of books is ranged simply and methodically according to their *natural* order, and in print (this last is most important) – that you can really set to work upon a proper basis. It is only by having such a Catalogue constantly under one's eye, by turning backwards and forwards readily, that one is able to see thousands of little things, which must escape otherwise.[21]

Care and Survival

What if we turn from questions of access and library management to questions concerning the understanding of books as objects and of their history? Just as some of the issues raised previously, with roots in the nineteenth century, are of immediate contemporary importance, so too the study and history of reading, which form so large a part of the discipline now called book history, depend on skills and processes developed at about the same time. For the study of reading must depend on the study of what is read. Among others, it depends on matters such as the historical evidence of book ownership and on the physical properties both of individual copies and of the shared features of multiple copies in an edition. It also depends on relationships between manuscript and print, on the documented interests of people whether in their correspondence, their publications or in larger personal or public archives. It depends on copy-specific information, and it depends on matters in common, including how the visual and physical attributes of books can be best understood and conveyed.

All these depend on care and survival. Theft and its close relation forgery are endemic, and always destructive of the contexts on which all historical evidence relies. Curatorship is not just about the care of individual objects. It is also about the care of their relationships one to another. On a larger scale, during the last few years public attention has been drawn increasingly to the destruction of books, whether by war, by terrorism, or by natural disasters.[22] The deliberate burning of the university library at Leuven in 1914 was no new phenomenon.[23] Within then-living memory, at Strasbourg in 1870 German bombardment had destroyed the Bibliothèque Municipale, and in 1871 the Bibliothèque de la Ville at Paris was burned down during the Commune. More recently, the looting and destruction of the national library at Baghdad in 2003, the efforts to save as much as possible of the ancient manuscripts at Timbuktu threatened by fundamentalist Muslims,[24] and accidental disasters such as the burning of the city library at Norwich in 1994, or the burning of the university library at Cape Town (involving considerable loss to South Africa's history) in 2021 are but some that have commanded news headlines. Books are also booty, whether plundered from Italy, the Vatican, Germany, Austria and the Low Countries by Napoleon's agents at the beginning of the nineteenth century, from France by Nazi forces in the Second World War, or from Poland and Germany by Russians in the same war.[25] One can look back to the Vikings in the ninth century,[26] for the main features of destruction and mobility are the same. Books move not only through trade and private relocation. More subtly, and quite apart from ordinary thieves, terrorists, warmongers and revolutionaries have realised that libraries enshrine a people's history, and that to destroy libraries is to attempt to destroy identity. In 1992 the national library at Sarajevo was deliberately targeted and destroyed for this reason.

Yet while some books are valued, many more are neglected. Across Europe, there remain today libraries that are poorly maintained, and little attended. Surveys such as the *Directory of rare book and special collections in the United Kingdom and the Republic of Ireland*,[27] and the vastly more detailed *Handbuch der historischen Buchbestände in Deutschland, Österreich und Europa*, edited by Bernhard Fabian,[28] have unearthed collections that lay disregarded and all but forgotten. In 1999 an exhibition at the Grolier Club of New York presented much that was unfamiliar from private libraries that had passed to the National Trust in Britain.[29]

At Antwerp, in 2004 an exhibition was organised of books in often ignored nearby religious libraries.[30]

In the nineteenth century, national, local and amateur interests prompted a new mood of exploration. In France, the post of *Inspecteur Général des Bibliothèques Publiques* was inaugurated in 1839. In England, less inclined to be centralised, ignorance and improvidence prompted Beriah Botfield to publish his *Notes on the cathedral libraries of England* in 1849, and a few parish and school libraries subsequently attracted attention from William Blades and others. Such investigations were forerunners of the gradual discovery of a host of disregarded libraries; and they appeared even as the interests of collectors and scholars alike were moving beyond the traditional concern for a canon of major early editions and authors, to wider considerations of a much greater variety of publications and subjects. What once seemed trivial attracted growing and innovative attention. These and other developments helped and encouraged examination of the more general surviving bibliographical evidence for increasingly ambitious interpretations of a multifaceted past.

Revolutions

In 1998 – about a quarter of a century ago – there was a conference at Lyon on *Les trois révolutions du livre*. It attracted sufficient attention to be followed in 2002 by a major exhibition with the same title at the Musée des Arts et Métiers in Paris.[31] The three revolutions identified were the invention and early spread of printing in fifteenth-century Europe; the industrialisation of book manufacture in the late eighteenth and early nineteenth centuries; and the application of computer methods to manufacture and presentation of books at the end of the twentieth century – what was referred to as the *dématérialisé* book. Roger Chartier has argued for a slightly different trio, drawing attention to the invention of the codex.[32]

Such a summary division into a tripartite process is useful not only because it promotes, raw and undigested, some of the most obviously distinct features in the history of the manufacture of books but also because it provokes debate. Yet it can be no more than a summary, and as a summary it is extremely selective.

Most obviously, even if the invention of the codex is identified as a key feature, and hence draws attention to the importance of the presentation of the written word, it pays very limited attention to the ways in which one medium overlaps with another. Manuscript and print have not only existed side by side for centuries but also depend on each other. The so-called printing revolution was complex, unequally focused and long drawn-out. So too with the mechanisation of the book: it was no sudden change, and even in its most basic elements took about a century to evolve. The recent developments of digital environments have happened rapidly in some respects, much more speedily and unpredictably than even the most optimistic and committed prophets might have foreseen; but they have taken hold and been further developed erratically, more for some kinds of books and publishing than for others, more for some audiences than others, and more in some markets than others, while the details of presentation and use are still far short of accepted norms.

All these changes have one feature in common. They concern the production, manufacture and hence by implication the circulation of words, numerals and images. They are not only defined by changes in their management or with understanding and interpretation. Yet in their own ways each of these elements also underwent its own revolution.

Within less than a century of Gutenberg, questions became pressing. How were printed books, produced in numbers that quickly became incalculable, to be recorded and discovered? How were they to be described? How were they to be distinguished one from another? How were they to be understood or valued? Which books were identified as being more important? At the time of publication? Within a generation or two? Within a century or two? In some ways, these are simple issues. Few people seem to have asked a slightly different question: how much the world, as communities, could actually afford to discard. Changes in the organisational and visual presentation of texts, in the identification of certain texts with certain authors, in the financial, social and legal status of texts and authors, all developed with the mutations enabled and made necessary by the advent of printed editions; but many of the features associated with print were in fact already present in the preceding manuscript environment.

Print and, most importantly, the varying awareness of the distinctive features of the printed book, in its appearance, its structure and its materials, brought a revolution that went far beyond the technology of invention. It involved new ways of reading, new ways of interpreting the page and new kinds of shared experiences that might be multiform, as much combative as submissive, as much contrasting as uniform. The physical uniformity of several copies of the same printed page is not in itself a guarantee of uniform reception. In fact, people can react to the same stimuli in wildly differing ways. This is obvious enough in different reactions to argument, statements or works of imagination. The commonly accepted credo concerning physical properties of books, that 'forms effect meaning',[33] has to be considered in contexts of the variety and circumstances of readers, the variety of their education and experience, and their psychological or physical reactions.

Comprehensive retrospective lists of earlier books, those out of print, have been an aim of scholars since Conrad Gesner's work in the sixteenth century,[34] but they too only matured in the nineteenth century, to be developed since into ambitious databases, at first nationally and now, also, internationally. For collectors, scholars, librarians and booksellers alike, the bibliographic record was refashioned wholesale in the successive editions of Jacques-Charles Brunet's *Manuel du libraire et de l'amateur de livres*, first published in 1810 and of which a third edition appeared in 1820. Faced with what he termed 'une révolution soudaine' in interests in medieval literature and *livres gothiques*, in 1834 he issued three volumes of *Nouvelles recherches bibliographiques* to supplement the earlier editions. Then he reverted to successively expanded editions of his *Manuel* until the appearance of a final *Supplément* in 1878.

The modern book trade, reliant on instant access to details of what is available, has been made possible by the joint efforts of publishers to gather into one place information on hundreds of thousands of books. This has usually centred on listing publications in individual countries, but is now increasingly international. In the late sixteenth century, printed catalogues listing new books from printers and publishers across much of Europe were produced for the bi-annual book fairs at Frankfurt.[35] Influenced by all the variations in anticipated market demand and international access, they were never intended to be comprehensive. On a vastly larger scale, collaborative efforts to bring together publishers' catalogues came of age only in the 1870s. In Britain, Joseph Whitaker published in 1874 the first edition of the *Reference catalogue of current literature*, assembling and indexing the catalogues of dozens of publishers. In the United States, the first *Publishers' Trade List Annual* appeared in 1873. In Belgium, the Cercle de la Librairie assembled a *Recueil alphabétique de catalogues* in 1884. In France, H. Le Soudier published the first *Bibliographie française; recueil de catalogues des éditeurs français* in six volumes in 1896.[36]

Although several of these themes individually have an earlier history, it is argued here that they coalesced in fundamental and definitive ways for the first time in the nineteenth century. Questions of access and management, questions of public and private presentation, questions of choice and care, questions of what seemed most material or significant from the past, questions of appearance and visual relationships between different periods, questions of how to understand the past and put this understanding to use, questions of what could be discovered from the surviving past, questions of how far the past could be considered stable, questions of relationships between manuscript and printed records and questions of specificity and generality.

All these and more lay behind a revolution that was both bibliographical and social. It was sometimes expressed simply in financial terms: the cash price of a particular book or class of books had gone up or down. Certainly for many people, driven by hope as well as knowledge, the need for successful investment was paramount. The various warnings to amateur collectors by idealists from the mid-century onwards against a venal approach are sufficient reminder of this, while reports of prices fetched at auctions, printed in newspapers and specialist journals, reflected and further encouraged a mercenary view. Taken as a whole, the reality was much more involved, even confused.

This book, concerned with fundamental changes in several aspects of the management and use of books and reading, is a reminder of the fluidity of how we communicate and participate in knowledge. Focusing on northwest Europe, and particularly on Britain and France, it considers how access, interest and knowledge of old books and of some aspects of the written past changed between the trade, scholars and the general reading public during a critical half-century.

2 | Re-Shaping the World

At one level or another, by one means or another, for one reason or another, a higher percentage of the population of western Europe was engaged with books and other forms of the printed word in the nineteenth century than at any time previously. In this as in most things, the various countries were not equal. Experience varied from region to region, from town to town and among different social groups. It depended on literacy rates, on transport and communication, on manufacturing capability, on education and on the requirements of everyday life whether in government, religion or social assumptions and practices. At one end of the spectrum were people struggling to read simple words, dependent more on pictures than on the alphabet. At the other end were some of the richest people of their times, possessing extensive libraries on which they lavished their fortunes. Most forms of learning, from the very beginner to advanced research, depended to some degree on the printed word. Schoolbook publishing, by established firms such as Longman and by newcomers such as Macmillan, or Hachette in France, became highly profitable. Practical experience was increasingly supplemented by manuals and handbooks: by paper and print. To feed a population that was growing not only numerically but also in its demands and needs, the number of printing firms, and with them numbers of publishers and booksellers, increased prodigiously, in some countries as limiting legislation was modified or removed.[1] In 1841 the British census recorded 50,000 men and women occupied in the paper, printing, books and stationery trades. By the census of 1891 this figure had risen to 256,000.[2] Technical innovations, accompanied by the gradual removal of taxes, brought many prices down. They also meant that books could be more ambitious in their design and presentation.

In the foreword to his pioneering and influential study of Victorian book design (1963), Ruari McLean commented that 'more exciting things happened in book design between 1837 and 1890 than in any other comparable period in the history of the world's printing; and most of them happened in London.'[3] Unlike McLean, who was able to concentrate on one side of the English Channel and North Sea, the market and appreciation of older books was heavily influenced by overseas interests, collegiality, trade and scholarship. An international perspective is essential.

Whether in manuscript or print, books had never been uniform in their production standards, or in their prices. Technological revolutions did not change this. Indeed, differences were enhanced. Just as comment on social or educational needs, opportunities and attainment became ever more common, so also the variety of printed matter became ever more evident. Much of this social and industrial revolution in the world of print has been long studied, and is generally understood. Changes in typography, in printing, in illustration, and in binding have been widely chronicled. So too has the transformative development of magazine and newspaper publishing, which used far more paper than did book production. In 1872 it was reckoned that domestic paper manufacture had almost doubled in twenty years: only a worldwide dearth of raw materials for a time held back further expansion.[4] For books and periodicals alike, differences in paper manufacture and quality were fundamental to prices and to publication. Many of the publishing firms established in this period lasted well into the twentieth century.

The scarcely less influential, and no less complex, revolution in the world of older printed books has received much less attention. Ever since the end of the fifteenth century, there have been more second-hand printed books in circulation than new ones. Some kinds of books have always been naturally valued more than others, and the names of the major collectors are well recorded. Yet the trade in a great range of second-hand books has been comparatively little examined by historians.[5] Antiquarian books have commanded more attention, the word antiquarian itself carrying connotations of values beyond the merely cheap.

A Period of Transition

The mid-nineteenth century was a period of rapid and sometimes bewildering social, political, religious, military, financial, industrial and legal change. For older books and manuscripts it also witnessed a bibliographical, geographical, educational and personal re-forming of the worlds of production, collecting, libraries, the book trade and bibliographical study, all aspects of access to books. This re-forming amounted to a revolution in practice and in outlook, and on it is based the world that is now undergoing a still greater transformation.

While by no means exact, the year 1830 reflects the time by which machinery had become an accustomed part of printing and paper-making, processes such as stereotyping and lithography were everyday, and cheap publishing at the hands of Charles Knight and others was creating new markets.[6] Historians of book collecting tend, naturally enough, to emphasise 1812, the date of the record-breaking sale of the Duke of Roxburghe's library. The subsequent foundation of the Roxburghe Club inspired the Société des Bibliophiles François in 1820.[7] The Philobiblon Society followed in 1853.[8] The membership of all was strictly limited, and included some of the most influential collectors of the day. For most purposes of the trade in early manuscripts and printed books, the end of the Napoleonic wars, the easing of international exchange and the disproportionate wealth of Britain compared with France were of much wider significance.

Except in retrospect, thanks to Queen Victoria's jubilee in 1887, the period with which this book is primarily concerned was not self-defining. Indeed, while many people were aware of aspects of change in the world of books, not many thought to single out these years as a bibliographical entity. Some people looked back to earlier years, sometimes wistfully, sometimes simply to observe facts such as changes in taste, in the prices of different kinds of books or in the ways books were sold. Naturally enough, few people attempted to predict the future, though several who were forward-looking established various social arrangements that were to dominate the bibliographical world in the years to come. A new self-consciousness in taste for book design characterised much of the world of bibliophily in Third Republic France and late Victorian Britain alike, but this was for contemporary productions. It affected the taste for older books, but for their study only obliquely.[9]

For Britain, self-awareness was consolidated at the end of the period by the beginning of the publication of two defining national monuments, James Murray's *New English dictionary* (1884–) and Leslie Stephen's *Dictionary of national biography* (1885–), as well as by the perceptions engendered in the jubilee year. In France, the half-century was bounded by two vast projects that helped to define French national identity. In 1837 Louis-Philippe, in a country far from unified or certain of itself, opened in part of the palace of Versailles a lavishly decorated Musée Historique. The building had been little used since the Revolution, and the newly constituted Galerie des Batailles, with paintings depicting famous battles since the fifth century, offered both a focus and a refreshing distinctiveness, recalling past glories.[10] Fifty years later, construction of the Eiffel Tower began in January 1887, so inaugurating one of the indelible features of

Paris. Similar public phenomena featured in other countries in Europe as well, the associated varieties of local experience and language, and the various pulls of major conurbations, whether Paris, Munich, Berlin or elsewhere, often creating different patterns of loyalty.[11]

Developments such as railway networks (including the need for common time-keeping[12]), uniform postal charges and the establishment of wider newspaper industries drew countries together in fresh ways, both independently and internationally. More reliable and faster journey times thanks to trains and cross-Channel steamers, allied to faster postal services, made connections between London and dealers on the continent ever easier. During this period, the best journey time between London and Paris was reduced from about two days to sometimes under ten hours. Improving communications whether by train, by faster shipping, or by the new electric telegraph, and an increasing custom of travel by people for whom a foreign tour would formerly have been unimaginable, brought new interdependence for individuals and organisations alike.

For all of Europe, communications were revolutionised with considerable periods of international stability. While ever-expanding series of popular guidebooks were intended primarily for tourists and sight-seers, they also helped bring the continent closer to hand in other ways. Baedeker's guides, initially to German-speaking regions, appeared from 1828.[13] John Murray launched his *Hand-books* in 1836,[14] and Adolphe Joanne launched his series for French speakers in 1841.[15] The increasing popularity of continental travel for English speakers was reflected in the unprecedentedly long lists of English-language reprints of popular authors from major publishers such as Baudry and Galignani in Paris, or Tauchnitz in Leipzig, the last eventually dominating this market.[16]

I propose to present the markets and tastes for second-hand books beyond the high spots and leading figures of the Roxburghe drama. Instead, I look in turn at some of the changes that occurred roughly during these years of the mid-century, and how some aspects of the appreciation, presentation, management, study and understanding of manuscripts and early printed books changed unequivocally, in ways that became standard parts of modern scholarship, practice and connoisseurship. The bibliographical revolution identified by Morison was of a particular and focused kind. It related to only one aspect of the study and use of books. It was only one part of a much wider and greater revolution, affecting not only historical questions concerning the analysis of earlier printing. A much more influential revolution developed over a few decades in the mid-nineteenth century and affected many more people.

Histories of book collecting tend to focus, naturally enough, on the more prominent owners and their possessions. That, indeed, was the title and purpose of Seymour de Ricci's seminal book in 1930, *English collectors of books & manuscripts, 1530–1930, and their marks of ownership*. Rather than following de Ricci and focusing largely on major individuals, the following pages also consider some of the more broadly sociable aspects: most obviously in the formal activities and organisation of societies and thereby the organisation of what became an ever more popular activity; of manuals to help beginners and advanced students alike; of the gradual development of a specialist periodicals trade for collectors; of the trade itself in some kinds of second-hand books; of price guides; of the public display and presentation of books; of the changing nature of canons of collecting; of the development of interest in modern literature and in modern manuscripts; of the development of collecting among what we may broadly speaking, albeit inadequately, call the middle classes and nouveaux riches; and of access to libraries both long-established and newly founded. Underpinning all of this were questions respecting the history of books, their survival and identification, access to them, and particularly of their manufacture.

All underwent fundamental and long-lasting changes within the space sometimes only of a generation. Further features include the evolution of an understanding of national collections and their relationship to private interests and responsibilities. How were large libraries to be organised and used? What was the public face of collecting? The overriding interests of major private collectors were related ever more to the national collections being formed at this time, while a growing specialist literature nurtured, and reflected, the management, perception and use of books old or new.[17]

What caused and fed an extraordinary change in attitudes specifically to older books in the mid-nineteenth century? Change was observable almost regardless of subject. For new books, it was not simply that literacy at various levels of accomplishment was increasing. It was not simply a growing class of people with sufficient spare resources, whether of time or money, to spend on what for others was a luxury. It was not simply that new books could be manufactured ever more cheaply thanks to cloth bindings, cheaper paper, and quicker methods of printing and binding. Print was inescapable thanks to the omnipresence of newspapers, magazines, penny readings, timetables, official and commercial forms, handbills, advertisements pasted to walls and a host of other daily uses. Amidst all this, books were distinct, as publishers in Britain and abroad recognised in packaging them often within gilt or coloured covers.[18]

Our period coincides closely with the life of Henry Bradshaw (1831–86), one of the most influential bibliographers and librarians of the century. He was appointed to his first post in Cambridge University Library in 1856, and died thirty years later. As University Librarian from 1867, he was more effective in explaining and presenting the collections especially of manuscripts and early printed books than he was in daily management. He left much unfinished. He agreed to contribute an article on the invention of printing to the *Encyclopaedia Britannica*, but nothing came of it, and it was left to Edward Gordon Duff to draw on the unpublished draft when he wrote his monograph on *Early printed books* (1893).[19] When he addressed the Library Association on early printed Bibles, it was expected that he would provide a copy of his paper for publication. He never did. His lifelong interest in the history of Irish printing, inherited from his father, was the background to an eagerly anticipated lecture he gave to assembled librarians at Dublin in 1884. But he seems to have lectured with few notes, so nothing appeared.[20] Yet, through his correspondence, a small group of pamphlets and his friendships his influence was immense, not only on the study of early printed books but also on editing Chaucer, on the history of liturgy, on many palaeographical matters and on all manner of antiquarian subjects. With some reluctance, he was drawn into a leading part in the Library Association during its formative years. He knew himself to be a wretched letter-writer in that he was rarely prompt in his replies, but his surviving letters are constantly filled with detailed help. Although he destroyed much of his correspondence, the hundreds of surviving letters in Cambridge University Library (most of them still under-explored) attest to his wide and valued reputation.

The Mid-Century

When in 1891 the typefounder Talbot Baines Reed (1852–93)[21] considered the career of William Blades, he cast his mind back to the early days of the Roxburghe Club, founded twelve years before Blades's birth in 1824. In those days,

Emulated by the example of these aristocratic enthusiasts, other more humble enquirers, such as Timperley, Hansard, and Johnson[22] were exploring the same field, and helping one another to conclusions. There was more zeal than knowledge. There was a great deal of fine writing, entertaining anecdote, and expensive book-making; there were sweeping generalizations, and a touching confidence in second-hand evidence. But in all the school, although it included one or two practical printers, no one had the courage to defy authority, and question all bibliographical dogma until he could verify it for himself. The little boy at Clapham [Blades] was destined to inaugurate this desirable revolution, and apply to the study of Early Printing a sturdy agnosticism which would have horrified Dibdin and scandalized the choice spirits of the Roxburghe Club.[23]

Like Reed, Blades brought practical knowledge to his subject. He was partner in one of the most prominent London firms of printers, with a reputation for keeping abreast of modern technical innovation. Both men combined a strong historical sense with ways of considering the history of printing that were firmly based on their training; yet in their correspondence and in their associations both also engaged with those responsible for the care of books. Reed became Secretary of the new Bibliographical Society. Blades was one of the first members of the Council of the new Library Association. These were not appointments simply for show. They reflected commitment, as bridges connecting different approaches to the knowledge of old books.

In the mid-century, the list of readily available and authoritative books on the history of printing looked meagre to at least one knowledgeable observer. An article in *Notes and Queries* commented:

For about thirty years, the study of the history of early printing has been commonly neglected, frequently despised ... It is unquestionable that books on bibliography, which once were highly rated, have latterly become (at least to those who have them already) provokingly cheap. In fact, unless some measures be adopted to revive a taste for this important branch of learning, the next generation will be involved in decrepitude and darkness with respect to typographical antiquities.[24]

It was signed by R.G., who was also responsible for several other articles in the journal on matters concerning early printed books. A century previously, the subject had been treated by authors such as the bookseller and bibliographer Prosper Marchand (The Hague, 1740), the antiquary Joseph Ames (1749) and the lawyer and bibliophile Gerard Meerman (The Hague, 1765), all writing for clienteles who were at least comfortably off. At the simplest level were various brief guides to skills and careers. In 1809 John Baxter, a printer and bookseller at Lewes, published a slim pocket-sized book on *The sister arts*. For 1s.6d., readers were told about paper-making, printing and bookbinding, with an account of the history of the invention of printing in the fifteenth century, its introduction into England and then a brief obeisance paid to Baskerville and to two men still at work, Thomas Bensley and William Bulmer. Much of it was selected word for word from

Caleb Stower's *Printer's grammar* (1808), to which readers were referred for further information. Baxter's modest publication, which seems to have been reissued later but with the same date, was intended for general readerships at an elementary level, not for specialists. By the mid-nineteenth century there were appearing numerous accounts of printing, its social and political benefits and the heroes in its development, from Gutenberg to Caxton to Benjamin Franklin. In Britain and France alike, it was a topic to be met in books, periodicals and newspapers. It was one for people of all ages, for Sunday school prizes as well as for reading in later life.

The books of Thomas Frognall Dibdin were expensive when published. Ordinary paper copies of *The library companion* (1824), intended as an introduction, cost 27s, the equivalent of about two weeks' wages for a manual labourer. Ordinary paper copies of his edition of Ames's *Typographical antiquities* (4 vols., 1810) cost 14 guineas. The three-volume *Bibliographical Decameron* (1817) cost 9 guineas.[25] Leather bindings added further to costs. While some of his comments were quoted in standard reference books by Lowndes and others, for most people his work survived more by repute than by use, as his name became associated with trends in collecting and scholarship that within little more than a generation had passed into history.

If his work was beyond the pockets of many people, some of the topics of which he wrote, especially concerning the history of printing and of books, proved to be of long-lasting and – for some – consuming interest. By the 1820s, some of the most readily available introductions to the history of printing lay not in the works of Dibdin, but in a handful of publications ostensibly intended primarily for professional printers but which in fact contained a mass of historical and more general bibliographical information.

Several audiences were addressed by John Johnson (1777–1848) in his *Typographia, or the printer's instructor*, published by Longman in two compact volumes of small type in 1824.[26] Much of it was likewise derived from Stower; but Johnson's decision to dedicate it to Earl Spencer and the Roxburghe Club, and the availability of copies also on further sizes of large paper, made plain that this was at least as much intended for private libraries as for professional printers. Ordinary copies were priced at 30s, those in the larger duodecimo format at £3, and the largest, in octavo, at 4 guineas.[27] The first volume was entirely historical. Johnson had been a partner in the Lee Priory Press, the private establishment enabled by Sir Egerton Brydges.[28] This was closed in 1823, and though he remained resentful of his treatment there, he remained respectful towards the bibliophile traditions embodied in the Roxburghe Club, using minute type in a display of Spencer's family tree to demonstrate skills in typesetting. All too aware of encroaching mechanisation in printing, he lamented the ways in which work was now hurried through the press with such speed that it valued men's skills less. For much of his historical part, in which he was helped by Richard Thomson, Librarian of the London Institution, he drew on Dibdin; for the technical part he paid especial tribute to John Smith's manual of 1755. In 1824 Johnson was in his late forties. He had been trained as a compositor, in a world of printing that had since much changed, and he found the new developments little to his taste. In devoting far more space proportionately to the history of printing than had been customary in previous manuals, Johnson was doing more than paying obeisance. He was also drawing a contrast between the achievements of the past and what to him was an unwelcome present. The inventions of the steam press and stereotyping were not in themselves to be welcomed, and in his final chapter he mounted his attack:

We allude to the very peculiar and most extraordinary transactions which have taken place in the profession (particularly within the last twenty years) since the partial introduction of the *Stereotype* process; and latterly, that of *Steam* and *Hand Machines* for the purpose of printing, instead of following the old, sure, and beaten track, by means of Presses, which are, unquestionably infinitely superior in every point of view: and we boldly assert, that there are presses now in use, as far superior to the machines, as is the meridian sun's bright rays, when placed within the murky clouds of night.[29]

Johnson found reason to complain concerning not only the quality of work produced but also the effect that these new methods had on employment. Stereotyping meant that there was less work for compositors. But, grumble as he might, he could not stop change. When his book was reviewed in the *Gentleman's Magazine*, it was criticised for its flamboyant typographical design, in particular its 'gingerbread decorations surrounding each page': Johnson took considerable trouble with the ornamental borders on the pages of the large-paper issues. Much more important was the simple fact that the editor thought it worthwhile to review a book on a technical subject. In this way its existence came to the attention of a much larger market but while the first volume was reluctantly tolerated, the second, on technical matters, was panned for its inaccuracies and hostility to recent advances, as well as for its style: 'Thus inverting the telescope of reason, and reducing all objects to the diminutive scale of his own eye, he would arrest all further progress of an art as yet in its infancy.'[30]

Johnson's work marked a change. It was imbued with some of the bibliomaniac preoccupations of early members of the Roxburghe Club, a mood that was already weakening after its first heady days. Apart from his first historical volume, in the second, on technical matters, he included detailed instructions for printers, the topics including typefaces, different languages, composition, the management of printing houses, the parts and use of the press including iron presses, the skills requisite in printing, the work of warehousemen in managing paper, the wages payable for different skills, and lists of printing offices and suppliers in London. In some respects he was more comprehensive than any of his predecessors. While his work found plenty of use among printers, it also found a place in many private libraries, whose owners could choose which format they preferred.

Published a few months later, Thomas Hansard's *Typographia* (1825) also depended much on Stower, and likewise also included a considerable historical section; indeed, this was given precedence over the practical part of the book in the chosen sub-title, *An historical sketch of the origin and progress of printing*. Equally aware of what he called 'great alterations and improvements', Hansard's object was to make his book 'acceptable, generally, to men of letters, and essentially so to members of the art'.[31] Its price was 3 guineas, and it was markedly more up to date than Johnson, whom Hansard in effect superseded. Neither Johnson nor Hansard was reprinted, though (as was customary in this literature) both were drawn on by subsequent writers.

In France, matters took a different turn. In the years since 1790, manuals had appeared frequently: by Martin Boulard (1791), Antoine Momoro (1793), Louis Bertrand-Quinquet (1799), Bonaventure Vincard (1806, 2nd ed. 1823) and Joseph Gillé (2nd ed. 1817). During a period of great changes in the industry, each was quickly overtaken. Then in 1825 appeared a small octavo *Traité de la typographie* by Henri Fournier, including a brief survey of the history of the subject.[32] Born near Tours in 1800, Fournier had only recently ceased his training with the Paris printer Firmin-Didot, and acquired his *brevet d'imprimeur* in 1824. Fournier now printed his own book, and dedicated it to the man who had taught him. No further edition was published until a slightly revised version in 1854, printed not in Paris but in Tours. Unlike the English manuals, it was unillustrated, and it was republished several times, in 1870, 1904 and, by now much revised, as late as 1925. Like another manual by Marcellin-Aimé Brun, also first published in 1825, Fournier's was pirated in Belgium the following year. It was the dominant authority, and its many admirers included the much-respected Paris printer Jules Claye in 1871 even though the two men held diametrically opposed views on type design.[33]

One alternative to the information available in printers' manuals was offered especially by William Chambers and Charles Knight. Both men were prolific publishers, and both sought to make printing cheaper and more widely available. While both lauded the importance of printing, and like Johnson and others before them attributed some aspects of contemporary well-being to its invention and subsequent pursuit, they wrote from limited historical knowledge. In depending on a few already existing summaries, they could offer no fresh approaches, or fresh ways of understanding how early printed books might be more rigorously studied, and better understood.

Their own understanding was grounded on modern practices. As professional printers and publishers they grasped the details of manufacture, and often revelled in the technical changes that were taking place. Johnson might lament some of them, but both the Chambers brothers and Charles Knight exploited stereotyping: the first so that they could print the large numbers required of *Chambers's Edinburgh Journal* in both London and Edinburgh from the same setting of type.[34] Knight later recorded that sales of the *Penny Magazine* reached 200,000 in 1832.[35] Among the earliest subjects to be presented in the *Penny Magazine* (founded in that year) were accounts of printing, of paper-making and of bookbinding.[36] *Chambers's Edinburgh Journal*, founded a little before the *Penny Magazine*, and priced at 1½d., was likewise committed to cheap printing.

Such publications were instrumental in encouraging awareness of the history and significance of printing. Caxton's house (Figure 2) still stood in Westminster. Knight worked enthusiastically to promote knowledge of two heroes in printing, Caxton and Gutenberg. He travelled to Mainz in order to join in the anniversary celebrations of Gutenberg in 1837. He wrote about Caxton most substantially in the first volume of his shilling series *Weekly volumes for all readers* (1844); and he took an active, and critical, part in the debate concerning a possible memorial to Caxton in 1847. But there was little suggestion in his works of the serious study of early printed books more generally. It was mostly a world of penny readings, of mechanics' institutes at best. Even for those of middling wealth, with a modicum of spare cash, there was no hint of collecting as a way of following curiosity, and only a small minority of Knight's readers ventured into the country's older libraries. Antiquarian societies, in London and increasingly across the rest of Britain, answered and encouraged some needs, but they all required

Figure 2 Caxton's reputed house in the Almonry, Westminster. From George Cooke, *Views in London and its vicinity* (1834), after a drawing by Samuel Prout. The building was demolished in 1845. By permission of Laurence Worms.

subscriptions and not all possessed libraries. To be an antiquary involved an interest in old books, but mostly as sources of information, not as objects of study in themselves. For most of the literate population, as distinct from the wealthier parts for whom Dibdin had laid the foundations of taste, the real changes in attitudes, practices and habits that might be described as broadly bibliological came only from the 1850s onwards. They were prompted partly by the development of public libraries, and more particularly by the editorial choices in the ever-increasing numbers of periodicals.

If the commentator 'R.G.' of 1851 in *Notes and Queries* chose his thirty-year limit deliberately, that coincided with the publication of works such as Dibdin's several books, or, in the Netherlands, Abraham de Vries's *Bijdragen tot de geschiedenis der uitvinding van de boekdrukkunst* (Haarlem, 1822), a study dominated by claims that the first printer was Laurens Coster, in Haarlem. De Vries was appointed in charge of Haarlem city library in 1821, and in the 1840s two of his works were published at The Hague in French: *Éclaircissemens sur l'histoire de l'invention de l'imprimerie* (1843) and *Arguments des Allemands en faveur de leur prétention à l'invention de l'imprimerie* (1845). They were not much circulated in England. The supposed anniversary of the invention of printing by Coster was cause for major celebration at Haarlem in 1823, and further fuelled the legends and arguments as to priority.[37] Gutenberg in turn was celebrated in German and French cities in 1837–40, again stimulating arguments that were frequently as much based on local or national pride as on bibliographical or historical evidence: 'In effect, as the Grecian cities contended for the birth of Homer, so do the German cities for that of printing.'[38]

Hain's *Repertorium bibliographicum* was of far greater value. Listing over 16,000 books either printed in, or dated to, the years before 1501, it had appeared in four volumes in 1826–38, and immediately became the standard work of reference for fifteenth-century printed books. A small group of monographs and reference books took matters forward chronologically. William Parr Gresswell's *View of the early Parisian Greek press* (Oxford, 1833) dealt with the Estienne dynasty of printers in the sixteenth century, as well as with much general background to French humanism. Renouard's *Annales de l'imprimerie des Alde*, published originally in 1803–12, was in its third and final edition (1834) and the second edition of his *Annales de l'imprimerie des Estienne* was published in 1843. Wider interests were served with the founding by Charles Nodier in 1834 of the *Bulletin du Bibliophile*, which still thrives. In Belgium, the foundation of a new periodical, the *Bulletin du Bibliophile Belge*, in 1845 encouraged interest in the history of printing, drawing a constant supply of informed scholarship from writers such as Frédéric de Reiffenberg (1795–1850), of the new Bibliothèque Royale de Belgique.[39]

For printing in the British Isles there was little modern work to help. C.H. Timperley's *Dictionary of Printers and Printing* (1839, republished with his *Printers' manual* as *Encyclopaedia of literary and typographical anecdote* in 1842) was very largely derivative, and it was never intended as a major work of analysis. It began life as a lecture delivered to the Warwick and Leamington Literary and Scientific Institution in 1828, and was proposed from the first as a summary of the subject more affordable than the expensive works of Dibdin. From this modest beginning it grew in the second edition to a fat book of over 1,000 pages, dealing with the history of the subject right down to the nineteenth century, and it was a constant source of reference. For the history of illustration, alike in continental Europe and Britain, and again taking the tale down to modern times, more detailed information was available in John Jackson and W.A. Chatto's liberally illustrated *Treatise on wood engraving, historical and practical* (1839).[40]

What if we consider a period beginning half-way through the century, bibliographically? In terms of monographs, and bearing in mind the foundations such as those just mentioned, the 1850s saw a group of French works that all found considerable readerships, and in some cases were of primary importance in establishing new paths in the history of books and printing.

First, in 1851 Ambroise Firmin-Didot produced one of the fullest extended accounts of the history of printing to have been published so far. It appeared initially in volume 26 of the *Encyclopédie moderne* (44 vols., 1846–63), printed by Didot Frères, and was then printed separately, with its own title-page, as *La typographie*. Occupying no fewer than 366 columns of small type, with four accompanying illustrations of modern machinery, it surveyed everything from ancient China to the Applegarth cylinder press installed at *The Times*. Firmin-Didot brought to his subject the technical knowledge of his family firm, and the commitment of a collector of early books and manuscripts. A classicist by training, he traced the origins of the concept of printing to the ancient world, quoting Plutarch, Cicero, Pliny and others, and moved on to the history of playing cards and xylography (woodcut books) before reaching the testimonies of the late fifteenth century by Ulrich Zell and Trithemius. Only then did he reach Gutenberg, where he provided a summary of the documentary evidence from Strasbourg treated by Johann David Schöpflin in 1760.[41] In addressing the claims of Gutenberg, he also considered the remarks by Fournier le jeune in the eighteenth century and Eugène Duverger in the nineteenth. Haarlem and the Coster claims were examined, and rejected. The claims by Mentelin's relatives and supporters were given almost four columns, and consideration was given also to Bamberg. But at the centre stood Gutenberg, Fust and Schoeffer, and not least the colour printing in the 1457 Psalter. Firmin-Didot set particular value on examining books not in facsimile, but in originals, even if his dream of assembling known examples now dispersed among libraries and collectors was not realistic. As a typefounder, he understood the value of minute comparisons, to detect difference, and wear as chronological evidence. Without that, there could only be more or less plausible conjectures. Much of his work was based on earlier well-known authorities, but much more was among less familiar literature.

The greater part of his essay was taken up with the major printers of Italy and the rest of Europe. He found space for the beginning of engraved illustration in England, for the beginning of printing by subscription, for Baskerville, for more recent fine printing, and for some of the work exhibited at the Great Exhibition in June 1851 – a date that provides a *terminus ad quem* for his work. France, naturally, received especial attention, and here Firmin-Didot began with thirteenth-century manuscripts, printing early documents in his support. His chronological account of the following centuries was long, and detailed. Not surprisingly given his earlier work on a new edition of Henri Estienne's Greek thesaurus (1831–), particular notice was paid to the achievements of the Estiennes in the sixteenth century. In treating more recent times, he was detailed in his horrified account of machine-breaking by French printers. For the last century or so, there were many similarities in his choice of topics and of prominent people to the method adopted in and for Britain by Timperley, on whose work Firmin-Didot drew for some of his detail. In his last few pages he turned to the principal French centres outside Paris, before a brief final technical summary; but by then he had expressed his own belief in the proven efficacy of printing. It allowed people to live free from the ignorance and prejudices that characterised war, and in universal concord accompanied by a generous spirit of emulation.

If Firmin-Didot was perhaps over-optimistic in these views, buried midway in the small type of a long discourse, he had nonetheless produced a *tour de force*: not only extensive and detailed but also mingling documentation and quotation from original sources with some highly pertinent opinions on how research on the earliest books should be conducted. In this, he was the forerunner of Blades. His work was not translated.

Two more specialist histories appeared in rapid succession. The first was by Auguste Bernard (1853) on the origin of printing in the West, 'Imprimé par autorisation de l'Empereur à l'Imprimerie Impériale'. The other was a more general one by Paul Dupont (1854), who confessed that his two volumes were less a history than a preparation for such a work, and devoted considerable space also to the trade and to techniques. Both works were advances in their subject.[42] L.-C. Silvestre's album of *Marques typographiques* (1853–67), reproducing hundreds of printers' marks from early books, proved fundamental to the study of an aspect of books that had never hitherto been so consistently, or so widely, applied. In a very different way, and exploring a subject that was so new it hardly existed, Charles Nisard's *Histoire des livres populaires* (1854, 2nd ed. 1864), prompted by political motives, proved influential in bringing people to understand aspects of cheap printing that had never been so well organised or presented.

These books were all French. Britain was producing no such literature. Charles Knight's *The old printer and the modern press* (1854) was at least as much concerned with contemporary political and social issues as it was with the history of printing. Samuel Leigh Sotheby's three-volume *Principia typographica* was not published until 1858, expensive and in a very limited edition.

Three events of 1847 each in its own way marked a significant date in the study and understanding of books, their making, circulation, reading and retention. The death of Thomas Frognall Dibdin signalled the close of an era of a particular kind of bibliophily and bibliographical study; the publication by Augustus De Morgan of *Arithmetical books from the invention of printing to the present time* heralded a new approach, underpinned by bibliographical method, to the historical study of a subject; and the establishing of a Royal Commission on the British Museum led to a report that laid the foundations and expectations of much of the Museum library's subsequent development as a national centre of memory and of humanist scholarship. We return in more detail to each of these later.

Also in 1847 realities were sinking home after several heady months of financial speculation in railways with little or no hope of ever being built. The consequent lost investments brought much misery to people who often had no previous experience of financial risk. A commercial crisis of the same year brought failure for dozens of merchant companies and banks in Britain and, no less importantly for trade, the continent. Several causes were to blame, including a poor harvest in 1846, the ensuing need to import more food than usual, a shortage of cotton, and over-extension of credit overseas. The crisis was by no means past, with failures especially in the East India and American trades, when in February 1848 Louis-Philippe, King of France, abdicated, and the Prime Minister François Guizot resigned. The European uncertainties and political chaos of the following months brought further collapse. In March and April 1848, over forty banks failed in France, Belgium, the Netherlands and Germany.[43]

In 1853, when a group of wealthy bibliophiles gathered to form a new select club, known as the Philobiblon Society,[44] the events of 1848, the year of revolutions, were fresh in people's memories. They affected some members of the society directly, most obviously the duc d'Aumale who was exiled like the rest of the French royal family. Almost twenty years later the Franco-Prussian war of 1870–1, which took Aumale back to France to re-enter French domestic life after his exile in England, brought further turmoil, not only directly in France but also in British attitudes already coloured by the several French governments of the mid-century. Unnerved by the unrest, and seeking stability in England, in December 1870 the Paris bookseller Edwin Tross sent stock for auction in London.[45] Another bookseller, Antoine Bachelin, publisher of *Le Bibliophile Illustré*, did the same the following July. In France, legislation restricting printers was eased.

With some obvious exceptions, ordinary financial and commercial events did not necessarily have an immediate impact on most of the world of the book trades whether new or second-hand. Nor did they necessarily affect confidence in this sphere. The book trades were helped fundamentally by successive reductions in postal charges, including a flat rate of sixpence a pound for parcels at the end of the 1840s and the introduction of the halfpenny postcard in 1870–1. They depended on customers, but often assumed very long periods of credit.

Bibliomania

For many people there was a further, and longer-term, challenge. Were there too many books? The same question had been asked ever since at least the sixteenth century.[46] To nineteenth-century educationists, set on extending literacy and the promotion of reading as the means to improvement, this perhaps seemed an inadequately framed question. Everything depended on the nature of what was being considered, in a world where cheap, misleading and unwholesome publishing was a matter of widespread concern in political, educational, religious and medical circles alike.

Nor was the question applicable only to what has been termed the undergrowth of literature. It also applied to survivals from the past as well as to the present.

Qualities of difference applied as much to older materials as to that hot off the press. The figure of the uncritical bibliomaniac had been recognised and satirised in print in the fifteenth century, and he (it was usually male) became a familiar figure, of fun or of despair. Booksellers, readers, collectors and commentators in the seventeenth and eighteenth centuries were ever more self-aware, as the quantity of printed matter increased and as criteria were established to determine the desirability of some kinds of books over others. The bibliomaniac was unable to distinguish. Like many others, the French Hebraist Nicolas Barat (d.1706) was alert to the dangers: 'La Bibliomanie, ou la passion d'avoir un grand nombre de livres, est une maladie commune à bien des gens, surtout en France.'[47] While he considered it an especially French malady, certainly the word did not come into familiar use in England until after his death. 'Beware of the bibliomanie', Lord Chesterfield warned his son in 1750.[48]

In the nineteenth century, Jean Baptiste Félix Descuret based his more detailed remarks on his observations as a physician:

Gardons nous de confondre avec les bibliomanes ces hommes doués d'esprit et de goût qui n'ont des livres que pour s'instruire, que pour se délasser, et qu'on a décorés du nom de bibliophiles ... Le bibliophile devient souvent bibliomane quand son esprit décroît, ou quand sa fortune augmente ... Le bibliophile possède des livres, et le bibliomane en est possédé.[49]

In 1809 Dibdin wrote at more length, in his *Bibliomania, or book madness*, addressing his book to one of the most prominent of all sufferers, Richard Heber.[50] No one chronicled what was widely acknowledged to be an age of bibliomania better or more enthusiastically than Dibdin. The foundation of the Roxburghe Club in 1812 epitomised the phenomenon among a select group of wealthy individuals. Dibdin, an original member, was at its centre. In his much-reduced last years, and after his death in 1847, his daughter Sophia reflected several times on the demise of the animated pleasures that members had found in their collecting activities. To her, deeply attached as she was to her father, the change in mood coincided with his retirement from the scene. Dibdin resigned from the club in 1843, having dedicated the 1842 edition of his *Bibliomania* to the Earl of Powis, as its president. Powis's death in 1848, which put an end to hopes she had of some financial support from the club, was all the more of a blow.

In the Advertisement to the 1842 edition of *Bibliomania*, Dibdin summarised some of the more obvious reasons for what he perceived as a change in the national mood:

I apprehend the general apathy of Bibliomaniacs to be in great measure attributable to the vast influx of Books, of every description, from the Continent – owing to the long continuance of peace; and yet, in the appearance of what are called English Rarities, the market seems to be almost as barren as ever. The wounds, inflicted in the Heberian contest, have gradually healed, and are subsiding into forgetfulness.[51]

In alluding to 'Heberian' wounds he had in mind the series of auction sales, conducted mostly in London but also in Ghent and Paris, of the library of Richard Heber. It was uncertain how many books Heber had accumulated in England and abroad: Dibdin speculated more than 164,000 volumes.[52] Such a wealth, released into the market within the space of little more than three years, was a mixed blessing. In Paris, his nearest equivalent was the lawyer and prolific translator Antoine-Marie-Henri Boulard (1754–1825), characterised and caricatured as a quite exceptional bibliomaniac, whose books were sold in 1828–34. He was thought to have possessed half a million books.[53]

Short of money, and ill for several years, Dibdin suffered a stroke in 1845. In a prospectus for his *Reminiscences*, circulated in 1834, the proposed work was described as 'probably the last of its author'.[54] Then two years later, when it was published, in the preface he referred to 'circumstances which have suddenly come upon me as in the hour of darkness and difficulty'.[55] In fact his *Bibliographical tour of the northern counties of England and in Scotland* had still to come. Though dated 1838, it was not published until 1839;[56] and it concluded with a further remark about his plight, 'the long hours of a painful illness' on his return from his northern excursion.[57] This indeed proved to be his last major work.[58]

His death aged seventy-one, on 18 November 1847, was widely reported, usually in identical wording: 'after a long illness of paralysis on the brain'. The notices in the East Anglian papers were to be expected, as he had been an incumbent of Exning in Suffolk, while as a member of St John's College it was natural for *Jackson's Oxford Journal* to carry a notice. There were also notices in Liverpool and Scottish papers, as well as in *The Times* and in *John Bull*. There were few obituaries. The longest, in the *Gentleman's Magazine*, was highly critical of the inaccuracies in his writings, and misprints in his *Reminiscences*.[59] The notice was adapted and printed at length in the Leipzig journal *Serapeum*.[60] In France, the *Bulletin du Bibliophile* reported his death promptly, but regretted the disorganisation that marred so much of his work, and it could not avoid mentioning the affronts felt by several people whom he mentioned in his account of his travels in that country.[61] In Brussels, the *Bibliophile Belge* recalled his visit in 1842, the support given to him by the prominent book collector and diplomat Sylvain van de Weyer, and the dinner celebrating the occasion. His work, however, remained generally little referred to on the continent,[62] and his reputation remained a mixed one. When in 1868 – two decades after his death – Gustave Brunet published an assessment in *Le Bibliophile Français*, he was cautious about much of his work, and Dibdin's remarks on French matters still rankled.[63]

Sometimes lavish in their production, and adorned with illustrations, most of Dibdin's major bibliographical works defied reappearance. His uncompleted revision of Joseph Ames's *Typographical antiquities* (1810–16, not reprinted) was found untrustworthy. His youthful handbook, *An introduction to the knowledge of rare and valuable editions of the Greek and Roman classics* (1802), revised and enlarged in 1804 and 1808, then rewritten in 1827, was not republished thereafter. His *Library companion* (1824), much criticised and even ridiculed, was not published again after he had revised it in 1825. *Bibliomania* (1809) proved more successful, enlarged in 1811 and then further extended and improved in 1842. With the exception of the *Tour of the northern counties*, the last ten years of his life had seen only minor new pieces, such as sermons and notices of courses of lectures. He was no longer essential reading. Many of his books sold slowly. In 1848, the year after his death, the bookseller Henry G. Bohn's catalogue recorded his books' decline in the clearest possible way: in prices. While extra-illustrated copies, copies with special plates, copies on large paper and copies in expensive bindings all held their prices, ordinary copies were to be had substantially cheaper than originally. *Bibliomania* (1842) was offered at half its original price. His edition of Ames, published at 14 guineas, was offered at 6.[64]

Bibliomania was simultaneously to be wondered at, and feared. While England produced the internationally celebrated examples of Heber in printed books, and Sir Thomas Phillipps in manuscripts,[65] French writers seemed especially aware, even nervous. In what was for many years a standard manual on librarianship in France, 'L.A. Constantin' sought to present a balanced view, but he was nonetheless critical.[66] The concern persisted, and in 1862 the liberal journalist Edmond Texier remarked:

La bibliomanie est, à mon avis, une des plus dangéreuses, et la plus despotique, parce qu'elle n'est jamais satisfaite. . . . Le vrai bibliomane croit, comme Alexandre, que rien n'est fait tant qu'il reste quelque chose à faire, qu'il possède peu de chose tant qu'il peut envier les trésors d'un autre.[67]

The Paris reprint in 1865 of the short anonymous book *De la bibliomanie*, originally published with a fictitious imprint in 1761, thus touched a contemporary chord. In his preface to the new edition, Paul Chéron, librarian and miscellaneous writer, had no need to dwell over-long on themes that seemed all too modern.[68] Bibliomania required neither great wealth nor knowledge. It stood at an extreme, and it ignored some of the most critical aspects of those who used, sold, collected, organised and studied books for more particular and better defined reasons. Moreover, as bibliophile enthusiasm failed to keep pace with bibliographic knowledge, bibliomania persisted as a malaise. In 1878, the twenty-seven-year-old Octave Uzanne assembled a group of his mostly lightweight essays, and remarked 'Aujord'hui, malheureusement, Bibliophile et Biblomane sont presque synonymes.'[69] For John Ruskin, in such a world the status of books did not always seem obvious:

I say first we have despised literature. What do we, as a nation, care about books? How much do you think we spend altogether on our libraries, public or private, as compared with what we spend on our horses? If a man spends lavishly on his library, you call him mad – a bibliomaniac. But you never call any one a horse-maniac, though men ruin themselves every day by their horses, and you do not hear of people ruining themselves by their books. Or, to go lower still, how much do you think the contents of the book-shelves of the United Kingdom, public and private, would fetch, as compared with the contents of its wine-cellars?[70]

Like others, it was easy for him not to be optimistic. Much less well understood or noticed is the revolution that took place during this same period in the study of the history of books and printing, and with it practices and policies respecting the care and use of books ancient and modern, that brought permanent changes in national outlooks and practices concerning value and access.

3 | Books in Abundance

How many books existed by the beginning of Queen Victoria's reign in 1837? How many new titles and new editions were published each year? In Britain? In France? Elsewhere overseas? No one knew the answers to such questions, and there was no way of discovering them.[1] For books published in the past, in 1838 staff at the British Museum, the largest library in the country, counted the number of volumes in the collection, and arrived at 235,000. Antonio Panizzi and his colleagues knew that this was only a tiny representation of almost four centuries of the world's printing. In 1845 the young American bookseller Henry Stevens provided a list of 10,000 American books not in the library,[2] and in the same year Panizzi assembled a report making an impassioned plea for more money so as to make up deficiencies across all disciplines and regions of the world. The Trustees presented it to the Treasury and were awarded an annual grant of £10,000 for the purchase of both new and old books.[3] It was a help, but it was not a sufficient answer for Panizzi.

Purchases on the whole were for works published overseas. The deposit provisions in the new Copyright Act of 1842 were designed to improve the collection of books published in Britain, and they also introduced a requirement for books published in British possessions overseas likewise to be deposited in the Museum. The latter met with very limited success.[4] For domestic publications, the process of collecting copyright deposit copies for the Museum was simplified by taking the duty away from Stationers' Hall, which had been at least partially responsible over many generations, and centring it firmly on Bloomsbury.[5] Numbers of volumes improved, but not dramatically.

By 1849 it was estimated that the Library contained 435,000 volumes thanks to purchases, deposits and gifts. Thomas Grenville's bequest of 1846 brought 20,240 volumes.[6] If Panizzi remained impatient to grow the library collections, and made good use of the increased purchase grant, there still remained a glaring challenge.

Total figures gave only the most approximate of guides. They depended not least on different ways of counting, sometimes of volumes or of titles, sometimes of books or sets of books. With some adjustments they have remained a standard approach to measuring libraries even into our own times, despite the advent of large commercial collections of books in microform, the invention of 'volume equivalents' and most recently the advent of online provision not just to purchased sets of works but also to universal access and to time-limited access by subscription.[7] As a guide to size, numbers can now be near meaningless without appropriate definition. For the nineteenth century, obsessed with statistics for all manner of management and social and personal improvement, numbers were of critical interest.[8] Professionals and amateurs alike compared libraries; they compared cities; and they compared countries. Yet numbers could differ dramatically even for the same library. In 1848, Edward Edwards, then on the staff of the Museum, stated that the British Museum contained 350,000 volumes,[9] while as just mentioned, only the next year an official estimate was 435,000.

Figures varied; but one thing was clear. The national library was nowhere near as large as its most obvious rival, in Paris, which had seen a 40 per cent increase in its funding between 1825 and 1842.[10] A figure obtained by the British Ambassador concerning the Bibliothèque Royale (Impériale) in 1850 suggested that there were 700,000 volumes and 500,000 *pièces en brochures*.[11] In 1847 it had been reported that the library contained 500,000 volumes,[12] and in evidence to the Select Committee on Public Libraries in 1849 Edward Edwards stated that the figure was 824,000 volumes. He added that the royal library in Berlin contained 480,000 volumes, and the royal library at Munich 600,000.[13] A few years later he stated that Berlin contained more than 500,000 volumes.[14] St Petersburg was said to be only slightly smaller, with an estimated 446,000 volumes thanks to Russia's having in 1795 seized from Poland the library assembled by the Zaluski brothers in the eighteenth century.[15] Edwards was considered an expert, as the author of *A statistical review of the principal public libraries of Europe and America*, but even his figures sometimes varied between what he published here, in 1848, and what he provided to the Public Libraries Commission a few months later.

If Edwards's figures, the widest-ranging survey we have, need to be treated with some caution, and much was clearly guesswork or at best rough estimates, the comparative totals that he offers do provide some indication of the relative sizes of the libraries concerned.

When Edwards calculated the number of books in the national and other largest libraries, added them into local or other totals and then set them beside the sizes of populations, he arrived at figures holding very little meaning. It was scarcely any use to learn that, according to his calculations, in Great Britain and Ireland there were just 43 volumes to each 100 inhabitants, compared with 80 in Russia, 125 in France, 268 in Tuscany and 2,353 in Brunswick. The figures for cities were no more helpful: 803 volumes per 100 inhabitants in Weimar, 6,750 in Munich, 143 in Paris and so forth. The only point he wished to make, based on these figures, was that Britain lagged seriously behind: London with just 20 volumes per hundred inhabitants. The numbers, applied to make a well-meaning social point, were based on irrelevantly applied and incomplete evidence. Quite apart from questions of access, the considerable collections accumulated in Munich from local ecclesiastical and other libraries included quantities of duplicates of early books, while ducal collections augmented with private libraries characterised other parts of Germany. They were scarcely applicable to modern questions of social well-being.

Beyond library walls, the trade's management of new books was undergoing a transformation, albeit one that remained imperfect. Volumes of the *London catalogue* had been issued periodically since the end of the eighteenth century, listing new and recent publications. In 1837 the bookseller Sampson Low founded the *Publisher's Circular*, providing a weekly list of new books and replacing the older *Monthly Literary Advertiser*, founded in 1805 by another bookseller, William Bent. *The Bookseller* followed in 1858. All these were trade publications, designed more to help booksellers and publishers than librarians or private readers. All were manifestly incomplete, weak especially on smaller publishers, on most pamphlet literature, and the book trade outside London. Basing himself solely on Sampson Low's *British catalogue*, the economist J.R. McCulloch noted that in 1849–52 an annual average of 2,796 new works were published, and 903 reprints, compared with an average of 2,149 and 755 in each category for a period of four years a decade earlier.[16] In 1844 Charles Knight was especially interested in the numbers of periodical issues. He noted that in this year there were about sixty weekly periodicals issued in London alone, and he estimated that there were about fifteen million copies printed annually just of the more important journals. Incomplete as it was, this suggested an overall figure far in excess of books.[17]

Britain was bibliographically better served in this respect than other countries. The political divisions of Germany, and specifically the variable arrangements for legal deposit in different regions, meant that the enumerative works of Wilhelm Heinsius, Christian Gottlob Kayser and Johann Conrad Hinrichs in Leipzig could never be adequate for a publishing industry larger than anywhere else. The *Börsenblatt für den Deutschen Buchhandel* (1834–) presented a mixture of listings with articles about the trade. In France, the strong eighteenth-century bibliographical tradition characterised in the work of Gabriel Martin, Jean-Baptiste Osmont, Guillaume-François Debure and others formed the background to the *Bibliographie de la France*, published from 1811 onwards. But this was selective in its listings, and weak on publications alike in Paris and in places remote from the capital.[18] In the Netherlands a group of booksellers in 1833 organised a regular *Nieuwsblad voor de Boekhandel*, which in turn became Brinkman's *Cumulative catalogus* from 1846. These and other collaborative projects, all responding to the changes in the book trade, literacy and government since the Napoleonic era, spoke to the same need, and the same questions. What was published, and by whom? The questions faced booksellers, and they faced others who were interested in what in 1827 the Comte Daru called a *statistique intellectuelle*.[19]

This was the bibliographical environment of new publications in which older ones survived. In the 1830s, books from the sixteenth and seventeenth centuries could be purchased cheaply, provided some obvious authors and genres were avoided – notably a few names in English literature, many books printed in black letter, and ambitious illustrated books. Later incunabula, from the 1490s, could be found for a few shillings. Eighteenth-century books were commonplace, part of ordinary stock-in-trade. A combination of developments meant that the second-hand trade was awash as never before. In Britain, on the very crudest of calculations the output from publishers more than doubled between the mid-1770s and the mid-1790s, partly as a result of the legal confirmation in 1774 of limited terms of copyright, which thus removed restrictions on printing older authors. Much of this increase was among books in smaller formats, octavo and duodecimo.[20] As second-hand books they were unavoidable within a generation. Abroad, the flood of books released into continental and British markets following the dispersal of Jesuit libraries consequent on the closing of the order in 1773, the secularisation or suppression of monasteries in Germany and Italy, and the abundance of books coming into the market in revolutionary and post-revolutionary France, all contributed to a copiously supplied world. To these were added the even greater flood of more recent books, many printed for audiences for whom low prices were of paramount importance, and manufactured on steam printing presses, on machine-made paper and in mass-produced bindings.[21]

Manufacture: Printing, Paper and Type

As a part of widespread fascination with all kinds of manufacturing processes in an industrialised world, one consequence of this unprecedented abundance, where books were omnipresent if not necessarily owned in quantity, was a general interest in their fabrication and in their history.

Books lasted longer than other forms of print; they could be organised on shelves; and they could be organised by price. But books, newspapers and the rest depended on the inventions of printing and of paper. The invention of printing had been much developed and extended since the fifteenth century, and modern methods, many of them transformative, held their particular interest, especially in a period that was preoccupied with inventions of all kinds. Printing was celebrated in popular books about inventions and discoveries, often given pride of place, at the beginning. The early heroes of what had developed into an extensive, powerful and influential industry, people such as Johann Gutenberg, William Caxton, Nicolas Jenson and Aldus Manutius, were internationally lauded. In the words of one much-circulated opinion intended for popular consumption, letterpress printing 'may undoubtedly be esteemed the greatest of all human inventions'.[22] In speeches from the rostrum and sermons from the pulpit, printing was celebrated as the means of political, social and religious enlightenment. For some, Caxton's introduction of printing to England was second only to the coming of Christianity.[23] The sentiment was not restricted to Westminster, for in the more secular surroundings of Paris the retired bookseller Edmond Werdet referred similarly to the invention of printing more generally: 'la découverte de l'Imprimerie, cette *seconde déliverance de l'Homme*'.[24]

Paper, 'that most commodious, portable, and invaluable substance, which preserves and transmits *thought* through succeeding centuries, and to remote countries',[25] offered further attractions, not only as an invention but also as the application of natural products to industrial use. The development of machine-made paper during the century for an ever-expanding list of new needs and purposes, domestic, commercial or industrial, has been less studied than has the succession of inventions in printing, but it was hardly less important.[26] In 1855, Richard Herring (1829–86), a paper agent and wholesale stationer in London, drew together his lectures given in 1853 at the London Institution on *Paper & paper making, ancient and modern*. Published by Longman, and short as it was, it was the fullest book in English thus far. By 1863 it was in its third edition. Herring arranged for an introduction by the incumbent of his parish, the Rev. George Croly, whose preaching in the City of London each Sunday attracted a large following: as a miscellaneous author and minor poet, Croly was prominent, well used to writing on a variety of subjects, and in 1840 had contributed the historical and descriptive notes to David Roberts's *Holy Land*. His interest in paper-making had been fired when he and Herring visited Whatman's Turkey Mill in Kent.[27] After remarks on early printing, with the cacophony of European events of 1848 fresh in his mind, Croly turned in particular to newspapers, 'the most influential of all human works', 'an intellectual railroad, given to our era, to meet the increased exigencies of intellectual intercourse'. In his opinion, the press ventilated away ill humours and saved England from political catastrophe.[28]

Croly was no historian, whether of Gutenberg or of the contributions of continental printers of newspapers, pamphlets and placards to political movements associated with 1848; but this was the context in which Herring's book was presented, where paper was key in the partnership between social and religious well-being. In this respect, and regardless of political or religious persuasions, the sentiments were akin to those of others who saw public salvation in the advent of print, and now its modern applications.

Herring's own work began with an account of the development of early writing surfaces, preceding the invention of paper. From this he moved on to the work of James Whatman in the eighteenth century, and to the invention of machine-made paper. The death in 1854 of Henri Fourdrinier, a key figure in its development, in his late eighties and 'comparatively a beggar', stood in marked contrast to the honour accorded to the memory of Caxton. Yet without paper, large-scale printing would be impossible. Herring's second chapter was almost wholly taken up with a technical account of the paper-making machine, before he turned to the application and history of watermarks. In his third he was much concerned with duties and taxes on paper, before in his final pages addressing the development of wallpaper. His professional employment as a paper supplier contributed to the more technical aspects of his book: the myriad different sizes of sheets, the chemistry of paper, and the advantages and disadvantages of the materials from which it could be made. At the end of his book he included thirty specimens, many of them alluded to in the text. They were but a tiny representation of the grades, sizes, colours and weights of paper available.

As public lectures at the London Institution, the purpose was to share knowledge. Yet, Herring reflected, 'it is not at all improbable that many into whose hands this book may fall will be disposed to charge me with ... concealing secrets connected with paper making'.[29] He warned his audience of the dangers of misunderstanding the chemicals used in manufacture: that paper could rapidly deteriorate, and fracture within a very short time, and that the reward for the pursuit of cheapness was self-destruction. There was nothing new in this. He reminded his readers of Thomas Hansard in 1825, who had written, 'Whole piles of quire-stock are already crumbling to dust in the warehouses of booksellers, never to come to light as books: and many a volume designed to enrich the library of its possessor, and to descend as an heir-loom to posterity, now presents to the mortified owner its elegant print surrounded by a margin of tan colour.'[30] Writing always in a manner accessible to amateurs, those who had no previous knowledge of the subject, Herring offered as much a corrective and reminder as a professional handbook.

Within a very short time he was taken to task not for his notes on industrial processes but for his inadequate understanding of the history of watermarks. Samuel Leigh Sotheby, whose three-volume *Principia typographica*, based on his father's work, was finally published in 1858, owned a large collection of examples.[31] On the basis of this, joined to an examination of fifteenth-century block-books, Sotheby was able to offer not just many times more than Herring's single plate of reproductions but also some basic observations on links between manufacture and (to a rather lesser extent) dates. Much of his information was misplaced, and much of it was based on very approximate comparisons, but it offered a more orderly summary than anything that had appeared hitherto. In the following decade, Étienne Midoux and Auguste Matton, an archivist, appealed for a more precise study of watermarks, drawing on dated or datable examples from French archives, and they offered six hundred reproductions.[32] There was to be no comparably detailed examination or analysis of watermarks until the authoritative work of C.M. Briquet at the end of the century.[33] Meanwhile there was much confusion in how their study might relate to where books were printed, and little understanding of the trade's structures. While in 1878 Tibulle Desbarreaux-Bernard gave several pages to the study of watermarks in his long introduction to the catalogue of the incunabula at Toulouse, the matter remained undeveloped.[34]

Links between the past and the present were nowhere more obvious than in developments in type design, where archaism met contemporary ideas. Typefounders always, to a greater or lesser degree, build on the work of their predecessors, if sometimes in deliberate contrast. This historical consciousness was apparent in the efflorescence of so-called Elzevir faces in the eighteenth and nineteenth centuries and in the imitation of Caslon's eighteenth-century work by the mid-nineteenth-century founders Miller and Richard.[35] But little notice had been taken by modern typefounders of most of the earliest types, from the fifteenth century. Nicolas Jenson, in Venice, was an exception, lauded among others by Philip Luckombe in 1771, by Dibdin in 1817, and by C.H. Timperley in 1839.[36] Henry Noel Humphreys wrote of Jenson's types being 'more perfect in form than those of any previous printer'.[37] They were not, however, the first choice among the few people interested in reviving the earliest types. At the Chiswick Press, some work was done for Charles Whittingham in a roman face cut in the 1850s by William Howard modelled on one used by Johann Froben at Basel: William Morris was among those whose work was printed in what became known as Basel.[38] A facsimile of one of William Caxton's types was also cut for the Chiswick Press, and seems to have been used mostly in printing facsimile leaves to make up imperfect copies for the antiquarian book trade.[39] The early Venetian face associated principally with Jenson was only revived when Morris worked with Emery Walker and the punch-cutter Edward Philip Prince to create his Golden type for the Kelmscott Press in 1890–2.[40]

Few commercial British publishers were as instrumental in directing attention to the typographical past as was Alphonse Lemerre in Paris.[41] *Le livre du bibliophile* (1874), a pamphlet of only about fifty small pages, was written mostly by Anatole France, who was employed by Lemerre in various editorial capacities. Lemerre had taken over a shop in the Passage Choiseul between the rue des Petits-Champs and the rue Saint-Augustin in 1862, and with the help of money brought by his wife developed an influential publishing business. His premises attracted a group of self-conscious avant-garde poets who became known as Parnassiens. Verlaine's first book was published there in 1864, and a lively trio of books *Le Parnasse contemporain* appeared in 1866–76. Alongside this, Lemerre launched several series devoted to earlier writers, especially of the sixteenth century such as Ronsard and Du Bellay. In accordance with French biblio-phile expectations, he had his books printed on various qualities and colours of paper including *papier d'Hollande*, Whatman, *papier de Chine*, and *papier vélin teinté*. In 1868 he launched a *Petite Bibliothèque Littéraire*, small-format books emulating the Elzevir publications of the seventeenth century. He had these printed by Jules Claye, with ornaments in a renaissance style.

His books' appearance was important to Lemerre, both in their small formats and in his search for typographic appropriateness. Claye had obtained a supply of the type inspired by the Elzevirs used by the printer Louis Perrin at Lyon for his own work, and in the 1870s managed to obtain the punches and matrices as well: they were bought by Lemerre himself in

1880.[42] Claye's equipment, and his ability to print with the so-called Elzevir types, made him a natural choice:

Ces caractères, fort beaux en eux-mêmes, nous donnent, pour le cas qui nous occupe principalement, c'est-à-dire pour la réimpression des vieux écrivains, l'avantage d'un archaïsme en harmonie avec les textes. Leur emploi dans cette circonstance concourt à produire cet effet de couleur locale si justement recherché de nos jours.[43]

As France and Lemerre pointed out, the term *Elzévirien* was not a precise one, but was applied to a variety of typefaces from the sixteenth, seventeenth and even eighteenth centuries. Antiquarian interests had unearthed some examples, including an incomplete set of early punches and matrices discovered by Perrin in the Lyonnais typefounder Rey. Meanwhile in Paris, Pierre Jannet produced his own version, while the best of the contemporary revivals were by Théophile Beaudoire from the Fonderie Générale (1858) and from the Fonderie Deberny.[44]

The search for these old-faced types coincided with the revived interest in Caslon's types in England. In Lemerre's hands it became something more than a circumscribed interest restricted to a few publications. He sought what he considered typographical appropriateness for a considerable range of earlier texts, which enjoyed substantial sales. The first edition of *Le livre du bibliophile* was printed by Claye on a hand-press, the hundred copies issued on various papers as well as on parchment and thus focused on one aspect of the bibliophile market.[45] A commercial edition followed in the same year, machine-printed and with no limitation: this in turn was reprinted in a slightly revised form. Unlike Édouard Rouveyre's later *Connaissances nécessaires à un bibliophile* (1877, etc.), it was not concerned with the enumeration of early editions, or many of the practicalities of their care. Instead, and much more briefly, it set out to present 'les conditions que doit, à notre avis, nécessairement remplir une édition pour être digne d'estime', focusing in particular on editions of earlier writers.

Lemerre's attention to earlier texts in his other publications was evident in the contents of this book. To a generation increasingly aware of textual differences between older and modern editions of medieval and renaissance texts, he offered a summary reminder, both in his publications and, now, with brief examples, in *Le livre du bibliophile*. His work coincided with the philological preoccupations reflected in newly organised disciplines in journals devoted to the study of medieval and renaissance literature. In 1866 Paul Meyer (then in the Département des Manuscrits in the Bibliothèque Nationale), Charles Morel and Hermann Zotenberg founded the *Revue d'Histoire et de Littérature*, and in 1872 Meyer joined with Gaston Paris to found the international language journal *Romania*.[46] Meyer was a frequent visitor to Britain in search of early French manuscripts, and besides developing friendships there were many shared linguistic and literary interests. The parallel in England was the Early English Text Society, founded in 1864 by F.J. Furnivall, W.W.Skeat and Richard Morris, though it made no pretence to typographical distinction.

New Attitudes

Numerically, visually, geographically, chronologically and technically, this was the bibliographical background to a profound change in the ways that older books were valued and studied. The shifts were at least twofold.

First, and more obviously, for collectors there was a shift away from the overriding concerns of older generations for the earliest editions of classical texts, epitomised in the work of printers such as Aldus Manutius in Venice but also in the early presses of the Rhine valley, of Rome, Lyon and Paris. The textual and philological foundations of classical authors represented by the earliest printers remained of critical importance to modern scholarship, while bibliophile interests developed an increasingly varied momentum elsewhere. A similar shift towards diversity occurred in the textual and bibliophilic treatment of more recent and modern literature. In this, Shakespeare remained as always to the fore, making headlines in the newspapers not only with theatrical performances. The shift resonated bibliographically in editions of Shakespeare, including facsimiles of the early quartos and of the First Folio (1623),[47] and in newspaper reports of prices fetched at sales. Illustrated editions proliferated.[48] Readers were asked to study prices in relation not simply to rarity but also to the condition of copies: books were characterised by their imperfections. Prices went inexorably up, and the best copies rose most of all.[49] Yet, while Shakespeare dominated the English-speaking world, he did not monopolise it.

Second, while the vastly increased presence of older books did not, and could not, in itself make obvious what might be of importance in amending or adjusting the history of the printed book and its influence, it did prompt a growing critical awareness of the extent of what had gone before. The great retrospective bibliographies of the first half of the nineteenth century, by Brunet, Ebert, Lowndes, Watts, Quérard and others, and the determination on the part of national libraries especially in Britain and France to gather in as much as possible, brought also further challenges. How was this mounting bibliographical tradition to be treated, not just *in toto* but also *in parvo*, the analytical study of early books and printers, even of individual books? The change in attitude happened within little more than a generation. Much of this work was pursued by people on the staff of major libraries: most prominently and influentially by Henry Bradshaw (1831–86) at Cambridge, by Léopold Delisle (1826–1910) at Paris, by J.W. Holtrop (1806–70) and his successor M.F.A.G. Campbell (1819–90) at The Hague. In London, William Blades, a printer, and Talbot Baines Reed, a typefounder, brought their professional knowledge to the study of the history of printing. Alongside them, and following in the wake of men such as Guillaume-François Debure (1731–82) and Antoine-Augustin Renouard (1765–1853), there developed a tradition of scholarly bookselling, exemplified in the work of Bernard Quaritch (1819–99) in London, Jacques-Joseph Techener (1802–73)[50] and Anatole Claudin (1833–1906) in Paris,[51] and Frederik Muller (1817–81) in Amsterdam.[52]

These phenomena, namely changes in collecting preoccupations, the analytical study of early books and printers, and the traditions of scholarly bookselling, are addressed later in this book.

4 | Celebrating Print

Early printers in Europe became an ever more prominent focus of public celebration. In 1823, Haarlem celebrated Laurens Coster as the first. In confirmation of continuing faith in his priority, a fresh statue of him by Louis Royer was erected in the marketplace in 1856 (Figure 3): it was reproduced that year on a widely circulated medal as the town and his supporters also celebrated him that year on stage and in song.[1] The coincidence of the celebrations with the publication of Holtrop's landmark catalogue of the incunables at The Hague was inescapable. Coster remained at the centre of Dutch claims to the invention of printing in Europe, extolled abroad as well as at home and we return to him further later.[2] In 1837 Mainz celebrated Gutenberg, marking the occasion with a statue by Bertel Thorvaldsen. Following established conventions for centennial observations dating from the seventeenth century, the year 1840 brought a flurry of Gutenberg celebrations, in Mainz, Leipzig, Dresden, Frankfurt, Vienna, Zurich and other towns and cities of German-speaking Europe.[3] Strasbourg, part of France, celebrated him amidst noisy popular rejoicings by erecting a statue by David d'Angers in Place Gutenberg (Figure 4).[4]

Two years later, anxious to maintain another's claim to be the inventor, nearby Sélestat erected a bust of their own local hero Johann Mentelin by Anne-Catherine Sichler-Valastre, and added an inscription, 'Mentel de Schlestadt inventeur de l'imprimerie'. At Frankfurt, Gutenberg was later joined by Fust and Schoeffer in an elaborate monument erected in 1858 in the Rossmarkt in the city centre: a further series of fourteen extra portrait heads of printers on the monument included William Caxton and Aldus Manutius. Of more recent heroes, Giambattista Bodoni (1740–1813) was commemorated in his lifetime with a medal engraved at the behest of the Parma magistrates,[5] and posthumously in 1872 with a statue by Gabriele Ambrosio at his birthplace, Saluzzo in Piedmont. There, the occasion was marked by the publication of a new celebratory biography by Jacopo Bernardi, dedicated to Vittorio Emanuele II, King of Italy. Whether in Piedmont, Sélestat, Strasbourg or elsewhere, and for various reasons, printing and politics were as inseparable as they had been for centuries. At Strasbourg, Gutenberg faced the cathedral not in alliance, but quite

Figure 3 Laurens Janszoon Coster. Commemorative medal issued in 1856. From William Blades, *The pentateuch of printing* (1891).

possibly more subtly in competition, perhaps recalling a scene in Victor Hugo's *Notre Dame de Paris* (1831), a novel much admired by D'Angers: 'Ceci tuera cela', the power of print will overcome the power of the church.[6]

William Caxton

In England, by far the most important name was William Caxton, long celebrated in popular and scholarly literature alike. But when did he begin to print in Westminster? Was he the first in England? The answer to the first question was not clear, and that to the second question was obscured. In the seventeenth century a politically motivated royalist named Richard Atkyns had credited the beginning of printing in England to one Frederick Corsellis, who was lured to England from Haarlem and then established at Oxford.[7] One difficulty was that no one could find the document Atkyns claimed to have identified in Lambeth Palace Library to support this account. Atkyns's purpose was to demonstrate that printing had long been exercised under royal prerogative, but he was on treacherous bibliographical and historical ground.[8] For Oxford, a book dated 1468 seemed to prove that a printer was at work there by then. In 1812 a slim publication by S.W. Singer, bookseller and literary antiquary, sought to confirm this, and to

Figure 4 Statue of Gutenberg by David d'Angers, erected at Strasbourg in 1840. From the *Magasin Pittoresque*, July 1840.

deny what had long since been demonstrated in 1735, by the Cambridge scholar Conyers Middleton, to be a misprint for 1478. For most people, Middleton's study left no room for doubt as to Caxton's priority.[9] Singer himself later admitted his error.[10]

The dating of Caxton's first work in England presented further differences. When a memorial to him was installed in St Margaret's church, Westminster, by the Roxburghe Club in 1820, the inscription (probably composed by Dibdin) was suitably cautious, with a comma. He was supposed to have introduced printing to England in 'A.D. 1477, or earlier'. Previous authorities had said 1474.[11] The question of how further to celebrate him was resurrected in 1847, with a suggestion by Henry Hart Milman that a fountain should commemorate him, perhaps illuminated at night. The example of Roman fountains came to mind. It did not suit everyone. Charles Knight, one of the most knowledgeable people in the country concerning Caxton's life, was adamant that a statue was needed, not a monument that might refer to many other blessings beside the art of printing:

We did not illustrate the memory of an orator by symbols of oratory, nor of a general by trophies of war. We wanted to show posterity what manner of man he was. The Germans had erected at Mayence a monument to Gutenberg. It was a bronze statue with bas-reliefs on the pedestal – not symbolical, but descriptive of his art.[12]

The creation of Victoria Street, running from Victoria station to Westminster Abbey, offered another opportunity, and in 1851 Milman suggested a proper statue in cast iron in front of the Abbey, but despite popular support, and an offer from the Coalbrookdale Iron Company, it came to nothing.[13] Another fruitless suggestion was that there should be an elaborate edition of many of Caxton's own writings. The debate, kept alive by Beriah Botfield, continued through 1851 and into 1852 in the pages of *Notes and Queries*. It was not until 1882 that a stained glass window in his memory was installed in St Margaret's, to a design by Henry Holiday and depicting Caxton flanked by Bede and Erasmus.[14]

Opinions as to dates canvassed among learned people, never completely unanimous, differed from those in some popular circles. *Chambers's Information for the people* enjoyed a very large circulation among the same classes that Charles Knight sought with his *Penny Magazine*: it was later claimed by its publishers to have sold in its various printings upwards of 170,000 sets.[15] Originally published in the 1830s, the account of the beginning of printing in England persisted in muddle in its later reprints. Accurately enough, it dismissed the suggestion that Caxton was established in Westminster Abbey in 1471: his press was never in the abbey, and this was far too early a date. Instead, the writer sought a compromise, based on the work of Atkyns, and on the early Oxford date:

The existence of the book before-named establishes beyond a doubt that books were printed at Oxford by Corsellis several years before Caxton set his press to work at Westminster, and therefore that that city has the honour of having been the first seat of the art in England; but Caxton was the first who introduced the printing with *moulded metal types*, the works by his predecessor having been executed merely with wooden ones. It is by our early writers not having attended sufficiently to this line of demarcation between the two stages of the art that the misunderstanding has, as far as we can judge, after much careful investigation, solely arisen.[16]

The suggestion that the Oxford printer had used wooden types was a further irrelevance, and it must be doubted that the writer had even seen the book of '1468', of which there was a copy in Cambridge University Library.

The date of 1474 persisted in many people's minds, even after the publication of Blades's two-volume study of Caxton in 1861–3. It was only with the commemorative exhibition of 1877[17] that a new date began to be fixed in public consciousness – that in turn to be displaced by further documentary research in the twentieth century which pointed to 1476. In the end there was no statue or other monument to mark the anniversary.

Fresh Approaches: Henry Bradshaw

In November 1869 an auction was held in Ghent of the library of the late Jean De Meyer who had died there in April at the age of seventy-five. Bibliophile and numismatist, De Meyer had assembled a library especially remarkable for its fifteenth-century printed books. The sale was organised by Camille Vyt, a local bookseller, who divided the library into 1,265 lots, concluding with a single one of about 300 pamphlets, minor works, local printing and imperfect books. It was the tidying-up of a library assembled with great care. The sale caught the attention of Bradshaw, working hard in Cambridge to build up the collections of Low Countries printing. Vyt had been in business since 1855, but this was his most important sale so far and he engaged expert help. The catalogue was compiled anonymously mostly by Ferdinand Vander Haeghen, whose seven-volume *Bibliographie Gantoise* was published in 1858–69. He was appointed University

Librarian of Ghent also in 1869.[18] Bradshaw clearly knew who was responsible, referring to him as 'the accomplished scholar' just a sentence after he had alluded to Vander Haeghen's *Bibliographie Gantoise*. It seemed in striking contrast to the work of others:

> The auction catalogues issued by the first houses in England and France are a standing disgrace to the two countries so far as this class of books is concerned; and yet there are no signs of any change for the better.

Vander Haeghen's catalogue was of a sufficiently high standard, and the early printed books were of such interest that Bradshaw became so engaged as to compile an index classified by printer, 'at first simply for my own convenience'. Then – unusually for a person who was normally so reluctant to rush into print – he had his work printed, along with some introductory remarks and several important and more detailed appendices. The pamphlet (Figure 5) was much more than a work of convenience. Working with Holtrop's achievements before them, Bradshaw was engaging with a scholar of shared interests, developing his own methods of work, in setting the presses in order, and pushing forward knowledge of the history of early Low Countries printing. It is small wonder that he opened his publication with more general observations, beginning

> It very rarely happens that a sale catalogue is drawn up with such care and knowledge as regards early printed books as to render the formation of such an index as the present in any way possible, unless after a careful verification by the books themselves. Indeed Ghent is almost the only place where there seems to be any attempt to give the attention to this subject which nevertheless is rendered all the more necessary from the very high prices which almost any good specimens of early printing are sure to bring.[19]

'The method of arranging these early books under the countries, towns and presses at which they were produced is the only one which can really advance our knowledge of the subject.'[20] Consequently, in an exercise inspired by Holtrop's 1856 catalogue of the incunabula at The Hague, Bradshaw applied what he called his 'natural history' method, 'the only one which can be productive of really valuable results':

> Each press must be looked at as a *genus*, and each book as a *species*, and our business is to trace the more or less close connexion of the different members of the family according to the characters which they present to our observation. The study of palaeotypography has been hitherto such a *dilettante* matter, that people have shrunk from going into such details, though when once studied as a branch of natural history, it is as fruitful in interesting results as most subjects. The Librarians

9

BELGIUM (1473).

ALOST (1473).

Th Martens (2d Press, 1487):

115 Horologium aeternae sapientiae. Ab. 1486–7. 4o. [50
BRH 57. VI 20. At Cambridge.

116 Another copy. [51

255 Juliani Pomerii Praenosticata. Ab. 1486–7. 4°. [52
Not in BRH. VI 18. At Cambridge.

210 Formula vivendi canonicorum. 4°. [53
Not in BRH. VI 17. At Cambridge (this copy).

138 Pectorale dominicae passionis. 4°. [54
BRH 144. VI 15. At Cambridge (this copy).

122 Sermones super *Salve regina*. 9 Jul. 1487. 4o. [55
BRH 59. VI 24. At Cambridge.

114 Angeli de Clavasio Summa Angelica de casibus conscientiae.
4 Jul. 1490. Folio. [56
BRH 60. MT 46. VI 27. At Cambridge.

LOUVAIN (1474).

Joh de Westfalia, late of Alost (1474):

237 Regimen sanitatis Salernitanum. Ab. 1480. 4o. [57
Not in BRH, not 586. At Cambridge (this copy).

217 Antidotarius animae. Ab. 1483–4. Folio. [58
BRH 113. At Cambridge.

Joh Veldener, late of Kuilenburg (1484–85):

137 Alphabetum divini amoris. 8°. [59
BRH 590. MT 47. At Cambridge (this copy). See Note E.

234 Herbarius. Ab. 1484–85. Ed. A. 4°. [60
Not in BRH, not 539. At Cambridge (this copy). See Note E.

Egid van der Heerstraten (1486):

8 Joh Beetz super decem praeceptis decalogi. 19 Apr. 1486.
Ed. A. Folio. [61
BRH 137. MT 55. At Cambridge (this copy).

Lud de Ravescot (1488):

103 Petri de Rivo Opus responsivum, 1488. (1488.) Folio. [62
BRH 132. MT 57, 58. At Cambridge.

BRUSSELS (1476).

Fratres communis vitae (1476):

172 Aegidii Carlerii Sporta fragmentorum, 1478; et Sportula fragmentorum, 1479. Folio. [63
BRH 242.

Figure 5 Henry Bradshaw, *A classified index of the fifteenth century books in the collection of M.J. De Meyer, which were sold at Ghent in November 1869* (Macmillan, 1870).

at the Hague have done very good service, and the *Catalogus* of 1856 is far the most valuable contribution to this class of literature which we have, so far as extent is concerned; but they are still very far from recognising the *natural history* method, if I may call it, as the only one which can be productive of really valuable results.[21]

He had his eye particularly on early printing in Zwolle, for which Holtrop's *Monuments* (1856–68) had proved inadequate, but the method was of much more general application.

Bradshaw had his pamphlet printed almost wholly for private distribution.[22] While his approach became familiar to a small group of enthusiasts in England and the continent, and his rearrangement of the incunabula on the shelves of what he called his 'typographical museum' in Cambridge University Library, became gradually known,[23] it was only when the pamphlet was included in Bradshaw's *Collected papers*, published in 1889 and thus three years after his death, that it became widely available. It was transformative, a turning point in the study of early printing.

His analysis of the early printed books in the De Meyer sale was the only occasion on which Bradshaw publicly presented his method *in extenso*. In June 1871 he returned to type analysis in more detail when he published another pamphlet, a *List of founts of type and woodcut devices used by printers in Holland in the fifteenth century*.[24] With its focus on the northern Low Countries, it was geographically more limited in scope, but it set out in further detail how, having sorted presses according to their imprints and typefaces, it was then possible by considering dated books to arrange undated ones made by the same printer in broad chronological order, as further types were acquired or earlier ones discarded. In this he was following the method of William Blades, who with the help of facsimiles prepared by G.I.F. Tupper in 1861–3 had published an analysis of the progressive additions by William Caxton to his equipment, and hence its use in his books:

A large number of purely conjectural dates would disappear from our catalogues, and instead of speculating as to what the date of a book may possibly be, that date would be assigned which best serves to connect the book with some well-defined characteristics of other books which bear a positive date, and the reason for assigning a date to a book would be self-evident, instead of being (as now) left to the conjecture of the reader of the catalogue.[25]

All this offered a new precision to bibliographical study, and hence not only to understanding the placing and dating of books but also to a new awareness of the relationships between different parts of the book trade. Bradshaw built on the work and methods of Holtrop and Blades, to create a credible historical basis for future scholarship.[26]

Bradshaw never showed a detailed interest in early Italian or French typefaces. He concentrated on the Low Countries, and on the lower Rhine valley. In this, the existence of Holtrop's *Monuments* was the key. It provided an orderly measure against which to set a defined group of early books and their printers. As he remarked in his analysis of the De Meyer sale, there was no equivalent for Germany, France, Italy or Spain, and he doubted whether one for France was even feasible.[27] Holtrop's work not only led directly to his focus on a particular group of books but also inspired him in his collecting of these books for Cambridge University Library. Without Holtrop, Cambridge would not now possess a collection of Low Countries incunabula comparable with the Royal Library in The Hague.

What had been vague in discussing the early history of printing had been given form when in 1856 Holtrop published his catalogue of the incunabula in The Hague and listed the books not, like Ludwig Hain in his *Repertorium bibliographicum* (1826–38), in alphabetical order of author or title, but instead in order of presses, country by country, town by town and press by press.[28] The principle with some variations seems to have been first applied to a collection in Britain when in 1876 Robert Sinker, advised by Bradshaw, compiled his list of incunabula in the library of Trinity College, Cambridge.[29] Instead of setting out the countries in the order adopted by Bradshaw, reflecting the order in which printing had been first established, Sinker was less influenced by bibliographical evidence. He set England first (in place of Germany), then Holland and Belgium together, before proceeding to Germany, France, Italy and Spain. For him, national and proprietorial pride was presumably irresistible, subduing bibliographical facts, but the principle of topographical and printers' distinctions was established.

With the notable exception of his early work on woodcuts associated with Caxton, at least as represented in his few publications, Bradshaw took only limited interest in early woodcut illustration.[30] In 1867 he wrote:

I have often thought of drawing up a technical list of the woodcuts used to illustrate the printed books of the first few generations of the art; discriminating the single cuts and series according to the works they were originally designed to illustrate, and tracing their origin, as well as their subsequent history, which sometimes shows the most grotesque application of a cut to a subject very remote from the mind of the original engraver.[31]

Like so many of his projects, it fell by the wayside. Instead, W.M. Conway, a young graduate of Trinity College, profited from his work, and from his bibliographical practices. Conway's *The woodcutters of the Netherlands in the fifteenth century* was published by Cambridge University Press in 1884, an extraordinary achievement just five years after he had graduated: the book in fact covered modern Belgium as well as the Netherlands. It owed its origin, its method, its compilation and its publication to Bradshaw, who steered it through to its subsidised publication.

After learning about early intaglio printing in the Fitzwilliam Museum, Conway was drawn to early woodcuts, and (as he told it) then met Bradshaw, who readily shared his knowledge, as he did with other aspirants such as J.H. Hessels.[32] Where Bradshaw analysed type, Conway turned to the woodcuts, and explained, 'Thus it became necessary to change the list of prints found in fifteenth century books to a list of blocks cut in the fifteenth century, care being taken to note in the case of every block the various occasions of its use.'[33] The change was as instrumental in the bibliographical study and analysis of the use of illustration as anything offered by Holtrop or by Bradshaw on typefaces. Conway's approach depended on both men, while he was also able to take advantage of Campbell's *Annales de la typographie néerlandaise au XVe siècle*, published in 1874. With immense energy, he surveyed copies in Britain, the Low Countries, France and Germany, and constructed a portrait of an industry where woodcuts, made by different artists and used by different printers, were handed down from generation to generation, and shared and borrowed among the trade.[34] Such work was impossible at this time for any region other than the Low Countries, for the bibliographical foundations did not exist. Conway later claimed that his book enjoyed only an extremely limited circulation, that copies were not sent out by the Press, that even Quaritch did not learn of it until much later, and that the remaining stock was destroyed.[35] It was not until Thierry-Poux's *Premiers monuments de l'imprimerie en France au XVe siècle* appeared in 1890, followed at the beginning of the new century by the first volume of Anatole Claudin's detailed survey of the early French presses, that real progress was made in France. These were, however, in nowhere near the same detail as Holtrop, Bradshaw, Campbell and Conway had achieved for the Low Countries.[36]

Gutenberg vs Coster

Who invented printing in the West? So fundamental a question seemed to most people to have a simple answer. Gutenberg was the hero of the hour.

In fact, matters were not so straightforward. First, as had long been recognised, Gutenberg worked in collaboration with two others, Johann Fust and Peter Schoeffer. The more that surviving books from the early years in Mainz were examined, the more complicated the bibliographical questions of attribution became. This apart, much more ink was spilled over a quite separate issue. Was printing in fact invented not in Mainz, but by a man named Laurens Coster, in Haarlem? National and local rivalry descended into a prolonged and ill-mannered argument between two men that, in the end, added very little to scholarship and nothing to public enlightenment.[37]

The history of printing depends ideally on a combination of different kinds of evidence as contexts in which to set printed matter. Quite apart from authorship, material evidence, whether of typefaces, page design, format or paper, may be difficult to interpret, but it is subject to other comparative and contextual checks. Documentary evidence may be printed or it may be written. It may be official, public or private. The evidence of dates on books is usually fundamental, though not all books are dated, and some books, whether deliberately or by mistake, are inaccurately dated.

In a book of 1816, later much quoted, William Young Ottley wrote concerning the invention of typography of the 'chaos of contradictory testimony and discordant opinion with which that important question is enveloped'.[38] In the continuing bitter arguments, the examination of material evidence heralded a revolution in bibliographical method. As debate shifted from the more obvious historical records and acquired a new focus, questions of type and eventually of paper took centre stage. They still left uncertainty, but some aspects could be set at rest.

The problem lay partly in a celebrated passage in a book known as the Cologne Chronicle, *Die Cronica van der hilliger Stat van Coellen*, printed in 1499 and thus close enough to the events it described for it to be reliant on personal memories. The anonymous author explained that he had his information from Ulrich Zell, who had introduced printing to Cologne. In translation, it read in part:

This right worthy art was invented first of all in Germany, at Mainz, on the Rhine. . . . And the first book that was printed was the Bible in Latin, and this was printed with a letter as large as that now used in missals. Although this art was invented at Mainz, as far as regards the manner in which it is now commonly used, yet the first prefiguration (*Vurbyldung*) was invented in Holland from the Donatuses which were printed there before that time . . .

But the first inventor of printing was a Burgher at Mainz, and was born at Strassburg, and called Yunker Johann Gutenberg.[39]

The statements about Gutenberg and Mainz were clear enough, but they were obscured by the remark about the *Vurbyldung* in Holland, and the copies of Donatus's grammar printed there. In any case, few people had access to the original, and although Dibdin had given considerable attention to the chronicle in his account of the Spencer library, he omitted the German and offered an imperfect translation of part of it.[40]

For these Dutch manifestations, there was a rather later claim in a book that was otherwise valued for its historical responsibility. The humanist and physician Hadrianus Junius, or Adriaen de Jonghe (1511–75), spent a large part of his life in Haarlem and composed *Batavia*, the first extended account in print of the north-western Low Countries. It was published posthumously in 1588, and included a long passage about Laurens Janszoon Coster who lived in the town. This consisted almost wholly of a tale said to be derived from a local bookbinder. According to the story as recounted by Junius, Coster's invention of casting letters was stolen by Johann Fust, who thereupon fled ultimately to Mainz where he established himself as a printer. It is difficult to distinguish scraps of fact from among the tangle of hearsay and tradition. In 1476 the bookbinder employed to bind the account books of Haarlem Cathedral used parchment fragments of a grammar by Donatus, a schoolbook, to strengthen bindings. Thus there is a *terminus ad quem*. Though there may well have been some early experiments in Haarlem, the many fragments of printing gathered since under the convenient heading of Costeriana are now dated some years after Gutenberg's work. While most of the names associated with the earliest printing were well established (Coster being the exception), many of the dates were not.

The claims of Haarlem to priority were noisy and long established, celebrated locally in monuments. They were based on statements made in the fifteenth and sixteenth centuries, and were supported by the existence of a number of undated fragments that were recognised as being from early Dutch presses. In 1856–68 J.W. Holtrop published facsimiles of most of those then known, and attributed them to Haarlem.[41]

At Haarlem itself, an exhibition in the stadhuis offered supposed evidence of Coster's activities, including block-books said to date from 1428 and a Dutch *Speculum humanae salvationis* attributed to 1440. Together with them was shown a specimen of the wooden lettering said to have been used by Coster. Visitors were told that his work dated from 1420–5 – long before Gutenberg's earliest experiments. The printed catalogue of the public library, published in 1848, included substantial accounts of these and other books associated with Coster.[42]

Outside Haarlem, most popular opinion supported the claims of Gutenberg. In a little book published in the Bibliothèque des Chemins de Fer (1853), Alphonse de Lamartine, more widely remembered as a poet and politician, uncompromisingly called him on the title-page 'inventeur de l'imprimerie'.[43] For Edmond Werdet in the 1860s, retired from a long career as a bookseller, Gutenberg's was 'l'oeuvre immortelle'.[44] In popular books about inventions, he was the hero. The theatre director Franz von Dingelstedt published a fanciful account of him, soon printed in French translation at Geneva and then into English, all for the benefit of bibliophiles.[45] In America, Emily Pearson of New Hampshire wrote a longer book about him, quickly adopted as a Sunday school prize, that invented conversations to vary the dullness or absence of facts.[46] Most of these books were more or less imaginative, as they embroidered the details of Gutenberg's life, but there was no doubting who was first. In 1828 Charles Knight, writing for the Society for the Diffusion of Useful Knowledge, was explicit. He dismissed Coster, whose claims could not stand 'the test of accurate investigation', and stated firmly that printing with moveable type was invented by Gutenberg, in Mainz, about 1438.[47] Charles Tomlinson (1808–97) was widely published on an array of scientific subjects and, in a pioneering appointment, taught experimental science at King's College School in London. He likewise dismissed any claim for Coster's priority, in a fat two-volume *Cyclopaedia of useful arts* that followed hard on the Great Exhibition of 1851: 'We are, however, on a careful examination of the confused mass of evidence before us, disposed to reject the claims of Coster, and to admit those of Gutenberg, Fust, and Schöffer, in the order in which we have written them down.' He drew attention to inconsistencies in the Coster tradition, and added a great deal of detail, repeating traditions concerning Gutenberg's experiments with plaster and with carved wooden letters. More plausibly, he attributed to Gutenberg the 'leading idea', 'the production of moveable types in metal'. To this trio of Fust, Schoeffer and Gutenberg was due 'the honour of having invented the art of printing with moveable metal types, produced by casting in metal moulds formed with steel punches'.[48]

Knight's suggested date was disputable, but while Gutenberg prevailed, Haarlem persisted. The Coster legend, a mixture of tradition, wishful thinking and disputes over how to translate or interpret some of the sources, had supporters beyond the Netherlands. In England, the connoisseur William Young Ottley (1771–1836), the auctioneer Samuel Leigh Sotheby (1805–61), the antiquary and naturalist Henry Noel Humphreys (1810–79) and the printer William Blades (1824–90) were all advocates.

So was the historian Auguste Bernard (1811–68) in France. It was a powerful group, albeit one of varied talents, but they shared the disadvantage of not having examined and analysed for themselves much of the surviving evidence scattered across the libraries of Europe.

Into this long-standing controversy came Jan Hendrik Hessels, a man as vigorous as he was committed to discovering the truth. Born at Haarlem in 1836, and trained as a bookseller with Frederik Muller in Amsterdam, he joined the staff of Cambridge University Library briefly in the 1860s. In circumstances that are not clear, in 1869 Bradshaw withdrew his special privileges for the library, and he subsequently spent many of his days there simply as a reader.[49] His relations with Bradshaw were complicated, made the more so because of their shared interests in early printing from the Low Countries.[50] In 1870 Bradshaw confessed to Campbell in The Hague, 'I always admired his powers of hard work – but his utterly insubordinate spirit can only give pain and annoyance to everyone with whom he works.'[51] He brought formidable energy to all that he did, whether working in the Library or pugnaciously engaging in bibliographical discussions that could develop into sometimes acrid arguments: a later acquaintance in Cambridge called him 'a most conceited and contentious person', not an easy colleague.[52] Hessels was interested also in manuscripts, and was an Old English scholar and philologist of some distinction. He further published the early archives from the Dutch church in London including the still standard edition of the letters of Abraham Ortelius then in its care.[53] For the purposes of the present study, his main published work concerned early printing at Haarlem and Mainz and the origin of printing with moveable type. The Gutenberg celebrations in the 1840s and 1850s reanimated the question.

In autumn 1871, Hessels issued an abridged translation of a study by Antonius Van der Linde of the Haarlem legend,[54] and supplied the fullest list thus far of the so-called Costeriana, fragments of early printing classified according to types with reference to Holtrop's *Monuments typographiques*.[55] Though Van der Linde dedicated his book to Holtrop, he had not pursued these details: Hessels now quietly dropped the dedication. In his introduction, Hessels could not resist commenting not only on the legend but also on those who supported it: 'The history of the Coster-legend, and the exposal of all that has been said or written on the subject, is not calculated to inspire anyone with a high opinion of the scholarship of those who have written on it.'[56] More positively, in viewing the work of Van der Linde, Hessels was able to reflect that the removal of Costerianism 'is, therefore, a revolution in bibliography, which promises a surprisingly plentiful harvest to a renewed, strictly scientific, exclusively historical and typological investigation'.[57]

Bradshaw too found Van der Linde an impressive change, and was complimentary about his 'lucid statement of facts lately published'.[58] For him, it was a welcome difference from past, and less informed, opinions: 'If the Dutch antiquaries interested in these matters would but bestow upon the investigation of downright facts a tithe of the energy which they have devoted to speculation upon possibilities for more than a century past, our knowledge would be in a very different state at present.' He treated Hessels with studied politeness, and saw no grounds for attributing the earliest printing to Haarlem. Typographical evidence pointed to Utrecht and to later dates.[59] When, in the wake of Van der Linde's study, he contemplated the possibility of three hundred years of cobwebs being swept away, he was firm: 'If we keep hard facts before our eyes, and discourage frivolous speculation, we are all the better prepared to catch the true significance of any fresh fact, the moment it is presented to us.'[60]

Like Hessels, Antonius Van der Linde (1833–97) had been born in Haarlem. He left the Netherlands to study for his doctorate in philosophy at Göttingen, and later joined the staff of the royal library in Wiesbaden.[61] This was the base where he assembled his work on Gutenberg,[62] whom in 1871 he called 'the immortal inventor of typography' ('De onsterfelijke uitvinder van de typografie').[63] In his view the Coster legend was exploded. 'All these secondary questions could not be clearly stated and impartially examined, so long as Costerianism clouded our heads with the prejudice of a plurality of the invention.'[64]

Van der Linde worked himself up to his conclusion:

At Haarlem, therefore, we have to do away with the following monuments: 1. The statue on the Market-place; 2. The memorial-stone in the front of the Coster-house; 3. The slab in the cathedral, in remembrance of the 'fourth jubilee' of 1823 (although the celebration of the first, second and third was never thought of!); 4. The memorial-stone in the Hout, with the arms of the sheriff and the year 1423; Finally, the deceptive Coster-museum ought to be abolished and the books themselves incorporated with the town library.

Let the votaries of dead conservatism, which would leave things in being, not because they are *good* and *true*, but because they *exist*, make no illusions of their cynicism of characterless indifference. 'That statue looks well there!' so the 'ostriches' of the solved question console themselves. But they forget that henceforth there can be no longer any pretence of a Coster-question, but of a Coster-*scandal*, which our national honour demands should be stopped as soon as possible; they forget that henceforth not only every scientific, but also every honest man, will disavow the exposed fraud; they forget that in our time of telegraphs and railways, international intercourse and reading, there is no longer place for shuffling tactics; . . . they forget that the bronze statue of 1856 is henceforth *impossible*, on account of the cause which it represents; that it is a shame to our nation, on account of the immorality of its origin; they forget that we could say with erect head to the foreigner: We were deceived, but the deception has no hold on us; for we ourselves have torn with strong hand the tissue of lies, and thrown the rags at the feet of the blockheads and deceivers.[65]

Van der Linde betrayed his ignorance of his home town in claiming that local Coster celebrations had never been thought of previously. In 1740 an elaborate and large medal had been struck in his honour, one of several made at that time,[66] and in the same year Isaac and Joannes Enschedé published at Haarlem a volume celebrating the tercentenary by Johann Seiz, editor of the *Oprechte Haarlemsche Courant*.[67] This apart, Van der Linde placed great emphasis on a scientific approach, 'a purely scientific treatment'. The same word was used in the original Dutch, 'wetenschappelijke', a term describing a way of thinking, of scholarly investigation, not necessarily only in the natural sciences.[68] It was a term much in vogue in several humanities subjects. Bradshaw employed the same word on other occasions. Questions and answers were to be determined by the disciplined use of evidence. Lord Acton later summed it up in his inaugural lecture as Regius Professor of History at Cambridge:

If men of science owe anything to us, we may learn much from them that is essential. For they can show how to test proof, how to secure fulness and soundness in induction, how to restrain and to employ with safety hypothesis and analogy. It is they who hold the secret of the mysterious property of the mind by which error ministers to truth, and truth slowly but irrevocably prevails. Theirs is the logic of discovery.[69]

Hessels found much to criticise when he came to read Van der Linde's later work. In particular, while he had admired his work on early printing in 1871, by the end of the decade Hessels thought very differently. When asked in 1880, not by a more obviously scholarly journal but by the *Printing Times and Lithographer*, to review Van der Linde's new book, he found himself quickly mired in a work which he found wanting in many respects. Readers were warned of what was to come by the tone of Hessels's opening sentence: 'Dr. Van der Linde, the latest author on the Invention of Printing, is a Hollander by birth, but a German by bias and inclination.' A few sentences later the same theme of betrayal was developed:

Dr. Van der Linde's pen is sharp and venomous. His '*Haarlem Legend*' is written in language as bitter as wormwood, and that of his present book is no less strong. Woe be to those who dissent from his views. Whether his antagonists are men of importance or not known at all, he attacks them all with the same relentless severity. His large views and cosmopolitan spirit induce him to ridicule on all occasions a country of such small proportion as Holland. That his countrymen ever claimed the honour of the invention of printing is to him not an error of judgment but a capital offence. That the Dutch never worshipped him for his vituperative language – that they did not at once at the appearance of his 'Haarlem Legend' destroy the statue erected to Laurens Janszoon Coster, the supposed inventor of printing – is to him the worst of all crimes they could perpetrate.[70]

Hessels paid fulsome tribute to Bradshaw, with whom he had shared many of the questions respecting the earliest printing in Mainz and whose own work had been only partially summed up in two brief pamphlets, on the De Meyer sale (1870) and the *List of the founts of type and woodcut devices used by printers in Holland in the fifteenth century* (1871): 'These few pages have done more good for the study of early-printed books than all the ponderous volumes under which the question of the invention of printing is buried.'[71] As for Van der Linde's own study of Gutenberg, Hessels was devastating. Work had been copied from others without acknowledgement. His arrangement was confusing. His own work on some of the documents was defective. He was inept and sometimes incompetent in transcribing. He was a person of 'singular credulity'.[72] It did not help that he was also a grateful admirer of the American printer Theodore Low de Vinne (1828–1914), whose book on the invention of printing, published in New York in 1877, paid fulsome attention to Van der Linde's dismissal of the Haarlem claims:[73]

Everywhere but in Holland and Belgium, Dr. Van der Linde's exposure of the spuriousness of the legend has been accepted as the end of all debate. Coster must hereafter be regarded as one of the heroes of fiction and not of history. With the downfall of Coster, fall also all the speculations concerning an early invention of printing in the Netherlands by an unknown or unnamed printer.[74]

It was not simply a question of one town versus another. There were national interests as well. The group of fragments associated with Coster in Haarlem was varied; and although tradition and typographical similarities associated them together, could they have been printed at different times, in different places? As for Mainz, while Gutenberg was usually credited with the early indulgences and books, by 1882 both Bradshaw and Hessels had concluded that there were in fact two presses: Schoeffer had printed the 42-line Bible, and another, perhaps Gutenberg, had printed the *Catholicon* of 1460.[75]

The differences between Hessels and Van der Linde concerning priority were charged with personal animosity. Hessels had two advantages. First, he had the benefit of frequent discussions in Cambridge with Bradshaw, whom he repeatedly acknowledged sometimes even with a degree of obeisance. Second, he showed considerable energy in travelling round Germany and France within the space of a few months, searching out and checking original documents and examining some of the books or fragments under discussion for himself. In this respect, he shared Bradshaw's own approach and enthusiasm for foreign libraries, and in seeing things for himself.

The question posed by Hessels in 1882 with his title *Gutenberg: was he the inventor of printing?* remained unsettled in his own mind:[76] 'I regret that, after all my labour, I have not found anything which enables me to answer this question with either yes or no.'[77] By 1887, Bradshaw having died in the previous year, he felt able to nail his colours firmly to the mast, in a series of articles written for the *Academy* and then gathered into another monograph *Haarlem the birth-place of printing, not Mentz*. Once again he focused his attention on Van der Linde, whom he found an all too easy target and whom he now attacked with renewed venom: 'wholly untrustworthy from an *exegetical* as well as from a *bibliographical* point of view'.[78]

By now Hessels was in a decreasing minority. In Haarlem, Coster was a matter for tourists as well as for local inhabitants, as the argument spread even to widely read guidebooks. By 1888, in more than a dozen lines of small print the Leipzig publisher Baedeker offered a summary for tourists:

The controversy as to whether Coster or Gutenberg was the real inventor of printing may now be definitely settled in favour of the latter. Recent investigations in the town records have, indeed, proved that a certain Laurenz Janszoon Coster lived at Haarlem in 1451–55 as a wine-dealer and tavern-keeper, and that he left the town in 1483; but no mention has been found of any printing-office in his possession. In any case, the works printed by this Coster, if such ever existed, cannot go back so far as 1454 (the oldest date of the Mayence printer), since the story of Coster, which came into vogue about 1560, expressly states that he was a grandfather when he made his first attempts. No works printed at Haarlem are known with a date either before or shortly after 1454. It is, however, certain that Haarlem was the first town in Holland at which printing was practised.[79]

The attempt to allow Haarlem some comfort as the first Dutch printing town was sadly mistaken. No press was established there until Jacob Bellaert worked there in 1483, long after printing had been introduced at Utrecht.

Most people discarded what had become known as Costeriana as the earliest printing, and Bradshaw himself had dismissed the Haarlem claims in a brief note in 1871. In this international bickering, although Hessels remained loyal to his home town, the question of Haarlem became less significant: the dates, most probably from the 1470s, were more important. While Bradshaw himself inclined to Utrecht,[80] his authority was by no means universally accepted, and his work was not always remembered even in Cambridge.

Yet if questions remained, in the 1880s and at the end of the century, they had now been placed on a fresh footing. Particulars of the various specialist debates of Holtrop's and Bradshaw's generations concerning the early history of printing with moveable types did not achieve a wide general circulation. Despite notices in the press, and some reviews, they were not studied closely beyond the small group of people that interested itself in the key minutiae of such matters. Deeply committed to the history as well as the practice of printing, Blades overstated the case when in 1887 he proclaimed that 'Next to religion, there is perhaps no subject that has excited more personal animosity and hatred than this – Who invented movable types?'[81] Bradshaw's contributions were originally published and circulated all but privately. Though he assembled notes, including acute observations on the 42-line Bible, he never wrote at length about Gutenberg. Hessels's translation of Van der Linde in 1871 achieved only a slightly wider circulation, published by Blades, East and Blades (i.e., the firm of the printer William Blades, biographer of Caxton), and it could never be accounted a best-seller.

The early years of the annual lectures established under the will of Samuel Sandars (d.1894) at Cambridge were overseen by Bradshaw's pupil Francis Jenkinson, as University Librarian. The first lecturer was Sir Edward Maunde Thompson, Principal Librarian of the British Museum, who spoke about Greek and Latin palaeography. Then the electors chose Charles Middleton-Wake. He delivered four lectures on 'The invention of printing', a topic that had so much concerned Bradshaw. Whatever his qualifications as an art historian, with standard publications on Rembrandt (1878) and Dürer (1893), he was no historian of early typography, and he lacked any appropriate analytical skills. Perhaps the electors hoped for some further enlightenment, ten years after Bradshaw's death. It did not come. While Middleton-Wake was more than willing to deny even the existence of Coster, he was determined not to pronounce priority in favour of either Haarlem or Mainz. His conclusion, based largely on a reading of Hessels, was a confession of judicious ignorance: 'The arguments on every side must, to so large an extent, be founded upon *inference*.'[82] Instead, he advanced the novel suggestion that the invention of printing (defined as printing with moveable types) should be attributed to the Brethren of the Common Life, perhaps more specifically at their house at Groenendael, near Brussels.[83] His improbable suggestion did not take root. More widely, discussions and analysis by other scholars depended on a mixture of the study of early documents, on provenances and places where fragments were found, and on type analysis.

Debates surrounding the early Mainz presses were also very far from resolved. For most people by the third quarter of the nineteenth century, the question of who invented printing with moveable type seemed settled. By the late 1880s the evidence appeared conclusive. But what exactly did Gutenberg print? Could he properly be celebrated as the inventor of printing? The significance of the 42-line Bible as the first major book to be printed had been established in the eighteenth century,[84] yet there remained many questions. In ordering the British Museum catalogue of fifteenth-century printed books, Robert Proctor followed Bradshaw in attributing early Dutch prototypography to Utrecht.[85]

In their different ways, and by no means always in agreement, Holtrop, Campbell, Bradshaw, Blades, Hessels and Van der Linde had inaugurated a new generation of scholarship. At a meeting of the Library Association in Birmingham in 1887, William Blades summarised the arguments of the past seventeen years, and pointed to the need for further German work.[86] In fresh hands the topic moved away from worrying about the priority of one town over another, to distinguishing the various presses working at Mainz in the 1450s and to analysing an ever-increasing group of surviving fragments that were gradually discovered. With the work of Paul Schwenke and Karl Dziatzko, German scholarship injected new life into what in some respects had become a cul-de-sac.[87] Gutenberg was not necessarily named as the printer of the 42-line Bible, though his name remained as the inventor in the popular imagination. He was celebrated on innumerable picture postcards in Germany, and in 1900 the traditional supposed anniversary of his birth was commemorated in exhibitions and publications. The Prussian Royal Library published a volume by Schwenke on the 42- and 36-line Bibles, and Mainz produced a Festschrift.[88] At Paris, the Imprimerie Nationale and the Bibliothèque Nationale combined to publish a special *Hommage*.[89]

Meanwhile Hessels could not disregard the question whose answer had eluded him in 1882, and in a long article on the early history of printing under the heading 'Typography' in the generally authoritative eleventh edition of the *Encyclopaedia Britannica* (1911) argued at length for the priority of Coster, and the so-called Costeriana: 'The invention of printing with movable metal types took place at Haarlem between the years 1440 and 1446 by Laurens Janszoon Coster.' By then he remained an all but lone voice, speaking from the past and determined not to be misled by modern and better scholarship. While many of the details were probably unfamiliar to most readers, it was as if the discussions that had animated scholarly discussion for two centuries, and the many discoveries that had been made in that time, were as naught. In this as in few other aspects of the bibliographical world there remained a division between rarely questioned popular assumptions and the preoccupations of scholarly analysis, not so much in establishing historical facts as in the significance attached to questions that might or might not any longer exist.

Libraries

5 | Access: National Collections

The common word 'access' means many things, and it is employed in many contexts. It is both a noun and a verb. We speak of roads or footpaths giving access to places, of gates giving access to gardens. 'Access land', marked on some maps, signifies open land over which, subject to certain conditions, we have a right to roam. We may seek access to a person. We speak of 'accessing' databases on computers. Libraries provide instructions on how to access their buildings and their stocks, and perhaps how to access ebooks or databases when you are off-site. In e-publishing, much is made of 'open access', designed to give readers free access to work that would otherwise have to be bought or rented from a supplier. The fact that it is simply a way of seeking to transfer costs does not affect the purpose of publication. A further use, now little seen, denotes an increase, or growth. In that the nineteenth-century book trade and libraries saw great increases, they also saw an access. The word is thus applicable in several senses to some of the key developments discussed in these pages.

We have become so accustomed to the word that we rarely give much thought to its implications. It relies on there being some target to access, whether a building, a road, the contents of a museum, paintings and sculpture in an art gallery, content in or via a computer, or books in a library. For books, access may involve purchase, borrowing, stealing, reading or simply looking: all these activities feature in the following pages. Whatever the method, the aim here is a physical object that is either known or thought to contain some desired content.

Access to a library therefore implies something more than just going through the door, or opening a web page. It may imply that there is (all being well) a catalogue; that it may be possible to ascertain what is not there as well as what is; that it will be possible to consult holdings; and that there will be help available if needed. In other words, we make certain assumptions, though anyone who has worked in a range of libraries, with a diversity of management attitudes and practices, will know that such assumptions are not invariably justified.

Thus access may be easy or difficult. It may or may not be rewarding. This has always been true, but in the nineteenth century many such matters came to a head as libraries experienced unprecedented growth, more libraries were established than ever before, and more readers made more demands of them than ever before. This growth faced audiences at all income levels, involved increases in literatures of all kinds, and was enabled by developments in manufacture and in transport and by changes in public finance and in taxation. As public awareness and education developed, so too did expectations. The following pages explore some of these phenomena, their circumstances, the challenges they created and the consequences.

We may also speak of a text, whether book, pamphlet, or journal article, being 'accessible', meaning that we can understand it with little difficulty. That in turn raises questions of how we are to understand what is before us: how it is to be interpreted. Simply to access a book, in terms of finding it on a shelf, is but the beginning. What does it mean? How does it relate to other works on the subject? Where does it sit in the history and development of its subject? Are its age or appearance significant? Such questions are assumed. Ever since the sixteenth century, and for some purposes centuries earlier again, people have worked to create an arsenal of aids to reading. Readers' companions, readers' guides, dictionaries, bibliographies and a plethora of other reference works have been designed to improve understanding and bibliographical navigation, whether in choosing and acquiring books, or searching for them in some other environment. For early books the questions were gradually extended, to investigations concerning their histories, the materials and means of their manufacture, the ways in which they had been sold, all with the purpose of increasing understanding of a large part of the printed inheritance.

In other words, access, understanding and meaning went, and go, hand in hand. How did this relationship develop in circumstances of considerable material and educational change, and what are its implications?

Libraries and Their Catalogues

Whether by purchase, copyright deposit, gift, war, confiscation, revolution or other means of acquisition, libraries across much of western Europe grew at unprecedented speeds in the first half of the nineteenth century. The increases were driven partly by increases in the number of new publications, and partly by the relocation and re-ordering of older collections. These increases provoked debate, either explicit or by implication. What should be kept, and what might be ignored? What was only of short-term, or ephemeral, interest? What could be rejected? What was irrelevant to current needs and definitions?

The aftermath of the French Revolution witnessed first a rejection of much relating to religion, heraldry and genealogy, only for some of this attitude to be replaced a few years later by a renewed attention to the country's and family history. In Paris, one of the most knowledgeable observers of the book trade remarked by 1879 that books in Latin, once so sought after, were now 'à peu près invendables', at least in France: people wanted books in their own language.[1] In England, at Lincoln Cathedral Thomas Dibdin persuaded the Dean and Chapter to part with a group of exceptionally rare early printed books that seemed to have no place in a nineteenth-century library. It was one of three groups of sales of early printed books between 1811 and 1817. For 80 guineas Sir William Bolland, another member of the Roxburghe Club, obtained through the auctioneer Benjamin Wheatley a volume of poetical tracts from Lincoln including *The rape of Lucrece* that alone sold later for 100 guineas.[2] The Cathedral's parting with some of its rarest books, and their replacement with modern works, brought opprobrium.[3] In London, the British Museum sold off quantities of so-called duplicates in an ill-considered series of sales between 1769 and 1832, and thus disposed of many rare or unique books.[4] Reflecting changed reading habits and tastes since it was founded in 1684, Archbishop Tenison's parochial library at St Martin in the Fields was auctioned by Sotheby's in 1861: it had been neglected for some years, and the sale, including medieval manuscripts, raised the modest total of £1,410.[5] In 1830–5, seeking to focus more on the sciences, the Royal Society sold manuscripts from the Arundel collection (given in 1667) to the British Museum,[6] and in 1872 sold off an assortment of miscellaneous literature. The trade in early books, involving the re-focusing and mobility of collections, was by no means limited to the private market.

Whatever the international pecking order, all libraries faced an ever-growing difficulty in making their collections known to readers. With growth and reorganisation came the need for up-to-date catalogues and, more specifically, new approaches to cataloguing. Old summary practices were no longer adequate. Some writers found cause to pillory earlier efforts. In 1837 Augustus De Morgan poked fun in a long essay contributed to the *Companion to the almanac*, an organ of the Society for the Diffusion of Useful Knowledge. In France, Gustave Brunet was inspired by the first (and only) volume of the new catalogue of the printed books in the British Museum, published in 1841, to ridicule the catalogue of the library of Lincoln's Inn and to highlight the misdeeds of other authorities.[7] In May

1843 the *Quarterly Review* led with an article written anonymously by John Holmes, of the Manuscripts Department in the British Museum.[8] He surveyed some of the questions raised by a group of recently published library catalogues. These were obviously a help to people not actually in the libraries concerned.

Yet even for readers in reading rooms, dependent on only locally held guidance, matters were not necessarily straightforward. Göttingen University Library was described in 1841 as 'la bibliothèque la plus complète, la mieux organisée, la plus utile de l'Europe'.[9] It had grown from about 65,000 volumes in 1765 to 300,000 in 1836, not including manuscripts. Its catalogue was handwritten, and ran to no fewer than two hundred volumes. At Copenhagen, the catalogue just of foreign publications was in 199 folio volumes: Danish publications were reported to be not catalogued at all, but kept in a separate room.[10]

Nor was it to be assumed that readers would always have access to the catalogues. The information gathered for comparative purposes by the Commission investigating the British Museum in 1836 recorded not only that the Bibliothèque Royale in Paris was in a state of disorder, with the cataloguing of large numbers of publications still not tackled by the staff, but also that even for those books that were catalogued, readers were only allowed to consult the catalogue under supervision.[11] The alphabetical catalogue in the royal library in Berlin was thought not to be accessible to readers at all. Nor were the catalogues in the Ambrosiana or Brera in Milan. At Munich, readers depended on 'special indulgence from the librarians', just as at Copenhagen it depended 'wholly on the Librarian's will'. At Göttingen, despite its reputation, things were scarcely better, for the catalogue could only be consulted 'if properly asked for'.[12]

It was assumed by the British Museum commissioners, as by most others, that a catalogue, whether printed or manuscript, detailed or a simple inventory, for a library was a *sine qua non*: 'Une bibliothèque sans catalogue, c'est le chaos.'[13] Yet, while most people assumed that a catalogue was a necessity, memories rankled. At the beginning of the century Napoleon's agents had used published catalogues of pictures and books as guides in picking out the treasures they most wished to confiscate for France.[14] Or, as the director of the Ambrosiana was reported to say, a printed catalogue was an invitation to thieves. The library had suffered much at the hands of Napoleon's thefts during the French occupation of Lombardy.[15] In a continuing tradition, a reluctance to publish shelf-marks in widely available catalogues persists among some librarians in the twenty-first century.

To link a reader to a catalogue was one thing. To link a catalogue to the order of books on the shelves, and hence to a reader, was quite another. The system of printed request slips developed after much wrangling by the British Museum was widely admired, for being clear and unambiguous. So seemingly simple an arrangement was far from universal, and readers in other libraries were constantly frustrated at the mistakes and waste of time that were regular parts of life. In about 1860 Edward Everett Hale, a minister from Boston, visited Europe, and spent time studying in the British Museum, where Panizzi, 'that prince of librarians', was a cordial host.[16] Approvingly, he found the system of asking for books the same as that in the Astor Library in New York. The contrast with the frustrations he endured in the national library at Paris could hardly have been greater:

I may tell you how I tested the Imperial Library in Paris, and how it failed. I went to one of the cases to which readers had not access, and copied the name of one of Lepsius's books, which I could see through the wire door: I did this simply to test the administration. Then I sent this in, in form, as my order. After two or three messages to me about what they had and what they had not, which ended in my directing them to bring me all Lepsius's works they had, they brought me two old pamphlets of his, but said they were in despair to find they had not in the collection the book whose title I had just before read there, within thirty feet of the librarian-in-chief. At the British Museum, on the other hand, I do not remember a mistake in the delivery – which was also the very rapid delivery – of all the hundreds of books which I had occasion to consult there during my stay in London.[17]

For some libraries – and they were a minority – the challenge lay in the increasing need for bibliographical particularity even as the number of books increased. The question lay at the centre of what might otherwise be regarded as a spat between stubborn, if influential, men respecting the daily activities of readers in the British Museum. Hale had the good fortune to arrive after much of the dust had settled.

Panizzi's position at the Museum gave him unique responsibilities, and De Morgan expressed considerable admiration for him. There was no denying the accountability of a national library with respect to cataloguing:

The catalogue of a noble library like that of the Museum, is not merely a book-finder, or at least ought not to be so. It should be the corrector, so far as its contents are concerned, of all those noisome and pernicious errors which our article has shown to exist; which deprive the dead of the fame they have fairly earned, tend to render the living callous to the sense of literary justice, and cultivate habits of inaccuracy among those who have to teach the rest of the world.[18]

As has been so frequently (and expensively) discovered since, it was difficult to judge how long large cataloguing projects might take. In 1839 the Bibliothèque Royale in Paris was awarded a special grant for editing and publishing a catalogue of its printed books.[19] While some progress had been made by 1847, the project met with criticism, and the task was far from complete.[20] Faced with mounting heaps of uncatalogued materials, the Library hit on an ingenious way of arranging books on the shelves in such a way that they could be found without the need for a catalogue. Matters were interrupted by the Revolution of February 1848. When Jules Taschereau took charge of the Library in 1852, cataloguing was given a new stimulus, with a scheme for *Catalogues méthodiques*, printed subject catalogues covering wide fields.[21] One on the history of France was published in eleven volumes in 1855–79, with an index following much later, in 1895.[22] Another for medical sciences was published in three volumes in 1857–89. There the programme came to an end. They did not answer the need for a catalogue of the entire library, and there were predictable qualms about how some subjects might be fitted into such a scheme. Quite apart from this painfully slow programme of publication, such catalogues had strictly limited uses. They became almost immediately out of date. Newspapers as different as *Le National* and *La Presse* took a critical interest, and Paulin Paris, who described himself as 'Membre de l'Institut, Conservateur-adjoint au Département des Manuscrits', wrote a pamphlet surveying the practical difficulties.[23] The whole was reorganised again under Léopold Delisle, who was appointed to succeed Taschereau in 1874, and after much debate the first volume of the new general printed catalogue, organised alphabetically by authors, was published in 1897. Nevertheless, it omitted works for which the author was not known.[24]

As Paris considered the Bibliothèque Royale in the 1840s, the Commission even then sitting on the British Museum faced a barrage of ideas and suggestions concerning how, in the wake of the aborted project of 1841, a catalogue of the books there might be assembled, and whether it was sensible to publish it. The Royal Commission appointed in 1847 spent many days considering the catalogues of printed books in the Museum, and the subject was rehearsed again at length by Edward Edwards in his *Memoirs of libraries* in 1859.[25]

In the end, and a generation later, the decision to print the catalogue rather than continue it in manuscript was forced on the Museum. With the volumes of the handwritten catalogue in the Reading Room by 1875 numbering two thousand, quite apart from those for maps and music, space was quickly running out,[26] and as Superintendent of the Reading

Room Richard Garnett was faced with an impossible task respecting public access. He fought, ultimately successfully, for several years. It was not until January 1880 that the printing of the catalogue was begun in earnest.[27]

By then the question of printing it had become linked to hopes not so much for a union catalogue, as a universal catalogue, of all publications extant. Charles Wentworth Dilke had argued for this in 1850, in the course of a review in the *Athenaeum* of the 1850 report on the Museum.[28] The Society of Arts took up the cause in the 1870s. It was far too ambitious.[29] In the end this grandiose proposal was watered down, but not until after it had been considered by the newly founded Library Association. It was encouraged by an outsider, Cornelius Walford, actuary and historian, who presented his own scheme more specifically devoted to English books first to the Society of Arts, and then at the first annual meeting of the Library Association in October 1878. He estimated that there would be about three million entries, and he offered a detailed sample description, running to about 150 words, of a single eighteenth-century book.[30] Such were not proposals likely to be thought realistic.

Though better based, and innovative in the proposed introduction of photographs of title-pages to accompany descriptions in the catalogue, so as to provide bibliographically precise details, the yet more ambitious proposals by the bookseller Henry Stevens stood even less chance of immediate success.[31] They came a quarter of a century after the question had been posed by Albert Blor, a lawyer writing from Dublin, 'May not photography be usefully applied to the making of catalogues of large libraries?'[32] Although the topic reappeared periodically, it was not taken up for a century, when in the 1980s images were gathered systematically in the compilation of the *Eighteenth-century* (subsequently *English*) *Short-Title Catalogue*.

When in 1877 Stevens addressed a conference of librarians in London, he was reflecting a change in mood as well as in practice:

Bibliography is fast becoming an exact science, and not a whit too soon. It is high time to separate it from mere catalogue-making. It is becoming a necessity to the scholar, the librarian, and the collector (they are not always identical).[33]

His solution was for libraries of older books to have two catalogues, one with bibliographical details, the other simply a finding list. This was hardly practical, but his proposal for the first was innovative in both conception and suggested execution. Through a Central Bibliographical Bureau, librarians and amateurs might subscribe to detailed catalogue records which would be shared. 'Such a bureau, or clearing-house, under Government protection', he believed, 'might from the beginning be made self-supporting, or even remunerative, like the Post Office.'[34] Each catalogue record was to be supported by a reduced photograph of the title-page, so that detailed comparisons between copies in different libraries might be made. Bibliographically it was not foolproof, for there may be many differences elsewhere in a book, while few libraries had the necessary photographic resources to submit records; but the proposal spoke of fresh approaches and enhanced understanding of the history of books. It went far beyond the ordinary printed catalogues of libraries that had become such a feature for research, for establishing rarity or simply for finding books.

Besides a universal catalogue, Dilke also argued for a more specialist one, of English books down to 1640.[35] He was not the first to try to seek a practical, if very partial, alternative to the Museum's ever-growing and ever less manageable general catalogue. Many years previously Panizzi had suggested to the Museum Trustees that there should be a separate catalogue of the fifteenth-century books. He had further discussed the matter with J.W. Croker, and both men raised the subject when they appeared before the commissioners preparing the 1850 *Report*.[36] Preoccupied with larger matters, the commissioners chose not to pursue either this or a catalogue of the vast collection of pamphlets concerning the Civil War and its aftermath, gathered by George Thomason. Instead, and no doubt partly inspired by the brief catalogue by S.R. Maitland of early books at Lambeth Palace, which aroused considerable curiosity among the mid-century commissioners, attention focused on early English books.

With the appearance in 1884 of George Bullen's *Catalogue of books in the library of the British Museum printed in England, Scotland and Ireland and of books in English printed abroad, to the year 1640* three decades of arguments between the Trustees, the Treasury and members of the staff in the Department of Printed Books came to a partial end. Even as Richard Garnett worked towards a general catalogue of the printed books, Bullen worked with an assistant on this more specialist one. In three octavo volumes it not merely gathered within a convenient space a detailed list of these books scattered all over the library. The Museum thus set before the public a part of the collection otherwise not easily determined. Though by no means perfect,[37] in its geographical, linguistic and chronological boundaries it also defined the scope of many aspects of English literary, religious, social and scholarly history for well over a hundred years yet to come. Meanwhile, from Cambridge, Henry Bradshaw appealed for the names of printers to be supplied in another separate catalogue of fifteenth-century books. By 1875 the beginnings of a dedicated catalogue of incunabula existed on slips, but it was not taken forward at this stage. Instead, Bullen's *Catalogue* took priority.

   As finally published, and in its various subsequent revisions, the general catalogue of printed books in the British Museum remained unchallenged anywhere in the world for almost a century. As a general reference, it had no equal for its size, its range or for the depth of its coverage. It became the authority to which other catalogues and cataloguers deferred. Nevertheless, and as those who called for various kinds of union catalogues realised, it was not comprehensive. In discussions that focused first on books in the languages of Britain, and then on the other major European languages, it obviously did not encompass the world. For the study of older books, some further supports were necessary. In a movement already evident in the specialist catalogues of Bullen and in surveys of incunabula, the focus increasingly shifted to identified classes of publications, defined either by region or by period. As will be seen in the following, individual scholarly achievement was translated into more general leadership, tending to be from the national and some other major libraries.

6 | The British Museum Commission, 1847–1850

We have touched on changes in attitudes and approaches in the professional management of collections of books, be it in libraries or in the book trade, and among what may broadly be called bibliophiles and collectors. They share overlapping and interdependent historical interests, whether in organisation and preservation or in the application of the past to contemporary preoccupations. These interests are linked intimately by personal and bibliographical ties, embodied in the physical realities of the books in question. With these elements in common, we turn now to resources, the more detailed description of early printed books in the mid-century, and to how bibliographical generalities were developed into more particular analysis partly by new ways of considering books themselves and partly by linking this to documentary evidence whether in the public domain or in private archives.

The work of the mid-century British Museum Commission in addressing readers and books alike lies at the heart of the nineteenth-century response to what was generally recognised as a much wider crisis. It attracted comment from all kinds of readers, besides those who had never thought of reading there. Though the numbers of readers were minute in relation to the population at large, many of the topics and principles were of general application. It was a matter of international interest. The Museum's library found eager admirers and equally eager detractors, and was debated in detail through the equivalent even of a microscope. As a body controlled by Trustees, established originally in the eighteenth century and among whom the government enjoyed only a minority representation, it was responsible for a substantial share of public funds in the form of parliamentary grants. Within two decades, the Museum was the subject of three parliamentary enquiries. Of these, the first two were especially concerned with the running of the Library. That of 1847 was also appointed with more general duties:

for the purpose of inquiring into the Constitution and Government of the British Museum, into the Administration of its Funds, and the Organization, Arrangements, and present Condition of the several Departments of that

Establishment, with the view of ascertaining in what manner that National Institution may be made most effective for the advancement of Literature, Science and the Arts.[1]

Under the chairmanship of the Earl of Ellesmere, owner of one of the finest collections of early books and manuscripts in the country, between July 1847 and June 1849 the Commission took evidence from members of staff, Trustees, readers, various scholars and professional members of the book trades before it reported in 1850. Although it surveyed all the departments, by far the majority of its time and energy focused on the departments of manuscripts and of printed books, the responsibilities respectively of Sir Frederic Madden and Antonio Panizzi. The jealousies between these two gifted and capable men frequently seemed trivial, and it is often surprising to see them taking up the time of the commissioners. Among other matters, they rehearsed their bickerings about keys to cases and about the fact that due to historical accident they each were responsible for volumes in media that might in ordinary circumstances seem the responsibility of the other. Even their squabbles about their official housing were brought to the commissioners. The commissioners also heard evidence concerning payments to staff right down to the last sixpence. There were more substantial organisational matters as well. The new buildings then being completed posed novel challenges in that space had not been fully allocated, or even designed: the placing of ancient sculpture was equally part of the commissioners' concerns, as they heard evidence from Sir Richard Westmacott. Most time was taken up with the Department of Printed Books. The title of the head of the Museum, Sir Henry Ellis, was Principal Librarian, though his evidence principally concerned the more general running of the Museum. In the course of his presentation and that of others, it emerged that the Museum's Secretary since 1828, Josiah Forshall, was ill. This was not entirely responsible for breakdowns in communications, but it contributed to a deeply unsatisfactory state of affairs, where in particular the Trustees only heard directly from the Keepers with extreme rarity. On occasions considered serious by some senior staff, Forshall blocked attempts to address them.

Insofar as the Department of Printed Books was concerned, there were six major issues: the management of the Reading Room; access to the catalogues; whether to print the catalogue or whether to print catalogues of some parts of the collection; how to catalogue anonymous books; acquisitions policies and practice; and how to cope with the increasing numbers of books entering the Museum.

Readers depended on two principal catalogues. In 1813–19 the Museum had published a seven-volume catalogue of the printed books. To this was added that of the King's Library, given by George IV: it was compiled by F.A. Barnard and J.H. Glover in 1820–9, and published in five folio volumes. Copies of both were in the Reading Room, and fresh additions to the collection were added in manuscript to a copy of the first. By the late 1840s this had become bulky, and confused. Readers sometimes found difficulty in distinguishing the correct shelf-mark, written in manuscript on overcrowded pages, for the book they wanted. Outside the Museum, the catalogue of the King's Library was scarce, whereas there were plenty of copies of the 1813–19 catalogue. After much debate, the first volume of what was intended to be a new catalogue of printed books was published in 1841, but this project was almost immediately abandoned. It covered only the letter A, and apart from the heading for 'Academies' was criticised variously for being misleading, wasteful, incomplete and inaccurate. So the commissioners heard opinions concerning the relative merits of a manuscript or printed catalogue.

Amidst much else, quite apart from questions of how much bibliographical detail was desirable (a topic that took up much time) were questions concerning whether a printed catalogue would recover its costs or, in practical terms more seriously, how it might be extended as further books were added to the library. In considering the more obvious printed catalogues of the larger libraries in Britain, such as the currently appearing volumes of the Bodleian Library which were no more than an amalgam of old catalogues, or the catalogue of the London Library, compiled by J.G. Cochrane and published in 1842–4, none found favour. Characteristically forthright on cataloguing as on most other matters, Augustus De Morgan was particularly voluble in his detailed denunciation of well-known examples. Of the Bodleian catalogue he claimed, 'Nothing better illustrates the manner in which learning may exist without any care to promote a sound knowledge of its sources, than the emanation of such a catalogue from such a university.' 'I believe that for one entry which is unobjectionable, there are two at least which contain inaccuracy, confusion, or incompleteness.'[2] The commissioners' final report favoured a manuscript catalogue, and so disappointed many people.

Some parts of the collection suggested themselves for separate catalogues. In 1836 Panizzi himself had suggested one of the fifteenth-century books.[3] The commissioners were shown a copy of a brief catalogue recently published of the early English printed books in Trinity College, Cambridge (1847), and also considered a similar one for English and foreign ones in

Lambeth Palace library, compiled by S.R. Maitland in 1843.[4] Early books could be considered rare; and by such catalogues people could learn the whereabouts of examples. Potential for the same selectivity could be claimed of other kinds of books in the Museum, for one of the perceived difficulties lay in the fact that the Museum contained both common and rare books, catalogued indiscriminately. The example in Paris of Van Praet's much-appreciated published catalogues of books printed on parchment raised the topic for the Museum. These were dealt with speedily, as the Trustees had at some time previously made clear their suspicion of the extravagance of buying books on parchment.[5] The collection of mid-seventeenth-century English pamphlets assembled by George Thomason, and given to the nation by George II, covering in near comprehensive depth the period of the Civil War and Commonwealth, presented a quite different, and more serious, challenge. They had not been entered in the old printed catalogue, and had only been added in manuscript subsequently. Despite much discussion, it was decided against printing a special catalogue: one was published only in 1908, compiled by a team supervised by G.K. Fortescue. For the present, nothing came of the further suggestion that the very considerable number of French Revolution tracts presented by J.W. Croker should be treated to a separate printed catalogue: one finally appeared at the end of the century.[6]

All this apart, what was the Museum to contain, as the national library? Panizzi spoke of the imperfections of copyright deposit. Following a discussion concerning the gaps among William Wordsworth's publications in the Museum, all of them issued in London, he added:

Of the works published in the provinces, I believe we get a certain number, but nothing in comparison to the number which is published; of the works printed out of England, I mean in Scotland and Ireland, I believe we get almost none at all; and of the works published in the colonies, to which the copyright extends, we get none at all.[7]

His evidence was at odds with that given to the Commission over a year previously by Forshall. The rule was that copyright deposit books were received by the Secretary's department, and after registration they were passed to Panizzi's responsibility. Panizzi himself had no control over what was sent in. When cross-questioned at some length by the Lord Advocate and Richard Monckton Milnes, Forshall had claimed that London publishers supplied 98 per cent of what was published.[8] Thus Panizzi found himself in a position not of his choosing: 'I am perpetually pestered by people who find fault with me because there are not these books, and I have no means of claiming them.'[9]

So much for the books. Opinion was divided as to whether or not newspapers were appropriate. Panizzi stated that he had bought a collection recently, that the Scottish collection was very incomplete and that, despite discouragement from the Trustees, the Museum purchased some foreign ones. There were, he said, none deposited from the colonies.[10] In speaking of the other printed materials, Thomas Carlyle paid especial tribute to the Thomason Tracts, which he had used extensively for his work on Oliver Cromwell.[11] On those that appeared during the French Revolution and the following years, J.W. Croker was adamant. His collections of pamphlets and other ephemera illustrated the point: that newspapers were sometimes valueless in reporting the events of these years, which were much better documented in cheap print: 'I think an effort ought to be made by the British Museum to buy everything they can of that sort, for it is really a most curious collection, and nobody can ever understand the real history of that revolution who does not read the ephemeral papers that came out at that time. The newspapers are nearly valueless.'[12] The following witness, the Rev. George Edward Biber, pointed to the deficiency in tracts and pamphlets relating to theology and theological controversy.[13]

Underlying all this were much larger and more general questions. To what extent should the Museum collect apparently minor publications, whether of the past or the present? How far should it expect to increase by purchase its holdings of early books? How was the ever-growing collection in the Museum, the result of purchases, gifts and copyright deposit, to be organised and controlled? Hence, how were readers to gain access? Further, notwithstanding the constantly increasing stocks, were these the most appropriate? Panizzi argued for larger purchase grants, but it was not always easy to see where they should be directed. When in the early 1860s William Blades came to study William Caxton, and concluded that he had worked with Colard Mansion in Bruges, he could find only one minor book printed by Mansion in the Museum. He had to depend on foreign libraries.[14] To make good this deficiency and to counter Blades's public complaint, three of Mansion's major works were bought between 1860 and 1865.[15]

The challenge was by no means unique to the Museum. Foreign libraries faced the same, and their practices were often enquired after. When asked about the printed catalogues of major overseas collections, the Berlin bookseller Adolphus Asher, one of the two principal suppliers of German books to the Museum, could think only of Jacob Quensel's catalogue of the books in the cathedral at Uppsala (1751). This was hardly relevant to nineteenth-century London, and he knew of no intentions to print any of the modern major libraries. The whole topic was closely related to questions of access. In the Museum, readers consulted the catalogues for themselves and were expected to do so. Elsewhere, as we have seen, they often had to ask the librarians, though as Asher remarked, 'The last revolutions have brought a revolution among other things in that system, and at present the readers are allowed to consult the catalogues in Vienna.' He assumed the same was true of Berlin; but it was certainly not true of Munich.[16] The political and social revolutions of 1848 had reached even into library management, but had achieved only so much.

It was not only a question of access to library catalogues. Witness after witness to the Museum commissioners offered his opinions as to how books should be described. Some favoured very short entries, some long. There was no agreement about how anonymous books should be entered. Early printed books presented repeated difficulties, sometimes in their title-pages, sometimes in their imprints, sometimes in their gathering together several texts not necessarily by the same author. While De Morgan was particularly detailed, he was also the most realistic when he remarked that 'One of the most difficult things that one can set himself to do is to describe a book correctly.'[17] Knowingly or not, he was repeating a point made some years earlier by John Holmes: 'There are few things which at first sight appear more easy than the compilation of a catalogue of printed books.' Like De Morgan, Holmes poked fun at some of the nonsenses perpetrated by cataloguers who confused authors and the variety of forms of name.[18]

In an attempt to gather not only opinion but also possible ways of proceeding to recommendations in the wake of experience with the abortive first and only printed volume of the new catalogue, published in 1841, the commissioners turned to people responsible for different kinds of catalogues: for bookselling, for auctions, for small libraries and for specialist libraries. Not surprisingly, there was little agreement when people addressed the Museum's catalogue. There was a world of difference between the catalogue of an institution containing hundreds of thousands of books, dating from the fifteenth century to modern times, being used by all manner of people from the deeply scholarly to the casual novice, and catalogues of smaller collections, often composed for specialist or already knowledgeable audiences.

Thus the short titles and brief details such as those in Maitland's catalogue of the early Lambeth books met a quite different need from the fuller details sometimes required in the Museum catalogue. In the view of John Payne Collier, 'the Rev. S.R. Maitland has not permitted himself to be seduced from his object, that of giving a most useful and comprehensive index, by any vanity of bibliographical display'.[19] Such an opinion was never likely to commend itself to Panizzi in defending the Museum practice, and in dealing with closely similar editions of the same books. When, arguing that books could be catalogued more speedily, Collier submitted a selection of books of his own cataloguing, dating from the sixteenth to the nineteenth centuries and in various Western languages, Panizzi handed the descriptions to one of his senior assistants, who demonstrated faults in each one. Panizzi was merciless. 'Had I seen these titles under any other circumstances than the present, I should have concluded that the object was to show how nearly worthless would be a catalogue, the proposed advantages of which were short titles, drawn up and printed within the shortest possible period of time.'[20] In a long summary (it must have taken well over an hour), he demolished Collier's descriptions, producing each book and showing to the commissioners how each description was either insufficient or inaccurate for the purpose of identifying the books.[21]

Faced with repetitive and what must have frequently seemed excruciating detail, the commissioners listened to discussions of cataloguing and of the Museum's catalogues of printed books. Opinions were often at odds with each other, and the topics absorbed more time by some of the country's most senior public men than was ever again to be the case. The focus was, at least for most of the time, on the Museum, but the questions were much wider, and emerged repeatedly in other contexts over the following years. How were early printed books to be described, so that there was no ambiguity? How were they to be recognised? Going into further and more specialist detail, Panizzi cited some of the ways employed at the Museum for early books, including identifying separate printings by comparing broken pieces of type, and different settings on various pages. Given that not infrequently authors were published under different names, or forms of their name, how were these to be described? All were pertinent questions, but De Morgan perhaps summed matters up best when he insisted on the consistent application of rules.[22] Witnesses were able to show how even in the 1841 catalogue, Panizzi's new ninety-one rules had not always been followed exactly; but these rules in turn were to prompt many more attempts to codify similar sets in Britain, continental Europe and America alike.

'Of all the malcontents within or without the Museum, those who complained of the *Catalogue* were the most noisy.'[23] It was by no means the only object of study. The 1850 report on the British Museum, coming hard on the heels of another report on the Museum only fifteen years earlier, was short in its summary but comprehensive in the number and range of witnesses, and in the time given to them. Most attention since then has naturally focused on Panizzi, the attacks on him, his defenders and the many days of evidence as he responded in turn to myriad principles and details. At its heart were not so much more general questions respecting the Museum, though each was given attention, as the constant arguments, sometimes serious and sometimes no more than bickering, between Panizzi and Madden. In the course of it all, a picture emerged of an institution in crisis, where communication and consultation were poor, not least between the Trustees and the staff, and where the mid-nineteenth-century bibliographical conundrums were only partly understood and tackled. It was not only a question of numbers. It was also a question of how printed matter was to be organised and used.

Augustus De Morgan

In view of De Morgan's outspoken remarks, it is worth visiting his own contribution to retrospective bibliography. Augustus De Morgan (1806–71) was educated at Trinity College, Cambridge, where he graduated in 1827 as fourth wrangler.[24] His biographer in the *Dictionary of national biography*, Leslie Stephen, attributed this slightly lower place than expected in the mathematical firmament to his dislike of competitive examinations and to his fondness for what he called discursive reading. Prevented by religious scruples from considering a Fellowship at the College, as might have been expected, after dallying with a career in law instead he was appointed, in 1828, as the first Professor of Mathematics at the new University College London. He remained in this post for almost all his career, until he resigned in 1866. It did not bring him riches, and for many years he wrote copiously for the weekly *Athenaeum*, sometimes reviewing two books in a single issue. He also contributed about 850 articles for Charles Knight's *Penny cyclopaedia*, besides writing for the *Quarterly Journal of Education*, the *Encyclopaedia metropolitana* and the *Companion* to the *British Almanac*. By no means everything was on mathematics, a subject on which he assembled a considerable library, most of which is now in the Senate House in London.

In an article innocuously entitled 'Mathematical bibliography', published in the *Dublin Review* in 1846, De Morgan offered various examples of cataloguers' mistakes and a discussion of how matters might be improved.[25] He was especially concerned with the tendency for mistakes to be repeated by later cataloguers and bibliographers, and his 'general impression' was that mathematical bibliography was 'somewhat imperfect'.[26] Ostensibly, according to the two books listed at the head of his article, his subjects were Hain's *Repertorium bibliographicum* (1826–38), on which he wrote extremely briefly, and Panizzi's catalogue of mathematical books in the Royal Society, 'the best scientific catalogue of which we know'.[27] In fact, the latter part of his article was taken up with an account of the inefficient and time-wasting procedures in the Reading Room of the British Museum for any reader wishing to order a book. The catalogue, he argued, had to be sufficiently detailed not only with respect to bibliographical information. Only thus would readers' and staff time be saved, and mistakes or unnecessary guesses be avoided. Further, for the Museum, the practice of allocating separate numbers to each volume was relatively new. Panizzi's predecessor as Keeper of Printed Books, Henry Baber, had favoured simply a shelf number, so that newcomers could be inserted in their appropriate places in the classification scheme. When in 1838–42 the library was moved from Montagu House into Smirke's new building, most of the books were given new pressmarks, in a continuous series where previously these had reflected the rooms in which they were placed. The move, the wholesale re-numbering and entering all the new pressmarks in the catalogues were accomplished speedily and with great efficiency,[28] but it remained that the books themselves were inadequately catalogued.

De Morgan's separate publication *Arithmetical books from the invention of printing to the present time* became better known. Published in 1847 by Taylor and Walton, conveniently close to University College in Gower Street, it was a landmark not just for its authority but also for its method. Others had written previously on the history of the subject, most recently John Leslie at Edinburgh in 1820 and Guglielmo Libri more generally on science in Italy. George Peacock's contribution on Arithmetic in the *Encyclopaedia metropolitana* formed one of the bases of De Morgan's work. Now, in 124 pages, De Morgan surveyed the printed literature from the 1490s to the fifth edition of his own *Elements of arithmetic* in 1846, beginning with the Grenville copy of Filippo Calandri's *Aritmetica* (Florence: Lorenzo Morgiani and Johannes Petri, 1491/2).[29] He was proud of having personally inspected at least one copy of almost every book described, and he dedicated his work to Peacock, his old teacher at Trinity.[30] Each entry was annotated, often explaining the significance or otherwise of a work, and adding a miscellany of bibliographical information. The assessments were frank, if often idiosyncratic. Gaspar Schott's *Cursus mathematicus* (Würzburg, 1623) was dismissed as including a 'shabby arithmetic, which, considering the magnitude of the course, reminds us of Falstaff's halfpennyworth of bread'. Robert Heath, part author of *The practical arithmetician* (1750), 'was a person who made a noise in his day, and in so doing established a claim to be considered a worthless vagabond'.

More seriously as a bibliographer, De Morgan noted on comparing his own copy with that in the Museum that there were two variant settings of some pages of Pacioli's *Summa de arithmetica, geometria, proportioni et proportionalita* (Venice, 1494): 'one of those phenomena which so frequently occur in very old printed books'.[31] Not surprisingly, formerly common books that had been much reprinted gave him especial trouble. The earliest edition he could offer of Francis Walkingame's *Tutor's assistant* ('by far the most used of all the school-books, and deserves to stand high among them') was the twenty-eighth, 1798. By the mid-nineteenth century, the variety of publishers and places of publication meant that there was much confusion as to how many editions had actually appeared: seventy-one, as claimed by a London publisher in 1831, or fifty-one according to a Derby imprint of 1843 (pp. 80–1). The book had originally appeared in 1751, published by subscription. If Walkingame was challenging, Cocker was even more so. Edward Cocker's *Arithmetic* enjoyed a greater vogue and offered a wealth of bibliographical puzzles in the various editions and adaptations published between the seventeenth and nineteenth centuries. De Morgan claimed to have seen a copy of an edition of 1677 in a sale, and the earliest he possessed was of 1685. As for the content, in an exceptionally long entry of more than six pages he demolished any claim that Cocker was solely responsible: 'The famous book itself I take to be a compilation or close imitation in all its parts' (p. 58), 'I am of opinion that a very great deterioration in elementary works on arithmetic is to be traced from the time at which the book called after Cocker began to prevail' (p. 62).

Quite apart from questions respecting such well-known books were the innumerable ones surrounding editions of earlier books. Robert Recorde's *Ground of artes* had already been the subject of remark by De Morgan in the *Companion to the Almanac* in 1837,[32] and he was thus revisiting old questions in 1847. Early editions of this several times reprinted book are exceptionally rare. In his *Arithmetical books* he entered it under 1561, and followed it with a note: 'That this book was published about fifteen-forty there is internal evidence: and Tanner gives it that date. Dr. Peacock has fifteen forty-two. But I have never seen any edition earlier than this.' Modern scholarship now attributes the first edition to 1543, followed by editions in 1549, 1551 and 1552.[33]

Like others, and pursuing a theme that was to occupy librarians and bibliographers with increasing energy over the following few decades, De Morgan explained his use of the ordinary terms 'folio', 'quarto', 'octavo' and 'duodecimo'. While he acknowledged that these had their origins in the practices of printers, he explained that he preferred to follow the usage of modern publishers, who ignored printers and instead used the terms to describe the sizes of books: 'A publisher thinks more of size than of the folding of the sheet when he talks about octavo or quarto' (p. xi). This made nonsense of early books whose leaves might have been cut down from a larger size, or printed on a particularly small sheet; and it equally made nonsense of modern books. His own book illustrated the point: 'In the book now before the reader, which is a half-duodecimo (or what I call a *duodecimo in threes*) the first sheet which follows the prefatory matter, B, has B on the first leaf, and B2 on the third; which is enough for the folder's purpose' (p. xi).

Accordingly, when in his book he referred simply to format, he referred 'entirely as to size, as completely as in a modern sale catalogue, the maker of which never looks at the inside of a book to tell its form'. He also ignored paper sizes, such as imperial, crown, demy and so forth. Thence, he sought to explain the make-up of each gathering:

When the modern word occurs with the addition of *in twos*, or *in threes*, &c. the addition expresses the number of *double leaves* which belong to one letter of signature; and which I believe would be found, if the books were taken to pieces, to be in each quire or gathering. Thus, *folio in ones*, or *quarto in twos*, or *octavo in fours*, or *duodecimo in sixes*, would in each case be unnecessary repetition ... But *folio in twos* would mean the folio size with two double leaves in one quire, *folio in fours*, with four double leaves. Thus a book of the octavo size, with the quarto signatures, is *octavo in twos*: had it been larger, I should have called it *quarto*.

By this means there is something as to size, and something as to signatures, in every description.

It was a cumbersome method, quite apart from its refusal to take account of the size of the sheet, even for early books. Moreover, the description could be further abbreviated, in a way he used for a supplementary list of works more briefly described: 'Here 2+2, 4+4, 6+6, mean quarto in ones, octavo in twos, duodecimo in threes' (p. 97). In other words, the terms could be both imprecise and abstruse in his hands.[34]

On other matters he could be observant. He called the chainlines in hand-made paper 'waterlines', thus ignoring the ordinary established technical terminology and, again, creating his own invention. But his note that they did not necessarily follow the patterns of the majority, where a folio usually had vertical chainlines, was a useful warning to his readers to exercise caution. Pacioli's edition of Euclid (Venice: Paganinus de Paganinis, 1509), a folio, has horizontal chainlines.[35] While he worried much about some matters, others were altogether excluded. He gave no paginations, so there was no way of establishing the length of any publication, and he only rarely named publishers or booksellers. Despite his concern for some aspects of bibliographical description, he thus neglected two of the most obvious.

But he was eager to repeat one point: that this was not a work concerned wholly with major authors:

It is then essential to true history, that the minor and secondary phenomena of the progress of mind should be more carefully examined than they have been. We must distinguish between the progress of possibilities and that of actual occurrences. Our written annals show us too little of what might have been, and too little what was.[36]

Or, more specifically, 'The public is beginning to demand that civil history shall contain something more than an account of how great generals fought, great orators spoke, and great kings rewarded both for serving their turn.' Hence the need also to consider 'second and third rate works in large numbers' (p. vii). Or again, as he summed the matter up to Peacock in his preface, 'The most worthless book of a bygone day is a record worthy of preservation' (p. ii). As De Morgan readily confessed, his own work was very far from complete; but his admixture of major and minor contributions, original and derivative, all within a single chronological order, promulgated this critical point: that historical understanding could not depend only on the most celebrated works of innovation and invention but should also depend on 'the minor works which people actually use, and from which the great mass of those who study take their habits and opinions' (p. vi).

Thus, quite apart from his subject-matter, De Morgan offered two key lessons for future work: the need to consider books as physical objects, bibliographically, and the need for better attention to the mass of minor publications that underpinned and extended knowledge.

De Morgan's pioneering and well-meaning contributions alike to the listing of books and to their description enjoyed a mixed reception. We return next to some of them, including a continuing discussion of formats.[37] They were, however, but two aspects of how to organise and present books, whether singly or in large libraries. As we have seen, the

British Museum Commission dealt with both in large matters of policy and in minutiae. In the following chapter we turn to questions of management and organisation; how poor stewardship exposed libraries to risk; limitations in response to theft; the ways in which the bibliographical record was attacked; and how individual books as well as collections were damaged irretrievably.

7 | Libraries in Confusion

Unlike several of the developments so far discussed, there was nothing new in book thefts. For centuries, booksellers, libraries and individuals have all suffered to a greater or lesser degree, and the purpose of the thefts has not necessarily been venal. In three notorious cases discussed in this chapter the motives were mixed, where scholarly and monetary greed were mingled and where in all cases the victims proved to be less than vigilant. The libraries concerned were all, to a greater or lesser extent, neglected and poorly supervised. The cases were distinctive, involving some of the most prominent institutions in Britain, France and Spain, and with the notable exception of one or two people, few emerged with their reputations wholly untarnished. All affairs had considerable aftermaths, and all involved people in England. While these and other lesser cases might seem to be no more than prominent examples of a continuing tradition of greed and misery, they claim attention here because they lie on the cusp of two library worlds, between disorganisation and neglect on the one hand, and on the other a growing consciousness of the need for better management and oversight. Nothing could better illustrate the urgent need for system, attention and up-to-date catalogues.

Trinity College, Cambridge

The medieval manuscripts in Trinity College, Cambridge, were checked in 1784. When in 1838 they were next checked there was thus a considerable margin of uncertainty in the discovery that several medieval volumes were missing.[1] It was not until five years later that Sir Frederic Madden in the British Museum noticed that one of a group of volumes recently purchased by the Museum from the bookseller Thomas Rodd had formerly belonged to Trinity. Then it quickly emerged that some others, also bought recently, were from the same source. Suspicion fell on a former undergraduate named James Orchard Halliwell, who had entered the college in 1837 and who had shown an especial interest in the manuscript collections, paying particular attention to broadly mathematical and scientific subjects.[2] After a brief time at Trinity he moved to Jesus College, choosing to change colleges like many other students. He took no degree, and shortly after going down was obliged to sell the collection of about three hundred manuscripts he had by then assembled from various sources.

Prompted by Madden, Trinity College supplied a list of seventeen medieval and later manuscripts known to be missing from its library, and of these Madden was able to identify several either as having been bought by the Museum, or else still in the hands of Thomas Rodd the London bookseller. He further noted that the manuscripts had been tampered with: 'In no single instance is a volume in its genuine state.' Altogether a dozen volumes, containing considerably more texts, seem to have been stolen in the 1830s. Ownership marks had been removed, and volumes containing several texts were broken up and rebound. But while both the College and Madden became convinced that Halliwell was the culprit, the evidence against him was weak in that the College was unable to prove when the volumes – and parts of volumes – might have left the library. Legal proceedings were dropped, but only after Halliwell had gone into print with a deceitful pamphlet in his own defence, and after he had written a letter to *The Times* that is best described as misleading.[3]

The case failed mainly because, lacking proper records, Trinity was unable to prove when it had lost the books. Furthermore, thanks to the legislation governing the Museum, the Trustees found themselves unable to restore the College's property. They seem to have taken no further steps. Halliwell went on to become a prominent Shakespeare scholar, the case was formally closed in May 1847 and most people outside a small circle forgot about the matter.

French Libraries

Just a month after the Halliwell case was closed, a far greater scandal began to unravel in France, and it likewise turned on disorder in library care. The neglected state of many French libraries was no secret. In 1842 a French guide to careers included a chapter on librarianship. It was not an easy path to enter without a patron. In smaller places especially, the post was simply given to a person who displayed literary tastes or an interest in local history. Pay was poor, and the position was often regarded as a sinecure:

> Les livres et les lecteurs étant peu nombreux, l'ordre n'est que trop aisément entretenu, et comme on ne vote guère de fonds pour des acquisitions nouvelles, il ne survient presque aucun changement dans les catalogues.[4]

Such conditions invited exploitation, and the considerable bibliographic riches of manuscripts and rare books, now dispersed among *bibliothèques municipales* in the aftermath of the Revolution, added further to the risk.

The condition of libraries had long been a bone of contention, both in government and among private individuals. In 1831 Ludovic Vitet, Inspecteur Général des Monuments Historiques de France, presented a damning report to the Interior Minister on libraries and monuments in the north of France.[5] Only one or two libraries could offer an adequate catalogue of their printed books; the situation for manuscripts was even worse: 'Pour la plupart des villes de France, tout est à faire.'[6] At Laon, one of the richest collections of early manuscripts that he considered, physical conditions were better than in some places. But the manuscripts were 'singulièrement négligés'. At Valenciennes, home of the early medieval manuscripts from the rich abbey of St Amand, they were 'dans un abandon déplorable'.[7] Few places had the skills to understand the manuscripts and early printed books that had been saved from religious houses. With no catalogues either of manuscripts or printed books, there were no readers. Much of France was ill-served. In his view both local and central authorities were to blame, and action was required by both. In such circumstances, for those who wished to do so it was clearly all too easy to abstract books.

When, in his first exercise as Inspecteur Général, Félix Ravaisson paid a series of visits in the west of France, he found a very mixed situation.[8] At Rennes, he was encouraged to find a well-run and well-used library, developed by a succession of dedicated librarians during the past twenty years. It was quite the opposite at Tours, where the rich collection of early manuscripts had suffered in the aftermath of the Revolution and had been dumped in a damp basement for twenty years, while some had been sold and many had been lost or stolen. It was not clear what exactly was in the library. While the collection at Tours was the richest, it remained that there were many other libraries that had suffered similarly. At Angers, books had been sold for a song, there was no catalogue, and the storage conditions lent themselves only to confusion. Local authorities took varied interest in collections, content sometimes to leave them in the hands of former members of religious orders, and sometimes to ignore them altogether. At Avranches, the books had suffered from damp like so many other collections, but matters were now improved, with investment and proper accommodation. At Caen, the library was well run, with a knowledgeable staff, and was well suited to receiving books allocated from elsewhere by the Minister.

Many libraries were ill-managed. So too were archives. When in 1835 Jules Michelet toured collections in south-west France on the instructions of the Ministre de l'Instruction Publique, and in preparation for writing about the Hundred Years War, he discovered a very mixed picture. At Bordeaux he found the precious records of the parlement in a poor state, covered in dust, some eaten by rats, wet thanks to the broken windows, and with the floor so rotten that not everything was accessible. At Limoges the water used to extinguish a fire in 1823 had done further damage. Interest in their care was often limited, whether to a single person or to someone now very aged. Few were listed.[9]

Such are some examples of the confused state of French libraries into which Count Guglielmo Libri introduced himself.

Count Libri

For many bibliophiles and others interested in the world of older books, the year 1847 was most remarkable for the auction in Paris of part of the library of M. L****, offered over thirty days in June at the maison Silvestre. It was widely advertised, including a news report in the London *Daily News* and a detailed notice in the *Bibliophile Belge*.[10] The quasi-anonymity fooled few of those interested, who recognised the owner as being none other than Count Guglielmo Libri (1802–69). Learned, industrious, sociable, combative, evasive and (as it proved) dishonest, Libri had arrived in France as a political refugee from Italy towards the end of 1830. There he became a member of the Institut, editor of the *Journal des Savants* and (in 1843) professor at the Collège de France. The four published volumes of his *Histoire des sciences mathématiques en Italie* (1838–41) established his international reputation as a well-known scholar, but he was also an ambitious book collector on a very large scale. As much dealer as collector, in Paris he became a part of the bibliophile circle including Paul Lacroix, Sainte-Beuve, Mérimée and the bookseller Jacques-Joseph Techener. He corresponded with booksellers in London and Italy, Germany and Spain, as well as in France, and by 1847 had amassed perhaps 40,000 volumes, including early manuscripts, autographs, incunabula and later printed books down to modern times. His methods in improving his books, for which he found help among Parisian binders, now seem unorthodox, but at the time there was less widespread concern for restoring early books with inked-in additions or even forged inscriptions, or old paper used for replacement leaves.[11]

Though he resented being thought a dealer, in fact much of his library was financed thanks to buying and selling, and the book trade was well used to him. Several of his sales were presented under pseudonyms. Between 1835 and 1846 he sold autographs anonymously and printed books at a dozen sales.[12] As a knowledgeable bibliophile ostensibly keen to promote the well-being of French libraries, he ingratiated himself with François Guizot, and as a scholar of Italian literature he became a friend of Panizzi. His evident concern for French provincial collections made him seemingly a well-suited choice in 1841 as secretary of the Commission charged with compiling a catalogue of manuscripts in French libraries. The Commission originated in an *ordonnance royale* of 3 August 1841, following a report by Abel-François Villemain referring to a call for such a catalogue as long ago as 1809.[13] In 1849 Libri contributed the preface to the first volume of the new *Catalogue général des manuscrits des bibliothèques publiques des départements*,[14] in which he had also drafted the descriptions for the Faculté de Médecine at Montpellier and for Albi. He further wrote the introduction for Autun. The sections on Autun and Laon were finished in 1846, when Libri ceased to be a member of the Commission. His tasks were assigned to Félix Ravaisson, who became Inspecteur Général des Bibliothèques.

By the mid-1840s there were suspicions among a few people that Libri was using his position not merely to gain access to libraries but also to abstract books from them: Léopold Delisle later recorded that he was known to have been active in Dijon, Lyon, Grenoble, Carpentras, Montpellier, Poitiers, Tours and Orléans.[15] By 1847 these worries were widespread. He was suspected of stealing manuscripts in Florence, and in London Thomas Rodd shared with Frederic Madden his suspicions of further thefts.[16] Libri's attempt to sell an exceptional collection of manuscripts to the British Museum collapsed after prolonged negotiations, as he meanwhile also tried to sell the same collection to Turin. It included an astonishing number of early manuscripts, including the sixth- or early seventh-century illustrated Pentateuch from Tours (now known as the Ashburnham Pentateuch): with the panache of a scoundrel he had altered the provenance of this manuscript, so as to suggest that it came not from Tours but from Grottaferrata. In the end the collection was sold, surreptitiously, to the Earl of Ashburnham.[17] As early as five or six years previously, books had been found to be missing from the library at Troyes, though no formal report of this seems to have been made until 1847. In 1844 Libri sold to the British Museum the Troyes copy of Le Fèvre's *Recueil des histoires de Troyes*, printed by Caxton.[18] There were further problems at

Carpentras. There, in 1840 he had been allowed to borrow a copy of Theocritus printed by Aldus Manutius in 1495, bound in parchment and uncropped. Its condition was believed to be unique, and after failing to answer requests for its return, Libri had sent a more ordinary copy instead. A copy of Castiglione, *Il cortegiano* had also disappeared. They proved to be but the beginning of many questions.

While the sale of his major collection of mostly Italian books in June 1847 was therefore not without its suspicions and anxieties,[19] it proved to be a success. It was buoyed up with a preface by Libri himself extolling a selection of the best. This emphasised not simply rarity, but also condition, 'une condition irréprochable' thanks to the skills of restorers in France and England, notably Bauzonnet, Trautz and Duru in Paris, and Clarke in London. On a rare copy of Boccaccio (Lot 2259), he explained that apart from the fifteen facsimile leaves by Harris, which had cost 900 francs, a further 150 francs had been spent on cleaning the pages.[20] There were books, he reported, that had once belonged to François Ier, Grolier, Diane de Poitiers, Charles V, de Thou and others. The catalogue explained that the owner's library, consisting of about 25,000 volumes, was to be put gradually on sale. After lauding the Italian rarities, Libri turned to other early books, including the *Catholicon* (1460, sold for 1,505 francs to Molini), the La Vallière copy of Cicero *De oratore* (1469), a group of Aldine editions and the first book printed at Paris (Gasparino Barzizza, *Epistolae* [1470]). Libri concluded his preface with a note about the importance of blank leaves, which were so often missing from early books but which were an integral part of a complete copy. The catalogue offered many examples of corrections to existing descriptions and explained the crucial presence in Libri's copies of these leaves. He disingenuously failed to add that they had sometimes been inserted by the restorers and had nothing to do with the books as first published.

Techener, editor of the *Bulletin du Bibliophile*, later remarked that several people gossiped during the sale about some of the books having been stolen from public libraries.[21] Notwithstanding this chatter, the trade bid energetically. While the Florence Homer (1488) was not offered, it was bought after the sale by Payne and Foss for 1,500 francs. The Carpentras copy of Theocritus was sold to Payne and Foss for 635 francs, and the Castiglione to Tilliard for 519 francs, passing thence to Nicolas Yemeniz. Molini obtained the Foligno Dante for 1,325 francs. Most books were sold successfully, in a sale dominated by Payne from London, Tilliard from Paris, Franck from Germany and Molini from Florence. Other private English buyers were also active, as were the British Museum and the

Bibliothèque Royale. Altogether the 3,025 lots offered produced the equivalent of 116,000 francs. The *Bulletin du Bibliophile* printed an extended account of the sale, but not until a report dated 6 November.[22]

Despite gossip, it seems that no one was prepared to say anything publicly, until in March 1848 a specially commissioned report was found among the office papers of Guizot, no longer Minister following the February revolution. Dated 4 February that year, it was quickly published in *Le Moniteur*, and so came to wider public attention. Faced with scandal and legal proceedings, in the same month Libri fled to England where he presented himself as a political refugee after the Revolution. A summary of the report was printed on 22 March in the *Morning Chronicle*, and in the Dublin *Freeman's Journal* the following day.[23] Thus London booksellers became involved in what quickly emerged as a major series of thefts from libraries across France and also in the Mazarine, the Arsenal and even the Bibliothèque Royale. In Brussels, the report seemed to explain how someone of quite ordinary means could afford to assemble so rich and extensive a library.[24] Meanwhile in Paris a search had revealed 30,000 volumes in his old apartments. More were recovered from a bookbinder.[25] The extent of Libri's thefts became clearer as these parts of his collection were examined.

Safely in London, Libri responded vigorously to the accusations printed in *Le Moniteur*, and issued an eighty-six page retort.[26] Copies were made available through the major London booksellers including Rivington, Pickering, Barthès & Lowell, and Rodd. Advertisements were taken out in the newspapers, and a separate edition was published in Paris. English opinion, sympathetic to a political exile, was generally in his favour, and a review in *The Examiner* summed up the mood: 'It is no more than justice to him to say that he proves the attempt to blacken his character in the *Moniteur* to have been mean, illiberal, and cruel.'[27] In France there was dismay that so much had either been sold to English customers, or had been otherwise exported across the Channel. There was much sympathy for him not just in Britain. In Berlin, the keeper of the Royal Library Carl Heinrich Brandes wrote a summary of Libri's apologia, and published it in the Leipzig *Serapeum*.[28] Brandes was not least concerned at the disorganised state of French libraries.

While opinion was divided in London, Libri never returned to face his accusers in France, where in 1850 he was condemned in his absence to ten years' solitary confinement with hard labour.[29] Instead, having managed with the help of the bookseller Hector Bossange to export eighteen further cases of books to England, he set about organising more sales. The manuscripts sold to Ashburnham, some of considerable value, had sometimes been altered, in order to mislead as to their provenances, and Libri continued to attend similarly to the books he sold subsequently. In Paris there were plenty of bookbinders willing to alter books as required. It emerged that he had caused early notes of provenance to be changed or erased,[30] though the widespread practice of washing books as a part of restoration perhaps dulled people's senses in this respect. Sometimes outright forgery was used. More commonly, books from French libraries were either sent to Italy to be rebound, or were rebound in London in Italian styles.

Historical curiosity could easily give rise to the recreation of historical records, sometimes for monetary gain, sometimes for more complicated reasons. In 1839 Alphonse Chassant, working at Évreux, produced a small manual *Paléographie des chartes* as a substitute for more unwieldy earlier studies. Like most such manuals, it was both a help and a hindrance, in that it was as useful for forgers as for honest enquirers. By 1876 it was in its seventh edition, published now in Paris by the same bookseller who also published his *Les nobles et les vilains du temps passé*, treating of 'la noblesse et les usurpations nobiliaires'. In 1851 Ludovic Lalanne and Henri-Léonard Bordier, two of those most responsible for exposing Libri, were candid about the extent to which manuscripts were altered or forged, and inscriptions changed or added.[31] Writing with the benefit of hindsight, and perhaps also in the hope that such matters were by 1888 a thing of the past, Delisle later reflected on this darker aspect of the Paris trade. It was encouraged by families wishing to create their past, perhaps to have evidence of ancestors' part in the Crusades, so that their names could be added to the roll-call in the museum at Versailles.[32]

Delisle wrote with characteristic energy, fervent in his campaign against Libri. In accusing the Paris book and manuscript trade in such absolute terms, he was no doubt right. However, he also failed to address a more general truth: that there is a spectrum of activities in the treatment of old books, between cleaning, conservation, minor improvement, major changes, replacement and outright forgery. The same has been a practice for years, and the more recent use in some quarters today of the term 'honest copy' to describe a volume that has been left in its old, often worn, state is a reflection of this continuing daily experience.[33]

Forgeries apart, Libri also assembled a series of stolen autographs that he had mounted in albums *à l'anglaise*, thus enabling him to pass them off without further enquiries about provenance.[34] All this meant that buyers were wise to proceed with caution. While Libri proceeded to sell many printed books at auction in Paris,[35] between 1849 and 1864 Sotheby's also presented nine auctions, at first anonymous and then explicit from 1859. In spring that year came a *Catalogue of the extraordinary collection of splendid manuscripts, chiefly upon vellum* (Figure 6).[36] Following his practice in 1847, Libri dressed it up with a long preface, this time in both French and English, followed by a list of almost three hundred reference works said to have been consulted and a pioneering series of facsimiles of many of the most interesting lots. The catalogue explained that the eight-day sale had been arranged as a consequence of Libri's ill health, and his need to leave London. This did not prevent his striving to ensure a good result. In a confidential exchange with Quaritch, he offered Quaritch modest inducements to invest, of up to five per cent reduction in price if he spent £4,000 or more. Quaritch was cautious. He was irritated to find that in one case, where he had charged 16 shillings, Libri or his agent had changed a note in the volume from this price to 6 guineas – in order to suggest an inflated value. Quaritch also made a note to himself that in some of the manuscripts that had passed through Libri's hands original ownership stamps had been obliterated, and fictitious ones inserted.[37]

On the whole, the quality in 1859 was lower than in some earlier sales, and bids reflected this. Most of the prices attained were modest, and the total for the sale reached only £6,783.[38] In Paris, Claudin followed this and some later sales carefully, printing summaries and reporting a large selection of prices in his monthly *Archives du Bibliophile*. Further sales followed in August (this time including early printing and a series of historic bindings), spring and summer 1861, July 1862 and June 1864, the last including a number of *objets de vertu*. A further anonymous sale by Puttick and Simpson followed in 1865.[39] It was unclear to bidders how much was honest and how much was not. Whether through genuine ignorance or through malice, for example, not all the books said to have come from the collection of Maioli in fact did so. In his subsequent brief history of bookbinding, Édouard Fournier remarked on the extraordinary price paid by the bookseller Villeneuve, £91, for a book from this collection: 'le seul Maioli authentique de cette vente, qui en étulait dix ou douze'.[40] In 1864, following ordinary trade custom, Libri constantly quoted the high prices achieved for copies of printed books in sales over the past thirty or forty years, but the sums buyers were now prepared to pay were often well below these. Though there were a few high prices, in general even rare books went cheap. The second-hand and antiquarian market was weak and suspicious, and buyers with deep pockets were difficult to find.

Libri died at Fiesole in 1869.

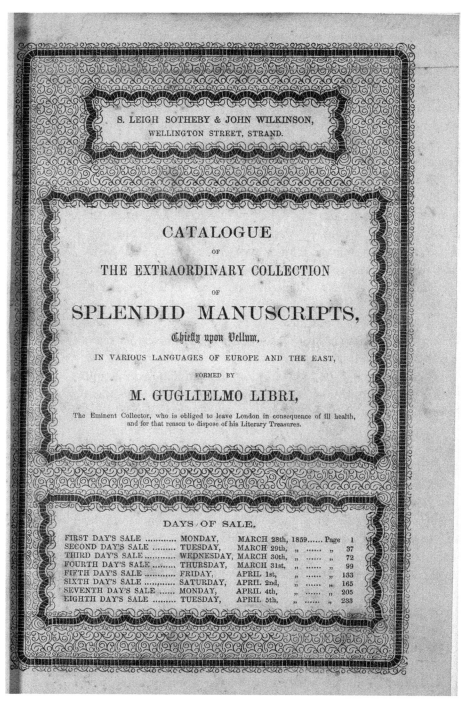

Figure 6 *Catalogue of the extraordinary collection of manuscripts, chiefly upon vellum ... formed by Guglielmo Libri ... Sotheby's, 28 March 1859 ...*

Attention had been drawn in a very public way to the disorganised state of French libraries. Even the Bibliothèque Royale was not immune to staff dishonesty; and as autograph collecting became an ever more popular pastime, with interest focused increasingly on celebrated names from the past, so the risks – and the losses – increased. The two most knowledgeable investigators of what became a national scandal dated a change in 1835, the year of an anonymous sale of autographs consigned by Libri. They noted the sudden appearance on the market of major names, where before there had been few such examples offered for sale. It was no longer petty theft, and libraries were the major victims. In 1848, by then no doubt with the Libri affair in mind, but also drawing on his further knowledge, Techener commented that 'Les richesses littéraires de nos dépots publics demeurent ignorées pour la plupart et souvent exposées à des soustractions dont on n'a que trop d'exemples.'[41] In 1851 thefts had become so widespread that it could be described as nothing less than 'une criminelle industrie'.[42]

Libri was by no means the only person to take advantage of poor, or non-existent, library management. He was also not the only person to employ nefariously the skills of Parisian facsimilists and forgers.[43] The affair raised many questions, and when in 1888 Delisle came to write an account, he painted a depressing picture of the disorganised state of the libraries where Libri had taken advantage: of books miscatalogued, of librarians who were incompetent and of other thefts that had in fact been taking place for decades.[44] Other people noted further invitations to theft. In a failure of ordinary curatorship, documents in archives had no marks of ownership. Libri brought many books and manuscripts to England, to be absorbed by English collectors, and thus further weakened France's bibliographical inheritance. The exceptional collection including stolen manuscripts sold by Libri to the Earl of Ashburnham in March 1847 was returned to the Bibliothèque Nationale in the 1880s.[45] For Delisle, Administrateur Général of the Library from 1875, Libri's activities meant decades of attempts to recover what had been purloined from French libraries.[46] The manuscripts collected by Joseph Barrois, and sold to Ashburnham, presented their own problems, of faked provenances and dubious circumstances surrounding the acquisition by Barrois of several volumes from the French national library.[47] For booksellers, the partnership of Payne and Foss, so much implicated in purchases at the point where the Libri scandal was beginning to erupt, ended with the auction of their stock in 1850.[48] In the end more generally and influentially, Libri had sown confusion across both France and England. Quite separately and more constructively, though the puffery irritated some people, the catalogues for the auctions, with their extended introductions and annotations, suggested new ways in which major collections might be sold.[49]

Tolerating Theft

Nowhere in Europe was there any kind of even local register of what books had been stolen, or what was missing. Booksellers might be warned to be alert for stolen goods; and in a world that depended largely on word of mouth rather than a more systematic exchange of information such as was initiated by the international antiquarian book trade in the later twentieth century, collectors might be stung. More often than not, catalogues of collections were inadequate, if they existed at all. Publication was not necessarily a defence. In 1829 Frédéric de Reiffenberg, then University Librarian at Leuven, described an extremely rare copy of the 30-line indulgence, printed at Mainz in 1454 and found by him in the binding of a book in the library. He included a facsimile in an article that was published prominently in the *Mémoires* of the Académie Royale in Brussels. The university was abolished in 1835, and the library was handed over to the newly founded Catholic University. At some point during these confused years the indulgence was acquired by Techener in Paris, who passed it to Payne and Foss in London, who then sold it to Earl Spencer. According to a knowledgeable later commentator, Spencer refused a request by the Belgian government to return what was clearly recognised, if not acknowledged, as stolen property.[50] It seems inconceivable that Techener, as a well-informed bookseller, did not know the history of what he was handling. Perhaps neither he nor Payne and Foss wished to know. The indulgence remains now in Manchester.[51]

When in 1851 Ludovic Marie Chrétien Lalanne (1815–98), Librarian of the Institut, and Henri-Léonard Bordier (1817–88), appointed to the Archives Nationales in that year, published their *Dictionnaire de pièces autographes volées aux bibliothèques de la France*, they were prompted by a specific scandal, the Libri affair; but their work had much wider implications. Given sufficient commitment and industry, a guide to thefts could be possible. Their work was by no means comprehensive, and it had involved three years of research on a specific challenge. They had searched the catalogues of 171 sales since 1822 that had included autographs, and estimated that well over 58,000 autograph pieces had been sold during that period. They concentrated on France, and on Paris, but they also included information from London: the problem was an international one. They had inspected archives in the Bibliothèque Nationale, the Paris Observatoire, the Archives Nationales and the Institut, as well as some libraries outside Paris, discovering that thousands of letters and other documents had been removed, sometimes accompanied by an effort to disguise the fact, and that subsequent rebinding had sometimes obscured matters further. Their industry was immense. In the Bibliothèque Nationale alone they reckoned to have examined up to 900 volumes. The Dupuy, Colbert and Baluze collections, among the richest and most important in the library, were only some that had suffered, and they restricted themselves to archives dating from before 1789.[52] They set out their findings in detail, in a dictionary of about 230 pages listing names of authors, to which were added notes of when many of these papers had appeared at auction – all too often among the property of Libri. There were a few successes to report, such as the pursuit through the courts of a document signed by Molière, but mostly it was a catalogue of national losses.

The *Catalogue général des manuscrits des bibliothèques publiques de France* launched originally by François Guizot went a long way to rectify a world of neglect, at least for manuscripts, though it proved a slow project. Only seven volumes were published between 1849 and 1885.[53] At Valenciennes, Jacques Mangeart compiled a fine catalogue independently, published in 1860: much had been done by then to improve the library and reading room, but the manuscripts and the printed books remained muddled together on the shelves.[54] Meanwhile many libraries remained without a proper survey or inventory.

The Biblioteca Colombina

The last example in this chapter of a library under attack dates from forty years or so later, and also concerns a collection that was the victim of inattention. The Biblioteca Colombina, in the care of Seville Cathedral, had for many years suffered from poor oversight. Hernando Colón (1488–1539), natural son of Christopher Columbus, collected one of the largest and most extensive libraries in Europe. Ambitious to encompass all books on all subjects, he pursued his goal by correspondence and in travels, and at his death left about 15,000 books. They came eventually into the care of the cathedral, but over the centuries this uniquely extensive collection was the repeated target of thefts, and was much neglected, to the loss of several thousand: about 3,000 survive today. Many of the remaining volumes were in poor condition, and though the Colón books were not stored separately, they were mostly identifiable by inscriptions. In 1885 scandal broke when it was discovered that volumes stolen in the previous year had found their way into the Paris trade, having (so it was reported) been partly used as packing material for furnishings sent from Spain.

As different parts of the trade woke up to the value of some of the books – some still marked with ownership stamps or inscriptions, while in others they had been clumsily removed – so collectors clustered, and details began to emerge. Books all too obviously from the library were bought by collectors including Baron Pichon (1812–96), President of the Société des Bibliophiles François. At the Bibliothèque Nationale, where even then Delisle was labouring to recover books from Libri's collection, a fifteenth-century *chansonnier* from Seville was purchased in 1885.[55] The affair caused some puzzlement, for the casual treatment of the stolen books suggested that the thief or thieves had only confused, if any, ideas of their value. It was reported at length by the *Revue Critique*, with details of some of the titles,[56] and again by Henry Harrisse in a short book *Grandeur et décadence de la Colombine* (Paris, 1885): Harrisse had become familiar with the library in writing his studies of Columbus father and son.[57] For English readers, further accounts were published in the *Library Journal* and *Book-Lore*. As for the cathedral authorities, little seems to have been done to recover the lost books, the librarian in Seville even denying an interest.[58] Volumes later found their way into the hands of the London trade and of well-known collectors including Charles Fairfax Murray who bought many of Pichon's books and possessed fifteen or sixteen examples.[59] In the words of a summary account presented to English readers, 'Assuming it to be true, the spoliation can only have been accomplished through the culpable neglect of the proper custodians. The thieves are evidently ignorant as well as dishonest, and may have done as much injury by stupid mutilations as by dishonest appropriations.'[60]

While the Colombina thefts remained an enigma in most respects, in that the books ended up in Paris initially at the cheap end of the trade before serious bibliophiles sought them out, the motives of Libri and of Halliwell were mostly financial. Other aspects were very similar in every case. All the thieves in these three cases took steps to disguise the origins of their spoils, whether with rebinding, erasure or alteration of ownership marks or simply cutting evidence out. In no case was the extent of the thefts fully established. None of the thieves sought to make use of the stolen books to further scholarship. So far as is known (Seville perhaps being the exception), none worked within a group of thieves, though both Libri and Halliwell employed binders to conceal provenance. Insofar as there was any complicity, it was fortuitous. All involved libraries in disorder, and a book trade that can at best be described as sometimes inattentive.

8 | Collaboration

Riding through all the discussions about the ordering of library catalogues, whether they should be of authors or of subjects, whether or not they should be printed and if so whether or not they should be sold or given away, were larger questions. What constituted the national book stock? Which parts were more important than others? In France, what was to be considered part of the *Patrimoine*?[1] How were libraries to be organised? What was their relationship to each other? How did organisation within and among libraries help or impede readers and any national research endeavours? How, therefore, did library provision reflect not just national pride but also the effectiveness of countries' knowledge economies? The size of any library when compared with others was a very crude measure. Its success in terms of how its contents were made available, and how far those contents reflected scholarly and research needs, came to be seen as more important and appropriate comparators. This became further pertinent as readerships changed in a world where social, financial, industrial, political and educational upheavals were everyday matters.

Much of this argued for a union catalogue, one that would not only save the time of people who might otherwise have to travel from library to library in quest of books without knowing where they were, but also one that would benefit the national consciousness. We have already seen some of the interest in this in discussions arising from the catalogue of the British Museum library.[2]

Union catalogues of printed books were slow to develop. A joint catalogue for Oxford libraries was first suggested in 1652, and a compilation was even advertised in the front of the Bodleian Library's published catalogue of 1738. The idea was revisited in the 1790s, but met with little response. It was bruited again in evidence given by the ornithologist and geologist Hugh Edwin Strickland to the Oxford University Commission in 1852, with a suggestion that books in college libraries but not in the Bodleian should be added to the Bodleian's own catalogue.[3] Nothing, again, came of it. In America, Charles Coffin Jewett, Librarian of the Smithsonian Institution, unsuccessfully proposed one for American libraries.[4] In Cambridge, projects for the colleges and university were contemplated in the mid-seventeenth and early eighteenth centuries. The matter was raised again in evidence to the Royal Commission on the University in 1852, and the subject was revisited in the 1880s.[5] Nothing came of any of these.

While printed books were often mentioned, in practice the emphasis had been on manuscripts.[6] As noted earlier, Edward Bernard assembled a union catalogue of manuscripts in England and Ireland in 1697, Bernard de Montfaucon's *Bibliotheca* had appeared in 1739, and in 1830 Gustav Haenel published a survey of library holdings in a large part of Europe, though not Germany or the Italian peninsula.[7] Though none was complete, all offered invaluable access. In France, where the first volume of a systematic series of catalogues of manuscripts appeared in 1849, it was not until 1886 that René Goblet, Ministre de l'Instruction Publique, addressed the question of printed books formally, and sought a union catalogue of incunables to sit alongside that of manuscripts.[8] By then there were a few printed catalogues of the early printed books at Toulouse (1878), Nancy (1883), Dijon (1886) and elsewhere. More generally applicable rules for their cataloguing were finally drawn up by Delisle in 1886, in response if not to an entirely new mood, then at least one revisiting old truths:

Ce qui justifie le traitement particulier dont ils sont l'objet, c'est que beaucoup d'entre eux ont presque la même autorité et sont à peu près aussi rares que les manuscrits. C'est encore et surtout parce qu'ils nous fournissent le moyen d'étudier l'origine encore obscure et les premiers développements d'un art sur lequel repose en grande partie la civilisation moderne.[9]

Despite his plea for a union catalogue that would serve both scholars and library management, early printed books remained poorly served until Marie Pellechet (1840–1900) took them in hand. Having cut her bibliographical teeth on a study of liturgical books from Autun, and with catalogues of the incunables at Dijon and Versailles completed, she was thinking ahead to a national union catalogue of incunabula when in 1893 she published a detailed account of those at Lyon. The first volume of her union catalogue, compiled in an extraordinarily short space of time and the only one to be published in her lifetime, covering just *Abano–Biblia*, appeared in 1897.[10]

If it seemed that Great Britain had less obvious a need of such projects, and most of the public libraries were outside London, the universities and the cathedrals were less well endowed with collections of early books and manuscripts, it remained that it was difficult to know what rare books existed, or where. In this respect the nineteenth century was an age of discovery on both sides of the Channel, as collections and rarities were gradually reported, and recorded. The need for a fuller international bibliography of incunabula, to replace Hain, and to include locations of copies, was pressed by W.A. Copinger in England and by Konrad Burger and Karl Dziatzko in Germany. It finally led to a meeting in 1904 at which what was to become the *Gesamtkatalog der Wiegendrucke* was launched, beginning with a full survey of German libraries.[11]

Various reasons were advanced for these projects, including their potential advantages as a means of avoiding buying expensive duplicates. They also reflected scholarly needs and aspirations, and methods of work as they had developed. Union catalogues, allied to increasingly efficient and speedy travel, made more comparisons possible, and therefore expected. The contrast between the detailed discussions of Bradshaw and Campbell concerning early Low Countries books following the publication of Campbell's *Annales* in 1874, and the summary inadequacies of Delisle's instructions for describing incunables, exposed all too clearly the weaknesses inherent in different approaches. A flurry of more general catalogues of printed books in libraries across France in the mid-nineteenth century was inspired not only by local pride. While they were by no means all of an equally high standard, they nonetheless brought routes for access. Sometimes they simply met local needs for straightforward reading. Sometimes they recorded books not to be found easily elsewhere. The same pattern emerged in the Netherlands (Amsterdam, Deventer, Gouda, The Hague, Haarlem, Nijmegen, Utrecht, etc.) and in Belgium (Antwerp, Bruges, Brussels, etc.). Libraries hitherto neglected or even forgotten sometimes offered more than antiquarian interest. On the north side of the Channel, in 1849 Beriah Botfield offered his *Notes on the cathedral libraries of England* as a contribution to 'the awakened interest in the curiosities of English literature'.[12] By that date there were summary printed catalogues of the libraries at Carlisle (1783), Canterbury (1802), Ely (1815), Norwich (1819, 1836), Rochester (1839) and Peterborough (1842). Although necessarily selective, Botfield's was the first extended survey of the cathedral libraries, for William Clarke in 1819 had provided notes on only Canterbury.[13] 'Among much that is obsolete', wrote Botfield, 'there is more that is valuable, and amid much that is trifling there is more that is important.'

Botfield provided sometimes long lists of the more notable early books in the libraries he described. It was not always an encouraging picture, and at Lincoln, 'this sadly bereaved repository', it was least encouraging of all. Not only had it been the practice to allow interested visitors to cut out illuminations from medieval manuscripts, in exchange (it was said) for a few shillings to the verger, but also rare printed books had been sold, and there were now no more Caxtons in the library. 'The guardians of the temple slept, and Mammon prevailed.'[14] The money had been used to buy modern books. In 1830 Gustav Haenel noted that manuscripts at both Salisbury and Lincoln had been damaged by damp.[15] Such comments drew public attention to needs, even if public opinion was muted. As for parochial libraries, while a few were well cared for, such as those at Beccles, Whitchurch and St Margaret's, King's Lynn, others were treated in a similar cavalier manner with no thought to their history or their content.[16] At Boston in Lincolnshire, a parish library founded in 1635, two or more cartloads were recorded as having been sold to a local dealer. At Swaffham in Norfolk, the books were reported to be in a desperate state, covered in mouse and bat droppings and with covers ripped off. At Wimborne, the neglected library had lost about 10 per cent of its stock in a hundred years.[17]

Access could be another matter entirely. Not all cathedral libraries were equally welcoming. At Rochester in the 1870s there was no librarian, and no library hours were offered. At Peterborough hours were limited to an hour on Saturday afternoons. While St Paul's Cathedral in London actively discouraged visitors, partly hiding behind the fact that there were other nearby libraries and that Sion College library, only a few hundred yards away, was available for clergy, other places such as Norwich or Gloucester claimed to be more accommodating. Few were used more than minimally; but in the work of Botfield, of the cathedral commissioners of 1854, and in a detailed survey offered to the infant Library Association compiled in the 1870s by the Rev. Herbert E. Reynolds of Exeter Cathedral, efforts were made to draw attention to these often neglected resources.[18] There was little attempt to co-ordinate information. Deans and Chapters remained firmly independent and had no interest in any kind of joint catalogues. By 1880, the date of the publication of the catalogue of Salisbury Cathedral library, catalogues for Lincoln, Lichfield, Worcester and Chichester had been added to the tally mentioned previously. None could claim bibliographical versatility. It was only in the mid-twentieth century that there emerged enough agreement for steps to be taken to compile a union catalogue of the early printed books in the cathedrals.[19]

The position among the Oxford and Cambridge colleges was mixed. At Cambridge, T.H. Horne produced a comprehensive two-volume catalogue of the printed books in Queens' College library in 1823, and in 1829 C.H. Hartshorne gathered his sometimes discursive notes into a more general book, *The book rarities of the University of Cambridge*. A selective account appeared in 1843 of some of the rarer books in St John's College.[20] Brief catalogues of the early books in Gonville and Caius were published in 1850.[21] The work in these was very variable. At Oxford, Magdalen College library was recorded in a three-volume catalogue in 1860–2, and the first of several volumes appeared for Merton in 1879.

By 1877, when a group of librarians visited various institutions in London, they were shown printed catalogues from Aberdeen, Birmingham, Blackburn, Bradford, Coventry, Edinburgh, Liverpool, over a dozen libraries in London, Manchester, Newcastle-upon-Tyne, Penzance, Plymouth and Rochdale, quite apart from a long series of American collections and a selection from continental Europe.[22] Copies were distributed widely among libraries. While by no means all these publications contained significant holdings of early books, and their primary purpose was often simply local, they represented a means of bibliographical access that had become assumed.

Beside all this there emerged a further question. How could libraries collaborate and co-operate so as to improve each other? Union catalogues, and printed catalogues of individual libraries, offered one way, but they presupposed that each library held and assembled its stock independently.

Delisle accepted what became widely, albeit not generally, received wisdom concerning the interdependence of French libraries, based on national supervision and organised from Paris. It had been a key element of discussions since soon after the Revolution, and though the concept then had achieved only very limited practical application, the idea remained a powerful one. In the early nineteenth century, a national union catalogue was proposed, and started, but it quickly ran into the ground: in the event, one was only tackled properly for manuscripts, in the 1840s.[23] Delisle later looked at the purchasing policies of the Bibliothèque Nationale, wishing to avoid unnecessary and expensive duplication. Buying was to be within the context of the other great Parisian libraries, particularly the Arsenal, the Mazarine and Ste Geneviève: 'Quand nous savons qu'un livre de ce genre [i.e., 'd'une incontestable utilité'] existe dans une de nos grandes bibliothèques, nous nous abstenons de l'acheter.'[24] He gave examples of early printed books that were by no means as rare as was claimed, but which were not obviously recorded. In a process that dated from at least the seventeenth century, many of the manuscripts and rarer or more important books held in libraries in the provinces had gravitated to Paris, whether for the royal library, or (for many years) for powerful political or ecclesiastical figures, or as a result of the Revolution.[25] The same principle prevailed in the reorganisation of libraries following the Revolution. In 1841, Ravaisson, inspecting libraries in the western part of France, argued repeatedly that libraries should exchange books, so as to reduce duplication and strengthen those less well supplied.[26] In his own suggested scheme for exchanges, Delisle was more interested in Paris. He followed this tradition, arguing for the central dominance of the Bibliothèque Nationale as the recipient of rare books it did not possess, but were to be found in other libraries.[27]

Exchanges not just between libraries but also between libraries and booksellers offered ways forward in markets where purchasing funds were inadequate. Though it became of key importance for the University Library at Cambridge, matters there began modestly enough. Recognising that the ordinary funds for purchase were very limited, in the 1860s the bookseller Henry Stevens worked with University Librarian J.E.B. Mayor and with Bradshaw to acquire early printed books for American libraries and provided modern publications in exchange. Within a few years, the arrangement was extended to improving the Library's stock of incunables.[28]

Thanks initially more to the energies of individuals than to government policies, international exchange became familiar to some. In France, Alexandre Vattemare (1796–1864) was ambitious, and influential. He is mentioned barely more than in passing in the *Histoire des bibliothèques françaises*, in connection with the exceptional American collection assembled thanks to his initiative at the Bibliothèque de la Ville in Paris. His influence was considerably wider, and his ideas were wider still.[29] He made his name and his fortune as a ventriloquist, and in the course of his international travels noticed the poverty of many libraries. Counter to this were the accumulations of duplicates to be seen on a vast scale at Munich but also apparent in lesser numbers elsewhere. From this developed his idea that libraries and public bodies might exchange duplicates with each other, thus enriching both parties. In the 1830s he worked towards agreements between French libraries and Russia, Denmark, Austria, England and Sweden, but his ideas bore fruit most in the United States, where in the 1840s reports to Congress summarised achievements thus far.[30] By 1850, French contributors included not only several government departments but also the cities of Metz, Nantes, Bordeaux and Marseille, as well as several private citizens. They parted with books printed from the sixteenth century onwards, including not only printed state papers but also everything from classical authors to theology, botany and medicine. Columbia College, the New York state hospital, the city of New York and the state of Connecticut (some to be deposited at Yale) were just some of those who benefited. The scheme was extended to include on appropriate occasions examples of natural history specimens, prints, coins and medals. Thus encouraged, Vattemare turned his attention to establishing exchange arrangements in Belgium and the Netherlands.[31]

While libraries in France parted with eighteenth-century books as well as more recent ones, there were other variations on this theme. Arrangements were made for forty-four sets to be presented, in the name of the state, of the *Natural history of New York*. This was a vast project published initially in Albany, of which the first of what was to be thirty volumes appeared in 1842: the project was not completed until 1894. The state's list of recipients, which included the Sultan of Turkey and the Pope, was noticeable in omitting any in the British Isles. It was pointed out that while the numbers of books in American libraries were not as great as those in Europe, the country was rich in natural resources, of which specimens might be provided. In 1851 the Smithsonian Institution in Washington established a system of exchanges for its own publications, receiving in return those of institutions or individuals overseas, mostly in Europe and gradually across the world. The scheme was subsequently extended to include a limited number of government documents.[32] It was not universally welcomed, and it took the British Treasury almost three years in 1879–82 to agree to a comprehensive exchange arrangement involving the British Museum. Arrangements with other countries soon followed, to be followed in turn by the 1890s with various learned institutions.[33]

Arising from all this, the principle that books might be exchanged between libraries for their mutual advantage was established, and with it developed arrangements for formalised inter-library loans. In Cambridge, Bradshaw was on several occasions willing to lend even rare early printed books internationally from the university library, usually (but not, it seems, invariably) subject to the University's formal agreement. In 1874 he wrote to M.F.A.G. Campbell at the Royal Library in The Hague concerning a fifteenth-century book:

Would it be possible for you to let me see your *Wech van salicheit*, printed by Gl at Utrecht? I am very anxious to be able to make out the connexion between it and the *Wech van salicheden* on the one side and the *Wech der syelen salicheyt* on the other. . . . I have persuaded the Library authorities here to allow any such books to go out freely where it is desirable. Formerly it was a very tedious process. . . . When a book is small enough to go by registered book post, there cannot well be any danger at all. They sent me a book from Munich the other day to examine, and I returned it the next day.[34]

Campbell supplied the book by return of post, and Bradshaw was able to send him a detailed bibliographical summary of the editions. On another occasion, working on editions of the *Rosarium BVM* printed at Antwerp in the 1480s, Bradshaw had in his hands copies from both The Hague and Berlin. When he borrowed a copy from The Hague in 1877, he only returned it in 1880 after reminders from Campbell.[35]

Not every library was in a position to be so accommodating. Sir Thomas Bodley had expressly forbidden loans in his new library in the early seventeenth century, and neither the British Museum nor the Bibliothèque Nationale enjoyed the freedoms of Cambridge and The Hague. Nonetheless, for centuries it had been possible for private scholars to borrow manuscripts from some libraries. The risks involved became disastrously evident in 1880, when fire broke out in Theodor Mommsen's house at Charlottenburg. He not only lost most of his huge library and a mass of working notes on the history of Rome gathered over many years but also manuscripts he had borrowed from other libraries including Cambridge, Brussels, Halle, Vienna, Berlin and Heidelberg. He was able to save some of what he had borrowed, but not everything: a medieval manuscript of Jordanes's *Getica* and other texts from Trinity College, Cambridge, were among the losses.[36] The fire was reported in *The Times*[37] and in many other newspapers, and people were quick to point out the moral: that while manuscripts might be lent to other libraries, they should not be lent to private individuals, however respected or eminent. Cambridge University Library had repeatedly lent manuscripts and rare printed books to individuals,[38] but now it was noted that the Bodleian lent only to libraries.

Understandably, opinion was divided. Ten years later the librarians and others gathered at Antwerp turned their attention to loans.[39] After considering arrangements for the international exchange of official publications, and noting the laborious processes involved in loans of manuscripts among French libraries, where requests had to be via the Ministre de l'Instruction Publique, discussion turned to ordinary printed books. For this, there was much to be said in favour, provided the books concerned were not in demand by readers, or were fragile, or were especially rare. Charles Ruelens, of the Bibliothèque Royale in Brussels, was adamant that dangers to manuscripts outweighed advantages to scholars. He recalled the example of a copy of Nicolas de Cusa lent to Germany, which had been returned to Brussels smelling strongly of tobacco and showing signs of having been in a beer cellar. Another manuscript had been returned with its illustrations cut out. Another had been rediscovered only by chance. Ruelens suggested alternative strategies, now that travel was so much cheaper and easier. For example, a youthful cadre of copyists could be recruited to copy out manuscripts required: the fact that transcripts were not necessarily all that was needed seemed to escape him. On the other hand, Willem Du Rieu, university librarian of Leiden, took a more positive approach. No doubt he was encouraged by remembering that the manuscript lent by Leiden to Mommsen had been rescued and returned safely.

The Mommsen affair, involving one of Europe's most celebrated scholars, rattled the library world and was still being quoted a decade and more later. It put librarians on their guard. But over the course of about half a century important principles had been worked out. Proceedings that had been ad hoc were regularised, as governments and libraries worked towards formal arrangements respecting not only the exchange of government publications but also of printed books and of manuscripts. In Brussels, a new Commission des Échanges Internationaux produced a handbook in 1875 listing publishing societies whose works might be drawn on.[40] The rudiments for an international exchange programme were put in place in 1886, with a convention in Brussels on the international exchange of official documents and scientific papers. This well-meaning project soon foundered, not to be revisited until the twentieth century,[41] but the point had been made. For most of those attending the Antwerp conference, there seemed no reason why the principle should not be extended to all kinds of publications. Whether between libraries or nations, exchanges of printed books promoted the advance of learning – a principle at the heart of the Smithsonian Institution's activities – but they were also a means of improving and distributing stocks of early books. Access was increased, and money could be saved.

Trading and Collecting

9 | The Trade in Second-Hand Books

In Britain, for trade, libraries and collectors alike, the period between the 1830s and the 1880s is bounded by two dominant series of events in the auction world. In April 1834 Sotheby's offered the first part of the library of the late Richard Heber. He represented the epitome of bibliomania, with houses full of books in different countries and reckoning to possess multiple copies of books as a matter of course. This first sale alone took twenty-six days, and it was followed by a series of further sales releasing into the market many tens of thousands of books whose overwhelming numbers and range were to affect the world of second-hand and antiquarian bookselling for the next thirty years. At the other end of the period, the Settled Lands Acts of 1882 and subsequently, legislation introduced in the wake of several years of agricultural depression, made it possible to release inherited property, and turn it into cash for reinvestment or even survival. Between 1868 and 1879 the price of wheat slumped from 63s.9d. a quarter to 43s.10d., and 1879 was recorded as the worst harvest known: the yield per acre was only just over half what it had been in the previous year.[1] A decline in rents over the next several years of agricultural depression affected some parts of the country very differently from others, though landlords who also possessed London property or industrial interests were shielded from the worst effects on annual income. The consequences for the book trade were dramatic, as a series of major inherited libraries were put up for sale. British legislation helped define an era. It was followed by the release into the market of old and well-stocked libraries containing many treasures, yet also a great quantity of quite ordinary common books.

The years 1881–3 brought to auction the Sunderland library from Blenheim Palace (Figure 7). One of the greatest collections of the eighteenth century, it had been formed originally by Charles Spencer, third Earl of Sunderland, in the reigns of George I and George II, and had been moved from Sunderland House in Piccadilly to the new Blenheim Palace. By the 1870s the family was acutely short of money. The celebrated collection of Marlborough gems, bought in 1766, was sold in 1875, and in 1880 the Blenheim Settled Estates Act gave freedom for further sales. No time was lost in the library, the first of five auctions by Puttick & Simpson

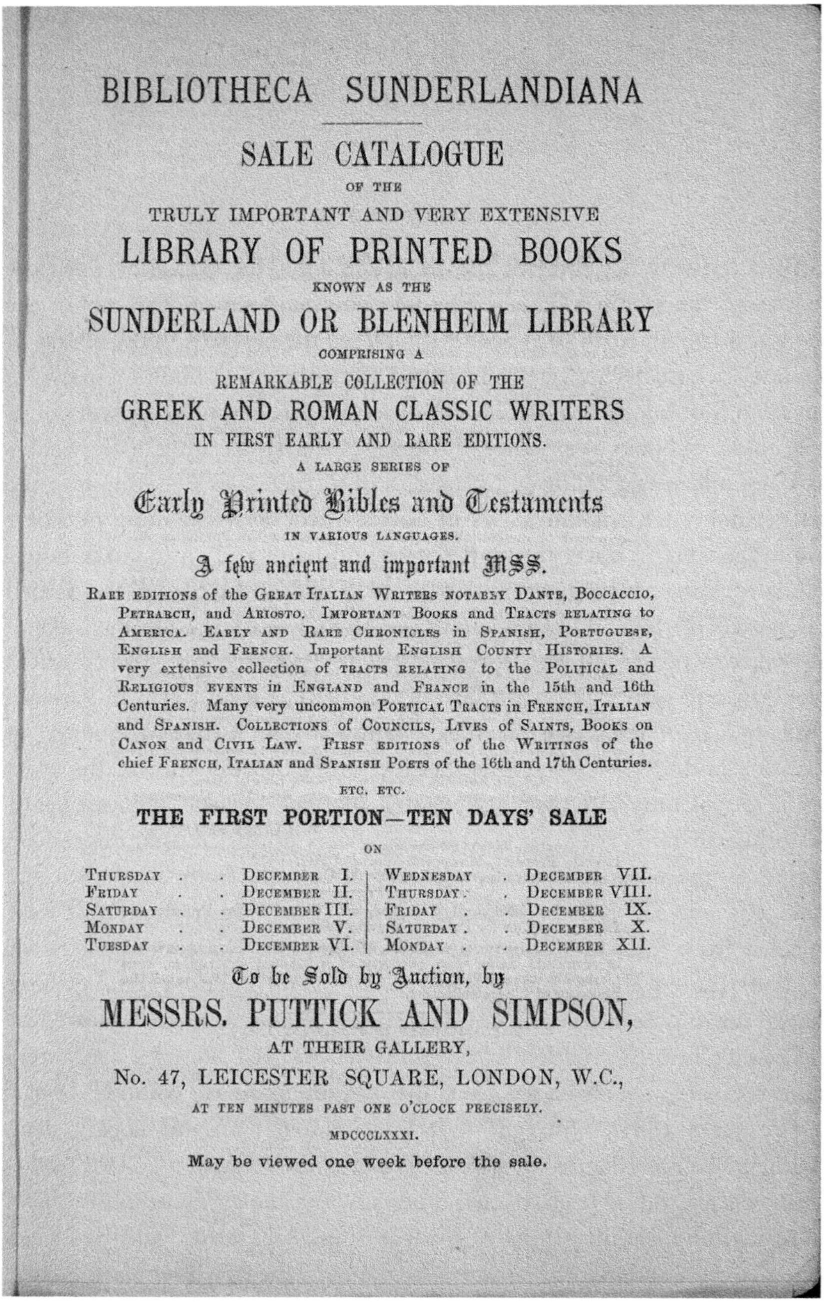

BIBLIOTHECA SUNDERLANDIANA

SALE CATALOGUE

OF THE

TRULY IMPORTANT AND VERY EXTENSIVE

LIBRARY OF PRINTED BOOKS

KNOWN AS THE

SUNDERLAND OR BLENHEIM LIBRARY

COMPRISING A

REMARKABLE COLLECTION OF THE

GREEK AND ROMAN CLASSIC WRITERS

IN FIRST EARLY AND RARE EDITIONS.

A LARGE SERIES OF

Early Printed Bibles and Testaments

IN VARIOUS LANGUAGES.

A few ancient and important MSS.

Rare editions of the Great Italian Writers notably Dante, Boccaccio, Petrarch, and Ariosto. Important Books and Tracts relating to America. Early and Rare Chronicles in Spanish, Portuguese, English and French. Important English County Histories. A very extensive collection of tracts relating to the Political and Religious events in England and France in the 15th and 16th Centuries. Many very uncommon Poetical Tracts in French, Italian and Spanish. Collections of Councils, Lives of Saints, Books on Canon and Civil Law. First editions of the Writings of the chief French, Italian and Spanish Poets of the 16th and 17th Centuries.

ETC. ETC.

THE FIRST PORTION—TEN DAYS' SALE

ON

Thursday .	. December I.	Wednesday	. December VII.
Friday .	. December II.	Thursday .	. December VIII.
Saturday .	. December III.	Friday .	. December IX.
Monday .	. December V.	Saturday .	. December X.
Tuesday .	. December VI.	Monday .	. December XII.

To be Sold by Auction, by

MESSRS. PUTTICK AND SIMPSON,

AT THEIR GALLERY,

No. 47, LEICESTER SQUARE, LONDON, W.C.,

AT TEN MINUTES PAST ONE O'CLOCK PRECISELY.

MDCCCLXXXI.

May be viewed one week before the sale.

Figure 7 *Bibliotheca Sunderlandiana. Sale catalogue of the library of printed books known as the Sunderland or Blenheim library . . . To be sold by auction by Puttick and Simpson,* 1881.

taking place over ten days in December 1881. Major paintings by Rubens, Raphael and Van Dyck left the house soon afterwards. Other owners followed with their own sales. The years 1882–4 brought to auction part of the library of William Beckford (1760–1844), in the Hamilton Palace sales;[2] 1883, books and manuscripts from the Towneley family library in Lancashire; 1884, the Thorold books from Syston Park and the library of the Earl of Gosford; 1885, the Earl of Jersey's books from Osterley Park;[3] and 1886, the residue of the collection assembled in the eighteenth and early nineteenth centuries by Michael Wodhull (1740–1816). The more recently formed library of John Fuller Russell was also offered in 1886 in this extraordinary series of major sales all within a very short period, and further sales were to follow.[4]

The antiquarian trade, suddenly over-supplied, was faced with the need to support prices and existing investments in stock, so as to avoid the collapse that had occurred earlier in the century. In this, Bernard Quaritch was a key figure.[5] In 1888 he issued a fat catalogue of early printed books, many of which came from these recent sales. It was remarkable for the numerous books that would ordinarily be considered rare, but were available here in sometimes multiple copies. Repeatedly, he drew attention to the lower prices that he was asking, compared with those achieved at auctions either very recently or some time previously. With two copies in stock of the Complutensian polyglot Bible (1514–17), one exceptionally fine and the other, slightly wormed, from the Sunderland sale, he offered the first for £200 and the second for £110, adding that it had cost £195 at the sale.

I am not concerned here with the conduct or detailed outcomes of these sales; nor am I much concerned with the immense influx of American investment in early books and manuscripts then and in the years following, though there was already significant activity here, exemplified in the dedicated work of the London-based New England bookseller Henry Stevens (d.1886).[6] The exodus of books to the United States was viewed sometimes with alarm. For those who took notice, it provoked a reaction rooted in various kinds of nationalism, just as earlier in the century France had viewed with dismay the exodus of books from that country in the wake of revolution and war. Three major American collectors died within a few years of each other: John Carter Brown of Rhode Island died in 1874, George Brinley of Connecticut in 1875 and James Lenox of New York in 1880. A new generation quickly took their place.

The changes in taste, provision and opportunities were easily noticed. Not all comment was accurate, such as Edward Arber's entirely unjustified anxiety in 1884 that the numbers of collectors and resources were both diminishing: 'It sometimes seems to me that literary culture is dying out. The day of great private collectors is gone: there are no books to be had.'[7] Given the extraordinary libraries that were even then coming to auction partly as a result of the settled estates legislation, his remarks about supply could hardly have been more mistaken, while a new generation of major as well as lesser collectors was coming forward. In some other respects there had been little less than a transformation.

Auctions

The trade depended fundamentally on auctions. In Britain, the book auction trade was dominated by London, where matters were organised mostly round the major houses of Leigh & Sotheby, Puttick & Simpson, Christie & Manson and Southgate & Barrett.[8] Although there were naturally exceptions, auctions elsewhere in the country tended to be smaller, and even very large libraries were transported to London for sale. The fullest census so far assembled, which is by no means comprehensive geographically, suggests that across the country there were over six thousand auctions involving larger or smaller collections of books between 1850 and 1883. There remains no census of lesser sales in the provinces of which the only surviving record is often no more than a newspaper advertisement. Auctions provided a speedy way of selling libraries, and they also offered booksellers an efficient means of disposing of unwanted stock as well as of acquiring new stock.[9]

Some observers found a change in behaviour at auctions. In offering advice to librarians on how to purchase second-hand and old books, Edward Edwards claimed that whereas in the 'palmy days' of thirty or forty years previously (the date of his writing suggested that he was thinking of about 1820) it had been wise to place commissions through agents, now it was safe to bid in person – always provided that one kept one's wits about one, and avoided being run up by other people in the room.[10] Others noted changes in auction-room practice, but came to a different conclusion: that it was no longer the ordinary custom to bid in person, as had the major collectors in the heyday of bibliomania, but instead, that now booksellers held the field.[11]

In Paris, this became more organised with the introduction of *commissaires-priseurs* as a means of controlling the trade in old books, parallel to legislation controlling new publications. Two locations became the focus for sales, the maison Silvestre and the hôtel Drouot.¹² They were not conducted in quite the same way in London and Paris. Matters proceeded more quickly in London, where – so it seemed to the Paris bookseller Joseph Techener – behaviour was generally better:

> L'ordre parfait et le calme qui règnent dans les ventes de livres en Angleterre, forment un contraste bien frappant avec le tumulte qui accompagne la plupart des ventes qui ont lieu dans notre pays. En Angleterre, le silence le plus absolu et l'attention la plus soutenue sont indispensables pour suivre les enchères qui marchent avec la rapidité de la vapeur. Trois cent articles sont ordinairement vendus en deux heures et demie.¹³

As Techener frequented the London sales, he was writing with first-hand knowledge. Auctions were not relished by everyone. In 1847 the well-established Paris bookseller Jules-Joseph Hébrard complained of their malign influence. Prices could be sometimes considerably higher than in shops; collectors sometimes seemed to prefer the excitement of a sale to a conversation with a knowledgeable bookseller; a bookseller would accept back an imperfect copy, whereas at auctions there was very limited time to return one. He resented the interfering and expensive necessity of the new *commissaires-priseurs*. It seemed to him that the French trade, so long dominant in Europe, had sunk below that in the Netherlands or Germany.¹⁴

The London auction seasons of the mid-1840s were punctuated by the long series of sales from the library of Joseph Walter King Eyton, FSA (d.1872), benefactor of the Society of Antiquaries and of Birmingham City Library. Three occurred in 1847 alone. Eyton came from an old Shropshire family, but had spent his life mostly in Birmingham and London. Sotheby's added notes on many of his large number of modern privately printed books. There were plenty of grand copies, but whereas in Paris some laudatory preface could have been expected, Sotheby's added none. Instead, there was much detail about bindings and about presentation copies. For the immense library of Stowe House in Buckinghamshire, sold over twenty-four days by Sotheby's in January–February 1849, likewise no prefatory matter was added. Puffing prefaces were rare, and those for the Libri sales were thus all the more noticeable.

The Libri affair¹⁵ was a reminder, if any was needed, of the close relationship between French and English booksellers, French and English auctioneers, and French and English collectors. Libri's sale to the Earl of Ashburnham of a major collection of manuscripts, many of them purloined from French libraries, understandably rankled in Paris. His subsequent sales in London added further to damage his reputation as one who, charged with improving French libraries, had defrauded them.[16] When his books came to auction at Sotheby's, Techener, Anatole Claudin and Tross were among the bidders seeking to return the exiled volumes to France. The colossal exodus of books and works of art across the English Channel following the French Revolution and its aftermath remained a defining aspect of trade, and for many years English collectors and dealers were in a powerful position, able to pay better prices than their continental equivalents. In November 1847 Techener took some pleasure in recording that French black-letter books once collected by English collectors had been bought back by the late Louis-Aimé Martin (1782–1847) and were now to be offered for sale in Paris.[17] Traffic had not all been one way. The sheer numbers of books in the Heber sales of the 1830s meant that there were opportunities for French buyers, and the Prince d'Essling (1799–1863) was prominent among them. In return, when some of Essling's books were auctioned at Paris in 1847, Payne was among the most active participants.

Changing Times

The year 1847 saw sales in France from the libraries of the Prince d'Essling in May, of books from Libri's collection in June, and in November of both Louis-Aimé Martin and the Marquis de Coislin. All were exceptionally rich, and the year was viewed as

véritablement une de ces années d'abondance qu'un sort de jaloux et parcimonieux ne nous accorde que de loin en loin.[18]

The mood was to change dramatically in February of the new year, when revolution in several countries brought temporary upset to the book trade.

Quite apart from the international political turmoil and unrest of 1848, there was a strong sense of an ending, of crisis, and growing from this a sense of both survival and renewal. The bookseller and literary scholar F.S. Ellis (b.1830) was too young to recall these years in detail, but they passed into his and London's professional memory as a period when book prices were at their lowest ebb.[19] Now they were further threatened by political upheaval and uncertainty. Yet the February Revolution in France, and the ending of the July monarchy, seemed within a few turbulent weeks to demonstrate the resilience of French life. Though it inevitably brought uncomfortable reminders of the chaos following 1789, this had not been repeated. In May 1848 Techener republished the third and most influential of the abbé Grégoire's reports on vandalism, originally issued in 1795, but it was little more than a reminder.[20] The trade, temporarily disrupted, soon recovered. A triple issue of the *Bulletin du Bibliophile*, published in March 1848 and covering the three months since the start of the year, signalled that a tumultuous first quarter was now past. One obvious measure was in auction activity. As the year 1849 developed, it became clear that in both Paris and the provinces sales were becoming more frequent, and that owners in other countries were also willing to consign their books for sale. Prices for the better and rarer books continued to rise, and new collectors were coming forward.[21] Ever anxious, Techener viewed with relief the evidence of recovery, as book collectors led by Nicolas Yemeniz in Lyon and the duc d'Aumale in London showed continuing enthusiasm, and auction prices were not damaged at least when the better and more expensive books were considered. He became even romantic:

Les livres rares et précieux, les volumes sortis des presses célèbres, ou reliés par des artistes en renom, attirent infailliblement les bibliophiles, ainsi que les fleurs odorantes et fraîches attirent les abeilles, ainsi que l'aimant attire le fer.[22]

Having escaped the worst of the revolutionary upheavals in mainland Europe, it was hardly to be expected that the London trade would be much affected. Auction prices seemed buoyant. Notwithstanding the gloom expressed by some people, the doldrums following the Heber sales seemed to have been broken with the several sales of the exceptional library of the late Benjamin Heywood Bright of Bristol, in 1845.[23] The major Libri sale of early 1849 came as encouragement.

The changes were partly more insidious. In Paris, there were discussions concerning the future of printing for the state, and with them a threat that the Imprimerie Royale (variously the Imprimerie Impériale or Nationale), dating back to 1640, should be closed. The proposal was met with vigorous defences that led directly to detailed published histories.[24] Although in 1861 François Antoine Duprat prefixed his remarks on the Imprimerie Impériale with allusions to Caxton, Aldus Manutius and others, his purpose was clearly more than historical. The first in his list of printing heroes was Johann Mentelin, who had been printing at Strasbourg by 1460. With Alsace now part of France, Mentelin was arguably the country's first printer (preceding the first press in Paris by ten years) and thus to be deployed in a political argument. For their very different purposes, Duprat in France, Charles Knight in England, and the promoters of Coster in the Netherlands and of Gutenberg in Germany were all using the history of printing as a support in wider political campaigns.

Had the world, asked Techener in 1850, arrived at 'une époque de transformation'?[25] Many brief periods have produced groups of changes, but they have not always been articulated as did Techener. He wrote of the world of books, yet the question applied at least as much to other aspects of social, economic and political life, and it applied not only to France. Among the Paris booksellers, the long-established, influential and revered firm of Debure was at an end. The sale of the library of Marie-Jacques Debure, who had died in June 1847, was arranged to take place in March 1848, but the events of February made this impossible, and it finally took place a year later, in March 1849. His older brother Jean-Jacques Debure died in 1853, and meanwhile their cousin Laurent-François Debure (1775–1864) had retired in 1846, the last member of the family to deal in books. In the Netherlands, the Leiden bookselling and printing firm of Luchtmans, with a history dating from the seventeenth century, came to an end in 1848.[26] In London, Thomas Rodd, bookseller to the British Museum and one of the most prominent people in the trade, died in 1849. In 1850 Payne and Foss closed their business, and sent to auction what was reckoned by some to be the most important collection of early books in the European trade.

With the benefit of a few further years' reflection, another major bookseller at Paris in 1862 advanced a thoughtful and informed view of how matters were changing. Eugénie-Marie Laurent, widow of the bookseller Pierre-Louis Deflorenne (d.1852) and recently remarried to Antoine Bachelin, put her name to the introduction to a new periodical, *Le Bibliophile Français*. Like the *Archives du Bibliophile* launched in 1858 by her colleague in the book trade Anatole Claudin (Figure 8), it was a mixture of news, sales reports, advertising and opinion, linked to the pair's regular catalogues of recently acquired second-hand books. These quasi-magazines, over half-full of lists of books, were a convenient way of also circulating offers of books. The opening sentences of the introduction to her fresh venture remarked explicitly on some of the changes that had occurred:

Depuis quelques années, la librairie antique, rare, artistique et curieuse a pris un développement extraordinaire.

Le goût des belles et bonnes éditions s'est étendu de l'aristocratie nobiliaire à cette autre aristocratie de la science et du talent qui n'est plus l'apanage de quelques privilégiés, mais qui, de nos jours, compte des membres nombreux dans tous les rangs de la hiérarchie sociale.[27]

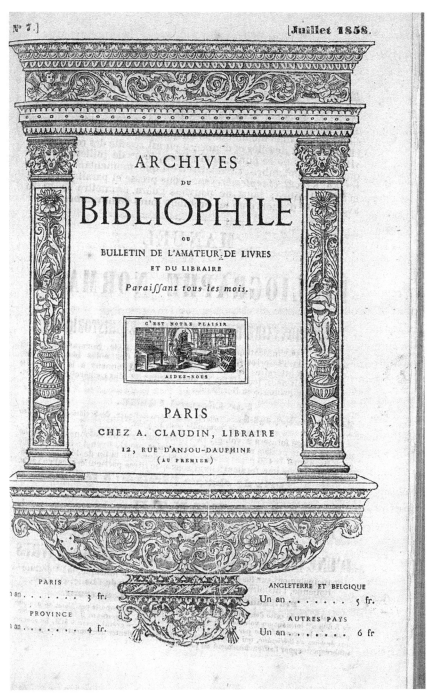

Figure 8 Anatole Claudin, *Archives du Bibliophile*, founded in 1858. The series continued until 1908.

Accompanying this social development was a shift from concentrating on the best printers of the past, such as the Aldus and Estienne dynasties, to a concern for illustration. Artistic and literary importance worked together. Moreover, it required a particular kind of attention:

> On conçoit dès lors quelle importance a dû prendre la bibliographie par suite de cette nécessité: le cercle des bibliophiles sérieux s'est aggrandi de plus en plus, l'érudition s'est popularisée et la formation des bibliothèques particulières est devenue la conséquence obligée de cette gravitation des esprits lettrés vers le beau, le vrai, l'utile et l'agréable.
>
> Toutefois pour former ou compléter des bibliothèques, il ne suffit pas d'être amoureux des livres; il ne suffit même pas d'être érudit, il faut encore connaître les maisons de librairie qui font leur spécialité de la vente des anciens ouvrages, à quelque genre qu'ils appartiennent.[28]

What she said of France and of the Paris trade applied no less to Britain. The world of books was passing though a period of adjustment, as increasing numbers of people, and different classes of people, took an interest in books and collecting. Some kinds of books were becoming difficult to find. For reasons not always to do with rarity or price, people were also turning their attention to genres different from those that had been the preoccupations of past generations.

At the end of the following decade Paul Lacroix ('Le Bibliophile Jacob') reflected on a similar theme: of how much had changed in the past twenty-five years. The number of second-hand and antiquarian booksellers had greatly increased, partly to meet the increased numbers of collectors. But the number of rare old books could not increase, and so collectors turned to other fields. More despairingly, he spent much of his opportunity in disparaging those who broke up books for their separate parts, making more money by selling the pictures.[29] Although he did not enter into details, the fashion for extra-illustration, cutting out parts of books in order to paste them into others, only added to the scale of this re-ordering of print. The demand for such work was sufficient to support several dealers in London who specialised in preparing special copies, frequently got up in expensive bindings.[30]

The Book Trade and Changing Tastes

The trade in antiquarian, rare and second-hand books was a complicated one. The terms were overlapping and interpreted variously by different people. On the one hand there were some guides, notably Jacques-Charles Brunet's *Manuel du libraire et de l'amateur des livres*, originally published in 1810 and much enlarged subsequently.[31] Joseph-Marie Quérard's *La France littéraire* (1827–39), though less ambitious in its range, added further detail.[32] For early English books, William Thomas Lowndes's *Bibliographer's manual* (1834) was increasingly seen to be inadequate, and in 1857–64 was replaced by a revision by Henry G. Bohn. Alongside these established and widely available authorities began to appear a new generation of guides for collectors, more limited in their bibliographical ambitions but adding a further array of notes and suggestions intended to help in the creation and maintenance of collections.

In England, France, Germany, the Low Countries and much of western Europe, part of the trade was well organised, with printed catalogues. Not surprisingly, some were better than others, and in 1841 it was remarked in a widely read manual:

On doit généralement regretter le peu d'ordre et de précision que présentent la plupart des catalogues de librairie; les titres y sont tronqués ou altérés, les noms estropiés, les dates omises, quelquefois le même ouvrage est annoncé par plusieurs catalogues sous des titres absolument différents.[33]

There was a world of difference between prominent, generally prosperous and self-promoting sections of the market and the great mass of lesser booksellers. Thanks not least to uniform postal charges, the 1840s saw a considerable increase in printed catalogues from dozens of lesser traders both in London and the provinces, who issued lists in small type on cheap paper of eight or sixteen pages. They responded to a demand, and they helped to develop a wider market. Unlike the more substantial catalogues from major firms, these ephemeral pamphlets, playing a hardly less vital part in their own constituencies, have attracted little attention from later acquisitions librarians, and as a consequence have now become rare.[34] Besides these, large segments of the trade were made up of smaller businesses that never produced catalogues, that depended on personal visits and correspondence, and that never expected or sought the kinds of wealthy or international clienteles enjoyed by the most prosperous businesses in the major cities. They worked in small shops, or eked out a living on street stalls (Figure 9). In these respects little had changed for generations.

For some people, quite apart from providing a modest income, with little need for investment by those unable or unwilling to establish themselves at expensive addresses, or to borrow in order to buy, or to maintain large

Figure 9 Outside a bookseller's shop. Etching by George Cruikshank, from Charles Dickens, *Oliver Twist* (1838).

warehouses, the hierarchy of trade offered one great advantage. For those with patience, knowledge and luck, the lower ends could occasionally produce books of great rarity. Stories circulated of Lord Macaulay's and Gladstone's frequenting street stalls as well as bookshops, to the benefit of their private libraries. They were by no means the only people to think it worthwhile.[35] At the beginning of the 1850s, Henry Mayhew reckoned that there were about twenty stalls scattered across London: it was probably an underestimate.[36] He also noted some of the changes that had occurred in the kind of older material that was offered:

There has been a change, and in some respects a considerable change, in the character or class of books sold at the street-stalls, within the last 40 or 50 years, as I have ascertained from the most experienced men in the trade. Now sermons, or rather the works of the old divines, are rarely seen at these stalls, or if seen, are rarely purchased. Black-letter editions are very unfrequent at street book-stalls, and it is twenty times more difficult, I am assured, for street-sellers to pick up anything really rare and curious, than it was in the early part of the century.

He then continued:

One reason assigned for this change by an intelligent street-seller was, that black-letter or any ancient works, were almost all purchased by the second-hand book-sellers, who have shops and issue catalogues, as they had prompt sale for them whenever they could pick them up at book-auctions or elsewhere.[37]

Some parts of London were especially known for street barrows, in Whitechapel, Shoreditch, Farringdon Road, and New Cut in Lambeth. In Manchester, Shudehill remained familiar, but it was only one area of several.[38] In Newcastle-upon-Tyne, people went to Grainger market. More regularly, and in much larger quantities, these same cheaper parts of the trade also provided resources for further up the financial and bookselling scale. In Paris, the *bouquinistes* by the Seine were a fertile hunting ground for a rich range of early books as well as later ones. They attracted collectors from overseas as well as from Paris, wealthy and poor alike.[39] In a hierarchy of resources the trade structure in most countries of western Europe was reminiscent of Jonathan Swift's observation, that 'Big fleas have little fleas upon their backs to bite them, and little fleas have lesser fleas, and so *ad infinitum*.'

At the bottom of this food chain was the waste-paper merchant, collecting for recycling. An 1872 directory recorded over eighty waste-paper merchants in London alone.[40] In 1895 William Roberts recorded that before the cheapening of paper (that is, about thirty years previously), a bookseller could rely on receiving 30s. per hundredweight, which was a useful inducement to dispose of unsold and unfashionable folios and quartos. But by the 1890s the price had dropped to half a crown (2s.6d.). As Roberts ruefully commented, 'There is a certain amount of danger in the wholesale destruction of books, for posterity may place a high value, literary and commercial, on the very works which are now consigned to the paper-mill.'⁴¹ Books become rare for all kinds of reasons, but once destroyed they could never be rediscovered.

Of those who could not afford the better booksellers, one example may serve, the more valuable because his library has survived mostly intact and in the condition he left it, now in the University of Otago. The Rev. William Shoults (1839–87) entered St John's College, Cambridge, in 1856. A high churchman by instinct and in practice, and with serious scholarly interests mostly relating to his calling, he was never a wealthy man and held various curacies mostly in the poorer parts of London. By the end of his life he had gathered several thousand books dating from the fifteenth century onwards, bought in London from minor dealers for modest sums and often from the street barrows. They demonstrate how customer knowledge could be deployed to advantage for particular interests, and they included thirty-seven incunabula.⁴² He does not seem to have frequented the more expensive West End booksellers, though some from his shelves are now of significant value. Because he had little money, many of his books are worn and were often well used even before he bought them. As a collection they thus present an unusually graphic picture of one part of the book trade, evidence of the often shabby state of millions of books on sale whose bindings had been left untouched since, or immediately after, their publication. It is all the more valuable in that they belonged to a scholarly person who had neither the means nor the inclination to spend much on his books, and they now provide an exceptional (and all too rare) portrait of the realities of the nineteenth-century book trade outside the circles for whom repair, rebinding and redecoration were essential parts of book collecting and bibliophily.⁴³

So far as can be seen, Shoults had little interest in modern literature, though it is possible that his widow retained some books when she parted with his working collection. By the late nineteenth century, when he was buying his books, second-hand booksellers were emerging who chose to specialise in more recent books, rather than older ones. It was a market completely different from that which was so familiar in the mid-century, as criteria for prices, editions and titles were ordered into a new and unfamiliar canon. We return later to some of these questions.

Booksellers

If auctioneers were short of time, and possessed an advantage in selling to a clientele whether trade or private that mostly already had some knowledge, for some booksellers it was different. Their catalogues could be read at more leisure, books could be examined for periods longer than a hasty few hours just before a sale, and new customers had always to be sought. So, when Henry George Bohn, bookseller in York Street, Covent Garden, issued in 1848 the first of what was intended to be three volumes of his new catalogue, he addressed another challenge. The date on his premises gave the building date of 1636, though it had been much changed since. Occupying two adjoining houses, the fascia offered an 'English and foreign library of the fine arts natural history & belles lettres.' The world could judge his importance accordingly. At 7 shillings, quarter-bound in red leather with red cloth sides, the catalogue itself was not cheap. At a time when many prices had noticeably weakened, it was a document as much of record as of books for sale. Bohn offered references to Brunet and other standard bibliographies, and extra observations occasionally. The copy of Maioli, *De gradibus medicinarum* (Aldus Manutius, 1497), for example, had no details about its condition save that it was a 'fine copy', 'excessively rare, £1.5s.':

This is one of the rarest volumes in the Aldine Series and is printed uniformly with Leonicenus. It is deficient in some of the most complete collections. In the fine Aldine collection at Syston Park there is only a Manuscript fac-simile, and there was no copy in the Libraries of Hibbert, Dent or Hanrott. The author was a distinguished book collector, and his name is known to Collectors by the fine condition of the books which bear his motto on the sides.[44]

No explicit reference to Renouard, the obvious standard authority, was thought necessary, nothing about the binding. The comparison with Leonicenus's *Libellus de epidemia* was presumably derived from Renouard's note.[45] Blurbs can seem informative or irritating, in the mid-nineteenth century as much as at other times, and Bohn did his best. In other parts of the catalogue he offered Thomas Hobbes to the accompaniment of a quotation from Pepys's diary, and Spanheim on numismatics (1706–17) supported by Edward Gibbon. He quoted Hallam's *Introduction to the literature of Europe* to help Montaigne to a purchaser. Judging by his choice of advocates, he clearly imagined a clientele of somewhat varied education. Very occasionally there was a note of a binding: the first edition of Newton *Principia mathematica* (1687) was offered for 6 shillings, 'hf. bd. calf'. Sometimes there were price comparisons. Three copies of Sloane's *Natural history of Jamaica* (1707–25) were offered at between £5.15.6 and £7.17.6 ('old English red morocco, gilt edges'), with a note that the Heath, Dent and Willett copies had sold, some years previously, for 19 guineas, 17 guineas and £16.5s.

respectively.[46] The catalogue was a large and general one, stretching from the fifteenth to the nineteenth centuries, and it was presumably compiled by several people over several months. Uniformity in such circumstances was hardly to be expected, and while there were many efforts to direct customers, there were in this catalogue many more books of which few will have heard and for which there was no guidance.

On this and other occasions, the immense catalogues, running to several hundred pages, published by Thomas Thorpe in 1842, by Henry G. Bohn in 1841 and 1848 and, later, by Quaritch were not necessarily catalogues of books currently for sale in the ordinary sense. Some were drawn partly from much briefer lists that were the true mechanisms for selling recently acquired books. Quaritch issued a monthly *Museum* in the 1850s, and later slim 'rough lists'. The large catalogues, such as those from these dealers and the two volumes issued in Paris by Techener in 1855 and 1858, running to several hundred pages, were to a great extent commemorative vanity publications, designed to show off the wealth and range of what might, or might no longer, be available from a leading seller. The hundreds of smaller printed catalogues that appeared each year were more useful for customers' everyday inspection, and more useful to booksellers who wished to see prompt sales for what they had bought. In both France and Britain a few booksellers such as Claudin in Paris and Willis & Sotheran[47] in London exploited variations in postal rates to issue their catalogues in the guise of periodicals, containing usually lightweight articles on broadly antiquarian subjects to accompany lists of stock.

In Paris, Édouard Rouveyre proved to be one of the most enterprising of a new generation of booksellers. Born in 1849, he established himself as an independent bookseller in 1872, while still in his early twenties. From a succession of addresses on the Left Bank near to the Palais de l'Institut, he issued a series of publications aimed at bibliophiles, including *Le Bibliophile; recueil des notices bibliographiques, philologiques et littéraires*, a monthly begun in 1873 to accompany his catalogues. In the same year he offered a *Guide du librairie bouquiniste, ou liste et adresses de plus de deux mille bibliophiles et amateurs français et étrangers*. Further guides followed, most notably in 1878 the first edition of *Connaissances nécessaires à un bibliophile*. The first two editions sold 2,500 copies in a few months,[48] and the book grew rapidly from under a hundred pages to a fifth edition in 1899, by which time it stretched to ten elaborately illustrated volumes. What had begun as a guide not simply to books but also to such practical matters as dealing with vermin, how to mend worm-holes, and how to clean books was dedicated in its second edition (1878) to the memory of Brunet and finished as almost an encyclopaedia.

All book collectors relied on the retail book trade, whether wealthy like many members of the Roxburghe Club or Philobiblon Society, or operating on small budgets like the thousands of people who did not necessarily account themselves collectors. By the 1860s and 1870s, there was a very clear break in the generations. By then there were also clear differences in practices.

As we have already noted, several of the leading London antiquarian and second-hand booksellers died or changed within a few years of each other. Thomas Rodd died in 1849 and Thomas Thorpe in 1851. Their stocks were auctioned off in sales over the following months. Payne and Foss ended their partnership in 1850. William Pickering was bankrupt in 1853.[49] All had been major buyers in the 1830s at the sales of Richard Heber, whose books still populated the shelves of the London trade in great quantities. Joseph Lilly died in 1870, and a series of auctions followed in 1871–3; William and Thomas Boone died in 1870–3, William having retired in 1860.[50] Henry George Bohn (b.1796), who did not die until 1884, sold off much of his stock at auction in 1868–72. F.S. Ellis, trained by Stewart, who died in 1883,[51] founded his own business in 1860, and then in 1872 acquired the Boones' premises and goodwill: he became agent for the British Museum.

Newcomers among the booksellers included Francis Edwards and Uriah Maggs, both on a modest scale in 1855. Of these and other arrivals, the most prominent was Bernard Quaritch. Born in Saxony in 1819 and trained partly in Paris by Théophile Barrois, he travelled regularly on the continent in search of stock, and through his friendships with booksellers such as Frederik Muller in Amsterdam, and Techener in Paris, he ensured that London was central to the international trade. After employment in London with Bohn from 1842, he opened his shop in Castle Street, near Leicester Square, in 1847, before in 1860 moving to better premises and a much better address in Piccadilly.[52] Castle Street disappeared with the later development of Charing Cross Road.

Bohn was proud of being the largest dealer of antiquarian books in London. His crown was inherited by Quaritch. Though linked in these ways, the two men dealt with utterly different environments. More than any other individual, Quaritch helped to create a new generation of bibliophiles. His name is often linked to wealthy collectors, but it is as important to remember that many of the books he sold were modest, that his prices were not necessarily extravagant and that he offered a large stock of remainders. Book collectors of lesser means, as well as people with very deep pockets, found purchases there. He benefited from the recovery in prices after the slump of the 1840s. He encouraged and supplied new generations of collectors in North America, as their tastes gradually developed for more than Americana and their buying of early European books became ever more ambitious. Thanks to his dominant position he was the effective fixer of values and prices for much of the antiquarian trade. As agent for the British Museum, the Bodleian Library and the Cambridge University Library, he was instrumental in shaping the most important national collections. For some of the most active private collectors he occupied a similar position of trust. As publisher, he provided collectors and the general public alike with resources to understand early printed books better. In his catalogues he established new standards that reflected a world that Bohn never knew. Quaritch's *General catalogue* of 1868 occupied over 1,100 pages and contained 14,701 entries – not counting the long list of remainders. It also included a list of several hundred desiderata representing both his own wants and those of his customers. This list ranged from the nearly trivial, and fragments of books to make good his own copies, to the Gutenberg Bible – a book that he first handled in 1858.[53]

In his catalogue of 1868 he had the benefit of incunabula bought at the recent Enschedé sale at Haarlem, where he acted for Lord Crawford as well as buying stock for himself.[54] Throughout, his catalogue descriptions of the more interesting books were consistently fuller than those of his predecessors, with better notes on condition, notes of missing leaves, descriptions of illustrations and often (for the early books) of type, notes of printers as well as of dates and places of publication for the early books, besides references (often corrected) to the usual authorities such as Brunet or Lowndes and an unusually wide range of less familiar names. He was not afraid to offer his own further opinions. 'A public institution should secure the above copy', he wrote of Audubon's *Quadrupeds of North America*. 'No public library can do without this important work', he commented on a complete run of the *Journal of the Asiatic Society of Bengal*. On the other hand, Heywood's *Generall historie of women* (1657) was 'a very ridiculous jumble'. Quaritch, working in his second language, was sometimes in the habit of allowing his staff not to mince their words.

Like Bohn before him and others such as Dulau in Soho Square, Quaritch was more than a bookseller. They supported their incomes, and in so doing sought ways of developing their customer base, by publishing programmes. Some of these books were aimed at a middle market. John

Obadiah Westwood's *Palaeographia sacra pictoria*, published by Henry Bohn in 1845, cost 90s. Henry Shaw's *Encyclopaedia of ornament*, published by Bohn in 1857, cost 60s. on large paper. Quaritch in particular diversified, and by the 1880s was supporting significant parts of the scholarly market in his collaborations with various societies. For those who sought information on early books, he offered attractive picture books. These books did not always sell well. *Monuments inédits ou peu connus*, a collection of elaborate chromolithographed plates designed to accompany a sale from the library of Libri, was published by Dulau in 1862, priced new at 9 guineas. Two copies were offered by Quaritch in 1868 at £4.15s and £5.[55] Lacroix's luxurious and wide-ranging *Le moyen âge et la renaissance*, in five volumes (Paris, 1848–51) was priced by Quaritch in 1868 at £18 in half morocco or £27.10s bound in full morocco by Leighton. In a market always largely defined by price differentials, such elaborate productions, sometimes more gift books than original contributions, stood in sharp contrast to less ambitious volumes on similar subjects costing only a few shillings.

These are only the leading names, and all are of London. In the early 1850s there was no guide to the British trade until Hodson's *Directory* appeared in 1855, its purpose as much a guide to the new as to the old trade.[56] It was also intended not least as a guide to the provinces. The first public appeal for a guide specifically to the second-hand trade of which I am aware appeared in *Notes and Queries* in July 1855. The anonymous correspondent was especially keen to learn of booksellers outside London. 'The utility of such a list', he remarked, 'to persons engaged in collecting for any particular object or course of reading is so obvious that, if it does not already exist, may I ask the help of "N. & Q." towards its formation?' His plea was partly answered in the two following months, when two lists appeared, offering details of 106 booksellers in thirty-three provincial towns in Britain and Ireland.[57] No further guide appeared until 1870, when John Power included a much-extended list in his *Handy-book about books*. By then he offered the names and addresses of 161 businesses in London alone, and further names in 150 provincial towns and cities in England, Wales, Scotland and Ireland. They ranged in size from large firms to the smallest, owned and staffed by a single person. Even so, and hardly surprisingly, the list was incomplete. Details of dozens more were given also of firms in continental Europe, the Americas, Asia, Africa, Australia and New Zealand. In a further development, after a brief guide was privately published in Nottingham in 1886, edited by Arthur Gyles in fulfilment of a promise made in *The Bibliographer* and in *Book-Lore*,[58] the first edition of what became for many years the standard source, James Clegg's *Directory of second-hand booksellers*, appeared in 1888, published not in London but in Rochdale. This was the work not of a collector but of a bookseller and printer, well placed as a specialist in printing booksellers' catalogues.

10 | Private Collectors and the Public

Leisure and Loyalties

Most of the changes so far discussed have concerned matters that are broadly bibliographical, notably changes in the trade, changes in library management and changes in taste. In themselves, they are not sufficient answer to the reasons why this happened. They are symptoms and results, not the cause. For causes we have to cast our net more widely, to changes in social structure, changes in patterns of wealth, changes in education and changes in the environment, to name but a few. For the French book collector and authority on early prints and bookbindings Henri Béraldi, much was the result of a new-found passion for the past, as a substitute for (in his view) failings in modern design. His focus was on bookbindings, but he had a more general point in mind. 'En 1860', he wrote, 'nous sommes décidément le siècle de la copie.'[1] For him as for many others, it was a time driven by historical and archaeological study. All these explanations can be very difficult to evaluate. If, for example, we posit changes in the pursuit of leisure, we mean only some kinds of leisure, not necessarily the increasingly popular day trips on the railway to the seaside. Perhaps we are closer if we look at educated leisure, such as visits to museums or art galleries. The 1851 exhibition had an exceptional influence on visitor figures in London, which therefore brings imbalance. It was reckoned that this exhibition attracted over six million visitors between May and October. In turn, a version of it was perpetuated in south London at the Crystal Palace from 1854, while the South Kensington museums were born from its exhibits and ideas: the South Kensington (later the Victoria and Albert) Museum opened in 1857 and the Natural History Museum in 1881. The South Kensington Museum, which mingled science and art, was open for part of the week to the general public, and on other days only for students. By 1881 the monthly average of general visitors on free days was almost 76,000, and in that year it welcomed over one million visitors altogether. On Easter Monday alone there were 31,900 visitors.[2]

Museums and art galleries are not libraries, though in many places the three were combined within a single building. Libraries tend to count not visitors but the numbers of books they contain, that are lent or that are consulted; and for those possessing earlier collections, there may be no distinction between old and new. This limits the relevance of some visitor statistics, except that, most importantly, they are one measure of leisure activity, where education could be combined with pleasure.

If we look at general visitor numbers to the British Museum, we find that they rose by about fifty per cent between the late 1850s and the early 1880s. The new Reading Room, opened in 1857, brought a proportionately much greater increase in readers. It replaced the old arrangements, 'the great manufactory of books' where people were engaged in 'grinding down the matter of old books in order to make new ones' (Figure 10). There, women readers had gradually increased in numbers, but the fact that facilities were shared by newspaper readers and by schoolboys had added to the crowd.[3] The ordinary public was given a chance to see some of the collections for the first time when permanent exhibitions of printed books and manuscripts were installed in the galleries in 1851.

Many of the statistics associated with museums and libraries need to be treated with caution. Sunday opening, for example, was an opportunity for more people to inspect collections that they could not see in the working week. The advent of public libraries brought a debate to the fore. They were intended for public instruction and enjoyment, and many of the people who had most to gain had very little free time. Against this stood the traditional values of Sunday as a day of rest and for the worship of God. Further, since an open library required staff to work, not to open was to protect what in 1859 Edwards called 'the most blessed privilege of the poor man, from dependence on the mere will and pleasure of the richer man'.[4] By the 1880s the question was a pressing one, for some people made more urgent by a decline in church-going among the working classes. Initially in his work on public libraries, Thomas Greenwood tried to remain neutral,[5] but by the time he came a little later to write about museums he stated his position clearly:

Museums and Picture Galleries belong to the nation, and not only to a portion of it. Consequently the convenience of the people as to when their institutions shall be open should be taken into account.... People must be brought under the influence of pictures and other beautiful objects and books. ... If people are to get the full benefits from the study of books, pictures, and the contents of Museums such places ought to be opened for certain hours on the Sunday.[6]

A few libraries and museums opened on Sundays, and others experimented, but there was no general movement to do so. Not until 1896 did

Figure 10 The old reading room, British Museum. After a watercolour by Thomas Hosmer Shepherd (1793–1864).

the British Museum (but not the Reading Room) or the National Gallery open on Sundays. Nor did legislation mean immediate action. Local authorities were slow to take up the opportunities offered for the support of museums in legislation of 1845 and 1850. A programme of loans from the South Kensington Museum to institutions across the country helped to ensure a distribution of works of art. But even when museums were opened, their hours were restricted, and visitor numbers could be minute. While museums in major conurbations such as Birmingham, Sheffield and Glasgow all welcomed comfortably over 200,0000 visitors each in 1877, others attracted far fewer.[7] For public libraries, it was several years before some large towns adopted the Act of 1850.

The reasons for this uneven expansion of support for, and interest in, public collections are to be found partly in new patterns of education, wealth and leisure, and partly in redefinitions of public property. The mid-century legislation to allow the creation of rate-supported museums and libraries gave a new meaning to public ownership. It brought opportunity. Rates were to be set locally, and the consequent debates were conducted locally. Westminster could propose, and it could legislate. It did not insist. This extension of responsibility, to ever more complicated structures of local authorities, emphasised the influence of individuals' private purses. To agree to be taxed was to agree to invest, and thus to own. The structures of older institutions such as subscription libraries, where ownership was shared among a limited group of individuals each of whom had a direct financial investment, were developed into a public model, affecting the whole rate-paying local population. Every individual, and every group, who used libraries, or visited exhibitions or museums, had their own purposes, and these were coloured to a greater or lesser extent by a sense not just of curiosity or sociability but also of ownership.

It was reflected in the gifts that found their ways into local museums and libraries. The gathering of collections, to be shared for a common good, was an expression not just of social concern, a sometimes paternalistic wish for educational, recreational or moral improvement of the kind so frequently manifest in the founding of mechanics' institutes, whose libraries were mostly in a serious state of decline in the second half of the century as public libraries took their place.[8] Rather, it was a further expression of this sense of corporate ownership, where ownership was defined locally, where it was not restricted to any single group of people but was something held in common. On occasion a major benefaction helped shape the subsequent development of the collection or institution as a whole. It was not simply a matter of wealth, though the major national collections attracted collections of very considerable value, magnificently so in the case of donors such as Thomas Grenville at the British Museum, or John Forster at South Kensington.

At a local level, this phenomenon was quite different in character from gifts to the major national collections, which until the mid-nineteenth century meant principally the British Museum, some cathedrals and the university and college libraries at Oxford and Cambridge. For members of ecclesiastical and academic communities it could seem only natural to bequeath collections to their associated libraries. Issues of local loyalties are also to be found in other libraries, and the concomitant assembling of collections. Unusually, Martin Routh (1755–1854), President of Magdalen College, Oxford, bequeathed most of his books to the young University of Durham in 1854, having failed in 1847 to reach agreement with Queen's College in Oxford for the purchase of his library for £10,000. Routh had taken an interest in the new university since its foundation.[9] In 1856 Edward Maltby (1770–1859), Bishop of Durham, added many books on his retirement. The subscription library at Penzance, Chetham's library in Manchester, Brighton Public Library and Edinburgh University Library all received extensive gifts or bequests from J.O. Halliwell-Phillipps. At Dundee, Andrew Wighton (1804–66), a local grocer, bequeathed his uniquely important collection of Scottish and other national music for the new public library. At Wisbech, Chauncy Hare Townshend (1798–1868), a friend of Dickens, bequeathed his library (including the manuscript of *Great expectations*) to the town museum.[10] At Warrington, John Fitchet Marsh (d.1880) deposited his music collection in the local museum and library.[11] Bookplates and gift inscriptions record dozens of smaller gifts to other libraries outside the charmed circles of universities and cathedrals.

While definitions of the middle classes are notoriously difficult, and ever shifting with fluctuating social assumptions, education and income, it remains that the mid- and late nineteenth century saw an enormous expansion in this part of the population.[12] The 1850s witnessed fresh debates over what were frankly referred to as the middle classes. New schools were founded,[13] public 'middle-class' examinations were introduced,[14] and the professions became ever more firmly defined. The decennial censuses, with their attention to increasingly detailed statistical analysis, helped further to define sometimes inchoate groups. At one end of this fragmented class were professions such as banking and medicine, and successful industrialists. Clinging to the other was an army of poorly paid clerks. The differences were reflected in the range of sizes and styles of new houses, in the contrasts between different suburbs, between inner and outer suburbs, in the variety between places and individual streets where people chose to live, in available spare time. Within their houses came new kinds of ready-made furniture, supplied by an increasing number of manufacturing companies. New kinds of shops catered for furnishings, decoration and equipment, and they offered reminders of what else might be added. This consumer revolution fed sometimes bitter arguments about style and taste.

The point here is not the nature of these arguments, but that there was sufficient money to buy these various chattels. In his *Hints on household taste* (1868), Charles Eastlake included a separate chapter on the library, assuming that the middle-class homes of which he wrote were of sufficient size to accommodate such a room. Robert Kerr, Professor at King's College London and architect of Bearwood, the baronial pile built for John Walter, proprietor of *The Times*, included chapters on the library in his *The gentleman's house; or how to plan English residences* (3rd ed., 1871). Less ambitiously, architects such as Edward Lushington Blackburne, showed how it could be accommodated into floor plans in suburban villas.[15] Eastlake thought fit to suggest some bulky, not to say ungainly, furniture. Whatever the size of the room, whether separate or part of other spaces, bookcases could be designed economically and make allowance for other pieces of furniture: the modern revolving bookcase, for instance, the largest standing about five feet high and capable of housing about 130 volumes, was invented by John Danner in Ohio in about 1876, and quickly found favour in Britain, where the publisher Nicolas Trübner imported an example, and sent it to *Nature* for comment.[16] Behaviour itself could be compared, in books of etiquette, and the running of households for those unfamiliar with the task was made easier thanks not only to the well-known *Book of household management* by Mrs Beeton but also to a host of similar manuals.[17]

A middle-sized house did not imply a middle-sized library. Nor did a large house imply a large one. Some of the very largest houses, belonging to some of the wealthiest people in the country, had quite modest ones. Amidst these webs of social capital and social behaviour came innumerable opportunities for refinement and imitation. Books were just one aspect of this culture of comparison. Pictures had always been hung on walls, but now there appeared a literature about how and where to hang them. The guidance on this offered for middle-class homes had little enough relevance to the hanging of major works of art in public galleries, but the general topic became one for debate as the newspapers followed arguments about the order of hanging in the new National Gallery, or in the pioneering Manchester Art Treasures Exhibition. In the market for mass-production, the mid- and late nineteenth-century trade in lithographs, plain or coloured, brought choice on an unprecedented scale, while the engraved and chromolithographed reproductions published by bodies such as the Art Union of London (founded 1837) and the Arundel Society (founded 1849) helped to assure purchasers of the quality and personal taste that they chose to share with their visitors.[18] So it was with books. In 1895 William Roberts contemplated the reality:

There can be no doubt about the fact that Englishmen as a rule do not attach sufficient importance to book-buying. If the better-class tradesman, or professional man, spends a few pounds at Christmas or on birthday occasions, he feels that he has become a patron of literature. How many men, who are getting £1,000 a year, spend £1 per month on books? The library of the average middle-class person is in ninety-nine cases out of a hundred the cruellest possible commentary on his intelligence, and, as a matter of fact, if it contains a couple of volumes worthy of the name of books, their presence is more often than not an accidental one. A few volumes of the *Sunday at Home*, the *Leisure Hour*, *Cassell's Magazine*, or perhaps a few other monthly periodicals, carefully preserved during the twelve months of their issue, and bound up at the end of the year – with such stuff as this is the average Englishman's bookcase filled.[19]

Obviously only a minority was interested in old books, but here too education and taste were social markers. Hence came the demand for manuals about book collecting by people such as John Power and J.H. Slater.[20] Prices could be unpredictable, but for the minority of the population interested in such matters that was part of the delight, where competition, practised with prudence, could bring its own rewards.

This naturally developed over several years. In her memoir of her husband Sir Charles Eastlake, Lady Eastlake dated at least part of this change to the 1830s, as she reflected on the change of patronage for her husband's paintings, and the increasing demand for his work:

The patronage which had been almost exclusively the privilege of the nobility and higher gentry, was now shared (to be subsequently almost engrossed) by a wealthy and intelligent class, chiefly enriched by commerce and trade ... To this gradual transfer of patronage another advantage very important to the painter was owing: namely, that collections, entirely of modern and sometimes only of living artists began to be formed. For one sign of the good sense of the *nouveau riche* consisted in a consciousness of his ignorance upon matters of connoisseurship. This led him to seek an article fresh from the painter's loom, in preference to any hazardous attempts at the discrimination of older fabrics. Thus such gentlemen as Mr. Sheepshanks and Mr. Vernon, who were the first founders of this class of collections, contended, and often with success, for the possession of fine modern pictures, with patrons of rank and distinction.[21]

Where concern for paintings led, concern for books followed, though not with the same obvious distinctions as Lady Eastlake suggested in her observations on the art market. There was not such a defined link between social rank and taste as she claimed; but the equivalent need by anyone coming anew to buying paintings (of any date) emerged for bibliographical help in books and their history.

When left undistinguished and without further definition, the term 'middle classes' is not always helpful, encompassing a wide range of social and financial distinctions. For Dianne Sachko Macleod in her *Art and the Victorian middle class*,[22] it comprised a mixture of people who mostly owed their livelihoods to commercial and manufacturing success. They were not necessarily entirely self-made: many of them were from at least a second generation of established financial and social comfort. They included people such as the engineer and armaments manufacturer Sir William (Lord) Armstrong, the oil merchant Elhanan Bicknell, the insurance underwriter Theophilus Burnand, the pen manufacturer Joseph Gillott, the barrister and literary figure John Forster and the calico printer Frederick Craven. Macleod's focus was on them as collectors of paintings, and to some extent of drawings or prints. Forster was also a serious book collector.

Others, with whom she was not concerned, collected antiquities, coins, ceramics, and geological, botanical or zoological specimens. Yet others collected books and manuscripts. Among all these various interests and more, some people founded museums or art galleries. Others gave or bequeathed their collections to existing institutions: John Forster (d.1876), John Jones (d.1882) and Constantine Ionides (d.1900) bequeathed their collections to the South Kensington (later Victoria and Albert) Museum. John Sheepshanks (d.1863) gave over five hundred pictures to the then young Museum in 1857, during his lifetime. Robert Vernon (d.1849) gave pictures to the new National Gallery in 1847 – and was disappointed not to receive a title in acknowledgement of his generosity. Richard Newsham (d.1883) bequeathed his pictures to the recently opened Harris Library and Museum in Preston. For many years Philip Rathbone (d.1895), from a family prominent in the insurance business, dominated the purchase of paintings for the Walker Art Gallery in Liverpool.[23] Others again left their collections to their successors. Many collections were sold and dispersed after their creators' deaths. There is little uniformity and, however defined, the middle classes were certainly not defined by any passion for collecting. They spilled across into lesser landed gentry and into the titled classes. Investment in land and in building large houses was an obvious way not just of managing surplus money. It also offered social advancement, though newcomers were not necessarily welcomed among established circles, whether in town or country. For some professional groups of people, such as many clergy, lawyers, bankers and Oxbridge dons, it was nonetheless easier to find a degree of acceptance even without noticeable wealth, albeit within carefully defined limits.

Systems of patronage operated at all levels, but one way of overcoming, or at least moderating, social distinctions was the learned society. The Burlington Fine Arts Club, founded in 1866, comprised a body of people identified not by class or wealth, but by interest. Its members included both artists and connoisseurs.[24] The much older, and much larger, Society of Antiquaries chose as its president in the mid-nineteenth century Lord Mahon, later Earl Stanhope, who served from 1846 to 1876.[25] Membership of these and many other bodies was by election, which conferred social recognition, or at least acceptance, on members in acknowledging a common cause. Similarly, if at a sometimes less ambitious level, non-metropolitan societies were defined by matters of mutual interest. Founded in 1813, the Society of Antiquaries of Newcastle-upon-Tyne claimed to be the oldest provincial antiquarian society. The Spalding Gentlemen's Society was founded in 1710, the Manchester Literary and Philosophical Society in 1781, the Louth and Lincolnshire Archaeological Society in 1844, and the Norfolk and Norwich Archaeological Society in 1846. A series of county archaeological societies were founded over the next few years.[26] It was generally assumed that such societies would possess a library, built up from donations and from subscriptions, and often including relevant early printed books.

Many of the book collections formed in the mid-nineteenth century were the work not of members of the aristocracy but of members of the professional middle class whose wealth was sometimes self-made and sometimes partly inherited from the immediately previous generation: it was not necessarily from longer family commitments. Equally, libraries formed within a generation rarely lasted beyond the next, and were more often sold or dispersed on the death of their creators: dispersal could be earlier, if illness intervened. Much of the library formed by Dawson Turner (1775–1858) was sold by Turner himself in his declining years.[27] The same happened to Thomas Corser (1793–1876) and his library, sold shortly before his death.

Some examples of the better-known libraries reflect this single-generation pattern of collecting. It was by no means a new feature, but the collections formed in short spaces of time suggest how patterns developed, reflecting availability and taste besides wealth. As active buyers and prominent figures, they all contributed to some of the changes in mood as well as in practice during the middle years of the century.

Private Libraries and Private Tastes

Private collections that have survived more or less intact, sometimes in families but no less importantly in institutions, whether large libraries such as Grenville's in the British Museum, John Forster's and Alexander Dyce's in the Victoria and Albert Museum, or smaller collections, each offer their own records in the books now to be studied on their shelves. The purposes in their gathering can be interpreted by the survivals, mindful of the myriad reasons that lead people to collect, including curiosity, financial investment, the pursuit of particular interests, personal rivalry, a wish to be remembered by posterity, or public good. They document changes in taste, varying among both individuals and groups, according to debate and fashion, where some are more prominent than others. Such considerations were not new to the mid-nineteenth century.

In dozens of cases, for those libraries no longer intact, virtually the only record that we have today is the catalogue when they were auctioned. Some details may be further identified thanks to bookplates, inscriptions or bindings, but most are now anonymous. The great majority of collections are no longer identifiable. For a few, there are catalogues privately printed at the expense of their owners, usually (but not universally) in a very few copies: editions of fifty or fewer were common. The year 1726 was the date of the earliest known privately printed catalogue of an English private library, and by the 1830s the genre had produced major catalogues notably of the Spencer library by Dibdin (1814–22), and of those of the Duke of Sussex (1827–39, unfinished), Samuel Parr (1827) and Frances Currer (1833).[28] Bibliographical and other details in these and in other smaller inventories varied. Such catalogues not only record collecting tastes, opportunities and wealth but, in some instances, also record how books were regarded: their physical characteristics, who bound them, and where and when they were obtained. In such notes are to be seen some of the same changes of emphasis that we have witnessed in the commercial and scholarly worlds. A few of these private catalogues had a further purpose, beyond the ordinary limits of private circulation among family or friends. They were designed to add to the national bibliographical record either in their details or because, like the Grenville, Forster and Dyce collections, they recorded holdings in national institutions.

In his survey of book catalogues, Archer Taylor was principally concerned in his discussion of private library catalogues with their use as subject guides.[29] The nineteenth century (which occupied less of his attention than earlier periods) witnessed changes of emphasis in discussing particular copies. While there were some encyclopaedic catalogues, others were of a different nature. The catalogue of the Chatsworth library, published privately in four volumes in 1879, offered only summary entries. It recorded a library with much earlier roots, but was not least a monument to the enthusiastic collecting of the 6th Duke of Devonshire (1790–1858), whose purchases at the Roxburghe sale in 1812 had passed into bibliographical legend: at that sale he had paid £1060.10s. for a copy of the *Recuyell of the histories of Troy* with a unique engraved frontispiece perhaps depicting Caxton himself.[30] The *myrour of the world* cost £351, and at sales between 1812 and 1815 he bought further Caxtons. These and other prices were recorded at the end of the printed catalogue, together with lists of books published on parchment and those in Grolier bindings. The incunabula had been further enriched with the purchase of most of the books of Thomas Dampier, Bishop of Ely, following his death in 1812. Entries recorded formats, and for some books (only) offered the briefest of notes on binding materials, such as 'o.c.' [old calf] or 'gr.mor.g.e'. There was very little further information about earlier provenances or named binders.

If the Chatsworth catalogue, traditional in most of its details, was strictly limited in its purpose, a record and a guide for those who might wish simply to find books, others showed wider and more elaborate ambitions.

Thomas Corser (b.1793) was third son of a banker in Whitchurch, Shropshire. After education at Manchester Grammar School and Balliol College, where his interests in early English literature were formed and encouraged by Henry Cotton of the Bodleian Library, in 1826 he married the eldest daughter of James Lyon, rector of the wealthy living of Prestwich. He became incumbent of Stand, Lancashire, in 1826, and held the living, worth £270 p.a., for half a century. The house was not large, and his books were stored away in all sorts of corners.[31] In 1828 he added to it the vicarage of Norton, Northamptonshire, worth the same amount. Here the Shropshire connection was critical, for Norton was in the gift of Beriah

Botfield, book collector and wealthy as owner of the valuable Old Park Iron Works, founded in 1790 and at one point the second largest in Britain. Corser placed his son in the parish as curate, so that he could concentrate on his life in Lancashire, where he helped found the Chetham Society in 1843. At Stand he gathered an exceptional collection of early English literature, which was described and illustrated with extensive quotations, in the eleven volumes of *Collectanea Anglo-Poetica* (1860–83). These were published not privately but by the Chetham Society, thus achieving a considerable circulation. Though Corser attached notes of formats, provenances, binders and binding materials, his purpose was primarily to record the achievements of early English printed poetry.

His inspiration came partly from two works. The *Bibliotheca Anglo-poetica*, a catalogue of books offered by Longmans in 1815, was compiled by Acton Frederick Griffiths. Corser managed to buy what he called a 'large portion' of it, after the books had been through others' hands. The other was John Payne Collier's *Catalogue bibliographical and critical of early English literature; forming a portion of the library at Bridgewater House, the property of the Rt. Hon. Lord Francis Egerton*, published in 1837. After Corser suffered partial paralysis in 1867, and became increasingly unwell, most of his books were auctioned at London and Manchester in 1868–76; he died in 1876, and the series was completed by his friend James Crossley.[32]

Corser's primary concern was for English poetical literature, copiously reflected in the long extracts included in his catalogue. Though also dominated by early English printing, the interests of Henry Huth (1815–78) were much broader. His library was passed to his son Alfred Huth, who continued to add to it until his own death in 1910.[33] The Huths were bankers, and after spending most of the years 1833–49 abroad in the United States, Mexico, France and Germany, Henry returned to work in London. From the City he made daily forays to the West End booksellers. The sales of the libraries of George Daniel in 1864 and of Corser in 1868–73 brought opportunities that he seized. His early purchases included several rare Spanish books, bought in Mexico, and he retained his Hispanic interests. He acquired the Henry Perkins paper copy of the Gutenberg Bible, sold in 1873, but he paid most attention to the sixteenth and early seventeenth centuries, assembling a collection of early English printing of unique stature. Alfred Huth bequeathed a choice of fifty books to the British Museum,[34] and the rest of the library was finally sold between 1911 and 1920 in a series of nine auctions at Sotheby's. Though inspired by the sparse bibliographical notes in the printed catalogue of Thomas

Grenville's library, these details were developed in the hands of W.C. Hazlitt, to whom the making of the catalogue of Huth's collection was first entrusted, so as to include formats, collations, provenances, notes of illustrations and dedications, and occasional notes about typography, as well as about binding materials. Unlike Corser's catalogue, the notes offered little of a literary nature in this library that was by no means limited to poetry.

The five volumes of the catalogue, completed by F.S. Ellis in 1880, found a place on libraries' reference shelves not because they recorded current locations: that was hardly possible after the auction sales. Instead, they were valued for their bibliographical detail and for including descriptions of many books of outright rarity.

In their very different styles and purposes, the multi-volume catalogues of the libraries of the Duke of Devonshire, the Rev. Thomas Corser and the banker Henry Huth represented the changing assumptions and aims among some of the country's leading private collectors. None was entirely new. Many of the Chatsworth books had been bought in the second decade of the century. Corser drew heavily on a collection sold in 1815. Huth, active in his daily pursuit among booksellers, was able to buy from the major sales of the mid-century. Amidst the multitude of printed catalogues of private libraries that were published in this period, some of comparable size and many much smaller, emerge the differing approaches to how books were to be described, and decisions as to how much tangential detail might be added. Corser was most concerned to record texts, literary detail, in a world where the Spenser, Chaucer and Percy Societies, private reprints and the Early English Text Society contributed so much to the study of early English poetry. Huth, and those who worked with him, exhibited a concern not only for rarity but also for the particularities of individual copies. Attitudes to private libraries changed both in owners' tastes and in how they were to be presented and to what purpose.

Books in Detail

11 | Writing in Books

Provenance

An interest in provenance, details of those who, whether individuals or institutions, had owned books formerly, was likewise no new phenomenon.[1] Classical and antiquarian scholars valued books not just for their associations but also for their annotations. Other names, written inside books, were noted much more rarely, with the obvious exception of William Shakespeare whose variously forged signatures by W.H. Ireland were not infrequent occurrences.

In 1835 Sotheby's offered amidst much fanfare the library of Georg Kloss, a physician from Frankfurt. The collection included annotated books that Samuel Leigh Sotheby attributed to the Reformation theologian Philip Melanchthon. They raised many hopes, not least those of Sotheby himself. Those hopes proved false, for the books were not Melanchthon's, and Kloss himself later complained of the error.[2] But the episode was a demonstration of how much annotation, as distinct from simply an ownership note, had the potential to become a central attraction. For the worlds of scholarship, such matters as textual collations or comment could be of critical significance, and had long been valued accordingly. In that manuscript notes added to the historical and intellectual portraits of owners, they represented more than a simple link to the past.

In France, Louis-Aimé Martin, latterly on the staff of the Bibliothèque Ste Geneviève, was one of several collectors who paid attention to prominent earlier owners, including literary figures. His library, sold in 1847–8, included books annotated by Tasso, Racine, Montaigne and Rabelais, and occasioned articles in the *Bulletin du Bibliophile* by Arthur Dinaux on further examples.[3] At a more ordinary level, signatures as marks of ownership were no more than autographs, to be cut out and preserved with their contexts stripped away. Ben Jonson signed his name on the title-pages of his books. Once chopped out by an autograph dealer or collector, as often happened, a signature was of no value whatsoever in this respect, while the value of the now damaged book was diminished. As Samuel Leigh

Sotheby pointed out in 1861, the word 'autograph' meant two things: either a signature or a complete document. Only the second was in his view worthwhile.[4]

Signatures, autograph letters and documents, and annotated books each held their attraction to amateurs and historians alike. The sale of books from Thomas Gray's library in 1846 contained many annotated by him, including his copy of the Strawberry Hill Press edition of the *Odes*, dense with notes about his sources. It fetched the high price of £105.[5] More generally, while headline interests were in named individuals, and especially famous people, there was also a gradual change in attitude to more ordinary annotation, including that by people who either were of less obvious account, or who remained completely anonymous. Annotation of all kinds was in Edward Edwards's mind when he wrote of a 'remarkable incontinence of penmanship'.[6]

The fashion in the earlier part of the century, and still to be found in some circles at the end, was for books that were clean: for washed copies, where disfiguring annotations were removed by various, sometimes alarming, methods. Names of owners and scribbles by readers were cleaned off. If used wrongly, chemicals used in cleaning could destroy the book itself. Binders did not always recognise the significance of what they trimmed off in their efforts to improve appearances. In such processes part of a book's history was destroyed. In 1847 readers of the *Bulletin du Bibliophile* were reminded of the copy of Montaigne's *Essais* at Bordeaux, annotated by Montaigne himself, that had been cropped of some of its notes by a 'relieur barbare'.[7]

By the 1850s a new mood was developing. It was not universal, for many collectors continued to insist on what were thought of as clean copies, and there was in any case no clear boundary between what was merely dirty, or accidentally soiled, and what was of possibly lasting interest.

Amidst all this, when in 1862 the facsimilist Frederick G. Netherclift offered a book on autograph collecting, he was able to summarise:

> Daily experience teaches the frequenter of old book-stalls, that great value and interest are attached to works containing marginal notes and other memoranda, when traced to be from the pens of eminent and distinguished persons.[8]

Other craftsmen produced forged signatures – a much easier task than the creation of entire documents. For many more people than those who haunted the bookstalls, the controversy arising from John Payne Collier's accounts of an annotated copy of the Second Folio of Shakespeare (1632) in 1852–3, first in the *Athenaeum* and then in a separate publication, aroused both interest and passions, in an activity that for a more ordinary book might have seemed mundane.[9] The volume offered novelty, a recent history that was full of circumstantial if rather odd detail and, most importantly, apparently a wealth of new evidence about the country's greatest writer. The handwriting was said to date from soon after publication, and included hundreds of amendments to the printed text. Much of the publicity occasioned by the volume was distinctly negative, as (with good reason) Collier's allegations were not all believed, and the debate rattled on in articles and pamphlets for the next decade and more.[10] More generally, and quite apart from Shakespeare, it provoked curiosity in annotations not just in theological works or in classical texts but also in works that were widely familiar. One immediate result was Samuel Leigh Sotheby's *Ramblings in the elucidation of the autograph of Milton* (1861), written by his own admission in the wake of the Collier controversies and liberally illustrated with facsimiles.

Much more traditionally, save that it was pioneering in its self-appointed task, in 1864 H.R. Luard's *Catalogue of adversaria and printed books containing MS. notes preserved in the library of the University of Cambridge* accompanied the programme to produce a six-volume printed catalogue of the Library's manuscripts. Indeed, the books listed – by no means all of their kind in the Library, notwithstanding Luard's claim – had all been assigned to the manuscript shelves. Among Luard's many interests, in classics, in medieval English history (he was an industrious editor of volumes in the Rolls series) and in English literature, he devoted further time to preserving the memory of the classical scholar Richard Porson. It may be that the existence of a volume gathering Porson's adversaria, edited by James Monk and Charles Blomfield,[11] was part-inspiration for his wider consideration of the Library's annotated books. A substantial part of the descriptions was occupied with an account of the adversaria of Peter Paul Dobree (1782–1825), Porson's successor but one as Regius Professor of Greek, a selection of which had been published in 1831–5. Many of the other annotations listed were anonymous, a clear declaration that names were not everything. Despite his hopes, Luard's example was not followed by other libraries, and the more general concept of adversaria, learned or otherwise, failed to arouse immediate interest in the general reading public.

The increased attention paid to earlier ownership was born out of all these concerns, but it was selective attention. The wide-ranging kinds of adversaria recorded by Luard were less noticed. Moreover, few catalogues paid the degree of attention to earlier ownership of books, especially those recorded in their bindings, as did that of the Lyon collector Nicolas

Yemeniz. The sale catalogue of his library prepared by the Paris booksellers Bachelin-Deflorenne in 1867 included not only details in many of the entries but also indexes for named binders and of books having belonged to prominent people in the past.[12]

As wider interest in earlier ownership developed in the last two decades of the century, so catalogues reflected this supplementary way of studying books. The Sunderland library from Blenheim Palace, formed in the first half of the eighteenth century, was untainted by more recent fabrications, and the introductions to each of the five parts of the sale in 1881–3 drew attention to what seemed primarily of interest – rare editions of early printed books, *editiones principes* of major authors, books printed on parchment, and books with obvious celebrated provenances: 'some fine bindings with Arms of former owners, including one or two of Grolier, Maioli, and Laurini, the famous binders and collectors, whose names are dear – in more senses than one – to modern bibliophilists'. This tasting menu was but the start. In fact, the catalogues recorded much more. The team led by John Lawler who compiled this catalogue was keen to demonstrate the care taken, not only with notes of bindings and provenance but also with other matters:

> We have taken the trouble to COLLATE all the most important books which occur in the Catalogue. This must give it a value for future reference, which it would not otherwise possess, as the collations given are those of actual copies in the Library. Where any differences are recorded by bibliographers they are noted.

It was a brave statement, and hardly surprisingly it was not one that was regularly followed. In their descriptions, the methods and approach owed part to the sale catalogues prepared by Libri some years previously. There was also the usual smattering of notes claiming rarity, and of the more notable prices fetched for other copies at previous sales. For reference books, the compilers seem to have had little more to hand than Dibdin's catalogue of the Spencer library and Brunet's *Manuel*. The notes of provenance revealed rather more: not just of famous names and collections but also a miscellany of others. So, here indeed were Grolier and Maioli as well as the historian Étienne Baluze, the statesman Pierre Séguier and the poet Philippe Desportes. There were dozens of books noted from the library of the Dutch scholar Hadrian Beverland (1650–1716), exiled in England after his books on sin and lust proved too much for some of his countrymen. Among more prominent English names were William Cecil and Matthew Parker. Some less familiar sixteenth-century British names included James Abetoun, Archbishop of Glasgow (1571), Sir Thomas Smith (1513–77), Sir

William Pykerynge (1516–75) and William Crashawe (1572–1626). But here too were notes of an assortment of scholars, including a copy of Euclid given to John Mill by Richard Bentley. There were books from Ben Jonson's library and John Donne's copy of Conrad Gesner's *Bibliotheca universalis* (1545). Two volumes bore the signatures of the Norfolk collector Thomas Knyvett (d.1618). No further details were added about these names. While the notes of these earlier owners tended naturally to be of names that were most legible or recognised, the selection was considerably more catholic than usual in such catalogues. Not all the obvious names were noted: notwithstanding a clear signature, the provenance of a volume once the property of Elizabeth I's Greek tutor Roger Ascham was not noted here and remained for Quaritch to publicise it later.

The same interest in provenance was to be seen in some of the published catalogues of libraries. In 1889 Marie Pellechet drew attention to provenances in her catalogue of the incunables at Versailles, and in her introduction summarised the principal sources of the collection – mostly institutional but also including the gifts in his final years of the recently deceased bibliographer J.P.A. Madden. Many of the books, confiscated in the wake of the decrees of 1789 and 1792, and by no means limited to the fifteenth century, had arrived at Versailles only indirectly, finally placed at the disposition of the town in 1803. Next, in 1893 she included a provenance index in her catalogue of the incunables at Lyon, a collection likewise partly made up of confiscations. To her chagrin, she was unable to add a more detailed history of the collection.[13]

If name recognition depended on individual enthusiasms, for most people the criteria had barely changed. When in 1892 Michael Kerney compiled the entry about the Sunderland library for Quaritch's *Dictionary of English book-collectors*, he not only provided an extensive list of the more prominent lots but also added a much briefer one of books 'bearing marks of distinguished ownership'. Apart from Cecil (of whom he noted just two volumes, out of at least five in the sale), Sir Thomas Wotton and half a dozen monarchs, there were no British names. Quaritch bought the bulk of the Sunderland books and had a special bookplate printed to be inserted in each of his purchases. This was not only an innovative way of commemorating a notable occasion but also a practical way of advertising the firm. It also signalled a wider attention to provenance, otherwise unrecorded since the Sunderland books bore no bookplates of their own.

The *Dictionary* contained names from the fourteenth century onwards. Not all the books listed had passed through auctions. Those of John Shirwood (d.1493) given to Corpus Christi College, Oxford, by the

College's founder Richard Foxe were listed, by the young Robert Proctor, from the library shelves. Those of Thomas Cranmer (d.1556) had been identified mostly in the British Museum and other libraries. For other early names, such as Gabriel Harvey, Ben Jonson, John Dryden, Richard Smith and Humphrey Dyson, Quaritch partly relied on earlier catalogues. For others he could write from experience. The focus was on Quaritch's own years of business. He had bought many of the non-scientific books once belonging to Bilibald Pirckheimer (d.1530) from the Royal Society. Michael Wodhull's (d.1816) books had been finally dispersed at auction only in 1886. The note contributed by Frederick Clarke about Sir Peter Lely (d.1680) depended on just one book. More comprehensively, W.C. Hazlitt supplied an account of the books assembled in Lincolnshire by Maurice Johnson of Spalding (1687–1755) and his family. Some of the library had been sold in a house sale, and others went to Sotheby's in 1898: the circumstances of the house sale provided Hazlitt with an opportunity to make sly comments about booksellers' rings on such occasions. Of longer-term significance, Quaritch provided scarcely any information as to the current whereabouts of the dozens of manuscripts and printed books listed. Even by the end of the century, the nascent interests in provenance had usually not passed beyond the recording of names. Any additional features of individual copies, to be discovered by further inspection, lay beyond what were still strictly limited bounds of curiosity.

12 | Bookbinding

Books from the library of Jean Grolier (d.1565) had been long valued for the association of his name tooled on distinctive and attractive bindings, and generally on books of readily identifiable interest.[1] Books once in the sixteenth-century French royal library or the gaudier of those once in the English royal library held similar appeal. So did books belonging to some popes and leading members of the church or nobility. Royal, noble and senior ecclesiastical provenances were always to be valued, with the inevitable result that bindings were specially manufactured for this part of the market. It was the bibliographical equivalent of sophistication in other articles; for example, in the ways that furniture could be made up from diverse pieces.[2]

Bindings, often armorial, were an essential element in guiding and developing this taste for prominent people from the past. In a view of two-dimensional ornament, it was a short step from illuminated manuscripts to the decoration of bookbindings, from the inside to the outside. Age and provenance were important, but the key was ornament, and particularly if it was gilt or coloured.

At Cologne, between 1853 and 1865, the auctioneer Heinrich Lempertz issued a series of fascicles illustrating various book arts, including gothic and renaissance examples.[3] At Paris in 1861, Techener issued the first parts of another folio album, with etched illustrations by Jules Jacquemart. This series was to run to a total of fifty plates, many reproducing books from the Techeners' own stock.[4] The prospectus for the project claimed that no work previously had been devoted to bookbindings.[5] This was not true, for earlier work had appeared in London as well as in Cologne;[6] but it was certainly the case that in the 1860s a group of albums reproducing bindings gave notice of new possibilities and new approaches.

Linked to the sale of some of his books and manuscripts, in 1862 Guglielmo Libri assembled a large folio album of chromolithographs depicting some of the most visually appealing items. Coming hard on the heels of other work, its purpose was explained in the introduction:

In faithfully reproducing these ancient chefs' d'oeuvre, not only are they fixed and a longer life secured to them, but connoisseurs are furnished with precious elements for an artistic history of Books, and to every one is rendered accessible the study of Monuments preserved in so many different countries.[7]

Setting aside the questionable claim that a printed reproduction on paper would last longer than many of the objects depicted, and also setting aside the claim to faithfulness, a claim that even then was being challenged by the photographic processes developed for the reproduction of books and works of art,[8] there was an important point here. Copies and facsimiles enabled comparison, between libraries and between countries.

The volume offered reproductions of bookbindings, 'the most beautiful models of one of the principal branches of the art of ornamentation'. Partly on these grounds, examples were shown at the 1862 international exhibition. Libri added:

In the plates composing this collection, may be studied the most beautiful models of one of the principal branches of the art of ornamentation. Not only will admirable models be found there of an art which has had the merit to attract to such a degree the attention of Albert, Duke of Bavaria [and others], but these plates may serve as a sure guide to those amateurs who in these days eagerly seek, at their weight in gold, bindings, of which by comparison with undoubted specimens, it is worth while to be always able to discuss the authenticity ... The more such publications are multiplied, the better we shall be able to understand the history of an art which forms one of the principal branches of ornamentation, but of which the products are incessantly tending to deterioration and total loss.[9]

Not everything in the album was genuine, including several examples of treasure bindings which were in fact *remboîtages*, confections built round perfectly genuine manuscripts.[10] In view of his own liberties with bookbindings, Libri's remark on authenticity perhaps betrays his inclinations more than he intended.

A paper read to the Society of Arts by the publisher Joseph Cundall (1818–95) and issued in 1848[11] concentrated on decorated, or ornamental, bindings. So did those of Edward Edwards in a considerable section on the subject in his *Memoirs of libraries* (1859), adding coloured illustrations imported from Brockhaus in Leipzig.[12] By the time that Cundall came to write again in a short book published in 1881 he still spent most of his energies on decorated bindings, but he also looked at some that were blind-stamped. His book, dedicated to Henry Cole with whom he had worked as a publisher, began in ancient Assyria, and proceeded via Greece and Rome to modern times. He was most attracted by elaborate work, and the more notable examples of medieval bindings were given generous treatment. In the sixteenth and seventeenth centuries Italy and France naturally occupied the lion's share of space, with an emphasis that became customary on major collectors as well as on binders when their names were known. But he also offered a little on German and Low Countries stamped bindings, as well as further attention to some of the more elaborate early English sixteenth-century blind-tooled examples: in considering panel stamps he quoted the work of John Reynes and Thomas Berthelet, among others, 'of a bold and effective character but with little pretension to good art'.[13] For continental and English examples alike, he referred on many occasions to documentary records of binders or their work, unfortunately failing to provide proper references. Cundall's influence was considerable and warmly acknowledged in 1889 by Henry Wheatley when he assembled an album of reproductions of bindings from the British Museum.

Study of the subject changed little between the 1840s and the 1880s. It was in stark contrast to the developing analytical study of early printers. The difference was at least threefold. First, while the aesthetic merits of some printed works, and the type on which they were based, were widely acknowledged in, for example, the books of Jenson, Aldus or Baskerville, these were not the criteria that dictated the overall history of printing to the exclusion of most work. Students of binding focused on the most elaborate work. Students of the history of printing did not all do so: much of the sixteenth-century work considered by Ames and his successors was very ordinary, even poor, while in France Charles Nisard, and in England Charles Hindley, concentrated specifically on some of the cheapest popular work.[14] Second, most aspects of the history of printing were not recognised as part of the history of decoration, or even often of the applied arts. Printing was a mechanical process, albeit one dependent on human skills and taste. Third, and perhaps most important, by the 1870s the study and analysis of distinctions between the earliest printing types were beginning to be properly established, in work led by J.W. Holtrop, Henry Bradshaw and William Blades. The two aspects, aesthetic and historic, were to be married in the work of William Morris, who combined historical analysis and decorative taste in the types developed for the Kelmscott Press (founded in 1891).[15] The work of binders attracted very little such detailed analysis. Instead, there was a focus on finishing, the tools that were employed for decoration, and there was much generalised writing. With a notable exception in the work of W.H.J. Weale, discussed later, the implications were not to be addressed for almost another generation.

Édouard Fournier (b.1819), in a career mostly as a journalist, produced a book nearly every year between 1847 and his death in 1880, several of them on the history of Paris. In 1852 he published a glossily illustrated history of medieval manuscripts and of printing, written in conjunction with Paul Lacroix and Ferdinand Seré.[16] He was no specialist; nor was he expert in bookbinding, the subject of his *L'art de la reliure en France aux derniers siècles* (1864). But he was well informed and had strong opinions on modern work. His opening words were self-deprecating and very much to the point:

> Nous ne prétendons pas écrire ici l'histoire si attendue de la Reliure. Plus elle est à faire, moins nous voulons l'entreprendre. Notre but, plus modeste, est simplement d'indiquer comment, depuis le moyen âge, le livre, profane ou sacré, fut toujours trouvé digne de devenir un joyau, et le devint en effet sous la main soigneuse d'ouvriers, la plupart inconnus, dont cet art de la parure des livres fut la brillante industrie.[17]

Much of his book was taken up with a survey of collectors, but as a historian of printing he was alert, like those who worked on Costeriana and found fragments of early printed books in bindings, to what could be found not just in decoration but also in the materials of which bindings were constructed.

Traditions and hearsay about the history of binding resisted eradication. The seventeenth-century embroidered bindings associated with Nicholas Ferrar's community at Little Gidding were repeatedly attributed to the supposed nuns living there.[18] On other occasions readers were solemnly told that monks became binders for amusement in the Middle Ages and that Thomas Maioli was a binder. Bookbindings were 'examples of monkish industry and art'.[19] In contrast to all this, some of the most thoughtful voices were in France, in the work of Fournier and in that of Le Roux de Lincy in his *Recherches sur Jean Grolier, sur sa vie et sa bibliothèque* (1866). For the rest, the pickings tended to be picturesque and meagre.

While special copies of the series of six catalogues of sales in Paris from the library of Ambroise Firmin-Didot (d.1876),[20] published by the firm of the same name from 1878 onwards, were illustrated with photographs from illuminated manuscripts and decorated bindings, the descriptions offered little that was new. Moreover, like other collectors, Firmin-Didot had made use of repairers and binders skilled in the art of facsimile and forgery, including Adam Pilinski (1810–87) and Louis (or Théodore[21]) Hagué (1823–91): while some of the descriptions were commendably frank, others were equally noticeably ambiguous or vague.

Bindings lent themselves naturally to exhibitions, and the more elaborate contemporary creations featured regularly at the major international occasions. These were not necessarily times to revel in the past, nor were they necessarily occasions focused on books. The exhibition of bookbinding and leatherwork at the South Kensington Museum in 1874[22] was mostly concerned with contemporary work, though a few earlier specimens were shown, lent by Earl Spencer, the Duke of Devonshire, R.S. Turner, Durham Cathedral and others. Further space was occupied by exhibits of saddlery, harness, spurs and other uses of leather.

With a more obviously bibliographical, not to say bibliophile, focus, at a meeting of the Society of Arts in 1880 those attending were able to inspect an exhibition of over eighty bindings from the sixteenth century onwards, many of them lent by the South Kensington Museum.[23] They formed the backdrop to a long paper read by Henry Wheatley, and an ensuing detailed discussion in which Henry Bradshaw was to the fore, emphasising the need for a proper chronological treatment of the subject. This was only partly met by Wheatley in his paper, for he rehearsed old ground in familiar ways.[24] He offered little by way of analysis or of attempting to relate different parts of Europe to each other, insisting on structuring his remarks country by country, and he persisted in considering it as a fine art and as a manufacture. As a lecture given before the Society of Arts (more fully for 'Encouragement of Arts, Manufactures and Commerce'), it was only fitting that he should remark on the quality, and lack of quality, apparent in much modern work. It seemed to him that binding flourished more in France than in England, and he concluded with remarks on binding as a mechanical art, before offering a few practical points on care and presentation. He gave himself no space to comment on Joseph Zaehnsdorf's recently published manual on *The art of bookbinding*, of 1880. Among his audience were George Bullen of the British Museum and James Weale, both of whom who offered some additions and corrections. Part of the discussion turned almost inevitably to the costs of binding, and Quaritch was vociferous in his defence of the necessarily expensive charges by Francis Bedford, whose skills in repair were unequalled: 'the greatest artist in bookbinding that England, or any other country, had ever produced'.[25]

Bradshaw was not primarily an expert on binding, but he offered one way forward for its study:

What he should like to see above everything ... would be a collection of specimens historically arranged, showing the different styles at the different dates. Such a thing might be arranged in the British Museum, or perhaps even better at one of the Universities. For instance, at the University Library, Cambridge, they had books which were given them in 1424. Most of the valuable books had been rebound, but some remained in their original condition; and he wanted to be able, when he took a book in his hand, to tell almost the decade in which it was bound.

He had given some attention to the early English binders, and had been much assisted by the fragments used in the binding. He understood now that care was taken in the Museum, when such fragments were taken from a book re-bound, to state what book they came from; but formerly this precaution was neglected, and even now it was so in many places. He had recovered specimens of Caxton and De Worde, simply from finding printers' waste in the binding. He found, in one book, a fragment printed by Lettou, the first printer of the City of London; and on going to Oxford, and looking at some other books by the printer, he recognised the same tooling at once. With very little difficulty, he could trace the change from 1480 to 1490 to 1500, and then a totally different style again in 1510 and 1520. If an exhibition could be formed, showing the sequence of patterns and style, it would be very useful; because, in binding books, if you imitated at all, it was very desirable to imitate the right style of the period. He only knew one man who had done anything in this way, and that was the librarian at Ghent. It was also very important that more attention should be paid to the forwarding; many binders looked upon books merely as pieces of furniture, with a magnificent outside. He remembered a specimen of Paris binding in the British Museum, which showed the falsification sometimes resorted to. It was one of those beautiful Bruges books which were exceedingly costly, in which missing leaves had been supplied. The binder, having an idea that the old printers always put a blank at the beginning, when there was no title – the fact being that this particular printer never did – forged a blank leaf, of the same paper as the body of the book, and even put a 'set-off' on it to make it look real. On examining it with a glass, however, it was seen to be a set-off from one of the facsimile leaves in the book, and not from the first page at all.[26]

For a small group of people, it was all too evident that the subject of the history of bookbinding was sorely neglected. As interest grew, so the need became greater. By 1883, a series of almost a thousand examples of fine bindings offered by Quaritch was prefaced by some more general remarks:

A good work on the history of Bookbinding has yet to be written. Arnett's treatises are jejune and out of date, and were based on defective material; while everything that has been written on the subject since is below criticism. We might except from this harsh judgment 'La Reliure' of Messrs. Marius-Michel, which is a thoroughly good book from its own point of view;[27] but unfortunately the authors are 'doreurs' not 'relieurs,' and suffer from bias like the man who cried 'There is nothing like leather!' He was not a binder, but they are 'finishers,' and their opinion is that nothing merits mention in connexion with the art of bookbinding beyond the process of decorating the sides and back of the leather with ornaments in gold. It is truly an elegant and artistic employment, requiring discrimination, taste, and skill; but alas! even of Marius-Michel, as of all other modern workmen, English and foreign, it must be said that they are mere eclectic copyists.[28]

In light of what later emerged in Quaritch's dealings with Hagué,[29] it is unclear how many of the books in the catalogue were genuine, and how many were modern adaptations or inventions. Hagué had worked for the duc d'Aumale and also in London with Zaehnsdorf, but he had also worked less openly, forging an unknown number of bindings.[30] The trade was diseased by them, though not everyone was prepared to admit it. In 1891, writing under the *nom de plume* of J. Verax, Anatole Claudin contributed a long article to the *Bulletin du Bibliophile*. Much of his essay was occupied by Hagué (whom he did not name), but he went on to allude to collectors who had been duped in Geneva and to a centre of activity in Bologna. It was a warning not only to collectors but also to booksellers, Claudin's colleagues in the trade.[31] Not everyone was as reticent. To the scholarly collector Henri Béraldi, Hagué was 'le célèbre truqueur', famous as a faker.

By the time that Quaritch issued his larger catalogue of 1889 devoted to bookbindings and provenances, he was able to advertise a selection of illustrated albums, few with notes of any substance. They included a collection of 116 plates, *La reliure ancienne et moderne*, introduced by Gustave Brunet (Paris, 1878); the Leipzig *Abbildungen* (1881); Marius-Michel, *La reliure française* (1880 and 1881); four portfolios of bindings from the library of James Gibson Craig (twenty-five copies only, Edinburgh, 1882); and a volume by Henri Bouchot on *Les reliures d'art à la Bibliothèque Nationale* (1888: copies also available on japon paper, bound in asses' skin). Whatever pleasures bibliophiles may have drawn from handling such compilations, these publications added little to the history of the subject.

For so long as the history of bookbinding was considered as little more than the history of a decorative art, it had little to offer in the development of the history of books and their making more generally. Sections on bookbinding were included in several of the major international exhibitions of industrial arts, and thus by implication it was a process of manufacture. But the subject could involve much more than this. A binding in a showcase could only display one aspect of a book: its outside decoration. It could not, for example, display forwarding, the processes that took place before the cover was finished. Thus, nothing could be seen of the quality or nature of work that was hidden.

The specialised catalogue from Quaritch issued in 1889[32] was preceded by a long introduction, signed by Quaritch himself though it may well have been partly written by a member of his staff, perhaps Michael Kerney.[33] Following the precedent set in the catalogue of 1883, it was both an introduction and a substantial account of the subject, one of the most substantial to have been published so far. It offered three reasons to value bindings: first, as preservatives; second, for the display of decorative art; and third, a sentimental one. 'The same feeling which formerly prompted veneration for bits of the True Cross, for the relics of saints and martyrs, the pollex of St. Sebastian or the coxa of St. Margaret, inspires the modern book-lover with reverence for the volumes, whether well or ill bound, which are stamped with the emblems of his nobler predecessors.' Despite this, there was no satisfactory history of the subject: John Hannett's brief small-format *Inquiry into the nature and form of the books of the ancients, with a history of the art of bookbinding* of 1837 was not uninteresting, but it was absurdly pretentious in its scope. As for blind-tooled bindings that flourished from *c.*1200 to after 1600, and commercial gilt bindings of the sixteenth and seventeenth centuries, these belonged 'undoubtedly to the genus of decorative bookbinding, but their mechanical qualities exclude them from the artistic species now in view, in which the craftsman worked with a free hand and with a distinct application of skill to every individual volume. Whatever was artistic in the decorative designs on stamped bindings was due to the engraver, not to the bookbinder.' It is unclear how the distinction was not equally applicable to later work, where the finisher depended no less on the skills of the person who made his tools, but the person who wrote this was determined to remain committed to what had become convention.

Quaritch's catalogue, in a larger format than usual, though without illustrations, was organised by country and by period, with bindings by or attributed to the same binder or collector assembled under appropriate heads. After a section on Italian bindings from the fifteenth century to modern times there followed a much longer one on French ones. This occupied over half the catalogue, beginning with a long series from 'the great age of binding', 1530–75. After this the specimens were divided in more detail: the De Thou library, the Eve family, Le Gascon and so on. In the mid-eighteenth century, the binders A.M. Padeloup took almost nine pages and Derome le jeune eleven. In the section on English work, Roger Payne took three. The modern London binders were all well represented. As always, the emphasis was on decoration. Since the books were divided geographically and chronologically according to bindings, various indexes were necessary: of authors and titles, languages, subject-matter, unique books, those printed on parchment, owners and libraries, and finally binders. Among the last was Hagué. Some of his work was signed, but some was not, and it remained unclear to what extent his work was also represented among the books offered as older bindings: descriptions did not hesitate to laud the quality or the rarity of the bindings, while on the other hand some examples were offered in their unrestored states, with spines missing or with the boards separated from the text-block. In all, the catalogue offered over 1,500 books. It not only reflected the exceptional riches of Quaritch's stock but also represented an extraordinary labour on the part of his staff. It further showed, in the index of provenances, how the study of bindings could be used in understanding the history of collecting and of reading by hundreds of people in the past who had no great claim to fame or fortune, and who were often known by nothing more than their initials.

Changes in the study of bindings came only at the end of the 1880s, though the subject remained plagued by forgeries. A review in 1890 in the *Revue de l'Art Chrétien* drew attention to three recent works: the catalogue from Quaritch, a collection of facsimiles, also published by Quaritch, and an album of reproductions of bindings in the British Museum, assembled by Henry Wheatley.[34] The reviewer pointed out that wider public interest in the study of bindings had developed only in the past two or three years, but that there was thus far nothing that dealt with medieval bindings in a serious manner. He found the facsimiles made by Griggs in the Quaritch album praiseworthy, not least for including examples of Flemish, German and English stamped bindings: it was a measure of expectations that he found the facsimiles, 'printed', in the words of Quaritch, 'in colours and gold to the exact semblance of the originals', to be so satisfactory. On the other hand, Wheatley's book on bindings in the British Museum, with an inadequate text and photographs by 'le nouveau procédé orthochromatique', printed in monotint by Messrs Aron Frères in Paris under the superintendence of Léon Gruel, was essentially what the reviewer called 'un livre pour une table de salon' – a coffee-table book. It had the considerable advantage of reproducing the bindings as photographs, but while modern technical reproduction techniques made for looks and verisimilitude, they could not disguise the poverty of the text. The title of the Quaritch album (which included reproductions of several unacknowledged forgeries) made one thing clear. The history of bookbinding was a branch of the decorative arts, and it remained so for many influential people even in the early twentieth century.[35]

Duff and Weale

The study of early blind-stamped bindings was taken up in 1891 in the brief contributions by Edward Gordon Duff to an exhibition of the history of binding organised by the Burlington Fine Arts Club. Duff, then aged just twenty-eight (he was to be appointed librarian to Mrs Rylands in 1893, thus becoming responsible for her new library at Manchester), was to prove a pioneer in this as much as was Weale, and he was to assemble his own substantial private collection of examples.[36] The exhibition, which attracted about 3,000 visitors,[37] was by far the largest historical display of bindings to have been organised in Britain, and it was the work of a group of people. Duff and Sarah T. Prideaux wrote the introduction, dividing their work between stamped bindings and gold-tooled examples. As Prideaux pointed out, 'no doubt it will be used by many students for purposes of comparison from the historical point of view'.[38] This was wishful thinking, and unrealistic, for the catalogue was utterly unsuited to such a purpose. Only a few copies were printed on large paper, with 114 lavish illustrations. Most copies were unillustrated, and the notes on most of the bindings were exiguous. They had little long-term value, while Prideaux herself remained wedded to the traditional values of the subject. Her preoccupations were all too clear in her concluding remarks: 'In all departments of decorative art we see the same inability to escape from the traditions of the past, but in none has there been such servile copying of the old models as in the decoration of books.'[39]

Duff was direct and to the point two years later: 'Too little attention has been paid, in this country at any rate, to the fact that some knowledge about early bookbinding is essential to the student of early printing.'[40] The two disciplines were inseparable not just on account of their both being applicable to a single object, a volume, but also because they each offered evidence in understanding the other. Although most attention naturally focused on decorative work, and there was increasing awareness of the evidence to be gained from scraps of printed paper or manuscripts used in construction, Duff also recognised how further evidence might be deployed:

Even a study of the forwarding of a binding is of great help. The method of sewing and putting on headbands is quite different in Italian books from those of other countries. Again, all small books were, as a rule, sewn on three bands in England and Normandy; in other countries the rule is for them to have four. The leather gives sometimes a clue, *e.g.* in parts of France sheepskin was used in place of calf. Cambridge bindings can often be recognised from a peculiar red colouring of the leather. So little has been done as yet to classify the different peculiarities of style or work in these early bindings, that it can hardly be expected that much should be known about them; at present the study is still in its infancy, but there is no doubt that, if persevered in, it will have valuable results.[41]

He was in advance of his time, and it was to be many years before concerted efforts were made to drag the study of bookbinding out from what has been called its decorative arts ghetto.[42] Duff himself did not pursue the question in detail, at least publicly, and while he assembled his own pioneering collection of early stamped bindings, most of his energies over the next several years were devoted to his bibliography of fifteenth-century English printing.[43]

James Weale was the author of a helpful catalogue of some of the music exhibition at the Albert Hall in 1885; but his current reputation depends more on his work on the history of bookbinding. Influenced in his tastes by Pugin, he was a person of wide learning and several enthusiasms from gothic architecture to early Flemish painting to the history of liturgy.[44] While a young man, Weale made his reputation as a pioneering scholar of Flemish art, and organised two influential exhibitions, one on religious applied arts at Mechelen in 1864 and another more specifically on paintings at Bruges in 1867.[45] Much of his adult life was spent in Bruges, where he brought up his family and battled for the retention of the town's old buildings when there were powerful interests arguing – all too often successfully – for their destruction. His guide to the town, published first in 1862, was key in the development among tourists and the international community of interest in a place that had in many respects been little changed since the Middle Ages. His influence on the study of early Flemish art was recognised only belatedly, in honours bestowed on him by Belgian academies. In 1879 he returned to London. His first brief study of early bindings was published in 1890 in a two-part article in the *Revue de l'Art Chrétien*, on bindings from the Middle Ages.[46] It began with the treasure book cover at Monza given to the church of S. Giovanni by Queen Theodolinda at the end of the sixth century, and then opened the second part with an account of the Stonyhurst Gospel of St John, the earliest known binding in decorated leather. He reminded his readers that when it had been brought to London and considered in 1806, it had been dated to the reign of Elizabeth I.[47] When it was displayed again at the 1862 exhibition at South Kensington this glaring mistake had been corrected.

On his return to London, Weale was appointed to care for the library of the South Kensington Museum. The appointment was a mixed success, and ended in a public row. On being invited by a departmental select committee to give evidence about the library, he spoke frankly about the shortcomings of the collection, of the poor catalogue, of policies for binding new arrivals, of the staff and of his superiors. The story circulated widely of how he had once peremptorily and noisily ejected a visitor who had dared to enter in order to sell obscene prints, and it was used to illustrate his short temper. More curiously, when – inevitably – he was dismissed, one of the allegations against him was that he had been too ready to help readers.

He was dismissed in 1897, but during the few years at the Museum he had compiled a detailed catalogue of early bindings and of rubbings. The second volume of this was published first, in 1894, and the first, being the historical introduction, four years later, after he had left the Museum. Both were published bound in cheap paper wrappers, in a style utterly unlike the generally expensive albums of reproductions on the subject that had appeared hitherto, or the bound volumes describing some other major parts of the Museum's collection.[48] Such was the museum's reluctance to promote his efforts. Whatever their outward garb, the volumes' importance could not be denied. In the later words of E.Ph. Goldschmidt, they 'stand in exactly the same relation to our present-day knowledge of the history of bookbinding as Newton's *Principia* to modern physics'.[49]

Just as Holtrop, Bradshaw and Blades had transformed the study of the history of printing types, and its applicability to the history of books and reading more generally, so Weale and Duff were pointing forward for the study and application of the history of bookbindings. Previous to Weale's two-volume catalogue of the bindings and rubbings of bindings published in 1894–8, a portfolio of illustrations of rubbings in the Museum had appeared in 1860.[50] His more systematic account was little less than a revolution. Cundall, Hannett and Edwards had written briefly and more generally, always with an emphasis on the more obviously decorated, gilt and coloured examples. Others, sometimes using the latest techniques of colour or monochrome reproduction, had produced albums of pictures, with texts that added little of substance. Weale now supplied the first really substantial survey of a considerable part of the subject, especially well informed on England and the southern Low Countries, somewhat less so on France and Germany, and distinctly less so on Italy. His focus was still on decorated bindings, but unlike his predecessors he was not bewitched by the most ostentatiously ornamental ones: 'Although I have visited many libraries in different parts of France, I have not come across a single specimen of ornamented leather binding anterior to the thirteenth century.'[51] Thus concentrating still on ornamentation as a key, his history was not comprehensive even in its selective geographical coverage, but it was an immense advance on all previous work, founded on comparative examination of hundreds of bindings and attention to documentary sources. He offered very few pictures of bindings, instead using line illustrations to show something of the structures of early examples and a few pictures of library shelves to demonstrate chaining arrangements in Hereford, Florence and elsewhere. More importantly, he included dozens of reproductions of early binders' stamps and of the decorative tools used by later practitioners. He was concerned with binders and bindings, across much of Europe, down to the end of the eighteenth century. It was not a grand album, and its brown paper wrappers belied the considerable riches of Weale's work.

He provided details of 325 bindings in the Museum and of 915 rubbings of bindings. The books had accumulated since the 1850s, and included a number bequeathed by Alexander Dyce. The rubbings were mostly the fruit of his own assembling. Sections were arranged geographically. For both books and rubbings much more detail was provided than was customary in accounts of bindings, and the rubbings in particular were almost all documented as to the ownership of the originals as well as with sufficient bibliographical detail to identify each copy. In only a few instances were details lacking, noticeably so in the case of unidentified manuscripts in the Bibliothèque Mazarine. Not surprisingly, given Weale's long residence in Bruges, the libraries of Amsterdam and the southern Low Countries were especially well represented, including those of some private collectors. In England, Weale had gathered copiously from the British Museum, both printed books and manuscripts, and he drew also from several cathedral libraries. A handful came from Cambridge libraries, thanks no doubt to Bradshaw. It was by far the widest and largest survey of bindings to have been gathered so far, and was the more remarkable in that it had been accomplished by a person whose first interests had not lain in such work. Weale offered verbal descriptions of each binding, the vast majority of them blind-tooled. He also added notes of early provenances for many of them. As a demonstration of bibliographical method, as well as in its scope, it was fundamentally innovative. While some of his attributions to particular localities have not stood the test of time, one omission obvious from the beginning was in his failing to supply references to places where the bindings had been reproduced in the existing literature.

The results of Weale's and others' studies only emerged into more public awareness a few years later. George Dunn (1864–1912) was in many ways a private and retiring person. Trained as a barrister, his private wealth meant that he had no need to practise. Instead, he pursued his hobbies, including photography, astronomy, old clocks and book collecting. His name became familiar to a select few for the photographs he made from his own copies of incunabula, circulated as the Woolley photographs and named after his house near Maidenhead. They were edited in conjunction with his near contemporary Robert Proctor (1868–1903) and were chosen because no other facsimiles of these particular typefaces were available. In his book collecting, he relished incunabula that presented bibliographical problems that he could share with Proctor.[52] With Duff (1861–1924), he was also one of the first who sought out early stamped bindings. The extent and nature of his book collections were revealed when they were auctioned over seventeen days in 1913–17, with catalogues that included details of many of the bindings. Most of his early law collection, in manuscript and print, was bought *en bloc* by Harvard Law School just before the first sale in February 1913. At the other sales the British Museum, Cambridge University Library, Charles Thomas-Stanford and E.P. Goldschmidt all bought heavily. With the Dunn sales the study of early stamped bindings may be said to have been established, a trend confirmed in the successful Gordon Duff sales of 1925.

Conservation and Fragments

One of the most lasting changes came in attitudes to the condition of old books. How much was acceptable or tolerated from the past? How much should the old be replaced? The widespread demand for facsimile leaves to make good imperfect copies was one reflection of a world where complete and perfect copies of the more important early printed books were becoming ever more scarce in the face of increased demand. Another, and more complex, reflection lay in the treatment of old bindings. We have already seen something of the extensive trade in the restoration of earlier work, and the skilled craftsmen willing, whether in Paris or London, to doctor them according to owners' wishes. The matter was by no means straightforward, for the bindings of books bore a multiplicity of values, most obviously as evidence of past owners or as examples of exceptional artistry and skill. It was not a foregone conclusion that a worn or shabby early binding should be discarded. Much, too, depended on an acceptable link between an interesting provenance and an interesting book. The temptation was therefore a powerful one, to transfer a remarkable binding from a dull book to one that had some easily demonstrable claim to fame. Such questions involved much more than decisions as to whether or not to retain an existing binding, rather than replace it with a new one, usually in more expensive modern materials and ornamented with appropriate lavishness.

The transition in taste and practice was a slow one, and many examples can be found in earlier periods where it had been preferred to retain an old binding for little more reason than that it was simply old. Yet few people appreciated the extent to which old bindings could be of value. For most, a new and costly binding on a rare old book not only added to its value but also signified how much a book was esteemed. Charles Nodier, writing in about 1814 and ever the guide to French bibliophile taste, had found it difficult to understand the 'manie incroyable' of the English for ancient bindings which he considered 'une nouvelle crise dans la bibliomanie'.[53]

There were few conventions in the treatment of older bindings, and the varying states in which volumes have come down to us make clear that opinions differed. In 1815, William Roscoe was becoming deeply involved in the repair and conservation of the manuscripts at Holkham in Norfolk. They derived from two principal sources: the library of the lawyer Thomas Coke at the start of the seventeenth century, and the much larger and more varied collection assembled by Thomas Coke in the eighteenth, partly but by no means wholly on his grand tour. Many of the bindings were in a poor state. In a letter to Thomas Coke, 1st Earl of Leicester, Roscoe reflected on how early bindings on manuscripts should be treated:

> I would observe that in case the ancient binding be in any tolerable condition, it is better to preserve it, than to change it for the finest modern binding that can be put upon it. Of these you will therefore judge of your own inspection, & will send only such as really require, for their preservation, to be rebound. There may however be some cases in which, altho' the ancient binding ought not to be changed, it should be repaired; & these you will also readily distinguish & may send of them among the rest. It will only be in very particular & indispensable cases that we shall think ourselves justifed in paring the edges of the leaves, as it not only deprives them of that appearance of antiquity that adds greatly to their value, but gives an idea that more has been cut off than is perhaps really the case.[54]

The first extended manual on bookbinding to be published in England was John Hannett's *Bibliopegia* (1835, 2nd ed. 1836).[55] This was addressed to binders, not to collectors, connoisseurs or even booksellers. It had little to say on the treatment of older books beyond a warning not to crop the edges of books being repaired. It was to be two decades before James B. Nicholson (1820–1901), working in Philadelphia, wrote another on the subject. His *Manual of the art of bookbinding* (1856) depended heavily on Hannett, but the title-page addressed a much larger audience: 'the whole designed for the practical workman, the amateur, and the book-collector'. His book was not published separately in England, though plenty of copies seem to have circulated there. On the subject of whether or not to replace old bindings, he was explicit:

Never destroy an old binding upon an old volume if the binding be in tolerable condition. An old book should not be rebound, unless it is essential to its preservation; and then it should be, as far as possible, a restoration.[56]

Obviously much was left to the binder, or the client: 'tolerable' carried many shades of meaning. Individual collectors and booksellers made different judgements, and there were never general agreements or accepted general criteria.

The opposite effects achieved by the most imaginative, and frequently (but not necessarily the most skilled) binders presumably depended on whatever instructions they were given. Hannett described a copy of Caxton's *Recuyell of the historyes of Troye* that had received special attention in what he called the Etruscan style – we do not know the condition of the book before the binder John Whittaker set about his work:

This style is where, instead of covering with gold, the book is ornamented with gothic or arabesque compartments, or imitations of Greek borders and Etruscan vases, in their proper colours; which, when well executed, have a good effect. The Marquess of Bath possesses a copy of 'Caxton's Recuyell of the Historyes of Troye,' bound in this coloured manner by *Whittaker* of London, who some years ago brought the style to considerable perfection. The back represents a tower, in imitation of stone, on the battlements of which is a flag bearing the title, and on a projection of the tower the name of the printer is impressed. On the sides are Trojan and Grecian armour, in relief, round which is a raised impression of the reeded axe. The insides which are also of russia, are ornamented with drawings, in India-ink, of Andromache imploring Hector not to go out to fight, and the death of Hector. The edges of the leaves are gilt, on which various Grecian devices are presented.[57]

Very few of his readers will ever have seen this book, but the point was clear: an old book was always liable to fall victim to the inspired imagination of modern connoisseurs.

The notion of conservation, in the sense of preserving as much as possible as an integral part of any repairs, was not familiar. When Sébastien Lenormand compiled his little manual on binding in the series *Encyclopédie-Roret*, he included a section headed 'conservation', but this was entirely concerned with insects and damp.[58] The considerable skills available apparently especially in Paris, and by no means unknown elsewhere, were focused on matters such as cleaning (whether of pages or bindings), discreet paper repairs, or making up lost decoration on leather bindings (including commissioning copies of tools if necessary[59]). Such procedures were generally seen not as part of any overall philosophy concerned with the historical interest of old bindings but simply as technical exercises requiring specialist skill.[60]

Previous writers interested in the history of playing cards, thought to be among the earliest examples of printing, had long realised that a principal source of survivals lay in their being pasted together to form the boards of books. In 1858 Paul Lacroix drew attention to the consequent importance of examining old *cartonnages*.[61] It was not a new activity, but as it was mostly pursued by binders much that was unearthed in this way remained unrecognised. In Cambridge, John Bowtell (1753–1813) bound some of the most important early books in the University Library. He kept many fragments, and on his death they passed to Downing College, Cambridge, part of the library for the new college.[62] John Lodge, University Librarian from 1828 to 1845, compiled a large scrapbook in which he placed ephemera and fragments from bindings. He does not appear to have known in detail what was included.[63] At St Albans, and most romantically of all, in 1858 William Blades found a battered and water-damaged volume in the old grammar school. On inspection, its covers were found to contain a multitude of fragments from Caxton's press. He described his discovery:

It was in a most deplorable state, covered thickly with a damp sticky dust, and with a considerable portion of the back rotted away by wet. The white decay fell in lumps on the floor as the unappreciated volume was opened. It proved to be Geoffrey Chaucer's English translation of 'Boecius de Consolatione Philosophiae,' printed by Caxton, in the original binding, as issued from Caxton's workshop, and uncut!! On examining the amount of damage it had sustained, I found that the wet, which had injured the book, had also, by separating the layers of paper of which the covers were composed, revealed the interesting fact that several fragments, on which Caxton's types appeared, had been used in their manufacture. After vexatious opposition and repeated delays the Acting Trustees were induced to allow the book, which they now prized highly, to be deposited in the care of Mr. J. Winter Jones, of the British Museum, for the purpose of rebinding. On dissecting the covers they were found to be composed entirely of waste sheets from Caxton's press, two or three being printed on one side only. The two covers yielded no less than fifty-six half-sheets of printed paper, proving the existence of three works from Caxton's press quite unknown before.[64]

The Museum was able to buy the volume in 1871, and the fragments were gathered together separately. Then, as there were already three other copies of this book in the Museum, the carcass was sold.[65]

In Oxford, the antiquary Philip Bliss (1787–1857) bought bundles of discarded fragments from the local binders, and at Corpus Christi College the undergraduate Robert Proctor, already considerably knowledgeable about early printing, and assisted by a friend, systematically removed fragments, with at least the connivance of the Librarian.[66] In France, Fournier quoted several instances of how printed or manuscript fragments had been found in bindings that were vastly more interesting than the texts that they covered.[67] Reflecting current connoisseurship, early printed images commanded his especial interest. Delisle, Holtrop and several private collectors all made fortunate discoveries, sometimes of what proved to be among the most valued items in their collections.

As Bradshaw and Nicholson before him pointed out, the materials used to construct a binding, in particular fragments of parchment or paper, manuscript or printed, could provide key historical evidence. Bradshaw had a much better understanding of the implications of binders' and printers' waste than others who simply saw them as quarries for unknown or rare texts.

Edward Edwards, writing in the 1850s – and thus some time earlier than Bradshaw – had focused on only one aspect:

> In destroying old covers take care to examine their linings, for on some ancient boards are pasted rare leaves, woodcuts, and other matters, of little value in their day but worthy of preservation now.[68]

It was a view rooted in traditional bibliographical values. It emphasised the separate objects that might be rescued in this way, whether images or fragments of rare printing, such as indulgences. Edwards clearly had no understanding of how the context of particular fragments in particular places could contribute to the larger geographical or chronological history of the manufacture and trade of books. When in 1870 Bradshaw acquired an illuminated copy of Boethius printed at Ghent in 1485 and still in its early stamped binding, he noticed that parchment strips had been used to strengthen the sewing. He took the volume apart, and found fragments of an indulgence printed at Oudenaarde early in 1480. His excitement on this occasion seems to have been more at the discovery of an unknown edition than at any possible implications of how a Ghent book came to include printing from a town a little to the south and also on the River Scheldt.[69] On another occasion, he found at Jesus College, Cambridge fragments of indulgences printed at London in 1480, used in the binding of a Cologne Bible of the same year. On also inspecting a book printed by Lettou in the early 1480s, he was able to attribute the binding of both books to him.[70]

Following the Caxton exhibition of 1877, Bradshaw took to Cambridge a copy of Caxton's *Mirror of the world* belonging to the Baptist College at Bristol. He kept it for more than two months, and (with the College's permission) removed from the binding a cancelled copy of a sheet from the *Fifteen Oes* printed by Caxton in about 1490–1. On the basis of this fragment of a short book he was able to prove the printer's order of proceeding in setting up the pages, and that the whole of a quire had not been set at once. It was a small but significant contribution to understanding the practices in Caxton's workshop, and in the pamphlet he printed on the subject, published as his *Memorandum* no. 5, he reflected further on the use of printers' waste in determining those responsible for binding. For Bradshaw, the survival of manuscript or printed fragments in a binding represented much more than simply the preservation of an object. Such objects were to be considered *in situ* as well as independently. Context was as important as object. He could not resist a more general conclusion as he thought of the arguments over Coster:

When applied to foreign early printing, it is evident that if only Dutchmen and Germans could be persuaded to work patiently and methodically upon some such lines, the results would be infinitely more satisfactory and more fruitful than the baseless and frivolous speculations which disfigure even the best books at present written on the subject.[71]

Further, while the bindings commissioned for prominent collectors of the past enjoyed extra social cachet and financial value, the strictly limited nature of this self-selecting group of owners obscured the wider interests of bindings as evidence of past ownership and fashions. In this, Quaritch's catalogue of 1889, with its vastly extended range of information about earlier owners, was pioneering, setting the study of provenance on a new footing. Besides this, the further exploration of tooled decoration, beyond the more gaudy gilt and coloured examples and into the complexities of late medieval blind-stamped work, as partly pursued by Weale, not only extended the subject but also raised questions of geographical relationships between places of printing, binding, sale and ownership. In practice, the questions and approaches that began to be explored in the 1880s proved to be transformative, as what had been considered simply as an aspect of ornamentation was harnessed into a central discipline for understanding the history of books, their making, their use, their value, their circulation and their ownership.

These were lessons that few of Fournier's successors, concentrating on the history of external decoration, remembered to emphasise. There was a difference between him and men such as Bradshaw or Weale. Where Fournier enthused over individual pieces, Bradshaw and Weale understood a larger principle: that even quite ordinary fragments could tell you much about the history of a volume more generally. As Weale summarised it after years of experience and discussion with others whose views on the physical properties of books were not limited to their covers:

> Old books often contain waste sheets or fragments of manuscripts, or of printed books, either as lining to the boards, or as guards in the middle of the gatherings, or employed instead of boards, pasted together to form the sides of the cover. When this waste is printed matter, care must be taken to distinguish between printers' and booksellers' waste. The first is almost always a safe indication of the local origin of the binding, especially if all the waste is that of one printer; the second is very untrustworthy. I have met with books bound in Lyons the covers of which consisted entirely of waste sheets of books printed in Paris, books bound in England with waste sheets of books printed on the Continent, and of books bound abroad containing English waste ... It is easy to understand that an English publisher, sending his books abroad to a foreign bookseller, would pack them in waste sheets, and that, paper being valuable, these would often be used up by the recipient when binding. The discovery inside the cover of an English bound book of a number of sheets of Netherlandish, German, and French books, with the binder's name and address written on them, opened my eyes to this fact.[72]

The habit of delving into bindings, and taking them apart, could be an informative archaeological exercise in excavation. But if the context of such fragments was ignored, then evidence was lost. In 1886 Léopold Delisle, better known for his work on manuscripts than on printed books, had responsibility for both in his post at the Bibliothèque Nationale. In this capacity he compiled some notes for the cataloguing of incunabula. To him, early bindings were of interest especially because they might contain fragments of early and possibly significant manuscripts. For that reason, when manuscript endleaves were found in printed books these were to be removed with care, preferably by a skilled conservator.[73] The practice was widely followed, but as notes were made only infrequently to link the different parts of the dismembered volumes much essential evidence was thereupon lost. The study of manuscript binding fragments became a part of the study of manuscripts, and printed books were separate. The essential integrity of volumes, and the evidence they could thus convey of their history, circulation and reading was thereby destroyed. It was to remain the case for many decades to come that when binders set a fresh cover on a book, they might occasionally put aside fragments that seemed to have some curiosity value. In simply gathering such fragments into uncatalogued boxes, libraries that should have been more historically aware allowed this evidence to be dispersed and forgotten.[74]

The temptations were considerable. Comparatively few early printed books were left undisturbed if they seemed worn in some way, and the upper echelons of the trade in London, Paris and elsewhere meanwhile helped to ensure that much that has come down to us bears little relation to the condition when in the hands of early readers.

Valuing Early Bindings

In the 1850s Nicholson assumed that, subject to condition, bindings were if possible to be left intact. If we look at the treatment accorded to a single well-known book, frequently offered for sale and with copies owned by a wide variety of people in Britain and overseas alike, it is possible to begin to judge how far Nicholson's remarks heralded limited change.

Two obvious candidates suggest themselves as offering the possibility of a continuing survey: Shakespeare's First Folio (1623) and Hartmann Schedel's Nuremberg Chronicle (1493). In 1824 Dibdin offered a list of thirty copies of the First Folio known to him,[75] and though copies of the First Folio recur in the trade through the century, many of these are reappearances of the same copies. With the notable exception of a small handful, notably that sold at the George Daniel sale in 1864, when it fetched an exceptional price of £716.2s.,[76] most were imperfect in some way and were either made good by pen facsimiles or by abstracting leaves from other copies. A copy offered by Willis and Sotheran in 1857, with the title reprinted and the Droeshout portrait inserted, was priced at £63.[77] Scarcely any copies were in even near-original bindings. Exceptional copies made high prices, the Henry Perkins copy fetching £585 in 1873.[78] 'Unfortunately,' said the sale catalogue of Sir William Tite's library in 1874 in presenting the First Folio, 'for most persons desirous of possessing a copy the yearly increasing price renders it almost unattainable, except by those Collectors to whom its present money value is of slight consequence. Mr. Gardner's copy sold for £250, G. Smith's for £410, Earl of Charlemont's for £455, and G. Daniel's for £714.'[79] The Daniel price was not beaten until the 1890s, and even then poor copies could still be had for under £100.[80] Fine or poor, copies were almost always in later bindings, and thus offer only limited comment on attitudes to what has come to be called conservation repair.

The Nuremberg Chronicle, printed by Koberger at Nuremberg, remains the most common surviving incunable volume of all. It recurred constantly for sale, much more frequently than the Shakespeare First Folio, was in constant demand, and came in a variety of bindings. By no means all booksellers' and auctioneers' catalogues provide even approximate details of bindings, but there are sufficient to gauge the range of preferences that developed between the 1830s and the 1880s. They may be summarised as follows.

It was printed first in Latin and then shortly afterwards in German. The latter proved more popular at first. Of perhaps 1,500 copies of the Latin edition about one-third remained unsold in 1509, whereas only forty-nine remained of the German. But it was the Latin edition that subsequently caught collectors' attention. Copies were available either plain or coloured.[81] Over nine hundred copies are recorded today, many of them unsurprisingly imperfect in one way or another. Many further copies have been cut up so that leaves can be sold separately, usually for the sake of their woodcuts. Over the years, as old bindings have been replaced, few copies now survive in their fifteenth- or early sixteenth-century state.

In his catalogue of the Spencer library, Thomas Dibdin devoted no fewer than twenty-six pages to it.[82] Quite apart from the materials of the binding, collectors were concerned with the height: a sign that former binders had been careful and that as much as possible survived of the original sheets. Internal condition was crucial, and so was the condition of the paper. Thus bibliophile criteria were selective. Dibdin described Spencer's copy as being 'of extraordinarily-white colour', compared with others 'of a tawny or even dingy tint'.

Booksellers were not necessarily concerned with all these criteria, and sometimes gave no condition details at all; but in their catalogues can be traced something of the changing fortunes of this most sought-for book, reflecting in turn the changing tastes and preoccupations of successive collectors.

It was a common book. In 1743 Thomas Osborne's catalogue of the Harleian library (1743) said simply and accurately 'Liber Chronicarum, Auctore Hartm. Schedel Norimb. 1493'. By the mid-nineteenth century more was needed. As a book that was widely available, and yet a key volume for collectors, details were essential in making choices among copies, the two principal criteria being money and condition. Provenance was usually less important, but interests in this also developed. Condition, size and appearance, particularly of bindings, were essential. The few copies in their earliest bindings were increasingly valued.[83]

Bindings were easy to describe at a very elementary level. The names of the better workshops were widely known, and they were key to prices. Henry G. Bohn offered two copies in his catalogue of 1831, one bound by

Clarke in Turkey morocco with gilt edges, price 9 guineas, and the other, a little wormed, for just 3 guineas.

At the auction in 1840 of the library of Sir William Bolland, one of the first members of the Roxburghe Club, his copy ('very large and sound' according to Dibdin[84]) was sold for £4.12s. to the bookseller Thomas Rodd. Five years later, George Willis, bookseller in Covent Garden, offered the coloured copy formerly in the collection of the Duke of Sussex for £5.10s.

Beriah Botfield, assembling one of the most lavish collections of early printed books in his time, bought his copy for 6 guineas from Payne and Foss at some date before 1849, and retained the contemporary Netherlandish binding of blind-stamped calf.[85] The growing perception that old bindings could offer more than decoration was by no means a smooth development, but catalogue descriptions reveal something of how priorities were worked out: when it was appropriate to retain an old binding, when an old one could be replaced, and what was a suitable replacement. Henry G. Bohn offered a copy in 1848 bound in what he described as 'Old morocco, tooled', for £8.18s.6d. In 1857 Willis and Sotheran offered an inferior copy ('slightly injured by damp, and two leaves of Index added in MS.'), bound in old calf, gilt, for £2.15.[86] Five years later the same firm offered another in stamped parchment for 5 guineas.[87] Bernard Quaritch established himself as the leader of a new generation of booksellers with his *General catalogue of books, arranged in classes* (1868). Prices had increased. There he offered no fewer than five copies, priced between 9 guineas ('quite perfect', in 'stamped hogskin', and 16⅝ ins tall) and £30 (also 'quite perfect, brown morocco extra, with gilt edges', by Bedford). This was 18¼ inches tall, and had an early sixteenth-century provenance: Bedford had stripped off the original oak boards. Then in his fat *Supplement* of 1875–7 Quaritch offered two more copies, one for £25, 'very tall', in 'brown pigskin extra, gilt edges, a masterpiece of Bedford's', and the other bound by Rivière in brown morocco extra with gilt edges, 'very fine and very large', for £27. Assuming that copies were in reasonable condition, early bindings were rated less than the work of the fashionable Bedford or Rivière. The copy belonging to Henry Perkins sold at auction in 1873 fetched no more than an average price, at 10 guineas in oak and stamped leather. Three years earlier the Glasgow insurance broker William Euing had paid Pearson in Pall Mall the same price for his tall copy in eighteenth-century calf.[88]

In 1888 Quaritch was again able to offer five copies of the Chronicle, at prices from £15 (for copies noticeably cut down) upwards. This was the price also asked for a copy in stamped pigskin. Sir Mark Masterman Sykes's copy, bound in morocco by Derome, was priced at £42. The copy once belonging to Adolf von Anhalt, Bishop of Merseburg, and given by him to Merseburg Cathedral in 1520, was exceptionally tall, described in 1887 as 'the finest and largest copy in existence'. It was in a modern binding, by Bedford, and was offered at £84, with a note that for the binding alone Bedford had charged £15 twenty years previously.[89] It did not sell immediately, and was reduced by 1897 to £63. In that year Quaritch was offering two further copies. One, in a Rivière binding of pigskin imitating an old German pattern, was £27. This had no provenance. The other, for £30, had formerly belonged to the Tudor politician Sir Richard Southwell and was still in its sixteenth-century English binding.[90]

Opinions differed. Some people preferred modern work, others earlier. F.S. Ellis, who shared many tastes for earlier work with his friend William Morris, recorded approvingly of the Earl of Ashburnham that

> With the instinct of a true antiquary he dearly loved to have his books in the original covers; an ancient book washed and smartly rebound was an abomination unto him. The skill of Messrs. Lewis, Clark, Bedford, or Rivière, when applied to the destruction of an old cover and the manufacture of a new one in its place, he held in hearty detestation.[91]

Ashburnham was a difficult man, not easy to please and of what Ellis called an 'overbearing temperament'. Quaritch recounted how he and the earl fell out over the prices of some manuscripts, and those who calculated his profits on the sale of his manuscripts found little to admire. But in his taste for early bindings he was ahead of many of his contemporaries.

Books on Show

13 | Reproduction

For readers at all levels, the advent of new techniques of reproduction for print and manuscript transformed the study of old books, introducing them to audiences for whom they were unfamiliar. Many of the more elaborate facsimiles were produced in extremely limited editions, and some had a value more antiquarian than literary; but the principal stimulus was a new market among those curious yet unable to buy original editions.

Chromolithography

The development of chromolithography by Godefroy Engelmann, Charles Hullmandel and others in the 1830s was the key component in a revolution in printed colour.[1] While on the one hand the process was adopted in a myriad of cheap illustrated books, on the other it was employed in all manner of expensive publications. Some of the better and more elaborate work was finished by hand. It was soon realised that the process had applications to the reproduction of early works of art, notably at first for illuminated manuscripts and then, very quickly later, for the reproduction of bookbindings. Some were over-ambitious. In France, between 1832 and 1869 the Comte de Bastard issued a series of *Peintures et ornements des manuscrits ... pour servir à l'histoire des arts du dessein depuis le IVe siècle de l'ère chrétienne jusqu'à la fin du XVIe*. It was a puzzle. One calculation suggested that for the twenty parts published, each containing eight coloured plates, subscribers would have to pay almost £1,500. Perhaps fortunately for what the same later commentator called the 'luckless or insane subscriber' it was never completed, for the cost would have amounted to about £10,000.[2] There was reason to claim that it was 'the most sumptuous, unique, and costly work that has ever been produced'; but it was hardly practicable, and not everyone was impressed. While the quality of the reproductions was much admired, and examples were shown at international exhibitions at London and Paris, its effectiveness was vitiated by a lack of accompanying text (never published), by the confusion in the ordering of plates that defeated librarians in their attempts to bind up copies, and by the fact that there were very few copies that could be considered complete even as to the plates. A partial copy sold at auction fetched just £200.[3] Many years later Léopold Delisle sought to bring some order into this potentially useful collection in an article summarising the contents.[4]

Joseph-Balthazar Silvestre's album *Paléographie universelle*, in four volumes (1839–41), another atlas folio, proved similarly disjointed. At a normal price of £75, unbound in parts, it too was not cheap. The 250 copies sold slowly, the King of France was said to have bought sixty-six copies for libraries, while many found buyers in Germany and Russia. English sales were turgid, allegedly amounting initially to just ten copies.[5] By 1848, when Henry G. Bohn advertised that he had purchased the remaining stock of fourteen copies, he was offering each at 50 guineas. Readers found Frederic Madden's revised and supplemented English version of Silvestre's work (1849–50) preferable. Others took a wider view of medieval art. Alexandre du Sommerard, who lived in what is now the Musée de Cluny where he created the Musée des Antiquités Nationales, issued in 1838–47 a more modest, and more modestly priced, group of volumes on *Les arts au moyen âge*. The coloured copies, with the several hundred illustrations heightened as appropriate with gold and silver, commanded especial attention.[6] Soon afterwards Paul Lacroix, *conservateur* at the Bibliothèque de l'Arsenal, gathered five substantial volumes on *Le moyen âge et la Renaissance: histoire et description des mœurs et usages, du commerce et de l'industrie, des sciences, des arts, des littératures et des beaux arts en Europe*, with extensive sections on illuminated manuscripts, bindings and early printed books. It was published in 1846–51 by subscription at the considerable price of 375 francs, and was slow to sell as the principal investors, including Lemercier as printer, soon found to their cost.[7] Lacroix's later derivations from this series were priced lower than some other publications, ambitious in their own ways, and enjoyed better success.

Photography

The mid-century bibliographical revolution was marked by no means least in a revolution in visual literacy. Chromolithography was admired, and much used, also in the hands of less ambitious people than those just mentioned. But it was a hand process, which depended on tracing and hand-copying. Though it presented a far greater technical challenge, photography offered more. William Henry Fox Talbot's *Pencil of nature* appeared in parts in 1844–6. As over the next few years photography made its way into books and into publishing, it hence made its way also into an essential position in the wider understanding of history and the visual arts.[8] Henry Bradshaw in Cambridge and J.W. Holtrop in The Hague were just two people who turned to photography when wishing to make comparisons in their correspondence.[9] By 1880 the photographer Léon Vidal expressed what was by then a generation-old commonplace:

> Une des applications les plus intéressantes de la photographie est la reproduction fidèle et incontestable des monuments et documents historiques ou artistiques.[10]

Depending on the process involved at a time of considerable experiment, some images could be published in larger numbers than others. Just twenty-five copies were made of the special illustrations for Stirling-Maxwell's *Annals of the artists of Spain* (1847) and twelve copies for his *Cloister life of Charles V* (1853). The 157 callotypes prepared for the four volumes of the illustrated record of the Great Exhibition of 1851 were on a quite different scale. These early productions were highly priced. Sets of photographs by Roger Fenton of the Crimean War, published in Manchester by Agnew, cost 60 guineas.[11] But as new techniques of reproduction were developed, so costs came down, prompting series of compilations of landscapes such as William and Mary Howitt's *Ruined abbeys and castles of Great Britain and Ireland* (1862–4). Photographs began to replace tracings and hand copies for manuscripts, in Fenton's photographs from the Codex Alexandrinus for the Epistles of Clement of Rome (1856), or in the single photograph inserted as a frontispiece in F.H. Scrivener's account of the ninth-century Codex Augiensis in Trinity College, Cambridge (1859). By the mid-1870s there were many guides to photographic techniques, some directed explicitly at amateurs, and there were numerous articles to be found in general periodicals.[12] Within a very few years, photographs had become an everyday part of life not just for portraiture, as in the early Daguerreotypes, but for all manner of other purposes as well. A fundamental change came when in 1882 (once again, a date towards the end of our period) Georg Meisenbach patented the half-tone screen for printing photographs, and so laid the foundations of cheap mass reproduction.

Meanwhile in 1860 George Stephens, an Anglo-Saxon scholar working in Denmark, had this to say:

> Photographic facsimiles of *old* manuscripts, especially in dialects where so much depends on grammatical niceties, on terminations, where an e or an ae . . . &c. &c.

can make all the difference, are undoubtedly to be preferred to the best lithographic imitations. In modern manuscripts, or where all is as plain as a pikestaff, the latter are well enough, and where the number printed is large, are also incomparably cheaper. But we must not sacrifice truth and use to show or price. The pretty mechanical copper or stone fac-simile is *inevitably*, to very great degree, the work, the reading or guess or caprice, of the *artist himself.* It is thus amusing to see how greatly 2 or 3 or 4 mechanical facsimiles, taken by different men, often differ, not only in the general air and character, but also, what is much more important, in the details. Very nice wars are sometimes carried on by learned critics, each one standing on his own facsimile. By the aid of the wonderful discovery of Photography all this is impossible. Nature reflects herself. What there is, we have. The resemblance is perfect. It is true that Photography has its disadvantages, when thus applied to literary remains. The older the parchment is, and thus the more anxious we may be to obtain a perfect copy, the darker will it be, and often stained and spotted and cruelly torn and twisted *injuria temporum*. But all this is most unfavourable to the art. Dark and yellow and brownish surfaces give, as we know, a blackish ground, and the letters are no longer so visible as might have been hoped, while every wound or tear or jag and wrinkle produces a corresponding streak or chasm, or line of light or shade. Even a powerful press applied to the parchment is only a partial remedy. But still the great fact remains. Photography is Nature. Altho not all we could wish, it is infinitely better, especially for ancient remains, than the *clear* and *elegant* copy.[13]

Beside such remarks are to be set the experiments at about the same time of Colonel Henry James at the Ordnance Survey, first with maps and then, publicly and triumphantly, in a full – and cheap – facsimile of the Domesday Book, based on the transfer of photographic images to lithographic plates. As images they were still crude and because the images were doctored before they were printed, they were not necessarily entirely accurate as reproductions. But it was an enormous advance, both in technique and in engaging public enthusiasm.[14] The advent of photolithography helped to induce Henry Noel Humphreys to compile his large folio volume *A history of the art of printing*, published by Quaritch in 1867 and replete with a hundred plates containing many more images, including some in colour:

The very best of the so-called fac-similes, executed by hand, can never reproduce the general aspect of a page of print of any special epoch with anything like the accuracy of a photo-lithograph, by which means an entire page can be accurately reproduced at one quarter the expense that a few lines would cost, if executed by hand; and it is this facility of copious illustration which has been one of my chief reasons for undertaking an outline history of the origin and development of the printing press during the first eventful century of its existence.[15]

As his title-page eagerly announced, the plates were printed by Day & Son, one of the most skilled practitioners in the business.[16] Humphreys was keen to promote their work, not only on the chromolithographs but also on some of the other more prominent facsimiles in a collection of reproductions that he claimed to represent his subject more extensively than any hitherto published. As an example, he cited the large reproduction from the Gutenberg Bible, 'such a specimen as no previous work on the subject can boast of, and which would not now have been produced but for new processes which scientific and artistic discoveries have placed at my disposal'. Humphreys presented his book as one for the general reader, the person to whom Latin, French and German would be unfamiliar. He believed his account of printing from about 1430 to 1530 to be the first of its kind, a continuous and readable narrative, sufficiently free of technical details to be readily intelligible. Whatever the technical achievements, his book was castigated for its text. In a highly critical review, 'WB' (perhaps William Blades) in *The Book-Worm* plainly called it an 'unsatisfactory volume'.[17] It followed his earlier books including *The illuminated books of the middle ages* (1849) and *The coinage of the British empire* (1855). As an author well experienced in exploiting colour reproductions for popularising volumes, his grasp of historical and bibliographical detail was of lesser importance.

Photography was only a partial answer. In a trio of articles published in *The Academy* in 1884, J.H. Hessels pondered a group of twenty-two monographs and albums of facsimiles published over the previous twenty-five years in England, Germany, France and Italy.[18] He had several criticisms. First, the reproduction of one or two pages from a manuscript could never give a proper impression of the whole. Such reproductions, done well, could certainly be a help: he singled out the work of E.A. Bond and Edward Maunde Thompson with the Palaeographical Society in particular.[19] But, in general, signs of abbreviation, signatures, punctuation, ruling and the quality of the parchment were all neglected. Reproduction techniques themselves were of very varying reliability:

> Photography has not been brought to such perfection that original MSS. and careful editors can as yet be discarded. And when we wish to undertake the reproduction of any more MSS., it would be well, I think, to speak a little more cautiously as to the 'preservation' of precious monuments by this process.[20]

He was especially critical of Henry Sweet's edition of a facsimile of the Epinal glossary, published by the Early English Text Society and reproduced by photolithography. Marks on the original were not all reproduced, and other, new, marks had been introduced.[21] Sweet himself had given Hessels his cue, having in his preface alluded to the considerable difficulties encountered in preparing the facsimile:

> When after long delays, I obtained proofs of the facsimiles, I found that they had been very largely touched by hand, in spite of my very definite instructions to the contrary: the photolithographer confessed to having put in nearly the whole of the last few pages by hand. It was nearly two years before I succeeded in obtaining what professed to be ungarbled facsimiles ... As will be easily seen, they fail in reproducing its less distinct portions.[22]

Overall, Hessels's remarks were restricted to Greek and Latin manuscripts, where Wilhelm Wattenbach's manuals were of obvious use. Looking further at what needed yet to be done, he remarked on the inadequacy of palaeographical terminology, particularly – but by no means only – after the eighth century.

Facsimiles made possible wider participation, whether among scholars working on early manuscripts or among a public eager to take advantage of the cheap photolithographed county volumes of James's Domesday Book. Responses to facsimiles of early printed books came likewise from a variety of readers.[23] The mixture of scholarly and amateur interests was epitomised, not surprisingly, by reprints of Shakespeare, notably the reduced facsimiles of the First Folio published by Lionel Booth in 1862–4, and by Chatto & Windus in 1876, besides a series of quarto facsimiles prepared by William Griggs. They formed a timely accompaniment to the new edition of the complete works edited at Cambridge, first published in 1863–6 and providing for the first time properly detailed collations with former editions.

All this is not to say that photography was immediately understood, or widely adopted. It took the Trustees of the British Museum over seventy years to accommodate themselves to an invention that seemed by turns to be expensive, threatening to the books, and awkward to manage. Little thought seems to have been given to how the conveniences of readers might be enhanced. At first all was well. In 1853 the Trustees agreed to construct a photographic studio on the roof of the Museum. Roger Fenton was appointed official photographer to the Museum as a whole, until this arrangement ended in 1859. He handed back all his negatives, and his equipment was put into store: it was finally sold off in 1876. No further official appointment to this post was made until 1927.[24] Half a century after *The pencil of nature*, the British Museum library still resisted the general introduction of photography. Instead, readers and other customers had to employ their own people. There were some, more enlightened, who saw matters differently. In 1884, shortly after the appearance of Hessels's criticism, Richard Garnett spoke out from the Department of Printed Books, where George Bullen was the Keeper. His audience was the annual meeting of the Library Association, held on this occasion in Dublin, and his cue was the recent decision that the Irish portion of the Ashburnham papers should be transferred from the British Museum to the Royal Irish Academy. After remarking on the advantages to be obtained by making photographic copies, and sharing them among libraries, he turned to some everyday realities:

Photographic reproduction has not as yet been regarded as a duty incumbent upon a public library, and has not, accordingly, been provided for out of public funds.[25]

In Garnett's view, in place of a library, or an individual, employing a private photographer, the library should itself employ one on its staff. The resulting work, with the accompanying advantages for scholarship, exchanges of documents nationally and internationally, conservation and sheer convenience would more than compensate for any cost, while there would be considerable savings in staff time:[26] 'The photographic reproduction of national property should be the concern of the nation.'[27]

Fifteen years later, by now Keeper himself, Garnett returned to the subject, nothing having been done in the meanwhile:

The most perfect unanimity exists within and outside the Museum with respect to the benefit which the adoption of photography as a department of the regular work of the institution would confer alike upon it and upon the public. Nevertheless, not a single step has been taken since the writer brought the subject forward in 1884, preceded as this had been by the successful introduction of photography at the Bodleian Library in connection with the Oxford University Press. Government seems to be unable to perceive the public benefit to be derived from the cheap reproduction and unlimited multiplication with infallible accuracy of historical documents and current official papers.[28]

Instead of a department, the Museum persisted with outside contractors, with the unavoidable extra costs this involved. In very different vein, at the South Kensington Museum Charles Thurston Thompson (1816–68), brother-in-law of Henry Cole, became the official photographer in 1856. It was the first appointment of its kind, and after Fenton's separation from the British Museum he was also made responsible for some Museum work.[29] So the national library, subservient to successive governments and lacking the resolve, perseverance, energy, imagination or influence to force a change, remained for the moment in the past.

14 | Exhibitions

In 1870 the penny guide to the showcases of printed books in the British Museum listed about 250 exhibits, from fifteenth-century block-books to specimens of bookbinding bequeathed by Felix Slade in 1868.[1] Apart from the old royal library and the library of George III, it included many exceptional specimens from the Cracherode and Grenville bequests. It also revealed recent purchases among early printed books, including no fewer than eighteen complete or fragmentary block-books bought since 1835. A book printed at Canton in 1671 on bamboo paper, the first to be printed there by Europeans, had been bought in 1844, and the first edition of *Robinson Crusoe* in 1852. One of the earliest books printed in the Americas, in 1543–4, came from the library of the late Maximilian, Emperor of Mexico, in 1869.

In representing print in the context of the history of human knowledge more generally, the Museum as a whole was at an advantage. However, while it could offer permanent exhibitions, whether of books or antiquities, it could not easily present them in the contexts of modern achievements. For this, the multitude of temporary exhibitions, across the country and across Europe, presenting old and new objects side by side, offered another perspective. They also reached audiences unfamiliar with the fixed presentations whether in London or Paris.

Exhibitions were, and are, inescapably selections. They could not be comprehensive, and in most cases they were chosen with specific purposes in mind. Thus they were ways of directing understanding, whether of historical phenomena such as the spread and influence of printing, or of the history of manufacture and of decorative arts, or on how inherited ideas and skills were to be compared with current manufacturing and design, and modern tastes. At first sight, it might seem odd to place medieval manuscripts and early printed books in exhibitions designed apparently primarily to celebrate modern achievements. But in concept and in practice these were but two aspects of the same group of questions: how was the present, a period of rapid and bewildering change, to be related to past achievements? Where did the modern world come from, and what inferences could be drawn for the modern good? All were driven by the same stimuli: of purpose, choice and audience.

In 1840, as part of the celebrations of Gutenberg, the book trade in Leipzig organised an exhibition that combined early printed books with modern printing techniques where the recent development of electrotyping was given prominence. The historical part was by no means only about Gutenberg, for early printing in Italy was also given space, as was the work of Christophe Plantin in sixteenth-century Antwerp, while modern mass production was represented in the firms of Tauchnitz and Wigand. It was the first large-scale celebration to encompass such a chronological and thematic range concerning printing.[2] The mid-century became a time of exhibitions of all kinds.[3] Some were international, some were national. Some, now much less remembered, were local. Apart from the innumerable small and usually short-lived occasions designed for special and closely defined clienteles, there were also much larger ones, lasting for weeks or even months. Here a much wider, and sometimes international, public could become familiar with what in the past had been reserved for the few.

Loan exhibitions of the size so often seen by the 1850s depended on the generosity of individuals, and their willingness to lend. They did so on scales never witnessed hitherto, spectacularly so for the Manchester Art Treasures exhibition in 1857.[4] Motives, as usual, were mixed, including emulation of other collectors and a wish to display as well as share wealth or taste. Public and private interests were combined. For the many exhibitions involving books, some collectors were prominent. The Queen lent repeatedly, sometimes the same book. Loans came on various occasions from long-established family collections, including the Duke of Devonshire and Lord Leicester. Earl Spencer proved exceptionally generous. Others came from people who were even at the time gathering their libraries, such as Sir William Tite, the Rev. John Fuller Russell and George Offor. The Caxton exhibition of 1877 would have been impossible without the exemplary participation as a lender of its instigator, William Blades.

Most of the temporary exhibitions were short-lived, mounted for just a few days despite the very considerable demands of selection, requests for loans, agreements, transport, security and display. In 1861 a large loan exhibition of antiquities and works of art at Ironmongers' Hall in the City of London opened in the evening on 8 May, with a reception attended by about six hundred people. On the following three days it opened again each morning, attracting several thousand more, and on the last day the Prince Consort paid a private visit. Then it closed. Apart from the treasures of the Company itself, dozens of people from across the country had lent objects of all kinds. The commemorative two-volume catalogue, partly illustrated in chromolithography, ran to 642 quarto pages (copies were also printed on large paper), and was only published eight years later.[5] It included descriptions of the exhibits, organised under forty-four heads including not just ironwork but also Egyptian antiquities, paintings, illuminated manuscripts, ivory carvings, plate from the London livery companies, and a selection of elaborate bookbindings from medieval to modern times chosen for the sake of their outward embellishment. The catalogue included the first extended account to be published of the fourteenth-century Litlington Missal, in Westminster Abbey.[6]

The Ironmongers' exhibition was exceptional in its range and in its wealth, as a privately organised occasion, with loans from the Queen as well as from well-known collectors including William Tite, George Offor and Felix Slade. Its original purpose was to celebrate recent innovations and successes in the use of iron, before the idea of a much more heterogeneous display took root.

Exhibitions were organised for many reasons. When the French art historian and journalist Louis Clément de Ris visited the London exhibition of 1862, he was dismayed to be reminded of how much of France's inheritance had fallen into the hands of English collectors, but also cheered to think how much that was superior still remained in Paris. It led him to reflect further: that the London exhibition should be followed by one in Paris, drawing on French collections from across the country.[7] On this occasion as on others, national interest and international competition were obvious stimulants and were manifest in two more apparent purposes: to show the achievements either of individuals or of industrial processes; and to provide opportunities for the sale of some of the work on show. This could include substantial commercial interests, and much thought was given to financial profits. The South Kensington Museum made regular purchases at the several international exhibitions that followed 1851, while some of the best work in the Paris exhibition of 1867 found its way into the fashionable shops of London's West End. Not everything was simply on loan. For some people, these sales inspired misgivings, though as was pointed out there were plenty of precedents. In the words of Henry Cole, writing from greater experience than anyone else, and in the wake of a series of international exhibitions during the 1870s:

It is not to be doubted that without the motive of sale being allowed to have free action, an exhibition of new objects in the present day, either of Fine Art or industry, could not be efficiently made, and if made would not be approved by the public. By degrees convenient arrangements have been adopted at the Royal Academy and other Fine Art exhibitions, at agricultural and other exhibitions, where prices of objects may be learnt and sales effected. The motives of the French and Belgian commissioners in erecting their supplementary buildings was avowedly to promote the commercial interests of France and Belgium. The more the public at large learn to appreciate works of Science and Art, the more they desire to possess them, and the greater should be the facilities of purchase.[8]

Commercial and financial considerations might thus colour the purposes for which older examples, such as early printed books, or old bindings, were sometimes included among modern work. The purpose was not simply historical or antiquarian. It was to provide comparisons and contrasts, where the modern was at least as important as the old. Yet when they were included, books formed a tiny part of these exhibitions, where the products of industry and invention dominated; and when paintings were included they attracted far more attention than old or new books or manuscripts. To a greater or less extent books figured on general occasions; and in the great mixture of exhibitions, varying from the local and amateur to the largest international, their distinctive purposes were not always clear. The mid-century saw the concept take the world by storm, not least enthusiastically among local amateur groups for whom an exhibition became a focus of identity. The Great Exhibition of 1851 (where modern books were little noticed, and there were no early ones) was but the most famous, and in the public mind at least therefore the most important.

Industrial arts and skills, described sometimes as 'useful arts', occasionally admitted of unexpected objects. The 1862 International Exhibition included the Koh-i-Noor diamond belonging to the Queen, shown as a specimen of diamond cutting:[9] how many people who saw it valued the opportunity as an occasion to admire technical skill, rather than a natural wonder or an aspect of royal wealth, can only be guessed. Organisers, exhibitors and visitors frequently had different purposes in mind. An experienced British bookbinder who visited the universal exhibition at Paris in 1867 found it impossible to judge the quality of the bindings on display because he could not see inside the books: they were exhibited simply for the sake of their external decoration.[10] Nonetheless, the British presence at the exhibition was impressive. Apart from printers, publishers and binders, on this occasion early printing crept in with a group of books exhibited by one of the largest antiquarian booksellers in London, C.J. Stewart: all were presumably for sale.[11]

It can be difficult to grasp the scale and complexity of some of these mid-century exhibitions. As an accompaniment to the industrial exhibition of 1862, the South Kensington Museum organised one devoted to works of art since medieval times. A general invitation to 'noblemen and gentlemen, eminent for their knowledge of art' to offer objects for loan was issued in March that year, and the exhibition opened just three months later: its execution was in the hands of J.C. Robinson, superintendent of the art collections at the Museum. Held from June to November, it brought together upwards of nine thousand exhibits, from about five hundred lenders. Not surprisingly, its organisation was a challenge, and not everything was assembled until the last moment. A provisional catalogue was issued in separate parts, and then all were gathered together into a volume published subsequent to the exhibition, in January 1863.[12] The purpose on this occasion was to exhibit decorative arts, and thus not paintings or drawings (unless they were designs for such work). So the contents proceeded from sculpture to decorative furniture and metalwork through to clocks and watches, ornamental cutlery, porcelain, glass, musical instruments 'remarkable as objects of artistic decoration' and textiles. This was but a selection; sections 30–31, and thus towards the end, comprised illuminated manuscripts and bookbindings.

Major exhibitions of inventions and the applied arts thus provided opportunities to compare past and present. Of the manuscripts in 1862, the Duke of Devonshire lent the tenth-century Benedictional of St Æthelwold (now British Library MS Add.49598) and Lady Stourton lent the late fifteenth-century Hastings Hours (now British Library MS Add.54782). Both Stonyhurst College and Lichfield Cathedral contributed their greatest manuscript treasures, and St Paul's Cathedral lent the Book of Penalties relating to non-performance at Westminster Abbey of prayers for the soul of Henry VII and others in the royal chapel. The section on bookbindings included about 130 examples, and was the largest exhibition of its kind so far seen in London. It depended overwhelmingly on modern collectors. They were led by the Earl of Gosford, Felix Slade, Earl Spencer and R.S. Turner. Sir Thomas Gage lent a manuscript of 1609 by Esther Inglis for the sake not of the astonishing calligraphy or decoration but of its green velvet binding worked with gold thread and seed pearls.[13] The selection of bindings was mainly Italian, French and English, with a few German and Flemish examples.

In keeping with the rest of the exhibition, the emphasis was always on decoration: on gilt or painted examples, on embroidered examples (including one attributed as usual to the nuns of Little Gidding), and if there was a distinguished provenance that was a bonus. The St Paul's loan inspired particular attention:

This remarkable volume is sumptuously bound in a rich velvet forel, studded with silver gilt roundels, enamelled with the royal arms and badges, upon a ground party per pale and vert argent, green and white, being the colours of the Tudor livery. To this deed are hung by silken cords, green and white twisted together, and put into silver skippets bearing on them other enamels, the seals of the contracting parties and witnesses; the one shown is that of the chapter of Canterbury cathedral, and of the early part of the 13th century. It is a splendid specimen of English die-sinking, most likely done by the hand of some Canterbury monk. The die of the seal is the 13th century English work, the enamels are early 16th century, and are also English work.[14]

Blind-stamped bindings were almost wholly excluded, the few exceptions including an undated copy of Grafton's *Chronicles* in oak boards covered in stamped leather and further ornamented in the late seventeenth century,[15] an elaborate Italian sixteenth-century example lent by Walter Sneyd,[16] and two books from Germany. A pair of block-books bound in pigskin was lent by Lord Spencer, the binding bearing the date 1467;[17] and a copy of Euripides (Basel, 1551), dated 1561, was described as being in 'Dutch hogskin'.[18] Though in date the exhibits ranged from the fifteenth to the eighteenth centuries, they represented a selective and restrictive way of looking at the history of the subject that was to persist until the twentieth century. As so often, the bindings most valued were those bearing gilt or coloured decoration. A further exhibition of historic bindings was offered in connection with the international exhibition of 1874, when among twenty-nine contributors the Dean and Chapter of Durham lent seventeen examples, Earl Spencer thirty-one and R.S. Turner thirty-seven.[19]

The exposition universelle held at Paris in May–November 1878 was an affirmation of the recovery of France to prosperity and authority following the shame of her defeat at the hands of Prussia in 1870–1, and the destruction of much of her capital city at the hands of the mob. Not only was it larger and more grandly conceived than the previous universal exhibition held at Paris in 1867 but also was larger than any held previously, anywhere. More visitors came than in 1867, despite the attempts of some clergy to dissuade people from attending a display that was unmarked by any religious dedication of the kind that was customary on such occasions. The exhibition, on the same site as in 1867, was dominated by the enormous, if not universally admired, Palais du Trocadéro, built specially for the exhibition on the site of the old Palais de Chaillot, and straddled the Seine.[20] It attracted an estimated 13 million visitors, for many of whom the lasting memory was of the hot air balloon, later sold to the manager of the Princes Theatre in London.

The fine and applied arts were only one small part of this event, and though very large in itself the exhibition of *art ancien* was smaller again. Within this enclave, and placed among other work, was gathered a selection of some of the manuscripts and printed books: others were to be found elsewhere on the site. The exhibition was organised by Adrien de Longpérier, formerly keeper of antiquities at the Louvre, while the subsequent catalogue was edited by Baron Alphonse de Ruble, historian of Paris and a noted bibliophile. He was aided by Léopold Delisle and a small group of leading librarians and archivists. Their catalogue, published after the exhibition had closed, was a souvenir, and a selective one at that: those who wished for a complete record were referred to the *Catalogue officiel*. Thus visitors did not have the same information at their command.

Though the exhibition as a whole was an unequivocal statement by France, it was also an international one, including the work of nations well beyond Europe. In the gathering of books made in France, Germany, Italy and England, the exhibition of manuscripts and early printed books reflected this dual nature. Loans came from provincial libraries and from private individuals, not from any of the Parisian national libraries. The bibliothèques municipales at Troyes and Rouen lent some of the earliest books, including a seventh-century copy of Gregory's *Liber pastoralis*. Loans from Rouen provided opportunities to show books from Anglo-Saxon England. Unlike other catalogues of exhibitions of manuscripts and early printed books, where entries were brief to the point of being abrupt, some of the Paris catalogue was generous in its detail. Much was due to Delisle, who commanded the necessary scholarship. So the Troyes Gregory was introduced with references to Mabillon, allusion was made to the manuscript's provenance from the Oratorians at Troyes, and a reference was given to the French *Catalogue général des manuscrits*. The Bible executed under the guidance of Theodulf, Bishop of Orleans in the late eighth/ninth century, and by 1878 at Le Puy, was given a page of small type, comparing it with the twin manuscript (MS Lat.9380) in the Bibliothèque Nationale. The so-called Gospel book of Charlemagne, in an elaborate treasure binding, received three pages, the description including a summary of opinions as to its origin as well as an extended discussion of recent literature on the binding; the book was the sole loan in the exhibition from its owner, the Marquis de Ganay.[21]

The catalogue listed eighty-four manuscripts down to the fifteenth century, many of the highest interest. No such exhibition had occurred previously. The ensuing section on printing began with two block-books, the first a French translation of the *Ars moriendi* believed to be unique.

This commanded almost two pages in the catalogue, as befitted what the writer of the catalogue entry considered to be the first book printed in French, dating from the first half of the fifteenth century and thus earlier than Gutenberg. The volume had been only recently discovered, and described by Brunet in his *Manuel du libraire*. It was easy to jump to wished-for conclusions, and in the absence of any kind of bibliographical evidence, readers and visitors to the exhibition were misled as to its date: modern opinion, guided by the evidence of watermarks in the paper, suggests that most surviving such block-books were printed in the 1460s or 1470s.[22] Brunet himself had written with some circumspection, where others were more precipitate:

Je ne chercherai pas à fixer ici la date de ce précieux monument, parce que mes conjectures à ce sujet ne me donnent rien de bien positif; mais les personnes qui pensent que les livres d'images en bois, tels que l'*Ars moriendi*, les *Biblia pauperum*, etc., ont précédé l'invention de l'imprimerie, ou tout au moins qu'ils ont été faits à la naissance de cette découverte, ne balanceront pas à regarder le présent *Art au morier* comme le plus ancien livre français imprimé qui soit connu jusqu'à présent.[23]

The copy of the Gutenberg Bible, on parchment, was lent by the bookseller Antoine Bachelin-Deflorenne, who had bought it with a group of manuscripts from a Spanish collector in the previous year.[24] Most of the early printed books were lent by two collectors in Lorraine, Charles Dugast-Matifeux (1812–94) and Benjamin Fillon (1819–81),[25] with Ambroise Firmin-Didot and Baron Seillière prominent among the others: Seillière lent the only Caxton in the exhibition, a copy of Cristine De Pisan *The fayttes of armes and of chyvalrye* (1489), described inaccurately as 'un des premiers livres imprimés en Angleterre' – that is, more than a decade after Caxton had set up his press in Westminster.[26] He also provided one of several books from Antoine Vérard, a copy of Boccaccio (1498) printed on parchment: it came from the Libri collection, and had been given to Seillière by the exiled duc d'Aumale 'en témoignage de gratitude et d'affection' in 1856.

The fifteenth century further included examples of the early printing types recently recovered from the River Saône in Lyon, by then belonging to Anatole Claudin,[27] and ended with a group of Books of Hours. The survey continued into the sixteenth century with a similar selection of grand and illuminated manuscripts, the initial section concluding with two writing books, by Pierre Hamon and Guillaume Legangneur. Then came a rare specimen of *dermotypotemnie*, based on cut parchment and the subject of a recent pamphlet by Ernest Aumale.[28] It had the merit of being simultaneously a work of art in its own right, and was thus suitable for the exhibition as a whole as an example of human ingenuity. Most of the rest of the selection of books and manuscripts, from the sixteenth to eighteenth centuries, focused on bindings. While there were occasional forays into notabilia, such as Nicolas Jarry's *Guirlande de Julie* (1641), for which an extended note of provenance was provided, most books were described with no more detail than might be expected from a competent bookseller's catalogue.

Though this exhibition souvenir offered extra space, and was sometimes used accordingly, it was not systematically exploited for everything. The advertising at the end, addressed wholly to bibliophiles, offered a clue. The catalogue was published by Léon Techener, publisher also of the *Bulletin du Bibliophile*.[29] Where other parts of the huge exhibition could readily claim to have some relevance and appeal to a mass audience, the selection of manuscripts and early books offered here was intended for people who were already committed to the subject, many of them Techener's existing customers. Yet, on the other hand, it was a project with high ambitions, in presenting to a world far beyond that of the bibliophile establishment so extensive an account of highlights in the history of manuscripts and printed books. Conventional though it was in the selection of exhibits, it also sought new audiences among the assorted crowds that attended. Situated among an immense international exhibition, and notwithstanding the bedrock of fashionable bibliophily, no clearer place could be have been chosen for demonstrating books' central importance in appreciating the world's inheritance.

Visitor numbers to exhibitions were unpredictable. Season tickets were available, but for the big London exhibitions most people paid a shilling. Experiments were made with pricing, even to the extent that the entrance fee in the last two weeks of the 1874 exhibition was just one penny. Not surprisingly, cheap weeks were popular, but the numbers did not produce much income.[30] Whereas the international exhibition of 1871 was a considerable (and unexpected) success, those over the following three years showed an alarming decline, from 1.14 million visitors to 467,000 in 1874. Worse still, gross receipts collapsed from £76,000 in 1871 to £16,000 in 1874. Understandably, the annual programme was abandoned.[31] Faced with losses in those of 1872, 1873 and 1874, the Prince of Wales told Henry Cole that 'Exhibitions are over & Museums take their place.'[32] Even Cole, who had encouraged and fought for them, had to accept this unavoidable conclusion.

Cole's caution against a continuing, ever more ambitious and ever more expensive, series of international exhibitions was necessarily level-headed; but it did not stem public enthusiasm. More followed in Australia, Paris, Philadelphia, Amsterdam, Antwerp and elsewhere, sometimes several a year, some privately financed and some by governments. But none offered so much about early books as did Paris in 1878.

Old or Modern?

Books were different from paintings and other works of art. Old Master paintings were distinguished as a separate genre. Though the year 1700 was sometimes chosen, and though it was unclear where the exact chronological boundary lay, yet there was a clear division between a taste for Old Masters and a taste for modern painters. The five volumes of Ruskin's *Modern Painters* (1843–60), offered originally as an encomium of Turner, before Ruskin turned then to other artists, served as a partial reminder of distinctions, while for many people the difference was simply between those who were alive and those who were dead.

The fine art dealers Zanetti and Agnew were established at Manchester in 1817. Zanetti retired in 1828 and Thomas Agnew focused with great success on contemporary paintings, to meet the demands of a monied clientele in Lancashire and the north-west. The firm opened a London office only in 1860, and when a year later Thomas retired, the *Art Journal* commented that 'the principal support of British art proceeds from wealthy Lancashire'.[33] Others could only agree. It was some of these same wealthy Lancastrians who helped in 1857 to guarantee the cost of mounting what became the largest and most influential of all exhibitions of a mixture of Old Masters and modern works. In Liverpool, the collection of older works of art assembled by the banker William Roscoe passed after his bankruptcy in 1820 to the possession of the Liverpool Royal Institution. There was thus a clear break between ancient and modern when from 1871 the city began to purchase works by contemporary artists, and in 1877 the Walker Art Gallery was opened thanks to the generosity of Alderman Andrew Barclay Walker. With knowledgeable buying, and notwithstanding some arguments and disappointments, by 1895, when Philip Henry Rathbone, one of its most influential and active advocates, died, the gallery housed one of the finest public collections of paintings by living artists in the country.[34] During that period, the gallery concentrated entirely on modern works, thus emphasising the distinction between ancient and modern. The accidents of history that created so clear a boundary in Liverpool between ancient and modern were not generally replicated. In reality, each generation overlapped or merged with the next. At Manchester in 1887, attention focused on paintings executed in the reign of the Queen. In 1888, the Grosvenor Gallery in London took a different approach in presenting a century of English art, thus reaching back to Gainsborough and Reynolds, and into the nineteenth century with Lawrence, Constable, Mulready, Bonington and Turner.[35] Boundaries could in practice be difficult to define.

For books, and specifically for printing, distinctions between old and contemporary were of a different kind. If there was a canon of taste for early books, albeit one that was subject to change, there was none for contemporary ones. There was admiration for innovation in colour printing, dominated by colour lithography, but few individual books or printers commanded the kind of adulation accorded to some contemporary painters. Insofar as there was any single group, it was of major colour-plate books: hand-coloured aquatints in Audubon's *Birds of America* (1827–38), Thomas Shotter Boys's pioneering book in chromolithography *Picturesque architecture* (1839), hand-coloured lithographs in the works of John Gould and in John Hooker's *Rhododendrons of Sikkim-Himalaya* (1849–51), and a host of others. These were very expensive, but others were not. Where prices ranged from a few pounds to several hundred, as they could also for contemporary paintings, there was plenty of room for collectors of all kinds.

The distinction was more often a different one. It was concerned with technological advance, and for many people this was associated with a clear political and social message: printing, made ever cheaper, was an essential component of modern political well-being. Hence, modern improvements, an expanding periodical and newspaper trade, and cheaper books had a moral dimension to them. The Caxton exhibition of 1877, always intended as an opportunity to present the early history of printing to a general public, was hardly less significant for the exhibits of modern printing techniques and equipment that formed the very substantial second part of the show.[36]

Big exhibitions, whether international or more focused like that celebrating Caxton in 1877, were complicated to organise, often expensive to house, and always liable to personal friction. While their overall success became increasingly difficult to measure as each competed with its predecessors, different parts attracted different interests, and different kinds of people. The sheer size of them made comprehensive absorption impossible for visitors.

While the Caxton exhibition, to which we return later,[37] could be accounted a special case in its clear focus on linking a specific anniversary to the modern trade, museums and libraries became the dominant places in which to present exhibitions of books in a longer term. The Prince of Wales's prescient comment to Henry Cole could hardly have been more accurate.

The British Museum introduced temporary exhibitions that could be focused on historical themes. It was not feasible to re-arrange the massive objects in the Assyrian collections, or many of the Greek and Roman antiquities: understandably, these departments stood by their permanent displays. Printed books and manuscripts were different, easy to move and endlessly applicable to different approaches and subjects. Apart from the permanent exhibitions introduced in both departments in 1851 there also developed a programme of temporary displays, often marking anniversaries: of Luther in 1883, Wycliffe in 1884, music in 1885, the Stuarts in 1889 (marking the bicentenary of the abdication of James II), and many others subsequently.[38] In France, anniversary exhibitions were held for Corneille in 1884 and for Racine in 1899.

It remains today that casual visitors to many historic libraries must place themselves in the hands of custodians, who work at their own paces. To those accustomed to more freedom, this could prove tiresome. The Vatican had long made its manuscripts available (though not all were catalogued), but the instinct for self-protection was powerful, and when combined with reluctant staff the result could be distinctly unwelcoming, even obstructive. The author of Murray's guide to Rome in 1881 thought it appropriate to add a comment for those who were not studying in the library. Visitors were

> hurried through it by a servant, more intent on receiving his fee than anything else. The selected collections of the most valuable MSS. formerly exhibited to the public are seldom shown except by special permission; the sight of the Medals and Coins is still more difficult. As to the Library of printed books and the *Stanze Borgia*, so interesting for their paintings by the great artists of the 16th century, they are closed. The library authorities at the Vatican would do well to imitate the liberality shown and facilities granted in other countries to the foreign visitor, *e.g.* at the British Museum, in the Imperial Libraries in Paris and Vienna, and in those of Florence, Venice, Milan, Turin, &c.[39]

It was as if access was resented. When it was granted, it came at a cost. The principle of allowing visitors to wander at will in the British Museum was different.

At Paris, preparing for the international exhibition of 1878, the Bibliothèque Nationale introduced a permanent exhibition of manuscripts and printed books for the first time,[40] taking a wide view of the history of printing and including some of the earliest printing in Mexico. The guidebook published in 1881 began with thirty-odd block-books before showing fragments from the earliest Mainz printing, two copies (one on parchment) of the Gutenberg Bible, a long series of subsequent printing at Mainz and Strasbourg, and later French books from the earliest presses down to a unique copy on parchment of the Didot edition of Racine (1801). Almost three hundred decorated bindings dated from the sixteenth to eighteenth centuries. In all there were over 670 objects on display, comfortably more than the equivalent in the British Museum.[41]

The importance of setting ancient and modern side by side, so clearly a part of the Leipzig exhibition of 1840 and of British thinking in the 1877 Caxton exhibition, if not, yet, universally in practice, was recognised in the first exhibition of both kinds of books organised by the Cercle de la Librairie in 1880 in its prominent new building designed by Charles Garnier in the boulevard Saint-Germain. The Cercle had been founded in 1847 under the presidency of J.-B. Baillière. In 1880, an immense effort was made to gather the first books printed from over 130 towns and cities across France: the books were all lent privately, mostly from the remarkable collections assembled by Anatole Claudin, Techener and Ambroise Firmin-Didot.[42] The purpose was as much modern as historical, and the second part of the catalogue listed about ninety contemporary French printers and publishers, besides a handful from abroad. It also offered 110 full-page advertisements, many of them in full colour and elaborately decorative. Those responsible for this part – printers, paper-makers, ink suppliers and providers of decorative ornaments – were all named. Copies were bound in various materials and to various designs by different binders, who thereby advertised their own skills.

Similarly in Amsterdam a year later, the new association of Dutch booksellers organised an exhibition of the work of binders, paper-makers, printers, typefounders, publishers and others connected with the printing trades. Most of the exhibition focused on contemporary work; but in the contributions by Beijers of Utrecht and Nijhoff of The Hague various earlier work appeared, some as specimens of binding. Nijhoff also showed early books for the sake of their printing, beginning with examples from the earliest Dutch printers and further including later work from German, French and British presses. The typefounders and printers Enschedé exhibited early equipment, including a wooden press.[43]

In Amsterdam as in Paris, the organisers issued an elaborate catalogue featuring exuberant displays of printing. There was no equivalent in Britain to these French and Dutch organisations, and apart from the Caxton celebration there were no equivalent exhibitions that set old and new so clearly together.

Exhibiting Books Alone

The exhibitions of manuscripts and early printed books organised after 1851 in the British Museum, and the success of the first public libraries in accumulating collections after the legislation of 1850, suggested how older books could be shared more widely. While there were no appropriate trade organisations, nor societies specifically dedicated to the study of books and manuscripts, and connoisseurship was the preserve of very restricted groups of people, there were other ways in which the taste might be pursued. Audiences were still strictly limited. Since the eighteenth century, the Society of Antiquaries had always included the study of historic and illuminated manuscripts among its activities. In 1755 it published facsimiles from the twelfth-century Eadwine Psalter at Cambridge. In 1832 the society's *Monumenta* included a series of engraved facsimiles, including the tenth-century Benedictional of St Æthelwold. In the early 1860s it offered several exhibitions on different topics, including civic plate and seals. These were short-lived affairs, and the practice was soon suspended, the Society meanwhile offering two relating to books: of illuminated manuscripts in June 1861, followed by printed books a few months later. At each of them, appropriate lectures were delivered by William Tite, Vice-President of the Society.[44] The Queen was among the lenders to the manuscripts exhibition. Tite, whose collecting tastes were later described as 'omnifarious', was by no means infallible, not just in dating manuscripts (no one was) but also in slips such as recording that the Meermann Museum in The Hague was in Belgium, rather than the Netherlands. More importantly, if not very profoundly, he tackled the widespread and inaccurate use of the word 'Missal' to describe all manner of medieval liturgical books and showed their different purposes and contents.

He wore his preferences on his sleeve. When he came to deliver a lecture for the exhibition of printed books a little later, he was frank: 'The Exhibition which is placed before you to-night, is of a far less fascinating and attractive character, *externally*, but it is of the highest intrinsic value.'[45] Then he continued:

It really represents the Progress of Humanity in Religious-knowledge, Literature, Science, and the Arts of Life. On merely glancing at the Typographical treasures before you, every one must feel the powerful force of the words of Foxe the Martyrologist ... 'Hereby tonges are known, knowledge groweth, judgment increased, books are dispersed, the Scripture is read, Stories be opened, Times compared, Truth discussed, Falsehood detected and with finger pointed out, And all this through the benefit of printing.'

Tite appealed to sixteenth-century authority. Charles Knight, in his work on Caxton, had appealed a few years earlier to the contemporary political and social world. Both men, one a widely respected antiquary as well as a well-known architect, the other a successful publisher, justified the study of early books by appeals to present needs. In itself, bibliophily was not sufficient: it had to have some modern relevance.

For practical reasons, Tite restricted his remarks mostly to his own books, and did not comment on others loaned by colleagues. His paper therefore reflected his collection, but the whole exhibition offered just short of eighty books, beginning with a block-book *Apocalypse*, four Caxtons and a group of other early English printers. Tite paid especial attention to a series of French printed Books of Hours. There followed a handful of other early continental books, a group of Bibles beginning with Coverdale's of 1535, a section of Shakespeare including the First Folio and an uncut copy of *Richard II* (1634[46]), and a concluding miscellany finishing with a copy of *Paradise lost* made up with three title-pages dated 1667, 1668 and 1669. As usual, the exhibition was open to members of the Society of Antiquaries and their guests, not to the general public; it seems to have lasted only a few days.

It confirmed a taste among antiquaries for such occasions, and the Royal Archaeological Institute followed suit a decade later with a project led by a person of very different calibre. William John Loftie was one of many who gravitated from Ireland to England. Born in Northern Ireland in 1839, he took his BA at Trinity College Dublin and was ordained in the Church of England.[47] After some years of parish work, latterly in London, he spent a quarter of a century, from 1871 to 1895, as assistant chaplain at the Chapel Royal, Savoy. This was a post that provided ample time for writing to supplement his income. He was a man of wide interests, who wrote knowledgeably about ancient Egypt and the early history of London, as well as local histories, the standard cheap guidebook to the Tower of London, a best-selling book about Windsor, a popular book on manuscript illumination[48] and monographs on several artists. His brief textual and bibliographical study of the English Bible in the century after 1611 was published by B.M. Pickering in 1872, printed by the Chiswick Press in its best antiquarian style.[49] He had a particular interest in the restoration of churches and was an early member of the committee of the Society for the Protection of Ancient Buildings, founded in 1877. For his bibliographical tastes and priorities we have to turn to the loan exhibition for which he was at least partly responsible in the Royal Archaeological Institute at London in 1871, a decade after the Society of Antiquaries' similar occasion.[50]

The Institute had already held exhibitions periodically, including ivory sculptures in 1863, and drawings by the late Charles Winston of early stained glass in 1865.[51] Like the exhibitions at the Society of Antiquaries, they were not generally open to the public, but were intended for members and their guests. Space in the society's premises was limited, and occasional use was made of a larger room at the Arundel Society. Loftie was elected to the Institute in 1870, and the subject of his exhibition was books printed before 1600. It was accompanied by a general lecture on early printed books given on 5 May by John Winter Jones, Principal Librarian and Secretary of the British Museum.[52] There was no separate catalogue, and a list of the exhibits, compiled by Loftie, was published a few months later in the *Archaeological Journal* in 1872.[53] Quite apart from the Society of Antiquaries a decade previously, the whole was partly at least in emulation of the Burlington Fine Arts Club nearby in Savile Row, which had been founded in 1866, and held regular exhibitions of a wide range of works of art, most recently of Raphael and Michelangelo in 1870: a more general one of Old Masters was organised in 1871. One of illuminated manuscripts was to be arranged in 1874.

The Royal Archaeological Institute's exhibition of 1871 was not widely remarked, or publicised. A former short lease having ended, the Society had in 1868 moved to a different address in New Burlington Street, where the exhibition was held. It lasted for just the first two weeks in May, an extraordinarily short time in view of the considerable work involved in borrowing books from several lenders. These were headed by the Queen, whose loans from Windsor included the 1457 Psalter and a group of books printed by Caxton. Aided by successive royal librarians, Bernard Woodward and Richard Holmes, the Queen was repeatedly generous in her support of exhibitions during these years.

The exhibition drew also on the trade: from Quaritch and from Frederick Startridge Ellis, then in partnership with G.M. Green. The Dean and Chapter of Westminster lent several crucial books, including volumes once having belonged to the antiquary William Camden. By far the largest lender was John Fuller Russell.[54] C.W. Standidge,[55] James

Yates[56] and Sir William Tite[57] were further major private contributors. Apart from books from the Society of Antiquaries and from Westminster, it was an exhibition dependent overwhelmingly on private collections.

The catalogue compiled by Loftie contained 261 entries, beginning with three block-books and ending with an edition printed by John Day of the Psalms in metre, translated by Matthew Parker ('c.1560', but in fact probably 1567),[58] 'often called the first book privately printed in England'.[59] The first entry of all, for a south German manuscript of the 1450s illustrated with woodcuts, was lent by Quaritch. It neatly represented the transition from manuscript to print, though nothing was made of this critical connection.[60] All of the nine books entered under the heading of Gutenberg were lent by Russell, though the attributions to Gutenberg's press were mostly fanciful.[61] While Loftie's entries were often confused, and his dates, especially for early printing, were sometimes no more than guesses, there was no disguising the impressive scale of this exhibition. He noted some of the more important provenances; for example, of Henry VIII, Latimer, Cranmer and Erasmus. An effort was made to include more than usual of the early printers, with early Hebrew printing from Lisbon and pioneering work from Breslau of 1504. The first press at Rome was represented by an illuminated copy of Suetonius (1472), lent by Standidge. Several books were represented by multiple copies, including two each of the Nuremberg Chronicle (1493), Higden's *Polychronicon* (Wynkyn de Worde, 1495) and the Coverdale Bible (1535, one of them from Windsor), and no fewer than four of the *Hypnerotomachia Poliphili* (1499). Though Loftie took a lead, it is by no means clear who helped him in the selection, while for the booksellers involved it must have represented an attractive marketing opportunity.

In introducing the catalogue, Loftie alluded to the playing cards offered in the Culemann sale of 1870 and to the St Christopher woodcut at Manchester dated 1423.[62] After these distractions he gave a little more space to the current controversies over Laurens Coster and the stories associated with him concerning the earliest printing.[63] In 1861 Jean-Philibert Berjeau had supported the claims of Coster to have invented printing at Haarlem.[64] As we have seen, others agreed, including some of the standard authorities of the past few decades: Ottley, Bernard, Sotheby, Noel Humphreys and William Blades among them. J.H. Hessels's translation of Antonius Van der Linde's attack on the claims appeared only in 1871, too late for Loftie to give it proper notice, but he made clear that he agreed with John Winter Jones in regarding the Coster tradition as a fabrication.[65]

For whom was this exhibition intended? In many ways it was a muddle, the result of enthusiasm rather than order. There were many gaps, and there were many treasures. The Queen had been persuaded to lend, and she lent key books. The overwhelming presence of Fuller Russell among the other lenders suggests that he was a leading light, and he too provided some remarkable rarities. Perhaps he brought in Standidge, Yates and Tite. Nothing seems to be known of how the books were shown, whether under glass or (risking security as well as safety for the often fragile originals) simply on tables and shelves.

This exhibition organised by the Royal Archaeological Institute in 1871, consisting only of old books, was a continuation of an earlier and more established tradition, in the private, self-limiting and sometimes exotic world of bibliophily. The whole was a complete contrast to the much larger and in the end, despite many setbacks, much better organised exhibition held at South Kensington just six years later, to commemorate Caxton.[66] From the outset of planning, this later exhibition was very much a public occasion, when (it seems) for the first time the great mass of the general public was offered a reasonably coherent account of the history of printing, and why it was to be considered important to the modern world. The personal enthusiasms of collectors were subsumed into a more public environment of display and determined popular education. Caxton was the inspiration, but the latter part of the exhibition, with its displays of modern printing equipment as well as modern books, drove home the message linking past and present.

It was both a national celebration, of Caxton and the beginning of printing in England, and an international one, of the early spread of printing. It was also a celebration of the technological history of printing, and of modern achievements. Lenders were extraordinarily generous, and more than one copy of many books were included. Most of the books relating to the history of printing were lent by William Blades, who also contributed his extensive collection of engraved portraits. Although in some ways it emulated the big international exhibitions, in comprehensiveness and in the conjunction of modern achievements with older traditions, Blades and his colleagues in the executive committee chaired by the typefounder Sir Charles Reed organised a quite different occasion. This was nowhere more manifest than in the printed catalogue, edited by George Bullen of the British Museum. It was copiously annotated, and the first section, on Caxton and early printing in England and Scotland, opened with an essay by Blades. Drawing on his study of 1861–3, he added a summary of Caxton's several types and their use in each book: such a determinedly technical approach was not an obvious route to a popular audience. Caxton's own books were presented in the same way, according to types, thus providing a structure in which to place the many undated books. His status as a national hero had been established for many years; but it was a reputation based on trust, on secondary literature, not on the physical evidence of seeing copies of his work. The mass of the general public had few opportunities to see many of his books. Now not only was there an extraordinary wealth of visual, physical, evidence but it was also shown in a manner that drew on the very latest scholarship. The significance of the different typefaces was easily absorbable by professional printers such as Blades, but it was a pioneering lesson in bibliographical practice for probably most people who saw these books for the first time. In this, the educational ambitions of the exhibition were unusually high.

The section on the holy scriptures, beginning with the Spencer copy of the Gutenberg Bible and the Windsor copy of the 1457 Psalter, was even more annotated, with long notes contributed by Henry Stevens. The exceptional copy of the Coverdale Bible of 1535, lent by the Earl of Leicester, was accorded a substantial essay in small type spread over more than two pages. Bullen, rightly, could not agree with Stevens's belief as to who – Coverdale or, as Stevens believed, Jacob van Meteren – translated it; but in the context of the exhibition and its presentation as a whole this was a minor matter.[67] Time and again, whether in Blades's continuing research on Caxton or in his systematic accumulation of materials relating to the history of printing, here was a subject, with its accompanying support, presented as a serious bibliographical as well as public endeavour.

The Caxton exhibition was a success on several grounds. It was open to all, and attracted a considerable number of visitors, if not as many as the organisers hoped. It at last provided the celebration that had eluded those who had advocated a national memorial in 1847. It encouraged others to promote more publicly the achievements of four centuries of printing. While Blades wrote authoritatively about Caxton, and Bradshaw was putting his ideas into practice at Cambridge, the case for informed historical and bibliographical study of early printed books was being presented to a general audience. Unlike popularising books, and while it could never be assumed that all visitors to South Kensington would be equally engaged, here was provision for an audience willing, and wishing, to be informed, varied alike in its education, wealth, age and inheritance. The catalogue itself found a ready market and was reprinted several times with various modifications.

While London and Paris were the sites of the major exhibitions, others took place elsewhere. An exhibition of ecclesiastical art at Derby, held in conjunction with the meeting of the Church Congress, offered loans again from J. Fuller Russell, this time including a Columbus letter (1494) and William de Machlinia's printing of the *Speculum Christiani* (c.1485). At Liverpool in 1882 the Liverpool Art Club organised one of bookbindings, six years after an exhibition of illuminated manuscripts.[68] Some exhibitions held abroad were also reported in London. In October 1883 the booksellers in Dresden, led by a local businessman Heinrich Klemm (1819–86), organised a particularly ambitious display of early printing, including the copy on parchment of the Gutenberg Bible recently exhibited at Paris and what was said to be a piece of Gutenberg's printing press.[69] Klemm had bought the Bible a little earlier from the Berlin antiquarian bookseller Albert Cohn. The exhibition was made possible partly thanks to Klemm's own collection, or bibliographical museum as he called it, and in 1884 the Bible was still in its early binding.[70] Another exhibition of archives and early printed books, this time specifically celebrating the links between the University and the book trade, was held at Orléans in May to June of 1885.[71] In 1887 Rouen celebrated the quatercentenary of printing in the city with an exhibition at the cathedral.[72]

An exceptional opportunity in London to display early books came in 1885, with the International Inventions Exhibition held at South Kensington. The site, used also for the exhibition of 1862, for the International Fisheries Exhibition in 1883 and the International Health Exhibition in 1884, sprawled over the area now occupied by the Royal College of Music, Imperial College and the Science Museum; that is, from south of the Royal Albert Hall to the rear of the Natural History Museum.[73]

Music and musical instruments had already figured in previous exhibitions overseas, as extensions to displays primarily of modern inventions. Visitors to that at Vienna in 1873 had been shown Mozart's violin and Haydn's cello. At Paris, making good hopes that proved too costly in 1867, in 1878 there had been early wind instruments and a psaltery, besides manuscripts by Rameau, Gluck and Mozart lent by Louis Viardot.[74] For 1885 in London, when a considerable attempt was made to introduce music from across the world, including a group of at least nineteen members of the King of Siam's court band,[75] a loan exhibition was gathered of early music and musical instruments. It was arranged by Alfred Maskell, art historian and photographer, working with his father and with Alfred Hipkins of Broadwood pianos who brought his detailed knowledge of early keyboard instruments to the selection for display. In the customary belief that numbers added to knowledge and enjoyment, over a hundred spinets and harpsichords alone were said to be included.[76]

The music exhibition was held not in the main site, but in the adjoining Albert Hall, where the manuscript and printed music were shown in the top gallery and the remainder in two large rooms at a lower level. Exhibits were borrowed from several other countries, the Belgian government proving especially generous in loaning gifts of Victor Mahillon from the museum of the Brussels conservatoire of music.

In many ways the exhibition was a challenge. Early music was little appreciated outside a small circle including people such as W.S. Rockstro, and his harpsichord pupil the young J.A. Fuller Maitland (1856–1936), who had graduated from Trinity College, Cambridge only in 1879. Maitland was to become a key figure in editing early music in the 1890s: his still standard edition of the Fitzwilliam virginal book, on which he worked with William Barclay Squire, appeared in 1894–9. From 1889 he was an influential chief music critic of *The Times*, and he became editor of the revised edition of Grove's *Dictionary of music and musicians* (1904–10). The 'historic concerts' for voice and instruments associated with the exhibition proved a success, including an assortment of music ranging from English madrigals to Palestrina's *Missa brevis* and a version of Allegri's *Miserere* – about which there was (not for the last time) some debate as to what was Allegri's and what was his editor's. It could hardly be said that a public exhibition in the upper reaches of the Albert Hall was easily found; but that could not excuse the poor attempts made to interpret unfamiliar themes. With more exhibits still arriving even after the opening, *The Times* was restrained in its comments: 'One cannot help feeling that the South Kensington authorities might have shown a little more alertness in dealing with the artistic and historical sides of their task.'[77] Not everything had even a rudimentary label, and a detailed catalogue of part of it was published only after it had closed. The preface to this made clear the displeasure felt by some. It was 'a great opportunity lost':

A wonderful treat to the few, it might and it ought to have been a source of instruction to the many. The relegation of the Collection to the Gallery of the Albert Hall was, perhaps, unavoidable, but pains should at least have been taken to make its importance known to the public.[78]

The catalogue was published not by the exhibition organisers, but subsequently in a small edition by Quaritch. The emphasis in it was on early western liturgical books, with a smaller section at the end devoted to treatises on music and some early scores. It included only a selection of what had been shown: manuscripts by Handel and Tallis, lent by the Queen, were omitted. So were manuscripts of Schubert, Mendelssohn and much else. Of those loans described, thirteen had been secured from the Queen. Private collectors included Earl Spencer, who lent fourteen, among them the 1457 Psalter, a number exceeded marginally by the musicologist James E. Matthew and the Munich bookseller Ludwig Rosenthal, each of whom lent fifteen. The Bodleian Library lent nine, and Cambridge libraries lent eleven: Henry Bradshaw and Francis Jenkinson personally lent one each. Some of the most remarkable arrivals were from Budapest, where both the national museum and the university library were generous. Other loans came from Cracow, from Mechelen (ten loans), Vienna and Utrecht. The earliest exhibits of all came from St Gallen, including a tenth-century Cantatorium containing the earliest neums with annotations and in a binding incorporating early ivory plaques, and two Troparies, one a tiny manuscript of the tenth and the other a finely illustrated one of the eleventh century.[79]

The detailed catalogue, the limited size of the edition (just 180 copies on two sizes of paper) no doubt reflecting anticipated interest, was by James Weale, who had supervised the selection of early printed books. At the same time Quaritch also published Weale's bibliography of missals for a similarly limited circulation. We have already considered his work in the South Kensington Museum on early bookbindings.[80] An independent income allowed him to travel in pursuit of copies of the books now being exhibited in London. He set great importance in comparing different copies of the same book. He had seen three copies of the 1457 Psalter, in Lord Spencer's collection, in Windsor and in the British Museum, and he now published the first detailed comparisons of the three. Of the then seven known copies of a Verona missal of 1480, all in Hungarian libraries, he had collated four.[81] Of the then three known copies of the Cracow missal printed by Peter Schoeffer at Mainz in 1484, he had collated two.[82]

Books were described in some depth, with notes of the number of leaves, of whether they were printed in red and black (an essential matter in a catalogue so much concerned with liturgical printing), of the numbers of columns, of the types used, of staves, of the make-up of the text, of collations for several exhibits, of illustrations, of ornamental initials and of dedications. Transcripts of title-pages and of colophons recorded lineation. Copy-specific details were added, including imperfections, manuscript additions, and notes of previous owners. Bindings were briefly described. Finally, where possible, came further bibliographical references. Indexes were added of manuscripts and printed books, and of lenders.

Self-confident, learned and innovative, Weale set new standards in an exhibition catalogue that was, despite the limited number of copies, intended – as it became – not least as a reference book in its own right.

Exhibitions came in all sizes, some extremely large. Some were professional, others were amateur. Some lasted just a few days, others for months. Of those for which there are catalogues, those catalogues were sometimes published after the event, and some of them became standard sources of reference. Despite their ostensibly public nature, not all were open to everyone, while others attracted audiences of many thousands. Some were commemorative, others were inspired independently. Some were provoked by international or local competition. Apart from those in the British Museum and the Bibliothèque Nationale, all of those mentioned in the last few pages had one thing in common: they showed early books, borrowed from a multitude of sources, in ways that offered a means of seeing what was usually hidden from view.

In ways that would have been inconceivable eighty or a hundred years previously, in a world defined by the bounds of privacy, books of all kinds had become established not only as a means of education and a record of achievement but also as a measure of public understanding and well-being, to be promoted and shown in the most prominent ways possible. The pride of ownership remained; but ownership was expressed and enhanced by the extension to the public sphere, sometimes limited and sometimes boundless, provided in exhibitions.

Another Generation

15 | Changes in Direction

To sum up so far. Among other matters we have noted changes in personnel, with the demise of a powerful generation of booksellers who had made their careers since the 1820s and 1830s, had lived through a major trade depression in the 1830s and who had also both benefited from, and been challenged by, the huge wealth of books emanating from the Heber sales of the 1830s in particular. We have noted debates on the founding, management and use of libraries, and the ways they were exploited for good or ill. We have noted some influential voices, reflecting on changes in taste and in the kinds of people who collect. We have noted a fresh confidence born of new bibliographical sources: now not just for the earliest printed books (Hain, etc.) but also for more modern ones, represented by the works of Lowndes in England, and Brunet and Joseph-Marie Quérard's *La France littéraire* (1827–39) in France. We have noted the emergence of a new discipline in the study of early printing. We have noted a new attention to the individuality of printed books, their copy-specific properties. We have noted some of the new visual resources available. We have noted how a world of exhibitions provided opportunities not only of education but also for considering the relationship of the past to the present specifically in the world of books. We have noted the willingness of private owners to share their treasures with the wider publics of exhibitions.

We can see also changes in direction as to what was collected. Here the contrasting bibliophile appeal of ancient and modern was reflected in the concerns of members of the Philobiblon Society, and only partly recorded in their discussions and a few surviving letters. The membership was tiny, but it represented a cross-section of interests among the wealthy, as a glance at the fifteen volumes of their published *Miscellanies* quickly reveals. These interests also emerge in what they chose to show their fellow-members. Some were of a well-established tradition: the Gutenberg Bible at the head of a mixture of the better-known incunabula, first editions of the Greek and Roman classics, and (fortified by Renouard's *Annales*) books from the Aldine press. Other members looked to a notably limited sampling of English literature: several owned Shakespeare's First Folio, but only one or two, such as the Earl of Ellesmere and Henry Huth, could offer much by way of the early quartos. Few members seem to have been interested in sharing with their fellows most other early English literature, save for two who showed their Chaucer manuscripts, the Ellesmere Chaucer now in the Huntington and another now in Yale.[1]

The first serious attempt to provide an adequately wide and informed reference source of British writers was published not in England but in Germany. Jeremias David Reuss was on the staff of Göttingen University Library, and thus had access to the best collection in Germany of British publications.[2] In 1791 there appeared his *Das gelehrte England oder Lexikon der jeztlebenden Schriftsteller in Grosbritannien, Irland und Nord-Amerika nebst einem Verzeichnis ihrer Schriften vom Jahr 1770 bis 1790, An Alphabetical register of all the authors actually living in Great-Britain, Ireland and in the united provinces of North-America, with a catalogue of their publications from the year 1770 to the year 1790.* It was published by Friedrich Nicolai (Berlin and Stettin, 1791) and, as George Forster reflected in his preface to the second volume, it was partly in answer to the lively interest evident among German readers for English authors. While Georg Christoph Hamburger (1726–73) and Johann Georg Meusel (1743–1820) had composed similar guides to contemporary German authors, there was no adequate equivalent for English. Notes were provided of current prices, and of German translations where appropriate: the two volumes were a guide to purchasing, as well as to reading, and Nicolai as a prominent English-language bookseller clearly had much to gain.[3] Reuss's work was very little known in England, even after a two-volume supplement appeared in 1804: it remains scarce in British libraries today, and it was not until 1816 that a much shorter equivalent was published in London. In that year there appeared *A biographical dictionary of the living authors of Great Britain and Ireland*, printed for Henry Colburn, proprietor of a fashionable circulating library near Hanover Square. The two unnamed editors were John Watkins and Frederic Shoberl (b.1775). They listed authors from all walks of life and in all subjects. They gave no details of publishers or prices. Neither Watkins nor Shoberl was a major member of the literary establishment. Shoberl, a Moravian from Yorkshire, was the translator of Gesner, Zimmermann, Sturm, Chateaubriand and others. John Watkins, from Devonshire, was a more general essayist, author also of *Scripture biography, or lives and characters of the principal personages recorded in the sacred writings* (1802).

Others, notably Robert Watt in his posthumously published and much more useful four-volume *Bibliotheca Britannica* (1824), were more general, dealing with the past as well as the present. None was concerned to list details of all successive editions, though Watt went to considerable trouble to supply the prices of those books in print. More restricted in his choice of books, but still reaching well beyond the obvious words of his title, William Thomas Lowndes provided in his *Bibliographer's manual of English literature* (1834) very erratic guidance to successive editions and to prices fetched at sales. None of these could serve collectors of recent books save in the most summary way.

Illustration

Much of the impetus for the collecting and study of modern authors came not from these compilations, but from illustrators. Few aspects of the appearance of books and journals in the mid-century were more prominent in change than illustration, in successive developments in wood-engraving, steel-engraving, lithography and photography. Charles Knight dated the modern age of cheap literature from 1827, the year of the launch of Constable's *Miscellany*, price 3s.6d. for each volume, and of the foundation of the Society for the Diffusion of Useful Knowledge. He believed that in that year there were about twenty wood-engravers in London who could be considered real artists.[4] Fifteen years later the trade had been transformed in a blossoming of illustrated journals. The heavily illustrated *Penny Magazine* (1832) and *Saturday Magazine* (1832), *Punch* (1841) and the *Illustrated London News* (1842) were followed in turn a little later by *Once a Week* (1859), the *Cornhill Magazine* (1860) and *Good Words* (1860). These and others, many of them cheaper, dependent on the skills of wood-engravers, made the illustrated journal familiar and artists such as Richard Doyle, John Tenniel, John Gilbert, John Leech and John Millais household names alike for books and journals. By the end of the 1860s there were eighty-five wood-engravers listed in the London directory alone, some being individuals working at home and others large firms employing many people.[5]

One artist of an earlier generation stood out. Of the work of Thomas Bewick (1753–1828), his volumes on British quadrupeds and birds, originally published in 1790–1804, were much reprinted in his lifetime; and after his death interest in most aspects of his work continued to grow. To some, the vignettes of rural early nineteenth-century Tyneside offered reminders of a world now lost, albeit one tinged with cruelty and poverty. To others, his ornithological illustrations were sources of inspiration. As stereotypes and electrotypes, his work was reproduced in new editions of works of natural history, notably Gilbert White's *Natural history of Selborne*. For wood-engravers, it presented a challenge, since the new machine presses did not permit the kind of detailed make-ready from which his work benefited. Different kinds of engraving were necessary.[6]

All this interest was fostered by the publication in 1862 of his autobiography, heavily edited by his daughter Jane.[7] Thomas Hugo's *Bewick collector* appeared in two volumes in 1866–8, followed by a volume of cuts by Thomas and John Bewick and others in 1870. His own collection was sold with an unusually detailed catalogue at Sotheby's in 1877, the British Museum having refused it.[8] The collection of Thomas Miller Whitehead had appeared at Christie's a few weeks earlier, and that of Edward Basil Jupp followed there in February 1878. In 1880 the Fine Art Society presented an exhibition of his work;[9] and a five-volume 'memorial edition' appeared in 1885–7, published by Quaritch, further evidence of how much enthusiasm had developed from Newcastle-upon-Tyne and become a national investment.[10] Reflecting a market greedy for his work, yet that only partly understood his imagination or the scale of his technical achievement, woodcuts were attributed to him that had nothing to do with him, or even with his workshop. His blocks were reproduced, and used in all manner of other books. Charles Hindley, pursuing his interests in cheap printing, bought blocks at the Hugo sale, and used them for his study of the ballad printer James Catnach.[11] Collectors were almost inevitably followed by forgers, most prominently a bookseller named Edwin Pearson.[12] His published concoctions alleged to be the work of Bewick fooled sufficient people for a sufficient length of time to be financially worthwhile: it is unclear how far his work fooled even the authoritative Hugo, who included several fakes in his survey. Pearson sold most of his collection of blocks and books at Sotheby's in 1868, and produced a several times reprinted edition of *Bewick's select fables* in 1871. It was a travesty of Bewick's work.

Bibliophiles enthused over Bewick's cuts of natural history and over his finely printed illustrations to the poems of William Somervile, Thomas Parnell and Oliver Goldsmith. Much more profuse, and much less understood, was a mass of jobbing work.[13] His legacy, and that of his workshop, was a taste that developed into a passion for wood-engravings, one that by its efflorescence in the 1860s became, in styles utterly unlike that of Bewick, what was in effect a new school of engraving that was a foundation for books and magazines.[14] Wood-engraved illustrations were on the one hand cheap, where their manufacture could be organised on industrial lines having little to do with the individuality that defined the work of

Bewick.[15] On the other, and just as with Bewick's work, the quality of their printing, the care that went into inking and to obtaining the right impression, the choice of ink and the quality of paper all contributed to effects that could vary from mediocre to acceptable to outstanding. By stereotyping, copies of blocks could be multiplied and further copies be printed at speed. The heavily illustrated publications of Charles Knight were printed from stereotypes in many thousands of copies and further stereotypes of the blocks were also sold overseas;[16] but then, for another kind of market, a selection of woodcuts from the *Penny Magazine* was published as a separate album, printed more carefully and to a higher standard.[17] Some of the more elaborate cuts in the *Illustrated London News* were similarly valued.[18] Large-scale mass-production made possible by machine printing was countered not by resorting to the older hand-presses (still very much part of most printing houses), but by slower and more careful presswork, where speed and cheapness were not driving principles.

While wood-engraving helped make illustration a part of everyday reading experience, the application of etching to steel or steel-faced plates transformed the use of intaglio methods in slightly more expensive books. Whereas earlier practitioners such as Gillray had worked on copper, the harder surface of steel, or steel-faced copper, enabled far greater numbers of impressions to be taken.[19] The enthusiasm among connoisseurs and collectors for Thomas Rowlandson (1756–1827) as a book illustrator depended on plates etched in copper, while the many copies of his pictures made by others reflected a contracting supply of the originals. Among the books Rowlandson had illustrated were William Combe's popular series of Dr Syntax's *Adventures* (1812–21), *The English dance of death* (1815–16) and *The dance of life* (1817). The taste for his work was encouraged and supported by the beginnings of a bibliography, in the work of the collector and journalist Joseph Grego.[20]

Following his father, George Cruikshank (1792–1878) began his career as a caricaturist before moving to book illustration: his etchings were a prominent feature of the first edition of *Oliver Twist*. Among artists sought by collectors, Cruikshank was to the fore, thanks partly to the range of his work, including his single-sheet caricatures as well as his extensive work in book illustration: he had all the merits of variety and visual attractiveness, and his work was readily available. The London auctioneers repeatedly advertised his work as being of especial interest, with sales sometimes within just a few weeks of each other. Blanchard Jerrold's *Life of George Cruikshank in two epochs* (1882) lent itself to extra-illustration, and many such copies survive today.

Thus not only were canons identified. By the 1880s they were also gradually documented in bibliographies and guides for collectors. It was illustrators such as Rowlandson, Cruikshank or 'Phiz' (Hablôt K. Browne), as much as the authors themselves, who attracted collectors of modern literature and hence gave a different status to living authors and to books quite recently published. As prices of some works increased during the 1880s, one feature emerged clearly in the mind of a contemporary commentator:

> The reason of this is not far to seek, for fashion, that stern arbiter whose decrees are slavishly enforced by the very slaves themselves, has declared in favour not so much of the author as of the artists who illustrated his works; and hence it is that in the minds of many, Dickens is quite a secondary personage when compared with 'Phiz'; and Surtees derives his reputation mainly from the labours of Leech.[21]

When Macmillan published Andrew Lang's popular book on *The library* in 1881, a chapter was added by Austin Dobson on nineteenth-century illustration. Or, as J.H. Slater, long experienced as an observer of collecting, put it a few years later:

> How the book-men, by whom is meant at the moment those who accumulate books from a mere love of possession, came to fix their attention on early editions at all is a matter for speculation. If a guess might be hazarded, it would be that they were first attracted by those containing plates by such well-known and popular artists as Rowlandson, Theodore Lane, H.K. Browne, Alken and many more, and that subsequently, when the fashion was firmly set, they extended their desires to other books not so illustrated, and that the same rules of procedure then began to operate with respect to them also.[22]

There was some truth in this, and the same sentiment was repeated by Michael Sadleir in considering nineteenth-century bibliography almost half a century later;[23] but it was not the whole truth about a motley development over several years.

Modern Authors

As for authors rather than illustrators, certainly the term 'first edition' had long been familiar, and was regularly used especially in booksellers' catalogues. It featured in the title to Dibdin's *Bibliotheca Spenceriana* (1814–15), and in 1836 Payne & Foss issued a catalogue using the term. Beriah Botfield was using a familiar term, when in 1861 he compiled his *Prefaces to the first editions of the Greek and Roman classics and of the sacred scriptures.* Classical scholars had for centuries been aware that the first edition, the *editio princeps*, was not necessarily the best: Aldus's texts, often composed from faulty manuscripts, the best that could be obtained, were sufficient witnesses of this. The same lessons had to be applied to modern authors, and Slater summed up the matter in the first page of his *Early editions* in 1894 – it is notable that he chose this title rather than the more obvious 'first editions':

> A late edition may, and in some cases should, be more complete than an earlier one; the errors in the first may be corrected in the second; additions, in the form of notes or otherwise, may have been made; yet notwithstanding these advantages it not unfrequently happens that the comparatively imperfect edition is the more sought after of the two.[24]

Hence collectors (and bibliographers) were to be interested not just in first editions but also in subsequent ones. Slater included selective lists of the publications of thirty-two modern authors. As he was writing in the 1890s, he included people such as Robert Bridges, Austin Dobson, Andrew Lang, Edmund Gosse and Robert Louis Stevenson. By the time these were at work, some bibliographical norms had been established. Some of Slater's earlier names were subjects in their day of pioneering bibliographical explorations, while for others, of the same period, he was himself a pioneer. His inclusion of the sporting journalist Pierce Egan (1772–1849) alongside major writers could only be justified by the celebrated and much-sought coloured illustrations. Of the mid-nineteenth-century authors, the novelists included W.H. Ainsworth, Dickens, George Eliot, Charles Lever, R.S. Surtees and Thackeray. Among the poets were Matthew Arnold, the Brownings, Shelley, Swinburne and Tennyson. Burns crept in from the eighteenth century. Two obvious omissions were Keats and William Hazlitt, but the list of absentees might be easily extended to include the Brontës, Disraeli, Mrs Gaskell and Trollope. Slater can never have intended to be comprehensive, and in the end his selection was not even representative.

In 1934 John Carter and Graham Pollard identified the key period for the emergence of interest in modern first editions as the decade 1885–1895.[25] Interest had taken root before then, but this was certainly the period in which it bloomed. The increasing enthusiasm for collecting modern authors, whether illustrated or not, brought with it a new phenomenon as people realised the need for accurate information respecting what they were seeking to collect. Thus the modern author bibliography developed, at first in publications that were sometimes little more than pamphlets, and then gradually becoming ever more comprehensive.

In linking interest in first editions of modern authors with illustration, Slater perhaps forgot that among the pioneering contemporary bibliographies were those for Tennyson (1866) and for Ruskin (1879). Both were by Richard Herne Shepherd (1840–95), a minor and industrious literary figure who made part of his living editing mostly lesser works by modern authors including Blake, Shelley, Lamb and Thackeray. In 1866 he issued *Tennysoniana*, published by Basil Montagu Pickering, who in the same year published an edition of William Blake's *Songs of innocence and experience* 'here for the first time printed in their integrity', in the words of the preface. As a foolscap octavo, *Tennysoniana* was designed to stand alongside Moxon's volumes of Tennyson's poems.[26] Its ambitions were comprehensive, experimental in the circumstances, and far beyond what might be expected of a listing:

Containing a full and Comprehensive Account of his Early and Suppressed Poems, and of the alterations made in successive editions; a Series of Parallel Passages between early and later Poems; a Comparison of In Memoriam and the Sonnets of Shakespeare; a List of Allusions to Holy Scripture and Classical Writers; an Account of the Tennyson Portraits; an Account of the Early Criticisms on Tennyson, by Arthur Henry Hallam [etc.] ... and a Bibliographical List of his Works from 1827 downwards.[27]

As Shepherd's study of Tennyson came from a major commercial publisher, Pickering, it may be assumed that he did not have an especially limited audience in mind. Tennyson's earliest works were mostly of well-known rarity. By the mid-1880s *Poems by two brothers* (1827) was fetching about 10 guineas, and the 1833 volume cost as much as £14.[28] The details Shepherd provided of the contents and literary echoes of some of the poems make clear that he was as much concerned for Tennyson's readers as for his collectors. The books by Tennyson that occupied Shepherd were not much illustrated until the appearance of a selection of his poems published by Moxon in 1857, elaborately illustrated by Millais, Maclise, Holman Hunt, Mulready and others, and an immediate popular success.

Shepherd was not the first person to attempt much of this. He had been forestalled by an article in the *Fortnightly Review*, by J. Leicester Warren.[29] This was far from accurate, as Shepherd was quick to point out, but it too represented a new approach to contemporary authors, where their successive editions were to be compared and changes noted, and their careers as writers documented. Neither list included details of the many American editions.

Tennyson himself did not welcome Shepherd's attention, and on being sent proofs of the 1866 volume wrote to Pickering:

While giving all due thanks for the kind intention of the Compiler, I must acknowledge that it will be entirely against my desire that they are published, if published, having myself an infinite dislike to the sort of book about anyone and finding moreover in this many mis-statements both as to facts and as to the Poems attributed to me.[30]

Shepherd was not to be so easily halted, but the assembling of the volume clearly gave him some trouble. Much in the end was omitted, not always for obvious reasons.[31] It met with a mixed reception, the *Pall Mall Gazette* opening cautiously in a generally favourable notice: 'A considerable harvest of pleasure may be reaped at a first reading from this modest little volume.'[32] This reviewer's attention focused particularly on Shepherd's detailed treatment of the relationship between *In memoriam* and Shakespeare's sonnets. Little heed was paid to the appendix, giving bibliographical details with summaries of Tennyson's habit of making changes in successive editions of some of his works. A revised and enlarged edition of *Tennysoniana* appeared in 1879, and reminded the world of a book that had not been universally welcomed. One reviewer commented:

For the production of such a work little is needed beyond some industry, a pertinacious love of trifling, and an utter absence of critical judgment, which gifts may serve, if superadded to an introduction to the poet's architect and a nodding acquaintance with his tailor. ... The author of all this Tennysonian flotsam and jetsam takes everything far too seriously, and lacks the knowledge to distinguish what is permanent and what is perishable. The time was not ripe for such a book, and Mr. Tennyson, to say nothing of the public, would have been more comfortable without it.[33]

Tennysoniana was the first of Shepherd's bibliographical compilations. The 1879 edition appeared at about the same time that Pickering took advantage of the publicity and sold his own collection of the poet, the auction marking a departure as one devoted to a contemporary author.[34] Shepherd followed with Ruskin in 1879, Dickens in 1880, Thackeray and Carlyle in 1881 and Swinburne in 1883. Some were followed by revised editions. A further revision of his work on Tennyson was published posthumously in 1896. His bibliography of Thackeray naturally made play with Thackeray's own illustrations, but in this respect it was incomplete and not always accurate. By the time he treated Dickens in 1880, the third volume of John Forster's *Life* had appeared (1874), with a list of his works including the names of illustrators. Shepherd was not a major book collector, but a person who fed from the fringes of the literary world.[35] His pioneering work on Tennyson was finally superseded by Thomas James Wise in his two-volume *Bibliography*, still incomplete and at times misleading, in 1908.

Wise recorded that between 1867 and 1876 Shepherd issued a series of pirated editions of early poetry by Tennyson, until his activities were stopped by the High Court.[36] In 1878 he printed Elizabeth Barrett Browning's early poems without permission. Later, Wise accused him, unjustly, of forgery. A succession of dismissive remarks about him in the *Athenaeum* prompted him to prosecute the magazine for libel. It was an unfortunate decision. In reports that were syndicated, thereby adding further to the damage, newspapers promptly repeated the words used: 'an insect', 'a vampire', 'a bookseller's hack', a competitor for the vacant office of hangman.[37] Shepherd's literary career was not without controversy; but his forwardness in promoting the bibliographical records of modern authors introduced a new aid in tracing authorial revisions and to understanding publishing and literary careers. It was more than simply an aid to book collecting. As by far the greatest part of *Tennysoniana* was taken up with literary questions, his work was perhaps most appreciated by those wishing to follow the evolution of Tennyson's writing. He invented a new genre in England, the bibliography of contemporary authors.

He did not invent a fresh taste for books in their original condition. Apart from the bindings on early books, discussed in previous chapters,[38] interests increasingly focused in the minds of some people on the appearance of books when they were first published. In England, this was most manifest in what became almost a fetish, not so much with cheap 'yellowback' paper-covered books designed for quick reading and a short life, as in the works – especially of Charles Dickens – issued in shilling monthly parts. The first editions of Dickens's books were printed in enormous numbers, and copies tended to be bound up into single volumes once the novel was complete.[39] Many fewer copies survive in their original wrappers, and fewer still with both the wrappers and the accompanying advertisement leaves intact. Other novelists published in the same way included Ainsworth, Charles Lever, Thackeray and Trollope, but none commanded the adulation of Dickens:

> It is only within the last few years this eager quest for early copies and first editions of Dickens's works has developed to such an extraordinary degree. Everything written by this master when in its 'first state' fetches extravagant prices. All sorts of refinements or variations are carefully noted to enhance the price.[40]

Understandably, some people looked on all this as little more than a fad. It was certainly no temporary one, for it became a theme of twentieth-century bibliographical study. One difference was that his early bibliographer Charles Plumptre Johnson recommended that collectors arranging to have their sets of part-novels bound up into volumes should take care to preserve one cover – not all, and certainly not all the accompanying advertising matter that was so much part of the economics of publishing.[41] The purpose was to preserve the illustration on the cover, not to preserve full bibliographical evidence.

It was easy to mock, and Percy Fitzgerald was one of several who called interest in paper covers this 'foolish craze'. He then illustrated his point with an anecdote concerning Baron Ferdinand de Rothschild, whose collecting career was cut short by his death at the age of thirty-seven. He visited the bookshops in the Passage Choiseul:

Where, we are told he met a class of fanatics devoted to the collection of illustrated romances published some sixty or seventy years ago. . . . These people he pleasantly satirised by purchasing a cheap copy of Hugo's poems in a villainous yellow paper cover, which he would not have bound or disturbed, but placed in a morocco case specially made for it. To some it seemed that this was genuine enthusiasm, but it was in truth a pleasant jest. He used also gravely to point out to them that they were neglecting a really important branch in not collecting the paper *backs* of these illustrated tomes, with their dates and inscriptions.[42]

Such exploits might cause some passing amusement, but they had no effect on collectors' enthusiasm. In 1885 Johnson, aware of some of the shortcomings in Shepherd's work, issued a small summary volume of *Hints to collectors of original editions of the works of William Makepeace Thackeray*, followed a little later by *Hints to collectors of original editions of the works of Charles Dickens*. In the latter he offered details beyond a simple list of editions. Variations in plates for illustrations were just one aspect of a bibliographical maze that was the result of so many copies having been printed as fast as possible in order to meet public demand. Matters were further complicated by the subsequent demand among collectors, which was sometimes met with simple forgeries, such as erasing the words 'second edition', or unidentified facsimiles. The fact that such crude dishonesty was worthwhile reveals much about the frequent lack of sophistication among buyers.

Among his warnings, Johnson drew attention to *Great Expectations*, first published in three volumes in 1861:

The whole first edition of this book was absorbed by the libraries, and it is, consequently, one of the most difficult of all Dickens's books to get in clean, uncut state. Other editions were printed, bearing on the title-pages an announcement of second, third, or other edition. These editions have been transformed into first editions by some dishonest person, who has printed title-pages as above, and has, no doubt, done a profitable trade with unsuspecting purchasers. The title-pages should be carefully inspected to see if they correspond as to paper, type, etc., with the remainder of the book.[43]

He noted that copies of the first edition were priced between £7 and £10; a third edition could be had for 25s.

Johnson's brief notes served their purpose as a guide in buying, but despite assorted notes on bindings and wrappers they offered little on the physical characteristics of the books under discussion. In this respect, Harry Buxton Forman's *Shelley library: an essay in bibliography*, published by the Shelley Society in 1886, was a very considerable advance, and suggested where emphases might change. Forman (1842–1917) had edited Shelley's poetry in four volumes in 1876–7, and the prose works in 1880.[44] In 1886 he turned to discussing the separate works, those published both in Shelley's lifetime and posthumously. He included, albeit not very systematically, notes of formats, of sheet sizes, of the quality of the printing (both misprints and presswork), of stereotyping, of paper colour and quality, and of variant imprints. He did not offer either collations or paginations in a systematic way, and clearly had no notion of the kind of work pursued by Bradshaw and others in debating how to present collations. Shelley's *Address to the Irish people* (Dublin, 1812) was, for example, described as:

A 'stabbed' octavo pamphlet, consisting of title-page and 22 pages of text, including the postscript, which occupies the last leaf. It is printed on three half-sheets, the title-page being the final leaf of the last half-sheet, and doubled back over the first two half-sheets. The pages have no headlines, but are numbered centrally; and no printer's name appears.

After a transcript of the title-page, set in display typography mimicking the original, he continued:

The type is exceedingly small and poor, and the paper very bad. Though just double the length of the second Irish pamphlet it has only two more leaves. The typography is moderately correct, though the punctuation, probably Shelley's, is eccentric.[45]

Most of the considerable extra space that he devoted to the circumstances of composition and publication was based partly on newspapers and contemporary letters. Altogether, it was an approach superficially quite unlike the treatment of early printed books, but it had an underlying similarity in the attention paid to physical characteristics. While he was unable to bring to his descriptions either the concision of Bradshaw or the professional printer's skills of Blades, his work nonetheless marked a considerable change in its particulars and preoccupations alike. No recent English author had been subjected hitherto to such minute bibliographical attention. While neither Shepherd nor Forman could be said to be either comprehensive or especially consistent, their various approaches to details of publication and reception offered not only guidance and criteria but also some foundations for the bibliographical structures of a new discipline in the treatment of modern books.

Bradshaw died a little before Forman's work appeared, and in that same year Forman became acquainted through the Shelley Society with Thomas James Wise. The Society was established in March 1886 with an inaugural address by Stopford Brooke.[46] It was quickly dominated by Wise, who within a few years was using it for his own profit.[47] Forman, with whom he will be for ever associated for forgeries of modern authors, held a senior position in the Post Office, and his literary work brought him few connections with the different preoccupations of the bibliographical establishment that we have explored so far. Forgers and bibliographers share one thing in common. Both are much occupied with the material aspects of books. Bradshaw, Blades and Reed were all concerned with differences in type design, while Bradshaw also gave considerable attention to the details appropriate for the physical description of books especially with respect to collational descriptions. Forman's interest in type and printers, if not as knowledgeable as those working on early printed books, was repeatedly apparent in his descriptions of Shelley's works; and in his work with Wise in creating type facsimiles or false editions he developed these concerns further. Their increasing care given to appearance, and the new historicist awareness among a more general audience for quasi-facsimiles, whether for honest or clandestine purposes, was a part of the bibliographical revolution, just as the Shelley Society type facsimiles reflected the changing concerns among readers for historically informed reconstruction. In all this, hopes and wishes ran ahead of reality.

Forman's bibliographical work was made available to a wider public, price half a crown. Meanwhile fashion for other books took its toll. The price of first editions of well-known works of English literature climbed upwards. By the end of 1886 the Kilmarnock Burns fetched 80 guineas at auction; and a bookseller was asking 50 guineas for a first edition of *Tom Jones* and £75 for a first edition of *The Vicar of Wakefield*.[48] Condition was crucial: both the latter were said to be uncut.[49] Such prices were comparable with those asked for early editions of classical authors, once the darlings of collectors and the rare book trade alike. The difference was that there was still little bibliographical knowledge about modern English authors.

Autographs and Literary Papers

We considered Libri's robberies, forgeries and other underhand activities earlier. Here we turn to the treatment of modern manuscript material by other individuals and institutions. As long ago as 1829, John Cochran, a bookseller in the Strand, had issued a pioneering catalogue almost wholly composed of manuscripts dating between the twelfth and eighteenth centuries. It was remarkable also in being perhaps the first English bookseller's catalogue to contain illustrations: a frontispiece and four further ones. The exceptionally full descriptions were the work of John Holmes who was in 1830 appointed to the Manuscripts Department of the British Museum. Cochran followed this up with a second catalogue in 1837, but neither met with great success, and much was subsequently sold off at auction.[50] His enterprise did not immediately prompt others to emulate him with any frequency. That took time.

Although many people spoke of themselves primarily as book collectors, autograph collectors or manuscript collectors, in fact many of those who considered themselves as primarily one or the other pursued interests in several markets. For people such as Dawson Turner and Monckton Milnes the manuscript record and the printed record were of equal interest. So it was also with some of the scholarly world. Henry Bradshaw worked at both printed books and medieval manuscripts, Irish and Chaucerian manuscripts as well as incunabula; Léopold Delisle is best remembered now as a palaeographer, historian and curator of manuscripts, but he was also instrumental in the study of incunabula in French libraries.[51] Among booksellers, Quaritch and Techener became prominent in dealing in both printed and manuscript matter. In this retail trade, while print and manuscript were often mingled within single catalogues, in some circumstances they were given independent emphasis.

All these fields, whether print or manuscript, witnessed fundamental changes in their pursuit. Because of the overlap in their study, their sale and their private or public collecting, the use and management of print and manuscript comment on each other. When in 1844 William Upcott exhibited a selection from his enormous collection of autographs at the

Liverpool Mechanics' Institution, it was part of that Institution's vigorous programme of public lectures, and thus very clearly a contribution to more general knowledge and education.[52] Printed books, medieval manuscripts and autographs could all participate in such an aim.

Attitudes to Autograph Collecting

Quite apart from the problem of forgeries, to which we shall return later, not everyone approved of autograph collecting. It was a hobby as cheap or expensive as one wished, since all that was necessary to form a passable collection was to write to eminent people and request their signatures. In 1836 Gabriel Peignot, an indefatigable author on all manner of topics connected with books, manuscripts and libraries, was frank: that opinion was divided as to the seriousness or otherwise of the pursuit: 'Les uns n'ont vu dans ce goût qu'une manie innocente à la vérité, mais frivole, puérile, inutile, une curiosité à-peu-près ridicule, qui ne s'attache à la célébrité d'hommes plus ou moins marquans que par un fil imperceptible, par un point peu important.'[53] Others, he thought, collected because they took an interest in handwriting, following remarks of the physiognomist Johann Kaspar Lavater (1741–1801) that handwriting is a guide to character: he called Louis XIV, Rousseau, Fénélon and Napoleon as witnesses. In advocating their more general potential as historical evidence, he gave prominence not to French writers but to John Lingard, whose multi-volume history of England since Roman times (1819, published also in Paris by Baudry), owed so much to the public records kept then in the Tower of London.

As for ordinary collectors, Thomas Carlyle for one was curt when a young lady wrote asking for his autograph: 'That is a weak pursuit, which can lead you to nothing considerable.'[54] Or, as his wife wrote to him in 1841: 'Also a letter from New York postage 8d ½ requesting to be favoured with your Autograph! How sick I am getting of these Yankees.' The demand did not diminish. In 1878 George Eliot wrote of 'how many letters I receive, from America specially where the collection of autographs seems to be a trade.'[55] On 12 August 1879 she wrote at more length to Charles Lee Lewes:

I am sorry to trouble you with the enclosed letter from an unconsciously impertinent American, but I think it is rather important that he should be set right. Will you send him an official letter to the effect that Mrs. Lewes (George Eliot), whom he has mistakenly addressed as Miss Marian Evans, has no photograph of herself and systematically abstains from giving her autograph. I send you the envelope as a specimen of what an American will do in the way of adventurous letter-directing.[56]

Increasingly, there was a supporting literature. In 1836, two books on the subject appeared. Peignot worked in Dijon. The other was by a Parisian who described himself as a member of the Institut Historique and a correspondent of the Académie of Évreux. He had been responsible for organising several sales of autographs in the past few years, and this experience made him realise how much a manual was needed. Pierre-Jules Fontaine published his work by subscription and assembled just over sixty collectors, connoisseurs, dealers and librarians in Paris alone, all willing to support his work. He found further people in Mons, The Hague, Leiden and Lisbon. Both Peignot and Fontaine knew they were writing in an unfamiliar field. 'La science des autographes est une science nouvelle et dont jusqu'ici aucun auteur n'avait tracé et défini les règles', wrote Fontaine.[57] The subject, and the emergence of a market thirsty for growth, had developed rapidly. Fontaine began a detailed account of recent sales with the Courtois sale of 1820, which had included an important group from Voltaire. Between 1830 and 1850 the number of sales with substantial groups of autographs escalated. The first retail catalogue of autographs to be issued by an English bookseller seems to have been one by Thomas Thorpe, in 1833.[58] Whereas the trade in printed books, and the many distinctions to be made between what was common and what was rare, and what was important and what was of more fleeting significance had been developed over several hundred years, the trade in autographs was barely a generation old. Its price structure was being developed, modified and adjusted almost with each sale.

In Germany, a *Handbuch für Autographensammler* by Johann Günther and Otto-August Schulz, published at Leipzig in 1856, was designed to meet an audience that had not only grown much in twenty years since the publications of Peignot and Fontaine but also demanded much more information collated in a form that could be ready assimilated. It offered accounts of different ways of collecting, suggestions from France, England and Germany of how collections might be organised, and directions on how to store large collections in albums and boxes. An important part of some of these handbooks was the price guide. Günther and Schulz also offered a survey of major collectors and dealers. As so much of the collecting world of autographs depended not just on the commercial trade but also on the willingness of amateurs to exchange with each other, their notes rather surprisingly listed Queen Victoria, Baron James Rothschild and the auctioneers Puttick & Simpson all under the same heading, without distinction.

The term 'autographs' encompassed much more than the signatures which became a principal goal for so many amateurs' albums later in the century. Besides letters it also comprised historical documents and entire archives. Because handwriting and personal history were so closely linked, for some people it further included annotated copies of printed books, presentation copies and books bearing the signatures of people of interest. Books once belonging to Racine, some heavily annotated and others simply bearing his signature, figured in a collection sold at Paris in 1834 and were widely available in the trade subsequently.[59] The collection of Mathieu Guillaume Thérèse de Villenave (1762–1846), housed in about six hundred boxes and portfolios, included books annotated by Guillaume Postel, Henri Estienne, Baluze, the abbé Rive and others, as well as a group of signed presentation copies.[60] In such an approach lay the germs of a wider interest in the history of provenance.

Not unnaturally, justification for collecting lay with the history of the pursuit, and here opinions were less divided. All the guides provided histories of the activity, Günther and Schulz beginning with Suetonius. Looking at England, Peignot found eighteenth-century evidence in Horace Walpole's proud possession of the death warrant for Charles I; but he considered that more general interest emerged in France in the first years of the nineteenth century, and that by 1812–15 it had become 'une passion, une fureur, une rage'.[61] The chronological coincidence was hardly remarkable. After the destructions following 1789, the re-emergence of historical concerns was all the more powerful, as people sought to recover not so much the past, as the records of what had been lost. In the 1880s Étienne Charavay considered that the taste in France for such collections could be traced at least to the Desprez de Boissy sale of 1803, when three volumes of letters from Henri IV, Sully, Villeroy, Louis XIII, Mme de Médicis and others had been sold by Barrois *aîné*.[62]

The craze frequently was characterised by a quite particular seriousness of a kind that had no equivalent in Britain. The French Revolution and its aftermath had released papers to the public in disorganised abundance, in quantities hitherto unequalled, emanating from private, ecclesiastical, administrative, governmental and all manner of other sources. Much was destroyed, either simply burned or sometimes used to contain the gunpowder used to fire artillery: France's enemies faced armies partly equipped with the torn fragments of manuscripts seized by frenzied mobs or, more insidiously, in systematic culls.[63] Collectors and agents who acted promptly managed to seize archives. Others had to be content with smaller groups, or just with individual documents. The purposes of those who cornered these papers obviously varied from individual to individual, but one major incentive lay in the knowledge that, signed by a well-known person or not, they represented a historical record. In their collecting there was space alike for the accumulator of trivia, for the mere hunter of signatures, and for the conscientious preserver of a part of the national record.[64] Literary papers further offered their own fascination.[65]

Many collectors numbered their papers by the thousand. When the collection of Baron de Trémont was auctioned at Paris in 1852–3, the sale took twenty-eight days. The Paris bookseller and scholar Auguste-Nicolas Laverdet (1805–65) produced detailed catalogues for the sales, and was succeeded as the most formidable of the dealers by Étienne Charavay (1848–99), whose father had moved from Lyon and opened a bookshop at Paris in about 1843.[66] Trained as *archiviste-paléographe* at the École des Chartes, Étienne helped organise the sales of the Yemeniz library and the library of Jacques-Charles Brunet in 1868, and many more followed. Some of his catalogues were notable for their illustrations, with héliogravures in the *de luxe* issues. When in 1887 he had printed the special post-sale catalogue of the collection of Alfred Bovet (1841–1900), one of the greatest of all French autograph connoisseurs and whose collection was sold in 1884–5, he worked with Bovet to ensure that this record of a unique event was presented in the best possible manner. Five hundred numbered copies were printed, of which 320 were for sale. Some 240 were printed on *vergé teinté*, sixty on *vélin blanc*, and twenty on large *Japon*. The *de luxe* copies, printed on paper specially made by Morel-Bercioux, were illustrated with héliogravures. The printer, the facsimilist, the compositor and the pressman were all named:

M. Alfred Bovet, obéissant à sa délicate nature de bibliophile, a voulu que son catalogue fût un modèle d'art typographique. Il appartient à l'école de ceux qui considèrent un livre comme un oeuvre d'architecture dont tous les éléments doivent se combiner de manière à présenter à l'oeil l'apparence de la grandeur et de l'harmonie.[67]

Whereas only a few years previously descriptions had been very summary, and only occasionally accompanied by facsimiles, in Charavay's hands collections could be shown off using the most elaborate resources of the printing trades employed more often for the production of expensive books. Charavay also formed his own private collection of autographs and of printed ephemera.[68] He took over the business from his father in 1869, and in turn gave it up to his younger brother in 1894. Between 1866 and 1892 he was the principal editor of the *Amateur des Autographes*, a journal founded by his father and uncle, and in 1874 he himself founded the *Revue des Documents Historiques*, in which he set high standards of production.

Words such as 'historical' and 'antiquarian' were readily applied to autographs. In contrast, how contemporary could you be as a serious collector? Living politicians, writers, artists and musicians were all likely to appear on the market. Further, autograph collecting ranged across everything from the signature of someone franking an envelope, through letters to historical archives. That was its pleasure, and that was its confusion, where the word was applied alike to signatures and to longer pieces.

When the collection of John Dillon was auctioned by Sotheby's in June 1869, prices were considered to be high.[69] An album of minor poems by Byron, enhanced with illustrations and in a red morocco binding, went for £27. This kind of special presentation ('a charming and matchless volume' in the words of the auctioneers) went far beyond the presentation of manuscripts by Byron and Robert Burns that John Murray produced from his firm's archives, for members of the Philobiblon Society to share when they came to breakfast with him.[70]

The manuscript of an unfinished work by another best-seller, Lord Macaulay, evoked considerable interest among the Philobiblon members when the publisher Thomas Longman shared it with his fellows, but the curiosity on this occasion had more to do with Macaulay's immensely popular *History of England* than with any consideration of its appropriateness as a part of a bibliophile's private library.[71] At least one member (Henry Bright, of the firm that owned the ship *Great Eastern*) interested himself in the manuscripts of contemporary novels, by Trollope, Nathaniel Hawthorne, Harriet Martineau and others.[72]

Prices for modern manuscripts crept upwards. Those of Sir Walter Scott's novels had been sold in 1831, at prices from £12 for the incomplete manuscript of *Ivanhoe* to £50 for *Rob Roy*, amidst prices at the sale that Dibdin and others found deeply disappointing,[73] and the taste for such material did not become generally established until several years later. In 1847 *Rob Roy* fetched £82 at the sale of John Wilks, MP for Sudbury. In 1855 the British Museum bought *Kenilworth* for £41, a price that was soon seen to be very reasonable. When Sir William Tite's considerable library (consisting mostly of early printed books) was sold in 1874, the manuscripts of *Peveril of the peak* (up from £50 in 1857) and *Woodstock* fetched £150 and £170 respectively. In contrast, a major English poem could command more interest: an autograph manuscript of Gray's *Elegy* reached £130 when it was sold in 1854.[74]

The 1831 sale of Scott's manuscripts seems to have been the first occasion in England on which major manuscript works of a living author were exposed to auction. Growing interest in literary papers showed itself in the succession of sales of papers from Thomas Gray, auctioned by Evans and by Sotheby's in 1847 and 1854.[75] Significant groups of papers from Robert Burns were offered by Wheatley in 1831 and by Puttick & Simpson in 1861. The posthumous sale at Sotheby's in June 1853 of papers from Thomas Moore was remarkable for the many small lots, of just two or three letters selling for a few shillings and clearly aimed at the autograph collector. It remained that there was much caution in such matters, and when later in the century Thomas James Wise importuned his contemporaries for materials to add to his collection, the sales were private ones, not public.

Proprieties and Priorities

This was not the same as a concern for contemporary or near-contemporary correspondence. In 1859 the auction of many of Dawson Turner's manuscripts included long files of letters to him from Thomas Dibdin (d.1847), almost the only example of its kind, for Turner's family retained most of his other incoming letters, including many from Dibdin. Among other nineteenth-century files of correspondence, and well over a hundred volumes of miscellaneous autograph letters down to the early nineteenth century, the sale included hundreds addressed to or from the classical scholar E.H. Barker (d.1839), William Cobbett (d.1835), George Crabbe (d.1832), James Gillray (d.1815) and David Wilkie (d.1841). They also included full-length novels and other works by William Godwin, including *Caleb Williams*, and manuscripts of the annual *Keepsake* between 1828 and 1843 in the autographs of the contributors. In all this there was naturally some sensitivity about privacy. The preface to the Turner catalogue explained:

It may with propriety be here stated that the very extensive series of letters addressed to the late Mr. Turner, and which it is well known he carefully preserved and bound, is in no way added to this collection. Not only have all such letters been carefully kept from risk of dispersion, but all these letters as, from any cause, would be likely to give a moment's pain to living persons, or to come, in any sense, into the category of private letters addressed to the late possessor, have been withdrawn.

Considerable pains have been taken to fulfil the directions of the Executors, and not less the wishes of the surviving members of the family on this point.[76]

Others, on other occasions, chose to ignore such questions.

Very considerably wealthier than Turner, though also eclectic in his interests, Alfred Morrison (1821–97) was helped and guided for some years by the London dealer Alphonse Wyatt Thibaudeau.[77] He used part of his inherited wealth to form an enormous collection of autographs and historical documents in the twenty years between 1862 and 1882: the speed with which he was able to gather his collection had as much to do with availability as with his financial resources.[78] At the same time he was also collecting paintings and prints, Chinese porcelain, Persian carpets, Greek antiquities and more besides. He used his printed volumes as more than a catalogue; for example, they published for the first time the correspondence between Nelson and Lady Hamilton. The first volume of his autographs catalogue was treated to a long notice in the *Bibliothèque de l'École des Chartes*, where Delisle welcomed Morrison's commitment in his collecting and now, in his programme for publishing, the care with which the catalogue had been compiled. More seriously, and ever alert, he was concerned at the number of pieces now in Morrison's collection that had been removed from the Bibliothèque Nationale, the Archives Nationales and other Paris archives.[79]

In France, a taste for literary manuscripts, as distinct from historical documents or autograph letters, was similarly slow to develop. An exception was Charles de Spoelberch de Lovenjoul (1836–1907), who had left his native Belgium as a young man and settled in Paris. Independently wealthy, he combed Europe with zest in his search for French nineteenth-century writers and formed a collection notable for the work of George Sand, Théophile Gautier and, above all, Balzac.[80] When in 1882 a group of manuscripts of Balzac's novels was sold in a hurried sale among the effects of his widow, it was said that the national library was not represented.[81] *Eugénie Grandet* sold for 2,000 francs (about £80),[82] and *Illusions perdues* for 2,050 francs.[83]

Forgeries

As with bindings and with printed books, forgery remained an activity against which collectors had constantly to be warned, and by which they were constantly duped. To some extent forgery could be countered most readily by the publication of facsimiles which could be compared; but there was an obvious weakness in this, as forgers had access to these same facsimiles, so their existence was not a foolproof defence. In 1788–93 John Thane, a printseller and engraver in Soho, published a three-volume collection of *British autography*. Demand for this work proved strong, and by the 1830s it was considered a book difficult to find. In 1829 John Gough Nichols compiled a large-format collection of reproductions of royal and noble autographs.[84] The taste for such evidence of personal individuality was exemplified in the decision of the British Association for the Advancement of Science to arrange an album of lithographed signatures of members attending the conference at Cambridge in 1833.[85] The four folio volumes printed by Delarue in 1843, *Isographie des hommes célèbres, ou collection de fac-simile de lettres autographes et de signatures*, included British, German, Italian and other examples as well as French.[86] The same international interest was reflected in a small album published three years later in Stuttgart: some copies of the *Sammlung historisch berühmter Autographen oder Facsimile's von Handschriften von berühmter Personen* were published with an English title-page whose design shows every sign of having been printed in London.[87] In 1848 Dawson Turner had printed in his home town of Great Yarmouth a *Guide to the historian, the biographer, the antiquary, the man of literary curiosity, and the collector of autographs, towards the verification of manuscripts, by reference to engraved facsimiles of handwriting*. The *Autographic Mirror* appeared between 1864 and 1866, with hundreds of reproductions in lithographic facsimiles, though not all were genuine.[88]

Works of art had long been a profitable field. Now the problem was extended. At Paris, the otherwise rich Bruyères-Chalabre sale of 1833 included several forged letters.[89] It was but one of several occasions in the 1830s involving supposed letters of Tasso, Montaigne, Mary Stuart and others.[90] Milnes too collected, and like many others was taken in by forgeries, whose growing numbers in the market and seeping into private houses were sure signs of serious collecting.

'No-one has of late been more exposed to fraud than the amateur collector of original writings', wrote F.G. Netherclift in his handy manual published in 1862, quoting a recent case where 40 guineas had been paid for a spurious letter from Henry VIII. He laid the blame squarely on Paris.[91] The 'Bibliophile Jacob' (Paul Lacroix), ever alert to the world of manuscript and book collecting, was just one who railed against forgeries, using the pages of *L'Amateur d'Autographes* to address Étienne Charavay.[92] As Lescure pointed out in 1865, forgery of literary and historical artefacts was a problem on a new scale, for the development of the collecting of autographs itself encouraged the development of a minor industry. Here as elsewhere, the boundary between facsimile and forgery was not always clear. He named three practitioners in Paris: Betbeder ('artiste peintre', rue Saint-Antoine 221), Bellot, and the Polish Adam Pilinski (rue des Noyes 31) who had for some years been producing 'des réproductions étonnantes de gravures, d'imprimés, de manuscrits'.[93] The problem was endemic in some parts of the Paris trade, all too willing to collaborate with dishonest profiteers, or seeking to gain from families who, contrary to the Revolution, now wished to establish a long and distinguished ancestry.[94] In England, the most celebrated forger was a man known as Major Byron, who claimed to be a descendant of the poet but who was really George de Gibler.[95] At various times Richard Monckton Milnes bought alleged autographs of Keats, Shelley and Byron, all in good faith.[96]

Vrain-Denis Lucas (1818–82) worked on a much more ambitious scale. The letters said to have passed between Pascal and Isaac Newton were early dismissed as forgeries by Sir David Brewster, author of the standard life of Newton (1831 and later editions), and by the mathematician Augustus De Morgan. Ever more voracious, Lucas played especially on the gullibility of one man, Michel Chasles. As he became increasingly creative, and Chasles and others became increasingly trusting, Lucas managed to sell letters purporting to be from the correspondence of Caesar and Cleopatra, as well as from Mary Magdalene, Judas Iscariot and others. Chasles seems not to have been concerned that such people wrote in French, or that the documents were on paper.[97] In the end, though they were generally dismissed as forgeries, many thousands of letters were involved, besides dozens of books bearing the supposed ownership inscriptions of Copernicus, Galileo, Rabelais, Newton and others. Lucas became the most notorious, but at the time there were plenty of other examples infecting even major collections. His work became a key element in a novel by Alphonse Daudet, *L'Immortel* (1888), translated and slightly abridged into English as *One of the 'Forty'* and published by Swan Sonnenschein in the same year. Alphonse Maze-Sencier, better known as a connoisseur of ceramics, paid special attention to them in the chapter on autographs in his more general book of 1885 about collecting and collectors.[98] Quite separately, in the 1880s books with Molière's name written on title-pages were a particular problem among the offerings of the bouquinistes on the Seine.[99] Though much of this now seems incredible, even risible in its audacity, at the time these and others were a critical difficulty. Chasles wasted perhaps 140,000–150,000 francs, which he never recovered.

Forgeries did not necessarily lead taste. They followed and encouraged it, answering needs or dreams, in Lucas's case partly feeding religious belief and a developing interest in the history of science. Likewise, in the 1840s and 1850s Constantine Simonides manipulated biblical criticism, with forgeries including Greek authors and an early copy of St Matthew's Gospel. His claim to have written the Codex Sinaiticus proved to be his reputational downfall.[100] In the 1850s John Payne Collier manipulated a mania for Shakespeare.[101] Collecting, scholarship, connoisseurship, belief and forgery were bedfellows, in literature, religion and the fine arts alike. Fontaine described some of the more elementary ways of detecting forgery, and quoted several examples since the sixteenth century. He also drew attention to a small book by Jacques Raveneau published at Paris: *Traité des inscriptions en faux et des reconnaissances d'escritures*, a book of sufficient interest to be printed in 1665, 1666, 1673 and 1691, and that had been castigated as a potential aid to forgers.[102] Raveneau, a professional calligrapher and concerned here with recent examples, has been overshadowed by Jean Mabillon's much more ambitious and scholarly work on earlier materials, *De re diplomatica* (1681). Both tackled similar challenges. Forged handwriting had been a problem for many centuries, but by the early nineteenth century there were new tools with which to counter it, to set beside the kinds of textual and palaeographical analysis that had enabled Edmond Malone to dismiss W.H. Ireland's forgeries. Now seen as amateur imitations of early handwriting, including supposed signatures of Queen Elizabeth I, Ireland's work took some people in.[103] The will to believe was as strong as reluctance to disbelieve. It was only partly relevant that, so long as reliable means of comparison were not widely available, such essays had a reasonable chance of success. Engraved copies of originals did not possess the same verisimilitude as the photographs of all kinds of documents and signatures that became widely available to later generations.

We have already considered annotated books.[104] Autographs took up little space in the home, and it is little wonder that their collecting became an ever more popular pastime. In the amateur market attention and purpose shifted away from consideration of manuscripts as part of historical archives, whose value lay in integrity as collections, to a focus on signatures, on letters and on what were essentially no more than fragmentary specimens. A letter of some content cost more than (say) one of casual social intercourse, but the focus on single documents became dominant. In a century that saw such an explosion in the numbers of letters written, they were readily available, and not necessarily in the hands of specialist dealers. In this, there was little difference from generation to generation.

The frontispiece of a leading popular book on the subject in 1894 displayed an advertisement from George Mackey, in Birmingham, 'Bric-à-brac dealer, &c.' He also offered coins, 'Japanese fine art work', enamels, armour, weapons, oriental and English china and pottery: 'In fact, examples of everything interesting to Collectors and Connoisseurs'.[105] Henry T. Scott, the author of the book, was a man of parts, qualified as a doctor and rector of the small village of Swettenham in Cheshire. Much of his book was taken up with facsimiles of signatures and a 'comprehensive price-list' of British, continental and American examples.

In offering a practical manual on the collecting and arrangement of autographs, Scott paid especial attention to the problem of forgeries. These short documents did not take long to manufacture and, as other people had long since discovered, there were plenty of collectors either unable or unwilling to determine whether or not their purchases were genuine. Scott was writing in the immediate aftermath of the unmasking of Alexander Howland Smith (known as 'Antique Smith') in Edinburgh, who had been responsible for unknown numbers of forgeries attributed to Burns, Scott, Edmund Burke and others: the market was tainted for years to come. While Smith's work fooled few people with any knowledge, there was also a further danger, with the application of photography: photographs of letters from Dickens, whose genuine examples commanded a premium, seem to have proved especially popular, and for those unacquainted with the surface characteristics of photographs they were easily passed off.

Scott's publisher Upcott Gill was also the publisher of another related book, *Character indicated by handwriting*. It was the work of Rosa Baughan, a leading writer on spiritualism who had launched her literary career in 1863 with an edition of Shakespeare's plays 'abridged and revised for the use of girls'. She later wrote a popular *Handbook of palmistry*, while her study of handwriting was sufficiently valued to be issued in a second edition just after the First World War. Her remarks on national styles of handwriting will have won her few friends on the continent:

The graceful '*insouciance*' of the French nation, its dislike of fixed work, and its inability to 'buckle to' to steady labour are shown in the rounded curves, the long and sloping upstrokes and downstrokes of the most ordinary type of French writing; the vanity and boastfulness of the nation are shown in the liberal amount of flourish in all the capital letters, and in the exaggerated ornamentation of the signatures of almost all French writers, whilst the delicacy of the lines of the letters, the fineness of the upstrokes and downstrokes, are all typical of the grace and refinement for which the nation is celebrated all over the world. The German hardness, practicality, and argumentativeness are all visible to the graphologist in the strange angular twists and upright lines in the cramped ordinary German handwriting.[106]

If such preoccupations were some distance from the historically inspired motivations of those collectors who had determined the purposes of the mid-century, they indubitably also took their inspiration from Lavater. His work had encouraged what in the hands of some people had become a craze having nothing to do with history. Instead, it fed the late nineteenth-century absorption with physiognomy, bone structure and such matters as the extent to which skull measurements reflected intellect. In the mind of Scott (and he was by no means the first thus to consider it) autograph collecting became also a means of financial gain to the owner.

Collecting in such a world offered little more than a trade, whether of books in the hands of writers such as Loftie,[107] or of letters in the hands of people such as Scott, or in those of people searching for evidence of characteristics. The objects themselves were of variable interest, but for all too many people mainly insofar as they had the potential to realise a profit.

The Challenge of Lesser Materials

Ephemera were always subject to different ideas and definitions. They ranged from single-sheet scraps to pamphlets, where the distinction between ephemera and more substantial work might depend more on content than on format or extent. Many children's books and much street literature encompassed in the term 'chap-books' were ephemeral in the sense that they often enjoyed a very short life. Like thousands of cheap publications costing just a few pence and printed in considerable quantities, these tend now to be rare. For years they attracted little interest in the national libraries, and hence they are under-represented in retrospective bibliographies. When in 1882 John Ashton produced his book about eighteenth-century examples, he claimed them as 'an epoch in the literary history of our nation', but complained of the difficulties in finding them in the British Museum and of the catalogue's inaccurate tendency to date them more by guesswork than research.[108]

In this world of differing definitions, the John Johnson collection of printed ephemera and the interests of the Ephemera Society today do not necessarily tally with all that might in the past have been considered as ephemeral.[109] While parts of the collections of Samuel Pepys and of John Bagford in the seventeenth and early eighteenth centuries can be readily recognised as constituting ephemera in the sense of being what cannot easily be organised, neither man counted most kinds of pamphlets in these parts of their interests.[110]

While casual disorganised accumulations were legion, some people were more systematic.[111] Dawson Turner, ever-organised and with the help of his family, gathered together much of his printed ephemera into several series of separate albums.[112] His filing system was not consistent however, and in the chronological series of his incoming correspondence, mostly now in Cambridge, some years include much more printed matter than do others. In Ghent, the ephemera assembled by the long-serving university librarian Ferdinand Vander Haeghen (1830–1913) ran to over a million items, focused mostly on the city: he sorted it according to his own classification scheme, and at the end of his life explained his purpose, one shared by many people elsewhere:

Ne détruisez jamais un document, imprimé ou écrit, quel qu'insignifiant qu'il soit. Après 7 ans, il vous intéressera. Après une nouvelle période de 7 ans, vous le jugerez tout à fait utile à conserver. 20 ans plus tard, il rendra service, il aura acquis de la valeur. En moins d'un siècle il deviendra précieux.[113]

In acknowledgement of growing interest, pioneers such as Charles Hindley (d.1893) and John Grand-Carteret (1850–1927) began to offer histories and surveys. Hindley's primary audience was a bibliophile one, and he made constant reference to Bewick. Anticipating a small market, his study of cheap printing by the Catnach Press published in 1869 was limited to 250 copies – 175 on fine and 75 on extra thick paper. Demand was immediate however, and in 1878 he issued a second study, *The life and times of James Catnach (late of Seven Dials), ballad monger*, in an edition of 500. The two books were separated by a more general survey *Curiosities of street literature* published by Reeves and Turner. Like Hindley, later and on a more ambitious scale, Grand-Carteret's interest was stimulated by images, and in a succession of books he published studies especially of caricatures. But his concerns were wider, encompassing such apparent trivia as visiting cards and exemplified in a study of French almanacs (Paris 1896). His wider-ranging *Vieux papiers, vieilles images; cartons d'un collectionneur* appeared in the same year. By then he had published an assortment of articles, had investigated obscure corners of the Département des Estampes in the Bibliothèque Nationale, and had found friends of shared interests including Georges Moreau of the publishers

Larousse.[114] Like all who wrote on the subject, Hindley and Grand-Carteret found it difficult to control an amorphous mass of paper, so much of which resisted organisation or bibliographical classification.

In practice, most pamphlet literature tended to be regarded as yet another category. Much of it was easier to control bibliographically. The importance of pamphlets had been recognised since at least the Reformation, and by the nineteenth century there were substantial collections formed of Lutheran materials. In the seventeenth century, millions of copies of newspapers, pamphlets and printed images spread news and propaganda about the Thirty Years War. By the end of that century, accumulations of pamphlets gathered in private libraries were familiar features at the end of auction sales if they were not put to other uses as waste paper. Such was their ubiquity that within little more than a generation there were whole sales and catalogues devoted to the genre. While political or religious upheavals tended to bring surges in production, they could be concerned with any subject. Some of the thousands gathered by the Earls of Oxford in the eighteenth century were edited as the *Harleian miscellany* by Samuel Johnson and William Oldys, in a project organised by the bookseller Thomas Osborne. It was first published in eight volumes in 1744–6, and then reorganised in a second edition of twelve volumes in 1808–11. In the early nineteenth century *The Pamphleteer* ran to twenty-nine volumes between 1813 and 1828, reprinting tracts first published separately. Quite apart from the political and other social subjects that dominated these series, pamphlets of all kinds were also a long-standing means of publishing popular literature. Cheapness was a virtue.

Some collections survived more or less intact. That assembled by Johan Duncan (c.1690–1753) numbered perhaps 20,000 items concerned with the Netherlands, mostly political, topographical and legal.[115] Following his death it was absorbed into the collections of the Royal Library in The Hague, and thus into the new national library in 1798. There it was joined by other collections, and was finally catalogued by W.P.C. Knuttel (1854–1921) in the late nineteenth and early twentieth centuries.[116] The Royal Library was by no means alone. Other large collections of pamphlets were sold by the Amsterdam dealer Frederik Muller, and another was assembled by Isaac Meulman, numbering about 10,000 and covering the years 1500–1713. The University of Ghent bought both the Meulman collection and the private collection of Muller himself.[117] At Groningen, between 1751 and 1842, the University bought several collections including materials dating from the sixteenth century onwards, finally assembled into a single catalogue published in 1944.[118]

Circulation figures could be enormous. It has been estimated that in the Netherlands between 800,000 and 2.4 million copies of these short publications were printed in 1672 alone.[119] As was only natural, some of the largest collections in different countries focused on major upheavals, whether the Lutheran Reformation in Germany, Mazarinades and the French Revolution in France, or the seventeenth-century Civil War in England. Some were collected at the time, others came later, often absorbing earlier collections. The French Revolution and its aftermath attracted the attention of collectors even as events unfolded, though the collections assembled at the time were mostly later broken up: that of the playwright and theatre director Guilbert de Pixérécourt was an exception, acquired by the Bibliothèque du Sénat.[120] Anne Louis François de Paule Lefevre d'Ormesson, briefly on the staff of the national library before he was guillotined in April 1794, worked likewise to assemble the printed detritus of the Revolution. A generation later, the historian and political writer Amédée Hennequin pursued a similar path. A wish to go to the sources similarly inspired the Comte de La Bédoyère (d.1862) to assemble his collection of pamphlets, newspapers and other lesser printed matter, thought to amount to about 100,000 pieces, alongside his more conventional bibliophile library: it was bought by the Bibliothèque Impériale in 1863.[121] J.W. Croker's collections relating to the French Revolution, acquired by the British Museum, have already been mentioned.

In Britain, to which so much migrated, Croker and Lord Crawford, whose collection is in Edinburgh, were just two who benefited. The Benedictine Father John Turner (1765–1844) was in Paris during the Revolution, and his collection is now in Reading University Library. Of earlier examples, the Borghese collection gathered between the mid-sixteenth century and c.1700 was a survival from the past, representative of a range of topics in the history of Rome. It remained together, to be absorbed into the library of Lord Crawford in the nineteenth century.

Broadside ballads had been of interest to collectors since at least the seventeenth century: both John Selden (1584–1654) and Samuel Pepys (1633–1703) possessed collections. Further enthusiasts followed in the eighteenth century, notably the Earl of Oxford who acquired John Bagford's collection. But little was published, and less still was in any sense organised. The various collections remained in private hands and were referred to according to their original or later owners. Selections only were printed. Richard Heber's collection was catalogued for William Christie-Miller in 1872. Halliwell-Phillipps catalogued the Chetham's Library collection in 1851 and sold his own collection of black-letter ballads to

William Euing in 1857.[122] The Roxburghe ballads, originally assembled by John Bagford, passed into the possession of the Duke of Roxburghe and then to Benjamin Henry Bright at whose sale in 1845 they were bought by the British Museum. Selections from them were published in 1873-4 (by Charles Hindley) and in 1876-8 (by Joseph Ebsworth). Henry Huth's appeared in 1867. Often each owner in turn added to the original core. The Crawford collection of seventeenth- and eighteenth-century English ballads had at its base the collection of the Earl of Jersey, sold at the Osterley Park sale in 1885.[123] Sir Frederic Madden also collected street songs and ballads, both early ones and, especially, current ones that – unlike most of his predecessors – he systematically sought out from contemporary printers across Britain. He amassed over 16,000 sheets, containing almost twice as many songs. Following Madden's death they were bought by Henry Bradshaw in 1873, probably in the hope (unrealised at the time) that they would appeal to the Cambridge authorities. The University Library bought them after Bradshaw's own death in 1886.[124] By then, early popular literature was finding a ready audience among scholarly editors, while Ashton, Charles Hindley and others provided for wider markets. In the words of a caption to an illustration in a work by Andrew Tuer, 'Antique ballads, sung to cries of old, Now cheaply bought at thrice their weight in gold.'[125] In all this, as with pamphlets, while attention was given to a few separate collections, there was little by way of overviews, and none of a bibliographical kind; but the drift from private to public ownership echoed the trade in early books more generally.

The trade was ever alert, both in leading and in following. For booksellers there was an obvious challenge: how to dispose of quantities of cheap stock that held no established interest as categories. This had been reflected in eighteenth-century catalogues, and political events now provided a valuable focus. Booksellers in Paris found in those of 1789, 1848 and 1870-1 the hooks on which to hang large offerings from the wealth of printed remains. In England, the bookseller John Russell Smith assembled what his catalogue of 1876 called *A unique and interesting collection of upwards of twenty-six thousand ancient and modern tracts and pamphlets*. All were on sale, separately. He followed it in 1878 with another, based partly on the collections of William Upcott, including 10,000 tracts and pamphlets illustrating the topography of the British Isles: the same catalogue added about 50,000 related prints and drawings. Librarians found it useful to distinguish pamphlets from larger publications. In 1840 the second volume of the catalogue of the London Institution was devoted to pamphlets. In 1857 the Royal Institution's catalogue included, more helpfully, a chronological list. In 1888–93 the South Kensington catalogue of John Forster's library separated pamphlets from books, probably simply because the larger number of pamphlets took longer to describe.

This increased awareness of the importance of an ephemeral, but in fact often crucial, literature had its effect on library policy. One of the subsequent recommendations made to the new public libraries created in the wake of the Public Libraries Act of 1850 was that an effort should be made to collect local literature of all kinds. A few libraries extended the principle to apply to other reference material of an apparently slight nature. In Manchester the public library bought a collection of pamphlets on political and commercial topics gathered by a German merchant resident in London in the mid-eighteenth century. Further collections were added over the next few years, some collected also in the eighteenth century and others more recently assembled. By 1855 the library contained 2,576 volumes of tracts. They were still not fully catalogued in the late twentieth century.[126]

In the early 1820s several tens of thousands of pamphlets in the British Museum remained uncatalogued for want of funds.[127] But how were the Museum's accumulations to be treated? In 1838 the Trustees decided that the pamphlets in the library of George III, hitherto kept in boxes, should be bound individually. Panizzi calculated that this could be done for 1s.8d. each, though he reckoned on there being only half the actual number of 20,000. To have bound them up into volumes would have been cheaper, but the distinction of individual works was more important. By the same line of reasoning, it was acceptable to break up the volumes in the Garrick collection of plays and those assembled by Sir William Musgrave (d.1800).[128]

In face of mounting costs, the system of binding pamphlets individually was formally ended by 1875, and henceforth they were gathered into volumes.[129] Other libraries moved in the opposite direction. In The Hague, the collection catalogued by Knuttel was eventually to be removed from its many bound volumes, and reorganised by Knuttel numbers. Though practical in some ways, it was not a solution that appealed to everyone.

As a genre, pamphlets and single sheets were elusive: elusive to find in that libraries gave them less attention than books, elusive in that booksellers realised they often had little commercial value in themselves, and elusive in that there was very limited bibliographical control. Yet they represented keys to public debate. In terms of titles, they comfortably outnumbered books. Their importance was sometimes obvious. Their management was much less so, hardly a surprise in that a pamphlet might be anything from four to twenty-four or thirty-two pages before it could be accounted a thin book. The range was further multiplied by the increasingly frequent practice of issuing offprints and reprints of articles from journals. All added to the weight of literature that included matter of great interest among much that was ephemeral in the sense of being of passing consequence and much that was more quickly recognised for its relevance to major past events. In evaluating this mass of printed matter other than books there was no clear path forward to which libraries could commit themselves. Initiatives tended to come not from library policies but from individuals.[130]

16 | Advice and Guidance

Guidance: Manuals

The events in continental Europe between 1789 and 1815 formed a natural watershed not only in politics but also in marking a boundary between the past and a modern world. The eighteenth century, ancien régime Europe, was separated from the present and the recent past by a break seemingly much more distinct and effective than any break between dates in the passing of one century to another. In paintings, it could offer a ready separation between old and modern. In furniture, dealers exploited the differences between the two centuries.[1]

To tastes for antiquarianism was added a wealth of discoveries of classical survivals from the Mediterranean, including the vases bought for the British Museum from Sir William Hamilton in 1772, the marbles of Charles Townley bought in 1805, and the Parthenon marbles brought to London by Lord Elgin and sold to the British government in 1816. These and other smaller groups not only enriched the visible archaeological wealth but through cheap as well as expensive publications they also helped in no small way to make these aspects of the past a matter of popular knowledge. The *Synopsis of contents of the British Museum*, first published in 1808, had run to sixty-three editions by the time of the last in 1856.

Changes in taste in architecture, in furniture, in furnishings and in paintings between the 1780s and the mid-nineteenth century have been much remarked and documented.[2] In searches for the past, architects and antiquaries such as Scott and Pugin in Britain, Arcisse de Caumont and Viollet-le-Duc in France, Pierre Cuijpers in the Netherlands and the lawyer and writer August Reichensperger in Germany recreated their own versions. It was always a compromise, a selective past coloured by and responding to modern taste and modern engineering and industrial skills. From the eighteenth-century Greek revival to the aggressive advocates of the Gothic revival in the nineteenth century, much of this evolved from a new familiarity with some chosen aspects.

This mid-ground, drawing on past and present, offered much in common with ways of looking at books. In quite separate developments, dependent mostly on technological innovations, newly published books, a part of furnishing as well as everyday needs, became very obviously different. The introduction of cloth bindings in the 1820s, the development of case binding, and the gradual exploitation of decoration in gilt, colour or blind embossing, transformed the appearance of books and, with them, the shelves on which they stood. For those who still wished their books to be bound in leather, an array of finishes to skins was available, and the widespread use of hollow backs gave a new feel to volumes in the hand.[3] In all this, the skills and ingenuity of binders could be as applicable to old as to new books. Within books, remodelling of type designs affected some, as so-called modern faces were introduced by founders and printers such as Didot in France, Bodoni in Italy, Unger and Walbaum in Germany, and Thorne and Fry in England. The invention of paper-making machines in France and England heralded changes in production. Shortages of raw materials for paper-making during the Napoleonic wars contributed to searches for new materials for its manufacture, and hence to a new texture and feel to finished products. Wood-engraving became the regular medium for economical illustration in books, pamphlets, handbills and magazines alike. Lithography, first just in black and then from the 1830s in chromolithography, transformed book illustration further. There had never been such a wealth from which to choose.

What of the choice of books from past generations? How should one choose? How far was a classical education a help? What about those who had no such education? For the top of the bibliophilic range there was considerable guidance on the kinds of books that had become established as those most desirable in a major private library where sufficient money was available. They remained led by first editions of the Greek and Latin classics, many (but by no means all) fifteenth-century books, the earliest Bibles, and books from major presses such as the Aldine dynasty, the Elzevirs,[4] or Baskerville. For British collectors, in modern literature Elizabethan and Jacobean black-letter books had their own clienteles, and Shakespeare was dominant. The later seventeenth century and subsequently offered less of interest. We shall return to this in a moment, and see how some of this changed for mid-Victorians.

Discursive, garrulous, opinionated and not always accurate, the first edition of Dibdin's *Library companion* (1824) offered in over 900 pages no more than a selection, albeit an extensive one, of books suited to a bibliophile or to a scholarly private library. In aiming to cater for many fields, one admitted gap was British topography, a subject well covered by the three volumes of William Upcott's *Bibliographical account of the principal works relating to English topography* (1818). Dibdin also declined to include heraldry or the fine arts, both having been surveyed by others. Nor did he attempt mathematical or scientific subjects. He expected collectors to focus, and he had in mind not least those who were setting out on their bibliophilic journeys: 'a guide to youth and a comfort to old age'. His interest on this occasion was predominantly in more recent or even modern books, early editions of classical texts having already been treated by him in his *Introduction to the knowledge of Greek and Roman classics* (3rd ed. 1808): he now provided few details of the earliest editions, or of their prices. Instead, he concentrated on the standard editions of a much greater range of authors, while also constantly reverting to enthusiastic remarks about copies on large paper, in special bindings, or on parchment. As a result of consulting with numerous collectors and with the major London booksellers, he was able to present a more than representative portrait of a particular kind of collecting. But it was a personal view, based on his own enthusiasms, not a systematic analysis. Few of his readers, for example, could aspire to possess an early edition of *Hamlet*, even were one to come onto the market. In any case, they would have found Dibdin of little use:

HAMLET. *Printed by J.R. for N. Landure, 1604.* Not in the Malone Collection, according to Mr. Boswell: nor, as far as I can observe, is it in the collections of Steevens and Bindley. Mr. Heber also still sighs for its possession. Its rarity may be therefore easily imagined. May I ask, if the Curators of the Bodleian Library (in which venerable and magnificent collection of books the MALONE TREASURES repose – but not *slumber*) will let slip any opportunity of securing it? They will not. They cannot. The second edition was published in 1605: also very rare: the third, no date, for *Smethwicke*: of which a copy brought 4*l.* 4*s.* at the sale of Bindley's library.[5]

Apart from the asides about the Bodleian Library and quasi-destitute collectors, almost every fact in this summary was wrong. The first edition was of 1603, not of 1604. Of the two surviving copies, that now in the Huntington Library had been found in a Suffolk house just the year before, and was sold to the London booksellers Payne and Foss in December 1824, too late for Dibdin to mention.[6] He corrected himself in the second edition. Thirty-odd years later a second copy, lacking its title-page, turned up in Dublin, and was eventually sold to the British Museum.[7] Dibdin could hardly be chastised for not knowing about 1603, but the mistakes for other editions were less responsible. In the imprint of the edition of 1604, the initials N.L. stood for the London bookseller Nicholas Ling, not the non-existent Landure. That dated 1605 was simply a variant title-page, with a different date from that of 1604. The first with the Smethwicke imprint was dated 1611, so Dibdin was presumably referring to Smethwicke's undated edition, of c.1625. A second and much enlarged edition of the *Companion* was published in 1825.

In 1850 the shelf of available reference books addressed to collectors in Britain was short. Dibdin apart (and none of his works had been reprinted since 1842), there was Edward Churton's very brief *The book collector's handbook*, published in 1845 and describing itself as 'a modern library companion'. It was little more than a bookseller's advertisement.[8] Most obviously there was Lowndes's *Bibliographer's manual of English literature*, dating from 1834 and recognised by the more knowledgeable as inadequate. In 1857–64 this was republished in a revised form by Henry G. Bohn, whose eponymous libraries of cheap editions were some of the most fruitful of all sources for thousands of owners from 1846 onwards seeking to add economically but effectively to the standard authors on their shelves.[9]

No further *vade-mecum* after Churton was to appear until 1862, when John Hill Burton issued a small handbook *The book-hunter*. Published first in Edinburgh, rapidly reprinted, published in New York the following year and still being printed as (by then) a classic of its kind in 1908, Burton's book transformed matters for those uncertain of themselves and anxious for a guide to a changing, strange and enticing world. Burton (1809–81) was a lawyer by profession, historian of Scotland and a frequent contributor to the Edinburgh-published magazines. His book originated with a series of articles published in *Blackwood's Magazine* in 1861. The physical appearance of his volume was important. Though of a small format, it was quarter-bound in cheap leather, with dark red cloth sides, reminiscent of Roxburghe Club books. He wrote in a rambling fashion, and his book contains little hard bibliographical fact. It tended to anecdote, hearsay and gossip. But it marked a change of mood:

One of the reasons why Dibdin's expatiations among rare and valuable volumes are, after all, so devoid of interest, is, that he occupied himself in a great measure in catering for men with measureless purses. Hence there is throughout too exact an estimate of everything by what it is worth in sterling cash, with a contempt for small things, which has an unpleasant odour of plush and shoulder-knot about it. . . .

Everything is too comfortable, luxurious, and easy – russia, morocco, embossing, marbling, gilding – all crowding on one another, till one feels suffocated with riches. There is a feeling, at the same time, of the utter useless pomp of the whole thing.[10]

In place of this, Burton offered much sound advice about the best methods of seeking out books, from street stalls to auctions. He drew repeatedly and approvingly from James Wynne's account of private libraries in New York, published in 1860. In his view, recent developments there such as the opening of the Astor Library in 1854 were reminders of how comparatively little had been done in Britain. 'What a lesson do these matters impress on us of the importance of preserving old books!'[11] Also in his view, government had done little in Britain, though he permitted himself a disquisition on provision for deposit of books in libraries under the successive copyright acts, and the consequent preservation of many books.[12] He chose to forget much that had been achieved over the course of three centuries and more, and blamed taxation, more specifically house and window duties, for the dispersal of collections. Writing in Edinburgh, he forgot – or chose to ignore – the recent extraordinary achievements of Panizzi at the British Museum, which could not have been accomplished without government support. For the various clubs and societies whose members paid for the printing of rare – and preferably nationally important – texts, he had little but praise. Roxburghe, Maitland, Spalding, Wodrow, Surtees, Chetham, Camden, Shakespeare, Percy, Hakluyt, Ray, Wernerian, Cavendish, Sydenham, Parker: such clubs were not just critical to the preservation and circulation of past knowledge but also a link between modern books and a taste for the past. Bibliophily encompassed both.[13]

Against a background of the new public libraries, Burton's proved to be the first of a popular kind of publication, as book collecting, and with it a desire to learn about old books, moved from the circles of the rich to those with more limited incomes. There was already a popular literature on Caxton and a few other early printers, some of it more imaginative than accurate. For the beginner, there was much less on how to go about collecting even of more modern books. Burton's work became widely read and was much reprinted, but ultimately it was of little practical value. Those who sought miscellaneous bibliographical information might also seek enlightenment in the *Gentleman's Magazine* or *Notes and Queries* but there remained little that was systematic, and less still that was practical, and few people possessed long runs of either journal.

The first person in Britain to attempt a manual of practical information, as distinct from the gossip of Burton or the bibliographical listings of Lowndes, was John Power.[14] Born in 1820, he trained as a civil engineer before turning to other interests. For some years he was on the editorial staff of the *Panama Star and Herald* until illness forced him to return to England.[15] Settled in London, he turned to the bibliography of Irish printing and Irish literature, and in his short-lived journal the *Irish Literary Inquirer* (1865) began to focus on a much larger project, a *Bibliotheca Hibernica*.[16] This was intended to provide for the first time a bibliography of Irish books down to the nineteenth century. Advertisements promised two volumes, of about 400 pages each. For a neglected field (and admittedly a minority interest: he had great difficulty in gathering subscriptions for the 350 copies proposed) this had much to recommend it. He engaged the interests of the young Henry Bradshaw, who contributed several brief articles to the *Irish Literary Inquirer* and was adding to the considerable library of Irish printing gathered by his father. A series of anonymous articles offered a history of Irish printing. The magazine closed, and the *Bibliotheca* never appeared.

Then in 1870, Power produced *A handy-book about books, for book-lovers, book-buyers, and book-sellers*. It was published opposite the British Museum by John Wilson, whose principal business was as a second-hand bookseller: among his specialities he listed works on Ireland. With its colour-printed, paper-covered boards, bearing designs copied from bindings exhibited in the British Museum, it looked very different from Burton's quarter roan (Figure 11). Its contents were also fundamentally different. The main sections provided a bibliography of the subject, a chronology of printing, a collection of useful recipes for cleaning books, a typographical gazetteer, a directory of booksellers in Britain and continental Europe and a dictionary of terms commonly met. The final section, headed simply 'Miscellaneous', offered articles on bookbinding, sizes and formats, publishing, paper sizes and qualities (including French and German equivalents for English terms), proof-correcting and other topics. Much of this section was taken from other publications, for Power made no claim to be original, but merely 'useful and interesting'. His book was not reprinted, and it soon became scarce.

Power died at St Leonard's on Sea in 1872. He offered book collecting as a new kind of world, one not rarefied such as that of Dibdin, nor restricted to the ancient classics such as Harwood's popular *View of editions of the Greek and Roman classics*,[17] nor restricted to English literature. His book appeared a little before the young firm of Chatto and Windus republished Dibdin's *Bibliomania*, and the two could hardly have been more different. Where Dibdin rambled and gossiped, Power was precise and focused, giving practical and direct advice also on a range of associated questions.

We have already met W.J. Loftie, working on an exhibition at the Royal Archaeological Institute in 1871.[18] As a populariser he did not restrict himself to books. Some of his tastes can be traced in his friendships.

Figure 11 John Power, *A handy-book about books* (1870). Top cover, with a facsimile by F.C. Price of a binding in the British Museum.

He was one of the first to appreciate the art of Kate Greenaway, while his interest in old buildings led him naturally to William Morris. Both are to be seen in a little book presented as the first of a series published by Macmillan, *Art at home*. His gave his volume, of just 100 pages and published in 1876, a long and revealing title: *A plea for art in the house, with special reference to the economy of collecting works of art, and the importance of taste in education and morals*. His subjects included ceramics, paintings, prints, furniture, medieval manuscripts and printed books. He peppered his chapters with anecdotes, true or invented, concerning collectors and fortunate individuals who had bought something cheap, and later sold it at a considerable profit: interest of 20 per cent per annum was quoted several times. His purpose was not only to encourage understanding and taste for the past but also to demonstrate how, with luck and a little knowledge, money could be made: 'The object of my book is to show that a very small expenditure on worthy objects of art is both good and pleasant in itself, and also a prudent piece of economy.'[19] In his discussions of books he quoted hardly any exact detail, and turned to black-letter ('printed before our ordinary type was in common use', p. 2) and early illustrated books: 'Modern illustrated books may be very briefly dismissed' (p. 73). As for early books:

> There has been a kind of run on early woodcuts of late years, and we are at length, after centuries of neglect, beginning to recognize the beauty of the early French school – that of Paris, from which issued so many devotional books in the fifteenth century, and the early part of the sixteenth, as well as of the later school, – and that of Lyons, from which issued so many exquisitely illustrated Bibles, Testaments, Dances of Death, Emblems, and other books, all now become exceedingly valuable, though once, not many years ago, to be had very cheap. (p. 74)

Loftie was nothing if not mercenary in his outlook and assumptions, a far cry from the kind of bibliophily where the shackles of money were rarely mentioned.

It was a theme by no means unique to this kind of modest collecting, or indeed of higher price structures. In 1863 the sale of Elhanan Bicknell's collection of paintings by Turner and other modern artists fetched almost three times what he had paid, and some of the paintings fetched more again: an oil by Turner of the Giudecca, bought for 252 guineas, fetched 1,650 guineas. If anything, the watercolours proved even better investments. A watercolour of Chartres Cathedral by Prout, bought for 6 guineas, reached 120 guineas. It was not only a matter for wonder and admiration in the popular press. The Bicknell prices also brought a comparison with

Lorenzo the Magnificent. Wise investment brought social cachet.[20] No less importantly, Loftie stressed that much-lauded Victorian virtue, of prudence. After his long sentence on early woodcuts he returned to his principal theme:

> If we could tell what will be the next fashion we might commence collecting now, and make a fortune when the tide turns. The French are busy at present with books illustrated with copper-plate vignettes, and chiefly belonging to the period before the Revolution. But we have little art to show for that period in England, and must come down to the times of Stothard and Westall for something original and good of native growth.[21]

Trading brought wealth, though it could not promise it. Given that early illustrated books were not much available any more at prices feasible for the ordinary buyer, unless he or she was blessed with unexpected good fortune, the collector who looked for new fields would be using knowledge more literary than artistic, and hence beyond Loftie's scope on this occasion.

Not everyone shared such obviously pecuniary ambitions. John Hill Burton, writing for an audience more familiar with early books and their values, was no less explicit, in his warning:

> The mercenary spirit must not be admitted to a share in the enjoyments of the book-hunter. ... If [he] allow money-making – even for those he is to leave behind – to be combined with his pursuit, it loses its fresh relish, its exhilarating influence, and becomes the source of wretched cares and paltry anxieties. Where money is the object, let a man speculate or become a miser.[22]

Concern for monetary gain was a constant theme in works about book-hunting. For some people it was alien: the interest of a book was greater than its cash value. For others, it was a means of livelihood. J.H. Slater's brief manual of a little later, *Round and about the book-stalls* (1891), was explicit. It was designed to point to 'those classes of books which are now but little thought of, but which should rise in value in the near future, and also to those books of present value which, though of mean appearance, are likely to be met with on the stalls of the dealers'.[23]

From the choice of books Loftie moved on more specifically to the choice of bindings, in particular warning his readers against craftsmen who trimmed margins (and sometimes thereby text), or who discarded endpapers and other endmatter that the collector especially valued. For those wishing to have their books rebound he offered not only warnings but also suggested examples, and in particular drew from two decorated blind-stamped examples from the fourteenth and fifteenth centuries in his own collection. He claimed to have used them as models for modern books on his shelves: 'The result is very pleasing ... What good effect may be produced by having the sides both ornamented but with different patterns, designed to harmonize with each other but not to match exactly.'[24]

In the end, Loftie said little to help his readers in creating a home furnished with early books, or even with fine ones. He managed to write about collecting without giving much detailed advice as to how to choose, where to buy, or how to apportion expenditure beyond the most obvious distinction between modern trinkets (he mentioned scarves and cigars as examples) and objects offering more lasting enjoyment.

He was writing for a general and broadly middling audience, about art in the home represented by more than books or bindings. His interest in early printing was revealed in an article he contributed to *Cassell's Magazine* on 10 September 1870. It was focused most on early English Bibles and on early liturgy. He possessed two bindings embroidered with gold and silver thread, attributed as usual then, and on no grounds whatever, to nuns at Little Gidding. In general, he spent little on rebinding his books, and many of his more important books were imperfect. His imperfect *Chronecken der Sassen* (Mainz: Peter Schoeffer, 1492) was still in its oak boards covered in stamped leather. A portion of his library was auctioned in 1873,[25] from which (for example) a mid-fifteenth-century Dutch Book of Hours is now in the Walters Art Gallery.[26]

Not surprisingly, a new popular manual for collectors sought to complement Power, rather than overshadow him. John Herbert Slater was a member of the Middle Temple, one among several lawyers who turned to book collecting for recreation; others included Slater's contemporaries Arthur Munby (1828–1910), minor poet and benefactor of Trinity College, Cambridge,[27] Richard Copley Christie (1830–1901) of Manchester, university professor and benefactor,[28] Samuel Sandars (1837–94), benefactor of Cambridge University Library and the Fitzwilliam Museum, and W.A. Copinger (1847–1910), Professor of Law at Manchester, author of the standard *Law of copyright* (1870 etc.) and one of the founders of the Bibliographical Society.[29] Unlike Munby, Sandars or Copinger, Slater made a career out of writing for a new generation of middle-income collectors, or book-hunters as (following Burton) he persisted in calling them. These were people who haunted bookstalls and small-scale dealers, rather than those who depended mostly on the major antiquarian booksellers. His gossipy mixtures of anecdote and advice, published in popular books and in magazines, found a ready market. What had become a fresh, if more modest, bibliophile tradition was given shape by Slater in his short handbook entitled *The library manual: a guide to the formation of a library, and the valuation of rare and standard books* (1883). In 1886 he established *Book Prices Current*, a record of prices achieved at auction.[30] With this, a coherent account of prices and the auction market was at last met. For the first time an organised structure was offered of the trade, and because it covered a large number of auctions systematically it was not restricted to high spots, or the more celebrated sales. It provided just the kind of reassurance needed by those venturing into book collections, and it was a very considerable time-saver for booksellers. No doubt it also offered comfort to those contemplating sale, though as always past performance was no guarantee of future results.

Slater's *Library manual* came from a publisher quite different from Chatto. By 1892 it was in its third and much enlarged edition. The publisher, Upcott Gill, specialised in handbooks on everything from gardening and field sports to keeping parrots and fancy pigeons to mechanics and photography. Slater dispensed quickly in twenty-five pages of small print with some of the more obvious needs for book collectors: the history of printing, technical terms, the relative values of books and hints on forming a library in a rational way. Apart from a summary list of booksellers, literary societies and private presses, the rest of his book was taken up with lists of books and their values. He divided these into six sections, giving more than a third to what he called 'scientific subjects', not just the natural sciences but also occult philosophy and law. Under English literature he included Lavater on physiognomy and Sir Isaac Newton, but his survey was more remarkable because it included a few authors who were still alive, including Ruskin and Tennyson. In neither case did he give any detail about some of their real rarities, and in the case of Tennyson he provided the merest generalities. For all authors he gave prices, frequently ignoring the earliest editions in favour of later ones costing only a very few shillings. This was a guide for ordinary readers and collectors who wished to possess authors, not necessarily those who insisted on first editions. There were also occasional warnings. The price of Ruskin's *Stones of Venice* (1851–3) was quoted at the extraordinarily high price of 16 guineas, with a warning about this and the other books listed: 'The works of Ruskin are steadily rising in price, and the above quotations may, if anything, be considered low.' It was a sign of a further development: that collectors were becoming willing to battle over recent or living authors, whose works seemed more accessible than dead ones and who seemed (however misguidedly) to require less bibliographical knowledge. While Thomas Wise

(1859–1937), forming the Ashley Library and assiduously courting contemporary authors, has become the best known name in this new development,[31] there were plenty of other collectors encouraged to focus as much on the present as the past. Such a market, and such tastes, were full of pitfalls, and many purchasers were to be ensnared by price fluctuations over the coming decades.

Slater's book soon went into a second edition, but it was full of errors, and was justly criticised by Ernest Thomas, the Secretary of the Library Association: 'The most slovenly production we remember ever to have seen.'[32] It presented another world, far removed from the expenses of older rarities. Slater was also no historian. In giving dates when printing had been first established in towns he gave Mainz as about 1440, Strasbourg and Haarlem as 1440, Oxford as 1468 and Westminster as 1474.[33] All these dates had been challenged many years before. Yet he went on to write several further popular books on book collecting. They were reminders of circles very different in their standards of knowledge and curiosity from those exemplified in a new generation that was even then well advanced in transforming the study of old books, in the work of William Blades, Henry Bradshaw, Talbot Baines Reed, Bernard Quaritch or some of the other collectors, scholars and librarians with whom they dealt. To the world occupied by Slater, with his interest in cheaper books and his indifference to accurate up-to-date information about the simplest historical and bibliographical facts, this kind of bibliographical scholarship was seemingly of little interest.

Guidance: Special Periodicals

The contrasting interests that were key to the change of course in mid-century collecting were not only reflected in the prices of early or rare books but also seen in the foundation of an increasing array of periodicals. The French *Bulletin du Bibliophile*, founded in 1834, was the fullest and most successful, while Auguste Aubry's *Bulletin du Bouquiniste*, founded in 1857, offered fare for those less wealthy. When in 1864 the Brussels bookseller F.J. Olivier launched what proved to be a short-lived project, *Annales du Bibliophile Belge et Hollandais*, he sought to remedy a neglect of Low Countries printing in the existing journals. The *Bulletin du Bibliophile Belge*, founded in 1845, welcomed the new arrival, albeit cautiously.[34]

Britain was not so well served. Those that began to appear in London in the 1860s were different from the by then well-established bibliophile journals of Belgium and France, but they depended on authors knowledgeable of the French traditions. At their head stood Jean-Philibert Berjeau (1809–91). He began his career as a legal clerk, before becoming involved in left-wing politics. In 1849 he fled France and a prison sentence, and settled in London. No monarchist, he was at the opposite end of the political spectrum to the greatest of all French bibliophiles at the time, the exiled duc d'Aumale, and few of his bibliographical or bibliophile publications are now among Aumale's library at Chantilly.

After a while, Berjeau turned his attention to publishing a series of facsimiles of early books, notably *Biblia pauperum* (John Russell Smith, 1859), *Canticum canticorum* (Trübner, 1860) and *Speculum humanae salvationis* (C.J. Stewart, 1861). Then in 1861 he founded a pioneering journal *Le Bibliomane*. Though published in London by Trübner, an immigrant bookseller from Germany, his choice of the French language showed that he clearly had an eye on the foreign market. The contents, however, were firmly Anglo-centric in reflecting the concerns of British collectors. It lasted for just two issues before being defeated by production costs, and in that time it included articles on Caxton, the first St Albans press, early woodcuts, watermarks and the 1457 Psalter, the last always a popular topic as the first printed book bearing a date of publication. After his project collapsed, in August 1861 he launched a successor, *Le Bibliophile Illustré*. Five hundred copies of each issue were printed, and in the course of the following four years twenty-five issues appeared, from four different publishers: successively, Trübner, John Russell Smith, William Jeffs and Eugène Rascol.[35] The first two, Trübner and Smith, had major bibliographical interests; the choice of Jeffs, a specialist in French books, marked an attempt to enlarge the market in what was by 1865 a much weakened journal. In its heyday it attracted some of the most prominent names in bibliography: J.W. Holtrop of the Royal Library in the Netherlands, John Bellingham Inglis (the first translator into English of Richard de Bury's *Philobiblon*[36]), Auguste Bernard, Henry Bradshaw,[37] Octave Delepierre and Paul Lacroix. A little after its demise, Berjeau issued from January 1866 yet another similar journal, *The Book-Worm*. These miscellanies of notes mostly on early printed books, fragments of gossip, occasional bibliographical queries and reports on some of the more important auction sales, never established sufficiently reliable and faithful readerships. Production standards gradually declined, from the coloured hand-made paper of the first to the cheap machine-made paper, in a smaller format, that marked the end of Berjeau's enterprises.[38]

The volumes of a new series of *Le Bibliophile Français* published by the Paris booksellers Bachelin-Deflorenne between 1868 and 1873 were of an entirely different quality, on *papier vergé* and copiously illustrated with bindings. The articles were mostly on earlier collectors, but there was a smattering of contemporary or more recent ones, including not only the duc d'Aumale but also Ambroise Firmin-Didot and Léopold Double. Paul Lacroix, who wrote about Double, was critical of his decision to sell his library in 1863, after assembling it in only about three years. The skilled reproductions of Double's two paintings by Vermeer offered some compensation to readers, but Lacroix had hit on an important point. Book collectors had many incentives, and these could as well be short term as long term. It was not necessary to invest a lifetime. While interests could easily weaken, or evaporate, and while personal disasters could curtail matters, for some there was also a question of financial investment, even speculation. The constant comments on prices and values in the literature of collecting at every level in England and France alike reflected criteria only partly concerned with the interest of books. They were also investments, with a cash value.

None of the British bibliophile journals at this time lasted very long, but as each one failed so lessons were learned for others that were started. When the publisher Elliot Stock issued the first number of *The Bibliographer* in December 1881, he had several advantages. First, as the publisher of facsimiles of early printed books he had the beginnings of a practical measure of the market.[39] Second, in Henry B. Wheatley (1838–1917)[40] he had an editor who both brought a range of acquaintances on whom to call and grasped better than most writers the kinds of information and comment that an audience of mixed tastes and skills might appreciate. Wheatley had learned the elements of bibliography in compiling a catalogue of the library of the Board of Trade in 1866. By 1881 he had been treasurer of the Early English Text Society since 1872, was a Fellow of the Society of Antiquaries, had written on the history of dictionaries and the history of London, had helped found the London Topographical Society, in 1877 had founded the Index Society and helped to found the Library Association, and in 1879 had moved from a post in the Royal Society which included responsibility for its library to become the Assistant Secretary of the Society of Arts. His appointment for a few years as external inspector of Cambridge University Library brought friendship with Henry Bradshaw, and his enthusiasm for Samuel Pepys was to lead in 1893–9 to a new edition of the diary. The auction sale of his library, sold over five days in April 1918, revealed much of his own collecting interests, led by an extensive collection of bookbindings and including a long series of autograph letters. The John Dryden collection was sold separately, while his several publications on decorated bookbindings showed both his strengths and his limitations in what was becoming an increasingly well-informed field.[41]

The Bibliographer offered a mixture of articles, reviews and news. For the first issue, Wheatley extracted from Bradshaw a study of the Antwerp printer Godfried van der Haghen, which Bradshaw had hitherto hesitated to publish. In the first volume there were offerings from William Blades on early English printers, a series of articles by W.M. Conway on the early woodcutters of the Netherlands (developed as a book in 1884) and a series by Nicholas Pocock on the Bishops' Bible. Wheatley himself wrote an appreciative trio of articles on Arber's transcripts of the Stationers' Company registers. W.H.J. Weale contributed a transcript of a letter from Christopher Plantin to Gabriel de Cayas. The journal was not only about print. Lucy Toulmin Smith gave summary reports on English manuscripts in Paris and Göttingen. An important part of most issues was dedicated to reports of the major London auctions of books, including in the first year the Sunderland, Beckford/Hamilton and Gurney sales, with long lists of prices and occasionally the names of prominent buyers. The reports provided an all too accurate assessment of the decrepit state of many of the books in the Sunderland library, where generations of exposure to sunlight had wrecked many of the bindings. It was also a journal about libraries, and public libraries featured increasingly prominently. Wheatley could be scathing about the state of some of the country's other libraries. That at Bath Abbey was castigated for its disgraceful state of neglect, where the books 'remain little better than lumber'.[42] All this was accompanied by reviews (generally of an amicable turn) and by brief news items.

Wheatley's venture, well-informed, international in scope and well connected, did not last. From time to time Ernest Thomas of the Library Association mocked it for its careless mistakes,[43] and in November 1884 the publisher Elliot Stock decided to bring it to an end. Wheatley re-focused on other projects, including a successful series of pocket-sized volumes for *The book-lover's library*: in a market that was sometimes ostentatiously bibliophile, volumes were offered on antique paper bound in cloth (4s.6d.), on hand-made paper, in Roxburghe-style half morocco (7s.6d.), or on larger hand-made paper, in the same style (£1.1s.), with only fifty copies being printed of the third.

The Bibliographer had shown a new way forward. It had published checklists of the works of people hitherto neglected including Henry

Sacheverell and Jonathan Swift, as well as more detailed bibliographies of best-sellers including Lewis Bayley's seventeenth-century *The practice of piety* (first published by 1612) in its several translations as well as the much-printed English original. It had provided detailed reports on major auction sales at a critical period as owners began to take advantage of the new freedom to sell inherited property following the settled estates legislation. It had campaigned not only in detailed reports of developments in the public library movement but also in drawing attention to the dismal state of parish libraries. Among its authors it could count some of the most respected and learned bibliographers of the day. It had printed informed obituaries of some of the major London booksellers and publishers including Henry Bohn, Nicolas Trübner and C.J. Stewart. Following his death, it had coped with the mixed reputation left by John Payne Collier. It had reported on some of the major issues of concern in the book world, from questions concerning the origin of printing to the sale of the Ashburnham manuscripts. In its miscellaneous notes each month it had chronicled a world defined by antiquarian books, their sale and their study, and each month it had brought within two covers the specialist interests of professional bibliographers beside those of enthusiastic bibliophiles.

Special Societies

An early call for a society to be devoted to the study of books was made in *Notes and Queries* in 1868. The author was William E.A. Axon (1846–1913), Lancashire antiquary, journalist for many years with the *Manchester Guardian*, a sometime member of the staff of Manchester Public Library, and a frequent contributor to the journal.[44]

In England we have many learned societies pursuing a course of steady usefulness, recording year by year new facts in science, throwing new lights on history, exposing old errors, and accumulating material for the future philosopher – for the future historian.

Everyone who has had to do with historical literature must have reaped benefits from the labours of the Society of Antiquaries, the Numismatic Society, and those others which are devoted to the promotion of historical knowledge; and every man of science must owe similar obligations to the Royal Society, the Chemical Society, &c. &c. The number of learned societies is now somewhat large, and each of them, in its own peculiar field of usefulness, has been of much service; and, with their example shining so clearly, it has often excited my surprise that there is not among them a Society of Bibliographers. . . .

Why, then, is there no society for its advancement? Let bibliographers consider this question. Lowndes, we are told by Mr. Bohn, complained that the bibliographer has no standing in England. A somewhat higher value is put upon these studies now, but the establishment of such a society as is here suggested would undoubtedly aid in giving to bibliographers still more of that position to which they are entitled in the republic of letters. When such an association *is* organised, there is plenty of work which it might usefully do. A General Literary Index would then be something of a possibility, the vexed question of cataloguing would, probably, find a solution, much light would be thrown upon literary history, special bibliographies of particular subjects might be brought out under its protection, and it would be able to accomplish for Europe that which the Smithsonian Institution does for America in the way of promoting friendly relations between different literary institutions and men.[45]

Perhaps drawing on assumptions made when he was a librarian, Axon saw bibliography as primarily a listing of books, a way of organising authors, titles and subjects. He did not think of it as a means of analysing or recounting the ways in which books were made, their materials, or their history, use and ownership. The title of Lowndes's *Bibliographer's manual* was a sufficient guide as to priorities and assumptions in the use of the word. Its wider application, to the study of books more generally, including details of their material properties, did not emerge until the work of Bradshaw and others in the 1860s to 1880s. For a short while the development of the two separate activities gathered under the same term each found a place in the new Library Association, founded in 1877, and in which Axon took an early interest. They proved too disparate in their aims. As the new professional association increasingly explored its central concerns in the management of libraries, so the study of bibliology (a French word, coined a hundred and more years earlier[46]) was the main concern of the Bibliographical Society founded in 1892 by W.A. Copinger, J.Y.W. MacAlister (one of the secretaries of the Library Association) and others.[47]

Axon had a general purpose in mind. Others were more focused. The Palaeographical Society, founded in 1873 by a group headed by E.A. Bond and Edward Maunde Thompson of the British Museum, existed to publish high-quality facsimiles of pages from early manuscripts and a few examples of lettering in other media.[48] Ten years later rumour reached Bradshaw of a proposed Palaeotypographical Society. 'It would be so easy', he remarked, 'to make a really good thing of it, and yet all experience goes the other way, and only inspires one with distrust.'[49] Nothing came of this, and only in the 1890s did a series of individual enterprises show a way forward, with

Konrad Burger's *Monumenta Germaniae et Italiae typographica* (Berlin, 1892–3), Olgar Thierry-Poux's *Premiers monuments de l'imprimerie en France au XVe siècle* (Paris, 1890) and Claudin's *Histoire de l'imprimerie en France au XVe et au XVIe siècle* (Paris, 1900–14). They came forty-odd years after Holtrop had begun to issue his *Monuments*.

Librarianship and Public Libraries

For most people in charge of libraries in the early and mid-nineteenth century, librarianship was not a profession. For all but a few scholars who found in it a productive niche it was an occupation, poorly paid and often all but self-taught. As such it could be resented. We have already seen the consequences of inattention in the French libraries raided by Libri. At Breslau, the University Librarian Hoffmann von Fallersleben (1798–1874), more widely remembered as a popular poet and historian of early German literature, regarded his appointment as on the one hand a sinecure, and yet on the other demanding service more oppressive than any corporal punishment devised in the army.[50] Friedrich Adolf Ebert (1791–1834), later distinguished as Librarian of Wolfenbüttel, as a young man considered university libraries to be 'dusty, desolate, and unfrequented rooms in which the librarian must spend a few hours weekly to discharge his duties – so that during this time he can be alone'.[51] Obviously not everyone viewed the task in such desperate terms, but many eighteenth- and early nineteenth-century custodians would have recognised themselves in his words. The variety of libraries, and the variety of employers institutional or private, expected a range of aptitude and approach varying from the professional to the amateur, knowledgeable or ignorant, paid or voluntary, part time or full time. Yet while the degree of skill required in managing a library also depended as much on the expectations and requirements of users as on individuals charged with collections, the most influential librarians have been those who have chosen to develop, and even exploit, their positions, whether for the increase of collections or for the increase of understanding.

The report of the Committee chaired by William Ewart on public libraries in 1849 was a call for action, for locally raised public money to be invested in libraries that would be accessible to all. The old circulating libraries, subscription libraries and what proved in many cases to be a short-term excitement engendered by the social and educational potential of libraries in mechanics' institutes, all demonstrated the need for more organised, more generally accessible and better-stocked collections. This applied in town and country alike, though in fact the first local authorities able to take advantage of the new legislation passed in 1850 and subsequently were all in towns or major cities.[52]

The new public libraries were a source of anxiety for many people. While their lending departments were used overwhelmingly by working and lower middle classes, they also attracted a sometimes high percentage of the professional classes, just the kind of clientele for whom Slater and Loftie mainly wrote.[53] Thomas Greenwood, author of a standard book on public libraries, dealt easily with the argument that these new libraries were not an unmixed good, and he drew attention to other institutions of society, whether workhouses, the police, roads or even marriage and food. If fiction was generally read more than other more serious work, it was (he argued) the better kind of fiction that had been deliberately chosen, not random pulp.[54] For those for whom public libraries were either inaccessible, or distasteful as possible sources of infection, Mudie's circulating library (founded in 1842 and offering a postal service) and that of W.H. Smith (founded in 1860) provided alternatives until they in turn foundered in the twentieth century. Even in places with established free public libraries, the commercial circulating libraries remained. In Manchester, where, apart from the central library, by 1900 there were branches across much of the city, the trades directory still listed fifteen circulating libraries, including an outpost of Mudie's.

The Public Libraries acts enabled local authorities in England to raise money from rates to pay not just for new books to be lent and circulated but also for the collecting of early books. The legislation was extended to Scotland in 1853. In this way, starting usually with local history, genealogy and topography, some libraries began to assemble what was eventually to become for some people one of their most valued features. The Guildhall Library in the City of London, founded in 1824–8 and with a history traceable from the 1420s, had always collected relevant local history as well as ranging more widely in early books.[55]

Long before the establishment of a public library at Liverpool, there had been proposals that the city should purchase the considerable collection of William Roscoe (1753–1831), biographer of Lorenzo de Medici and of Pope Leo X, when the bank in which he was a partner failed. It was known to contain many rarities and to be especially rich in early Italian literature. Although he was internationally celebrated as a collector and as a scholar, he had many local enemies who, dependent for their wealth on slavery, could not accept his vocal antipathy to it.[56] In a sale over fourteen days,

Roscoe's library was accordingly auctioned at Liverpool in 1816, the situation only partly saved by a group of his friends who bought many of the lots. When Roscoe refused these as a gift, they presented them to the Liverpool Athenaeum, founded in 1797.

The extension of the public libraries movement was irregular, spread over several decades even into the twentieth century. Local benefactors could have major effects, sometimes by encouraging new libraries by providing collections or money in advance of any vote, and sometimes by subsequent financial or other support. Of the largest libraries, and those which were able to take an extended interest in old as well as new books, Manchester and Liverpool were opened in 1852, Birmingham in 1861 and Leeds in 1870. The Mitchell Library at Glasgow opened in 1877. At Bristol, where the old city library dated from 1613, serious efforts were being made for a local collection in the new public library by 1855. These and others depended much on gifts and bequests, which might as often contain unwanted material as things of value. Out of this mixture of policy and chance grew accumulations of miscellaneous early printing available to a public unable to get to the great national libraries and shy of their dominance.

Henry Bradshaw used his presidency of the Library Association in 1882 to urge that local libraries should become centres for the gathering and study of local history, of works by local authors and of local printing:

If, as we are told, the library is destined to be the university of the future, there ought surely to be room on the staff of the library for some 'professor' of local antiquities of this kind, for some one whose very work will train him to be a centre of information upon all subjects bearing immediately upon the state and history of his own town or district.[57]

Like other Lancashire industrial towns, Wigan and the surrounding area expanded rapidly in the mid-nineteenth century. It depended mostly on coal-mining and on cotton mills. Of the local authorities that chose to spend part of their money on rare or early printed books, Wigan was remarkable from the inception of its library.[58] A combination of private benefactions, an energetic and imaginative librarian and a supportive local landowner (Lord Crawford) created a collection of quite exceptional importance. Only about seventeen miles from the central library in Manchester, it chose to assemble for its own locality an extraordinary collection, one that in many ways outdid its neighbour. The policy was made possible by a combination of benefactors and local bibliophily. In 1873 one of the leading local doctors, Joseph Taylor Winnard, left a

Figure 12 The reference collection, Wigan Public Library, c.1900. From H.T. Folkard, *Wigan Free Public Library, its rise and progress* (1900).

substantial sum for the purchase of books, his provision suggesting that there was already a local wish among some people for a library. In 1876 the Public Libraries Acts were adopted. A local cotton mill owner, Thomas Taylor (d.1892), JP and mayor of Wigan, provided money for land and premises. The new library was a building of which to be proud. Designed by Alfred Waterhouse, with an elaborately decorated exterior, it opened in 1878, its construction coinciding with the time that much of Waterhouse's energy was engaged in the design and erection of his Gothic masterpiece at Manchester town hall, opened in 1877.

The lending library was on the ground floor. Upstairs (Figure 12) was the reference library, containing the older or more valuable books in a large room whose shelved alcoves on two levels reminded some readers of college libraries. A posthumous portrait of Winnard, commissioned by the town, dominated one end. Tables were provided for readers down the middle of the room. Henry Tennyson Folkard (1850–1916), formerly at the Royal Academy in London, was appointed as Librarian. Advised by various specialists, he applied a mixture of bibliophily and wide general knowledge to create a reference library of unusual depth, though his detailed printed catalogue, on a scale unparalleled among public libraries, was never completed. When in 1883 members of the Library Association visited Wigan as part of their annual conference, he drew especial attention to the collections in bibliography, topography and the sciences, besides the set of the *Acta sanctorum* and Migne's *Patrologia* and the Great Bible of 1541: all had been among the library's earliest acquisitions.[59] At that stage, most of the acquisitions were of modern books, including several expensive illustrated works, but there was a smattering of publications before 1800. Agricola's *De re metallica* (Basel, 1561) was obviously pertinent to a community so many of whom were involved in mining. Following publication of the printed catalogue, Folkard expanded his ambitions, in both medieval manuscripts and printed books. The majority of the earlier books and more recent expensive works were bought subsequently, and Folkard installed glazed showcases in which to display some of the treasures. Eventually there were over seventy incunabula, and more than 3,600 English and foreign books of before 1800.

It is by no means clear how far Folkard was driven by bibliophily, and how far by a wish to provide for local education and leisure. For him, they were complementary. The books were used by readers well beyond the town's boundaries. Certainly the stock, including such locally relevant rarities as *Gleanings from the menagerie at Knowsley Hall* (1850),[60] developed far beyond what might ordinarily be expected. A utilitarian case might readily be made for Walton's polyglot Bible (1657), but the only Vulgate listed in the printed catalogue was a two-volume manuscript dated c.1250 that had formerly belonged to Adam Clarke and had featured at the Society of Antiquaries in 1879. It is no longer at Wigan.[61] When in 1900 Folkard produced a commemorative book on the library that was so much his creation, he remarked that the best way of demonstrating the value of the reference collection was to list a selection of its treasures: his list, as much concerned with standard reference works as with valuable early books, occupied over half the volume.[62] The collections were exceptional not only among local authorities but even nationally, and for a few decades the library offered readers one of the finest opportunities in the country.[63]

Leader in so many ways, in one crucial respect Britain lagged behind other countries. No one by 1850 had produced a manual of librarianship, and there was little sign of collaboration among librarians. The public libraries legislation proved of profound importance, but it was not at first supported in Britain by much literature explaining how libraries were to be built and run, how books were to be selected, how the book trade worked, how catalogues were to be compiled, or how books were to be arranged on the shelves. Their various activities and departments required new ideas in architecture. For most people who were given responsibilities for the new public libraries, these were matters to be explored. There was no manual until in 1859 Edward Edwards, very recently the Chief Librarian of Manchester, produced two fat volumes: *Memoirs of libraries: including a handbook of library economy.* The first volume and part of the second offered an extensive survey and history of libraries, in Britain, continental Europe and the United States. The remainder addressed the practicalities of running a library, including not only book selection and book-buying but also such matters as shelving and heating. His aim was encyclopaedic, and he was frank as to his purposes. By 1859 he could draw not only on his years in the British Museum Library but also, and much more immediately, his experience in running the pioneering new public library in Manchester. Short-tempered and not always tactful,[64] Edwards's career in neither London nor Manchester was a happy one. He was ejected from his Manchester position in autumn 1858, and his two volumes were published in the first month of 1859, priced at 48 shillings.[65] He wished not just to offer a history and a manual but also to raise the status of librarians: 'Librarianship, like schoolkeeping, has, in England, too frequently been made a respectable sort of "Refuge for the Destitute."'[66]

Notwithstanding the reservations mentioned previously, it was different in Germany, where Ebert and (at more length) the Danish librarian, historian and theatre director Christian Molbech had issued manuals in 1820 and 1828–9. At Munich, Martin Schrettinger (1772–1851), facing the challenge of vast quantities of books received into the royal library following the secularisation of monasteries, produced first a two-volume *Lehrbuch* and then in 1834 a single-volume *Handbuch*.[67] Of the next generation, in 1856 Julius Petzholdt (1812–91), founder-editor of *Anzeiger für Literatur der Bibliothekwissenschaft* and librarian at Dresden, published the first edition of his *Katechismus der Bibliothekenlehre*, a work on both the theory and the practice of librarianship, including library planning and different practices in cataloguing. He extended it in 1871 and then revised it for a third edition in 1877. By then there was a considerable literature in Germany about theory and practice. In 1863 Johann Georg Seizinger addressed both book and archive management.[68] Not all these books found favour, in what threatened to become an overload of professional advice among German speakers, and they never became familiar in Britain. In France, the establishment of *bibliothèques municipales*, and their development especially under

Guizot from the 1830s, were supported by L.-A. Constantin's little textbook on *Bibliothéconomie* (1839, new ed. 1841) in the series of *Manuels Roret*, though it was remarked in 1842 that appointments often still depended more on patronage than on skills.[69]

In America, following the Ewart report in England, a meeting of librarians was organised in 1853 by Charles Jewett (Librarian of the Smithsonian Institution) and W.F. Poole (Librarian of the Boston Mercantile Library), to confer 'upon the means of advancing the prosperity and usefulness of public libraries, and for the suggestion and discussion of topics of importance to book collectors and readers'. In adding book collectors and readers, the organisers extended any purpose that might have been intended in Britain. Although about eighty people attended, nothing further seems to have been heard until a similar conference in Philadelphia, shortly before the centennial exhibition held in the city in 1876. The US Bureau of Education report on *Public libraries in the United States* (1876),[70] coming seventeen years after the Ewart report, was naturally different in its approach. It reported on libraries already existing, it offered proposals on how their influence might be improved and extended, and it concerned itself with college and specialist libraries, as well as public ones, historical societies and art galleries. Though often impelled by cultural cringe, in fact it was the widest consideration of libraries ever attempted. As an appendix, it printed Charles Cutter's rules for a dictionary catalogue.

For a time, American and British professional interests marched hand in hand. In 1876 the young Melvil Dewey launched the *Library Journal*, published in New York by Frederick Leypoldt and in London by Nicolas Trübner. Soon it was able to describe itself as the official organ of the professional associations in both countries. Among the associate editors recruited from Britain were William Axon of Manchester, George Bullen and Richard Garnett of the British Museum, and H.O. Coxe of the Bodleian Library: it was clear where leadership lay in at least some aspects of the emergent profession.

By the time that a group of librarians, professional and amateur, met at the London Institution in October 1877, there was much to consider from the United States, and the conference included many American delegates. While the chief among them was Justin Winsor, Librarian of Harvard, who was elected Vice-President of the meeting, others also brought considerable experience. Delegates attended from France, Germany, Greece and Italy. Sir Redmond Barry, the moving spirit behind the already considerable Public Library of Victoria, came from Melbourne and contributed several papers. Guided by suggestions circulated before the meeting for possible topics, attention focused on different kinds of public or institutional libraries, library buildings, their contents, cataloguing and arrangement, on binding, and on borrowing. In the course of extended exchanges about the wisdom or otherwise of printing the British Museum catalogue, a call emerged for a General Catalogue of English Literature. The encouragement of bibliographical research meant in this instance the compilation of lists, not the physical study of books.

Axon, as Honorary Secretary of the Manchester Literary Club, took up a theme that emerged briefly in a paper on university libraries in the 1877 meeting, and in two more substantial papers in the American report of 1876, on professorships of books and reading. Axon was interested only incidentally in the history of printing, paper, binding and other physical matters. For him, the task of a professor of bibliography attached to a library would be to guide reading, in what the American report described as 'a trackless, if not a howling wilderness, in which a guide, philosopher, and friend will find ample occasion for his services'.[71] The general mood of the meeting seems to have been summarised by Ernest Thomas, who distinguished between bibliography, as listing 'the insides of books', and bibliology, their outsides. His words were reported: 'Whether they knew anything about their outsides – their bindings, places of publication, printers, width of margin, and the number of commas in the titles of each various edition was a matter of comparative indifference to him.'[72]

The *Library Journal* focused increasingly on the United States and in 1884 the Library Association launched the *Library Chronicle*. Reflecting the eclectic interests of members, the new journal offered a mixture of articles on historical subjects and on library management, and it contained a quantity of short news items concerning libraries and librarianship generally. Though Henry Bradshaw was a member and served a term as its president, the Association never showed sustained concern for his scholarly interests.

Two Approaches

The emergent tensions in the newly founded Library Association appeared partly in a debate about size-notation and its relationship to format, a topic growing from cataloguing needs but that was quickly confused as members spoke variously about modern or older books. Hence it was that when Bradshaw took his turn as president in 1882, he found it necessary to respond to what he regarded as an inadequate report on size-notation presented by a special committee to the Cambridge meeting that year. His final paragraph could not conceal his irritation, even despair:

> The truth is that, although Frenchmen seem to be generally taught these things as elementary facts, I am bound to say that I have not found, during the last twenty years, five Englishmen, either librarians or booksellers, who knew how to distinguish a folio from a quarto, or an octavo from a 12° or a 16°.[73]

He had complained of the same for many years, and his correspondence on incunabula with J.W. Holtrop, Librarian of the Royal Library in The Hague, had been all the more refreshing to him because they understood each other. England left him despondent. 'The authorities at the British Museum', he wrote in 1864, 'do not (most of them) know a folio from a 4° or an 8° from a 16°.'[74] A quarter of a century after Bradshaw complained of such ignorance of quite basic principles of books' construction, it was still considered worthwhile for William Blades to contribute an article on formats to the new journal *The Library*.[75] It was one small element of the division between those who concentrated on the contents of books, and those who concerned themselves with structures and materials. The notion of *bibliographie matérielle* that formed part of the basis of the massive work in France by Jules Cousin, University Librarian of Douai, *De l'organisation et de l'administration des bibliothèques publiques et privées* (Paris, 1882), was in fact much more complicated. Cousin summed it up initially, if somewhat superficially: 'La connaissance des livres au point de vue de leurs conditions extérieures: format, impression, papier, reliure, âge, etc.' He then continued: 'Elle est indispensable au libraire: c'est la clef du commerce des livres; elle est également nécessaire au bibliothécaire: sans elle, il marcherait souvent à l'aventure et sans guide.'[76]

A little later Albert Maire, trained by the palaeographer Émile Chatelain and now on the staff of the library of the Sorbonne, repeated the theme, slightly less precisely. Again he distinguished between bibliography as listing the content of books and their relation one to another, and *bibliographie matérielle*. Thus, *Bibliologie* encompassed knowledge of the history of books down to the present and *connaissance matérielle extérieure et intérieure*:

> Cette partie de la bibliographie s'attache à la description de la matière employée pour faire un livre, aux procédés typographiques et de gravure mis en usage, ainsi qu'à sa reliure et toute autre particularité pouvant le signaler à l'attention des amateurs ou des bibliographes.[77]

The development of new approaches to the bibliographical study of books lay at the heart of the nineteenth-century revolution. In its origins it included both the listing of books and their study as physical objects: what some people found useful to call an archaeology of the book. Such a study involved consideration not only of the materials and creation of books but also, by extension, tangible and visible evidence for volumes' circulation, collection, treatment at the hands of later owners, and reading. It included the study of paper, of typefaces, of printing-house practices, of the manufacture and of decoration of bookbindings. From the hands of printers, binders, publishers and booksellers, all led to the use of books at the hands of owners and readers.

Though much can be made of distinctions between physical, or material, bibliography and enumerative bibliography – the listing of books – in fact the two are complementary. Brunet had shown some understanding of this in his *Manuel*, yet by the last decades of the century the differences between the two approaches seemed ever greater, all too evident in the divergent courses taken by the Library Association and the Bibliographical Society. They seemed greater because each had developed so dramatically. In a series of debates that were far from straightforward concerning how books should be described, library catalogues emphasised how books were to be found. Increased attention to material, or physical, bibliography emphasised manufacture, circulation and use. To people such as Ernest Thomas, it seemingly had little to do with the contents of books. In fact, each depended on the other, and nowhere more so than in the hands of those responsible for addressing each, ultimately at the hands of readers. If, as was repeatedly remarked, access lay at the heart of use, so it also depended on material properties.

Henry Bradshaw and Léopold Delisle were the most influential scholars respectively of early printed books and of manuscripts in their two countries. While they shared many interests, in fact there were fundamental differences. Bradshaw never formally adumbrated in public a set of principles for the description of books, either printed or manuscript. To some extent only, he set them out by example. Delisle, as an administrator and instrumental in preparing catalogues of manuscripts, was required to produce them, and he did so for both manuscripts and printed books. The importance he attached to codicological questions, involving the material archaeology of codices, was set out in a brief document published in 1884.[78] Such questions had been first raised extensively by F.A. Ebert at Wolfenbüttel, in 1825, in the first volume of his manual on librarianship,[79] and were presented in the context of manuscripts; but his work was never translated, and – to his regret – Bradshaw did not know German.[80]

Bradshaw's own contributions to the study of fifteenth-century books depended on two concerns in particular. First, his wish to establish who printed particular books, and which books were printed by particular printers or, failing a name, by which anonymous press. For him, this depended first and most importantly on the identification of the typefaces used in each book, and on the different practices of printers in setting and assembling pages: what Bradshaw, working in 1870 on early Dutch presses, referred to as printers' 'habits', and Blades, writing a few years earlier, had called 'typographical particulars'.[81] In his revision of his study of Caxton (1877), which incorporated a great deal of new material from Bradshaw, Blades quoted Bradshaw's own words, that the bibliographer should 'make such an accurate and methodical study of the *types* used and *habits of printing* observable at different presses as to enable him to observe and be guided by these characteristics in settling the date of a book which bears no date upon the surface'.[82] Second was his perception that in the codicological evidence that any printed or manuscript book could offer lay clues to its textual composition, its manufacture and its history:[83]

To work out the history of the volume from the present to the past; to peel off, as it were, every accretion, piece by piece, entry by entry, making each contribute its share of evidence of the book's history backwards from generation to generation; to take note of every entry which shows either use, or ownership, or even the various changes in library arrangement, until we get back to the book itself as it left the original scriptorium or the hands of the scribe; noting how the book is made up, whether in 4-sheet, 5-sheet, or 6-sheet quires, or otherwise; how the quires are numbered and marked for the binder; how the corrector has done his work; ... how the rubricator has performed his part; what kind of handwriting the scribe uses; and, finally, to what country or district all these pieces of evidence point ... The quiet building up of facts, the habit of patiently watching a book, and listening while it tells you its own story, must tend to produce a solid groundwork of knowledge, which alone leads to that sober confidence before which both negative assumption and ungrounded speculation, however brilliant, must ultimately fall.[84]

With this quotation from Bradshaw himself, Duff closed his study of *Early printed books*. Bradshaw wrote here of manuscripts, but once a few obvious adjustments are made his words apply as much to printed books.

Thus volumes might be taken apart. We have already seen him dismembering bindings.[85] In 1875 Samuel Sandars presented an early sixteenth-century manuscript Dutch prayer book to Cambridge University Library. Bradshaw saw that it was misbound, and described what then happened:

I am afraid you will be shocked, but as I examined the manuscript you were good enough to give us, I found it was so precious and so interesting that I could not resist the temptation of taking it to pieces, which I did with the utmost care and gentleness. ... It would have been quite impossible to get at the truth about it without doing what I have done. ... Several leaves were cruelly misplaced, but I have made out the whole thing clearly now, and I shall be very glad to show you how prettily it all comes out.[86]

He gave little study to paper or to watermarks except insofar as they contributed to understanding a book's physical structure, and he showed severely restricted interest in early bindings.[87] Some years after the event, the mathematician Karl Pearson, student and then Fellow of King's College, Cambridge, recalled what was perhaps an amalgam of occasions:

As he handled the pages of some early folio, and described how two presses had been employed, one working away at this point, and the other at that; how the first stock of paper had been exhausted here, and the second there; how at this point the printer had thought to improve on his original, or had bought somebody else's cuts, or chopped up his own – the auditor felt himself carried back centuries, and saw the men of the past at their work.[88]

Delisle, coming to the study of early printed books as a secondary interest, an administrative necessity thanks to his official position, naturally followed his predecessors when in 1886 he codified their description. His requirements respecting format, type (roman or black-letter), *justification* (that is, page lay-out, including the number of columns on a page), illustrations and printers' marks were all derived from others. But then he went further, moving on from elements held in common among copies to copy-specific information. His requirement that copies on special paper or on vellum (parchment) should be noted accorded with long-established bibliophile traditions. Nevertheless, much of this was ill-developed. If books were in more than one size of type, that was not noted. No details were provided of the number of leaves or pages, or of collations. Few references were added to previous authorities such as Hain or Panzer. The catalogue of the incunables at Toulouse published eight years earlier was by no means perfect, but it showed a firmer grasp of matters than did Delisle.[89] Despite the fact that by Delisle's death in 1910 the new catalogue of the fifteenth-century books in the British Museum was transforming the description of these books, it was still thought worthwhile in Paris to republish Delisle's by now long out-of-date instructions. More helpfully, ways forward had been demonstrated in the succession of catalogues of incunabula prepared by Marie Pellechet, first in those for Dijon (1886), Versailles (1889) and Lyon (1893), and then in her much greater and more ambitious enterprise, a union catalogue of incunabula in French libraries.

17 | Standing Back

Previous chapters have mostly been concerned directly with books or manuscripts: with their handling in libraries, in the book trade and among readers. Here we turn to two less direct aspects, both of which reflected and influenced attitudes and understanding. Commemorations brought authors and their works to wide public attention, partly through reports in the newspaper and magazine press, and, when such occasions were marked by the erection of public statues, by a continuing visible presence. Whether (as here) of literary or related figures, or of politicians, clergy, military heroes, philanthropists, or people distinguished in the arts, they were, and remained, unavoidable reminders in stone or metal of a particular and selected past. To commemorate the past on paper it was traditional to write and print its history. There were, however, further remains and archival strata that invited investigation. As had been recognised for many years in the work of dozens of scholars, in these archival survivals lay the explanation, rationale and often the justification for modern religious, political and other aspects of social organisation. The book trades were no exception, but it was only in the late nineteenth century that they were the object of detailed, systematic exploration and publication.

Anniversaries and Memorials

The anniversaries of major literary figures have been often enough presented as an aspect of cultural, even national, memory.[1] In 1859 Robert Burns was commemorated worldwide in hundreds of speeches and gatherings having a distinctive Scottish voice; by the end of the century statues of him had been erected not only in several Scottish cities but also as far afield as Chicago and San Francisco.[2] Schiller, commemorated in a statue at Stuttgart since 1839, was in 1859 a widespread, if varied, focus for German nation-building.[3] The tercentenary of Shakespeare in 1864 was celebrated alike in Stratford-upon-Avon and London, arousing not a little jealousy between the two places.[4] In 1871, after the Boydell Shakespeare Gallery in London was demolished, the statue made for it by Thomas

Banks was removed to New Place in Stratford, albeit not without some local opposition. In Scotland, where statues of Sir Walter Scott stood prominently in Glasgow and Edinburgh, a major exhibition was organised in 1871 to mark the centenary of his birth.[5] Celebrations at Florence of the 600th anniversary of Dante's birth coincided with the struggle for the unification of Italy, and a statue of him was erected in the Piazza Santa Croce in 1865.[6] Florence became briefly the capital city of Italy in this year: the links between literature, history and politics could hardly have been more strongly expressed. In Switzerland, a bronze statue of Rousseau by James Pradier was erected in Geneva in 1835. Voltaire and Rousseau in 1878 were marked as two heroes in national memory, political at least as much as literary and overlain with religious disputes.[7] In 1880, Russia celebrated Pushkin, and the monument erected in Moscow by public subscription was followed by many more.[8] In their different ways, each of these emphasised social and political themes. They were contributions to identity, whether for emigrant Scots scattered all over the world or as an aid in defining a newfound unified Italy. While anniversaries provoked such commemorations, it was not always necessary for a date to be an excuse. The monument erected to honour Molière (1622–73) in Paris was erected in 1844, paid for by public subscription and took advantage of a site opposite his house that had become unexpectedly clear.[9]

The bust of Shakespeare in the parish church at Stratford-upon-Avon dated from between 1616 and 1623. The Temple of British Worthies at Stowe, designed by William Kent in the 1730s included Shakespeare and Milton. When a group of Byron's friends commissioned a posthumous statue from Bertel Thorvaldsen, their first thought was that it should be placed in Poets' Corner in Westminster Abbey. It only reached its final, and secular, home in the Wren library at Trinity College Cambridge, Byron's own college, after it had been refused (twice) at Westminster and deemed inappropriate for the college chapel, where it would have been in conclave with Isaac Newton. It never became a public statue in an ordinary sense, but joined a pantheon of busts of ancient and modern writers assembled in the eighteenth century.[10]

A sense of a literary past identifiable with specific individuals emerged not just in commemorative statues but also in associated locations. The Shakespeare celebrations drew renewed attention to his birthplace in Stratford-upon-Avon. Any physical evidence of connections with his family had long since departed from this house later owned by others, although it attracted casual visitors who were expected to leave gratuities. When it was offered to the highest bidder in 1847, a public campaign was launched to defeat the American showman P.T. Barnum, who wished to ship it over the Atlantic. The house was bought for £3,820, and was opened to the public under new arrangements, with a curator, by 1852. In Alloway, south of Ayr, Robert Burns had been marked for tourist pilgrimage since the beginning of the century. His two-room cottage was acquired by trustees in 1881, and turned into a museum. At Chalfont St Giles, there was a different threat, when it was rumoured that an American wished to buy Milton's cottage and ship it over the Atlantic. It was saved when a trust was established to create a museum and reading room.[11] In the Lake District, Dove Cottage was bought by a group of well-wishers and admirers of Wordsworth in 1890, and opened to the public the following year.[12] Presentation was all-important. 'You see', wrote Stopford Brooke concerning Dove Cottage, 'I have not made the place into a Museum, as some folks wanted me to do. I shall put up more pictures, and a few books, first editions, etc., of the poems, and that is all.'[13]

Each created a selective memory, focused on an individual. It is difficult to measure how much influence, if any, such places and circumstances had on public interest in the earliest editions of these authors. Exhibitions in writers' houses naturally included examples of their published work. The new owners of Shakespeare's birthplace began to gather exhibits when they bought a single leaf from *Venus and Adonis* (1594) at the George Daniel sale in 1864, and added *The merchant of Venice* (1600) three years later. Their copy of the First Folio was incomplete and in very poor condition, part of the assorted collection of books and other Shakespeareana from a local benefactor Anne Wheler (d.1870). Copies of the other three folios were presented in 1863. Only several years later were the trustees able to afford a complete copy of the First Folio, for £585 at the Ashburnham sale in 1898.[14]

What exactly was involved in this manufacture of cultural memory, and how effective was it in presenting a longer-term view, beyond the excitement of a few weeks or months? Certainly the various buildings and statues figured in editions of writers' works, sometimes as frontispieces, sometimes as title-page decorations, and sometimes more extensively. If the attention was gained of those responsible for assembling national or other large libraries, what of individuals? What bibliographical aids were provided? Publishing mechanisms, an interest in past manifestations in print, the arrangements and practices of the book trade both new and second-hand, and the treatment of inherited volumes, all contributed to the development of memory that always further depended on a diverse mixture of other inheritance.

Burns had some claim to be a special case. He enjoyed a uniquely enthusiastic following among Scots alike in the home country and among the diaspora. Bibliographically, he had been much reprinted, but the earliest editions were few, and the first edition of his poems, printed in a modest edition at Kilmarnock in 1786, was one of the famous rarities in literature. By the time of his death in 1796 just six editions had appeared, printed variously in London, Dublin, Belfast and Edinburgh, and not all that had been included in the Belfast edition was by him. By the centenary of his birth in 1859 there were dozens of editions, some costing as little as one penny and others for bibliophiles. There were editions illustrated by Bewick and other artists, and many contained accounts of his life. In 1866, James McKie, a bibliophile printer in Kilmarnock, hit on the idea of a type facsimile of the original edition, to be printed in what he described in the prospectus as 'Founts of the same Type, and *sorts*, with which the original Kilmarnock Edition was printed' and 'with paper made of the same antique quality, and done up in the original style, Paper Boards, Edges uncut', price 12s.6d. a copy. It was published in the same format and binding style as the catalogue of his private library, which included a bibliography of Burns based on his own collection.[15] Meanwhile in London, the West End booksellers Willis & Sotheran had become enthusiastic, and arranged with McKie for fifty copies of the type facsimile to be printed on large paper, at a price of 2 guineas. While this stretched the concept of a facsimile, it made very clear that Burns had a fashionable and wealthy following. Book collecting was not just about owning early editions but also about special and distinctive ones, where values might be at least as much social as bibliographical.

Scott's inheritance was equally self-conscious; but while he and Burns both offered comfort and encouragement to Scottish national identity, bibliographically they were utterly different. Scott's creation of his own image, the writer immersed in the physical memorabilia of antiquity (however much of it was phoney), the creator of a fine country house at Abbotsford and a man whose financial embarrassments both added further to his reputation and led to ever more publications, all created a portrait that thousands of readers found irresistible. He had a greater European following than almost any writer in English other than Shakespeare and Byron. The biography of Burns was soon told, and regularly figured in volumes of his poems. The first edition of J.G. Lockhart's much reprinted *Life* of his father-in-law Sir Walter Scott, published in 1837–8, occupied seven volumes. The first statue erected to his memory was not in Edinburgh, but in George Square in Glasgow, where John Greenshield's statue of 1837 was erected on top of a column once intended for George III, to join Flaxman's statue (1819) of the Glaswegian John Moore, hero of the battle of Corunna. The much more elaborate Scott monument, designed by George Kemp and dominating Princes Street in Edinburgh, came later, in 1840–6.[16]

Documentation

The archival documentation lying behind the production and sale of most early printed books for many years attracted little attention. While ambitious national general projects had been established, including the publication under the authority of the Public Record Office, beginning in 1856, of the British *Domestic state papers*, followed in 1858 by the first of the Rolls Series (so called because they were publications of the Master of the Rolls[17]) of chronicles, hundreds of smaller archives awaited discovery. Abroad it was the same, and often on a much larger scale. The *Monumenta Germaniae historica* was founded in 1819.[18] In 1846–7 the École des Chartes in France, founded originally in 1821, was reorganised and its funds trebled.[19] The first volume of the *Collections des documents inédits sur l'histoire de France* appeared in 1835, under the auspices of the Comité des Travaux Historiques launched by Guizot only a few months earlier.[20] Commercial and trade archives attracted less attention than political ones, and medieval ones at first attracted more attention than later ones. Modern interests were served by such ambitious projects as Wellington's despatches (12 volumes, 1834–9) and Napoleon's correspondence and other papers (32 volumes, 1858–69).

In contrast, the historical resources of the early modern book trades were unearthed and published only slowly in a development that took root and flourished in the last three decades of the century. In the early 1880s an occasional series in *The Bibliographer* noted the more prominent relevant documents in the *Calendar* of domestic state papers, but it was very selective. For those interested in the subject, two major resources were readily accessible by then. They were drawn from the Stationers' Company in London, and from the Plantin archives in Antwerp. Neither of the ambitious editions prepared from parts of these large archives in the late nineteenth century has been wholly superseded today.

Both Joseph Ames in 1749 and John Nichols in 1797[21] had used the London Stationers' Company archives. John Payne Collier was entirely correct in realising their importance, when in 1848–9 he printed extracts from the early register as publications of the Shakespeare Society.[22] But his inaccurate and misleading transcription did not even tally with his own account of his methods of selection,[23] and it was further infected by insertions of his own invention.[24] When almost three decades later in 1875 Edward Arber presented his much more comprehensive transcript, covering the years to 1640, he had a more general purpose in mind:

How far the Registers are deficient as a record of their total contemporaneous Literature, and the why and wherefore thereof? Who were the greatest publishers? Who were the greatest printers? What kind of books were generally issued by each publisher? . . . Meanwhile it is certain that this *Transcript* will inaugurate an era of yet still more scientific and exhaustive study and research into the Mind-World of that Age: and that from henceforward no one will pretend to be a master of this section of our literature who has not made its chief contents his own possession.[25]

Though involved and incomplete, the surviving Stationers' Company archives had the merit of mostly retaining their historic order. The books printed by Christophe Plantin and his successors from 1555 onwards had long been a target for collectors. In 1866 Charles-Louis Ruelens and Augustin De Backer's annotated *Annales plantiniennes*, partly modelled on Renouard's work on the Aldus dynasty and the Estiennes, at last gave some bibliographical shape to the early output.[26] The old wooden presses and typographical materials in the printing house remained much as they had for generations. The purchase by the city of Antwerp of the family's prominent renaissance town house and its contents, including three centuries of documentation, preceded the opening in 1877 of the first museum in the world devoted to the history of printing. It was followed in 1882 by Max Rooses's massive exploration of the firm's history and archives: an astonishing achievement in so short a time, it has still not been wholly overtaken by more recent work.[27]

The partly dispersed papers of Christophe Plantin and his successors were much more complicated than the London Stationers' Company, and when Rooses embarked on an edition of Plantin's correspondence between 1555 and 1589 (published 1883–1918), he faced a very different task.[28] While many of the letters had been preserved together, others were scattered. The sequence was incomplete: some letters or transcripts were in Plantin's hand, some in the hands of copyists. The surviving incoming correspondence was thin and patchy: Rooses estimated that there were only a few dozen incoming examples. There were several languages involved: French, Latin and Spanish. In all, it was a considerably more complicated editing task than that faced by Arber for the Stationers' Company. In most of his work, Arber's guiding principle was the diffusion of English literature,[29] but his comprehensive approach, to publish the registers more or less in their entirety, meant that he offered a much more general panorama.

Yet both archives possessed one thing in common. They offered the documentary basis of two critical parts of the sixteenth-century book trade: one domestic, in that the Stationers' Company usually had little interest in affairs beyond the shores of Britain, and the other spreading across large parts of western Europe. No one had published such systematic extended archives hitherto, and both editions remain standard today.

On a much more limited scale, J.P. Edmond searched the university and (with more success) town records for his work on early printers in Aberdeen. This was a more traditional approach, a search for particular information rather than the wholesale publication of records indifferent to whether they could be precisely attached to specific publications or episodes.[30]

One of Arber's principal motives in studying the Stationers' archives was to determine what had been published, including what had not survived. The same concern to recover bibliographical records inspired the first publication of a document dating from the 1470s–80s discovered in the archives of the monastery of San Jacopo di Ripoli at Florence at the end of the eighteenth century. Vincenzio Fineschi's *Notizie storiche sopra la stamperia di Ripoli le quali possono al'illustrazione della storia tipografica fiorentina* (1781) mostly listed the titles of books recorded in these accounts, with a few assorted details on the prices of paper and other printing necessities. Both of Fineschi's successors, Ferdinando Fossi in the 1790s and Francesco Roediger in 1887–9, used it for the same enumerative purposes, and it was only when Pietro Bologna turned his attention to the document in 1892–3 that serious attention was paid to its wider implications for the history of printing and the trade in printed books.[31]

By then, Horatio Brown's study of early Venetian printing had demonstrated the importance of archival research in ways not pursued by Arber. The son of Scottish parents and educated at Clifton and Oxford, Brown (1854–1926) was never a part of the circle of people in Britain who were transforming the study of early printing.[32] He had no bibliographical training, and his skills were more as a historian. Yet in fundamental respects he was pioneering in the study of early printed books. In 1879 he settled in Venice, and there devoted much of his time to the city's archives. Among the state papers in the Frari he found the records of the Venetian Inquisition, and these seem to have been the inspiration for his substantial book on *The Venetian printing press. An historical study based upon documents for the most part hitherto unpublished*, published by J.C. Nimmo in 1891. He was presumably drawn to Nimmo as the publisher also of his close friend John Addington Symonds, for Nimmo showed little other interest in the subject.[33] By 1891 the relevance of contemporary documentation to the history of the book trade had become recognised in Venice, where the wealth of surviving regulatory archives invited transcription and publication. Most importantly, these archives were readily accessible for public inspection. Rinaldo Fulin's *Nuovi documenti per servire alla storia della tipografia Veneziana* had appeared in *Archivio Veneto* in 1882, printing a notebook of book prices compiled by the bookseller and publisher Antonio Moretto at Padua in 1480.[34] Carlo Castellani's *La stampa in Venezia dalla sua origine alla morte di Aldo Manuzio seniore* was published in 1889.

Fulin, Castellani and Brown were all writing before the publication of Bologna's work on Florence. Although Brown alluded to the Ripoli accounts, and quoted from them, his reference was to Fineschi, in 1781. Brown drew his landscape more broadly than Bologna. Fulin, Castellani and their predecessors offered transcripts, eager to show that Germany was not the only country to be able to produce documentation on early printing. Brown offered more. He used over half of his book to publish several series of documents relating to the Venetian trade, a more extensive selection than any published hitherto. Among other materials, these included the laws of the Republic concerning printing and the book trade; a survey of monopolies and other privileges; the matriculation book and various other documents from the Guild of Printers; papers concerning relations between the Curia and the republic; and a list of prosecutions drawn from the archives of the Venetian Inquisition. While his trawl was not comprehensive, it demonstrated a fresh thoroughness in the history of the subject, an approach all the richer thanks to the extraordinary Venetian archives. It showed how these records permitted a contextual account beyond one dependent on the examination of surviving printed books and the more obvious immediately related documents. The last of the transcripts consisted of considerable extracts from the accounts of a Venetian bookseller of 1484, rediscovered in 1810. This had been written about briefly in 1885 by the director of the archives at the Frari, but Brown was the first to use it extensively.[35]

In 1895 Lord Acton reflected more generally on the great changes that had occurred in the nineteenth century in the opening up and publication of the national archives. Although only one among many, the opening of the Vatican archives was for him a key turning point, notwithstanding the fact that, as he pointed out, others were richer. All would lead to a revolution in knowledge. And yet, he wrote, 'We are still at the beginning of the documentary age.'[36] He pursued a similar theme a few months later, in proposing a new world history to be published by Cambridge University Press: 'All information is within reach, and every problem has become capable of solution.'[37] In setting the Plantin correspondence, the records of the London Stationers' Company, and documents from the Venetian archives before the public, the stage was similarly set for a wider reconsideration of the early book trade and of what had survived. In these and in further projects over the coming years, the understanding of early printed books was not only supplemented; as for Acton in his wider landscape, it was also enhanced, modified and altered sometimes dramatically.

18 | The Next Generation

The late 1880s brought a concatenation of events in the world of books that identifies these few years as a period of especially rapid and fundamental change. People were well aware of it at the time, and wrote about it explicitly. Henry Wheatley was one of the most experienced observers of a period marked by obvious difference. 'We must remember', he wrote in 1886, 'that year by year old and curious books become scarcer, and the number of libraries where they are locked up increase; thus while the demand is greater, the supply diminishes, and the price naturally becomes higher.'[1] Much the same could be said if one took a longer view, but Wheatley was addressing a single generation. In the same year Percy Fitzgerald was not only seeking to justify another book about collecting when he wrote in the preface to *The book fancier* that

Within the last few years there has been a revival of the old and elegant taste of the book-fancier, as well as of that passion or faith which is described with such aimiable enthusiasm in the little tract of Richard of Bury.

He went on to write expressedly of John Hill Burton, 'perhaps the first in our time to deal popularly with such matters', and Andrew Lang as 'the latest to illustrate this subject from his abundant stores of knowledge'.

Fitzgerald has been quoted several times already. Born in Ireland in 1834, he trained as a lawyer and after practising there he moved to London. He made little progress in this new environment until, by his own account, he was befriended by John Forster to whom he volunteered a quantity of material for Forster to use in the biography of Swift on which he was then engaged. Forster in turn introduced him to others, and Fitzgerald developed a career as a prolific journalist, contributing to *Household words*, *All the year round* and others. By the time his *Recreations of a literary man, or Does writing pay?* was published in 1882, he had written well over forty other books, an assortment of literary biographies, novels, histories, religious works, plays and accounts of the stage. He was to continue his pace, not dying until 1925.[2]

The book fancier quoted partly from his earlier work. It appeared amidst what had developed into a genre of writing for a new generation of book collectors and enthusiasts. They had little to do with the scholarly themes as pursued by Bradshaw and others in London, Cambridge, Oxford, Paris, The Hague, Berlin and elsewhere. Instead, this new genre appealed to people who might be collecting in their own modest ways, or who were curious about related subjects beyond their own opportunities or purses. Few people could expect to buy early editions of Shakespeare or Milton, but there was much pleasure to be had at a remove, as understanding of the changes in books and their contents gradually developed among the wider population. Half a dozen books were addressed to amateur bibliophiles, mostly consisting of lightweight gossip of the kind contemporaries liked to call 'agreeable'.

Lang's *The library*, 'with a chapter on modern English illustrated books by Austin Dobson', was published by Macmillan in May 1881 at 3s.6d. in the 'Art at home series' edited by W.J. Loftie. Discursive, informed and interspersed with practical suggestions about the care of books, it found a ready market, stereotyped for a reprint in July and also issued in a large paper edition the same year at 10s.6d. An enlarged edition on ordinary and large paper followed in 1892. Lang, former Fellow of Merton College, Oxford, had still to make his name as an anthropologist and supremely successful popular writer: by 1881 he had published some minor verse and was still known best as a minor journalist and translator of Greek texts. The first of his celebrated *Fairy books* for children did not appear until 1889.

If *The library* was slight by Lang's scholarly standards, presumably bringing useful income, it also proved to be the inspiration of a succession of like-minded books over the following few years, as authors and publishers tapped into a national mood. Lang himself gathered some of his essays together in *Books and bookmen* (1886), also for the middling bibliophile market and likewise available on large paper. In 1888 he adapted an anthology *Ballads of books* by the American Brander Matthews, Longmans issuing it under the same title. This particular corner had little to offer: 'It will not', wrote Lang, 'escape the reader that few very great poets have written like bibliophiles.' That did not prevent other anthologists in the next few years. More substantially, we have seen that in 1883 J.H. Slater produced his *Library manual*, the first of his brief handbooks offering information about prices and trends in collecting: even if they were aware, few people seem to have cared about his inaccuracies or omissions, for the books sold to a consistent audience.

Ireland's *The book-lover's Enchiridion: thoughts on the solace and companionship of books, and topics incidental thereto* (1883), an anthology of reflections on the pleasures to be obtained from reading and associated activities, began in the Old Testament with Solomon. It was the work of a Manchester printer, and prompted immediate further demand. A third edition, much enlarged, was published by October 1883, in an edition of 3,700 copies, and a fourth edition, again enlarged, appeared late the following year. Copies were to be had not only in ordinary cloth but also in parchment embossed in gold, price 10s.6d. (compared with 6s. for plain copies) 'suitable for an elegant gift-book'. Ireland worked hard to market his book, not only sending review copies to an unusually wide range of journals, and then printing the favourable notices, but also sending copies to well-known public figures in order to elicit further recommendations: the Crown Princess of Germany, James Russell Lowell, Oliver Wendell Holmes, John Morley, Frederic Harrison and Robert Louis Stevenson were among those to whom were attributed the commendations thereupon printed. His anthology proved a useful resource for speakers, including Sir John Lubbock, who milked it for a lecture delivered to the London Working Men's College in Great Ormond Street, and then included the lecture in his much reprinted collection *The pleasures of life*, which within fifteen months of first publication in June 1887 went through twelve editions and printings. A reprint of Burton's *Book-hunter*, published by Blackwood's in 1885 was an obvious next step for publishers in a thriving market.

In 1886 Elliot Stock launched his popular and wide-ranging series *The Book-lover's library*. Some of the volumes were valuable and original, while others were little more than lightweight pot-boilers. It was edited by the indefatigable Wheatley, and within a decade or so included some books that offered material of more than passing interest. It began with Wheatley's own *How to form a library*, and extended the field systematically, initially in 1887 with books on dedications and on modern methods of book illustration. In that year a new and enlarged edition of William Blades's impassioned and much quoted *Enemies of books* replaced the third and earlier editions that had been published by Trübner: it had first appeared in 1881, and in its several subsequent editions was to develop a larger, and probably more dispersed, readership than any other of the books mentioned here. In the persons of Wheatley and of Blades, there was a continuation and a connection with the older world of Bradshaw, who had worked with both men.

As a much more seriously scholarly project, in 1888 John MacAlister, recently appointed librarian of the Royal Medical and Chirurgical Society, founded a new journal, *The Library*, using it to present a mixture of bibliographical topics and news of occurrences in the wider world of libraries of all kinds.[3] For its first several years it was the organ of the Library Association, until it became clear that too many of the professional concerns of librarianship were incompatible within a single body, or within a single journal, with the work being developed by a new generation for whom the study of books meant something quite different. These formative years were further marked in 1888 with a new edition of Richard de Bury's fourteenth-century *Philobiblon*. This was the work of Ernest C. Thomas, who went to considerable lengths to consult the manuscript tradition: he claimed to have inspected all thirty-five manuscripts then known. His was the first edition to be published in England since that of Thomas James in 1598 and its editorial progress was marked by various bulletins by Thomas in the *Library Chronicle*, which he edited as Honorary Secretary of the Library Association. Better known by repute than in fact, *Philobiblon* was hardly a best-seller. In 1832 Thomas Rodd, one of London's leading antiquarian booksellers, had published a translation by J.B. Inglis. The only other modern edition of the original had appeared at Paris in 1856, and Thomas, ever critical, seized several opportunities to castigate it. Now he provided both an annotated text and a translation. Notwithstanding his using the pages of the *Library Chronicle* for his own purposes when he needed, he clearly preferred to keep his life in separate compartments. All correspondence with the journal was via the printer. In 1885 Stevens & Haynes published the second edition of his *Leading cases in constitutional law*. When he came to the title-page of *Philobiblon*, he was 'Barrister-at-law, late scholar of Trinity College, Oxford and Librarian of the Oxford Union.' He dated his preface from the seaside town of Sheringham, in Norfolk, and maintained his tart comments about others' work to the end, decrying the cheap and inaccurate reprint that had just appeared in Henry Morley's *Universal library*.

Mostly priced at a very few shillings and some also available on large paper or in special bindings, reflecting market tastes, these books came from several different publishers. While Elliot Stock remained the leading figure, other major firms also ventured into what had identified itself as a distinct clientele. Trübner, publisher of Blades, died in 1884. Now Macmillan, Routledge, Longman, Simpkin Marshall and Sampson Low all contributed to this particular kind of popular bibliophily. As a measure of national interest, whether in early books, modern books, or books more generally, this publishing trend was of only limited value. Notwithstanding work on Caxton, Edmond on Scotland and Brown on Venice, when early books were mentioned they came from a strictly circumscribed field.

In France, bibliophile taste had taken a quite different course,[4] while Claudin and others pursued the history of French printing. There was little to compare with the procession of popular books on bibliophile subjects that were published in England. The essays of Octave Uzanne, *Caprices d'un bibliophile* (1879) were addressed to similar audiences: in the words of its advertising, 'Ce n'est plus de la bibliographie aride, mais de la bibliophile amusante et gaie.'[5] But while publishers such as Champion, Lemerre and Rouveyre all took historically inclined interest, there was no dominating activist such as Wheatley, and no publisher as committed to this kind of popular bibliographical instruction as Elliot Stock. Blades's *The enemies of books* was translated and published as *Les livres et leurs ennemis* by Claudin in 1883. In Paris, the traditions established by the prolific Paul Lacroix found expression in his various essays, while a much more thoughtful contribution to the field, linking past practices to modern policy, was to be seen in Lemerre's slim *Le livre du bibliophile* of 1874.

The contrast between some of these publications and *The Library*, published by Kegan Paul, became ever greater, reflected in the impetus to found the Edinburgh Bibliographical Society in 1890, followed in London by the Bibliographical Society two years later.[6]

Libraries

For better or worse, some major libraries faced fundamental changes. In Oxford, Henry Octavius Coxe, Bodley's Librarian since 1860, much cherished and the author of several still essential catalogues of Oxford manuscripts, died in 1881 after a period of decline.[7] He was succeeded by the thirty-three-year-old Edward W. B. Nicholson, who in 1888 produced a sixty-six page report on the Library since 1882 that was largely taken up with reforms and steps towards modernisation intended to replace older, less organised and more easy-going ways.[8] Not the least of his problems was the confused and incomplete catalogue, the result of divergences in practices and policies over many years but still not to be wholly tamed under Nicholson. The challenge was only successfully met in the following century. As expenditure on books declined, so anxiety in the University mounted, and in 1888 an appeal was addressed to the Curators that the Library should pay more attention to foreign purchases and to filling in gaps in the collections from the second-hand market.[9] These were years for reflection. In 1887 Richard Garnett spoke to the Library Association about changes at the British Museum in the past ten years. Most of his remarks, generally confident in tone, concerned changes in cataloguing and in acquisition statistics, but he had soon afterwards to report that the government purchase grant to the British Museum was reduced by two-fifths, in all departments. Garnett summarised the result for printed books, where purchases had as a consequence to be confined to new books and periodicals, and that 'little or nothing can be done towards supplying deficiencies in the Library'.[10]

Beyond the national collections in these financially lean years, public libraries in 1887 presented a mixed picture. Many towns had still not adopted the legislation that permitted a penny rate. In local votes, Croydon and Gloucester both rejected it in that year. Croydon adopted it a year later, but in 1888 votes were lost at Glasgow, Taunton and Tunbridge Wells, while some parts of London finally agreed to promote what had been legislated for almost forty years previously. Meanwhile, in other authorities new library buildings were erected, in Swansea, Windsor, Cheltenham, Ipswich, Wimbledon and elsewhere. Swansea over-reached itself, and after building costs were defrayed there was no money to buy new books.[11] In Edinburgh, where discussions were also beginning to focus on the need for a national library, the foundation stone was laid by Andrew Carnegie for an ambitious new building for the public library. At Cardiff it was agreed to build an extension, besides a museum and art gallery. These were events of major local importance, sometimes to be marked by prominent public figures. The foundation stone of the new library in Bethnal Green was laid by the King of the Belgians, and at Swansea the new library, replacing that used since 1878, was opened by Gladstone.

In budgets of public money that were always tight, most effort had to be spent on collections of modern books, whether for reference or for borrowing, or for newspapers. Gifts, often of several thousand volumes, played a large part in development. After the widow of the physicist James Clerk Maxwell presented his books to Cambridge public library, they were divided up, Cambridge retaining a few hundred and the important Scottish parts being sent to the Mitchell Library in Glasgow and the public library in Edinburgh; the remaining duplicates were sold.[12] At Birmingham, the valuable Shakespeare Memorial Library was lost in a disastrous fire of 1879, when a large collection of Cervantes presented by the engineer William Bragge in 1873 was also destroyed. Both collections were partly rebuilt, and to them were added John Milton and Byron, each developed from private gifts. Like one or two others, including Manchester and Wigan, Birmingham interpreted its role as reaching far beyond the widely recognised duty to cover local history and topography, and the everyday needs of ordinary borrowing. Early printed books were placed within its remit.

Not everyone welcomed this hospitable attitude. At Liverpool, in 1887 Sir James Picton, Chairman of the committee charged with libraries, the museum and art gallery, presented a report on work accomplished since 1850. Income from rates had been reduced by about £900 a year, and ratepayers declined to sanction an increase to 1¼d. He reported dejectedly of his fellow-citizens that the town council had recently refused to grant £6,000 for the purchase of the collections of the late Joseph Mayer (d.1886). Mayer had already given his then collection of antiquities and ceramics to Liverpool in 1867, a year after he had endowed a library at Bebbington. In Picton's view, this refusal twenty years later would cripple the work of institutions founded only recently 'amidst the plaudits and acclamations of the community'. Together with his remaining collections of antiquities and works of art, Mayer's library was auctioned at Liverpool at the end of 1887.[13]

1886–1887

The major auction sales of the 1880s provoked a rash of newspaper reports, but for many in the library world other events in the opening months of 1886, a year characterised internationally by socialist and communist unrest, seemed far more significant. Within a few weeks, three of the most influential people in the bibliographical world died: Edward Edwards, secluded and impoverished in retirement on the Isle of Wight, died on 7 February; Henry Bradshaw died in his rooms in King's College, Cambridge, on 11 February; and Henry Stevens died on 28 February. None of these men had figured extensively in the work of the several authors of popular bibliophily, but their influence on public knowledge and on the public provision of books was no less absolute. Bradshaw's reach was international, and the range of newspapers and journals in Britain offering obituaries was some guide to his reputation, even if it did not mean that his published work had been as widely read. Notices appeared not only in the local Cambridge press and the professional library press but also in more general publications. Hessels and the liturgist F.E. Warren wrote in the *Academy*, and Arthur Benson in *Macmillan's Magazine*. The *Athenaeum*, the *Saturday Review* (by J.W. Clark), *The Times* and the *Daily Telegraph* all carried obituaries, and William Blades wrote in the *Printers' Register*. The publication three years later of his collected papers, edited by Francis Jenkinson, and particularly of his biography by G.W. Prothero, prompted their own reviews and further reflection.[14]

While Bradshaw and his memory were revered in Cambridge and among many outside, and some of his work appeared with that of others,[15] for most of the wider world his influence on the bibliography of early printing ripened only gradually. He had never sought a general public readership while alive, and his influence was in the end felt at a remove. His name was commemorated in the Henry Bradshaw Society, founded in 1890 for the publication of early liturgical texts. In the same year the first volume appeared of the *Transactions* of the new Guild and School of Handicraft, founded in east London on Ruskinian principles. It was edited by C.R. Ashbee, who graduated from King's College in the year of Bradshaw's death and acknowledged him in the dedication: 'in loving mindfulness of many lessons learnt, to the memory of Henry Bradshaw'. Among more bibliographical circles, Wheatley, friend and ally over several years, had lost the support for which he might have looked in launching his new project: 'I had hoped to dedicate this first volume of the Book Lover's Library to Henry Bradshaw, one of the most original and most learned bibliographers that ever lived, but before it was finished the spirit of that great man had passed away.'[16] Edward Gordon Duff, a far better scholar than Wheatley, was still an undergraduate at Wadham College, Oxford, and in 1893 dedicated his *Early printed books* to Bradshaw's memory. Duff had never met Bradshaw, in whose shadow he worked when he began to catalogue the incunabula in the Bodleian: Bradshaw had compiled a similar list in the 1860s, but fell out over it with the Librarian, H.O. Coxe.[17]

Of those who died that February, Henry Stevens had come into wide public prominence when in 1878 he issued his detailed catalogue of the Bibles exhibited at the Caxton exhibition the previous year. But it was Francis Fry (b.1803) who had for many years devoted much of his spare time to collecting and studying early English Bibles in particular. He died on 12 November 1886, only a few months after the others just mentioned.[18] Unlike Bradshaw, Edwards and Stevens, he was not a professional in the world of books. A member of the chocolate and cocoa manufacturing family in Bristol, and descended from the typefounders Joseph and Edmund Fry, much of his career had also involved such matters as railway investment and the Bristol water supply. In the course of thirty-odd years he assembled perhaps the largest collection of early English Bibles in private hands, comparable with the collections of the bookseller George Offor (1787–1864)[19] and Lea Wilson (1801–46).[20] In correspondence with

Stevens, James Lenox of New York and other collectors and scholars, he gave especial attention to William Tyndale (of whose New Testament of 1525 he published a lithographed facsimile in 1862), Cranmer and the King James version of 1611.

For his study of the Great Bible of 1539 and its successors, he examined 146 copies, and showed how, in the course of successive printings, sheets had become mixed as printers strove to make up the large number of copies required. The principle was valid, but it is now impossible to determine the true extent of this practice. Partly at Fry's hands (he was by no means the only culprit), surviving copies have been so supplemented, reorganised and rebound at the behest of booksellers and collectors in mistaken efforts to make as many perfect copies as possible that evidence of sixteenth-century practices has been lost. In concentrating attention on exchanging leaves, without taking account that in a folio volume printers print not one but two leaves together, evidence has been further confused.

As a bibliophile, Fry's own inclinations were also reflected in the provision he made for publishing some of his work. In what seems to have been a pioneering arrangement, which was later to develop into a practice of creating 'leaf books' that all too often involved the destruction of important early books, leaves emanating from the 1539 and later Bibles were added to his work on the Great Bible.[21] He arranged for a few copies of his study of the 1539 Bible to be printed on parchment priced at £20 (four times the price of ordinary copies), and of his account of the Coverdale Bible (1867) there were copies on both ordinary and large paper, as well as parchment.[22] Copies of the facsimile of what was then believed to be the unique perfect copy of Tyndale's New Testament were available on two sizes of paper and on parchment. In 1890 most of his Bibles were bought by the British and Foreign Bible Society,[23] but key bibliographical evidence all too often had been destroyed.

While in many ways the bibliographical, bookselling and bibliophilic worlds had always to look forward, in 1887 Talbot Baines Reed (1852–93) brought a sense of both closure and of the opening of a new chapter with his magisterial *History of the old English letter foundries*.[24] Ten years earlier, he had played a key part in organising the exhibition celebrating the anniversary of Caxton's first printing at Westminster. His work on the exhibition was an extraordinary achievement for a young man of only twenty-five. The chairman of the executive committee for this project was his father Sir Charles Reed, partner in the family firm of typefounders. The younger Reed sat on the sub-committee responsible for assembling the sections on typefounding, stereotyping and other equipment, and he wrote the catalogue entries for the first part of this. The task was slightly different from those who were charged (like Blades) with writing about Caxton, or (like Henry Stevens) with Bibles, or (like the printer Andrew Tuer) with the products of printing by steam. He had a long period to cover, and he did so using technical evidence. Though visual changes were a key ingredient, they were not the whole. So far as visitors to the exhibition were concerned, the lessons and the attractions were limited to what was visible in the showcases. Reed's own approach was subtle and informed. It was inspired by Blades, who in 1875 had gathered together a group of his pioneering articles published in the *Printers' Register* concerning early type specimens.[25] At the core of Reed's section in 1877 was a group of well over a hundred examples, some as sheets, others as books:

> A collection of type specimens contains, in proportion to its completeness, a history both exhaustive and simple. In any survey of the rise and progress of Typography the primary reference is naturally made to such an authority, not only as giving details of names, places, and dates, but as disclosing the development of an invention, the cultivation of an industry, and the advance of an art, by marked stages, from its crude beginning to its present refinement.[26]

In other words, contemporary evidence was key. It was not sufficient simply to work backwards. Only in this way could the significance of successive inventions be understood, and only in this way could changes in taste and design be followed. To a procession of specimens from Britain and abroad he added technical support: punches, matrices and type from Fell's press in seventeenth-century Oxford, eighteenth-century equipment from the Caslon foundry, and more recent equipment from Edmund Fry and from the Fann Street Foundry, in which his father was partner. A group of pieces of equipment said to have been used by the eighteenth-century punchcutter J.M. Fleischmann was lent by Enschedé, in Haarlem. The printers William Blades, Andrew Tuer and James Fenton all contributed to the exhibition of specimens from founders and printers, Enschedé being particularly generous in providing for the Netherlands and Belgium. The London Institution lent the then sole known copy of the specimen and sale catalogue of the uniquely important record assembled in the course of the eighteenth century by the founders John James and his father.[27]

All this came together in Reed's *History of the old English letter foundries*, a natural fit for Elliot Stock as publisher during the 1880s and 1890s of antiquarian and bibliographical books and journals. The book was written over several years, amidst other occupations as typefounder, novelist and founding editor of the *Boy's Own Paper*. By the mid-1880s the world of typefounding was facing what Reed knew to be a revolution, with the invention of new machines for typecasting and composition, and the application of pantographic engraving machines to replace hand-engraved punches.[28] A typecasting machine was patented by Frederick Wicks of *The Times* in 1881, and two years later he developed a typesetting machine. It was but the latest in a series of more or less successful machines designed to dispense with the labour of hand casting and hand composition. The printing exhibition at the Agricultural Hall in 1883 featured the Winder machine for composition and distribution. In 1886 the new Linotype composing machine was installed in the *New York Tribune*. 'At such a time,' wrote Reed, 'it seems not undutiful to attempt to gather together into a connected form the numerous records of the Old English Letter Foundries' (p. v).[29] The book was a considerable triumph for a person still in his mid-thirties, and in its revised form of 1952 it remains unsurpassed, the standard work on its subject. Reed overworked himself, in 1892 agreeing also to become the first secretary of the Bibliographical Society. He died the following year at the age of only forty-one.

In Britain, prior to Blades and Reed, no one employed in the printing or related trades had set down this aspect of the history of these subjects so clearly. Joseph Moxon in 1683–4 had written about punchcutting and typefounding, but not about the history.[30] Edward Rowe Mores in the eighteenth century was an amateur antiquary. In France, Fournier's *Manuel typographique* (1764–6) pre-dated him and was the work of a practising printer. Thirty years later, the bookseller A.M. Lottin presented a summary list of Parisian typefounders down to 1788, with notes of many of the specimens they issued.[31] But neither Fournier nor Lottin achieved anything like the depth or range of Reed.

Reed's work was exceptional in a more general way. He was distinctly unusual in attempting a detailed, original and comprehensive history that spanned the fifteenth to the nineteenth centuries. Few other writers, either in Britain or on the continent, attempted such a challenge concerning aspects of the history of printing and to do so in a profoundly scholarly manner. There was plenty, albeit of very varied quality, on the fifteenth century; there was much on the sixteenth; and there was a smaller group of works on the seventeenth and eighteenth. Timperley had produced an overall account, but much of his work was little more than a chronology.[32] Reed produced a coherent and continuous study, documented according to the best materials available to him, covering more than four centuries.

Blades and Bradshaw had corresponded over many years; and though Reed acknowledged help from both men in his account of English typefounders, there had been fewer exchanges with Bradshaw. All three were formative influences on the next generation, as well as long subsequently; but it was a generational gap, not a gradual imparting of knowledge through meetings over many years. Of those in this next generation most interested in early printing and typography, Robert Proctor met Bradshaw only briefly, on perhaps a single occasion, and Edward Gordon Duff seems only once to have exchanged letters.

As for others, the person apart from Blades whom the young Duff most valued in compiling his annotated album of facsimiles *Early English printing* (1896) was a fellow Scotsman, John Philip Edmond, whose work on Aberdeen printers he regarded as one of the 'best monographs we possess', alongside Blades on Caxton.[33] It was high praise from a person much inclined to be critical. Edmond (1850–1906) was a relentlessly hard worker. He had been librarian to Lord Crawford since 1891, eight years after their first acquaintance, his knowledge and enthusiasm for the history of Scottish printing winning him assured approval. In 1883 he was with his father's firm of bookbinders and stationers in Aberdeen, and for much of his analysis of the earliest printers there he was self-taught. *The Aberdeen printers, Edward Raban to James Nichol* appeared in four parts in 1884–6, including some copies on large paper. It was pioneering in its unusually detailed bibliographical descriptions of each of the books under discussion, and the preface made clear where his inspiration lay:

> To the late Mr. Henry Bradshaw, Librarian of the University of Cambridge, I owe more than I can find words to express. Encouragement at the commencement, direction while in progress, and commendation bestowed in unmeasured terms – all this I received from the friend whose opinion I valued above all others.

Edmond became devoted to the library at Haigh and then at Balcarres, working endlessly to catalogue the enormous and ambitious collection. He was profoundly upset when the medieval manuscripts were sold en bloc to Mrs Rylands in Manchester, and in 1904 he became Librarian of the Signet Library in Edinburgh, where he continued to encourage work on the catalogue of Lord Crawford's printed books being prepared for publication at Aberdeen.[34] Though notably hospitable in receiving visitors to the Crawford library, he did not seek to be in the midst of his profession, either as a bibliographer or as a librarian: he remained closer to the Library Association than to the Bibliographical Society, which he never joined.

Organisation

During the 1880s and 1890s, activities and processes that had been piecemeal in the 1830s, and had remained so for much of the past fifty years, were given new organisational garbs. Most of these have been mentioned already, and together they offer a portrait of a new world. Much of this involved imaginative ways of thinking and fresh social approaches. It did not necessarily grow easily, and some of what was achieved was opportunist.

For antiquarian and second-hand booksellers, Clegg's *Directory*, first published in 1886, became the trade standard for well over half a century. For book auctions and many booksellers, *Book Prices Current* became an essential desk reference. For collectors, thanks to the prolific enthusiasm of Wheatley and others, supported especially but by no means exclusively by the publisher Elliot Stock, there was a range of manuals and introductions setting out help and suggestions. For autograph and manuscript collectors, the indiscipline of the mid-century was provided with new authority and shape. For the emergent new cast of librarians in the wake of the 1850 Act and fresh self-confidence in the major libraries, the formation of the Library Association in 1877 offered a professional home, albeit thus far one not always clearly focused. The new Edinburgh Bibliographical Society focused not on library management but on early Scottish books.[35] For people whether amateur or professional, concerned with the history of printing and of the book, the foundation in London of the Bibliographical Society brought together those of like interests in a group that organised both meetings and a programme of publications. Its initial limited membership of a little over two hundred was later abandoned, and no limit was set on numbers.

The Bibliographical Society, with its limited funds committed elsewhere, felt unable to undertake the full and properly ordered publication of what might have been most useful: a bibliographical survey of British books down to the seventeenth century that had been a central occupation of W.C. Hazlitt ever since 1866. Keenly aware of the inadequacies of Lowndes's work, even in Bohn's revision, Hazlitt accumulated detailed notes on thousands of books, and latterly had free access to the unique riches of Huth's library. In 1867 his *Handbook* on the subject was but the beginning, as a disorderly series of supplements appeared over the following decades. Though acknowledged for their accuracy, the various *Collections and notes* were awkward to use. Never consolidated, and thus unwelcoming to readers, Hazlitt's work sat on the open shelves of reference libraries, but remained more admired than used.[36]

For access to libraries, a new generation of specialist catalogues both reflected demand and stimulated historical research: in the British Museum, Bullen on English books to 1640 and Fortescue on the Thomason tracts were prominent examples, part of a programme that also saw catalogues published of the Museum's oriental printed books.[37] The Museum's and the Bodleian's holdings of incunabula were listed with those of the Museum in Proctor's *Index*.[38] Printed catalogues of the major public libraries became common from one end of the country to the other. Overseas, the launch in 1897 of Pellechet's union catalogue of incunables in France showed what might be done not only to aid readers searching for books but also (as she and Delisle hoped) as a tool for national library management.

In 1890 the interests of many of those most concerned in the world of books came together in a *conférence du livre* held at Antwerp. It was occasioned by the anniversary of the death of Christophe Plantin in 1589, and the year also marked the opening of two major institutions that further established Antwerp's cultural hegemony: the Royal Museum of Fine Arts and the Museum of Antiquities. The first was in a prominent new building, under construction since 1879. The second was in a new extension to the Steen, the old castle. The conference became the principal occasion marking the year. It was attended by almost two hundred people, predominantly from Belgium but also with a few from the Netherlands, France, Germany and elsewhere. Of the handful from England, Francis Jenkinson came from Cambridge, the Guildhall Librarian came from London and the head of the public library came from Leeds. Talbot Baines Reed came as a typefounder, and William Roberts as editor of *The Bookworm*. The list of delegates included librarians, archivists, bibliographers, printers, bookbinders, booksellers, educators, artists, lawyers and bibliophiles. Max Rooses, as Secretary-General, was instrumental in organising the occasion. While the conference could not be comprehensive in addressing all the delegates' assorted interests, it covered a great deal, including how the contents of books should be arranged, problems of theft and restitution, the international loan of books, customs charges, the need for catalogues of manuscripts, and the creation of national and international bibliographies, as well as matters concerning manufacture, notably standards for typefounding and the improvement of bindings. Much time was spent on the advisability of printing library catalogues, and on the need for readers to have access to catalogues: in this, some librarians remained as reluctant as their predecessors had been fifty and more years earlier. In the published verbatim report[39] there was much that was useful, some relevant only to some countries, and some that was unnecessarily fretful. Little was said about social organisation, such as the establishment of learned societies and professional associations; but as a whole the occasion revealed the preoccupations and anxieties of a wide range of the professionally informed and some of the general public in the midst of rapid change.

A concern specifically with the history of printing was expressed quite separately and differently in a series of catalogues and bibliographies. In America, much of the library of the printing and paper historian Joel Munsell (1808–80) had been acquired by the New York State Library, which in 1858 included his collection in a substantial catalogue of its books on bibliography, printing and engraving.[40] Copies of the catalogue were circulated to public libraries in Britain as well. In Pittsburgh, John Marthens in 1874 published a brief bibliography of printing in his journal *The Quadrat*. In Germany, the catalogue of the more general library of the Börsenvereins der Deutschen Buchhändler published in 1869 included a short section on the subject.[41] In 1877 the American printing press manufacturer Richard Hoe had printed privately a brief bibliography,[42] but by then a much more ambitious project was under way. On a far larger scale, and of long-term consequence, Quaritch introduced to each other the printer Charles William Henry Wyman and Edward Clements Bigmore, agent for books for the American government. Like William Blades, both men were assembling notes for a bibliography of the history and practice of printing. Helped by a group of like-minded enthusiasts including Theodor Goebel in Stuttgart, Frederik Muller in Amsterdam, Louis Mohr in Strasbourg and T.L. de Vinne in New York, in January 1876 they published the first part of their work in the *Printing Times and Lithographer*, a journal edited by Wyman. Most of the extensive annotations to the entries were written by another printer, John Southward. Their full *Bibliography of printing* appeared in three volumes in 1880–6, published by Quaritch and was immediately recognised as the international authority: it remains unsuperseded.

In 1891, using money from City charities, an institute intended for training in printing was founded in the parish of St Bride, Fleet Street, a few yards from the centre of Britain's newspaper industry. The new building was not opened until 1894, but after William Blades died in 1890 an opportunity was seen to support the training purposes with a library devoted to the history and practice of the subject. Encouraged by C.J. Drummond, one of the trustees, the Charity Commission sanctioned the purchase of Blades's library, price £975. Of this, £500 was subscribed by John Passmore Edwards (1823–1911), philanthropist and owner of the

Liberal newspaper *The Echo*, who saw the Institute as 'a beneficial link in the chain of educational agencies destined to raise, bind, and strengthen the nation'.[43] When Talbot Baines Reed died in November 1893 a further opportunity presented itself to extend the collection. His books had been assembled not least for the *History of the old English letter foundries*, and they included early works, representative of major printers, that had no place in Blades's more technical collection. Thus the two complemented each other, and Passmore Edwards again contributed £500 for Reed's assemblage. It was a fortunate conjunction. The deaths within a few months of each other of two of the most influential Londoners in printing and in the history of printing, the founding of a place dedicated to teaching modern practical work, the recognition that history and modern practice related to each other, the presence among the trustees of a person of sufficient vision and energy to pursue this, and the existence of a notably committed benefactor combined to found what became one of the world's most important libraries for its subject.[44]

Caring for Books

The category of scholar-librarian encompasses a wide range of emphases. Dibdin was librarian to Lord Spencer and eventually became incumbent of St Mary's, Bryanston Square in London. Hessels was only briefly on the staff of Cambridge University Library. Weale, on the staff of the South Kensington Museum for only a few years, is remembered by many as a pioneer historian of Flemish painting more than as an authority on early bookbindings. Holtrop and Campbell were both in charge of national libraries; Bradshaw was University Librarian at Cambridge, highly successful in some ways quite apart from his bibliographical studies, though not a natural administrator. Madden, in charge of the manuscripts at the British Museum, also pursued a productive and influential career as writer. Bullen was Keeper of Printed Books at the British Museum and professionally active outside the Museum as well. Delisle was the most remarkable of all, not only on account of his exceptional scholarly output but also because he had responsibility first for one of the greatest collections of manuscripts in any library, and then as the library's head.

Somehow they found time to produce work that has remained even today of fundamental importance to their subjects. Panizzi would be included here, save for the fact that, in running not just the Library but also, from 1856, the whole of the British Museum, he had little time for his own work after his editions of Boiardo (1830–4) and Ariosto (1834) and his brief later study *Che era Francesco da Bologna?* (1858). In uniting specialist knowledge at the highest level, administrative ability, and authority by virtue of their positions, these and others with similar combinations of skills created an environment of unique efficiency. As a principle of management, the complementary skills and understanding of scholar and librarian-administrator remained widespread until the late twentieth century.

Increasing professionalism stumbled into more formal organisations, where knowledge and experience could be shared and training encouraged. Apart from the Library Association, the Museums Association was established at York in 1889, the Bibliographical Society in 1892 and the Booksellers Association in 1895. Book collectors, always a heterogeneous body, overlapped with some of these, but on the whole remained independent. Their number included most shades of wealth, and their interests were endlessly diverse. Bibliophile societies proved especially popular in France, as new tastes in books were shared sociably in what has been called 'la frénésie bibliophilique'[45] between 1871 and 1900. The Société des Amis des Livres was founded in 1874; the short-lived Société des Bibliophiles Contemporains in 1889; the Société des Cent Bibliophiles in 1895; and the Société des XX, with an emphasis on *livres d'artiste*, in 1897.

Of the British booksellers, Quaritch dominated, master not just of the London trade but also of much of Europe. As successor to the older firms of Payne & Foss, Bohn, Thorpe and others he outshone them all. His catalogues, compiled by his staff, were not only encyclopaedic, with offerings from the earliest incunables to books in oriental languages and the most recent remainders. They also set standards for pricing, and they often led taste, in for example his catalogue of 1889, which included a much greater range of information on provenances than was usual. As major collectors emerged in the United States, he strove simultaneously to retain his old world customers as well as add new names overseas. Like Henry Stevens, he was deft in addressing change, though this was not always achieved without disagreements.

But he was not a scholar in the ordinary sense. In some ways he was behind the times in the emergent literature. Of this generation, by far the most scholarly bookseller was Anatole Claudin in Paris, who after a long series of shorter publications on the history of French printing in Paris and the provinces crowned his career with a four-volume large folio *Histoire de l'imprimerie en France au XVe et au XVIe siècle* (1900–14), printed in the grandest manner by the Imprimerie Nationale, full of reproductions of typefaces and woodcuts and including plates in colour. It was unwieldy, beautiful and, thanks to its format and weight, ill-designed as a standard reference work needing to be much consulted.[46] Claudin had organised his first auction sale under his own name in 1856, having worked for a time with H. Pouchin, and between 1858 and 1908 there appeared a series of retail catalogues entitled *Archives du Bibliophile* – the title making clear that these were more than ordinary catalogues.

All these people, whether librarians or booksellers, had the advantage that they were handling a great variety of old books every day. They did not depend on catalogues and special reading rooms.

Librarians, often dependent on public money, tend to be shy concerning what is not done. Much of the first part of this book was about library access: how readers could determine what was available. It was concerned with the inadequacies of the catalogues of several prominent institutions. Many of these were addressed by the Royal Commission on the British Museum in 1850, with the evident implication that some better means should be found in London.[47] Challenges remained. When in 1897 a printed catalogue of the Bibliothèque Nationale was launched, it was decided not to include most anonymous work, and this decision held throughout the long history of the catalogue's publication: volume 150, taking it to the end of the alphabet, appeared only in 1981.

In that people tend to be wary of announcements that libraries are discarding materials, it is understandable that few public statements are made. One challenge for the libraries of copyright deposit lay in the fact that much ephemeral or near-ephemeral material arrived along with work of more obvious long-term interest. Cambridge fell foul of Thomas Carlyle who in his evidence to the British Museum Commission of 1850, said of unwanted books that 'They pile them up in heaps: if anybody happen to want any of them, they are brought out; if after a certain number of years nobody wants them, they are lying there, and you can light the fires with them.' He confused Trinity College (which had no such policy) with the University Library, but the allegation was damaging enough.[48]

At both Cambridge and Oxford, it was decided in the 1860s that slighter publications should not be included in the main catalogues. In December 1860 the Bodleian Curators defined these as theological tracts printed for parochial distribution; lives of eminent persons abridged from larger biographies; elementary school-books; works of fiction, including anonymous novels and tales, and reprints for railway-station circulation; and plays and poetical pieces that were anonymous or appeared to be of trifling importance.⁴⁹ The decision by Coxe at Oxford was overturned in the 1880s by his reforming successor Nicholson, a change not welcomed by everyone. While Nicholson argued that 'no printed matter which the Library receives under the Act is valueless to posterity', one of the Curators took the opposite view: 'All this rubbish is to be catalogued, at an expense perhaps of one shilling a slip, when the thing catalogued is not worth the tenth part of a farthing.'⁵⁰ Compromise of a kind was reached when in 1896 the Curators decided that it should not be catalogued in detail. Cataloguing was not the only consideration. By the 1920s it was also a question of space, when a committee recommended that intake should be limited, and that publications 'which could in no circumstances advance knowledge' should be discarded.⁵¹ In Cambridge University Library, accumulations of minor publications that were not already catalogued were gathered in the mid-1860s into a group, much of which remained undescribed until the late twentieth century, while a supplementary catalogue was launched for minor materials received henceforth.⁵²

So much for contemporary or recent minor publications. For earlier materials similar conditions could be found: of collections not catalogued, or dependent on older and inadequate catalogues – the Thomason tracts offer a prime example. Not only apparently minor publications were treated in this way. Until the late twentieth century many of the books bequeathed by Grenville in 1846 were not added to the catalogue if they duplicated copies already in the Museum. These and other similar conscious decisions of policy are quite different from the delays in cataloguing collections that are a familiar part of any large library's acquisitions, and quite different from the Private Case of the British Library, containing erotic or legally banned books, which for many years was scarcely known to exist.⁵³ In Paris, the creation of *l'Enfer* at the Bibliothèque Nationale in the late 1830s similarly did not become general knowledge until in 1913 Guillaume Apollinaire and others publicised it for the first time.⁵⁴ The challenges facing the staff at the national library in Paris during the nineteenth century, and the pamphlets at Manchester, have already been mentioned. They are far from unique among large libraries.⁵⁵

By the late nineteenth century many of the features familiar in the main catalogues of major libraries were established. Sets of cataloguing rules were formalised, albeit by no means uniformly. Some were derived from Panizzi's rules of 1841, others from Charles Cutter's of 1876. In the Bodleian Library new rules were introduced in 1883, replacing those in use since the seventeenth century.⁵⁶ The newly printed British Museum catalogue enjoyed a justified reputation for its exceptional accuracy, and in its various published manifestations over the next several decades was to be confirmed as the first place in which to look for bibliographical details. Yet here and elsewhere, questions of access remained as they had for generations and as they were to do so in the future.

Conclusion

19 | Then and Now

In his inaugural address of 1892 as President of the new Bibliographical Society, W.A. Copinger, lawyer, collector of early printed Bibles and bibliographer of incunabula, turned naturally to the world from which the infant society was being formed.

The fashion of the age changes – what satisfies one generation is wholly inadequate for the requirements of the succeeding generation. Dibdin and Lowndes did much admirable and useful work, but their methods lacked the accurate principle which is the very life of Bibliography as now understood. The influence of a Bradshaw has been experienced, and his teaching, and that of others who have trodden closely in his footsteps, have produced a desire for a higher degree of accuracy than sufficed for a nation in the infancy of its bibliographical life and love. This desire after a more exact and accurate knowledge is not confined to Bibliography – it is the spirit of the age, and to be discerned in every department of study.

Everywhere there is a reconsideration of old facts as well as a discovery of new. Our old histories of England no longer answer the requirements of the age – they have passed out of date. Many of our received, and in some cases cherished, ideas as to the character of individuals and the parts they played in historical events have been ruthlessly destroyed, as well by the strict investigation of records and contemporary documents as by the spirit of criticism which is absolutely necessary for the writer who would clear up the difficulties arising in great measure from the acceptance of so many things on trust. Is this not illustrated in another branch of literature by Dr. Murray's 'New Critical Dictionary on Historical Principles'?[1]

Richard Monckton Milnes as a book collector, John Herbert Slater as a compiler of guides, Henry Bradshaw and Léopold Delisle as scholar-librarians, Richard Garnett as a librarian, Joseph Techener, Anatole Claudin and Bernard Quaritch as booksellers, Paul Lacroix as a journalist and bibliophile, William Blades as a printer, and Talbot Baines Reed as a typefounder, all recognised from their different standpoints a succession of changes in the world of old books. Yet they and others all pondered one thing in common: the printed book or the manuscript composed of paper or parchment, designed to be held in the hand, placed on a shelf, and organised in ways that had been developed since the fifteenth century – and before that in the case of medieval manuscripts. It was a product designed and manufactured in various ways at different periods, modified most obviously with the application of mechanised processes in the nineteenth century, but remaining recognisably the same product, always dependent on the same physical skills, techniques and resources of its readers.

In rehearsing some of the conclusions of this book, we return to questions often asked and that have many answers. How do we own the past? If reading, and thereby a measure of understanding, in some sense includes ownership, then how far does ownership encompass access? What are the means by which we understand the past? They are questions often heard among archaeologists and anthropologists, among lawyers, politicians and curators arguing over repatriation and restitution. They deserve to be asked much more insistently about how we read books and, now, about digital environments; for questions of use, ownership, interpretation and preservation relate closely to questions of the use and nature of the past. The trick in such questions is what we mean by the past: whether in its artefactual survival, in its oral or visual memory, in its digital records, in its changing political and social structures, in its social conventions and traditions, or in the changing landscape. In the most literal sense, the physical past is owned by individuals, groups or public bodies, where books and manuscripts are just one aspect. But it is always a selective past: we choose what to remember, what to preserve and how to see it; and therefore, by implication, what to discard, what to neglect, and thus eventually to forget.

The editorial processes of people such as Arber working on the Stationers' records, or Bradshaw working on medieval manuscripts and early printed books, are as selective in their own ways as decisions as to how much should be preserved and studied of a ruined medieval castle. After Bullen's catalogue of pre-1641 books in the British Museum, it was a further generation before there was the beginning of a full organised retrospective bibliography of the books that lay at the heart of Arber's work. Even then, it was concerned only with what had survived, not what could be shown to have been lost.[2] Medieval and renaissance bindings were scarcely understood until E.Ph. Goldschmidt's analytical work in the 1920s forced wide scholarly attention on them more than simply as examples of decoration and applied art; and he offered only a beginning.[3] So too with collectors, and their freedom to choose what to collect, and so too with institutional libraries, as they focused or refocused their attention, generation by generation. The study and evaluation of the past, whether in scholarly preoccupations, in popular presentations such as exhibitions, in what has survived, in determining what is of unimpeachable authority, or in the various strata of collecting was, as it remains, an endlessly flexible process. The current debates about how to present matters on the computer screen, how to gather and organise them, and how to make them accessible are all part of this same series of selective decision-making.

An expanding readership in the nineteenth century not only brought more readers but also an increasingly well-informed, demanding and critical readership. This group was always international, for publishers, booksellers and customers alike; but the nineteenth century witnessed fresh cosmopolitan habits of thought and practice. Firms increasingly established major outlets and branches in different countries. French, German, Italian and American booksellers and publishers opened branches in London, and British firms opened overseas. Title-pages and imprints bore evidence of international collaborations, manufacture and funding; more travellers patronised more foreign bookshops; for visitors overseas, circulating libraries became a familiar part of tourism; and visits to foreign libraries became ever more habitual to, and feasible for, scholars. International issues and experiences became routine in ways and on a scale not before experienced.

Access depended on opportunity, on social assumptions and on catalogues. The introduction and expansion of the public library movement encouraged the use of books. For some people this brought anxiety about unfettered access by all kinds of readers, but the principle of universal access was accepted and maintained. For catalogues, the arguments surrounding the greatest catalogue of all, in the British Museum, had at their core questions of accuracy, of feasibility, of presentation (manuscript or printed?), of access and of how far it was a national record. From these questions arose ones concerning availability of catalogue records for other libraries as well, and related questions respecting union catalogues. The new cataloguing codes both sought uniformity, and also offered alternative means of access. One aim was always to combine conciseness with accuracy: to save the time of the reader: 'The main object of the good cataloguer should be to make the consultation of his work easy.'[4] In the opening words of a consideration of cataloguing prepared not by a librarian, but by one of the compilers of the *English catalogue*, the standard catalogue of the trade's output, who had gathered a sometimes entertaining assortment of examples good and bad: 'In the present state of dependence upon books for nearly all our information, the importance of ready access to great collections need scarcely be insisted on.'[5] Panizzi, Cutter, Bradshaw and lesser writers such as Wheatley and Blackburn each addressed what had become one of the greatest challenges of all. The many words shed on the subject of access from the mid-nineteenth century onwards, in a world that was itself becoming ever more organised, sought to bring order on a scale wholly different from similar concerns in the sixteenth century.

Some aspects in this changing world were less welcome. Theft and forgery were old familiars, but here too there were lessons and novel features. Whether out of lack of interest or investment, or thanks to being overwhelmed by numbers of books, or thanks to neglect or over-casual supervision, or thanks simply to ignorance, libraries were at risk. With increasing awareness of the value of older books came an increase in thefts, though money was not always the incentive. Nineteenth-century libraries were the targets of major thefts, well beyond the ordinary minor attritions of casual operators.

In other criminal activity, forgery had previously been more familiar in financial instruments (for which the penalty could be death[6]) and in the ambitions of literary or other textual inventors. In the nineteenth century the problem became acute also in bibliographical contexts: in the creation of forged bindings, of forged early printing, of forged modern editions, of forged provenances and of forged handwriting. All remain today, pitfalls for the trade and for customers, exemplified in the recent scandal over a forged copy of Galileo's *Sidereus nuncius* (1610),[7] in the temporary excitement over the so-called Hitler diaries in the early 1980s,[8] in the forged Freeman's Oath, the supposed first printing in the North American colonies,[9] in the deception of the Mormon church in the 1980s, and in a rash of forged documents in Texas.[10] The exposure of forgery still depends on knowing or seeing more than the forger, while conversely each forger learns from past errors. The modification of digital media, with its capacity for almost unbounded dishonesty as well as for more legal activities, has become a new challenge; but its exposure depends on similar understandings of what is technically feasible.

The study of the history of early printed books depended in the nineteenth century on at least three basic developments. First, as unfamiliar libraries were explored, so further examples of rare books came to light. This is to be seen most obviously, but by no means only, in the number of books described as being not listed by authorities that had been – and still were – taken as authoritative. Brunet's *Manuel du libraire*, extensive though it was, had never been intended to be comprehensive. For incunabula, the publication of Hain's *Repertorium* in 1826–38 offered a new confidence in that it recorded everything known. Not surprisingly, there were thousands of subsequent additions, many of them published in W.A. Copinger's *Supplement* of 1895–1902. For early English books, the standard remained Herbert's edition of Ames, likewise incomplete. Though the British Museum's collection was far from complete, Bullen's three-volume catalogue of 1884 offered a very considerable advance. There was no equivalent in France or most other foreign countries, though a start was made in the Low Countries in 1880 with the publication of the first fascicle of the project led by Ferdinand van der Haeghen towards a *Bibliotheca Belgica*.[11]

The second foundation lay in documentary evidence, and here progress was more selective. While such evidence for the earliest printing in the Netherlands and Germany was pored over, in Britain the publication in the 1850s and subsequently of the sixteenth- and early seventeenth-century domestic state papers prompted no immediate flowering of discoveries.[12] These had to wait for the publication of some of the Stationers' records in the 1870s and after.

Third was the study of the physical properties of books, including structure, bookbinding, printing types and paper. Notably, little interest was shown in the details of manufacture or of the environments in which books were printed. This was despite an apparently widespread curiosity in modern means of manufacture. The old standard printer's manuals by Stower, Hansard and others were little quoted in later literature, and their modern successors were in any case more concerned with contemporary practices. It was left to the next generation, headed by R.B. McKerrow in 1913, to lament 'the curious ignorance of the most elementary facts of the mechanical side of book-production during the Tudor and Jacobean period':

One is indeed constantly reminded that for those who have neither a practical acquaintance with the art of printing, access to a large collection of early printed books, nor friends experienced in such matters, adequate knowledge of the subject cannot easily be acquired.[13]

Blades, as a printer, was better equipped than many to understand the processes of printing, and Bradshaw repeatedly showed his grasp. But Blades had little experience of sixteenth-century methods, and so far as is known Bradshaw never worked either with type or with a press. Until 1913 there was no *vade-mecum* to help those seeking information on early practices.

For printing types, the basic equipment of all printers, everything depended on accuracy of representation and alertness to how type was employed. Holtrop's work on early Low Countries printing made possible the work of Henry Bradshaw. The hand-traced facsimiles made by George

Tupper for William Blades's two volumes on Caxton (1861–3) were of exceptional quality, and Blades's analysis remains fundamental today in a modified form. While these, and the skills of John Harris in making traced facsimiles of missing leaves, were universally admired, it remained for the critically informed application of photography to transform the study of early printing types. The palaeotypographical society of which Bradshaw heard rumours in 1883 did not materialise: the idea re-emerged when Robert Proctor and George Dunn collaborated in the collection known as the Woolley photographs of early printing types in 1899–1905, and when the short-lived Type Facsimile Society, guided by Proctor, issued its images in 1900–9. Both projects enjoyed very limited circulation, and only with the facsimiles included in the British Museum catalogue of incunabula shortly before the First World War did a general conspectus become widely available. Hand in hand with the study of individual designs went what Blades, Bradshaw and others called printers' habits: the ways in which type was chosen, set and arranged on the page. In this respect, computer applications and new imaging methods have transformed matters only to a limited extent.

For the study of ownership and provenance, while questions have become much broader the skills remain basically unchanged in their conception, albeit also gradually being transformed by the application of digital methods and the creation of large datasets.[14] As attention shifted in the nineteenth century from the more obviously prominent historical figures to people of interest for other reasons, priorities extended from recording signatures in books, or decorative bindings, to questions of how people read books, where they obtained them, how much was borrowed, how much was bought, how far readers' annotations can provide a guide to their responses and processes of thought. While manuscript marginalia had always commanded attention in some genres such as classical and antiquarian studies, outside these disciplines there was little set down *in extenso*. G.C. Moore Smith's generous selection of Gabriel Harvey's notes marked a new era, published in 1913 and the result of ten years' search for Harvey's books.[15] He provided a list of such books and manuscripts known to him, and in an ingenious typographical arrangement set the transcribed annotations next to the passages in the original editions. It offered an entry into the past of a kind new to English literature. But few people seem to have pursued annotated books for their own sake, and still in the 1920s Henry Clay Folger was thought to be unusual in his wider interest in such books.[16] The current Archaeology of Reading project, based at Johns Hopkins University,[17] is focused especially on the copious annotations by

John Dee and by Harvey. It has grown out of interests mostly developed not in the nineteenth but in the twentieth century: when in 1842 J.O. Halliwell edited Dee's diary and catalogue of his manuscripts, he showed no interest in the printed books (listed with his manuscripts in the same volume at Trinity College) or in their annotations.[18]

Access Today

Expectations and practices today have much in common with the ways they developed in the nineteenth century; but as computer applications become ever more abundant in book manufacture and publishing, in the organisation of libraries, in delivery to readers, and in managing large quantities of data, so further comparisons are inevitable. What we do today online depends also, and no less significantly or essentially, on a partial suppression of the past. Expectations based on past experience may be invalid. This applies on both micro and macro levels. Many of these pages have been concerned with individual books, how they may be accessed, how they are valued, how they may be understood. More generally, it was assumed that growth was desirable, that a large library represented public intellectual wealth and well-being. Now, as university, specialist and public libraries discard books in larger numbers than ever previously, on the often mistaken assumption that e-formats will be of sufficient quality as a substitute, proven values are being destroyed.[19] Some of the largest digitisation programmes have proved to be rich in promise, and poor in delivering even supposedly complete books. Missing, incomplete or blurred pages are commonplace. Beyond this, but related to it, is the separate challenge of ensuring that the evidence from which a digitised past is created is not destroyed. Digital files have an uncertainly limited life.[20] All too often, and completely independently of this reincarnation, new digitised existence has, for good or ill, presented the opportunity to discard or neglect the physical past.[21]

Visually, the germ of change lay in the nineteenth-century application of photography to books, the realisation that many of the attributes of a three-dimensional object could be acceptably represented in just two. It was a concept entirely different from the long-standing traditions of facsimiles and copies made by hand, whether letterpress, engraved or lithographed, in that it offered (even if it did not always provide) a new quality of assured accuracy. It was the foundation on which the concept of scanning became based, literally so in the millions of microfilm frames that became the basis of digitised files of both early printed books and manuscripts. To students of early modern Britain these are familiar in the translation of University Microfilms' series of early English books to EEBO (Early English Books Online),[22] while numerous libraries have digitised their old microfilms of manuscripts, offering these instead. Here in particular the lack of tonal range, and the lack of quality, in many old microfilms is a major disadvantage, sometimes to the point of illegibility, quite apart from the inherent lack of codicological information.

The drawbacks as well as the considerable advantages of microfilm, and the very poor quality of some if it, have been widely recognised. Unsatisfactory in visual quality though many of these transitions from film to digital files are, they take for granted the same background knowledge of readers. This can no longer necessarily be expected, as fewer people physically study large numbers of early books. McKerrow's lament of 1913 has come full circle. High resolution digital images have many advantages, but apparent ease of access on screen obscures features obvious when a volume is set before one. The transition eliminates some of the most basic properties of the manuscript or printed book. It ignores scale. It ignores the quality of the paper or parchment support. It ignores weight. It ignores all tactile qualities. It ignores nuances of colour and scent. It ignores codicological questions, and thus how volumes are structured and composed, whether in the printing house, by binders, by restorers, among different scribes, even composed among several copies drawn together to create a complete book out of an incomplete one. It ignores details of how books are bound.

All this may be quite apart from enforced reliance on the publisher of the filmed or digitised copy: that it is what is claimed. The UMI film of STC 13851 (*The good hows-holder*, 1607), for example, is from a reduced nineteenth-century facsimile, not from the unique surviving copy in the British Museum. Images of copies can also be distorted. Those of the Coverdale Bible (1535) offered by EEBO, based on a microfilmed copy in the British Library, are only partly legible thanks to poor exposure. Invaluable, time- and money-saving though the unique microfilm copy usually available may be, it inevitably ignores the fact that not all copies of early books are the same, different alike in the printing house and at the hands of binders. In other large commercial digitisation programmes, mismatches between descriptions and images are a familiar features.

Political, technological, economic or social, revolutions can rarely be said to be finished. Copinger echoed Bradshaw in summing up a course that had by 1892 been maturing for three decades:

There can be no doubt that Bibliography is now in process of development, and is fast becoming an exact science. It is high time, therefore, that it should be recognized as something very different from mere cataloguing.[23]

The revolution that developed in so many parts of the bibliographical world during the nineteenth century was to continue. In a direct line of descent its ideas and practices continue to influence how the study, use and care of old books are pursued. In a digital world, many new questions can be explored; but the foundations for such questions remain unavoidably keyed to the same kinds of evidence and resources that faced mid-Victorian generations. These help shape the questions that are asked; and with that they offer measures of how the past can be selected, interpreted and understood. Digital research brings opportunities, but it must also insist on the primacy of the nature of what is under consideration. That involves understanding what cannot – yet – be adequately translated.

More generally: just as during a critical half-century between the 1830s and the 1880s a cadre of librarians, scholars, booksellers and readers created and developed a revolution in the ways that books were accessed, read and studied, so in the twenty-first century a now much-extended group of those responsible for the preservation and exploitation of knowledge face a further challenge. The confusions and inadequacies exposed during the Covid pandemic face more than a technical revolution, more than one of new reading practices and more than one of interpretation. It is more than one of access – the theme of so much in these pages. In the context specifically of print and manuscript, to what extent must further skills be applied to relate material inheritance to the vagaries of computer applications on which we increasingly depend to access and understand the past? How far can the authority which has been vested in libraries since the early civilisations of the Middle East now be judged as core? As so many books and manuscripts become universally, if intermittently, available on screen, where does authority lie? In the face of commercially driven deliberate obsolescence, the challenges of digital sustainability, and the need for continuous reinvestment in hardware and software alike, the assumed stabilities of a world recorded and exploited on paper have been set aside. Is there in effect a difference not just in status but also in authority between what is available online and what remains only on paper? As libraries now face a world where their carefully curated digital recreations of their holdings can be manipulated by outside and unauthorised parties, so the artefactual survivals, and understanding them as artefacts become all the more vital.[24]

Notes

Prologue

1 https://libguides.kcl.ac.uk/covid (accessed 8 July 2020).
2 https://libguides.stir.ac.uk/c.php?g=530482 (accessed 11 July 2020).
3 John B. Thompson's extended study, *Book wars; the digital revolution in publishing*, was published as I was completing this book. It is not concerned with the extra stimulus brought by the Covid pandemic.

1 Introduction

1 Viardot, 'Les nouvelles bibliophilies', p. 343.
2 Mansel, *Paris between empires, 1814–1852*, pp. 141–64. For variations, ambiguities, misunderstandings and alliances, see Tombs and Tombs, *That sweet enemy; the French and the British from the Sun King to the present*.
3 Prétot, *Annuaire de la typographie parisienne et départementale*, pp. 142–3; Barber, 'Galignani's and the publication of English books' adds (pp. 284–6) a 'List of English newspapers and magazines published in Paris, 1814–50'.
4 In 1876 the remains of Louis-Philippe and his wife were removed to the Orléans necropolis at Dreux.
5 Cazelles, *Le duc d'Aumale*; Woerth, *Le duc d'Aumale; l'étonnant destin d'un prince collectionneur*; McKitterick, *The Philobiblon Society*.
6 Morison, 'On the classification of typographical variations'. For Blades more generally, see the introduction and bibliography of his work by Talbot Baines Reed appended to William Blades, *The pentateuch of printing*; James Moran, 'William Blades'.
7 Holtrop, *Monuments typographiques des Pays-Bas au quinzième siècle*; Bradshaw, *Correspondence on incunabula with J.W. Holtrop and M.F.A.G. Campbell* 2, pp. 492–3.
8 Bradshaw's annotated copy of Holtrop's *Catalogus librorum saeculo XV° impressorum. Quotquot in Bibliotheca Regia Hagana asservantur* is Cambridge University Library Adv.c.77.38.
9 His annotated copy is Cambridge University Library Adv.b.77.18–19.
10 R.A.B. Mynors, R.H. Rouse and M.A. Rouse (eds.), *Registrum Anglie de libris doctorum et auctorum veterum* (1991).

11 See *ODNB* and Thomas Tanner, *Bibliotheca Britannico-Hibernica* (1748), pp. xvii–xliii.
12 Bernard, *Catalogi librorum manuscriptorum Angliae et Hiberniae in unum collecti*.
13 Haenel, *Catalogi librorum manuscriptorum qui in bibliothecis Galliae, Helvetiae, Belgii, Britanniae M., Hispaniae, Lusitaniae asservantur*.
14 Wiegand, *Irrepressible reformer: a biography of Melvil Dewey*.
15 For some further cautionary remarks, see Alston, 'Charting the bibliographic sea; research and the art of navigation'.
16 McCrimmon, *Power, politics, and print; the publication of the British Museum catalogue, 1881–1900*; Chaplin, *GK: 150 years of the general catalogue of printed books in the British Museum*.
17 Hall, 'The guard-book catalogue of Cambridge University Library'; Chaplin, *GK: 150 years of the general catalogue of printed books in the British Museum*, pp. 104–5, 136–7 et passim.
18 *The National Union Catalog pre-1956 imprints: a cumulative author list representing Library of Congress printed cards and titles reported by other American libraries*.
19 *English short-title catalogue*: estc.bl.uk; *Universal short title catalogue*: www.ustc.ac.uk; *Incunabula short-title catalogue*: www.bl.uk/catalogues/istc/.
20 Bradshaw, *Presidential address to the Library Association, 1882*; McKitterick, 'Henry Bradshaw as librarian'; Ranganathan, *The five laws of library science*. The influence of S.R. Ranganathan (1892–1972) on Anglo-American librarianship has been fundamental.
21 Bradshaw to Holtrop, 21 March 1864: Bradshaw, *Correspondence on incunabula* 1, p. 49.
22 Among the now numerous books about the destruction of books and libraries, see, for example, Báez, *A universal history of the destruction of books, from ancient Sumer to modern Iraq*; Raven (ed.), *Lost libraries; the destruction of great book collections since antiquity*; Knuth, *Libricide; the regime-sponsored destruction of books and libraries in the twentieth century*; Knuth, *Burning books and levelling libraries; extremist violence and cultural destruction*; Polastron, *Livres en feu*. For further aspects, see Ovenden, *Burning the books; a history of knowledge under attack*.
23 Tollebeek and van Assche (eds.), *Ravaged; art and culture in times of conflict*.
24 For two accounts, see Hammer, *The bad-ass librarians of Timbuctu* and English, *The book smugglers of Timbuktu*.
25 In considerable literatures, see for example Savoy, *Patrimoine annexé; les biens cuturels saisis par la France en Allemagne autour de 1800*; Coeuré, *La mémoire spoliée; les archives des Français, butin de guerre nazi puis soviétique*.
26 The Stockholm Codex Aureus (National Library of Sweden MS A.135), an eighth-century Gospel book written probably in Canterbury, was looted by

Vikings in Kent and recovered on payment of a ransom. It entered the Swedish royal collection in 1690.

27 Ed. Moelwyn Williams (1985); 2nd ed., ed. B.C. Bloomfield (1997); 3rd and 4th eds., ed. Karen Attar (2016, 2021).

28 Online at https://fabian.sub.uni-goettingen.de/fabian.

29 Barker, *Treasures from the libraries of National Trust country houses*.

30 Delsaerdt and others, *Een zee van toegelaten lust: hoogtepunten uit abdijbibliotheken in de provincie Antwerpen*; Delsaerdt and Kayaert (eds.), *Abdijbibliotheken; heden, verleden toekomst* (Antwerpen, 2005); see also Isaac and Vandeweghe (eds.), *Répertoire des fonds anciens en Belgique / Repertorium van het oude boekenbezit in België*.

31 Barbier (ed.), *Les trois révolutions du livre; actes du colloque international*; Mercier and others, *Les trois révolutions du livre*.

32 Chartier, *Le livre en révolutions; entretiens avec Jean Lebrun*.

33 McKenzie, *Bibliography and the sociology of texts*, p. 4; Chartier, *Forms and meanings; texts, performances and audiences from codex to computer*. See also McKitterick, *The invention of rare books*, pp. 340–1.

34 Gesner, *Bibliotheca universalis*; Gesner, *Pandectarum universalium libri XXI*; see Fischer, 'Conrad Gesner (1516–1565) as bibliographer and encyclopaedist'; Serrai, ed. Cochetti, *Conrad Gesner*; Zedelmaier, *Bibliotheca universalis und bibliotheca selecta*; Sabba, *La 'Bibliotheca universalis' di Conrad Gesner*.

35 Thompson (ed. and trans.), *The Frankfort book fair; the Francofordiense Emporium of Henri Estienne*; Pollard and Ehrman, *The distribution of books by catalogue from the invention of printing to A.D. 1800*; Maclean, *Learning and the market place; essays in the history of the early modern book*.

36 Malclès, *Manuel de bibliographie*, 4th ed.

2 Re-Shaping the World

1 For France, see Casselle, 'Le régime législatif'; Mollier, 'La police de la librairie (1810–1881)'; Boscq, *Imprimeurs et libraires parisiens sous surveillance (1814–1848)*.

2 Mitchell, *British historical statistics*, p. 104.

3 McLean, *Victorian book design & colour printing* (1963), p. vii.

4 *Post Office directory of stationers, printers, booksellers, publishers and paper makers* (1872), preface.

5 For Britain, there is nothing for earlier centuries to compare with Mandelbrote (ed.), *Out of print and into profit*, but see McKitterick, 'Second-hand and old books', in McKitterick (ed.), *The Cambridge history of the book in Britain. 6. 1830–1914*, pp. 635–73. For the Low Countries, see Buijnsters, *Geschiedenis van het Nederlandse antiquariaat*, and Buijnsters, *Geschiedenis van antiquariaat en bibliofilie in België*. For France, see Gaviglio-Faivre d'Arcier, 'Les libraires d'ancien

et d'occasion'. For Germany, see Barbier, 'La librairie ancienne en Allemagne au XIXe siècle', and Jäger and Wittman, 'Der Antiquariatsbuchhandel'. For Italy, see, for example, Cristiano, *L'antiquariato librario in Italia; vicende, protagonisti, cataloghi*, pp. 19–43, and, for the second half of the nineteenth century, Cristiano, 'Biblioteche private e antiquariato librario'. For the United States, see the summary by Stern, *Antiquarian bookselling in the United States; a history from the origins to the 1940s*. See further Sachet, 'Selling Aldus in the UK (c.1630–2015): towards a checklist of British sale catalogues of books published by the Manuzio family'.

6 McKitterick (ed.), *The Cambridge history of the book in Britain. 6. 1830–1914*, pp. 1–4.
7 Barker, *The Roxburghe Club*; Husbands, *The early Roxburghe Club, 1812–1835*; Hesse, *Histoire des sociétés de bibliophiles en France de 1820 à 1930* 1, pp. 3–12.
8 McKitterick, *The Philobiblon Society*.
9 See, for example, Silverman, *The new bibliopolis; French book collectors and the culture of print, 1880–1914*.
10 See Gaehtgens, 'Le musée historique de Versailles'. The collections in the new museum, drawn partly from the Louvre, were rapidly supplemented with an assortment of objects gathered from elsewhere. By the 1880s much of the original quality had become obscured. 'The historical object of the foundation of the gallery having always been predominant, numerous works have necessarily been received without much regard to their artistic merit. The critical eye will therefore detect very inferior productions intermingled with the efforts of transcendental genius' (Baedeker, *Paris and environs* 7th ed., p. 286).
11 Loyrette, 'La tour Eiffel', in Nora (ed.), *Les lieux de mémoire* 3, pp. 4270–93. For some other aspects of France, see, for example, Weber's classic *Peasants into Frenchmen*; Lyons, *Le triomphe du livre*; Gerson, *The pride of place*.
12 Common time-keeping ('Railway time') was introduced on the Great Western Railway in 1840.
13 Hinrichsen, *Baedeker's Reisehandbücher, 1832–1944*.
14 John Murray, 'The origin and history of Murray's Handbooks for travellers', in John Murray IV, *John Murray III, 1808–1892*, pp. 39–49; Lister, *A bibliography of Murray's Handbooks for travellers*.
15 Nordman, '*Les Guides-Joanne: ancêtres des Guides Bleus*'.
16 Barber, 'Galignani's and the publication of English books in France from 1800 to 1852', and 'Postscript' by Barnes; Cooper-Richet and Borgeaud, *Galignani*; Todd and Bowden, *Tauchnitz international editions in English*.
17 McKitterick, *The invention of rare books*, ch. 19, 'Public faces, public responsibilities'.
18 McLean, *Victorian publishers' book-bindings*; McLean, *Victorian publishers' book-bindings in paper*; King, *Victorian decorated trade bindings, 1830–1880*; Malavieille, *Reliures et cartonnages d'éditeur en France au XIXe siècle*

(1815–1865); Utsch, *Rééditer Don Quichotte. Matérialité du livre dans la France du XIXe siècle* (with further references, pp. 58–68).
19 *Library Chronicle* 1 (1884), p. 103; Duff, *Early printed books*, pp. 19–20.
20 Prothero, *A memoir of Henry Bradshaw*, pp. 299–300.
21 On Reed, see especially Morison, *Talbot Baines Reed; author, bibliographer, typefounder* and Mosley, 'Talbot Baines Reed, typefounder and sailor'.
22 Timperley, *A dictionary of printers and printing*; Timperley, *Encyclopaedia of literary and typographical anecdote* 2nd ed.; Hansard, *Typographia*; Johnson, *Typographia, or the printer's instructor*.
23 Talbot Baines Reed, 'Memoir' prefixed to Blades, *The pentateuch of printing*, pp. ix–x. For bibliographical details of Dibdin's work, see Jackson, *An annotated list* and Windle and Pippin, *Thomas Frognall Dibdin*.
24 *Notes and Queries* no. 102 (11 October 1851).
25 Prices from the *London catalogue of books*.
26 A.F. Johnson, '*Typographia, or the printer's instructor*'.
27 Prices from the *London catalogue of books*.
28 Martin, *Bibliographical catalogue of books privately printed*, pp. 379–404.
29 John Johnson, *Typographia, or the printer's instructor* 2, p. 657.
30 Reviewed at length in the *Gentleman's Magazine* 94 (1824), pp. 341–3, 447–50, 537–42.
31 Hansard, *Typographia*, p. iv.
32 *BB* 1852, pp. 660–1.
33 Claye, *Manuel de l'apprenti compositeur*, pp. 149, etc. Fournier died in 1888.
34 Chambers, *Memoir of William and Robert Chambers*, pp. 237–8; Ordish, 'Chambers's Journal'.
35 Knight, *Passages in a working life* 2, p. 184.
36 'The commercial history of a *Penny Magazine*', *Penny Magazine*, monthly supplements, 1833; Dodd, *Days at the factories*.
37 See pp. 57–67. For lists of some of the associated publications, see *Catalogus der bibliotheek van de Vereeniging ter Bevordering van de Belangen des Boekhandels te Amsterdam* 1, pp. 99–101 and Hoffmann, *Chronological list of books and articles on the history of printing in Holland and Belgium*, pp. 38–42, 114–15.
38 Rees, *Cyclopaedia, or universal dictionary of arts* 28, art. 'Printing'.
39 Remy, *Aux origines de la Bibliothèque Royale de Belgique*.
40 2nd ed., with a new chapter by Henry G. Bohn (1861).
41 Schöpflin, *Vindiciae typographicae*.
42 Bernard, *De l'origine et des débuts de l'imprimerie en Europe*; Dupont, *Histoire de l'imprimerie*.
43 Evans, *The commercial crisis 1847–1848*.
44 McKitterick, *The Philobiblon Society*.
45 For Tross, see Kratz, 'Libraires et éditeurs allemands installés à Paris, 1840–1914', and Jeanblanc, *Des Allemands dans l'industrie et le commerce du livre à Paris (1811–1870)*.

46 Rosenberg, 'Early modern information overload'; Blair, *Too much to know; managing scholarly information before the modern age*.
47 Barat, *Nouvelle bibliothèque choisie* 1, 'Avertissement'. See also McKitterick, *The invention of rare books*, pp. 250–4.
48 Lord Chesterfield, *Letters* 1, p. 567.
49 Descuret, *La médecine des passions*, pp. 751–2. See also and more generally Desormeaux, *La figure du bibliomane; histoire du livre et stratégie littéraire au XIXe siècle*.
50 Dibdin, *The bibliomania; or, book-madness; containing some account of the history, symptoms, and cure of this fatal disease*. For details, see Jackson, *An annotated list*, pp. 19–22, and Windle and Pippin, *Thomas Frognall Dibdin, 1776–1847; a bibliography*, pp. 32–41.
51 Dibdin, *Bibliomania; or book madness* (1842), p. ix.
52 Hunt, 'The sale of Richard Heber's library'.
53 The final sale also included books from Heber. See further Stammers, *The purchase of the past*, pp. 114–15, 132–41.
54 Trinity College, Cambridge MS O.14.13 (64, 90); Windle and Pippin, *Thomas Frognall Dibdin, 1776–1847; a bibliography*, p. 175.
55 Dibdin, *Reminiscences of a literary life* 1, p. vii.
56 The copy given to Frances Currer, the dedicatee, is dated 19 April 1839: see Windle and Pippin, *Thomas Frognall Dibdin*, p. 185.
57 Dibdin, *A bibliographical, antiquarian and picturesque tour of the northern counties of England and in Scotland* 2, p. 1090.
58 His last years, and the difficult years after his death, when she and her mother were ill and impoverished, are chronicled in the letters written between 1839 and 1850 by his daughter Sophia ('Sophy') to Dawson Turner, now in Trinity College, Cambridge MSS O.14.22–49. She wrote repeatedly of the financial drain on the family in looking after him and of her unsuccessful pleas for support from others.
59 *Gentleman's Magazine* n.s.29 (1848), pp. 87–92, 338.
60 *Serapeum* 10 (1849), pp. 333–6, 363–8.
61 For a brief discussion of the differences between Dibdin and his French hosts, see Janssen, *Dibdin in Paris (1818)*.
62 *BB* 8 (1847), p. 508; *Bibliophile Belge* 4 (1847), pp. 434–5.
63 Brunet, 'T.F. Dibdin'.
64 Bohn, *Catalogue of books* 1 (1848); Bohn, *New, valuable, and most important books, offered at very reduced prices* [1848].
65 De Ricci, *English collectors of books & manuscripts, 1530–1930 and their marks of ownership*; Munby, *Phillipps studies*, abridged in Barker, *Portrait of an obsession; the life of Sir Thomas Phillipps, the world's greatest book collector*.
66 Léopold Augustin Constantin Hesse ('L.A. Constantin'), *Biblioéconomie*, pp. 12–15.
67 Texier, *Les choses du temps présent*, p. 147.

68 [Louis Bollioud de Mermet] *De la bibliomanie*, new ed. by Paul Chéron. For aspects of the continuing phenomenon, see Desormeaux, *La figure du bibliomane*.

69 Uzanne, *Caprices d'un bibliophile*, p. 66.

70 Ruskin, *Sesame and lilies*, pp. 74-5.

3 Books in Abundance

1 For some of the challenges in trying to establish how much was published in nineteenth-century Britain, see Eliot, *Some patterns and trends in British publishing, 1800-1919*. He notes a surge in the number of titles listed in the *Publishers' Circular* in the late 1840s and early 1850s, due largely to pamphlet literature: this later flattened out. For some of the similar difficulties in France, see especially de Conihout, 'Police de la librairie et mesure du livre au XIXe siècle; le dépôt légal, la *Bibliographie de la France*, et la bibliométrie'.

2 Orville A. Roorbach's pioneering *Bibliotheca Americana; catalogue of American publications ... from 1820 to 1848*, 'all American editions now on the market' (preface), was published in 1849. See also *The American catalogue of books, or, English guide to American literature ... with especial reference to works of interest to Great Britain* (Sampson Low, 1856).

3 Harris, *History of the British Museum library*, pp. 144-7.

4 Partridge, *The history of the legal deposit of books throughout the British Empire*, pp. 80-4; Sternberg, 'The British Museum Library and colonial copyright deposit'.

5 Eliot, '"Mr. Greenhill, whom you cannot get rid of"; copyright, legal deposit and the Stationers' Company in the 19th century.'

6 *Report of the Commissioners appointed to inquire into the constitution and government of the British Museum, with minutes of evidence* (1850), p. 261.

7 Perzanowski and Schultz, *The end of ownership; personal property in the digital economy*.

8 The Manchester Statistical Society was founded in 1833, and the Statistical Society of London in 1834. See Cullen, *The statistical movement in early Victorian Britain; the foundations of empirical social research*; Porter, *The rise of statistical thinking, 1820-1900*; Rosenbaum, 'The growth of the Royal Statistical Society'.

9 Edwards, *A statistical review of the principal public libraries of Europe and America*, p. 8. This paper was summarised also in *BB* 8 (1848), pp. 811-19. For Edwards, see Greenwood, *Edward Edwards, the chief pioneer of municipal public libraries* and Munford, *Edward Edwards, 1812-1886; portrait of a librarian*.

10 Pim den Boer, *History as a profession; the study of history in France, 1818–1914*, p. 72; but for further details see Foucaud, *La Bibliothèque Royale sous la Monarchie de Juillet*, pp. 38–41 *et passim*.
11 Edwards, *Memoirs of libraries; including a handbook of library economy* 2, p. 294. For further estimates, see Foucaud, *La Bibliothèque Royale sous la Monarchie de Juillet*, p. 118.
12 *Serapeum* 8 (1847), p. 336.
13 *Report of the Select Committee on Public Libraries* (1849), paras. 43, 56, 73.
14 Edwards, *Memoirs of libraries* 2, p. 417.
15 Edwards, *A statistical review of the principal public libraries of Europe and America*, p. 6. Edwards had delivered his paper first to the Statistical Society of London (*Journal* 11 (1848), pp. 250–81). His figure seems all the more unlikely as part of the Zaluski library had been returned to Poland in 1842. Further books were restituted subsequently, but an unknown number was retained in St Petersburg. Most of those returned to Poland were burned by German troops in 1944 as part of a large-scale destruction of Polish libraries: Bernhard Fabian (ed.), *Handbuch deutscher historischer Buchbestände in Europa. 6. Polen, Bulgarien* (Hildesheim, 1999), p. 30.
16 McCulloch, *A dictionary, practical, theoretical, and historical, of commerce and commercial navigation* (1859), p. 175.
17 Knight, *William Caxton, the first English printer*, pp. 233–4; Altick, *The English common reader*, chapter 14, quotes further statistics. *Mitchell's Newspaper press directory* was first published in 1846. See also *May's British & Irish press guide* (1874 etc.).
18 See again de Conihout, 'Police de la librairie et mesure du livre au XIXe siècle; le dépôt légal, la *Bibliographie de la France,* et la bibliométrie'.
19 Comte Daru, *Notions statistiques sur la librairie* (Paris, 1827).
20 St Clair, *The reading nation in the romantic period*; Suarez, 'Towards a bibliometric analysis of the surviving record'.
21 Altick, *The English common reader; a social history of the mass reading public, 1800–1900*.
22 William Chambers and Robert Chambers (ed.), *Chambers's information for the people*, revised ed. (1848), 'Printing', p. 705.
23 *The Times*, 14 June 1847.
24 Werdet, *Histoire du livre en France* 2, p. vi, Werdet's italics. For Werdet, see Felkay, *Balzac et ses éditeurs, 1822–1837; essai sur la librairie romantique*, pp. 219–49.
25 *Vegetable substances; materials of manufactures*, p. 129. Italics in original. This chapter was concerned mostly with the many experiments that had been made to form paper from different plants.
26 Coleman, *The British paper industry, 1495–1860*; de Fontenelle and Poisson, *Manuel complet du marchand papetier et du régleur*; Le Normand, *Manuel du fabriquant du papier, ou de l'art de la papeterie*; Planche, *De l'industrie de la*

papeterie; de Vries, *De Nederlandse papiernijverheid in de negentiende eeuw*; Clapperton, *The paper-making machine; its invention, evolution, and development*; André, *Machines à papier; innovation et transformations de l'industrie papetière en France, 1798–1860*.

27 Herring, *A few personal recollections of the late Rev. George Croly*, pp. 2–30.
28 George Croly, Introduction to Herring, *Paper & paper making, ancient and modern*.
29 Herring, *Paper & paper making* 2nd ed., p. 96.
30 Ibid., p. 98, quoting T.C. Hansard, *Typographia*, pp. 230–1.
31 His annotated collection of specimens and tracings is now in the British Library, shelf-mark C.135.k.1.
32 Midoux and Matton, *Étude sur les filigranes des papiers employés en France aux XIVe et XVe siècles*.
33 Sotheby, *Principia typographica*, 3. For subsequent work, cf. Briquet, 'Papiers et filigranes des archives de Gênes, 1154 à 1700'; Briquet, *Les filigranes*.
34 Desbarreaux-Bernard, *Catalogue des incunables de la Bibliothèque de Toulouse*, pp. xv–xxvi.
35 Ovink, 'Nineteenth-century reactions against the Didone type model'; Mosley, 'Recasting Caslon Old Face'.
36 Luckombe, *The history and art of printing*, p. 14; Dibdin, *The bibliographical decameron* 1, p. 397; Timperley, *A dictionary of printers and printing*, p. 130.
37 Humphreys, *A history of the art of printing from its invention to its widespread development in the middle of the 16th century*, p. 112.
38 Morris arranged for trial pages of his projected *Earthly paradise* to be set in this type in 1858. It had been first used in William Calvert, *The wife's manual* (Longman, 1854). More generally, see Johnson, 'Old-face types in the Victorian age'.
39 Freeman, 'Founders' type and private founts at the Chiswick Press in the 1850s'. Vincent Figgins's recutting of one of Caxton's types was used for a type facsimile of *The game of the chesse* in 1860.
40 Peterson, *The Kelmscott Press; a history of William Morris's typographical adventure*.
41 For Lemerre, see Jean-Paul Fontaine: http://histoire-bibliophilie.blogspot.com/2014/02/alphonse-lemerre-le-barbin-des-jeunes.html (accessed 30 January 2021).
42 Monfalcon, *Étude sur Louis Perrin, imprimeur lyonnais*.
43 [Anatole France] *Le livre du bibliophile* (Paris, 1874), p. 12.
44 Thibaudeau, *La lettre d'imprimerie*, pp. 376–84, 445–7.
45 In this book I have followed modern conservators' usage, and generally used the term 'parchment' rather than 'vellum', the word that was employed almost universally in the nineteenth century.
46 For Meyer, see the obituary and tributes in the *Bibliothèque de l'École des Chartes* (1917), pp. 429–46.

47 Murphy, *Shakespeare in print; a history and chronology of Shakespeare publishing*, pp. 239–42.
48 Sillars, *The illustrated Shakespeare, 1709–1875*.
49 Among the many accounts of the trade in early editions during the nineteenth century, see Fitzgerald, *The book fancier*, pp. 253–306.
50 Gaviglio-Faivre d'Arcier, 'Portrait d'un libraire d'ancien: Techener'; Jeanblanc, *Des Allemands dans l'industrie et le commerce du livre à Paris (1811–1870)*, pp. 268–9.
51 de Ricci, *Bibliographie des publications d'Anatole Claudin (1833–1906)*; Fontaine, 'Anatole Claudin', *Les gardiens de bibliopolis; cent soixante portraits pour servir à l'histoire de la bibliophilie*. For tributes at his funeral by Delisle and by Édouard Rahir, see *BB* 1906, pp. 144–50. For his interest in the first Scottish printers, and connections with northern France, see his letters in Dickson, *Introduction of the art of printing into Scotland*, pp. 77–92, but see also the correction in Duff, *Early printed books*, p. 175.
52 Keyser, *Frederik Muller en de oude boekhandel*; Keyser and others (ed.), *Frederik Muller (1817–1881): leven & werken*.

4 Celebrating Print

1 Hellinga-Querido and de Wolf, *Laurens Janszoon Coster was zijn naam*; Blades, *Numismata typographica*, no. 33.
2 Kuitert, 'The art of printing in the Dutch East Indies; Laurens Janszoon Coster as colonial hero'. He was still celebrated in pre-independent Indonesia in 1950. See p. 57.
3 For a list of many of the publications arising from these celebrations, see Kirchhoff, *Katalog der Bibliothek des Börsenvereins der Deutschen Buchhändler*, pp. 51–5. For Gutenberg celebrations more generally, see Estermann, '*O werthe Druckerkunst/ Du Mutter aller Kunst*'; *Gutenbergfeiern im Laufe der Jahrhunderte*.
4 A detailed account of some of the celebrations, particularly at Leipzig and Strasbourg, was published in the *Gentleman's Magazine* N.S.14 (1840), pp. 185–7. A long description of the statue at Strasbourg, and of the associated celebrations, appeared in the *Magasin Pittoresque* 8 (July 1840), pp. 217–20. The same publication also illustrated Thorwaldsen's statue at Mainz (ibid., 6 (1838), p. 89).
5 Blades, *Numismata typographica*, no. 63.
6 See Suzanne Braun, 'Le monument de Gutenberg', http://acpasso.free.fr/archives/photosdiverses/Le%20monument%20de%20Gutenberg.pdf (accessed 28 April 2020).
7 Atkyns, *The original and growth of printing collected out of history, and the records of this kingdome*.

8 Johns, *The nature of the book; print and knowledge in the making*, pp. 338–43, etc.
9 Singer, *Some account of the book printed at Oxford in MCCCCLXVIII, under the title of Exposicio Sancti Jeronimi ... in which is examined its claim to be considered the first book printed in England*; Middleton, *A dissertation concerning the origin of printing in England*. Middleton's book was reviewed favourably, for example, in the *Literary Magazine*, February 1735, pp. 122–5, and held the ground as the accepted standard account.
10 Sotheby, *Principia typographica* 3, pp. 18–19.
11 Barker, *The Roxburghe Club; a bicentenary history*, pp. 77–8. Cf. 'Thus much, however, is certain: that, previously to the year 1477 our Printer had quitted the Low Countries, and taken up his residence in the vicinity of Westminster Abbey' (Ames and Herbert, *Typographical antiquities; or the history of printing in England Scotland and Ireland* 1, p. xcviii). Ames in 1749, followed by Herbert in his revision of Ames in 1785, had said categorically that Caxton began to print in England in 1474. It is now accepted that he was at work in Westminster by the end of 1476.
12 Knight, *Passages in a working life during half a century*, p. 106.
13 *The Times*, 14 May 1847, 9; 14 June 1847; *The Builder*, 19 June 1847, pp. 285–6; *John Bull*, 19 June 1847; *Notes and Queries* 19 July 1851 (article by Bolton Corney).
14 It was paid for by the printers of London. At the invitation of F.W. Farrer, Dean of Westminster, a quatrain by Tennyson was added. The window was destroyed in the Second World War, but is depicted in Southward, *Progress in printing and the graphic arts during the Victorian era*.
15 Chambers, *Memoir of William and Robert Chambers*, p. 264.
16 Chambers and Chambers (ed.), *Chambers's information for the people*, revised ed., 'Printing', p. 707.
17 See pp. 178–9.
18 For Vander Haeghen, see Mansion, 'Ferdinand van der Haeghen'; Uyttenhove and Van Peterghem, 'Ferdinand van der Haeghen's shadow on Otlet: European resistance to the Americanized modernism of the Office Internationale de Bibliographie'.
19 Bradshaw, 'A classified index of the fifteenth century books in the De Meyer collection', *Collected papers*, p. 206.
20 Ibid., p. 221.
21 Ibid.
22 He listed the names of those to whom he expected to send copies in Notebook XVIII: see *Correspondence on incunabula* 2, pp. 390–1. For a translation of Van der Linde's review in the *Nederlandsche Spectator*, see Bradshaw, *Correspondence on incunabula* 2, pp. 405–8.
23 'Another compartment contains the museum of early printing, consisting of books printed between 1450 and 1500': Annual report of the Library Syndicate.

See also Bradshaw, *Correspondence on incunabula* 2, pp. 396–8 and McKitterick, *Cambridge University Library*, pp. 735–6.

24 Repr. in Bradshaw, *Collected papers*, pp. 258–80.
25 Ibid., pp. 259–60.
26 Myers, 'William Blades's debt to Henry Bradshaw and G.I.F.Tupper'. For a summary view of the relations between Blades, Tupper and Bradshaw, see Morison, 'On the classification of typographical variations', at pp. xix–xxi.
27 Bradshaw, *A classified index of the fifteenth century books in the De Meyer collection*, *Collected papers*, p. 222.
28 Holtrop, *Catalogus librorum saeculo XV° impressorum, quotquot in Bibliotheca Regia Hagana asservantur*. See also Jos van Heel (ed. and trans.), *Jan Willem Holtrop on the study of early printed books from the Low Countries (1856)*.
29 Sinker, *A catalogue of the fifteenth-century printed books in the library of Trinity College, Cambridge*.
30 Bradshaw, 'On the earliest English engravings of the indulgence known as the "Image of pity"'.
31 Ibid., p. 98.
32 See p. 56.
33 Conway, *The woodcutters of the Netherlands in the fifteenth century*, p. vi. See now Kok, *Woodcuts in incunabula printed in the Low Countries*.
34 For some of Conway's experience in the Low Countries, see Bradshaw, *Correspondence* 2, pp. 454–7.
35 Conway, *Episodes of a varied life*, pp. 53–6. The book remained in print for many years. For Conway's varied life as art historian, mountaineer, explorer and public servant, see Evans, *The Conways; a history of three generations* and the notice by Peter H. Hansen in the *ODNB*.
36 Claudin, *Histoire de l'imprimerie en France au XVe et au XVIe siècles*. There was no extended analysis of English woodcuts until Edward Hodnett's *English woodcuts, 1480–1535* (Bibliographical Soc., 1935), a study made possible by the appearance of Pollard and Redgrave's *Short-title catalogue* in 1926.
37 Hellinga-Querido and de Wolf, *Laurens Janszoon Coster was zijn naam*.
38 Ottley, *An inquiry into the origin and early history of engraving*, pp. 101–2.
39 'Item dese hoichwyrdige kunst vursz is vonden aller eyrst in Duytschlant tzo Mentz am Rijne ... Dat eyrste boich dat men druckde die Bybel zo latijn, ind wart gedruckt mit eynre grouer schrifft. as is die schrifft dae men nu Mysseboicher mit druckt. Item wiewail die kunst is vonden tzo Mentz, als vursz vp die wijse, als dan nu gemeynlich gebruicht wirt, so is doch die eyrste vurbyldung vonden in Hollant vyss den Donaten, die dae selffst vur der tzijt gedruckt syn. ... Mer der eyrste vynder der druckerye is gewest eyn Burger tzo Mentz. ind was geboren van Straiszburch, ind hiesch joncker Johan Gudenburch.' Text and translation from Pollard, *Fine books*, pp. 34–6.
40 Dibdin, *Bibliotheca Spenceriana* 3, pp. 282–3.

41 Holtrop, *Monuments typographiques des Pays-Bas au quinzième siècle*, pp. x–xi and plates 11–30.
42 *Catalogus Bibliothecae Publicae Harlemensis*, pp. 68–76; *A handbook for travellers on the continent*, 11th ed. (John Murray, 1856), p. 44; de Vries, *Lijst der stukken betrekkelijk de geschiedenis van de uitvinding der boekdrukkunst, berustende op het raadhuis te Haarlem*; Jaspers, *De blokboeken en incunabelen in Haarlems Libry*.
43 Lamartine, *Gutenberg, inventeur de l'imprimerie*.
44 Werdet, *Histoire du livre en France* 2, p. vi.
45 Dingelstedt, *Iean Gutenberg, premier maître imprimeur*. Transl. from German by Gustave Revilliod (Genève, 1858).
46 Pearson, *Gutenberg; or the world's benefactor*.
47 Knight, *Life of William Caxton*, p. 19.
48 Tomlinson (ed.), *Cyclopaedia of useful arts* 2, pp. 472–3.
49 Bradshaw, *Correspondence on incunabula* 2, p. 376.
50 Though Bradshaw recognised Hessels's skills, he also increasingly recognised his limitations, and had to put up with his difficult personality. See Bradshaw, *Correspondence on incunabula*, passim.
51 Bradshaw to Campbell, 5 May 1870: Bradshaw, *Correspondence on incunabula* 1, p. 145.
52 Venn, *Alumni*, quoting the Scott manuscripts in St John's College library. Hessels was given an honorary MA by the University in 1884, and became a member of St John's College in 1894. He died in 1926 at Bloemendaal, near Haarlem.
53 Hessels (ed.), *Ecclesiae Londino-Batavae archivium*.
54 Van der Linde, *De Haarlemsche Costerlegende wetenschappelijk onderzocht*, trans. by J.H. Hessels as *The Haarlem legend of the invention of printing by Lourens Janszoon Coster, critically examined*.
55 Hessels, 'Introduction' to Van der Linde, *The Haarlem legend*, pp. xi–xvi.
56 Ibid., p. xxv.
57 Ibid.
58 As the remark was made almost in passing, it is not clear that he had by this point seen Van der Linde's original Dutch: he may have been relying on Hessels.
59 See also M.-F.-A.-G. Campbell, 'La prototypographie néerlandaise (à Utrecht?)', in his *Annales de la typographie néerlandaise au XVe siècle*, pp. 517–18.
60 Bradshaw, *List of the founts of type and woodcut devices used by printers in Holland in the fifteenth century*, repr. in his *Collected papers*, pp. 258–81, at pp. 261–2.
61 In 1876 he sold his collection of books on chess to the Koninklijke Bibliotheek in The Hague for 3,000 Dutch guilders.
62 Van der Linde, *Gutenberg und Erdichtung aus den Quellen nachgewiesen*.

63 Van der Linde, *The Haarlem legend*, p. 12.
64 Ibid., preface.
65 Ibid., p. 169.
66 The medal of 1740 struck in his honour was by Martin Holtzhey; Blades, *Numismata typographica: or, the medallic history of printing*, no. 22.
67 Seiz, *Het derde jubeljaar der uitgevondene boekdrukkonst, behelzende een beknopt historis verhaal van de uitvinding der edele boekdrukkonst*, trans. as *Annus tertius saecularis inventae artis typographicae, sive brevis historica enarratio de inventione nobilissimae artis typographicae, in qua ostenditur, quo tempore, à quo & ubi locorum ea primum fuerit inventa*.
68 Van der Linde, *The Haarlem legend*, p. 1. Hessels changed the title for the English translation, avoiding the term of the original. Van der Linde, *De Haarlemsche Costerlegende; wetenschappelijk onderzocht* (The Hague, 1870).
69 Acton, *A lecture on the study of history, delivered at Cambridge, June 11, 1895*, pp. 54–5.
70 Hessels, *Gutenberg: was he the inventor of printing?*, p. 2. This part of Hessels's book was originally published in the *Printing Times and Lithographer*, February–May 1880.
71 Ibid., p. 3.
72 Ibid., p. 10.
73 Ibid., p. 128.
74 De Vinne, *The invention of printing*, p. 374.
75 Prothero, *A memoir of Henry Bradshaw*, pp. 368–9.
76 Hessels, *Gutenberg: was he the inventor of printing?*, p. 189. In France, Anatole Claudin wrote of his 'excellentes recherches': *Catalogue des monuments typographiques et d'un choix de livres rares et précieux provenant du cabinet de feu M. Benjamin Fillon*, p. 7.
77 Hessels, *Gutenberg: was he the inventor of printing?*, pp. x–xi.
78 Hessels, *Haarlem the birth-place of printing, not Mentz*, p. 9: Hessels's italics.
79 Baedeker, *Belgium and Holland. Handbook for travellers*, 9th ed. (Leipsic, 1888), p. 267. The mistake about Haarlem's priority persisted in later editions.
80 Bradshaw, *List of the founts of type and woodcut devices used by printers in Holland in the fifteenth century*, repr. in his *Collected papers*, pp. 258–81, at pp. 261–2.
81 Blades, 'On the present aspect of the question', p. 135.
82 Middleton-Wake, *The invention of printing*, p. 130: his italics. The lectures were published privately.
83 Ibid., pp. 171–4.
84 White, *Editio princeps; a history of the Gutenberg Bible*.
85 Proctor, *An index to the early printed books in the British Museum from the invention of printing to the year MD*, pp. 652–3. For further discussion of the early Dutch work, see especially the introduction by L.A. Sheppard to BMC 9

(1962), and Hellinga and Hellinga, *The fifteenth-century printing types of the Low Countries* 1, pp. 4–9.
86 Blades, 'On the present aspect of the question, Who was the inventor of printing?'. This includes an extended list of publications on the subject between 1868 and 1887, but oddly omits Bradshaw's brief intervention.
87 Needham, 'Paul Schwenke and Gutenberg scholarship: the German contribution, 1885–1921'.
88 Schwenke, *Untersuchungen zur Geschichte des ersten Buchdrucks*; Hartwig (ed.), *Festschrift zum fünfhundertjährigen Geburtstage von Johann Gutenberg*.
89 *À la mémoire de M. Jean Gutenberg. Hommage de l'Imprimerie Nationale et de la Bibliothèque Nationale*. For a summary list of celebratory publications across Europe, see *Trans Bibliographical Soc.* 10 (1910), pp. 245–6.

5 Access: National Collections

1 Lacroix, 'Le commerce des livres anciens'.
2 Roberts, *The book-hunter in London*, p. 69.
3 See further pp. 110–11. For these sales, see Hurst, *Catalogue of the Wren Library of Lincoln Cathedral; books printed before 1801*, pp. xi–xii. In 1977 the cathedral disposed of many nineteenth-century publications.
4 Harris, *History of the British Museum library*, pp. 20–1, 42–3 etc.
5 For its recent state, see *Report of the Select Committee on public libraries* (1849), paras. 2108–19; see also Hoare, 'Archbishop Tenison's library'.
6 Harris, *History of the British Museum library*, pp. 70–3.
7 Brunet, 'Quelques mots au sujet des difficultés que présente la catalographie'.
8 [John Holmes] 'Libraries and catalogues'.
9 Hesse ('L.A. Constantin'), *Bibliotéconomie, ou nouvel manuel complet pour l'arrangement, la conservation et l'administration des bibliothèques*. Nouvelle éd., 'Essai d'une statistique des bibliothèques publiques des pays étrangers de l'Europe', p. 214.
10 *Report of the Select Committee on the British Museum* (1836), p. 546.
11 Ibid., p. 547.
12 Ibid., p. 548.
13 Lacroix ('P.L.Jacob'), *Réforme de la Bibliothèque du Roi*, p. 63.
14 Savoy, *Patrimoine annexé; les biens culturels saisis par la France en Allemagne autour de 1800*.
15 Lacroix, *Réforme de la Bibliothèque du Roi*, p. 65.
16 Hale, *Ninety days' worth of Europe*, p. 182.
17 Ibid., p. 187.
18 De Morgan, 'Mathematical bibliography', p. 33.
19 Ledos, *Histoire des catalogues des livres imprimés de la Bibliothèque Nationale*, p. 154.

20 Lacroix, *Réforme de la Bibliothèque du Roi*; Ledos, *Histoire des catalogues des livres imprimés de la Bibliothèque Nationale*, p. 165.
21 For Taschereau, see Ledos, *Histoire des catalogues des livres imprimés*, pp. 168–88. For an English comment, see Edwards, *Memoirs of libraries: including a handbook of library economy* 2, pp. 873–7.
22 For critical remarks in London on the *Catalogue de l'histoire de France*, see the *Athenaeum*, 13 January 1855, p. 51, summarised in Ledos, *Histoire des catalogues des livres imprimés*, pp. 172–3.
23 Paris, *De la Bibliothèque Royale et de la nécessité de commencer, achever et publier le catalogue général des livres imprimés*.
24 Delisle contributed a detailed account of these developments, besides the earlier history of the Library, as an introduction to the first volume of the *Catalogue général des livres imprimés de la Bibliothèque Nationale* (1897).
25 Edwards, *Memoirs of libraries: including a handbook of library economy* 2, pp. 747–60, 851–68. See further pp. 81–3, 307–8.
26 McCrimmon, *Power, politics, and print; the publication of the British Museum catalogue, 1881–1900*, p. 42.
27 Garnett, 'The printing of the British Museum catalogue'. For further details of the prolonged discussions preceding the decision, and for subsequent progress, see Chaplin, *GK: 150 years of the general catalogue of printed books in the British Museum*. See also McCrimmon, *Power, politics, and print*: despite its title, this includes much on the previous decades.
28 *The Athenaeum*, 1850, pp. 499–502.
29 *Journal of the Society of Arts*, 15 and 22 February, 23 and 30 August, 6 September 1878; 'Report of the committee on a general catalogue of English literature', *Library Journal* 4, pp. 418–20. For further ideas put forward by the University Librarian at Ghent in the 1870s, see Uyttenhove and Van Peterghem, 'Ferdinand van der Haeghen's shadow on Otlet: European resistance to the Americanized modernism of the Office Internationale de Bibliographie', p. 92. For Bradshaw's hope that each nation would survey its own books, and the British Museum would each year print a list of books received by copyright deposit, see his letter to Ferdinand Vander Haeghen, 28 September 1877: J. Machiels, 'Henry Bradshaw's correspondentie met Ferdinand Vander Haeghen', pp. 609–10.
30 Walford, 'Some practical points in the preparation of a general catalogue of English literature'.
31 Stevens, 'Photobibliography; a word on catalogues and how to make them'; Stevens, 'Photo-bibliography; or, a central bibliographical clearing-house'.
32 *Notes and Queries* 7, no. 212 (21 May 1853), p. 507. See also Luther, *Microfilm; a history, 1839–1900*.
33 Stevens, 'Photo-bibliography', p. 80.
34 Ibid., p. 73.
35 Edwards, *Memoirs of libraries* 2, p. 867.

36 See p. 82. *Report of the Commissioners* (1850), paras. 8476 (Croker) and 9860-1 (Panizzi).

37 Reviewed at length, with some criticisms, by Henry R. Tedder in a paper delivered to the Library Association, and printed in *The Library Chronicle* 2 (1885), pp. 57-63. See also the anonymous review in the *Athenaeum*, 1885, p. 307, and one by W.E.A. Axon in the *Academy* 19 (1884), p. 212. For Bullen's catalogue more generally, see McCrimmon, *Power, politics, and print*, pp. 81-94.

6 The British Museum Commission, 1847-1850

1 *Report of the Commissioners appointed to inquire into the constitution and government of the British Museum* (1850), p. iii.

2 Ibid., Evidence, para. 8967. For more detail and background, see Harris, *History of the British Museum Library*.

3 *Report of the Commissioners*, Evidence, paras. 9860-1. In answer to a question from Lord Seymour, the chairman, 'If it were to be considered inexpedient to print a catalogue of all the books in the Museum, do you think it might be very expedient to print a catalogue of certain portions of those books; for instance, several witnesses have said, that if a catalogue of books printed before the year 1500 were printed, it would be very valuable for the country.'

To which Panizzi replied, 'As to the suggestion about printing catalogues, for instance of the books printed before the end of the fifteenth century, or catalogues of the tracts on the English Civil Wars, or catalogues of the tracts on the French Revolution, I have myself suggested that to the Trustees at various times.' (Seymour:) 'I find that was stated by you as early as 1836?' (Panizzi:) 'Yes, in a Report to the Trustees, dated February 1836.'

4 Ibid., paras. 7779-84.

5 Ibid., paras. 9112-15. Thomas Grenville's bequest of 1846 added substantially to such books. In the next few years the library bought a *Horae* (Pigouchet, 1501) and a Homer (Charles Whittingham, 1831), both on parchment.

6 Fortescue, *List of three collections of books, pamphlets and journals in the British Museum relating to the French Revolution*.

7 *Report of the Commissioners*, Evidence, para. 8996.

8 Ibid., para. 1444.

9 Ibid., Evidence, para. 9012.

10 Ibid., paras. 3974, 3976, 3979-80, 9193-4. See also Harris, *History of the British Museum Library*, pp. 345-6 etc.

11 *Report of the Commissioners*, Evidence, para. 4374.

12 Ibid., para. 8763.

13 Ibid., para. 8772.

14 William Blades, *Life and typography* 1, p. vii.

15 Boccaccio, *De la ruine des nobles hommes et femmes* (1476, bought 1860), Jean Boutillier *Somme rurale* (1479, bought July 1861) and Ovid *Metamorphoses* in French (1484, bought July 1865).
16 *Report of the Commissioners*, Evidence, paras. 6697–704.
17 Ibid., para. 5815. See also Augustus De Morgan, 'On the difficulty of correct description of books'. In his account of the *Report* in the *Edinburgh Review* 91 (1850), pp. 371–98, De Morgan also concentrated on cataloguing matters.
18 *Quarterly Review* 72 (1843), pp. 1–25: review article occasioned by the 1835 report on the Museum and six printed catalogues of printed books, most recently the first two volumes of the Grenville catalogue and vol. 1, A, of the Museum's 1841 catalogue.
19 *Report of the Commissioners*, Evidence, para. 5103.
20 Ibid., para. 9788.
21 Ibid., paras. 9789–841.
22 Ibid., paras. 5716–24.
23 [Richard Ford] Review of several reports and pamphlets concerning the Museum, 1835–50, p. 167.
24 That is, fourth in the first class in his final examinations in mathematics. De Morgan, *Memoir of Augustus De Morgan, with selections from his letters*.
25 De Morgan, 'Mathematical bibliography'. Despite its title, the journal, owned by the Roman Catholic Nicholas Wiseman, was published in London. De Morgan contributed several articles on mathematical and scientific subjects between 1837 and 1847.
26 Ibid., p. 27.
27 Ibid., p. 9. The preparation of this catalogue caused much friction between Panizzi and the Royal Society, and occasioned a spirited exchange of pamphlets. See Panizzi, *A letter to His Royal Highness the President of the Royal Society*; *Address of His Royal Highness the Duke of Sussex, the President, read at the anniversary meeting of the Royal Society, on Thursday, November 30, 1837*; *Observations on the address by the President, and on the statement by the Council ... respecting Mr. Panizzi*; Panizzi, *To S.P. Rigaud, Esq. M.A. F.R.S.*; *Defence of the resolution for omitting Mr. Panizzi's bibliographical notes from the catalogue of the Royal Society*. The argument was not least about payment to Panizzi for his work. See also Fagan, *The life of Sir Anthony Panizzi* 1, pp. 119–30.
28 Harris, 'The move of printed books from Montagu House, 1838–42'; Harris, *History of the British Museum library*, pp. 114–15.
29 In his Addenda he included an unspecified edition of *Algorithmus novus de integris*, which he noted as 'I think this is the oldest book in my list'. In fact it was one of several editions printed at Cologne c.1500.
30 In his Addenda he noted a number of early books described by Hain and others, that he had not seen.

31 De Morgan, *Arithmetical books from the invention of printing to the present time*, p. 2. A third setting was discovered subsequently. These later settings are now dated *c*.1502 and *c*.1507–9. See Clarke, 'The first edition of Pacioli's "Summa de arithmetica" (Venice, Paganinus de Paganinis, 1494)'.
32 [Augustus De Morgan] 'Notices of English mathematical and astronomical writers between the Norman conquest and the year 1600', pp. 35–7.
33 STC nos 20797.5 *et seq.*
34 De Morgan's fumbling attempts at collational descriptions were superseded. For Henry Bradshaw's clearer concept, and its gradual evolution, see Needham, *The Bradshaw method; Henry Bradshaw's contribution to bibliography*, Appendix, 'Henry Bradshaw and the development of the collational formula'.
35 Thomas-Stanford, *Early editions of Euclid's Elements*, pp. 22–3.
36 De Morgan, *Arithmetical books from the invention of printing to the present time*, p. 6.
37 See p. 276.

7 Libraries in Confusion

1 Winstanley, 'Halliwell Phillipps and Trinity College library'; Spevack, *James Orchard Halliwell-Phillipps; the life and work of the Shakespearean scholar and bookman*, pp. 124–43.
2 Munby, *The history and bibliography of science in England: the first phase, 1833–1845*.
3 *The Times*, 13 November 1845.
4 Charton (ed.), *Guide pour le choix d'un état, ou dictionnaire des professions*, p. 88.
5 Vitet, *Rapport à M.le Ministre de l'Intérieur sur les monuments, les bibliothèques, etc.* See also Casselle, 'Les pouvoirs publics et les bibliothèques'.
6 Vitet, *Rapport*, p. 70.
7 Ibid., pp. 81, 87.
8 Ravaisson, *Rapports au Ministre de l'Instruction Publique sur les bibliothèques des départements de l'ouest.*
9 Michelet, *Rapport au Ministre de l'Instruction Publique sur les bibliothèques et archives des départements du sud-ouest de la France.* See also Pim den Boer, *History as a profession; the study of history in France, 1818–1914*, p. 87; more generally, see Moore, *Restoring order; the École des Chartes and the organization of archives and libraries in France, 1820–1870.*
10 *Daily News*, 13 March 1847; *Bibliophile Belge* 4 (1847), pp. 297–8.
11 Delisle, *Catalogue des manuscrits des fonds Libri et Barrois, Bibliothèque Nationale*, pp. vi–vii; Maccioni Ruju and Mostert, *The life and times of Guglielmo Libri (1802–1869)*, p. 166; Centina and Fiocca, *L'archivio di Guglielmo Libri dalla sua dispersione ai fondi della Biblioteca Moreniana.* The

literature on Libri is considerable. Delisle's heartfelt account of the developing scandal remains the best, and he included a list of thirty-nine pamphlets, articles and other publications arising from the affair: see his *Catalogue* pp. xxx–xxxv. For a summary of the affair in the context of other aspects of French libraries, see Thomas, 'Détournements, vols, destructions', and for a further survey of Libri's career see also Norman, *Scientist, scholar & scoundrel; a bibliographical investigation of the life and exploits of Count Guglielmo Libri*.

12 Lescure, *Les autographes*, pp. 80–1. See the summary in Delisle, *Catalogue des manuscrits des fonds Libri et Barrois*, p. vii.
13 *Catalogue général des manuscrits* 1 (1849), preface.
14 The second volume, covering just Troyes, appeared in 1855, and the third in 1861.
15 Maccioni Ruju and Mostert, *The life and times of Guglielmo Libri*, pp. 203–8, 213–17; Centina and Fiocca, *L'archivio di Guglielmo Libri*, pp. 145–6; Delisle, *Catalogue des manuscrits des fonds Libri et Barrois*, pp. xiii, lxiii–lxxxxii.
16 Maccioni Ruju and Mostert, *The life and times of Guglielmo Libri*, p. 221.
17 Munby, 'The Earl and the thief'.
18 Recorded by S. de Ricci, *A census of Caxtons*, p. 6, as having been stolen in 1841. BMC IX p. 131 does not mention a Troyes provenance.
19 Maccioni Ruju and Mostert, *The life and times of Guglielmo Libri*, p. 227, describes the 1847 sale of printed books as having taken place over ten days from 28 July. But the printed catalogue (priced copy in Grylls collection, Trinity College) is dated 28 June, and the following twenty-nine days.
20 The pound was worth about 25fr., 57 cms. (McCulloch, *Dictionary* (1859), p. 582). See also Harris, 'The Ripoli *Decameron*, Guglielmo Libri and the "incomparable" Harris'.
21 Boucly, *Rapport addressé à M. le garde des sceaux Hébert, suivi du procès intenté par M.Libri*, p. 9. For an assessment of Jacques-Joseph Techener (d.1873), see *BB* (1873), pp. 244–56. See also Gaviglio-Faivre d'Arcier, 'Portrait d'un libraire d'ancien; Techener'.
22 'Revue de ventes', *BB* 8 (1847), pp. 383–406; another report was printed in the *Bulletin des Arts* 6 (1847), pp. 81–5, edited by Paul Lacroix.
23 *Morning Chronicle*, 22 March 1848; *Freeman's Journal*, 23 March 1848.
24 *Le Bibliophile Belge* 5 (1848), p. 34.
25 *Manchester Times and Gazette*, 28 March 1848.
26 *Réponse de M.Libri au rapport de M.Boucly, publié dans le Moniteur Universel du 19 March 1848*, advertised for example in the *Morning Chronicle*, 29 May and the *Examiner*, 3 June.
27 *The Examiner*, 10 June 1848; see also for example [Augustus De Morgan] 'The case of M.Libri', *Bentley's Miscellany* 32 (1852), pp. 107–15.
28 Brandes, 'Beleuchtung der Anklage gegen Libri wegen Beraubung öffentlicher Bibliotheken in Frankreich'; Brandes, 'G.Libri's Aufschlüsse über Verluste der öffentlichen Bibliotheken in Frankreich'.

29 The charges were fully reported by the Paris bookseller Edwin Tross, 'Der Prozess "Libri"'.
30 Maccioni Ruju and Mostert, *The life and times of Guglielmo Libri*, pp. 209–13. For examples of false provenances, see Delisle, *Catalogue des manuscrits des fonds Libri et Barrois*, pp. xiv–xvi.
31 Lalanne and Bordier, *Dictionnaire de pièces autographes volées aux bibliothèques publiques de la France*. See also Jammes, *Libri vaincu; enquêtes policières & secrets bibliographiques*.
32 Delisle, *Catalogue des manuscrits des fonds Libri et Barrois*, pp. xvi–xvii.
33 Carter, *Taste and technique in book-collecting*, pp. 124–5.
34 Delisle, *Catalogue des manuscrits des fonds Libri et Barrois*, pp. xviii–xx.
35 For a list of these sales, see ibid., p. xxvii.
36 Noticed at length by Claudin in *Archives du Bibliophile* 14 (1859), pp. 32–6.
37 Libri to Quaritch, 18 June 1859: Trinity College, Cambridge Add.MS 126.
38 Claudin provided a selection of French equivalent prices in *Archives du Bibliophile* 18 (1859), pp. 216–20, 288–90.
39 Libri fell out with Sotheby's: see Herrmann, *Sotheby's; portrait of an auction house*, pp. 42–3.
40 Fournier, *L'art de la reliure en France aux derniers siècles*, p. 60.
41 Techener, 'De l'amélioration des anciennes bibliothèques en France, et de la création de nouvelles bibliothèques appropriées au perfectionnement moral du peuple', p. 632.
42 Lalanne and Bordier, *Dictionnaire de pièces autographes*, p. 5.
43 On Barrois's employment of them see Delisle, *Catalogue des manuscrits des fonds Libri et Barrois*, pp. xxxviii–xxxix.
44 Ibid, pp. lxiii–lxxxii.
45 Ibid; Munby, 'The triumph of Delisle'. Delisle decided that the Ashburnham manuscripts should remain in the Bibliothèque Nationale, regardless of whence they had been stolen.
46 Delisle, *Catalogue des manuscrits des fonds Libri et Barrois*, Préface. For the more public parts of his sustained efforts, see Lacombe, *Bibliographie des travaux de M.Léopold Delisle*, Index, s.v. 'Libri'.
47 Collingham, 'Joseph Barrois. Portrait of a bibliophile XXVI'. See also Omont, *Catalogue des manuscrits Ashburnham-Barrois acquis en 1901*.
48 J.T. Payne's private library of select books was auctioned on 10 April 1878.
49 Maccioni Ruju and Mostert, *The life and times of Guglielmo Libri*, pp. 293–7.
50 Comment by Charles Ruelens in Rooses (ed.), *Compte-rendu de la première session de la Conférence du Livre . . . 1890*, pp. 121–2.
51 Reiffenberg, 'Note sur un exemplaire des lettres d'indulgence'; Bernard, *De l'origine et des débuts de l'imprimerie en Europe* 1, p. 172; de Ricci, *Catalogue raisonné des premières impressions de Mayence (1445–1467)*, pp. 48–9; now John Rylands Library Spencer 17250.1. I am grateful to Julianne Simpson for help here.

52 Auvray and Poupardin, *Catalogue des manuscrits de la collection Baluze*, pp. xiii–xv.
53 See Casselle, 'Les pouvoirs publics et les bibliothèques', at pp. 111–12.
54 Mangeart, *Catalogue descriptif et raisonné des manuscrits de la Bibliothèque de Valenciennes*, p. xi.
55 BnF MS Nouv. Acq. Fr. 4379 (42 leaves, formerly part of Bibl. Colombina 5-1-43).
56 *Revue Critique* NS 19 (1885), pp. 388–401, including a history of the library and its periodic neglect. See also ibid., NS 21 (1886), p. 518.
57 Also translated into Spanish as *Grandeza e decadencia de la Colombina* (Sevilla, 1886). See McDonald, *The print collection of Ferdinand Columbus (1488–1539)*, especially 1, pp. 126–44, and now Pérez Fernández and Wilson-Lee, *Hernando Colón's new world of books; toward a cartography of knowledge*, p. 186.
58 *Revue Critique* NS 20 (1885), pp. 78–81.
59 Quaritch, *Catalogue of the monuments of the early printers* (1888) offered (no. 36507) Manuel (King of Portugal), *Copia de una lettera del Re de Portogallo mandata al Re de Castella del viaggio & successo de India* (Roma, 1505), bought in Rome by Colón in 1515; Davies, *Catalogue of a collection of early French books in the library of Charles Fairfax Murray*, Index IV. For books from the Colombina library in the Rosenwald collection, see *The Lessing J. Rosenwald collection; a catalog of the gifts of Lessing J. Rosenwald to the Library of Congress, 1943 to 1975*. In 2020 at least one volume, ex-Pichon and Fairfax Murray, was advertised on sale in the trade (*Image du monde* (Paris, 1530), Davies, *Catalogue of a collection of early French books in the library of Charles Fairfax Murray*, 288).
60 *Book-Lore* 2 (1885), p. 56.

8 Collaboration

1 The question has been answered in many different ways since 1789. In a very large literature, see, for example, Oddos (ed.), *Le patrimoine; histoire, pratiques et perspectives*; '"Patrimoines"; dossier'; *Patrimoine des bibliothèques de France; un guide des régions*.
2 See pp. 36–8.
3 Oxford University Commission report (1852), p. 102; Craster, *History of the Bodleian Library, 1845–1945*, p. 274.
4 Jewett, *Smithsonian Institution catalogue system*; Goode (ed.), *The Smithsonian Institution, 1846–1896; the history of its first half century*, pp. 276–80. See also Borome, *Charles Coffin Jewett*.
5 McKitterick, *Cambridge University Library*, pp. 531, 748–9.

6 For a summary list of published finding aids for manuscripts and printed books in French collections, organised by library, see 'Chronique. Bibliothèques', *Bulletin des Bibliothèques et des Archives* 1884.1, pp. 66–91.

7 Bernard, *Catalogi librorum manuscriptorum Angliae et Hiberniae*; Haenel, *Catalogi librorum manuscriptorum qui in bibliothecis Galliae, Helvetiae, Belgii, Britanniae M., Hispaniae, Lusitaniae asservantur*. Haenel's work was extended to include Germany and France in a revised version published by J.P. Migne in 1853.

8 Ledos, *Histoire des catalogues des livres imprimés*, p. 212.

9 Delisle, 'Circulaire à MM. les Maires relative au catalogue des incunables des bibliothèques de France'.

10 Pellechet, *Catalogue général des incunables des bibliothèques publiques de France*. For Pellechet, see Baurmeister, 'De la dame-copiste bénévole à la bibliothécaire honoraire: Marie Pellechet à la Bibliothèque nationale', with further references; Barbieri, *Haebler contro Haebler; appunti per una storia dell'incunabolistica novecentesca*, pp. 47–58.

11 Crous, 'The general catalogue of incunabula'; Crous, 'The inventory of incunabula in Great Britain and Ireland'; Eisermann, 'The greatest of all such lists'. Much more ambitiously, in a related development, the Preussische Staatsbibliothek in Berlin joined with ten university libraries in Prussia to launch a *Gesamtkatalog der Preussischen Bibliotheken*. The scheme subsequently expanded to include Munich, Vienna and other libraries, and the first volume was published in 1931. It collapsed with the fourteenth volume in 1939. See Fuchs, 'The *Gesamtkatalog* of the Prussian libraries'.

12 Botfield, *Notes on the cathedral libraries of England*, pp. xiv, viii. It was welcomed enthusiastically in the *BB* 9 (1849), p. 233.

13 Clarke, *Repertorium bibliographicum, or some account of the most celebrated British libraries*.

14 Botfield, *Notes on the cathedral libraries of England*, p. 272; Thomson, *Catalogue of the manuscripts of Lincoln Cathedral Chapter library*, p. xxiii, with a list of mutilated manuscripts.

15 Haenel, *Catalogi librorum manuscriptorum qui in bibliothecis Galliae, Helvetiae, Belgii, Britanniae M., Hispaniae, Lusitaniae asservantur*, cols. 799, 907.

16 A series of contributions to *Notes and Queries* in 1852–4 provided a very mixed picture.

17 Tedder and Thomas (ed.), *Transactions and proceedings of the first annual meeting of the Library Association of the United Kingdom*, Appendix 2. The information about the condition of Wimborne was out of date by the 1870s, following some repairs in the 1850s, including partial replacement of the original chained fittings.

18 *First report of Her Majesty's Commissioners to inquire into the state and condition of the cathedral and collegiate churches* (1854); Tedder and Thomas

(ed.), *Transactions and proceedings of the first annual meeting of the Library Association of the United Kingdom*, Appendix 1.

19 Hands, 'The cathedral libraries catalogue'; Read, *A checklist of books, catalogues and periodical articles relating to the cathedral libraries of England*; Read, 'Cathedral libraries: a supplementary checklist'; Shaw and others (ed.), *The cathedral libraries catalogue*.

20 Cowie, *A descriptive catalogue of the manuscripts and scarce books in the library of St John's College, Cambridge* (Cambridge, 1843).

21 Collett, *A list of early printed books in the library of Gonville and Caius College, Cambridge*. This was published at the same time as his *Index of English books printed before the year MDC, now in the library of Gonville and Caius College, Cambridge*: the two are usually found bound up together.

22 Nicholson and Tedder (ed.), *Transactions and proceedings of the conference of librarians ... October 1877* (1878), pp. 243–6. For later use of printed catalogues of public libraries, see Bowman, 'The decline of the printed catalogue in Britain'.

23 See p. 105.

24 *Catalogue général des livres imprimés de la Bibliothèque Nationale* 1 (1897), p. lxxxi.

25 Balayé, *La Bibliothèque Nationale des origines à 1800*; Delisle, *Le cabinet des manuscrits de la Bibliothèque Nationale/Impériale*.

26 Ravaisson, *Rapports au Ministre de l'Instruction Publique sur les bibliothèques des départements de l'ouest* (Paris, 1841), pp. 21, 24–5, 38–9, etc.

27 For subsequent exchanges between the Bibliothèque Municipale at Besançon and the Bibliothèque Nationale, for example, see Waille, *Catalogues régionaux des incunables des bibliothèques publiques de France. 19. Franche-Comté* 2, pp. 224, 277–80.

28 McKitterick, *Cambridge University Library*, pp. 634–46, 663–4. In 1948 and 1957 further exchanges of incunables were organised with the British Museum: Harris, *History of the British Museum Library*, p. 599; for Cambridge acquisitions (and de-accessions in 1957), see the annual reports of the Library Syndicate, 1947–8 and 1956–7.

29 Varry (ed.), *Histoire des bibliothèques françaises. Les bibliothèques de la Révolution et du XIXe siècle*, p. 415. See further Tilliette, 'Alexandre Vattemare's international document exchanges and the collection of foreign official publications of the Bibliothèque Administrative de la ville de Paris; a historian's treasure trove' (IFLA general conference, Amsterdam, 1998): archive.ifla.org/IV/ifla64/151-133e.htm (accessed 8 November 2020); Richards, 'Alexandre Vattemare and his system of international exchanges'.

30 26th Congress, 1st session, House of Representatives, Report no. 586, 6 June 1840, 'Exchange of books'.

31 Vattemare, *Second annual report on international literary exchanges*; *Third annual report and letters on international exchanges made to the Governor of Connecticut*.
32 Winlock, 'The international exchange system', in Goode (ed.), *The Smithsonian Institution, 1846–1896*.
33 Harris, *History of the British Museum library*, pp. 349–50, 427–8.
34 Bradshaw to Campbell, 1 November 1874: Bradshaw, *Correspondence on incunabula* 1, p. 182. The printer has been sometimes wrongly thought to be Gerardus de Leempt: see Hellinga, *The fifteenth-century printing types of the Low Countries* 1, p. 47.
35 Bradshaw, *Correspondence on incunabula* 1, pp. 197, 200, 201, 202, 203, 204, 206, 228, 229.
36 Trinity College MS O.4.36. See Mandatori '"But the calamity was complete and total"; Mommsen, Giordane e i dotti inglesi', pp. 178–202.
37 *The Times*, 26 July 1880.
38 By agreements recorded in the University's Grace Books: see *A chronological list of the graces, documents, and other papers in the University Registry which concern the University Library*.
39 Rooses (ed.), *Compte-rendu de la première session de la Conférence du Livre, tenue à Anvers . . . 1890*, pp. 158–71.
40 *Introduction à la bibliographie de Belgique . . . dressé par les soins de la Section Littéraire de la Commission des Échanges Internationaux* (Brussels, 1875, rev. 1877).
41 UNESCO *Convention concerning the Exchange of Official Publications and Government Documents between States* (1958).

9 The Trade in Second-hand Books

1 *Whitaker's almanack* (1885), p. 439; Mitchell, *British historical statistics*, p. 195; Beckett, 'Agricultural landownership and estate management'.
2 Several sales were reported in *The Bibliographer* and (less fully) in *The Athenaeum*. Earlier sales of Beckford's books had taken place in 1804, 1808 and 1817.
3 Among various press reports of the sale, see *Book-Lore* 2 (1885), pp. 17–18.
4 For a summary, see de Ricci, *English collectors of books & manuscripts, 1530–1930, and their marks of ownership*.
5 For Quaritch, see especially the notice by Arthur Freeman in the *ODNB*. A long account of a conversation with him about his premises and practices is included in Fitzgerald, *The book fancier*, pp. 14–16.
6 Parker, *Henry Stevens of Vermont*.
7 Edward Arber to Lord Coleridge, 15 July 1884. Birmingham University Library, Edward Arber papers US4/1/58.

8 For nineteenth-century auctions, the *List of catalogues of English book sales, 1676–1900, now in the British Museum* has been superseded by Lenore Coral's list of auctions, 1801–1900, available online via the website of the Bibliographical Society of America. Unhappily, she died before finishing this: her own and subsequent papers and files assembled by Annette Fern are now in the Grolier Club library. See also Coral, 'Towards the bibliography of British book auction catalogues, 1801–1900'.
9 Cf. Powell and Wyke, 'At the fall of the hammer: auctioning books in Manchester, 1700–1850'.
10 Edwards, *Memoirs of libraries* 2, p. 644.
11 *The Athenaeum*, 18 January 1845, p. 70.
12 Lescure, *Les autographes*, pp. 63–108, 'Histoire de la salle Silvestre', provides a summary of autograph sales here.
13 Techener, 'Des ventes de livres en Angleterre'.
14 Hébrard, *De la librairie, son ancienne prospérité, son état actuel; causes de sa décadence, moyens de régénération*.
15 See pp. 92–102.
16 See pp. 97–8.
17 *BB* 6 (1847), p. 541.
18 *BB* 7 (1847), p. 535.
19 F.S. Ellis, recalling Lord Ashburnham as a collector, in Quaritch (ed.), *Contributions towards a dictionary of English book-collectors*, part X.
20 Grégoire, *Troisième rapport sur le vandalisme* (Convention Nationale, an III [1795].
21 *BB* 9 (1849), p. 256.
22 *BB* 9 (1849), p. 897. For similar remarks, see *BB* 9 (1850), p. 511. For Yemeniz (1783–1871), born in Greece and settled in Lyon, see Niepce, *Les bibliothèques anciennes et modernes de Lyon*, pp. 250–5, and Fontaine, *Les gardiens de bibliopolis; cent soixante portraits*, pp. 617–27. His library, with a catalogue based on the three-volume privately printed catalogue of 1865–6, was sold by Bachelin-Deflorenne in 1867 with a long introduction by Le Roux de Lincy.
23 The catalogue was summarised at length in three articles in *The Athenaeum*, January 1845, pp. 70–2, 93–5, 118–20.
24 Duprat, *Précis historique sur l'Imprimerie Nationale et ses types*; Duprat, *Histoire de l'Imprimerie Impériale de France*; Bernard, *Notice historique sur l'Imprimerie Nationale*; Bernard, *Histoire de l'Imprimerie Royale du Louvre*.
25 [J. Techener] 'Revue des ventes', *BB* 9 (1850), p. 712.
26 Smitskamp and others, *Luchtmans & Brill; driehonderd jaar uitgevers en drukkers in Leiden 1683–1983: catalogus van de tentoonstelling*; van der Veen and others, *Brill; 325 years of scholarly publishing*.
27 'Introduction', *Le Bibliophile Français* 1 (1862), pp. 1–2. See also Jimenes, 'Le Bibliophile Français et la librairie Bachelin-Deflorenne'.
28 Ibid.

29 Lacroix, 'Le commerce des livres anciens'.
30 Peltz, *Facing the text: extra-illustration, print culture and society in Britain, 1769–1840*. The fashion continued long afterwards.
31 For this and later editions, see Stoddard, *Jacques-Charles Brunet: le grand bibliographe*. For Jules Janin's obituary of Brunet, see *Le Bibliophile Français* 1 (1868), pp. 5–16.
32 For Quérard, see especially the obituaries in *BB* 1865, pp. 443–50.
33 'L.A. Constantin' (Léopold Augustin Constantin Hesse), *Biblioéconomie, ou nouvel manuel complet pour l'arrangement, la conservation et l'administration des bibliothèques*, p. 96.
34 For guides to some of the more substantial collections of booksellers' catalogues, see *Catalogus der bibliotheek van de Vereiniging ter Bevordering van de Belangen des Boekhandels te Amsterdam*, 4; Blogie, *Répertoire des catalogues de ventes de livres imprimés appartenant à la Bibliothèque Royale Albert Ier*; Faure (ed.), *Catalogues de libraires et d'éditeurs, 1811–1924: inventaire*.
35 Roberts, *The book-hunter in London*, pp. 149–67, 215.
36 Mayhew, *London labour and the London poor* 1, p. 292.
37 Ibid., p. 293.
38 'Felix Folio', *The hawkers and street dealers of the north of England manufacturing districts*, records that by the time he wrote much of the business formerly conducted at stalls in Manchester had migrated into shops (p. 81). See also Weatherley, *Recollections*.
39 Lacroix, 'Le commerce des livres anciens', pp. 63–78.
40 *Post Office directory of stationers, printers, booksellers, publishers and paper makers* (1872).
41 Roberts, *The book-hunter in London*, p. xxiii.
42 Just twenty-eight are now in the Shoults collection in Dunedin: Selwyn College, Dunedin, the owner of the library, sold eight in the 1930s.
43 I am most grateful to Donald Kerr for showing me the Shoults collection, for many conversations about it and for sharing his draft book.
44 Bohn, *Catalogue of books* (1848), p. 343. The book is not especially rare: ISTC records over fifty copies.
45 Renouard, *Annales de l'imprimerie des Alde*, p. 14.
46 Bohn, *Catalogue of books* (1848), p. 57.
47 In the 1850s Willis & Sotheran issued *Willis's Price Current* monthly, with a cover price of threepence.
48 Preface to third edition (1879).
49 Warrington, 'The bankruptcy of William Pickering in 1853'.
50 Smith and Benger, *The oldest London bookshop: a history of two hundred years*.
51 *The Athenaeum*, 29 September 1883, p. 402.
52 Preface to *A catalogue of books and manuscripts issued to commemorate the one hundredth anniversary of the firm of Bernard Quaritch* (1947); Arthur Freeman,

'Bernard Quaritch', *ODNB*; Barker, 'Bernard Quaritch'. For alterations to streets, see Edwards, *History of London street improvements, 1855–1897*.
53 Folter, 'The Gutenberg Bible in the antiquarian book trade', p. 300.
54 Hellinga, 'The Enschedé sale was most disappointing ...'; Barker, *Bibliotheca Lindesiana*, pp. 236–7; Jaspers, *De blokboeken en incunabelen in Haarlems Libry*, pp. 50–1.
55 Quaritch, *A general catalogue of books, arranged in classes, offered for sale* (1868).
56 *Hodson's Booksellers, publishers and stationers directory, 1855*. For a list of publishers and booksellers in central London, c.1846, arranged geographically, see Marston, *After work; fragments from the workshop of an old publisher*, pp. 323–30.
57 *Notes and Queries* no. 12 (1855), p. 47; 11 August, p. 96; 29 September, p. 242.
58 Gyles offered his *Directory of second-hand booksellers* at one shilling (cloth), 1s.6d. ('parchment, interleaved'), 3s. ('Large Paper, half rox. Morocco'), or 4s. for the last, interleaved.

10 Private Collectors and the Public

1 Béraldi, *La reliure du XIXe siècle* 2, p. 116.
2 *29th Report of the Science and Art Department of the Committee of Council on Education* (1882), C.3271, pp. 544–5.
3 McTurk, 'The reading room of the British Museum'.
4 Edwards, *Memoirs of libraries* 2, pp. 1044–5.
5 Greenwood, *Free public libraries, their organisation, uses and management*, pp. 246–7.
6 Greenwood, *Museums and art galleries*, pp. 199–200, in a chapter on 'The Sunday opening of museums'.
7 *25th Report of the Science and Art Department of the Committee of Council on Education* (1878), C.2098, p. 472.
8 'Mechanics' institutions'(1874). For earlier history, see Tylecote, *The mechanics' institutes of Lancashire and Yorkshire before 1851*. For further remarks on institutes, whose libraries retained their importance, see Greenwood, *Free public libraries*, pp. 37–8.
9 For Routh, see Burgon, *Lives of twelve good men* 1, pp. 1–115, 467–72; for his wishes for his library, see Middleton, *Dr. Routh*, pp. 253–6.
10 Gardiner, *History of Wisbech and neighbourhood, during the last fifty years, 1848–1898*, pp. 200, 414–16; notice by Rosemary Scott in the *ODNB*.
11 King, *Some British collectors of music, c.1600–1960*, p. 64.
12 Davidoff and Hall, *Family fortunes: men and women of the English middle class, 1780–1850*, pp. 23–4, give further references and offer a summary of internal divisions within the middle classes, between lower and higher ranks. In a

considerable literature, see for example Smith, *Conflict and compromise; class formation in English society, 1830–1914*.

13 For some of the new proprietary day and boarding schools, see the *Report of the Public Schools Commission* (1864).
14 For one comment on the new schools examining body established at Cambridge, see Jessopp, *The middle class examinations*.
15 Blackburne (ed.), *Suburban & rural architecture. English & foreign*.
16 *Nature* 18 (1878), p. 15; it was also available direct from America through Melvil Dewey, in Boston, price $18 plus £2.2s. carriage (advertised in Nicholson and Tedder (ed.), *Transactions and proceedings of the conference of librarians ... October 1877*, p. 242).
17 For a selection, see Attar, *A bibliography of household books published in Britain, 1800–1914*.
18 For further details of the various art unions, see *Report from the Select Committee on Art Unions* (House of Commons, 1845). The Art Union of London also published an *Annual*, with reduced reproductions of the pictures available, prices and names of prize-holders. See further Darcy, *The encouragement of the fine arts in Lancashire, 1760–1860*; King, *The industrialization of taste: Victorian England and the Art Union of London*; King, 'George Godwin and the Art Union of London, 1837–1911'.
19 Roberts, *The book-hunter in London*, p. xxi.
20 See below, pp. 225–6, 259–62.
21 Lady Eastlake, 'Memoir of Sir Charles Lock Eastlake', in Eastlake, *Contributions to the literature of the fine arts*, p. 147.
22 Macleod in her *Art and the Victorian middle class: money and the making of cultural identity*. She based her selection principally on a series of contemporary articles concerning collectors in the *Art Journal*.
23 Morris, *Victorian & Edwardian paintings in the Walker Art Gallery and at Sudley House*.
24 Pierson, *Private collecting, exhibitions and the shaping of art history in London: the Burlington Fine Arts Club*.
25 Evans, *A history of the Society of Antiquaries*.
26 Piggott, 'The origins of the English county archaeological societies', in his *Ruins in a landscape*, pp. 171–95.
27 McKitterick, 'Dawson Turner and book collecting', in Goodman, *Dawson Turner*.
28 *Catalogus bibliothecae Kingstonianae* (1726); Dibdin, *Bibliotheca Spenceriana* and *Aedes Althorpianae*; Pettigrew, *Bibliotheca Sussexiana*; *Bibliotheca Parriana*; *Catalogue of the library of Miss Richardson Currer*.
29 Taylor, *Book catalogues: their varieties and uses*.
30 Now in the Huntington Library.
31 Hazlitt, *Four generations* 2, pp. 260–1.

32 For Crossley as a collector, see Courtney, 'Mr. James Crossley', and Collins, *James Crossley*.

33 Hazlitt, *Four generations* 2, pp. 266–84; Hazlitt and Ellis, *The Huth library: a catalogue of the printed books, manuscripts, autograph letters, and engravings, collected by Henry Huth, with collations and bibliographical descriptions*. Copies of the catalogue were obtainable for 10 guineas. A revised edition of part of the catalogue was published later: Huth, *A catalogue of the woodcuts and engravings in the Huth library*.

34 *Catalogue of the fifty manuscripts & printed books bequeathed to the British Museum by Alfred H.Huth*.

11 Writing in Books

1 For many aspects of current interest, see Pearson, *Provenance research in book history: a handbook*.

2 *Catalogue of the library of Dr. Kloss ... including ... printed books with MS. annotations, by Philip Melancthon, which will be sold by auction, by Mr. Sotheby and Son ... May 7, and nineteen following days* (1835); Kloss, 'Ueber Melanchthons angebliche Handschriften, welche in dem Catalogue of the Library of Dr. Kloss verzeichnet sind'.

3 Dinaux, 'Livres annotés, signés et estampillés'. Autograph collecting is discussed in more detail on pp. 233–44.

4 Sotheby, *Ramblings in the elucidation of the autograph of Milton*.

5 'The library of Gray the poet', *Gentleman's Magazine* 1846, pt 1, pp. 29–33. The volume is now in the Pierpont Morgan Library, no. 16518.

6 Edwards, *Memoirs of libraries* 2, pp. 659–60.

7 Note by Arthur Dinaux, *BB* 8 (1847), p. 491.

8 Netherclift, *The hand-book of autographs*, p. 2.

9 Freeman and Freeman, *John Payne Collier: scholarship and forgery in the nineteenth century*, pp. 583–639, 720–824, 1221–5.

10 Ibid., pp. 1049–54.

11 Cambridge, 1812; revised ed. Leipzig, 1814.

12 *Catalogue de la bibliothèque de M.N. Yémeniz, précédé d'une notice par M. Le Roux de Lincy* (Paris, 1867).

13 Pellechet, *Bibliothèque Publique de Versailles. Catalogue des incunables et des livres imprimés de MD à MDXX*; Pellechet, *Catalogue des incunables des bibliothèques publiques de Lyon*.

12 Bookbinding

1 Le Roux de Lincy, *Recherches sur Jean Grolier: sur sa vie et sa bibliothèque*.

2 Hill, *Time's witness*, p. 158, quoting J.C. Loudon (1839).

3 Lempertz, *Bilder-Hefte zur Geschichte des Bücherhandels und der mit demselben verwandten Künste und Gewerbe*.
4 Techener and Techener, *Histoire de la bibliophilie. Reliures: recherches sur les bibliothèques des plus célèbres amateurs; armorial des bibliophiles*. For some of this history, see Breslauer, *The uses of bookbinding literature*.
5 Prospectus quoted (in translation) in 'Ancient ornamental book-binding', a review of the *Histoire de la bibliophilie* and other works, *The Fine Arts Quarterly Review* 1 (1863), pp. 172–9.
6 Cf. Hannett, *An inquiry into the nature and form of the books of the ancients*; Tuckett, *Specimens of ancient and modern binding, selected chiefly from the library of the British Museum*; Cundall, *On ornamental art, applied to ancient and modern bookbinding*.
7 *Monuments inédits ou peu connus, faisant partie du cabinet de Guillaume Libri, et qui se rapportent à l'histoire des arts du dessin considérés dans leur application à l'ornement des livres*, p. 4.
8 See p. 169.
9 Libri, quoted in 'Ancient ornamental book-binding', pp. 177–8.
10 A group of these treasure bindings was bought by Sir Thomas Phillipps, and later acquired by Pierpont Morgan. See Needham, *Twelve centuries of bookbindings, 400–1600*, pp. 52–4.
11 Cundall, *On ornamental art, applied to ancient and modern bookbinding*. For Cundall as a publisher and book designer, see McLean, *Victorian book design and colour printing*, 2nd ed., pp. 140–154, and McLean, *Joseph Cundall, a Victorian publisher: notes on his life and a check-list of his books*.
12 Edwards, *Memoirs of libraries* 2, pp. 959–80.
13 Cundall, *On bookbindings, ancient and modern*, p. 60.
14 Nisard, *Histoire des livres populaires*; Hindley, *Curiosities of street literature* (1871); Hindley, *The life and times of James Catnach (late of Seven Dials), ballad monger*.
15 Needham, Dunlap and Dreyfus, *William Morris and the art of the book*; Peterson, *The Kelmscott Press: a history of William Morris's typographical adventure*.
16 Fournier and others, *Histoire de l'imprimerie et des arts et professions qui se rattachent à la typographie, comprenant l'histoire des anciennes corporations et confréries depuis leur fondation jusqu'à leur suppression en 1789*.
17 Fournier, *L'art de la reliure en France aux derniers siècles*, p. 1.
18 The view persisted for a long time that the Ferrar community at Little Gidding was composed mostly of Anglican nuns. For a discussion of the bindings attributed to the community, see Hobson, *Bindings in Cambridge libraries*, pp. 122–4, and Nixon, *Five centuries of English bookbinding*, pp. 74–5.
19 Edwards, *Memoirs of libraries* 2, p. 959.
20 Wallon, *Notice sur la vie et les travaux de M.Ambroise Firmin-Didot*.

21 Now identified as Pierre-Étienne-Théodore Hagué: see http://histoire-bibliophilie.blogspot.com/2013/01/nouvelles-decouvertes-sur-le-relieur.html (accessed 1 January 2021). See further p. 169.
22 Reviewed in *The Times*, 24 June 1874.
23 Wheatley, *Bookbinding considered as a fine art, mechanical art, and manufacture; a paper read before the Society of Arts ... April 14, 1880*. Catalogue of specimens lent for exhibition, pp. 25–7.
24 Wheatley, *Bookbinding*. Although Bradshaw later agreed to a proposal by Wheatley that the two men should collaborate on an illustrated history of English binding, nothing came of it: see Prothero, *A memoir of Henry Bradshaw*, p. 330.
25 Ibid., Discussion p. 23.
26 Ibid.
27 Marius-Michel, *La reliure française, depuis l'invention de l'imprimerie jusqu'à la fin du XVIIIe siècle*; idem, *La reliure française commerciale et industrielle depuis l'invention de l'imprimerie jusqu'à nos jours*.
28 Quaritch, *Catalogue of works on the fine arts*, p. 1217. The catalogue of bindings, of which this forms a part, was issued first separately in July: see Henry B. Wheatley, 'Mr. Quaritch's catalogue of bookbindings', *The Bibliographer* 4 (1883), pp. 65–8.
29 Foot, 'Double agent: M.Caulin and M.Hagué; Foot, Blacker and Poole-Wilson, 'Collector, dealer and forger; a fragment of nineteenth-century binding history'.
30 Eudel, *Le truquage*, p. 264; Davenport, 'Forgeries in bookbinding'; Helwig, *Einbandfälschungen: Imitation, Fälschung und Verfälschung historischer Bucheinbände*; Nixon, 'Binding forgeries'. Hagué's work included new bindings bearing Grolier's name: see, for example, Davies, *Catalogue of a collection of early German books in the library of C. Fairfax Murray*, no. 386 (*Passio S. Ursulae* (Cologne, c.1503–11?)). For a colour reproduction of work attributed to him on a copy of Aegidius Carlerius, *Sporta fragmentorum* (Brussels, 1478–9), see H.P. Kraus catalogue 209, no 134, and for his work on Mazzochius, *Epigrammata antiquae urbis* (Rome, 1521), British Library C.48.h.10, see Jones (ed.), *Fake? The art of deception*, pp. 192–3.
31 'J. Verax' [Anatole Claudin], 'Les faussaires de livres'. More generally, see Béraldi, *La reliure du XIXe siècle* 2, pp. 125–36.
32 Quaritch, *A catalogue of fifteen hundred books remarkable for the beauty or the age of their bindings*.
33 Dring, 'Michael Kerney'.
34 *Revue de l'Art Chrétien* 1890, p. 162, reviewing Quaritch's *Catalogue of fifteen hundred books remarkable for the beauty or the age of their bindings, or as bearing indications of former ownership of great book-collectors and famous historical personages* (1889); *A collection of facsimiles from examples of historic or artistic bookbinding, illustrating the history of binding, as a branch of the*

decorative arts (Quaritch, 1889); Wheatley, *Remarkable bindings in the British Museum selected for their beauty or historic interest* (Sampson Low, 1889). The review was signed by W.H. de W., presumably Weale.

35 'Bookbinding is certainly a province of bibliography, yet it almost merges into a fine art, as do even more clearly book-illustration and illumination. Bibliography has to take cognizance of these subjects, but it can never make them altogether its own' (Greg, 'What is bibliography?').

36 Sold at Sotheby's, 16 March 1925. The catalogue prints his own notes on the bindings.

37 This was average for the Club's exhibitions. Two years earlier an exhibition of portrait miniatures drew an exceptional number of over 12,000, but during these years numbers varied between just over 1,000 and almost 4,000 for Japanese lacquer in 1894; Pierson, *Private collecting, exhibitions and the shaping of art history in London*, p. 165.

38 Burlington Fine Arts Club, *Exhibition of bookbindings*, p. xiv. The exhibition was summarised in *The Library* 3 (1891), pp. 287–91, and in the *Saturday Review*, 20 June 1891, pp. 740–1. For Prideaux, see Tidcombe, *Women bookbinders, 1880–1920*.

39 Burlington Fine Arts Club, *Exhibition of bookbindings*, p. lii.

40 Duff, *Early printed books*, p. 185.

41 Ibid., pp. 193–4.

42 The descriptions in Nixon, *Broxbourne Library: styles and designs of bookbindings from the twelfth to the twentieth century* are notable for their more than usual detail about matters other than decoration. See generally Pickwood, 'An unused resource: bringing the study of bookbindings out of the ghetto'; for further detail, see, for example, Pickwood, 'The interpretation of bookbinding structure: an examination of sixteenth-century bindings in the Ramey collection in the Pierpont Morgan Library'.

43 Duff, *Fifteenth century English books: a bibliography of books and documents printed in England and of books for the English market printed abroad*, repr. with supplementary materials by Lotte Hellinga as *Printing in England in the fifteenth century*

44 Brockwell, 'W.H. James Weale, the pioneer'; van Biervliet, *Leven en werk van W.H. James Weale, een Engels kunsthistoricus in Vlaanderen in de 19de eeuw.*

45 Weale, *Catalogue des objets d'art religieux du moyen âge, de la renaissance et des temps modernes: exposés à l'Hôtel Liedekerke à Malines*; Weale, *Tableaux de l'ancienne école néerlandaise exposés à Bruges dans la grande salle des Halles. Catalogue.*

46 Weale, 'La reliure au moyen âge'.

47 Milner, 'Account of an ancient manuscript of St. John's Gospel', p. 20.

48 Weale, *Bookbindings and rubbings of bookbindings in the National Art Library.*

49 Goldschmidt, 'The study of early bookbinding', p. 176.

50 Richardson, *Examples of ancient bookbindings: a portfolio of rubbings in the possession of the Art Library of South Kensington Museum*.
51 Weale, *Bookbindings and rubbings of bookbindings in the National Art Library* 1, p. lxvii.
52 Jenkinson, *A list of the incunabula collected by George Dunn arranged to illustrate the history of printing*: this includes the obituary notice from *The Times*.
53 Charles Nodier to Charles Weiss, 31 March [1814?], *Correspondance inédite*, p. 152. For Nodier, see, for example, Barrière, *Nodier l'homme du livre: le rôle de la bibliophilie dans la littérature*.
54 Reynolds, *A catalogue of the manuscripts in the library at Holkham Hall*. 1: *Manuscripts from Italy to 1500*. 1, p. 22. For more general remarks, see Pickwoad, 'The use of fragments of medieval manuscripts in the construction and covering of bindings on printed books'.
55 For this and earlier work see Pollard and Potter, *Early bookbinding manuals: an annotated list of technical accounts of bookbinding to 1840*. For Hannett (1803–93), see Morgan, 'John Hannett's *Bibliopegia* and *Inquiry*, and Salt Brassington's revision'.
56 Nicholson, *A manual of the art of bookbinding*, p. 294.
57 Hannett, *Bibliopegia: or, the art of bookbinding, in all its branches*, p. 87. This copy belonged once to Sir John Thynne, and was at Longleat by the 1540s. The second Longleat copy, formerly the property of Beriah Botfield, was sold at Christie's 13 June 2002.
58 Lenormand, *Nouveau manuel complet du relieur, dans toutes ses parties*.
59 The finishing tools of René Simier (1772–1843), one of the most prominent Paris binders, were sold by Lafon Castandet at the Hôtel Drouot, Paris, 2 June 2010.
60 See Bonnardot, *De la réparation des vieilles reliures*.
61 Lacroix, *Curiosités de l'histoire des arts*, p. 36.
62 Doyle, 'Two medieval calendars and other leaves removed by John Bowtell from University Library MSS'; McKitterick, *Cambridge University Library*, pp. 310, 313–14.
63 The volume passed into the hands of the Palgrave family, and then via an Ipswich bookseller to the typographer John Lewis: it is now in Reading University Library. A.F. Johnson later identified one piece as an indulgence printed by Thierry Martens at Antwerp in 1497: see Lewis, *Printed ephemera*, pp. 9 and 25, and Lewis, *Such things happen; the life of a typographer*, pp. 113–15. For a further fragment of printing by Caxton in the Lewis collection, and perhaps removed from a book in Cambridge University Library in the same period, see Delbecque, 'A newly discovered fragment of William Caxton's *Ordinale*'.
64 Blades, *The biography and typography of William Caxton, England's first printer*, 2nd ed., p. 215.

65 It is now in a modern binding in the Lessing J. Rosenwald collection, Library of Congress. See BMC XI, pp. 81, 108, 110.
66 Pollard, 'Memoir', in Proctor, *Bibliographical essays*, pp. xv, xviii–xix; Ker, *Pastedowns in Oxford bindings, with a survey of Oxford binding c.1515–1620*, p. xvi. Much of Bliss's collection was finally dispersed from 1984 onwards in a series of Quaritch catalogues (nos. 1036 etc.).
67 Fournier, *L'art de la reliure en France*, pp. 32–7.
68 Edwards, *Memoirs of libraries* 2, p. 985.
69 Oates 4003 (Boethius), 3872 (Indulgences). Bradshaw, *Correspondence on incunabula* 1, p. 147; 2, pp. 400–1. The illuminations have been attributed to Bruges: see Arnould and Massing, *Splendours of Flanders*, pp. 168–9.
70 Bradshaw, 'Notice of a fragment of the Fifteen Oes and other prayers printed at Westminster by W. Caxton about 1490–91, preserved in the library of the Baptist College, Bristol', p. 348.
71 Bradshaw, 'Notice of a fragment of the Fifteen Oes', p. 349. For the locations and interpretation of fragments of early Dutch printing, see Needham, 'Fragments in books: Dutch prototypography in the van Ess library' (with further general remarks); Hellinga, 'Fragments found in bindings and their role as bibliographical evidence'. For further comments on printer's and binder's waste used in bindings, see Duff, *Early printed books*, pp. 194–9, and White, 'Fragments of early Mainz printing in the R.E. Hart collection'.
72 Weale, *Bookbindings and rubbings of bindings in the National Art Library, South Kensington Museum* 1, pp. xix–xx.
73 Delisle, 'Circulaire à MM. les Maires relative au catalogue des incunables des bibliothèques de France', p. 8. See also Delisle, *Instructions pour la rédaction d'un inventaire des incunables conservés dans les bibliothèques publiques de France* (Paris, 1886) and the notice in the *Revue Critique* NS 22 (1886), p. 98; repr. with his *Instructions pour la rédaction d'un catalogue de manuscrits* (Paris, 1911).
74 For some efforts to preserve fragments in nineteenth-century Oxford, see also Ker, *Pastedowns*, pp. xiv–xv.
75 Dibdin, *The library companion*, pp. 809–16.
76 Bought for Angela Burdett-Coutts. Now Folger Shakespeare Library copy no. 5.
77 Willis and Sotheran, *Catalogue of superior second-hand books* (25 January 1857), no. 1.
78 Now Folger Shakespeare Library copy no. 69.
79 Catalogue of the books, manuscripts ... of the late Sir William Tite ... sold by Sotheby, Wilkinson & Hodge, 18 May etc. (1874), Lot 2713.
80 For summaries of prices of the First Folio at auction, see Wheatley, *Prices of books*, pp. 222–29, and West, 'Sales and prices of Shakespeare first folios: a history, 1623 to the present'.
81 Wilson, *The making of the Nuremberg chronicle*, pp. 229–37.
82 Dibdin, *Bibliotheca Spenceriana* 3, pp. 255–80.

83 Part of the following summary is from McKitterick, *The Philobiblon Society*, pp. 89–90.
84 Dibdin, *Bibliotheca Spenceriana* 3, p. 256.
85 Sold Christie's 13 June 2002, lot 60. For Botfield, see pp. 149–50.
86 *Willis's Prices Current* 25 March 1857, no. 204.
87 Willis and Sotheran, *A catalogue of upwards of fifty thousand volumes, of ancient and modern books*, p. 113.
88 Now Glasgow University Library BD9-a.2: Baldwin, *A catalogue of fifteenth-century printed books in Glasgow libraries and museums*, no. S16/2.
89 Quaritch, *Catalogue of the monuments of the early printers*, p. 4009.
90 Quaritch, *Monuments of typography and xylography*, nos. 110–13.
91 F.S. Ellis in Quaritch (ed.), *Contributions towards a dictionary of English book-collectors*, part X.

13 Reproduction

1 McLean, *Victorian book design and colour printing*, 2nd ed., pp. 115–39; Twyman, *A history of chromolithography: printed colour for all*.
2 Fitzgerald, *The book fancier*, pp. 218–19.
3 Robert Cutlar Fergusson auction, Sotheby's 28 February 1860, reported by Fitzgerald, *The book fancier*, p. 219.
4 Delisle, 'L'oeuvre paléographique de M. le comte de Bastard'. See also Bordier, 'Écritures, peintures et ornements des manuscrits'.
5 Bohn, *Catalogue of books* 1 (1848), New books at reduced prices, p. 15.
6 Quaritch, *Catalogue of works on the fine arts* offered the Hamilton Palace copy for £180.
7 Bouquin, 'Influence des relations entre éditeurs et imprimeurs-lithographes dans la genèse de l'illustration des livres au XIXe siècle', pp. 735–7.
8 See, for example, Roberts (ed.), *Art history through the camera's lens*; Hamber, *'A higher branch of the art': photographing the fine arts in England, 1839–1880*.
9 Bradshaw, *Correspondence on incunabula*.
10 Vidal, *La photographie appliquée aux arts industriels de la reproduction*. This was presented as a lecture in the previous year.
11 *Agnew's, 1817–1967* (1967), pp. 69–76.
12 Gernsheim, *Incunabula of British photographic literature, 1839–1875*.
13 Stephens, *Two leaves of King Waldere's lay, a hitherto unknown Old-English epic of the eighth century, belonging to the saga cyclus 'King Theodric and his men', now first published from the originals of the ninth century*, p. 14.
14 James, *Photo-zincography*; McKitterick, *Old books, new technologies: the representation, conservation and transformation of books since 1700*, pp. 103–5.
15 Humphreys, *A history of the art of printing*, preface.

16 For other aspects of Humphreys's work, see McLean, *Victorian book design and colour printing*, 2nd ed., pp. 99–114.

17 *The Book-Worm*, 1 March 1868, pp. 36–9.

18 'The palaeographical publications of the last twenty-five years'. To the list of twenty works listed at the head of the first article he subsequently added two more.

19 Reviewed also by Léopold Delisle in the *Bibliothèque de l'École des Chartes* 45 (1884), pp. 533–49.

20 *The Academy*, 20 September 1884, p. 186.

21 Hessels's own work was not above reproach. See for example, Nettleship, Review of *An eighth-century Latin-Anglo-Saxon glossary, preserved in the library of Corpus Christi College, Cambridge* by J.H. Hessels.

22 *The Epinal glossary, Latin and Old-English of the eighth century*, ed. with transliteration, introduction, and notes, by Henry Sweet, Preface. The photo-lithographs were prepared by Griggs, one of the most experienced firms in London.

23 Williams, 'Photo-facsimiles of *STC* books: a cautionary check list'; McKitterick, *Old books and modern technologies*.

24 Harris, *History of the British Museum Library*, pp. 226, 279, 354.

25 Garnett, 'Photography in public libraries', pp. 236–7.

26 Harris, *History of the British Museum Library*, pp. 430–1.

27 Garnett, 'Photography in public libraries', p. 252.

28 Garnett, *Essays in librarianship and bibliography*, Preface, p. x. For early photography at the Bodleian Library, see Craster, *History of the Bodleian Library, 1845–1945*, pp. 203–4.

29 Hamber, '*A higher branch of the art*': *photographing the fine arts in England, 1839–1880*.

14 Exhibitions

1 *Guide to the printed books exhibited to the public* (1870).

2 Morel, 'Ueber die Ausstellung auf der deutschen Buchhändlerbörse zu Leipzig während der Feier des Buchdruckfestes 1840'.

3 For some of the major international general ones, see Greenhalgh, *Ephemeral vistas: the Expositions Universelles, Great Exhibitions, and World's Fairs, 1851–1939*; notwithstanding the title, Démy, *Essai historique sur les expositions universelles de Paris* has details of dozens of exhibitions also in provincial France and across the world.

4 Finke, 'The art-treasures exhibition'; Pergam, *The Manchester Art Treasures exhibition of 1857: entrepreneurs, connoisseurs and the public*.

5 *A catalogue of antiquities and works of art, exhibited at Ironmongers' Hall, London, in the month of May 1861*. Some 100 large-paper copies were printed, price 5 guineas; small-paper copies cost 3 guineas.
6 MS 37: Sandler, *Gothic manuscripts, 1285–1385*, no. 150.
7 de Ris, *La curiosité; collections françaises et étrangères*, pp. 192–4.
8 Cole, *A special report on the annual international exhibitions of the years 1871, 1872, 1873, and 1874, presented by the Board of Management to Her Majesty's Commissioners for the exhibition of 1851*, p. xxxi.
9 *International exhibition, 1862; Official catalogue, industrial department*, p. xvi.
10 *Reports of artisans selected by a committee approved by the council of the Society of Arts to visit the Paris Universal Exhibition, 1867*, p. 374.
11 *Paris Universal Exhibition of 1867. Part II. Catalogue of the works exhibited in the British Section*, p. 74, appendix p. 19.
12 Robinson (ed.), *Catalogue of the special exhibition of works of art of the mediaeval, renaissance, and more recent periods, on loan at the South Kensington Museum, June 1862*. Revised ed.
13 Catalogue no. 7101; no. 37 in the list of her manuscripts in Barker (introd.), *Esther Inglis's Les proverbes de Salomon: a facsimile*, pp. 86–94.
14 Catalogue no. 7109.
15 Catalogue no. 7099.
16 Catalogue no. 7116, Johannes Lorichius, *Aenigmatum libellus* (1540).
17 Catalogue no. 7025. See also Sotheby, *Principia typographica* 1, p. 22.
18 Catalogue no. 7115.
19 Cole, *A special report on the annual international exhibitions of the years 1871, 1872, 1873, and 1874, presented by the Board of Management to Her Majesty's Commissioners for the exhibition of 1851*, p. 163.
20 Démy, *Essai historique sur les expositions universelles de Paris*, p. 250.
21 The cover is illustrated in *Choice examples of the engraver's art* (1890).
22 The volume was in possession of the comte Louis Van der Cruisse de Waziers, in Lille; Mertens and others, *Blockbücher des Mittelalters: Bilderfolgen als Lektüre*.
23 Brunet, *Manuel du libraire* 1, pp. 508–9.
24 White, *Editio princeps: a history of the Gutenberg Bible*, p. 255. This copy later belonged to Heinrich Klemm: see p. 213.
25 After various bequests, Fillon's early printed books were sold by Claudin at Paris in 1883.
26 This copy is now in the Bibliothèque Nationale de France.
27 Audin, *Les types lyonnais primitifs conservés au Département des Imprimés*, now on deposit in the Musée de l'Imprimerie at Lyon.
28 Aumale, *La dermotypotemnie; étude sur quelques livres, cum figuris et characteribus ex nulla materia compositis*. The catalogue described the exhibit: 'Chaque feuillet est doublé d'un morceau d'étoffe ou de carton foncé qui forme

transparent, et qui, lorsque la page est appliquée sur sa doublure, donne un relief éclatant au dessin ou au texte qu'elle présente.'

29 Léon Techener (1832–88) succeeded his father on Joseph's death in 1873. The third and final sale of his valuable private library took place in May 1889, with a catalogue prefaced by Émile Picot.

30 Cole, *A special report on the annual international exhibitions of the years 1871, 1872, 1873, and 1874, presented by the Board of Management to Her Majesty's Commissioners for the exhibition of 1851*, appendix LVI.

31 Ibid., p. xxxvi.

32 Bonython and Burton, *The great exhibitor; the life and work of Henry Cole*, p. 264.

33 *Agnew's, 1817–1967*, p. 8. For the taste for modern pictures among collectors in the north-west, see Morris, *Public art collections in north-west England*; for commitment to the fine arts in a broader part of the population, see Darcy, *The encouragement of the fine arts in Lancashire, 1760–1860* and Seed, '"Commerce and the liberal arts"; the political economy of art in Manchester, 1775–1860'.

34 Morris, *Victorian & Edwardian paintings in the Walker Art Gallery and at Sudley House: British artists born after 1810 but before 1861*.

35 Wedmore, 'A century of English art: the Grosvenor Gallery'; Staley, '"Art is upon the town!": the Grosvenor Gallery winter exhibitions'.

36 Bullen (ed.), *Caxton celebration, 1877. Catalogue of the loan collection of antiquities, curiosities, and appliances concerned with the art of printing*; Stevens, *The Bibles in the Caxton exhibition, MDCCCLXXVII*; Myers, 'The Caxton celebration of 1877'; McKitterick, *Old books, new technologies*, pp. 159–77. See further on pp. 211–12.

37 See pp. 297–8

38 Harris, *History of the British Museum library, 1753–1973*, p. 319. For the Luther exhibition, see the anonymous review in *The Bibliographer* 4 (1883), pp. 126–32, and the note by Karl Pearson, ibid., pp. 179–80.

39 *A handbook of Rome and its environs*, ed. A.J.S[trutt], 13th ed. (John Murray, 1881), p. 354. Strutt (1819–88) was a landscape painter who settled in Rome.

40 Olgar Thierry-Poux, Bibliothèque Nationale. Département des Imprimés. *Notice des objets exposés*; [Delisle] Bibliothèque Nationale. Département des Manuscrits, Chartes et Diplômes. *Notice des objets exposés*.

41 Bibliothèque Nationale, *Notice des objets exposés. Imprimés. Manuscrits. Estampes* (Paris, 1881).

42 *Cercle de la Librairie. Première exposition*. See also the detailed history of the Cercle in *Le Cercle de la Librairie de Paris à l'exposition du livre; catalogue*, prepared for the exhibition celebrating the third centenary of Christophe Plantin, Antwerp, 1890, and Fléty, 'Le Cercle de la Librairie; un siècle et demi d'histoire'.

43 *Vereeniging ter Bevordering van de Belangen des Boekhandels, Erste tentoonstelling*.

44 See the notice by S.P. Parissien in *ODNB*.
45 Tite, *An address delivered before the Society of Antiquaries ... December 12th, 1861, at an exhibition of printed books, to which is subjoined an address delivered on June 6th, 1861, at an exhibition of illuminated manuscripts*, p. 1. Evans, *A history of the Society of Antiquaries*, p. 306, records that the exhibition was in fact postponed until 9 January 1862, because of the death of the Prince Consort.
46 This copy is now in the Pforzheimer collection, University of Texas: see *The Carl H. Pforzheimer library. English literature, 1475–1700*, no. 896.
47 See the notice by W.B. Owen and Bernard Nurse in the *ODNB*. His books were sold at Sotheby's, 24 February 1873.
48 Loftie, *Lessons in the art of illuminating ... with practical instructions and a sketch of the history of the art*.
49 Loftie, *A century of Bibles, or the Authorised Version from 1611 to 1711*.
50 For details of the Institute's management, see the Council minute book, 1862–78, deposited in the library of the Society of Antiquaries.
51 Cf. Winston, *Memoirs illustrative of the art of glass painting*.
52 Jones, 'Early printed books'.
53 Loftie, 'Catalogue of a loan collection of books printed before 1600'.
54 See p. 121.
55 His books were sold at Sotheby's, 29 August 1877.
56 See the notice by Alexander Gordon and R.K. Webb in *ODNB*. Yates died in 1871, and books from his library were sold at Sotheby's, 24 June 1875.
57 He died in 1873, and his books were sold at Sotheby's in 1874–5: see p. 237.
58 STC 2729.
59 The first book listed in Martin's *Bibliographical catalogue of books privately printed* (1834) was not this, but Parker's anonymous *De antiquitate Britannicae ecclesiae et privilegiis ecclesiae Cantuariensis* (1572).
60 Schmidt, *Gedruckte Bilder in handgeschriebenen Büchern: zum Gebrauch von Druckgraphik* ... p. 263.
61 For example Hermannus Schildiz, *Speculum sacerdotum de tribus sacramentis principalibus* (Mainz: Printer of the 'Darmstadt' prognostication, c.1477–80), Goff S316, now in the Huntington Library, and Sifridus de Arena, *Determinatio duarum quaestionum* (Mainz: Printer of the 'Darmstadt' prognostication, 1476?), Goff S495. For Russell's copies, see Hessels, *Gutenberg: was he the inventor of printing?* pp. 108, 110.
62 John Rylands University Library of Manchester, Spencer 17249.
63 See pp. 57–67.
64 Berjeau, *Essai bibliographique sur le Speculum humanae salvationis, indiquant le passage de la xylographie à la typographie*.
65 See further p. 65.
66 McKitterick, *Old books, new technologies*, pp. 159–82.

67 Hope, 'The Antwerp origins of the Coverdale Bible: investigations from the 1884 *Athenaeum* controversy to the present day', in Arblaster, Juhász and Latré (ed.), *Tyndale's Testament*, pp. 41–4; Bullen (ed.), *Caxton celebration, 1877. Catalogue of the loan collection ... connected with the art of printing*, pp. 116–18. Thanks to Stevens's late submission, the final and fuller version of the catalogue differed substantially from the 'Preliminary issue'.

68 The report in *The Bibliographer* 3 (1882–3) pp. 14–16, presumably written by Wheatley, was based on the extensive account in the *Liverpool Mercury*.

69 Klein, *Über Gutenberg und das im ersten Druckhaus desselben aufgefundene Fragment seiner Presse*; Klemm, *Beschreibender Catalog des Bibliographischen Museums*, pp. 452–64. Supposed relics of Gutenberg's press were natural magnets for the curious. In 1860 Francis Fry was shown a 'precious relic', a bar of wood with Gutenberg's initials and the date 1441 said to have been unearthed beneath a building in Mainz in 1857 together with 'a few stone mulls, used no doubt for grinding the ink', and four Roman coins. Fry regarded the discovery as further confirmation that Gutenberg had invented printing, at Mainz. (Fry, *A brief memoir of Francis Fry*, pp. 65–9, printing a note by Fry dated 1 January 1861.)

70 *The Bibliographer* 5 (1883–4), p. 22; Klemm, *Beschreibender Catalog des Bibliographischen Museums*: for the Gutenberg Bible, including a description of its binding, see p. 11. More generally, see Rüdiger, 'Eine Büchersammlung im 19. Jahrhundert: über einige Provenienzen der Sammlung Heinrich Klemm'. Klemm had the original binding removed, and a modern one substituted. The Bible is now in the Russian State Library: see White, *Editio princeps: a history of the Gutenberg Bible*, pp. 254–8.

71 *L'Université et la typographie: exposition organisée par la Société Archéologique et Historique de l'Orléanais*.

72 Sauvage, *Souvenirs de l'exposition typographique de Rouen*.

73 For plans of the estate of the 1851 Commissioners, see *Survey of London*, 38. *The Museums area of South Kensington and Westminster*, p. 54.

74 Démy, *Essai historique sur les expositions universelles de Paris*, pp. 144–5, 195, 255.

75 *The Times*, 4 May 1885.

76 *Guide to the loan collection and list of musical instruments, books, paintings, and engravings, exhibited in the gallery and lower rooms, of the Albert Hall*.

77 *The Times*, 25 July 1885.

78 Weale, *Historical music loan exhibition, Albert Hall: a descriptive catalogue of rare manuscripts & printed books, chiefly liturgical*, preface. For one appreciative review, see that by W.H. Stone in *Nature*, 25 June 1885, p. 174. Stone had lectured on sound and music in a series of science lectures at South Kensington in 1876.

79 St Gallen mss 359 (called a Graduale and dated s.ix by Weale), 484, 376 (dated s.x by Weale).

80 See pp. 169–73.
81 ISTC now records twenty copies, including eleven in Hungary.
82 ISTC now records ten copies, most imperfect.

15 Changes in Direction

1 Huntington Library MS EL 26 C 9; Yale University Library MS Takamiya 32.
2 Fabian, 'An eighteenth-century research collection: English books at Göttingen University Library'; Fabian, 'Die erste Bibliographie der englischen Literatur des achtzehnten Jahrhunderts: Jeremias David Reuß' *Gelehrtes England*'; Jefcoate and Kloth, ed. Fabian, *A catalogue of English books printed before 1801 held by the University Library, Göttingen*. For German interest in English literature, see Fabian, *The English book in eighteenth-century Germany*.
3 Selwyn, *Everyday life in the German book trade: Friedrich Nicolai as bookseller and publisher in the age of enlightenment, 1750–1810*.
4 Knight, *The old printer and the modern press*, p. 244.
5 *Business directory of London* (1869).
6 For some of this, see Donald and Donald, *The art of Thomas Bewick*, especially pp. 181–223, '"Know your Bewick"; the Victorian inheritance', and Williams, *Thomas Bewick, engraver, & the performance of woodblocks*.
7 The complete text was first printed in Bewick, *A memoir*, ed. Iain Bain.
8 Hugo, *Bewick's woodcuts. Impressions of upwards of two thousand wood blocks*; Hindley, *The life and times of James Catnach (late of Seven Dials), ballad monger*, pp. xv–xvi.
9 Stephens, *Notes on a collection of Thomas Bewick's drawings and woodcuts, exhibited at the Fine Arts Society's rooms*. See also and more comprehensively Tattersfield, *The complete illustrative work of Thomas Bewick*.
10 For a summary of these and other occasions or comments, see Daxon, 'Thomas Bewick at 250: landmarks in the building of a reputation'.
11 Hindley, *The life and times of James Catnach (late of Seven Dials), ballad monger*. Of the 230 woodcuts in this book, he claimed forty-two to be by Bewick.
12 Tattersfield, *Dealing in deceit: Edwin Pearson of 'The Bewick Repository' bookshop, 1838–1901*.
13 Tattersfield, *Thomas Bewick, the complete illustrative work*.
14 Apart from the classic studies by White, *English illustration: 'the sixties', 1855–70* and Reid, *Illustrators of the sixties*, see Goldman, *Victorian illustration: the Pre-Raphaelites, the Idyllic School and the high Victorians* and Cooke, *Illustrated periodicals of the 1860s; contexts and collaborations*.
15 For an account of preparing large blocks by a team of craftsmen, see Jackson, *The pictorial press: its origin and progress*, pp. 315–25.

16 Knight, *The old printer and the modern press*, pp. 258–9. Knight claimed that such stereotypes were supplied for eleven different countries and languages: *Passages in a working life* 2, p. 223.
17 *One hundred and fifty wood cuts selected from The Penny Magazine; worked, by printing machine, from the original blocks.*
18 See Chatto, *The history and art of wood-engraving, with specimens of the art, ancient and modern, selected from 'The Illustrated London News'*.
19 Hunnisett, *Steel-engraved book illustration in England*; Hunnisett, *Engraved on steel: the history of picture production using steel plates*.
20 Grego, *Rowlandson the caricaturist*.
21 'The present value of Dickens's works', *Book-Lore* 5 (1886–7), p. 145.
22 Slater, *Early editions: a bibliographical survey of the works of some popular modern authors*, p. vii.
23 Sadleir, 'The development during the last fifty years of bibliographical study of books of the XIXth century', p. 150.
24 Slater, *Early editions: a bibliographical survey of the works of some popular modern authors*, p. v.
25 Carter and Pollard, *An enquiry*, pp. 99–109.
26 Though the title-page is dated 1866, in fact it was not published until April 1867: advertisements in the *Literary Examiner*, 6 April, the *Pall Mall Gazette*, 15 April, *The Times*, 17 April.
27 Advertisement prefixed to some copies of *Tennysoniana*.
28 Fitzgerald, *The book fancier*, pp. 155–6.
29 Warren, 'The bibliography of Tennyson'. Warren (1835–95) is better remembered as the minor poet Lord de Tabley.
30 Tennyson to Pickering, 14 May 1866. Tennyson, *Letters* 2, p. 436.
31 Henry Bradshaw signed his copy (Trinity College, Cambridge G.18.22) on 24 May 1867. It contains about thirty pages not in the partially reset standard copies, besides further cancelled leaves.
32 *Pall Mall Gazette*, 15 May 1867.
33 *The Examiner*, 26 April 1879.
34 Puttick & Simpson, 7 April 1879.
35 See the account by J.F.R. Collins in the *ODNB*.
36 Wise, *A bibliography of the writings of Alfred, Lord Tennyson* 2, pp. 7–21. But for Shepherd's relationship with Wise, see Barker and Collins, *A sequel to an enquiry*.
37 *Belfast News-Letter*, 30 May 1879; *Dundee Courier*, 30 May 1879; *Huddersfield Chronicle*, 31 May 1879. A fuller report of proceedings was printed in the *York Herald*, June 1849.
38 See pp. 171–4.
39 The first number of *Dombey and Son* was printed initially in 34,000 copies, and *Bleak House* sold about 35,000 copies: Patten, *Charles Dickens and his*

publishers, Appendix B, and (more summarily) Altick, *The English common reader: a social history of the mass reading public, 1800–1900*, pp. 383–4.
40 Fitzgerald, *The book fancier*, p. 179. See for example Dickson, *The Arents collection of books in parts: a complete checklist*.
41 Johnson, *Hints to collectors of original editions of the works of Charles Dickens* (1885). Noticed in *Book-Lore* 2 (1885), pp. 76–7.
42 Fitzgerald, *The book fancier*, pp. 117–18.
43 Johnson, *Hints to collectors of original editions of the works of Charles Dickens*, p. 33. See also Smith, *Charles Dickens in the original cloth*. Part 1, pp. 99–104.
44 Barker and Collins, *A sequel to an enquiry*, pp. 23–42.
45 Forman, *The Shelley library: an essay in bibliography*, p. 27.
46 Wise, *Catalogue of the Ashley library* 5, p. 128.
47 Barker and Collins, *A sequel to an enquiry*, pp. 47–8.
48 A summary list by Austin Dobson of editions of *The Vicar of Wakefield* was added to the type facsimile published by Elliot Stock in 1885.
49 *Book-Lore* 5 (1886–7), p. 53.
50 Payne, *Great catalogues by master booksellers*, pp. 43–7, prints Cochran's long preliminary advertisement, and quotes details of the slow sales, compiled by S.C. Cockerell, from the copy in the Grolier Club library.
51 See Lacombe, *Bibliographie des travaux de M.Léopold Delisle; Supplément*.
52 *Catalogue of the autograph room, entirely filled with the collection of Mr. William Upcott ... With portraits. Third exhibition, Liverpool Mechanics' Institution, June and July 1844*.
53 Peignot, *Recherches historiques et bibliographiques sur les autographes et sur l'autographie*, pp. 2–3. For Peignot, see Simonnet, *Essai sur la vie et les ouvrages de Gabriel Peignot*.
54 Thomas Carlyle, letter to an anonymous correspondent, 8 February 1872. Maggs catalogue 1231 (1997), no. 22.
55 George Eliot to William Griffiths, 25 July 1878: Christie's, 12 December 2018, lot 52.
56 Eliot, *Letters* 7, p. 193.
57 Fontaine, *Manuel de l'amateur d'autographes*, p. 1.
58 Munby, *The cult of the autograph letter*, p. 81.
59 Fontaine, *Manuel de l'amateur d'autographes*, pp. 156–65.
60 Ibid., p. 349. More generally, see Lalanne and Bordier, *Dictionnaire de pièces autographes volées aux bibliothèques publiques de la France, précédé d'observations sur le commerce des autographes*, pp. 36–54; see also Bodin, 'Les grandes collections de manuscrits littéraires', esp. pp. 170–2.
61 Peignot, *Recherches historiques*, p. 42.
62 See also Lescure, *Les autographes*, p. 62.
63 'Les parchemins existant dans les ci-devant chambres des comptes et autres dépôts publics, bibliothèques particulières, etc. ... qui se trouvent propres à faire des gargousses pour le service de l'artillerie des ports de la République,

soient mis à la disposition du ministre de la marine, etc.' (Decree of 5 January 1793, quoted ibid., p. 41.)

64 Stammers, 'The refuse of the Revolution; autograph collecting in France, 1789–1860' in Aementenos and others (eds.) *Historicising the French Revolution*. For this and further aspects, see Bertrand and others (ed.), *Collectionner la Révolution française*, and Stammers, *The purchase of the past: collecting culture in post-revolutionary Paris, c.1790–1890*, chapter 2, 'Archiving and envisioning the French Revolution (c.1780–1830)'.

65 Bodin, 'Les grandes collections de manuscrits littéraires'.

66 Gaviglio-Faivre d'Arcier, 'Les Charavay: une dynastie de marchands d'autographes'; David and Nougaret, *Collection des catalogues de vente d'autographes et livres anciens imprimés des libraires et des salles de vente: inventaire analytique*. Dawson Turner owned his catalogues nos. 1–23, 1845–7: see *Catalogue of the remaining portion of the library of Dawson Turner* (Puttick and Simpson, 16 May 1859, etc.), lot 2026. Turner's exceptional collection of several hundred sale catalogues of autographs occupied mainly lots 2013–48, most lots containing several catalogues.

67 Charavay, *Lettres autographes composant la collection de M. Alfred Bovet, décrites par Étienne Charavay*.

68 Some of his ephemera are reproduced in Grand-Carteret, *Vieux papiers, vieilles images: cartons d'un collectionneur*.

69 *The Book-Worm*, 1869, pp. 94–5.

70 McKitterick, *The Philobiblon Society*, pp. 85, 98.

71 Briggs, *A history of Longmans and their books, 1724–1990: longevity in publishing*, pp. 241–4.

72 McKitterick, *The Philobiblon Society*, pp. 96–7.

73 Lescure, *Les autographes*, p. 111; Dyson, 'The MSS. and proof sheets of Scott's Waverley novels'; Munby, *The cult of the autograph letter*, pp. 6–8.

74 For these and further details, see [H.H. Wood] 'Jottings from the note-book of an undeveloped collector', p. 498. For prices achieved by Scott's manuscripts, see *The Scott exhibition MDCCCLXXI; catalogue of the exhibition held at Edinburgh, in July and August 1871*.

75 For a report on the 1846 sale, see the *Gentleman's Magazine*, 1846, pt 1, pp. 29–33.

76 *Catalogue of the manuscript library of the late Dawson Turner ... sold by auction, by Messrs Puttick and Simpson ... June 6 and four following days* (1859), p. xix. For the general series of correspondence now in Trinity College, Cambridge, and for several other series, see Munby, *The cult of the autograph letter*, pp. 59–60 (notes by Warren R. Dawson).

77 For a crisis in his career, see Harding, 'The Colvin print theft and the rise and fall of A.W. Thibaudeau'.

78 *Catalogue of the collection of autograph letters and historical documents formed between 1865 and 1882, compiled and annotated under the direction of A. W.*

Thibaudeau, and various later volumes. See Munby, *The cult of the autograph letter*, pp. 76, 77–9.
79 *Bibliothèque de l'École des Chartes* 45 (1884), pp. 196–202.
80 For Lovenjoul, see Crampton, 'Charles de Spoelberch de Lovenjoul, 1836–1907', and Gaviglio Faivre d'Arcier, *Lovenjoul (1836–1907): une vie, une collection*.
81 *The Bibliographer* 2 (1882), p. 22. See also *BB* 1882, pp. 317–23.
82 Purchased by a private collector. Bought by the Pierpont Morgan Library in 1925.
83 Purchased, with several other Balzac manuscripts, by Lovenjoul and now with the rest of his collection in the Institut de France.
84 For a select list of volumes of facsimiles published in England between 1835 and 1866, see Munby, *The cult of the autograph letter*, p. 100. For French and further works, see Fontaine, *Manuel de l'amateur d'autographes*, pp. 34–50 and Lescure, *Les autographes*.
85 *Lithographed signatures of the members of the British Association for the Advancement of Science, who met at Cambridge, June M.DCCC.XXXIII: with a report of the proceedings at the public meetings during the week, and an alphabetical list of the members.*
86 For a list of contents, and a summary of those to be found instead in the fortnightly periodical *Amateur des Autographes*, see Lescure, *Les autographes*, pp. 198–210.
87 *A collection of 300 autograph letters of celebrated individuals of all nations, from the sixteenth to the nineteenth century* (Stuttgart, 1846).
88 For the forged Keats entry, printed in good faith, see Freeman, *Bibliotheca fictiva*, p. 247.
89 Fontaine, *Manuel de l'amateur d'autographes*, pp. 125, 126.
90 Lescure, *Les autographes*, pp. 281–3.
91 Netherclift, *The hand-book of autographs*, p. 2.
92 His essays were reprinted in Lacroix ('P.L. Jacob'), *Mélanges bibliographiques*, pp. 244–58, 269–78.
93 Lescure, *Les autographes*, pp. 28, 281.
94 Delisle, *Catalogue des manuscrits des fonds Libri et Barrois*, pp. xvi–xvii. See also Lalanne and Bordier, *Dictionnaire de pièces autographes volées aux bibliothèques publiques de la France, précédé d'observations sur le commerce des autographes* and pp. 104–5.
95 Ehrsam, *Major Byron, the incredible career of a literary forger*.
96 Freeman, *Bibliotheca fictiva: a collection of books & manuscripts relating to literary forgery, 400BC–AD2000*, pp. 48, 242, 247–8.
97 De Morgan's letter on the subject to *The Athenaeum*, 27 August 1867, was reprinted in *The Book-Worm*, 30 September, pp. 136–7. For Lucas, see especially Bordier and Mabille, *Une fabrique de faux autographes, ou récit de l'affaire Vrain Lucas* (with facsimiles of some forgeries), trans. as *Prince of*

98 Maze-Sencier, *Le livre des collectionneurs*, pp. 797–8.

99 Charavay, preface to *Lettres autographes composant la collection de M. Alfred Bovet, décrites par Étienne Charavay*, p. xvii. For further comment not just on forged books, bindings and manuscripts but also on a range of other works of art, see Eudel, *Le truquage*.

100 For Henry Bradshaw's exposé in *The Guardian*, see Prothero, *A memoir of Henry Bradshaw*, pp. 92–7.

101 Freeman and Ing, *John Payne Collier: scholarship and forgery in the nineteenth century*.

102 Fontaine, *Manuel de l'amateur d'autographes*, pp. 27–33; Sauvy, *Livres saisis à Paris entre 1678 et 1701*, p. 86.

103 Schoenbaum, *William Shakespeare; records and images*, pp. 117–36. For doubtful and spurious Shakespeare signatures, see ibid., pp. 99–109. A large group of his forgeries was sold at Sotheby's, on 19 August 1835, in the library of Charles Mathews, the comedian. One of his albums, later owned by Richard Monckton Milnes, is now in Trinity College, Cambridge. See also Arthur Freeman, 'William Henry Ireland's "Authentic original forgeries": an overdue rediscovery'.

104 See p. 155.

105 Scott, *Autograph collecting: a practical manual for amateurs and historical students*.

106 Baughan, *Character indicated by handwriting*, pp. 3–4.

107 See pp. 208–11.

108 Ashton, *Chap-books of the eighteenth century, with facsimiles, notes and introduction*, preface.

109 For a recent discussion see Russell, *The ephemeral eighteenth century: print, sociability, and the cultures of collecting*, Introduction. The diverse nature of the phenomenon is addressed in Rickards and Twyman, *The encyclopedia of ephemera*; for reflections in the context of the ESTC, see Alston, 'The eighteenth-century non-book; observations on printed ephemera', in Barber and Fabian (eds.) *Buch und Buchhandel in Europa*.

110 For Pepys's collections, see Latham (ed.), *Catalogue of the Pepys library at Magdalene College, Cambridge*. For Bagford, see Gatch, 'John Bagford, bookseller and antiquary'; A.W. Pollard's 'rough list' of the contents of the Bagford collection, first printed in the *Transactions of the Bibliographical Soc.* 7 (1902–4), pp. 23–35, is reprinted in Wolf, *Catalogue and indexes to the title-pages of English printed books in the British Library's Bagford collection*.

111 The categorised collection of Sarah Sophia Banks (1744–1818) included large numbers of tickets and visiting cards, besides much other matter and a group of coins and tokens: Griffiths and Williams, *The Department of Prints and Drawings in the British Museum: user's guide*, pp. 82–4; Leis, 'Sarah Sophia

Banks, "A 'truly interesting collection of visiting cards and Co.'"; Russell, *The ephemeral eighteenth century: print, sociability, and the cultures of collecting*, pp. 98–152.

112 Some of his collection of prospectuses, on lotteries, on the Great Yarmouth and Norwich railway and on an assortment of other topics, is now in the British Library, shelf-marks 8225.bb.78, 1889.d.14 and 1879.b.1. See Boneham, 'The Dawson Turner collection of printed ephemera and Great Yarmouth'.

113 Vander Haeghen, *Pièces volantes*; see also Uyttenhove and Van Peterghem, 'Ferdinand van der Haeghen's shadow on Otlet: European resistance to the Americanized modernism of the Office International de Bibliographie', especially pp. 91–2. See also Roersch, 'Notice sur Ferdinand van der Haeghen'.

114 For Moreau and Larousse, see Mollier and Dubot, *Histoire de la librairie Larousse (1852–2010)*.

115 Gruys, 'The Bibliotheca Duncaniana'. See also Reinders, *Printed pandemonium: popular print and politics in the Netherlands, 1650–72*.

116 Knuttel, *Catalogus van de pamfletten-verzameling berustende in de Koninklijke Bibliotheek*.

117 *Bibliotheek van Nederlandsche pamfletten. Eerste afdeeling. Verzameling van Frederik Muller te Amsterdam naar tijdsorde gerangschikt en geschreven door P.A.Tiele*; *Catalogus van de tractaten, pamfletten, enz. over de geschiedenis van Nederland, aanwezig in de bibliotheek van Isaac Meulman, bewerkt door J.K. Van der Wulp*; Gruys, 'The Bibliotheca Duncaniana', p. 33, notes 17–18.

118 Van Alphen, *Catalogus der pamfletten van de bibliotheek der Rijksuniversiteit te Groningen, 1542–1853*.

119 Reinders, *Printed pandemonium*, p. 18. 1672 was 'Het rampjaar', the disaster year, in which France invaded the Dutch Republic.

120 Stammers, *The purchase of the past*, pp. 113–14.

121 Thibaut, *Description historique et bibliographique de la collection de feu M. le comte de la Bédoyère ... sur la Révolution Française, l'Empire et la Restauration*; Tesnière, 'La postérité de la presse révolutionnaire à la Bibliothèque nationale de France'.

122 Spevack, *James Orchard Halliwell-Phillipps: the life and works of the Shakespearean scholar and bookman*, p. 285.

123 Both the Borghese and ballads collections are deposited in the National Library of Scotland.

124 McKitterick, *Cambridge University Library*, pp. 687–8.

125 Tuer, *Old London street cries and the cries of today*.

126 Bloomfield (ed.), *A directory of rare book and special collections in the United Kingdom and the Republic of Ireland*, 2nd ed. (1997), pp. 457–8.

127 Harris, *History of the British Museum library*, p. 58.

128 Ibid., p. 150; Kahrl and Anderson, *The Garrick collection of old English plays: a catalogue with an historical introduction*.

129 Harris, *History of the British Museum library*, p. 276.
130 In attempts to describe what are now millions of uncatalogued pieces of minor printed material in Britain, the Research Support Libraries Programme (RSLP) was founded in the 1980s with the aims first of ascertaining what was thus far unattended in libraries, and then of devising ways of making that known, whether through focused cataloguing of some subjects or, more recently, in agreed criteria for structured collection descriptions that can then be made available on the Web.

16 Advice and Guidance

1 Davis, *The tastemakers; British dealers and the Anglo-Gallic interior, 1785–1865*.
2 Wainwright, *The romantic interior: the British collector at home, 1750–1850*.
3 Middleton, *A history of English craft bookbinding technique*. For practices in French binding at this time, see Lenormand, *Nouveau manuel complet de relieur*.
4 Kraye and Sachet (ed.), *The afterlife of Aldus: posthumous fame, collectors and the book trade*. The continuing appeal of books published by the Elzevier dynasty is considered in Lang, *Books and bookmen*, pp. 3–17, and in Christie, 'Elzevier bibliography'. Christie's paper was occasioned by the publication of Berghman, *Études sur la bibliographie Elzevirienne*, supplementing Willems, *Les Elzevier*.
5 Dibdin, *The library companion*, pp. 805–6.
6 It was bought by the Duke of Devonshire and was later sold with the Kemble plays to the Huntington Library.
7 For the circumstances of discovery of both copies, see Freeman and Ing, 'Did Halliwell steal and mutilate the first quarto of *Hamlet*?' See also Fitzgerald, *The book fancier*, pp. 282–7.
8 Churton's stock-in-trade was auctioned on his premises in Holles Street, Cavendish Square, in 1851–2.
9 Cordasco, *The Bohn libraries: a history and a checklist*.
10 Burton, *The book-hunter etc.* (Edinburgh, 1862), pp. 153–4. The 'new edition' (1882), in a substantially larger format, included a memoir of Burton by his widow. A further portrait of Burton is given in Cooper, *An editor's retrospect; fifty years of newspaper work*, pp. 319–24.
11 Burton, *The book-hunter etc.*, p. 179. The Astor library was opened as a public library in 1854, and a printed catalogue was first published in 1857–61.
12 Partridge, *The history of the legal deposit of books throughout the British Empire*.
13 The publications of these and other clubs are listed, for example, in Hume, *The learned societies and printing clubs of the United Kingdom* and in Bohn, *Appendix to the bibliographer's manual of English literature* [Lowndes].
14 *Notes and Queries* 4th ser. 9 (1872), p. 417.
15 Crone, 'Our forerunner'.

16 A six-leaf specimen of the *Bibliotheca Hibernica: a manual of Irish literature* was issued in 1865: copy in Cambridge University Library, Hib.5.865.5. Power intended six numbers of the *Irish literary enquirer; or notes on authors, books, & printing in Ireland, biographical and bibliographcal, notices of rare books, memoranda of printing in Ireland, biographical notes of Irish writers, &c.* (1865). For Bradshaw's own Irish collection, see *A catalogue of the Bradshaw collection of Irish books in the University Library, Cambridge*. Despite the work of E.R. McClintock Dix (1857–1936), most of whose Irish books are now in the National Library of Ireland, there is still no modern retrospective and comprehensive bibliography specifically of Irish printing and publishing: for a partial survey see Sharpe and Hoyne, *Clóliosta: printing in the Irish language, 1571–1871: an attempt at narrative bibliography*.
17 Harwood, *A view of editions of the Greek and Roman classics*.
18 See p. 208.
19 Loftie, *A plea for art in the house*, p. 16.
20 Macleod, *Art and the Victorian middle class*, pp. 43–4. See also her chapter 4, 'Money and mainstream Victorian values'. For more details of the Bicknell prices, see Hall, *Retrospect of a long life: from 1815 to 1883*, pp. 197–8.
21 Loftie, *A plea for art in the house*, p. 74.
22 Burton, *The book-hunter* (1862), p. 92, quoted also in Wheatley, *Prices of books*, p. 19.
23 Slater, *Round and about the book-stalls: a guide for the book-hunter*, Preface.
24 Loftie, *A plea for art in the house*, p. 79.
25 He possessed seven manuscript *Horae* in all, including one given to the Cambridge antiquary William Cole in 1761.
26 Walters Art Gallery MS W 165. Defoer and others, *The golden age of Dutch manuscript painting*, pp. 188–9 and plate 52. For details, see https://searchworks.stanford.edu/view/kb564yr3366 (accessed 5 May 2019).
27 Hudson, *Arthur Munby, man of two worlds*.
28 Christie, *Selected essays and papers*; Leigh and others, *Catalogue of the Christie collection*.
29 McKitterick, *Cambridge University Library*, pp. 690–701.
30 Prices recorded in this publication, as also in other printed accounts and marked-up copies of auction catalogues, sometimes need to be treated with caution. The existence of organised, sometimes extempore, 'rings' of booksellers, who agree not to bid against each other at a sale, but to have a further private auction among themselves afterwards, was not made illegal until 1928. In 1881–2 both the Hamilton Palace and the Sunderland sales were ringed by a small group of leading booksellers from London and Paris. The practice is explained, and details are given of many nineteenth- and early twentieth-century booksellers who shared in it (including Quaritch and most of the major London firms), in Freeman and Ing, *Anatomy of an auction: rare books at Ruxley Lodge, 1919*. For an earlier example, see Hazen, 'The booksellers' "ring" at Strawberry Hill in 1842'.

31 Wise, *Catalogue of the Ashley library*.
32 Review by Thomas, *The Library Chronicle* 1 (1884), pp. 46–7.
33 Slater, *Library manual*, pp. 14–15.
34 *Bulletin du Bibliophile Belge* 20 (1864), p. 435.
35 For Trübner (d.1884), see especially Axon, 'In memoriam: Nicolas Trübner'; for Jeffs, see Atkinson, 'William Jeffs, Victorian bookseller and publisher of French literature'.
36 See the obituary by J.P. Berjeau, *The Bookworm* 5 (1870), pp. 178–82.
37 For Bradshaw's anonymous contributions, see Prothero, *A memoir of Henry Bradshaw*, pp. 109–10. Bradshaw also gave money to support the failing journal.
38 While Bradshaw appreciated Berjeau's well-meaning efforts, he thought little of him as a bibliographer. See Henry Bradshaw, *Correspondence on incunabula* 2, pp. 310–11, including the obituary printed in *The Bookworm*, 1892.
39 McKitterick, *Old books, new technologies*, pp. 131–2, 136–8.
40 See the notice by J.D. Lee in the *ODNB*.
41 Lee, 'The father of British indexing: Henry Benjamin Wheatley'.
42 *The Bibliographer* 1, p. 29.
43 *Library Chronicle* 1 (1884), *passim*.
44 See his biography by Brian Charles Hollingworth in the *ODNB*.
45 *Notes and Queries*, ser. 4, vol. 1 (1868), p. 26. For the Smithsonian and the distribution of subject bibliographies, see Goode (ed.), *The Smithsonian Institution, 1846–1896: the history of its first half century*, pp. 792–804.
46 McKitterick, *The invention of rare books*, pp. 232, 234–6. Cf. Peignot, *Dictionnaire raisonné de bibliologie*.
47 Francis, 'The Bibliographical Society: a sketch of the first fifty years'.
48 The society was dissolved in 1895. See its *Indices to facsimiles of manuscripts and inscriptions, series I and II* (1901). The New Palaeographical Society issued its first facsimiles in 1903.
49 Bradshaw to M.F.A.G. Campbell, 27 March 1883: Henry Bradshaw, *Correspondence on incunabula* 1, p. 219.
50 Quoted in Hessel, *A history of libraries*, p. 81.
51 Ebert, *Über öffentliche Bibliotheken, besonders deutsche Universitätsbibliotheken*, quoted in Hessel, *A history of libraries*, p. 81. On Ebert, see, for example, Nestler, *Friedrich Adolf Ebert und seine Stellung im nationalen Erbe der Bibliothekwissenschaft*, and Goldschmidt, 'Pioneer professional: Friedrich Adolf Ebert (1791–1834), librarian to the King of Saxony'.
52 Greenwood, *Free public libraries, their organisation, uses, and management*; idem, *Public libraries*.
53 Kelly, *A history of public libraries in Great Britain, 1845–1965*, pp. 82–3, based on Parliamentary returns for 1876 and 1877.
54 Greenwood, *Free public libraries, their organisation, uses, and management*, pp. 32–3.

55 *A catalogue of the library of the Corporation of London instituted in the year 1824*.
56 Aspinall, *Roscoe's library; or, old books and old times*, p. 22.
57 Bradshaw, 'Note on local libraries considered as museums of local authorship and printing'.
58 *Wigan Free Public Library: its rise and progress. A list of some of its treasures, with an account of the celebration of the twenty-first anniversary of its opening*.
59 Ernest C. Thomas (ed.), *Transactions and proceedings of the Library Association . . . at their sixth annual meeting . . . 1883* (1886), p. 194. Details of acquisitions in the reference library were provided by Folkard in his annual reports, 1879, etc.
60 In August 2021 a copy of this book from Wigan Public Library was on sale in the trade for $35,000.
61 Not in N.R. Ker, *Medieval manuscripts in British libraries* 5 vols (Oxford, 1969–2002), who lists the remaining manuscripts.
62 Folkard, *Wigan Free Public Library*.
63 Like most public libraries, that at Wigan has since sold off or otherwise disposed of most of its rare or early books. The extraordinary riches of the collections were summarised in a long entry in the 1997 edition of the *Directory of rare book and special collections*. In 1978–83 about 20,000 items were disposed of. A further 20,000 items were discarded subsequently. By 1995 there was no public access. Most discards went to the book trade, and some passed to the British Library. Further sales followed, as the collection assembled in the first years of the library was stripped. Judging by the prices later asked, and obtained, by booksellers, it must be doubtful that the local authority received the full value for those books that it sold. The building has since been adapted as the Museum of Wigan Life.
64 Munford, *Edward Edwards, 1812–1886; portrait of a librarian*, p. 137, quoting John King, one of Edwards's defenders in his battle with his opponents in Manchester.
65 Ibid., p. 140.
66 Edwards, *Memoirs of libraries* 2, p. 1063.
67 Schrettinger, *Versuch eines vollständigen Lehrbuchs der Bibliothek-Wissenschaft*; Schrettinger, *Handbuch der Bibliothek-Wissenschaft*. See also Remy, 'Un précurseur de la bibliothéconomie moderne: Martin Schrettinger (1772–1851)'.
68 Seizinger, *Theorie und Praxis der Bibliothekswissenschaft. Grundlinien der Archivswissenschaft*.
69 Charton, *Guide pour le choix d'un état, ou dictionnaire des professions*, pp. 90–1.
70 *Public libraries in the United States of America; their history, condition, and management*.
71 Axon, 'Professorships of bibliography'; F.R. Perkins on professors of books and reading, in *Public libraries in the United States of America* (1876), p. 235.

72 Comment by E.C. Thomas, *Transactions and proceedings of the first annual meeting of the Library Association*, pp. 138–9.
73 Bradshaw, 'A word on size-notation as distinguished from form-notation'. Arguments continued for several years. See Wheatley, *How to catalogue a library*, pp. 168–78, including reference to the cataloguing rules worked out by E.W.B. Nicholson in the Bodleian Library. See also McKitterick, *Old books, new technologies*, pp. 199–200. For French guidance, see, for example, Rouveyre, *Connaissances nécessaires à un bibliophile*, pp. 37–54.
74 Bradshaw to Holtrop, 21 March 1864: Bradshaw, *Correspondence on incunabula* 1, p. 49.
75 Blades, 'On paper and paper-marks'.
76 Cousin, *De l'organisation et de l'administration des bibliothèques publiques et privées*, pp. iv–v; see also pp. 120–1.
77 Maire, *Manuel pratique du bibliothécaire*, p. 291. See further Amory, review of Roger Laufer (ed.), *La bibliographie matérielle*.
78 Delisle, 'Note sur la rédaction des catalogues de manuscrits'. For later brief remarks on relations between palaeography and codicology, and on the connections between codicology and archaeological applications, see Masai, 'Paléographie et codicologie': 'En somme, la codicologie est une discipline *archéologique* tandis que la paléographie, la bibliologie et l'histoire de l'enluminure sont des sciences *historiques*. Le codicologue doit être au courant de l'histoire des écritures et de la peinture, un peu comme l'archéologue qui fouille le sol de Grèce ou de l'Italie doit connaître l'épigraphie et la céramique ou la numismatique' (p. 292).
79 Ebert, *Die Bildung des Bibliothekars* 2 parts. 1. *Handschriftenkunde*; cf. Gumbert, 'Ebert's codicology a hundred and fifty years old'.
80 'My total ignorance of German': Bradshaw to S.W. Lawley, 14 July 1881, 'Eleven letters from Henry Bradshaw to S.W. Lawley'.
81 Bradshaw, *A classified index of the fifteenth century books in the De Meyer collection* (1870), note D, 'Printing at Zwolle': *Collected essays*, p. 221.
82 Blades, *The biography and typography of William Caxton* (1877), p. 55. In turn, this was quoted by Reed, *A history of the old English letter foundries* (1887), p. 83.
83 Needham, *The Bradshaw method: Henry Bradshaw's contribution to bibliography*; Beadle, *Henry Bradshaw and the foundations of codicology*.
84 Quoted in Duff, *Early printed books*, pp. 211–12.
85 See p. 178.
86 Bradshaw to Sandars, 1875, respecting Cambridge UL MS Add.3016: quoted in Prothero, *A memoir of Henry Bradshaw*, pp. 336–7.
87 For some of his limited awareness of watermarks in the 1860s, see Bradshaw, *Correspondence on incunabula* 1, p. 124.
88 Pearson, 'Henry Bradshaw', *The Academy* 27 February 1886. Quoted in Prothero, *A memoir of Henry Bradshaw*, p. 328.
89 Desbarreaux-Bernard, *Catalogue des incunables de la Bibliothèque de Toulouse*.

17 Standing Back

1. Halbwachs, *Les cadres sociaux de la mémoire*; Jan Assmann, 'Collective memory and cultural identity,'; J. Assmann, *Das kulturelle Gedächtnis: Schrift, Erinnerung und politische Identität in frühen Hochkulturen*, trans. as *Cultural memory and early civilization: writing, remembrance, and political imagination*; A. Assmann, *Erinnerungsräume: Formen und Wandlungen des kulturellen Gedächtnisses*, trans. as *Cultural memory and western civilization: functions, media, archives*; Quinault, 'The cult of the centenary, c.1784–1914'.
2. Ballantine (ed.), *Chronicle of the hundredth birthday of Robert Burns*; Rigney, 'Embodied communities: commemorating Robert Burns, 1859'.
3. Rainer Noltenius, 'Schiller als Führer und Heiland: das Schillerfest 1859 als nationaler Traum von der Geburt des zweiten deutschen Kaiserreichs', in Düding and others (eds.) *Öffentliche Festkultur*; Duncan, 'Remembering Schiller: the centenary of 1859'.
4. Cox, *The tercentenary: a retrospect*. Some of the celebrations of 1863 are described in Hunter, *Shakespeare and Stratford-upon-Avon: a 'chronicle of the time'*; see also Foulkes, *The Shakespeare tercentenary of 1864*.
5. *The Scott exhibition MDCCCLXXI: catalogue of the exhibition held at Edinburgh, in July and August 1871*.
6. McKitterick, 'Putting the past on show. Old books and communal memory in the nineteenth century'.
7. Goulemot and Walter, 'Les centenaires de Voltaire et de Rousseau'; Bird, *Reinventing Voltaire: the politics of commemoration in nineteenth-century France*; Boudrot, 'Voltaire 1878: commemoration and the creation of dissent'; Paris, *Honneurs publics rendus à la mémoire de Jean-Jacques Rousseau*.
8. Levitt, *Russian literary politics and the Pushkin celebration of 1880*.
9. *Notice sur le monument érigé à Paris par souscription à la gloire de Molière. Suivie de pièces justificatives et de la liste générale des souscripteurs*.
10. Baker, 'The portrait sculpture'; Sinker, *The library of Trinity College, Cambridge*, pp. 125–32; Mole, *What the Victorians made of romanticism*, pp. 140–4.
11. *Library Chronicle* 4 (1887), p. 73.
12. Brooke, *Dove Cottage. Wordsworth's home from 1800–1808, December 21, 1799 to May –, 1808*; Gill, *Wordsworth and the Victorians*, pp. 243–6; Reavell and others, *Professor William Knight, 1836–1916: 'Wordsworthian discoverer, enabler and publicist'*.
13. Brooke to Mrs Crackanthorpe, 23 October 1897: Jacks, *Life and letters of Stopford Brooke* 2, p. 529.
14. *Catalogue of the books, manuscripts, works of art . . . at present exhibited in Shakespeare's birthplace*, pp. 30–4; *Catalogue of the books, manuscripts, works of art . . . which are preserved in the Shakespeare library and museum in Henley Street*.
15. *Title pages (and imprints) of the books in the private library of James McKie, Kilmarnock*.

16 Mole, *What the Victorians made of romanticism*, pp. 145–63.
17 Knowles, *Great historical enterprises*, pp. 100–34.
18 Bresslau, *Geschichte der Monumenta Germaniae historica*; Knowles, *Great historical enterprises*, pp. 64–97.
19 Moore, *Restoring order: the École des Chartes and the organization of archives and libraries in France, 1820–1870*.
20 Charmes (ed.), *Le Comité des Travaux Historiques et Scientifiques (Histoire et documents)*. For a convenient summary of major European national archives, but omitting Britain, see Guyotjeannin, 'Les grandes entreprises européennes d'édition et sources historiques des années 1810 aux années 1860'.
21 Nichols, *Illustrations of the manners and expences of antient times in England, in the fifteenth, sixteenth, and seventeenth centuries, deduced from the accompts of churchwardens, and other authentic documents*.
22 Collier (ed.), *Extracts from the registers of the Stationers' Company of works entered for publication between the years 1557 and 1570*. Vol.1. For his treatment of the archive, see Freeman and Ing, *John Payne Collier*, pp. 1197–1201, 1207–11.
23 'The present selection excludes only early dissertations upon medical and other sciences, old divinity, and such chronicles, and other works, as are well known in the various extant editions. All that relates to popular poetry and prose, plays, tracts, voyages, travels, and lighter literature, has been carefully preserved' (p. vi).
24 Freeman and Ing, *John Payne Collier*, pp. 493–502, etc.
25 Arber (ed.), *A transcript of the registers of the Company of Stationers of London; 1554–1640 A.D.* 1, p. 1.
26 Ruelens and De Backer, *Annales plantiniennes, depuis la fondation de l'imprimerie plantinienne à Anvers, jusqu'à la mort de Chr. Plantin (1555–1589)*.
27 Rooses, *Christophe Plantin, imprimeur anversois*. For Rooses (1839–1914), see Voet, *The golden compasses* 1, pp. 408–10, with further references, and Somers, 'De Plantijnstudies van Max Rooses', in de Schepper and de Nave (eds.), *Ex officina Plantiniana: studia in memoriam Christophori Plantini*, pp. 45–53.
28 Plantin, *Correspondance* 9 vols; *Supplément* (Antwerp, 1955).
29 Arber to Spedding, 7 March 1871: Birmingham University Library, Edward Arber papers US4/11/1130.
30 See further p. 300. Edmond subsequently turned his attention to earlier Scottish printing, in Dickson and Edmond, *Annals of Scottish printing, from the introduction of the art in 1507 to the beginning of the seventeenth century*: Edmond edited Dickson's unfinished work, and then wrote the rest of the book himself. Its publication at Cambridge by Macmillan and Bowes was thanks at least partly to Francis Jenkinson, whose help is acknowledged.
31 Bologna, *La stamperia fiorentina del monastero di S.Jacopo di Ripoli e le sue edizioni: studio storico e bibliografico*. The manuscript was not published in full

until over a century later: Conway, *The Diario of the printing press of San Jacopo di Ripoli: commentary and transcription*.
32. For his biography, see the account by John Pemble in the *ODNB*.
33. For Nimmo and Symonds, see Grosskurth, *John Addington Symonds: a biography*, pp. 254–6.
34. See now Peric, *Vendere libri a Padova nel 1480; il Quaderneto di Antonio Moretto*.
35. Cecchetti, 'La stampa tabellare in Venezia nel 1447 e l'esenzione del dazio dei libri del 1433'. For more recent work towards its full publication, see Dondi and Harris, 'Oil and green ginger. The *Zornale* of the Venetian bookseller Francesco de Madiis, 1484–1488'.
36. Acton, *A lecture on the study of history, delivered at Cambridge, June 11, 1895*, p. 19.
37. Acton, *Longitude 30 west; a confidential report to the Syndics of Cambridge University Press*.

18 The Next Generation

1. Wheatley, *How to form a library*, pp. 71–2.
2. He summarised his work in a privately published list: *An output: a list of writings on many divine subjects, of sculptures, dramas, music, lectures, tours, collections, clubs, and public donations, being a record of work done during a long and busy life, 1850–1912*.
3. Pollard, 'Sir John MacAlister: some reminiscences'; Godbolt and Munford, *The incomparable Mac: a biographical study of Sir John Young Walker MacAlister (1856–1925)*.
4. Silverman, *The new bibliopolis: French book collectors and the culture of print, 1880–1914*.
5. Notice included in Rouveyre, *Connaissances nécessaires à un bibliophile*, 3rd ed. (1879).
6. See p. 301.
7. Burgon, *Lives of twelve good men* 2, pp. 122–48.
8. Nicholson, *The Bodleian Library in 1882–7*; *Library Chronicle* 5 (1888), p. 199; Craster, *History of the Bodleian Library, 1845–1945*, pp. 152–71.
9. Craster, *History*, pp. 174–5.
10. Garnett, 'Changes at the British Museum since 1877'.
11. Swansea Public Library and Gallery of Art Committee, *Annual report, 1886–7*: summarised in *Library Chronicle* 5 (1888), p. 22.
12. Cambridge Public Free Library. Thirty-second annual report, 1886–7, summarised in *Library Chronicle* 4 (1887), p. 154.
13. *Library Chronicle* 3 (1886), pp. 144–5; 4 (1887), p. 52; Gibson and Wright (eds.), *Joseph Mayer of Liverpool, 1803–1886*.

14 Prothero's biography provided an opportunity for Ernest C. Thomas to add his own comment, and some extra detail: *Library Chronicle* 5 (1888), pp. 179–88.
15 Skeat's edition of Chaucer, much dependent on Bradshaw, appeared in 1894–7, and the statutes of Lincoln Cathedral, edited by Bradshaw with Christopher Wordsworth, in 1892–7. Wordsworth and Francis Procter's edition of the Sarum Breviary, with bibliographical contributions by Bradshaw, had appeared in 1879–86.
16 Wheatley, *How to form a library*, pp. vi–vii.
17 Prothero, *A memoir of Henry Bradshaw*, pp. 203–5.
18 Fry, *A brief memoir of Francis Fry, F.S.A.* (1887); Hall, 'Francis Fry, a maker of chocolate and Bibles', in Hunt and others (eds.) *The book trade & its customers*; David J. Hall in *ODNB*.
19 Offor's books, due to be sold at auction, were destroyed in the Sotheby's fire, 26 June 1865.
20 Lea Wilson, *Bibles, Testaments, Psalms and other books of the Holy Scriptures in English, in the collection of Lea Wilson*.
21 de Hamel and Silver, *Disbound and dispersed: the leaf book considered*, pp. 64–5.
22 Fry, *A description of the Great Bible, 1539, and the six editions of Cranmer's bible, 1540 and 1541*; Fry, *The Bible by Coverdale, 1535*.
23 Numbering over 1,200 volumes. See Herbert, *Historical catalogue of printed editions of the English Bible, 1525–1961, revised and expanded from the edition of T.H. Darlow and H.F. Moule*.
24 See p. 299. A.F. Johnson's new edition of *A history of the old English letter foundries* (1952), incorporating work by Stanley Morison, both omits passages from the original and adds further. Of contemporary reviews, J.H. Slater summarised part of the book in *Book-Lore* 5 (1886–7), pp. 138–44.
25 Blades, *Some early type specimen books of England, Holland, France, Italy, and Germany, with explanatory remarks*.
26 Bullen (ed.), *Caxton celebration, 1877. Catalogue of the loan collection ... connected with the art of printing*, p. 354.
27 A second copy was found by D.B. Updike in the Grolier Club of New York. The copy in the London Institution was sold and eventually joined the rest of Updike's typographical library in Providence Public Library. See Mores, *A dissertation upon English typographical founders and founderies*, ed. Harry Carter and Christopher Ricks.
28 For a selective summary, see Moran, *The composition of reading matter: a history from case to computer*.
29 Reed, *History of the old English letter foundries*, p. v.
30 Moxon, *Mechanick exercises on the whole art of printing (1683–4)*, ed. Herbert Davis and Harry Carter.
31 Lottin, *Catalogue chronologique des libraires et des libraires-imprimeurs de Paris depuis l'an 1470*, pp. 233–44.

32 Timperley, *A dictionary of printers and printing*; Timperley, *Encyclopaedia of literary and typographical anecdote*.
33 Edmond's annotated proofs of Duff's *Early printed books* are in Cambridge University Library.
34 For much of Edmond's work, see Barker, *Bibliotheca Lindesiana*. See also the obituary in the *Library Association Record* 8 (1906), pp. 199–201 and Webb, *John Philip Edmond: bookbinder, librarian and bibliographer of Aberdeen, 1850–1906: a short biography*.
35 Ferguson, *Some aspects of bibliography*; Johnston, 'The story of the Edinburgh Bibliographical Society'.
36 Browne, 'W.C. Hazlitt and his "Consolidated bibliography"'.
37 A catalogue of the British Museum holdings of Hebrew printed books was published in 1867, of Sanskrit and Pali in 1876, of Chinese in 1877 and of Bengali in 1886: Goodacre and Pritchard, *Guide to the Department of Oriental Manuscripts and Printed Books* (British Library Reference Division).
38 Proctor, *An index to the early printed books in the British Museum: from the invention of printng to the year 1500*.
39 Rooses (ed.), *Compte-rendu de la première session de la Conférence du Livre, tenue à Anvers ... 1890*.
40 *Catalogue of books on bibliography, typography and engraving in the New-York State Library*.
41 Kirchhoff, *Katalog der Börsenvereins der Deutschen Buchhändler*.
42 Hoe, *Literature of printing*.
43 J. Passmore Edwards to Drummond, 22 April 1892: *The Passmore Edwards and William Blades libraries of printing and the allied crafts*, p. 8. See also Edwards, *A few footprints*.
44 Southward, *Catalogue of the William Blades library*; Saint Bride Foundation. *Catalogue of the technical reference library of works on printing and the allied arts*.
45 Hesse, *Histoire des sociétés bibliophiles en France* 1, p. x, with further details of these societies.
46 de Ricci, *Bibliographie des publications d'Anatole Claudin (1833–1906)*.
47 See p. 76.
48 *Report of the Commissioners appointed to inquire into the constitution and government of the British Museum, with minutes of evidence* (1850) Evidence, para. 4499. There was no such arrangement at Trinity College, where the question did not arise. For the University Library, see McKitterick, *Cambridge University Library*, pp. 565–6.
49 Bodleian Library, Curators' Minutes, 11 December 1860.
50 Craster, *History of the Bodleian Library, 1845–1945*, pp. 52, 169.
51 Ibid., p. 319. 'Statutory power was eventually taken in 1938 to eliminate from the library material of no literary or artistic value or of an ephemeral nature, and is used with circumspection' (p. 319, note 1.).

52 McKitterick, *Cambridge University Library*, pp. 429, 651–2.
53 See Kearney, *The private case: an annotated bibliography of the private case erotica collection in the British Museum library* and *Supplement*; Cross, 'The private case; a history', in Harris (ed.) *The library of the British Museaum*. The Private Case is not restricted to erotica.
54 Apollinaire and others, *L'Enfer de la Bibliothèque Nationale*.
55 In 1981, readers at the British Library were warned that not everything was catalogued in the library of Thomas James Wise, sold by his widow to the British Museum in 1937. The gift by Henry Davis (1897–1977) to the Museum in 1968 of his exceptional collection of fine bindings was withheld from the general catalogue until some years after its arrival: some are (in 2021) still not included. A very rapid search today reveals uncatalogued collections of pamphlets in Ulster University Library (from a collector who died in 1953), Trinity College Dublin (c.13,000 paphlets and other transient literature relating to the period of the French Revolution), New York Public Library (the so-called pamphlet files), McMaster University Library (a collection on communism and socialism) and the American Antiquarian Society (with an estimated 75,000 uncatalogued).
56 Craster, *History of the Bodleian Library, 1845–1945*, p. 169.

19 Then and Now

1 Copinger, 'Inaugural address'.
2 For an account of the gestation and development of Pollard and Redgrave, *A short-title catalogue of books printed in England, Scotland, & Ireland and of English books printed abroad, 1475–1640* (Bibliographical Soc., 1926), see the Preface by the editors. Cf. Hill, *Lost books and printing in London, 1557–1640*.
3 Goldschmidt, *Gothic & renaissance bookbindings, exemplified and illustrated from the author's own collection*; but see also Goldschmidt's tribute to the all too brief publication of Theodore Gottlieb of Vienna (d.1929), 'this strangely suspicious and secretive man', *Bucheinbände. Auswahl von technisch und geschichtlich bemerkenswerten Stücken (aus der K.K.Hofbibliothek* (Vienna, 1910): 'Theodore Gottlieb: a reformer of the history of bookbinding'; for Goldschmidt, see R.O. Dougan, 'E. Ph. Goldschmidt, 1887–1954'.
4 Wheatley, *How to catalogue a library*, p. 3.
5 Blackburn, *Hints on catalogue titles, and on index enries*, p. v.
6 Handler, 'Forgery and the end of the "Bloody code" in early nineteenth-century England'.
7 Bredekamp, Brückle and Needham (eds.), *A Galileo forgery: unmasking the New York Sidereus Nuncius*.
8 Harris, *Selling Hitler*.
9 Gilreath, *The judgment of experts*.

10 Sillitoe and Roberts, *Salamander: the story of the Mormon forgery murders*; Bozeman (ed.), *Forged documents; proceedings of the 1989 Houston conference*; Taylor, *Texfake: an account of the theft & forgery of early Texas printed documents*.
11 Apers, 'Ferdinand van der Haeghen en het ontstaan der *Bibliotheca Belgica*'.
12 Lemon and Green (ed.), *Calendar of state papers, Domestic Series, of Edward VI, Mary, Elizabeth I and James I*.
13 McKerrow, 'Notes on bibliographical evidence for literary students and editors'.
14 For example, Paul Needham's index of owners of fifteenth-century printed books (https://data.cerl.org/ipi/_search) or David Pearson's guide to seventeenth-century English owners (www.bookowners.online).
15 *Gabriel Harvey's marginalia*, collected and ed. G.C. Moore Smith.
16 Sherman, '"Rather soiled by use"; renaissance readers and modern collectors'.
17 https://archaeologyofreading.org
18 Dee, *Private diary, and catalogue of his library of manuscripts*, ed. J.O. Halliwell; for Dee's catalogue, see Roberts and Watson (ed.), *John Dee's library catalogue*.
19 Stauffer, *Book traces*, pp. 138–55, with further references.
20 Digital loss is commonplace. For one attempt to avoid it, cf. the Digital Preservation Coalition (www.dpconline.org).
21 New Zealand, New South Wales, Canada and The National Archives have all published guidelines about the digitisation and subsequent destruction of public records on paper. Several practitioners have published guidance on how to scan books more quickly by cutting off their spines, and thus destroying them.
22 For some aspects of this, see Gregg, *Old books and digital publishing: Eighteenth-Century Collections Online*.
23 Copinger, 'Inaugural address'.
24 In November 2020 the Vatican Library announced that it was victim of frequent cyber attacks on its digitised collections, and had engaged a leading cyber AI company to protect it. The development was widely reported. www.cambridgenetwork.co.uk/news/vatican-library's-digitised-manuscripts---including-oldest-surviving-copy-bible---protected (accessed 15 November 2020); www.theguardian.com/world/2020/nov/08/vatican-enlists-bots-to-protect-library-from-onslaught-of-hackers; www.theartnewspaper.com/news/hacker-ai-vatican-library.

Select Bibliography

Unless otherwise stated, books are published in London.

À la mémoire de M. Jean Gutenberg. Hommage de l'Imprimerie Nationale et de la Bibliothèque Nationale (Paris, 1900)

Acton, Lord, A lecture on the study of history, delivered at Cambridge, June 11, 1895 (1905)
 Longitude 30 west: a confidential report to the Syndics of Cambridge University Press (New York, 1969)

Agnew, Geoffrey, Agnew's, 1817–1967 (1967)

Alphen, Gregorius van, Catalogus der pamfletten van de bibliotheek der Rijksuniversiteit te Groningen, 1542–1853 (Groningen, 1944)

Alston, Robin, 'Charting the bibliographic sea: research and the art of navigation', Alexandria 5 (1993), pp. 71–88
 'The eighteenth-century non-book: observations on printed ephemera', in Giles Barber and Bernhard Fabian (eds.), Buch und Buchhandel in Europa im achtzehnten Jahrhundert / The book and book trade in eighteenth-century Europe (Hamburg, 1981), pp. 343–60

Altick, Richard D., The English common reader: a social history of the mass reading public, 1800–1900 (Chicago, 1957)

American (The) catalogue of books, or, English guide to American literature ... with especial reference to works of interest to Great Britain (Sampson Low, 1856)

Ames, Joseph and William Herbert, Typographical antiquities: or the history of printing in England Scotland and Ireland, greatly enlarged by T.F. Dibdin, 4 vols. (1810–19)

Amory, Hugh, review of Roger Laufer (ed.), La bibliographie matérielle, PBSA 78 (1984), pp. 341–7

André, Louis, Machines à papier: innovation et transformations de l'industrie papetière en France, 1798–1860 (Paris, 1996)

Apers, René F., 'Ferdinand Van der Haeghen en het ontstaan der Bibliotheca Belgica', in Lode Baekelmans ter eere 1945 (Antwerp, 1946), 1, pp. 107–21

Apollinaire, Guillaume and others, L'Enfer de la Bibliothèque Nationale (Paris, 1913)

Arber, Edward (ed.), A transcript of the registers of the Company of Stationers of London: 1554–1640 A.D, 5 vols. (1875–7, 1894)

Arnould, Alain and Jean Michel Massing, Splendours of Flanders (Cambridge, 1993)

Ashton, John, Chap-books of the eighteenth century, with facsimiles, notes and introduction (1882)

Aspinall, James, Roscoe's library: or, old books and old times (1853)

Assmann, Aleida, Erinnerungsräume: Formen und Wandlungen des kulturellen Gedächtnisses (Munich, 1999), trans. as Cultural memory and western civilization: functions, media, archives (Cambridge, 2011)

Assmann, Jan, 'Collective memory and cultural identity', *New German Critique* 65 (1995), pp. 125–33

Das kulturelle Gedächtnis: Schrift, Erinnerung und politische Identität in frühen Hochkulturen (Munich, 1997), trans. as *Cultural memory and early civilization: writing, remembrance, and political imagination* (Cambridge, 2011)

Atkinson, Juliette, 'William Jeffs, Victorian bookseller and publisher of French literature', *The Library* 7th ser. 13 (2012), pp. 257–78

Atkyns, Richard, *The original and growth of printing collected out of history, and the records of this kingdome* (1664)

Attar, Dena, *A bibliography of household books published in Britain, 1800–1914* (1987)

Audin, Maurice, *Les types lyonnais primitifs conservés au Département des Imprimés* (Paris, 1955)

Aumale, Ernest, *La dermotypotemnie: étude sur quelques livres, cum figuris et characteribus ex nulla materia compositis* (Issoudun, 1867)

Auvray, Lucien and René Poupardin, *Catalogue des manuscrits de la collection Baluze* (Paris, 1921)

Axon, William E.A., 'In memoriam: Nicolas Trübner', *Library Chronicle* 1 (1884), pp. 42–6

'Professorships of bibliography', in Henry R.Tedder and Ernest C.Thomas (eds.), *Transactions and proceedings of the first annual meeting of the Library Association of the United Kingdom* (1879), pp. 104–7

Baedeker, Karl, *Belgium and Holland. Handbook for travellers*, 9th ed. (Leipzig, 1888)

Paris and environs, 7th ed. (Leipzig, 1881)

Báez, Fernando, *A universal history of the destruction of books, from ancient Sumer to modern Iraq* (New York, 2008, originally published in Spanish, Barcelona, 2004)

Baker, Malcolm, 'The portrait sculpture', in David McKitterick (ed.), *The making of the Wren library, Trinity College, Cambridge* (Cambridge, 1995), pp. 110–37

Balayé, Simone, *La Bibliothèque Nationale des origines à 1800* (Geneva, 1988)

Baldwin, Jack, *A catalogue of fifteenth-century printed books in Glasgow libraries and museums*, 2 vols. (Woodbridge, 2020)

Ballantine, James (ed.), *Chronicle of the hundredth birthday of Robert Burns* (Edinburgh, 1859)

Barat, Nicolas, *Nouvelle bibliothèque choisie*, 2 vols. (Amsterdam, 1714)

Barber, Giles, 'Galignani's and the publication of English books in France from 1800 to 1852', *The Library* 5th ser. 16 (1961), pp. 267–86, and 'Postscript' by James J. Barnes, *The Library* 25 (1970), pp. 294–313

Barbier, Frédéric, 'La librairie ancienne en Allemagne au XIXe siècle', *Bulletin du Bibliophile* 1984 (4), pp. 543–58

(ed.), *Les trois révolutions du livre: actes du colloque international de Lyon/Villeurbanne, 1998, Revue Française d'Histoire du Livre* 106–9 (2000)

Barbieri, Edoardo, *Haebler contro Haebler: appunti per una storia dell'incunabolistica novecentesca* (Milan, 2008)

(ed.), *Nel mondo delle postille: i libri a stampa con note manoscritte. Una raccolta di studi* (Milan, 2002)

Barker, Nicolas, 'Bernard Quaritch', *The Book Collector*. Special number for the 150th anniversary of Bernard Quaritch (1997), pp. 1–34
    Bibliotheca Lindesiana (Roxburghe Club, 1977)
    (introd.), *Esther Inglis's Les proverbes de Salomon: a facsimile* (Roxburghe Club, 2012)
    Portrait of an obsession: the life of Sir Thomas Phillipps, the world's greatest book collector (1967)
    The Roxburghe Club: a bicentenary history (Roxburghe Club, 2012)
    Treasures from the libraries of National Trust country houses (New York, 1999)
Barker, Nicolas and John Collins, *A sequel to an enquiry into the nature of certain nineteenth century pamphlets by John Carter and Graham Pollard: the forgeries of H. Buxton Forman & T.J. Wise* (1983)
Barrière, Didier, *Nodier l'homme du livre: le rôle de la bibliophilie dans la littérature* (Bassac, 1989)
Baughan, R., *Character indicated by handwriting* [1880]
Baurmeister, Ursula, 'De la dame-copiste bénévole à la bibliothécaire honoraire: Marie Pellechet à la Bibliothèque nationale', in Bruno Blasselle and Laurent Portes (eds.), *Mélanges autour de l'histoire des livres imprimés et périodiques* (Paris, 1998), pp. 295–301
Beadle, Richard, *Henry Bradshaw and the foundations of codicology* (Cambridge, 2017)
Beckett, J.V., 'Agricultural landownership and estate management', in E.J.T. Collins (ed.), *The agrarian history of England and Wales, 7: 1850–1914* (Cambridge, 2000), pp. 693–758
Bentley, G.E., Jr, *Blake books* (Oxford, 1977)
Béraldi, Henri, *La reliure du XIXe siècle*, 4 vols. (Paris, 1895–7)
Berghman, Gustav, *Études sur la bibliographie Elzevirienne* (Stockholm, 1885)
Berjeau, J.Ph., *Essai bibliographique sur le Speculum humanae salvationis, indiquant le passage de la xylographie à la typographie* (1862)
Bernard, Auguste, *Histoire de l'Imprimerie Royale du Louvre* (Paris, 1867)
    Notice historique sur l'Imprimerie Nationale (Paris, 1848)
    De l'origine et des débuts de l'imprimerie en Europe, 2 vols. (Paris, 1853)
Bernard, Edward, *Catalogi librorum manuscriptorum Angliae et Hiberniae in unum collecti* (Oxford, 1697)
Bertrand, Gilles and others (eds.), *Collectionner la Révolution française* (Paris, 2016)
Bewick, Thomas, *A memoir*, ed. Iain Bain (Oxford, 1975)
Bibliotheek van Nederlandsche pamfletten. Eerste afdeeling. Verzameling van Frederik Muller te Amsterdam naar tijdsorde gerangschikt en geschreven door P.A. Tiele, 3 vols. (Amsterdam, 1858–61)
Bibliothèque Nationale, Département des Imprimés [Olgar Thierry-Poux], *Notice des objets exposés* (Paris, 1878)
Bibliothèque Nationale, *Notice des objets exposés. Imprimés. Manuscrits. Estampes* (Paris, 1881)
Biervliet, Lori van, *Leven en werk van W.H.James Weale, een Engels kunsthistoricus in Vlaanderen in de 19de eeuw* (Brussels, 1991)
Bird, Stephen, *Reinventing Voltaire: the politics of commemoration in nineteenth-century France* (Oxford, 2000)
Blackburn, Charles F., *Hints on catalogue titles, and on index entries* (1884)

Blackburne, E.L. (ed.), *Suburban & rural architecture. English & foreign* (1867)

Blades, William, *The biography and typography of William Caxton* (1877, 2nd ed., 1882)

    The life and typography of William Caxton, 2 vols. (1861–3)

    Numismata typographica: or, the medallic history of printing (1883), repr. with an introduction by Henry Morris (Newtown, PA, 1992)

    'On paper and paper-marks', *The Library* 1 (1889), pp. 217–23

    The pentateuch of printing (1891)

    'On the present aspect of the question, Who was the inventor of printing?' *Library Chronicle* 4 (1887), pp. 135–43

    Some early type specimen books of England, Holland, France, Italy, and Germany, with explanatory remarks (1875)

Blair, Ann M., *Too much to know: managing scholarly information before the modern age* (New Haven, 2010)

Blogie, Jeanne, *Répertoire des catalogues de ventes de livres imprimés appartenant à la Bibliothèque Royale Albert Ier*, 6 vols. (Brussels, 1982–2003)

Bloomfield, B.C. (ed.), *A directory of rare book and special collections in the United Kingdom and the Republic of Ireland*, 2nd ed. (1997); 3rd ed., ed. Karen Attar (2016)

Boase, Frederic, *Modern English biography*, 6 vols. (1892–1921)

Bodin, Thierry, 'Les grandes collections de manuscrits littéraires', in Annie Charon and Élisabeth Parinet (eds.), *Les ventes de livres et leurs catalogues, XVIIe–XXe siècle* (Paris, 2000), pp. 169–90

Boer, Pim den, *History as a profession: the study of history in France, 1818–1914* (Princeton, 1998)

Bohn, Henry G., *Appendix to the Bibliographer's manual of English literature* [Lowndes] (1864)

    Catalogue of books, 1 (1848)

    New, valuable, and most important books, offered at very reduced prices (1848)

Bologna, Pietro, *La stamperia fiorentina del monastero di S.Jacopo di Ripoli e le sue edizioni: studio storico e bibliografico* (estr. da *Giornale Storico della Letteratura Italiana* 20) (Turin, 1893)

Boneham, John, 'The Dawson Turner collection of printed ephemera and Great Yarmouth', *Electronic British Library Journal* (2014), article 13

Bonnardot, A., *De la réparation des vieilles reliures* (Paris, 1858)

Bonython, Elizabeth and Anthony Burton, *The great exhibitor: the life and work of Henry Cole* (2003)

Bordier, Henri, 'Écritures, peintures et ornements des manuscrits', *Bulletin de la Société de l'Histoire de France* (1851–2), pp. 365–70

Bordier, Henri and Émile Mabille, *Une fabrique de faux autographes, ou récit de l'affaire Vrain Lucas* (Paris, 1870), trans. as *Prince of forgers* (New Castle, DE, 1998)

Borome, Joseph A., *Charles Coffin Jewett* (Chicago, 1951)

Boscq, Marie-Claire, *Imprimeurs et libraires parisiens sous surveillance (1814–1848)* (Paris, 2018)

Botfield, Beriah, *Notes on the cathedral libraries of England* (1849)

Boucly, *Rapport addressé à M. le garde des sceaux Hébert, suivi du procès intenté par M. Libri* (Paris, 1850)

Boudrot, Pierre, 'Voltaire 1878: commemoration and the creation of dissent', in Joseph Leerssen and Ann Rigney (eds.), *Commemorating writers in nineteenth-century Europe, nation-building and centenary fever* (Basingstoke, 2014), pp. 152–72

Bouquin, Corinne, 'Influence des relations entre éditeurs et imprimeurs-lithographes dans la genèse de l'illustration des livres au XIXe siècle', in Frédéric Barbier and others (eds.), *Le livre et l'historien: études offertes en l'honneur du Professeur Henri-Jean Martin* (Geneva, 1997), pp. 723–42

Bowman, J.H., 'The decline of the printed catalogue in Britain', *Library History* 22 (2006), pp. 67–99

Bozeman, Pat (ed.), *Forged documents: proceedings of the 1989 Houston conference* (New Castle, DE, 1990)

Bradshaw, Henry, *A classified index of the fifteenth century books in the De Meyer collection* (1870); *Collected papers*, pp. 206–36

   Collected papers, ed. Francis Jenkinson (Cambridge, 1889)

   Correspondence on incunabula with J.W. Holtrop and M.F.A.G. Campbell, ed. Wytze Hellinga and Lotte Hellinga [commentary etc. trans. from Dutch by H.S. Lake], 2 vols. (Amsterdam, 1966 [1968]–78)

   'On the earliest English engravings of the indulgence known as the "Image of pity"', *Cambridge Antiquarian Soc. Communications* 17 (1866–73), pp. 135–52; *Collected papers*, pp. 84–100

   'Eleven letters from Henry Bradshaw to S.W.Lawley', *Fasciculus Ioanni Willis Clark dicatus* (Cambridge, 1909), pp. 115–34

   List of the founts of type and woodcut devices used by printers in Holland in the fifteenth century (Cambridge, 1871); *Collected papers*, pp. 258–81

   'Note on local libraries considered as museums of local authorship and printing', in Ernest C.Thomas (ed.), *Transactions and proceedings of the fourth and fifth annual meetings of the Library Association of the United Kingdom held in London ... 1881, and at Cambridge ... 1882* (1884), pp. 237–8; *Collected papers*, pp. 404–5

   'Notice of a fragment of the Fifteen Oes and other prayers printed at Westminster by W. Caxton about 1490–91, preserved in the library of the Baptist College, Bristol', *Collected papers*, pp. 341–9

   Presidential address to the Library Association, 1882 (Cambridge, 1882); *Collected papers*, pp. 371–409.

   'A word on size-notation as distinguished from form-notation', *Collected papers*, pp. 406–9

Brandes, Carl Heinrich, 'Beleuchtung der Anklage gegen Libri wegen Beraubung öffentlicher Bibliotheken in Frankreich', *Serapeum* 9 (1848), pp. 201–8

   'G.Libri's Aufschlüsse über Verluste der öffentlichen Bibliotheken in Frankreich', *Serapeum* 10 (1849), pp. 314–28

Braun, Suzanne, 'Le monument de Gutenberg', http://acpasso.free.fr/archives/photosdiverses/Le%20monument%20de%20Gutenberg.pdf (accessed 28 April 2020)

Bredekamp, Horst, Irene Brückle and Paul Needham (eds.), *A Galileo forgery: unmasking the New York Sidereus Nuncius* (Berlin, 2014)

Breslauer, B.H., *The uses of bookbinding literature* (New York, 1986)

Bresslau, Harry, *Geschichte der Monumenta Germaniae historica* (Hanover, 1921)

Briggs, Asa, *A history of Longmans and their books, 1724–1990: longevity in publishing* (2008)

Briquet, C.M., 'Papiers et filigranes des archives de Gênes, 1154 à 1700', Atti della Società Ligure di Storia Patria 19, 1887 (Geneva 1888)

Les filigranes, 4 vols. (Geneva, 1907), repr. ed. Allan Stevenson (Amsterdam, 1968)

Brockwell, M.W., 'W.H. James Weale, the pioneer', The Library 5th ser. 6 (1951-2), pp. 200-11

Brooke, Stopford A., Dove Cottage. Wordsworth's home from 1800-1808, December 21, 1799 to May -, 1808 (1890)

Browne, Ronald, 'W.C. Hazlitt and his "Consolidated bibliography"', in Robin Myers and Michael Harris (eds.), Pioneers in bibliography (Winchester, 1988), pp. 73-85

Brunet, Gustave, 'T.F. Dibdin', Le Bibliophile Français 1 (1868), pp. 217-25

'Quelques mots au sujet des difficultés que présente la catalographie', Bulletin du Bibliophile 9 (1850), pp. 563-7

Brunet, J.-C., Manuel du libraire, 3 vols. (Paris, 1810); 5th ed. 6 vols. (Paris, 1860-5; Supplément, 1878)

Nouvelles recherches bibliographiques, 3 vols. (Paris, 1834)

Buijnsters, Piet J., Geschiedenis van antiquariaat en bibliofilie in België (Nijmegen, 2013)

Geschiedenis van het Nederlandse antiquariaat (Nijmegen, 2007)

Bullen, George (ed.), Caxton celebration, 1877. Catalogue of the loan collection of antiquities, curiosities, and appliances concerned with the art of printing (1877)

Burgon, John William, Lives of twelve good men, 2 vols. (1888)

Burlington Fine Arts Club, Exhibition of bookbindings (1891)

Burton, J.H., The book-hunter etc. (Edinburgh, 1862, new edition 1882)

Business directory of London (1869)

Cambridge Public Free Library. Thirty-second annual report, 1886-7

Campbell, M.-F.-A.-G., Annales de la typographie néerlandaise au XVe siècle (The Hague, 1874)

Carl (The) H. Pforzheimer library. English literature, 1475-1700, 3 vols. (New York, 1940)

Carter, John, ABC for book-collectors, 4th ed. (1966)

Taste and technique in book-collecting (Cambridge, 1949)

Carter, John and Graham Pollard, An enquiry into the nature of certain nineteenth-century pamphlets (1934)

Casselle, Pierre, 'Les pouvoirs publics et les bibliothèques', in Dominique Varry (ed.), Histoire des bibliothèques françaises. Les bibliothèques de la Révolution et du XIXe siècle (Paris, 1991), pp. 109-17

'Le régime législatif', in Henri-Jean Martin, Roger Chartier and Vivet, Jean-Pierre (eds.), Histoire de l'édition française, 3: Le temps des éditeurs (Paris, 1985), pp. 47-55

Catalogue (A) of antiquities and works of art, exhibited at Ironmongers' Hall, London, in the month of May 1861, 2 vols. (1869)

Catalogue (A) of books and manuscripts issued to commemorate the one hundredth anniversary of the firm of Bernard Quaritch (1947)

Catalogue (A) of the Bradshaw collection of Irish books in the University Library, Cambridge, 3 vols. (Cambridge, 1916)

Catalogue (A) of the library of the Corporation of London instituted in the year 1824 (1859)

Catalogue de la bibliothèque de M.N. Yéméniz, précédé d'une notice par M. Le Roux de Lincy (Paris, 1867)

Catalogue général des livres imprimés de la Bibliothèque Nationale (1897 etc.)

Catalogue général des manuscrits des bibliothèques publiques des départements (Paris, 1849 etc.)
Catalogue of books on bibliography, typography and engraving in the New-York State Library (Albany, 1858)
Catalogue of printed books in the British Museum, 1 (1841)
Catalogue of printed books in the library of the British Museum, 393 parts (1881–1900)
Catalogue of the autograph room, entirely filled with the collection of Mr. William Upcott . . . With portraits. Third exhibition, Liverpool Mechanics' Institution, June and July 1844 (Liverpool, 1844)
Catalogue of the books, manuscripts, works of art . . . at present exhibited in Shakespeare's birthplace (Stratford-upon-Avon, 1910)
Catalogue (A) of the books, manuscripts, works of art . . . which are preserved in the Shakespeare library and museum in Henley Street (1868)
Catalogue of the collection of autograph letters and historical documents formed between 1865 and 1882, compiled and annotated under the direction of A. W. Thibaudeau, 6 vols. (Privately pr., 1883–92)
Catalogue of the fifty manuscripts & printed books bequeathed to the British Museum by Alfred H.Huth (1912)
Catalogue of the library of Dr. Kloss . . . including . . . printed books with MS. annotations, by Philip Melanchthon, which will be sold by auction, by Mr. Sotheby and Son . . . May 7, and nineteen following days (1835)
Catalogue of the manuscript library of the late Dawson Turner . . . sold by auction, by Messrs Puttick and Simpson . . . June 6 and four following days (1859)
Catalogue of the remaining portion of the library of Dawson Turner (Puttick and Simpson, 16 May 1859 etc.)
Catalogus Bibliothecae Publicae Harlemensis (Haarlem, 1848)
Catalogus der bibliotheek van de Vereeniging ter Bevordering van de Belangen des Boekhandels te Amsterdam, 8 vols. (The Hague and Amsterdam, 1920–79): now in Amsterdam University Library
Catalogus van de tractaten, pamfletten, enz. over de geschiedenis van Nederland, aanwezig in de bibliotheek van Isaac Meulman, bewerkt door J.K. Van der Wulp, 3 vols. (Amsterdam, 1866–8)
Cazelles, Raymond, *Le duc d'Aumale* (Paris, 1984)
Cecchetti, Bartolomeo, 'La stampa tabellare in Venezia nel 1447 e l'esenzione del dazio dei libri del 1433', *Archivio Veneto* 29 (1885), pp. 87–91
Centina, Andrea del and Alessandra Fiocca, *L'archivio di Guglielmo Libri dalla sua dispersione ai fondi della Biblioteca Moreniana* (Florence, 2004)
Cercle (Le) de la Librairie de Paris à l'exposition du livre: catalogue (Paris, 1890)
Cercle de la Librairie, *Première exposition* (Paris, 1880)
  Recueil alphabétique de catalogues (1884)
Chambers, William, *Memoir of William and Robert Chambers* (Edinburgh, 1893)
Chambers, William and Robert Chambers (eds.), *Chambers's information for the people*, revised ed. (1848)
Chaplin, A.H., *GK: 150 years of the general catalogue of printed books in the British Museum* (1987)
Charavay, Étienne, *Lettres autographes composant la collection de M. Alfred Bovet* (Paris: Librairie Charavay Frères, 1887)

Charmes, Xavier (ed.), *Le Comité des Travaux Historiques et Scientifiques (Histoire et documents)*, 3 vols. (Paris 1886)

Chartier, Roger, *Forms and meanings: texts, performances and audiences from codex to computer* (Philadelphia, 1995)

Le livre en révolutions: entretiens avec Jean Lebrun (Paris, 1997)

Charton, Édouard (ed.), *Guide pour le choix d'un état, ou dictionnaire des professions* (Paris, 1842)

Chatto, William A., *The history and art of wood-engraving, with specimens of the art, ancient and modern, selected from 'The Illustrated London News'* (1848)

Chesterfield, Lord, *Letters*, 2 vols. (1774)

Choice examples of the engraver's art (1890)

Christie, R.C., 'Elzevier bibliography', *Library Chronicle* 5 (1888), pp. 117–23, repr. in his *Selected essays and papers* (1902), pp. 297–308

Selected essays and papers (1902)

'Chronique. Bibliothèques', *Bulletin des Bibliothèques et des Archives* 1884 1, pp. 66–91

Chronological (A) list of the graces, documents, and other papers in the University Registry which concern the University Library (Cambridge, 1870)

Clapperton, R.H., *The paper-making machine: its invention, evolution, and development* (1967)

Clarke, D.A., 'The first edition of Pacioli's "Summa de arithmetica" (Venice, Paganinus de Paganinis, 1494)', *Gutenberg Jahrbuch* (1974), pp. 90–2

Clarke, William, *Repertorium bibliographicum, or some account of the most celebrated British libraries*, 2 vols. (1819)

Claudin, Anatole ('J.Verax'), 'Les faussaires de livre', *Bulletin du Bibliophile* (1891), pp. 513–24

Catalogue des monuments typographiques et d'un choix de livres rares et précieux provenant du cabinet de feu M. Benjamin Fillon (Paris, 1883)

Histoire de l'imprimerie en France au XVe et au XVIe siècles, 4 vols. (Paris, 1900–14)

Claye, Jules, *Manuel de l'apprenti compositeur* (Paris, 1871)

Clergy list (1841, etc.)

Coeuré, Sophie, *La mémoire spoliée: les archives des Français, butin de guerre nazi puis soviétique* (Paris, 2007)

Cole, Henry, *A special report on the annual international exhibitions of the years 1871, 1872, 1873, and 1874, presented by the Board of Management to Her Majesty's Commissioners for the exhibition of 1851* (1875)

Coleman, D.C., *The British paper industry, 1495–1860* (Oxford, 1958)

Collection (A) of 300 autograph letters of celebrated individuals of all nations, from the sixteenth to the nineteenth century (Stuttgart, 1846)

Collections de Louis XIV: dessins, albums, manuscrits (Orangerie des Tuileries, Paris, 1977)

Collett, W.R., *Index of English books printed before the year MDC, now in the library of Gonville and Caius College, Cambridge* (Cambridge, 1850)

A list of early printed books in the library of Gonville and Caius College, Cambridge (Cambridge, 1850)

Collier, J.Payne (ed.), *Extracts from the registers of the Stationers' Company of works entered for publication between the years 1557 and 1570*, 2 vols. (1848–9)

Collingham, Hugh, 'Joseph Barrois. Portrait of a bibliophile XXVI', *The Book Collector* 33 (1984), pp. 431–48

Collins, S., ' James Crossley of Manchester', in Eddie Cass and Morris Garratt (eds.), *Printing and the book in Manchester, 1700–1850* (Manchester, 2001), pp. 137–52

James Crossley: a Manchester man of letters (Manchester, 2012)

Colomb de Batines, P., *Bibliografia Dantesca*, 2 vols. (Prato, 1845–6)

'Commercial (The) history of a *Penny Magazine*', *Penny Magazine*, monthly supplements, 1833

Conihout, Isabelle de, 'Police de la librairie et mesure du livre au XIXe siècle: le dépôt légal, la *Bibliographie de la France*, et la bibliométrie', in Alain Vaillant (ed.), *Mesure(s) du livre* (Paris, 1992), pp. 23–39

Conlin, Jonathan, *The nation's mantelpiece: a history of the National Gallery* (2006)

Conway, Melissa, *The Diario of the printing press of San Jacopo di Ripoli: commentary and transcription* (Florence, 1999)

Conway, Lord, of Allington, *Episodes of a varied life* (1932)

Conway, W.M., *The woodcutters of the Netherlands in the fifteenth century* (Cambridge, 1884)

Cooke, Simon, *Illustrated periodicals of the 1860s: contexts and collaborations* (2010)

Cooper, Charles A., *An editor's retrospect: fifty years of newspaper work* (1896)

Cooper-Richet, Diana and Emily Borgeaud, *Galignani* (Paris, 1999)

Copinger, W.A., 'Inaugural address', *Trans Bibliographical Soc.* 1 (1893), pp. 29–59

Copinger, W.A., *Supplement to Hain's Repertorium bibliographicum*, 3 vols. (1895–1902)

Coral, Lenore, 'Towards the bibliography of British book auction catalogues, 1801–1900', *PBSA* 89 (1995), pp. 419–25

Cordasco, Francesco, *The Bohn libraries: a history and a checklist* (New York, 1951)

Courtney, W.P., 'Mr. James Crossley', *The Bibliographer* 4 (1883), pp. 97–9

Cousin, Jules, *De l'organisation et de l'administration des bibliothèques publiques et privées* (Paris, 1882)

Cox, James, *The tercentenary: a retrospect* (1865)

Crampton, Hope, 'Charles de Spoelberch de Lovenjoul, 1836–1907', *Book Collector* 10 (1961), pp. 18–27

Craster, Sir Edmund, *History of the Bodleian Library, 1845–1945* (Oxford, 1952)

Cristiano, F., 'Biblioteche private e antiquariato librario', in G. Tortorelli (ed.), *Biblioteche nobiliari e circolazione del libro tra Settecento e Ottocento* (Bologna, 2002), pp. 79–115

L'antiquariato librario in Italia: vicende, protagonisti, cataloghi (Rome, 1986)

Crone, J.S., 'Our forerunner', *Irish Book Lover* 1 (August 1909)

Cross, Paul J., 'The private case: a history', in P.R. Harris (ed.), *The library of the British Museum: retrospective essays on the Department of Printed Books* (1991), pp. 201–40

Crous, Ernst, 'The general catalogue of incunabula' (a paper read 16 December 1912), *Trans Bibliographical Soc.* 12 (1914), pp. 87–99

'The inventory of incunabula in Great Britain and Ireland', *Trans Bibliographical Soc.* 12 (1914), pp. 177–209

Cullen, Michael J., *The statistical movement in early Victorian Britain: the foundations of empirical social research* (Hassocks, 1975)

Cundall, Joseph, *On bookbindings, ancient and modern* (1881)

On ornamental art, applied to ancient and modern bookbinding (1848)

Darcy, C.P., *The encouragement of the fine arts in Lancashire, 1760–1860* (Manchester, 1976)

Daru, Pierre Antoine, comte, *Notions statistiques sur la librairie* (Paris, 1827)

Davenport, Cyril, 'Forgeries in bookbinding', *The Library* N.S. 2 (1901), pp. 389–95

David, P. and C. Nougaret, *Collection des catalogues de vente d'autographes et livres anciens imprimés des libraires et des salles de vente: inventaire analytique* (Pierrefitte-sur-Seine: Archives Nationales, 2003)

Davidoff, Leonore and Catherine Hall, *Family fortunes: men and women of the English middle class, 1780–1850* (1987)

Davies, Hugh William, *Catalogue of a collection of early French books in the library of Charles Fairfax Murray*, 2 vols. (1910)

Catalogue of a collection of early German books in the library of C. Fairfax Murray, 2 vols. (1913)

Davies, James A., *John Forster: a literary life* (1983)

Davis, Diana, *The tastemakers: British dealers and the Anglo-Gallic interior, 1785–1865* (Los Angeles, 2020)

Daxon, Hugh, 'Thomas Bewick at 250: landmarks in the building of a reputation', *Bewick studies: essays in celebration of the 250th anniversary of the birth of Thomas Bewick, 1753–1828* (Newcastle-upon-Tyne, 2003), pp. 9–21

De Hamel, Christopher and Joel Silver, *Disbound and dispersed: the leaf book considered* (Chicago, 2005)

De Morgan, Augustus, *Arithmetical books from the invention of printing to the present time* (1847)

[De Morgan, Augustus], 'The case of M.Libri', *Bentley's Miscellany* 32 (1852), pp. 107–15

'On the difficulty of correct description of books', *Companion to the Almanac* (1853), pp. 5–19: reprinted with an introduction by Henry Guppy in the *Library Association Record* (1902), and then separately [Manchester, 1902]

'Mathematical bibliography', *Dublin Review* 21 (1846), pp. 1–37

'Notices of English mathematical and astronomical writers between the Norman conquest and the year 1600', *Companion to the Almanac* (1837), pp. 21–44

De Morgan, Sophia, *Memoir of Augustus De Morgan, with selections from his letters* (1882)

De Ricci, Seymour, *Bibliographie des publications d'Anatole Claudin (1833–1906)* (1926)

Catalogue raisonné des premières impressions de Mayence (1445–1467) (Mainz, 1911)

A census of Caxtons (Bibliographical Soc., 1909)

English collectors of books & manuscripts, 1530–1930, and their marks of ownership (Cambridge, 1930)

De Vinne, T.L., *The invention of printing* (New York, 1877)

de Vries, B.W., *De Nederlandse papiernijverheid in de negentiende eeuw* (The Hague, 1957)

Dee, John, *Private diary, and catalogue of his library of manuscripts*, ed. J.O. Halliwell (Camden Soc., 1842)

Defence of the resolution for omitting Mr. Panizzi's bibliographical notes from the catalogue of the Royal Society (1838)

Defoer, Henri L.M. and others, *The golden age of Dutch manuscript painting* (New York, 1990)

Delbecque, Erika, 'A newly discovered fragment of William Caxton's *Ordinale*', *The Library* 7th ser. 21 (2020), pp. 518–27

Delisle, Léopold, *Bibliothèque Nationale. Département des Manuscrits, Chartes et Diplômes. Notice des objets exposés* (Paris, 1878)

    Le cabinet des manuscrits de la Bibliothèque Nationale/Impériale, 4 vols. (Paris, 1868–81)

    Catalogue des manuscrits des fonds Libri et Barrois, Bibliothèque Nationale (Paris, 1888)

    'Circulaire à MM. les Maires relative au catalogue des incunables des bibliothèques de France', *Bulletin des Bibliothèques et des Archives* 3 (1886), pp. 1–42

    Instructions pour la rédaction d'un inventaire des incunables conservés dans les bibliothèques publiques de France (Paris, 1886, repr. Paris, 1911)

    'Note sur la rédaction des catalogues de manuscrits', *Bulletin des Bibliothèques et des Archives* 1 (1884), pp. 94–109

    'L'oeuvre paléographique de M. le comte de Bastard', *Bibliothèque de l'École des Chartes* 43 (1882), pp. 498–523

Delsaerdt, Pierre and others, *Een zee van toegelaten lust: hoogtepunten uit abdijbibliotheken in de provincie Antwerpen* (Antwerp, 2004)

Démy, Adolphe, *Essai historique sur les expositions universelles de Paris* (Paris, 1907)

Desbarreaux-Bernard, Tibulle, *Catalogue des incunables de la Bibliothèque de Toulouse* (Toulouse, 1878)

Descuret, Jean Baptiste Félix, *La médecine des passions* (Paris, 1844)

Desormeaux, Daniel, *La figure du bibliomane: histoire du livre et stratégie littéraire au XIXe siècle* (St-Genoulph, 2001)

Dibdin, Thomas Frognall, *A bibliographical, antiquarian and picturesque tour of the northern counties of England and in Scotland*, 2 vols. (1838)

    The bibliographical decameron, 3 vols. (1817)

    The bibliomania; or, book-madness; containing some account of the history, symptoms, and cure of this fatal disease. In an epistle addressed to Richard Heber, Esq. (1809, new and improved ed. 1842)

    Bibliotheca Spenceriana, 4 vols. (1814–15)

    The library companion (1824)

    Reminiscences of a literary life, 2 vols. (1836)

Dickson, Robert, *Introduction of the art of printing into Scotland* (Aberdeen, 1885)

Dickson, Robert and J.P. Edmond, *Annals of Scottish printing, from the introduction of the art in 1507 to the beginning of the seventeenth century* (Cambridge, 1890)

Dickson, Sarah Augusta, *The Arents collection of books in parts: a complete checklist* (New York, 1957)

Dinaux, Arthur, 'Livres annotés, signés et estampillés', *Bulletin du Bibliophile* 7 (1846), pp. 744–53, 887–93; 8 (1847), pp. 490–8

Dingelstedt, Franz von, *Iean Gutenberg, premier maître imprimeur. Transl. from German by Gustave Revilliod* (Genève, 1858), trans. English in the *Miscellanies* of the Philobiblon Society 5 (1859)

Dodd, George, *Days at the factories* (1843)

Donald, Diana and Paul F. Donald, *The art of Thomas Bewick* (2013)

Dondi, Cristina and Neil Harris, 'Oil and green ginger. The *Zornale* of the Venetian bookseller Francesco de Madiis, 1484–1488', in Malcolm Walsby and Natasha

Constantinidou (eds.), *Documenting the early modern book world: inventories and catalogues in manuscript and print* (Leiden, 2013), pp. 341–406

Dougan, R. O., 'E. Ph. Goldschmidt, 1887–1954', *The Library* 5th ser. 9 (1954), pp. 75–84

Doyle, A.I., 'Two medieval calendars and other leaves removed by John Bowtell from University Library MSS', *Trans Cambridge Bibliographical Soc.* 1 (1949), pp. 29–36

Dring, E.M., 'Michael Kerney', *Book Collector* special number for the 150th anniversary of Bernard Quaritch, ed. Richard Linenthal (1997), pp. 160–6

Duff, Edward Gordon, *Early printed books* (1893)

   Fifteenth century English books: a bibliography of books and documents printed in England and of books for the English market printed abroad (1917), repr. with supplementary materials by Lotte Hellinga as *Printing in England in the fifteenth century* (2009)

Duncan, Bruce, 'Remembering Schiller: the centenary of 1859', *Seminar: a Journal of Germanic Studies* 35 (1999), pp. 1–22

Dupont, Paul, *Histoire de l'imprimerie*, 2 vols. (Paris, 1854)

Duprat, F.A., *Histoire de l'Imprimerie Impériale de France* (Paris, 1861)

   Précis historique sur l'Imprimerie Nationale et ses types (Paris, 1848)

Dyce collection. A catalogue of the paintings, miniatures, drawings, engravings, rings, and miscellaneous objects bequeathed by the Reverend Alexander Dyce (1874)

   A catalogue of the printed books and manuscripts bequeathed by the Reverend Alexander Dyce, 2 vols. (1875)

Dyson, Gillian, 'The MSS. and proof sheets of Scott's Waverley novels', *Edinburgh Bibliographical Soc. Trans.* 4 (1960), pp. 13–42

Eastlake, Lady, 'Memoir of Sir Charles Lock Eastlake', in C.L. Eastlake, *Contributions to the literature of the fine arts* 2nd ser. (1870), pp. 1–192

Ebert, F.A., *Die Bildung des Bibliothekars*, 2 parts, 1, *Handschriftenkunde* (Leipzig, 1825)

   Über öffentliche Bibliotheken, besonders deutsche Universitätsbibliotheken (Freiburg, 1811)

Edmond, J.P., *The Aberdeen printers: Edward Raban to James Nicol, 1620–1736* (Aberdeen, 1886)

Edwards, Edward, *Memoirs of libraries: including a handbook of library economy*, 2 vols. (1859)

Edwards, Edward, *A statistical review of the principal public libraries of Europe and America* (1848)

Edwards, J. Passmore, *A few footprints* (1905)

Edwards, Percy, *History of London street improvements, 1855–1897* (1898)

Ehrsam, Theodore G., *Major Byron, the incredible career of a literary forger* (New York, 1951)

Eisermann, Falk, '"The greatest of all such lists", oder: Was Sie schon immer über den GW wissen wollten', in Christoph Reske (ed.), *Kontext Buch: Festschrift für Stephan Füssel* (Wiesbaden, 2020), pp. 65–81

Eliot, George, *Letters*, ed. Gordon S. Haight, 9 vols. (New Haven, 1954–78)

Eliot, Simon, '"Mr. Greenhill, whom you cannot get rid of": copyright, legal deposit and the Stationers' Company in the 19th century', in Robin Myers, Michael Harris and Giles Mandelbrote (eds.), *Libraries and the book trade* (Winchester, 2000), pp. 51–84

   Some patterns and trends in British publishing, 1800–1919 (1994)

English, Charlie, *The book smugglers of Timbuktu* (2017)

Epinal (The) glossary, Latin and Old-English of the eighth century, ed. with transliteration, introduction, and notes, by Henry Sweet (1883)
Estermann, M., *"O werthe Druckerkunst/ Du Mutter aller Kunst": Gutenbergfeiern im Laufe der Jahrhunderte* (Mainz, 1999)
Eudel, Paul, *Le truquage* (Paris, 1884)
Evans, D. Morier, *The commercial crisis 1847-1848: being facts and figures illustrative of ... the railway mania, the food and money panic, and the French revolution* (1848)
Evans, Joan, *The Conways: a history of three generations* (1966)
  A history of the Society of Antiquaries (Oxford, 1956)
Fabian, Bernhard, 'Die erste Bibliographie der englischen Literatur des achtzehnten Jahrhunderts: Jeremias David Reuß' *Gelehrtes England*', in his *Selecta Anglicana* (Wiesbaden, 1994), pp. 239-65
Fabian, Bernhard, 'An eighteenth-century research collection: English books at Göttingen University Library', *The Library* 6th ser. 1 (1979), pp. 209-24, repr. in his *Selecta Anglicana* (Wiesbaden, 1994), pp. 177-94
  The English book in eighteenth-century Germany (1992)
Fabian, Bernhard (ed.), *Handbuch der historischen Buchbestände in Deutschland, Österreich und Europa*, https://fabian.sub.uni-goettingen.de/fabian
Fagan, Louis, *The life of Sir Anthony Panizzi, KCB*, 2 vols. (1880)
Fasciculus Ioanni Willis Clark dicatus (Cambridge, 1909)
Faure, Chantal (ed.), *Catalogues de libraires et d'éditeurs, 1811-1924: inventaire* (Bibliothèque Nationale de France, 2003)
'Felix Folio', *The hawkers and street dealers of the north of England manufacturing districts*, 2nd ed. (Manchester, 1858)
Felkay, Nicole, *Balzac et ses éditeurs, 1822-1837: essai sur la librairie romantique* (Paris, 1987)
Ferguson, John, *Some aspects of bibliography* (Edinburgh, 1900)
Finke, Ulrich, 'The art treasures exhibition', in John H.G. Archer (ed.), *Art and architecture in Victorian Manchester* (Manchester, 1985), pp. 102-26
Firmin-Didot, Ambroise, *Essai sur la typographie* (Paris, 1851)
First report of Her Majesty's Commissioners to inquire into the state and condition of the cathedral and collegiate churches (1854)
Fischer, Hans, 'Conrad Gesner (1516-1565) as bibliographer and encyclopaedist', *The Library* 5th ser. 21 (1966), pp. 269-81
Fitzgerald, Percy, *The book fancier* (1886)
  An output: a list of writings on many diverse subjects, of sculptures, dramas, music, lectures, tours, collections, clubs, and public donations, being a record of work done during a long and busy life, 1850-1912 [1913?]
Fléty, J., 'Le Cercle de la Librairie: un siècle et demi d'histoire', *Arts et Métiers du Livre* 127 (1983), pp. 1-25
Folkard, H.T., *Wigan Free Public Library: its rise and progress* (Wigan, 1900)
Folter, Roland, 'The Gutenberg Bible in the antiquarian book trade', in Martin Davies (ed.), *Incunabula: studies in fifteenth-century printed books presented to Lotte Hellinga* (1999), pp. 271-351
Fontaine, Jean-Paul, 'Anatole Claudin', *Les gardiens de bibliopolis: cent soixante portraits pour servir à l'histoire de la bibliophilie* (Paris, 2015)
  Les gardiens de bibliopolis. Cent soixante portraits (Paris, 2015)

Fontaine, P.-J., *Manuel de l'amateur d'autographes* (Paris, 1836)

Fontenelle, Julia de and P. Poisson, *Manuel complet du marchand papetier et du régleur* (Paris, 1828)

Foot, Mirjam M., 'Double agent: M.Caulin and M.Hagué', *Book Collector* special number for the 150th anniversary of Bernard Quaritch, ed. Richard Linenthal (1997), pp. 136–50

    The Henry Davis gift: a collection of bookbindings, 3 vols. (1978–2010)

Foot, Mirjam M., Carmen Blacker and Nicholas Poole-Wilson, 'Collector, dealer and forger: a fragment of nineteenth-century binding history', in Mirjam M. Foot (ed.), *Eloquent witnesses: bookbindings and their history* (2004), pp. 264–81

[Ford, Richard], 'Review of several reports and pamphlets concerning the British Museum, 1835–50', *Quarterly Review* 175 (1850), pp. 136–72

Forman, H.Buxton, *The Shelley library: an essay in bibliography* (1886)

Forster collection. A catalogue of the paintings, manuscripts, autograph letters, pamphlets, etc. bequeathed by John Forster (1893)

Forster collection. A catalogue of printed books bequeathed by John Forster (1888)

Fortescue, G.K., *Catalogue of the pamphlets, books, newspapers, and manuscripts relating to the civil war, the Commonwealth, and Restoration, collected by George Thomason, 1640–1661*, 2 vols. (1908)

    List of three collections of books, pamphlets and journals in the British Museum relating to the French Revolution (1899)

Foucaud, Jean-François, *La Bibliothèque royale sous la Monarchie de Juillet* (Paris, 1978)

Foulkes, Richard, *The Shakespeare tercentenary of 1864* (1984)

Fournier, Édouard, *L'art de la reliure en France aux derniers siècles* (Paris, 1864)

    and others, *Histoire de l'imprimerie et des arts et professions qui se rattachent à la typographie, comprenant l'histoire des anciennes corporations et confréries depuis leur fondation jusqu'à leur suppression en 1789* (Paris, 1852)

France, Anatole, *Le livre du bibliophile* (Paris, 1874)

Francis, F.C., 'The Bibliographical Society: a sketch of the first fifty years', in *The Bibliographical Society, 1892–1942: studies in retrospect* (1945), pp. 1–22

Freeman, Arthur, *Bibliotheca fictiva: a collection of books & manuscripts relating to literary forgery, 400BC–AD2000* (2014)

    'William Henry Ireland's "Authentic original forgeries": an overdue rediscovery', http://blogs.harvard.edu/houghton/files/2012/08/Ireland.pdf (accessed 10 July 2020)

Freeman, Arthur and Janet Ing Freeman, *Anatomy of an auction: rare books at Ruxley Lodge, 1919* (1990)

    'Did Halliwell steal and mutilate the first quarto of *Hamlet*?', *The Library* 7th ser. 2 (2001), pp. 349–63

    John Payne Collier: scholarship and forgery in the nineteenth century, 2 vols. (New Haven, 2004)

Freeman, Janet Ing, 'Founders' type and private founts at the Chiswick Press in the 1850s', *JPHS* 19/20 (1984/86), pp. 62–102

Fry, Francis, *The Bible by Coverdale, 1535* (1867)

    A description of the Great Bible, 1539, and the six editions of Cranmer's bible, 1540 and 1541 (1865)

Fry, Theodore, *A brief memoir of Francis Fry, F.S.A.* (1887)

Fuchs, Hermann, 'The *Gesamtkatalog* of the Prussian libraries', *Library Quarterly* 4 (1934), pp. 36–49
Gaehtgens, Thomas W., 'Le musée historique de Versailles', in P. Nora (ed.), *Les lieux de mémoire*, 3 vols. (Paris 1997) 2, pp. 1781–1801
Gardiner, F.J., *History of Wisbech and neighbourhood, during the last fifty years, 1848–1898* (Wisbech, 1898)
Garnett, Richard, 'Changes at the British Museum since 1877', *Library Chronicle* 4 (1887), pp. 81–5
  Essays in librarianship and bibliography (1899)
  'Photography in public libraries', *Essays in librarianship and bibliography* (1899), pp. 234–52
  'The printing of the British Museum catalogue' in Ernest C.Thomas (ed.), *Transactions and proceedings of the fourth and fifth annual meetings of the Library Association of the United Kingdom held in London . . . 1881, and at Cambridge . . . 1882* (1884), pp. 120–8, repr. in his *Essays in librarianship and bibliography*, pp. 67–86
Garrick, David, *Letters*, ed. David M. Little and George M. Kahrl, 3 vols. (Oxford, 1963)
Gatch, Milton McC., 'John Bagford, bookseller and antiquary', *British Library Journal* 12 (1986), pp. 150–71
Gaviglio-Faivre d'Arcier, Catherine, 'Les Charavay: une dynastie de marchands d'autographes', in Patricia Sorel and Frédérique Leblanc (eds.), *Histoire de la librairie française* (Paris, 2008), p. 133
  'Les libraires d'ancien et d'occasion', in Patricia Sorel and Frédérique Leblanc (eds.), *Histoire de la librairie française* (Paris, 2008), pp. 128–39
  Lovenjoul (1836–1907): une vie, une collection (Paris, 2007)
  'Portrait d'un libraire d'ancien: Techener', in Patricia Sorel and Frédérique Leblanc (eds.), *Histoire de la librairie française* (Paris, 2008), p. 130
Gernsheim, Helmut, *Incunabula of British photographic literature, 1839–1875* (1984)
Gerson, Stéphane, *The pride of place: local memories and political culture in nineteenth-century France* (Ithaca, 2003)
Gesner, Conrad, *Bibliotheca universalis* (Zurich, 1545)
  Pandectarum universalium libri XXI (Zurich, 1548)
Gibson, Margaret and Susan M. Wright (eds.), *Joseph Mayer of Liverpool, 1803–1886* (1988)
Gill, Stephen, *Wordsworth and the Victorians* (Oxford, 1998)
Gilreath, James, *The judgment of experts* (Worcester, MA, 1991)
Godbolt, Shane and W.A. Munford, *The incomparable Mac: a biographical study of Sir John Young Walker MacAlister (1856–1925)* (1983)
Goldman, Paul, *Victorian illustration: the Pre-Raphaelites, the Idyllic School and the high Victorians* (1996, revised ed. 2004)
Goldschmidt, E.Ph., *Gothic & renaissance bookbindings, exemplified and illustrated from the author's own collection*, 2 vols. (1928)
  'The study of early bookbinding', in *The Bibliographical Society: studies in retrospect, 1892–1942* (1949), pp. 175–84
  'Theodore Gottlieb: a reformer of the history of bookbinding', *The Library* 4th ser. 10 (1930), pp. 274–81
Goldschmidt, Eva, 'Pioneer professional: Friedrich Adolf Ebert (1791–1834), librarian to the King of Saxony' *Library Quarterly* 40 (1970), pp. 223–35

Goodacre, H.J. and A.P. Pritchard, *Guide to the Department of Oriental Manuscripts and Printed Books* (British Library Reference Division, 1977)

Goode, George Brown (ed.), *The Smithsonian Institution, 1846–1896: the history of its first half century* (Washington, DC, 1897)

Goodison, J.W. and G.H. Robertson, *Fitzwilliam Museum, Cambridge: catalogue of paintings, 2: Italian schools* (Cambridge, 1967)

Gottlieb, Theodore, *Bucheinbände. Auswahl von technisch und geschichtlich bemerkenswerten Stücken aus der K.K.Hofbibliothek* (Vienna, 1910)

Goudie, Gilbert, *David Laing LL.D.: a memoir of his life and literary work* (Edinburgh, 1913)

Gould, Alison, *Reader Guide, 9: Named special collections in the Department of Printed Books* (British Library Reference Division, 1981)

Goulemot, Jean-Marie and Éric Walter, 'Les centenaires de Voltaire et de Rousseau', in Pierre Nora (ed.), *Les lieux de mémoire*, 3 vols. (Paris, 1997) 1, pp. 351–82

Grand-Carteret, John, *Les almanachs français: bibliographie, iconographie* (Paris, 1896)
   Vieux papiers, vieilles images: cartons d'un collectionneur (Paris, 1896)

Greenhalgh, Paul, *Ephemeral vistas: the Expositions Universelles, Great Exhibitions, and World's Fairs, 1851–1939* (Manchester, 1988)

Greenwood, Thomas, *Edward Edwards, the chief pioneer of municipal public libraries* (1902)
   Free public libraries (1886; 2nd ed. 1887)
   Museums and art galleries (1888)
   Public libraries, 4th ed. (1891)

Greg, W.W., 'What is bibliography?' *Trans Bibliographical Soc.* 12 (1914), pp. 39–53, repr. in his *Collected papers*, ed. J.C. Maxwell (Oxford, 1966), pp. 75–88

Gregg, Stephen H., *Old books and digital publishing: Eighteenth-Century Collections Online* (Cambridge, 2020)

Grego, Joseph, *Rowlandson the caricaturist*, 2 vols. (1880)

Grégoire, Abbé, '*Troisième rapport sur le vandalisme* (Convention Nationale, an III [1795])', *Bulletin du Bibliophile* 8 (1848), pp. 751–68

Griffiths, Antony and Reginald Williams, *The Department of Prints and Drawings in the British Museum: user's guide* (1987)

Grivel, Marianne, 'Le Cabinet du Roi', *Revue de la Bibliothèque Nationale* 18 (1985), pp. 36–57

Grosskurth, Phyllis, *John Addington Symonds: a biography* (1964)

Gruys, J.A., 'The Bibliotheca Duncaniana', in Marieke van Delft and others (eds.), *Collectors and collections: Koninklijke Bibliotheek, 1798–1998* (Zwolle, 1998), pp. 30–3

Guerzoni, Guido, 'The export of works of art from Italy to the United Kingdom, 1792–1830', in Susanna Avery-Quash and Christian Huemer (eds.), *London and the emergence of a European art market, 1780–1820* (Los Angeles, 2019), pp. 64–78

Guide to the loan collection and list of musical instruments, books, paintings, and engravings, exhibited in the gallery and lower rooms, of the Albert Hall (1885)

Guide (A) to the printed books exhibited to the public (British Museum, 1870)

Gumbert, J.P., 'Ebert's codicology a hundred and fifty years old', *Quaerendo* 5 (1975), pp. 336–52

Guyotjeannin, Olivier, 'Les grandes entreprises européennes d'édition et sources historiques des années 1810 aux années 1860', in Bruno Delmas and Christine Nougaret (eds.), *Archives et nations dans l'Europe du XIXe siècle* (Paris, 2004), pp. 135–70

Gyles, Arthur, *Directory of second-hand booksellers* (1886)

Haenel, Gustav, *Catalogi librorum manuscriptorum qui in bibliothecis Galliae, Helvetiae, Belgii, Britanniae M., Hispaniae, Lusitaniae asservantur* (Lipsiae, 1830)

Hain, Ludwig, *Repertorium bibliographicum in quo libri omnes ab arte typographica inventa usque ad annum MD. typis expressi*, 4 vols. (Stuttgartiae, 1826–38)

Halbwachs, Maurice, *Les cadres sociaux de la mémoire* (Paris, 1952)

Hale, Edward E., *Ninety days' worth of Europe* (Boston, 1861)

Hall, D.J., 'Francis Fry, a maker of chocolate and Bibles', in Arnold Hunt and others (eds.), *The book trade & its customers, 1450–1900: historical essays for Robin Myers* (1997), pp. 265–77

Hall, J.J., 'The guard-book catalogue of Cambridge University Library', *Library History* 13 (1997), pp. 39–56

Hall, S.C., *Retrospect of a long life: from 1815 to 1883* (New York, 1883)

Hamber, Anthony J., *"A higher branch of the art": photographing the fine arts in England, 1839–1880* (Amsterdam, 1996)

Hammer, Joshua, *The bad-ass librarians of Timbuctu: and their race to save the world's most precious manuscripts* (New York, 2016)

Handbook (A) for travellers on the continent, 11th ed. (John Murray, 1856)

Handbook of the Dyce and Forster collections in the South Kensington Museum (1880)

Handler, Phil, 'Forgery and the end of the "Bloody code" in early nineteenth-century England', *Historical Journal* 48 (2005), pp. 683–702

Hands, M.S.G. (Mrs MacLeod), 'The cathedral libraries catalogue', *The Library* 5th ser. 2 (1948), pp. 1–10

Hannett, John ('John Arnett', pseud.), *An inquiry into the nature and form of the books of the ancients* (1837)

('John Arnett', pseud.), *Bibliopegia: or, the art of bookbinding, in all its branches*, 2nd ed. (1836)

Hansard, T.C., *Typographia* (1825)

Harding, Robert, 'The Colvin print theft and the rise and fall of A.W.Thibaudeau', *Print Quarterly* 22 (2015), pp. 162–76

Harleian (The) miscellany, ed. Samuel Johnson and William Oldys, 8 vols. (1744–6)

Harris, Neil, 'The Ripoli Decameron, Guglielmo Libri and the "incomparable" Harris', in Denis V. Reidy (ed.), *The Italian book, 1465–1800: studies presented to Dennis E. Rhodes on his 70th birthday* (1993), pp. 323–33

Harris, P.R., *A history of the British Museum library, 1753–1973* (1998)

'The move of printed books from Montagu House, 1838–42', in P.R. Harris (ed.), *The library of the British Museum: retrospective essays on the Department of Printed Books* (1991), pp. 75–101

Harris, Robert, *Selling Hitler* (1986)

Harrisse, Henry, *Grandeur et décadence de la Colombine* (Paris, 1885)

Hartwig, Otto (ed.), *Festschrift zum fünfhundertjährigen Geburtstage von Johann Gutenberg* (Mainz, 1900)

Harvey, Gabriel, *Gabriel Harvey's marginalia*, collected and ed. G.C. Moore Smith (Stratford-upon-Avon, 1913)

Harwood, Edward, *A view of editions of the Greek and Roman classics* (1775; 4th ed. 1790)

Hazen, Allen T., 'The booksellers' "ring" at Strawberry Hill in 1842', *Studies in Bibliography* 7 (1955), pp. 194–8

Hazlitt, W.C. and F.S. Ellis, *The Huth library: a catalogue of the printed books, manuscripts, autograph letters, and engravings, collected by Henry Huth, with collations and bibliographical descriptions*, 5 vols. (1880)

Hazlitt, W. Carew, *Four generations of a literary family*, 2 vols. (1897)

Hébrard, J., *De la librairie, son ancienne prospérité, son état actuel: causes de sa décadence, moyens de régénération* (Paris, 1847)

Heel, Jos van (ed. and trans.), *Jan Willem Holtrop on the study of early printed books from the Low Countries (1856)* (The Hague, 2013)

Hellinga, Lotte, 'Fragments found in bindings and their role as bibliographical evidence', in David Pearson (ed.), *"For the love of the binding": studies in bookbinding history presented to Mirjam Foot* (2000), pp. 13–33, repr. with revisions as 'Fragments found in bindings: the complexity of evidence for the earliest Dutch typography' in Lotte Hellinga, *Incunabula in transit: people and trade* (Leiden, 2018), pp. 204–29

Hellinga-Querido, Lotte and Clemens de Wolf, *Laurens Janszoon Coster was zijn naam* (Haarlem, 1988)

Hellinga, Wytze, 'The Enschedé sale was most disappointing . . .' *Quaerendo* 5 (1975), pp. 303–11

Hellinga, Wytze and Lotte Hellinga, *The fifteenth-century printing types of the Low Countries*, 2 vols. (Amsterdam, 1966)

Helwig, Hellmuth, *Einbandfälschungen: Imitation, Fälschung und Verfälschung historischer Bucheinbände* (Zutphen, 1968)

Herbert, A.S., *Historical catalogue of printed editions of the English Bible, 1525–1961, revised and expanded from the edition of T.H. Darlow and H.F. Moule, 1903* (1968)

Herring, Richard, *A few personal recollections of the late Rev. George Croly* (1861)
  Paper & paper making, ancient and modern, 2nd ed. (1855)

Herrmann, Frank, *Sotheby's: portrait of an auction house* (1980)

Hesse, Léopold Augustin Constantin ('L.A.Constantin'), *Biblioéconomie, ou nouvel manuel complet pour l'arrangement, la conservation et l'administration des bibliothèques et des archives*, Nouvelle éd. (Paris, 1841)

Hesse, Raymond, *Histoire des sociétés de bibliophiles en France de 1820 à 1930*, 2 vols. (Paris, 1929–31)

Hessel, Alfred, *A history of libraries*, trans. Reuben Peiss (Washington, DC, 1950)

Hessels, J.H., *Gutenberg: was he the inventor of printing?* (1882)
  Haarlem the birth-place of printing, not Mentz (1887)
  'The palaeographical publications of the last twenty-five years', *The Academy* (20 September 1884), pp. 184–7; (4 October), pp. 221–2; (11 October), pp. 237–40
  (ed.), *Ecclesiae Londino-Batavae archivium*, 3 vols. in 4 (1887–97)

Hill, Alexandra, *Lost books and printing in London, 1557–1640* (Leiden, 2018)

Hill, M.J. and S. Hengchen, 'Quantifying the impact of dirty OCR on historical text analysis: Eighteenth Century Collections Online as a case study', *Digital Scholarship in the Humanities* 34 (2019), pp. 824–43

Hill, Rosemary, *Time's witness: history in the age of romanticism* (2021)

Hindley, Charles, *Curiosities of street literature* (1871)
  The life and times of James Catnach (late of Seven Dials), ballad monger (1878)

Hinrichsen, Alex, *Baedeker's Reisehandbücher, 1832–1944* (Holzminden, 1981)

Hoare, Peter, 'Archbishop Tenison's library at St Martin-in-the-Fields: the building and its history', *London Topographical Record* 29 (2006), pp. 127–50

Hobson, G.D., *Bindings in Cambridge libraries* (Cambridge, 1929)

Hodson's Booksellers, publishers and stationers directory, 1855: a facsimile, introd. Graham Pollard (Oxford, 1972)

Hoe, Richard M., *Literature of printing* (privately pr., 1877)

Hoffmann, F.L., *Chronological list of books and articles on the history of printing in Holland and Belgium, compiled 1856–1858* (Chicago, 1941)

Holmes, John, 'Libraries and catalogues', *Quarterly Review* 72 (1843), pp. 1–25

Holtrop, J.W., *Catalogus librorum saeculo XV° impressorum, quotquot in Bibliotheca Regia Hagana asservantur* (The Hague, 1856)

Monuments typographiques des Pays-Bas au quinzième siècle (The Hague, 1856–68)

Hope, Andrew, 'The Antwerp origins of the Coverdale Bible: investigations from the 1884 *Athenaeum* controversy to the present day', in Paul Arblaster, Gergely Juhász and Guido Latré (eds.), *Tyndale's Testament* (Turnhout, 2002), pp. 39–54

Hudson, Derek, *Arthur Munby, man of two worlds* (1972)

Hugo, Thomas, *The Bewick collector*, 2 vols. (1866–8)

Bewick's woodcuts. Impressions of upwards of two thousand wood blocks (1870)

Hume, A., *The learned societies and printing clubs of the United Kingdom* (1847, enlarged ed. A.I. Evans, 1853)

Humphreys, Henry Noel, *A history of the art of printing from its invention to its widespread development in the middle of the 16th century* (1867)

Hunnisett, Basil, *Engraved on steel: the history of picture production using steel plates* (Aldershot, 1998)

Steel-engraved book illustration in England (1980)

Hunt, Arnold, 'The sale of Richard Heber's library', in Robin Myers and others (eds.), *Under the hammer: book auctions since the seventeenth century* (New Castle, DE, 2001), pp. 143–71

Hunter, Robert E., *Shakespeare and Stratford-upon-Avon: a 'chronicle of the time'* (1864)

Hurst, Clive, *Catalogue of the Wren Library of Lincoln Cathedral: books printed before 1801* (Cambridge, 1982)

Husbands, Shayne, *The early Roxburghe Club, 1812–1835: book club pioneers and the advancement of English literature* (2017)

Huth, Alfred Henry, *A catalogue of the woodcuts and engravings in the Huth library* (1910)

International exhibition, 1862: Official catalogue, industrial department (1862)

Introduction à la bibliographie de Belgique ... dressé par les soins de la Section Littéraire de la Commission des Échanges Internationaux (Brussels, 1875, rev. 1877)

Irish literary enquirer: or notes on authors, books, & printing in Ireland, biographical and bibliographcal, notices of rare books, memoranda of printing in Ireland, biographical notes of Irish writers, &c. (1865)

Isaac, Marie-Thérèse and Frank Vandeweghe (eds.), *Répertoire des fonds anciens en Belgique / Repertorium van het oude boekenbezit in België* (Mons, 1989)

Jacks, Lawrence Pearsall, *Life and letters of Stopford Brooke*, 2 vols. (1917)

Jackson, John and W.A. Chatto, *Treatise on wood engraving, historical and practical* (1839); 2nd ed., with a new chapter by Henry G. Bohn (1861)

Jackson, Mason, *The pictorial press: its origin and progress* (1885)

Jackson, W.A., *An annotated list of the publications of the Reverend Thomas Frognall Dibdin* (Cambridge, MA, 1965)

Jäger, Georg and Reinhard Wittman, 'Der Antiquariatsbuchhandel' in Georg Jäger and others (eds.), *Geschichte des deutschen Buchhandels im 19. und 20. Jahrhundert. Das Kaiserreich, 1871–1918*, part 1, vol. 3 (Berlin, 2010), pp. 195–280

James, Henry, *Photo-zincography* (Southampton, 1860)

Jammes, André, *Libri vaincu: enquêtes policières & secrets bibliographiques* (Paris, 2008)

Janin, Jules, 'Brunet', *Le Bibliophile Français* 1 (1868), pp. 5–16

Janssen, Frans A., *Dibdin in Paris (1818)* ('t Goy-Houten, 2008)

Jaspers, G.J., *De blokboeken en incunabelen in Haarlems Libry* (Haarlem, 1988)

Jeanblanc, Helga, *Des Allemands dans l'industrie et le commerce du livre à Paris (1811–1870)* (Paris, 1994)

Jefcoate, Graham and Karen Kloth, ed. Bernhard Fabian, *A catalogue of English books printed before 1801 held by the University Library, Göttingen*, 7 vols. (Hildesheim, 1987–8)

Jenkinson, Francis, *A list of the incunabula collected by George Dunn arranged to illustrate the history of printing* (1923)

Jessopp, Augustus, *The middle class examinations* (1860)

Jewett, C.C., *Smithsonian Institution catalogue system* (Washington, DC, 1850)

Jimenes, Rémi, '*Le Bibliophile Français* et la librairie Bachelin-Deflorenne', *Nouvelle Revue des Livres Anciens* 2 (2009), pp. 59–64

Johns, Adrian, *The nature of the book: print and knowledge in the making* (Chicago, 1998)

Johnson, A.F., 'Old-face types in the Victorian age', *Selected essays*, ed. P.H. Muir (Amsterdam, 1970), pp. 423–35

 '*Typographia, or the printer's instructor*', in his *Selected essays*, ed. P.H. Muir (Amsterdam, 1970), pp. 416–22

Johnson, Charles Plumptre, *Hints to collectors of original editions of the works of Charles Dickens* (1885)

Johnson, J., *Typographia, or the printer's instructor*, 2 vols. (1824)

Johnston, George P., 'The story of the Edinburgh Bibliographical Society', *Journal of the Edinburgh Bibliographical Society* 1 (2006), pp. 109–17

Jones, J.Winter, 'Early printed books', *Archaeological Journal* 28 (1871), pp. 1–22

Jones, Mark (ed.), *Fake? The art of deception* (1990)

Kahrl, George M. and Dorothy Anderson, *The Garrick collection of old English plays: a catalogue with an historical introduction* (1982)

Kearney, Patrick J., *The private case: an annotated bibliography of the private case erotica collection in the British Museum library* (1981); Supplement (Berkeley, 2016)

Kelly, Thomas, *A history of public libraries in Great Britain, 1845–1965* (1973)

Ker, N.R., *Medieval manuscripts in British libraries*, 5 vols. (Oxford, 1969–2002)

 Pastedowns in Oxford bindings, with a survey of Oxford binding c.1515–1620 (Oxford, 1954)

Keyser, Marja, *Frederik Muller en de oude boekhandel* (Amsterdam, 1994)

Keyser, Marja and others (eds.), *Frederik Muller (1817–1881): leven & werken* (Zutphen, 1996)

King, A. Hyatt, *Some British collectors of music, c.1600–1960* (Cambridge, 1963)

King, Anthony, 'George Godwin and the Art Union of London, 1837–1911', *Victorian Studies* 8 (1964), pp. 101–30

King, Edmund M.B., *Victorian decorated trade bindings, 1830–1880: a descriptive bibliography* (2003)
King, L.S., *The industrialization of taste: Victorian England and the Art Union of London* (Ann Arbor, 1985)
Kirchhoff, A., *Katalog der Börsenvereins der Deutschen Buchhändler* (Leipzig, 1869)
Klein, Karl, *Über Gutenberg und das im ersten Druckhaus desselben aufgefundene Fragment seiner Presse* (Mainz, 1856)
Klemm, Heinrich, *Beschreibender Catalog des Bibliographischen Museums* (Dresden, 1884)
Kloss, G., 'Ueber Melanchthons angebliche Handschriften, welche in dem Catalogue of the Library of Dr. Kloss verzeichnet sind', *Serapeum* 2 (1841), pp. 369–77
Knight, Charles, *Life of William Caxton* (1828)
   Passages in a working life during half a century, 3 vols. (1865)
   The old printer and the modern press (1854)
   William Caxton, the first English printer (1844)
   (ed.), *London*, 6 vols. in 3 (1851)
Knowles, David, *Great historical enterprises* (1963)
Knuth, Rebecca, *Burning books and levelling libraries: extremist violence and cultural destruction* (Westport, CT, 2006)
   Libricide: the regime-sponsored destruction of books and libraries in the twentieth century (Westport, CT, 2003)
Knuttel, W.P.C., *Catalogus van de pamfletten-verzameling berustende in de Koninklijke Bibliotheek*, 11 vols. (The Hague, 1889–1920)
Kok, Ina, *Woodcuts in incunabula printed in the Low Countries*, 4 vols. (Houten, 2013)
König, Eberhard, *Biblia pulcra: die 48zeilige Bibel von 1462* (Ramsen and Rotthalmünster, 2005)
Kratz, Isabelle, 'Libraires et éditeurs allemands installés à Paris, 1840–1914', *Revue de Synthèse* 113 (1992), pp. 99–108
Kraye, Jill and Paolo Sachet (eds.), *The afterlife of Aldus: posthumous fame, collectors and the book trade* (2018)
Kuitert, Lisa, 'The art of printing in the Dutch East Indies: Laurens Janszoon Coster as colonial hero', *Quaerendo* 50 (2020), pp. 141–64
Lacombe, Paul, *Bibliographie des travaux de M.Léopold Delisle* (Paris, 1902); *Supplément* (Paris, 1911)
Lacroix, Paul, 'Le commerce des livres anciens', in É. Rouveyre and O. Uzanne (eds.), *Miscellanées bibliographiques*, 2 (Paris, 1879), pp. 63–78
   Curiosités de l'histoire des arts (Paris, 1858)
   ('P.L. Jacob'), *Mélanges bibliographiques* (Paris, 1871)
   ('P.L. Jacob'), *Réforme de la Bibliothèque du Roi* (Paris, 1845)
Lalanne, Ludovic and Henri-Léonard Bordier, *Dictionnaire de pièces autographes volées aux bibliothèques publiques de la France, précédé d'observations sur le commerce des autographes* (Paris, 1851)
Lamartine, A. de, *Gutenberg, inventeur de l'imprimerie* (Paris, 1853)
Lang, Andrew, *Books and bookmen* (1887)
Latham, Robert (ed.), *Catalogue of the Pepys library at Magdalene College, Cambridge*, 7 vols. and facsimiles (Cambridge, 1978–94)
Laufer, Roger (ed.), *La bibliographie matérielle* (Paris, 1983)

Le Normand, L.-Séb., *Manuel du fabriquant du papier, ou de l'art de la papeterie*, 2 vols. (Paris, 1833)

Le Prince, Nicolas, *Essai historique sur la Bibliothèque du Roi* (Paris, 1782)

Le Roux de Lincy, Antoine, *Recherches sur Jean Grolier, sur sa vie et sa bibliothèque* (Paris, 1866)

Le Soudier, H., *Bibliographie française: recueil de catalogues des éditeurs français* (1896)

Ledos, E.-G., *Histoire des catalogues des livres imprimés de la Bibliothèque Nationale* (Paris, 1936)

Lee, J.D., 'The father of British indexing: Henry Benjamin Wheatley', *The Indexer* 23 (2002), pp. 86–91

Leigh, Charles W.E. and others, *Catalogue of the Christie collection* (Manchester, 1915)

Leis, Arlene, 'Sarah Sophia Banks, "A 'truly interesting collection of visiting cards and Co."'", in Toby Burrow and Cynthia Johnston (eds.), *Collecting the past: British collectors and their collections from the 18th to the 20th centuries* (Abingdon, 2019), pp. 25–44

Lemon, R. and M.A.E. Green (eds.), *Calendar of state papers, Domestic Series, of Edward VI, Mary, Elizabeth I and James I* (1856–72)

Lempertz, Heinrich, *Bilder-Hefte zur Geschichte des Bücherhandels und der mit demselben verwandten Künste und Gewerbe* (Köln, 1853–65)

Lenormand, Séb., *Nouveau manuel complet du relieur, dans toutes ses parties*, nouvelle éd. (Paris, 1840)

Lescure, M.F.A. de, *Les autographes et le goût des autographes en France et à l'étranger … Ouvrage contenant la bibliographie analytique et critique des traités sur les autographes, des catalogues de ventes et des recueils de fac-simile français & étrangers* (Paris, 1865)

Lessing J. Rosenwald collection (The): a catalog of the gifts of Lessing J.Rosenwald to the Library of Congress, 1943 to 1975 (Washington, DC, 1977)

Levitt, Marcus C., *Russian literary politics and the Pushkin celebration of 1880* (Ithaca, 1989)

Lewis, John, *Printed ephemera* (Ipswich, 1962)

   Such things happen: the life of a typographer (Stowmarket, 1994)

'Library (The) of Gray the poet', *Gentleman's Magazine* 1846, pt 1, pp. 29–33

Libri, Guglielmo, *Réponse de M.Libri au rapport de M.Boucly, publié dans le Moniteur Universel du 19 March 1848* (1848)

Linde, Antonius, van der, *Gutenberg und Erdichtung aus den Quellen nachgewiesen*, 2 vols. (Stuttgart, 1878)

   De Haarlemsche Costerlegende wetenschappelijk onderzocht (The Hague, 1870), trans. and introduced by Hessels as *The Haarlem legend of the invention of printing by Lourens Janszoon Coster, critically examined* (1871)

List of catalogues of English book sales, 1676–1900, now in the British Museum (1915)

Lister, W.B.C., *A bibliography of Murray's Handbooks for travellers* (Dereham, 1993)

Lithographed signatures of the members of the British Association for the Advancement of Science, who met at Cambridge, June M.DCCC.XXXIII: with a report of the proceedings at the public meetings during the week, and an alphabetical list of the members (1833)

Loftie, W.J., 'Catalogue of a loan collection of books printed before 1600', *Archaeological Journal* 29 (1872), pp. 45–70

   A century of Bibles, or the Authorised Version from 1611 to 1711 (1872)

Lessons in the art of illuminating ... with practical instructions and a sketch of the history of the art (Vere Foster's Water-Colour Series) [1885]

A plea for art in the house (1876)

Lottin, A.M., *Catalogue chronologique des libraires et des libraires-imprimeurs de Paris depuis l'an 1470* (Paris, 1789)

Lowndes, W.T., *The bibliographer's manual of English literature*, 4 vols. (1834); revised and expanded by Henry G. Bohn, 4 vols. (1857–64)

Loyrette, Henri, 'La tour Eiffel', in Pierre Nora (ed.), *Les lieux de mémoire*, 3 vols. (Paris, 1997), 3, pp. 4270–93

Luckombe, Philip, *The history and art of printing* (1771)

Luther, Frederic, *Microfilm: a history, 1839–1900* (Annapolis, 1959)

Lyons, Martyn, *Le triomphe du livre: une histoire sociologique de la lecture dans la France du XIXe siècle* (Paris, 1987)

Maccioni Ruju, P. Alessandra and Marco Mostert, *The life and times of Guglielmo Libri (1802–1869)* (Hilversum, 1995)

Machiels, J., 'Henry Bradshaw's correspondentie met Ferdinand Vander Haeghen', *Archives et Bibliothèques de Belgique* 43 (1972), pp. 598–614

Maclean, Ian, *Learning and the market place: essays in the history of the early modern book* (Leiden, 2009)

Macleod, Dianne Sachko, *Art and the Victorian middle class: money and the making of cultural identity* (Cambridge, 1996)

Maire, Albert, *Manuel pratique du bibliothécaire* (Paris, 1896)

Malavieille, Sophie, *Reliures et cartonnages d'éditeur en France au XIXe siècle (1815–1865)* (Paris, 1985)

Malclès, Louise-Noëlle, *Manuel de bibliographie*, 4th ed. (Paris, 1986)

Mandatori, Gianluca '"But the calamity was complete and total": Mommsen, Giordane e i dotti inglesi', *Quaderni di Storia* 86 (2017), pp. 178–202

Mandelbrote, Giles (ed.), *Out of print and into profit: a history of the rare and secondhand book trade in Britain in the twentieth century* (2006)

Mangeart, Jacques, *Catalogue descriptif et raisonné des manuscrits de la Bibliothèque de Valenciennes* (Paris, 1860)

Mansel, Philip, *Paris between empires, 1814–1852* (2001)

Mansion, J., 'Ferdinand van der Haeghen', *Jaarboek der Koninklijke Vlaamsche Academie voor Taal-en Letterkunde* (1921), pp. 125–44

Marius-Michel, *La reliure française commerciale et industrielle depuis l'invention de l'imprimerie jusqu'à nos jours* (Paris, 1881)

La reliure française, depuis l'invention de l'imprimerie jusqu'à la fin du XVIIIe siècle (Paris, 1880)

Marston, E., *After work: fragments from the workshop of an old publisher* (1904)

Martin, John, *Bibliographical catalogue of books privately printed* (1834)

Masai, François, 'Paléographie et codicologie', *Scriptorium* 4 (1950), pp. 279–83

May's British & Irish press guide (1874, etc.)

Mayhew, Henry, *London labour and the London poor*, 4 vols. (1861–2)

Maze-Sencier, Alphonse, *Le livre des collectionneurs* (Paris, 1885)

McCarthy, William, 'What did Anna Barbauld do to Samuel Richardson's correspondence? A study of her editing', *SB* 54 (2001), pp. 191–223

McCrimmon, Barbara, *Power, politics, and print: the publication of the British Museum catalogue, 1881–1900* (Hamden, CT, 1981)

McCulloch, J.R., *A dictionary, practical, theoretical, and historical, of commerce and commercial navigation*, new ed. (1859)

McDonald, Mark, *The print collection of Ferdinand Columbus (1488–1539): a renaissance collector in Seville*, 2 vols. and CD (2004)

McKenzie, D.F., *Bibliography and the sociology of texts* (1986)

McKerrow, R.B., 'Notes on bibliographical evidence for literary students and editors', *Trans Bibliographical Soc.* 12 (1913), pp. 211–318, also reprinted separately (1914)

McKie, James, *Title pages (and imprints) of the books in the private library of James McKie, Kilmarnock* (Kilmarnock, 1867)

McKitterick, David, *Cambridge University Library: a history. The eighteenth and nineteenth centuries* (Cambridge, 1986)

'Dawson Turner and book collecting', in Nigel Goodman (ed.), *Dawson Turner: a Norfolk antiquary and his remarkable family* (Chichester, 2007), pp. 67–110

'Henry Bradshaw as librarian', *TCBS* 16 (2019), pp. 517–33

The invention of rare books: private interest and public memory, 1700–1840 (Cambridge, 2018)

Old books, new technologies: the representation, conservation and transformation of books since 1700 (Cambridge, 2013)

The Philobiblon Society: sociability & book collecting in mid-Victorian Britain (Roxburghe Club, 2019)

'Putting the past on show. Old books and communal memory in the nineteenth century', *Archivio Storico Italiano* 172 (2014), pp. 77–107

'Second-hand and old books', in D. McKitterick (ed.), *The Cambridge history of the book in Britain, 6: 1830–1914* (Cambridge, 2009)

(ed.), *The Cambridge history of the book in Britain, 6: 1830–1914* (Cambridge, 2009)

McLean, Ruari, *Joseph Cundall, a Victorian publisher: notes on his life and a check-list of his books* (Pinner, 1976)

Victorian book design & colour printing (1963, 2nd ed. 1972)

Victorian publishers' book-bindings (1974)

Victorian publishers' book-bindings in paper (1983)

McTurk, James, 'The reading room of the British Museum', in Charles Knight (ed.) *London*, 6 vols. in 3 (1851), 4, pp. 385–400

'Mechanics' institutions', *Chambers's Papers for the people* 23 (1874)

Mercier, Alain and others, *Les trois révolutions du livre* (Paris, 2002)

[Mermet, Louis Bollioud de], *De la bibliomanie* ('La Haie', 1761), new ed. Paul Chéron (Paris, 1865)

Mertens, Sabine and others, *Blockbücher des Mittelalters: Bilderfolgen als Lektüre* (Gutenberg-Museum, Mainz, 1991)

Michelet, Jules, *Rapport au Ministre de l'Instruction Publique sur les bibliothèques et archives des départements du sud-ouest de la France* (Paris, 1836)

Middleton, Bernard, *A history of English craft bookbinding technique*, 2nd ed. (1978)

Middleton, Conyers, *A dissertation concerning the origin of printing in England* (Cambridge, 1735)

Middleton, R.D., *Dr. Routh* (Oxford, 1938)

Middleton-Wake, Charles H., *The invention of printing* (1897)

Midoux, Étienne and Auguste Matton, *Étude sur les filigranes des papiers employés en France aux XIVe et XVe siècles* (Paris, 1868)

Milner, J., 'Account of an ancient manuscript of St. John's Gospel', *Archaeologia* 16 (1812), pp. 17–21

Milnes, Richard Monckton (ed.), *Life, letters and literary remains, of John Keats*, 2 vols. (1848)

Mitchell, B.R., *British historical statistics* (Cambridge, 1988)

Mitchell's Newspaper press directory (1846, etc.)

Mole, Tom, *What the Victorians made of romanticism* (Princeton, 2017)

Mollier, Jean-Yves, 'La police de la librairie (1810–1881)', in Patricia Sorel and Frédérique Leblanc (eds.), *Histoire de la librairie française* (Paris, 2008), pp. 16–26

Mollier, Jean-Yves and Bruno Dubot, *Histoire de la librairie Larousse (1852–2010)* (Paris, 2012)

Monfalcon, Jean-Baptiste, *Étude sur Louis Perrin, imprimeur lyonnais*, ed. Laurent Guillo with a postface by René Ponot (Paris, 1994)

Montfaucon, Bernard de, *Bibliotheca bibliothecarum manuscriptorum nova*, 2 vols. (Paris, 1739)

Monuments inédits ou peu connus, faisant partie du cabinet de Guillaume Libri, et qui se rapportent à l'histoire des arts du dessin considérés dans leur application à l'ornement des livres (1862, and supplement, 1864)

Moore, Lara Jennifer, *Restoring order: the École des Chartes and the organization of archives and libraries in France, 1820–1870* (Duluth, MN, 2008)

Moran, James, *The composition of reading matter: a history from case to computer* (1965)

  'William Blades', *The Library* 5th ser. 16 (1961), pp. 251–66

Morel, G., 'Ueber die Ausstellung auf der deutschen Buchhändlerbörse zu Leipzig während der Feier des Buchdruckfestes 1840', *Serapeum* 15 (1840), pp. 225–36

Mores, Edward Rowe, *A dissertation upon English typographical founders and founderies*, ed. Harry Carter and Christopher Ricks (Oxford, 1961)

Morgan, Paul, 'John Hannett's Bibliopegia and Inquiry, and Salt Brassington's revision', in David Pearson (ed.), *'For the love of the binding': studies in bookbinding history presented to Mirjam Foot* (2000), pp. 283–8

Morison, Stanley, 'On the classification of typographical variations', in John Dreyfus (ed.), *Type specimen facsimiles* (1963), pp. ix–xxix

  Talbot Baines Reed: author, bibliographer, typefounder (Cambridge, 1960)

Morris, Edward, *Public art collections in north-west England: a history and guide* (Liverpool, 2001)

  Victorian & Edwardian paintings in the Walker Art Gallery and at Sudley House: British artists born after 1810 but before 1861 (1996)

Mosley, James, 'Recasting Caslon Old Face', *Type Foundry* blog, 4 July 2010

  'Talbot Baines Reed, typefounder and sailor', *The Private Library* 6th ser. 4 (2011 [2012]), pp. 235–44

Moxon, Joseph, *Mechanick exercises on the whole art of printing (1683–4)*, ed. Herbert Davis and Harry Carter, 2nd ed. (Oxford, 1962)

Munby, A.N.L., *The cult of the autograph letter in England* (1962)

  'The earl and the thief', in *Essays and papers*, ed. Nicolas Barker (1977), pp. 175–91

The history and bibliography of science in England: the first phase, 1833–1845, to which is added a reprint of a catalogue of scientific manuscripts in the possession of J.O.Halliwell, Esq. (Berkeley, CA, 1968)

Phillipps studies, 5 vols. (Cambridge, 1951–60)

'The triumph of Delisle: a sequel to "The earl and the thief"', in *Essays and papers*, ed. Nicolas Barker (1977), pp. 193–205

Munford, W.A., *Edward Edwards, 1812–1886: portrait of a librarian* (1963)

Murphy, Andrew, *Shakespeare in print: a history and chronology of Shakespeare publishing*, 2nd ed. (Cambridge, 2021)

Murray, John, IV, *John Murray III, 1808–1892: a brief memoir* (1919)

Myers, Robin, 'The Caxton celebration of 1877. A landmark in bibliophily', in R. Myers and M. Harris (eds.), *Bibliophily* (Cambridge, 1986), pp. 138–63

'William Blades's debt to Henry Bradshaw and G.I.F.Tupper', *The Library* 5th ser. 23 (1978), pp. 265–83

Mynors, R.A.B., R.H. Rouse and M.A. Rouse (eds.), *Registrum Anglie de libris doctorum et auctorum veterum* (1991)

National Union Catalog pre-1956 imprints: a cumulative author list representing Library of Congress printed cards and titles reported by other American libraries, 754 vols. (1968–81)

Needham, Paul, *The Bradshaw method: Henry Bradshaw's contribution to bibliography* (Chapel Hill, 1988)

'Fragments in books: Dutch prototypography in the van Ess library', in Milton McC. Gatch (ed.), *'So precious a foundation': the library of Leander van Ess at the Burke Library of Union Theological Seminary* (New York, 1996), pp. 85–110

'Paul Schwenke and Gutenberg scholarship: the German contribution, 1885–1921', *PBSA* 84 (1990), pp. 241–64

Twelve centuries of bookbindings, 400–1600 (New York, 1979)

Needham, Paul, Joseph Dunlap and John Dreyfus, *William Morris and the art of the book* (New York, 1976)

Nestler, Friedrich, *Friedrich Adolf Ebert und seine Stellung im nationalen Erbe der Bibliothekswissenschaft* (Leipzig, 1969)

Netherclift, Frederick G., *The hand-book of autographs* (1862)

Nettleship, H., Review of *An eighth-century Latin-Anglo-Saxon glossary, preserved in the library of Corpus Christi College, Cambridge* by J. H. Hessels, *Classical Review* 5 (1890), pp. 382–4

Nichols, John, *Illustrations of the manners and expences of antient times in England, in the fifteenth, sixteenth, and seventeenth centuries, deduced from the accompts of churchwardens, and other authentic documents* (1797)

Nicholson, E.W.B., *The Bodleian Library in 1882–7* (Oxford, 1888)

Nicholson, Edward B. and Henry R. Tedder (eds.), *Transactions and proceedings of the conference of librarians . . . October 1877* (1878)

Nicholson, James B., *A manual of the art of bookbinding* (Philadelphia, 1882 printing)

Niepce, Léopold, *Les bibliothèques anciennes et modernes de Lyon* (Lyon, 1876)

Nisard, Charles, *Histoire des livres populaires*, 2nd ed., 2 vols. (Paris, 1864)

Nixon, Howard M., 'Binding forgeries', *VIth international congress of bibliophiles, Vienna, 20 September–5 October 1969* (Vienna, 1971), pp. 76–81

Broxbourne Library: styles and designs of bookbindings from the twelfth to the twentieth century (1956)

Five centuries of English bookbinding (1978)

Nodier, Charles, *Correspondance inédite* (Paris, 1876)

Noltenius, Rainer, 'Schiller als Führer und Heiland: das Schillerfest 1859 als nationaler Traum von der Geburt des zweiten deutschen Kaiserreichs', in Dieter Düding, Peter Friedemann and Paul Münch (eds.), *Öffentliche Festkultur: politische Feste in Deutschland von der Aufklärung bis zum Ersten Weltkrieg* (Reinbek bei Hamburg, 1988), pp. 237–58

Nora, Pierre (ed.), *Les lieux de mémoire*, 3 vols. (Paris, 1997)

Nordman, Daniel, 'Les Guides-Joanne: ancêtres des Guides Bleus', in Pierre Nora (ed.), *Les lieux de mémoire*, 3 vols. (Paris, 1997), 1, pp. 1035–72

Norman, Jeremy M., *Scientist, scholar & scoundrel: a bibliographical investigation of the life and exploits of Count Guglielmo Libri* (New York, 2013)

Notice sur le monument érigé à Paris par souscription à la gloire de Molière. Suivie de pièces justificatives et de la liste générale des souscripteurs (Paris, 1844)

Observations on the address by the President, and on the statement by the Council ... respecting Mr. Panizzi (1837)

Oddos, Jean-Paul (ed.), *Le patrimoine: histoire, pratiques et perspectives* (Paris, 1995)

Omont, Henri, *Catalogue des manuscrits Ashburnham-Barrois acquis en 1901* (Paris, 1902)

One hundred and fifty wood cuts selected from The Penny Magazine; worked, by printing machine, from the original blocks (1835)

One hundred years of book auctions (1907)

Ordish, T. Fairman, 'Chambers's Journal', *The Bibliographer* 4 (1883), pp. 57–65

Ottley, William Young, *An inquiry into the origin and early history of engraving* (1816)

Ovenden, Richard, *Burning the books: a history of knowledge under attack* (2020)

Ovink, G.W., 'Nineteenth-century reactions against the Didone type model', *Quaerendo* 1 (1971), pp. 17–32, 281–302; 2 (1972), pp. 121–44

Oxford University Commission, *Report* (1852)

Panizzi, A., *A letter to His Royal Highness the President of the Royal Society, on the new catalogue of the library of that institution now in the press* (1837)

To S.P. Rigaud, Esq. M.A. F.R.S. (1838)

Paris, Jean-Moise, *Honneurs publics rendus à la mémoire de Jean-Jacques Rousseau* (Geneva, 1878)

Paris, Paulin, *De la Bibliothèque Royale et de la nécessité de commencer, achever et publier le catalogue général des livres imprimés* (Paris, 1847)

Paris Universal Exhibition of 1867. Part II. Catalogue of the works exhibited in the British Section (1867)

Parker, Wyman W., *Henry Stevens of Vermont: an American bookdealer in London, 1845–'86* (Amsterdam, 1963)

Partridge, R.C. Barrington, *The history of the legal deposit of books throughout the British Empire* (1938)

Passier, Alphonse ('Wilhelm Eriksen'), *Les échanges internationaux littéraires et scientifiques, 1832–1880* (Paris, 1880)

Passmore Edwards (The) and William Blades libraries of printing and the allied crafts (1900)

Patrimoine des bibliothèques de France: un guide des régions, 11 vols. (Paris, 1995)

'"Patrimoines": dossier', *Bulletin des Bibliothèques de France* 49, 5 (2004), pp. 5–78

Patten, Robert L., *Charles Dickens and his publishers* (Oxford, 1978)

Payne, John R., *Great catalogues by master booksellers* (Austin, TX, 2017)

Pearson, David, *Provenance research in book history: a handbook*, new ed. (Oxford, 2019)

Pearson, Emily C., *Gutenberg: or the world's benefactor* (1870)

Pearson, Karl, 'Henry Bradshaw', *The Academy* (27 February 1886)

Peignot, Gabriel, *Dictionnaire raisonné de bibliologie*, 3 vols. (Paris, 1802–4)

    Recherches historiques et bibliographiques sur les autographes et sur l'autographie (Dijon, 1836)

Pellechet, Marie, *Bibliothèque Publique de Versailles. Catalogue des incunables et des livres imprimés de MD à MDXX* (Paris, 1889)

    Catalogue des incunables des bibliothèques publiques de Lyon (Lyon, 1893)

    Catalogue général des incunables des bibliothèques publiques de France, 3 vols. (Paris, 1897–1909). Repr. and extended with Pellechet's manuscript and Louis Polain's working notes, 26 vols. (Nendeln, 1970)

Peltz, Lucy, *Facing the text: extra-illustration, print culture and society in Britain, 1769–1840* (San Marino, 2016)

Pérez Fernández, José María and Edward Wilson-Lee, *Hernando Colón's new world of books: toward a cartography of knowledge* (New Haven, 2021)

Pergam, Elizabeth A., *The Manchester Art Treasures exhibition of 1857: entrepreneurs, connoisseurs and the public* (2011)

Peric, Ester Camilla, *Vendere libri a Padova nel 1480: il Quaderneto di Antonio Moretto*, introd. Neil Harris (Udine, 2020)

Perzanowski, Aaron and Jason Schultz, *The end of ownership: personal property in the digital economy* (Cambridge, MA, 2018)

Peterson, William S., *The Kelmscott Press: a history of William Morris's typographical adventure* (Oxford, 1991)

Pickwood, Nicholas, 'The interpretation of bookbinding structure: an examination of sixteenth-century bindings in the Ramey collection in the Pierpont Morgan Library', in M.M. Foot (ed.), *Eloquent witnesses: bookbindings and their history* (2004), pp. 127–70

    'An unused resource: bringing the study of bookbindings out of the ghetto', in R. Mouren (ed.), *Ambassadors of the book: competences and training for heritage librarians* (Berlin, 2012), pp. 83–93

    'The use of fragments of medieval manuscripts in the construction and covering of bindings on printed books', in Linda Brownrigg and Margaret M. Smith (ed.), *Interpreting and collecting fragments of medieval books* (Los Altos Hills, 2000), pp. 1–20

Pierson, Stacey J., *Private collecting, exhibitions and the shaping of art history in London: the Burlington Fine Arts Club* (2017)

Piggott, Stuart, 'The origins of the English county archaeological societies', in his *Ruins in a landscape* (Edinburgh, 1976), pp. 171–95

Planche, Gabriel, *De l'industrie de la papeterie* (Paris, 1853)

Plantin, Christophe, *Correspondance*, ed. Max Rooses and J. Denucé, 9 vols. (Antwerp, 1883–1918); *Supplément*, ed. M. van Durme (Antwerp, 1955)

Polastron, Lucien X., *Livres en feu* (Paris, 2007)
Pollard, Alfred W., *Fine books* (1912)
   'Sir John MacAlister: some reminiscences', *The Library*, 4th ser. 6 (1926), pp. 375–80
Pollard, A.W. and G.R. Redgrave, *A short-title catalogue of books printed in England, Scotland, & Ireland and of English books printed abroad, 1475–1640* (1926)
Pollard, Graham and Albert Ehrman, *The distribution of books by catalogue from the invention of printing to A.D. 1800* (Roxburghe Club, 1965)
Pollard, Graham and Esther Potter, *Early bookbinding manuals: an annotated list of technical accounts of bookbinding to 1840* (Oxford, 1984)
Porter, Theodore, *The rise of statistical thinking, 1820–1900* (Princeton, 1986)
Post Office directory of stationers, printers, booksellers, publishers and paper makers (1872)
Powell, Andy, Michael Heaney and Lorcan Dempsey, 'RSLP Collection Description', *D-Lib Magazine* 6 (2000)
Powell, Michael and Terry Wyke, 'At the fall of the hammer: auctioning books in Manchester, 1700–1850', in Peter Isaac and Barry McKay (eds.), *The human face of the book trade: print culture and its creators* (Winchester, 1999), pp. 171–89
Prétot, E.-M., *Annuaire de la typographie parisienne et départementale* (Paris, 1846)
Proctor, Robert, *Bibliographical essays* (1905)
   An index to the early printed books in the British Museum from the invention of printing to the year MD. With notes of those in the Bodleian Library, 2 vols. (1898–1906)
Prothero, G.W., *A memoir of Henry Bradshaw* (1888)
Public libraries in the United States of America: their history, condition, and management (Bureau of Education, US Dept of Interior, 1876)
Publishers' Trade List Annual (1873–)
Quaritch, Bernard, *A catalogue of fifteen hundred books remarkable for the beauty or the age of their bindings, or as bearing indications of former ownership of great book-collectors and famous historical personages* (1889)
   Catalogue of the monuments of the early printers (1888)
   Catalogue of works on the fine arts (1883)
   A collection of facsimiles from examples of historic or artistic bookbinding, illustrating the history of binding, as a branch of the decorative arts (1889)
   A general catalogue of books, arranged in classes, offered for sale (1868)
   Monuments of typography and xylography (1897)
   (ed.), *Contributions towards a dictionary of English book-collectors* (1892–1921)
Quérard, J.-M., *La France littéraire, ou dictionnaire bibliographique des savants, historiens et gens de lettres de la France*, 10 vols. (Paris, 1827–38)
Quinault, Roland, 'The cult of the centenary, c.1784–1914', *Historical Research* 71, 176 (1998), pp. 303–23
Ranganathan, S.R., *The five laws of library science* (Madras, 1931)
Ravaisson, Félix, *Rapports au Ministre de l'Instruction Publique sur les bibliothèques des départements de l'ouest* (Paris, 1841)
Raven, James (ed.), *Lost libraries: the destruction of great book collections since antiquity* (Basingstoke, 2004)
Read, E. Anne, 'Cathedral libraries: a supplementary checklist', *Library History* 4 (1978), pp. 141–63

A checklist of books, catalogues and periodical articles relating to the cathedral libraries of England (Oxford, 1970)

Reavell, Tony and others, *Professor William Knight, 1836–1916: 'Wordsworthian discoverer, enabler and publicist'* (Grasmere, 2016)

Reed, Talbot Baines, *A history of the old English letter foundries* (1887, Rev. A.F. Johnson 1952)

Rees, Abraham, *Cyclopaedia, or universal dictionary of arts*, 45 vols. (1819–20)

Reid, Forrest, *Illustrators of the sixties* (1928)

Reiffenberg, Baron Frédéric de, 'Note sur un exemplaire des lettres d'indulgence', *Nouveaux Mémoires de l'Académie Royale des Sciences et Belles-Lettres de Bruxelles* 5 (1829), pp. 5–12

Reinders, Michel, *Printed pandemonium: popular print and politics in the Netherlands, 1650–72* (Leiden, 2013)

Remy, Fernand, *Aux origines de la Bibliothèque Royale de Belgique. Étude sur son personnel et ses méthodes de travail, 1837–1850* (Brussels, 1960)

  'Un précurseur de la bibliothéconomie moderne: Martin Schrettinger (1772–1851)', *Archives et Bibliothèques de Belgique* 35 (1964), pp. 3–30

Renouard, A.A., *Annales de l'imprimerie des Alde*, 3rd ed. (Paris, 1834)

Report from the Select Committee on Art Unions (House of Commons, 1845)

Reports of artisans selected by a committee approved by the council of the Society of Arts to visit the Paris Universal Exhibition, 1867 (1867)

Report of the Commissioners appointed to inquire into the constitution and government of the British Museum, with minutes of evidence (1850)

Report of the Public Schools Commission (1864)

Report of the Select Committee on public libraries (1849)

Report of the Select Committee on the British Museum (1836)

Reynolds, Suzanne, *A catalogue of the manuscripts in the library at Holkham Hall*, 1: *Manuscripts from Italy to 1500. 1. Shelfmarks 1–399* (Turnhout, 2015)

Richards, Elizabeth M., 'Alexandre Vattemare and his system of international exchanges', *Bull. Medical Library Association* 32 (1944), pp. 413–48

Richardson, H.S., *Examples of ancient bookbindings: a portfolio of rubbings in the possession of the Art Library of South Kensington Museum* (1860)

Rickards, Maurice and Michael Twyman, *The encyclopedia of ephemera* (2000)

Rigney, Ann, 'Embodied communities: commemorating Robert Burns, 1859', *Representations* 115 (2011), pp. 71–101

Ris, Louis Clément de, *La curiosité: collections françaises et étrangères* (Paris, 1864)

Roberts, Helene E. (ed.), *Art history through the camera's lens* (Amsterdam, 1995)

Roberts, Julian and Andrew G. Watson (ed.), *John Dee's library catalogue* (1990)

Roberts, William, *The book-hunter in London* (1895)

Robinson, J.C. (ed.), *Catalogue of the special exhibition of works of art of the mediaeval, renaissance, and more recent periods, on loan at the South Kensington Museum, June 1862*, revised ed. (1863)

Roersch, A., 'Notice sur Ferdinand van der Haeghen', *Annuaire de l'Académie* (1913), pp. 89–110

Roorbach, Orville A., *Bibliotheca Americana: catalogue of American publications ... from 1820 to 1848* (New York, 1849)

Rooses, Max, *Christophe Plantin, imprimeur anversois* (Antwerp, 1882)

Rooses, Max (ed.), *Compte-rendu de la première session de la Conférence du Livre, tenue à Anvers . . . 1890* (Antwerp, 1891)

Rosenbaum, S., 'The growth of the Royal Statistical Society', *Journal of the Royal Statistical Society* Series A (General) 147 (1984), pp. 375–88

Rosenberg, D., 'Early modern information overload', *Journal of the History of Ideas* 64 (2003), pp. 1–9

Rouveyre, Édouard, *Connaissances nécessaires à un bibliophile*, 3rd ed. (Paris, 1879)

Rouveyre, É. and O. Uzanne (eds.), *Miscellanées bibliographiques*, 2 (Paris, 1879)

Rüdiger, Bettina, 'Eine Büchersammlung im 19. Jahrhundert: über einige Provenienzen der Sammlung Heinrich Klemm', *Leipziger Jahrbuch zur Buchgeschichte* 16 (2007), pp. 383–96

Ruelens, C. and A. De Backer, *Annales plantiniennes, depuis la fondation de l'imprimerie plantinienne à Anvers, jusqu'à la mort de Chr. Plantin (1555–1589)* (Paris, 1866)

Ruskin, John, *Sesame and lilies* (1865)

Russell, Gillian, *The ephemeral eighteenth century: print, sociability, and the cultures of collecting* (Cambridge, 2020)

Sabba, Fiametta, *La 'Bibliotheca universalis' di Conrad Gesner: monumento della cultura europea* (Rome, 2012)

Sachet, Paolo, 'Selling Aldus in the UK (c.1630–2015): towards a checklist of British sale catalogues of books published by the Manuzio family', in Jill Kraye and Paolo Sachet (ed.), *The afterlife of Aldus: posthumous fame, collectors and the book trade* (2018), pp. 145–56

Sadleir, Michael, 'The development during the last fifty years of bibliographical study of books of the XIXth century', in *The Bibliographical Society: studies in retrospect* (1949), pp. 146–58

Saint Bride Foundation. Catalogue of the technical reference library of works on printing and the allied arts (1919)

Sandler, Lucy Freeman, *Gothic manuscripts, 1285–1385 (Survey of manuscripts illuminated in the British Isles)*, 2 vols. (1986)

Sauvage, Abbé, *Souvenirs de l'exposition typographique de Rouen* (Rouen, 1887)

Sauvy, Anne, *Livres saisis à Paris entre 1678 et 1701* (The Hague, 1972)

Savoy, Bénédicte, *Patrimoine annexé: les biens culturels saisis par la France en Allemagne autour de 1800*, 2 vols. (Paris, 2003)

Schmidt, Peter, *Gedruckte Bilder in handgeschriebenen Büchern: zum Gebrauch von Druckgraphik . . .* (Cologne, 2003)

Schoenbaum, S., *William Shakespeare: records and images* (1981)

Schöpflin, Johann David, *Vindiciae typographicae* (Strasbourg, 1760)

Schrettinger, Martin, *Handbuch der Bibliothek-Wissenschaft* (Vienna, 1834)

Versuch eines vollständigen Lehrbuchs der Bibliothek-Wissenschaft, 2 vols. (Munich, 1808–29)

Schryver, A. de, M. Dykmans and J. Ruysschaert, *Le Pontifical de Ferry de Clugny* (Vatican City, 1989)

Schwenke, Paul, *Untersuchungen zur Geschichte des ersten Buchdrucks* (Berlin, 1900)

Scott (The) exhibition MDCCCLXXI: catalogue of the exhibition held at Edinburgh, in July and August 1871 (Edinburgh, 1872)

Scott, Henry T., *Autograph collecting: a practical manual for amateurs and historical students* (1894)

Seed, John, '"Commerce and the liberal arts": the political economy of art in Manchester, 1775–1860', in Janet Wolff and John Seed (ed.), *The culture of capital: art, power and the nineteenth-century middle class* (Manchester, 1988), pp. 45–81

Seiz, Johann Christian, *Het derde jubeljaar der uitgevondene boekdrukkonst, behelzende een beknopt historis verhaal van de uitvinding der edele boekdrukkonst* (Haarlem, 1740), trans. as *Annus tertius saecularis inventae artis typographicae, sive brevis historica enarratio de inventione nobilissimae artis typographicae, in qua ostenditur, quo tempore, à quo & ubi locorum ea primum fuerit inventa* (Haarlem, 1742)

Seizinger, Johann Georg, *Theorie und Praxis der Bibliothekswissenschaft. Grundlinien der Archivswissenschaft* (Dresden, 1863)

Selwyn, Pamela, *Everyday life in the German book trade: Friedrich Nicolai as bookseller and publisher in the age of enlightenment, 1750–1810* (University Park, PA, 2000)

Serrai, Alfredo, *Conrad Gesner*, ed. Maria Cochetti (Rome, 1990)

Sharpe, Richard and Micheál Hoyne, *Clóliosta: printing in the Irish language, 1571–1871: an attempt at narrative bibliography* (Dublin, 2020)

Shaw, David J. and others (eds.), *The cathedral libraries catalogue*, 3 vols. (1998)

Shepherd, Richard Herne, *Tennysoniana* (1866; 2nd ed. 1879)

Sherman, William H., '"Rather soiled by use": renaissance readers and modern collectors', in Sabrina Alcorn Baron and others (eds.), *The reader revealed* (Folger Shakespeare Library, 2001), pp. 85–91

Sillars, Stuart, *The illustrated Shakespeare, 1709–1875* (Cambridge, 2008)

Sillitoe, Linda and Allen D. Roberts, *Salamander: the story of the Mormon forgery murders* (Salt Lake City, 1988)

Silverman, Willa S., *The new bibliopolis: French book collectors and the culture of print, 1880–1914* (Toronto, 2008)

Simonnet, Jules, *Essai sur la vie et les ouvrages de Gabriel Peignot* (Paris, 1863)

Singer, S.W., *Some account of the book printed at Oxford in MCCCCLXVIII, under the title of Exposicio Sancti Jeronimi . . . in which is examined its claim to be considered the first book printed in England* (1812)

Sinker, Robert, *A catalogue of the fifteenth-century printed books in the library of Trinity College, Cambridge* (Cambridge, 1876)

The library of Trinity College, Cambridge (Cambridge, 1891)

Slater, J.H., *Early editions: a bibliographical survey of the works of some popular modern authors* (1894)

Library manual [1883]

Round and about the book-stalls: a guide for the book-hunter (1891)

Smith, Charles Saumarez, *The company of artists: the origins of the Royal Academy of Arts in London* (2012)

Smith, Dennis, *Conflict and compromise: class formation in English society, 1830–1914: a comparative study of Birmingham and Sheffield* (1982)

Smith, George and Frank Benger, *The oldest London bookshop: a history of two hundred years* (1928)

Smith, Nicholas, 'The Garrick papers: provenance, publication, and reception', *The Library* 7th ser. 21 (2020), pp. 293–327

Smith, Walter E., *Charles Dickens in the original cloth*, Part 1 (Los Angeles, 1982)

Smitskamp, R. and others, *Luchtmans & Brill: driehonderd jaar uitgevers en drukkers in Leiden 1683–1983: catalogus van de tentoonstelling* (Leiden, 1983)

Solkin, David H. (ed.), *Art on the line: the Royal Academy exhibitions at Somerset House, 1780–1836* (New Haven, 2001)

Somers, Marc, 'De Plantijnstudies van Max Rooses', in Marcus de Schepper and Francine de Nave (eds.), *Ex officina Plantiniana: studia in memoriam Christophori Plantini* (Antwerp, 1989), pp. 45–53

Sorel, Patricia and Frédérique Leblanc (eds.), *Histoire de la librairie française* (Paris, 2008)

Sotheby, Samuel Leigh, *Principia typographica*, 3 vols. (1858)

Ramblings in the elucidation of the autograph of Milton (1861)

Southward, John, *Catalogue of the William Blades library* (1899)

Progress in printing and the graphic arts during the Victorian era (1897)

Spevack, Marvin, *James Orchard Halliwell-Phillipps: the life and work of the Shakespearean scholar and bookman* (New Castle, DE, 2001)

St Clair, William, *The reading nation in the romantic period* (Cambridge, 2004)

Staley, Allen, '"Art is upon the town!": the Grosvenor Gallery winter exhibitions', in Susan P. Casteras and Colleen Denney (eds.), *The Grosvenor Gallery: a palace of art in Victorian England* (New Haven, 1996), pp. 59–74

Stammers, Tom, *The purchase of the past: collecting culture in post-revolutionary Paris, c.1790–1890* (Cambridge, 2020)

'The refuse of the Revolution: autograph collecting in France, 1789–1860', in Caroline Armentenos and others (eds.), *Historicising the French Revolution* (Newcastle-upon-Tyne, 2008), pp. 39–63

Stauffer, Andrew M., *Book traces: nineteenth-century readers and the future of the library* (Philadelphia, 2021)

Stephens, F.G., *Notes on a collection of Thomas Bewick's drawings and woodcuts, exhibited at the Fine Arts Society's rooms* (1880)

Stephens, George, *Two leaves of King Waldere's lay, a hitherto unknown Old-English epic of the eighth century, belonging to the saga cyclus 'King Theodric and his men', now first published from the originals of the ninth century* (Cheapinghaven, 1860)

Stern, Madeleine B., *Antiquarian bookselling in the United States: a history from the origins to the 1940s* (Westport, CT, 1985)

Sternberg, Ilse, 'The British Museum Library and colonial copyright deposit', *British Library Journal* 17 (1991), pp. 61–82

Stevens, Henry, *The Bibles in the Caxton exhibition, MDCCCLXXVII* (1878)

'Photo-bibliography: or, a central bibliographical clearing-house', in Edward B. Nicholson and Henry R. Tedder (eds.), *Transactions and proceedings of the conference of librarians ... October 1877* (1878), pp. 70–81

'Photobibliography: a word on catalogues and how to make them', prefixed to his *Bibliotheca geographica et historica* (1872)

Stoddard, Roger E., *Jacques-Charles Brunet: le grand bibliographe* (2007)
Suarez, Michael F., 'Towards a bibliometric analysis of the surviving record', in Michael F. Suarez and Michael Turner (eds.), *The Cambridge history of the book in Britain, 5: 1695-1830* (Cambridge, 2009), pp. 39-65
Survey of London. 38. The Museums area of South Kensington and Westminster (1975)
Sussex, Duke of, *Address of His Royal Highness the Duke of Sussex, the President, read at the anniversary meeting of the Royal Society, on Thursday, November 30, 1837* (1837)
Swansea Public Library and Gallery of Art Committee, *Annual report*, 1886-7
Tanner, Thomas, *Bibliotheca Britannico-Hibernica* (1748)
Tattersfield, Nigel, *The complete illustrative work of Thomas Bewick*, 3 vols. (2011)
  Dealing in deceit: Edwin Pearson of 'The Bewick Repository' bookshop, 1838-1901 (Bewick Soc., 2020)
Taylor, Archer, *Book catalogues: their varieties and uses*, 2nd ed., Rev. Wm P. Barlow, Jr (Winchester, 1986)
Taylor, W. Thomas, *Texfake: an account of the theft & forgery of early Texas printed documents* (Austin, 1991)
Techener, Joseph, 'Des ventes de livres en Angleterre', *BB* 9 (1850), pp. 709-11
Techener, Joseph and Léon Techener, *Histoire de la bibliophilie. Reliures: recherches sur les bibliothèques des plus célèbres amateurs: armorial des bibliophiles*, 10 parts (Paris, 1861-4)
Techener, Jules, 'De l'amélioration des anciennes bibliothèques en France, et de la création de nouvelles bibliothèques appropriées au perfectionnement moral du peuple', *BB* 8 (1848), pp. 631-8
Tedder, Henry R. and Ernest C. Thomas (ed.), *Transactions and proceedings of the first annual meeting of the Library Association of the United Kingdom* (1879)
Tennyson, Alfred, Lord, *Letters*, ed. Cecil Y. Lang and Edgar F. Shannon Jr, 3 vols. (Oxford, 1982-90)
Tesnière, Valérie, 'La postérité de la presse révolutionnaire à la Bibliothèque nationale de France', *Revue de la Bibliothèque Nationale de France* 10 (2002), pp. 47-50
Texier, Edmond, *Les choses du temps présent* (Paris, 1862)
Thibaudeau, Francis, *La lettre d'imprimerie*, 2 vols. (Paris, 1921)
Thibaut, François Noël, *Description historique et bibliographique de la collection de feu M. le comte de la Bédoyère ... sur la Révolution Française, l'Empire et la Restauration* (Paris, 1862)
Thierry-Poux, Olgar, *Notice des objets exposés* (Paris, 1878)
Thomas, Ernest C., 'Henry Bradshaw', *Library Chronicle* 5 (1888), pp. 179-88
Thomas, Marcel, 'Détournements, vols, destructions', in Dominique Varry (ed.), *Histoire des bibliothèques françaises. Les bibliothèques de la Révolution et du XIXe siècle* (Paris, 1991), pp. 267-70
Thomas-Stanford, Charles, *Early editions of Euclid's Elements* (1926)
Thompson, James Westfall (ed. and trans.), *The Frankfort book fair: the Francofordiense Emporium of Henri Estienne* (Chicago, 1911)
Thompson, John B., *Book wars: the digital revolution in publishing* (Cambridge, 2021)
Thomson, Rodney M., *Catalogue of the manuscripts of Lincoln Cathedral Chapter library* (Woodbridge, 1989)

Tidcombe, Marianne, *Women bookbinders, 1880–1920* (1996)

Tilliette, Pierre-Alain, 'Alexandre Vattemare's international document exchanges and the collection of foreign official publications of the Bibliothèque Administrative de la ville de Paris: a historian's treasure trove' (IFLA general conference, Amsterdam, 1998): archive.ifla.org/IV/ifla64/151-133e.htm (accessed 8 November 2020)

Timperley, C.H., *A dictionary of printers and printing* (1839)
   Encyclopaedia of literary and typographical anecdote (1842)

Tite, William, *An address delivered before the Society of Antiquaries … December 12th, 1861, at an exhibition of printed books, to which is subjoined an address delivered on June 6th, 1861, at an exhibition of illuminated manuscripts* (1862)

Todd, William B. and Ann Bowden, *Tauchnitz international editions in English, 1841–1955: a bibliographical history* (New York, 1988)

Tollebeek, Jo and Eline van Assche (eds.), *Ravaged: art and culture in times of conflict* (New Haven, 2015)

Tombs, Robert and Isabelle Tombs, *That sweet enemy: the French and the British from the Sun King to the present* (2006)

Tomlinson, Charles (ed.), *Cyclopaedia of useful arts*, 2 vols. (1854)

Tross, Edwin, 'Der Prozess "Libri"', *Serapeum* 11 (1850), pp. 315–20

Tuckett, Charles, *Specimens of ancient and modern binding, selected chiefly from the library of the British Museum* (1846)

Tuer, Andrew, *Old London street cries and the cries of today* (1885)

Twyman, Michael, *A history of chromolithography: printed colour for all* (2013)

Tylecote, Mabel, *The mechanics' institutes of Lancashire and Yorkshire before 1851* (Manchester, 1957)

UNESCO *Convention concerning the Exchange of Official Publications and Government Documents between States* (1958)

Université (L') et la typographie: exposition organisée par la Société Archéologique et Historique de l'Orléanais (Orléans, 1885)

Utsch, Ana, *Rééditer Don Quichotte. Matérialité du livre dans la France du XIXe siècle* (Paris, 2020)

Uyttenhove, Pieter and Sylvia Van Peterghem, 'Ferdinand van der Haeghen's shadow on Otlet: European resistance to the Americanized modernism of the Office Internationale de Bibliographie', in W. Boyd Rayward (ed.), *European modernism and the information society: informing the present, understanding the past* (2008), pp. 89–104

Uzanne, Octave, *Caprices d'un bibliophile* (Paris, 1878)

van der Veen, Sytze and others, *Brill: 325 years of scholarly publishing* (Leiden, 2008)

Vander Haeghen, Ferdinand, *Pièces volantes* (Ghent, 1912)

Varry, Dominique (ed.), *Histoire des bibliothèques françaises. Les bibliothèques de la Révolution et du XIXe siècle* (Paris, 1991)

Vattemare, Alexandre, *Second annual report on international literary exchanges* (Albany, 1850)
   Third annual report and letters on international exchanges made to the Governor of Connecticut (New Haven, 1852)

Vegetable substances: materials of manufactures (Library of Entertaining Knowledge) (1833)

Venn, J.A. and J. (ed.), *Alumni Cantabrigienses: a biographical list of all known students, graduates and holders of office at the University of Cambridge, from the earliest times to 1900*, 10 vols. (Cambridge, 1922–54)

Vereiniging ter Bevordering van de Belangen des Boekhandels, *Erste tentoonstelling* (Amsterdam, 1881)

Viardot, Jean, 'Les nouvelles bibliophilies', in H.-J.Martin and others (eds.), *Histoire de l'édition française, 3: Le temps des éditeurs* (Paris,1985), pp. 343–63

Vidal, Léon, *La photographie appliquée aux arts industriels de la reproduction* (Paris, 1880)

Vitet, Ludovic, *Rapport à M.le Ministre de l'Intérieur sur les monuments, les bibliothèques, etc.* (Paris, 1831)

Voet, Leon, *The golden compasses*, 2 vols. (Amsterdam, 1969–72)

Vries, Abraham de, *Lijst der stukken betrekkelijk de geschiedenis van de uitvinding der boekdrukkunst, berustende op het raadhuis te Haarlem* (Haarlem, 1862)

Waagen, G.F., *Treasures of art in Great Britain*, 3 vols. (1854)

Waille, Marie-Claire, *Catalogues régionaux des incunables des bibliothèques publiques de France, 19: Franche-Comté*, 2 vols. (Geneva, 2019)

Wainwright, Clive, *The romantic interior: the British collector at home, 1750–1850* (New Haven, 1989)

Walford, Cornelius, 'Some practical points in the preparation of a general catalogue of English literature', in Henry R. Tedder and Ernest C. Thomas (ed.), *Transactions and proceedings of the first annual meeting of the Library Association of the United Kingdom . . . 1878* (1879), pp. 9, 54–64

Wallon, H., *Notice sur la vie et les travaux de M.Ambroise Firmin-Didot* (Paris, 1886)

Warren, J. Leicester, 'The bibliography of Tennyson', *Fortnightly Review* 2 (1 October 1865), pp. 385–403

Warrington, Bernard, 'The bankruptcy of William Pickering in 1853: the hazards of publishing and bookselling in the first half of the nineteenth century', *Publishing History* 27 (1990), pp. 5–25

Weale, W.H. James, *Bookbindings and rubbings of bindings in the National Art Library, South Kensington Museum*, 2 vols. (1894–8)

Catalogue des objets d'art réligieux du moyen âge, de la renaissance et des temps modernes: exposés à l'Hôtel Liedekerke à Malines (Brussels, 1864)

Historical music loan exhibition, Albert Hall: a descriptive catalogue of rare manuscripts & printed books, chiefly liturgical (1886)

'La reliure au moyen âge', *Revue de l'Art Chrétien* (1890), pp. 194–9, 293–6

Tableaux de l'ancienne école néerlandaise exposés à Bruges dans la grande salle des Halles. Catalogue (Bruges, 1867)

Weatherley, James, *'A bread and cheese bookseller': the recollections of James Weatherley of Manchester, c.1790–1850*, ed. Michael Powell and Terry Wyke (Manchester, 2021)

Webb, John, *John Philip Edmond: bookbinder, librarian and bibliographer of Aberdeen, 1850–1906: a short biography* (Aberdeen, 2011)

Weber, Eugene, *Peasants into Frenchmen: the modernization of rural France, 1870–1914* (Redwood City, CA, 1976)

Wedmore, Frederick, 'A century of English art: the Grosvenor Gallery', *The Magazine of Art* (1888), pp. 168–71

Werdet, Edmond, *Histoire du livre en France*, 5 vols. (Paris, 1861–4)

West, Anthony James, 'Sales and prices of Shakespeare first folios: a history, 1623 to the present', *PBSA* 92 (1998), pp. 465–528; 93 (1999), pp. 74–142

Wheatley, Henry B., *Bookbinding considered as a fine art, mechanical art, and manufacture: a paper read before the Society of Arts . . . April 14, 1880 . . .* Repr. from the *Journal of the Society of Arts* (1882)

 How to catalogue a library (1889)

 How to form a library (1886)

 Prices of books (1898)

 Remarkable bindings in the British Museum selected for their beauty or historic interest (1889)

Whitaker, Joseph, *Reference catalogue of current literature* (1874 etc.)

White, Eric Marshall, *Editio princeps: a history of the Gutenberg Bible* (Turnhout, 2017)

 'Fragments of early Mainz printing in the R.E. Hart collection', in Cynthia Johnston (ed.), *A British book collector: rare books and manuscripts in the R.E. Hart collection, Blackburn Museum and Art Gallery* (2021), pp. 155–64

White, Gleeson, *English illustration: 'the sixties', 1855–70* (1897, revised 1903)

Whitehead, Christopher, *The public art museum in nineteenth century Britain: the development of the National Gallery* (2005)

Wiegand, Wayne A., *Irrepressible reformer: a biography of Melvil Dewey* (Chicago, 1996)

Wigan Free Public Library: its rise and progress. A list of some of its treasures, with an account of the celebration of the twenty-first anniversary of its opening (Wigan, 1901)

Willems, Alphonse, *Les Elzevier* (Bruxelles, 1880)

Williams, Franklin B., 'Photo-facsimiles of *STC* books: a cautionary check list', *SB* 21 (1968), pp. 109–30

Williams, Graham, *Thomas Bewick, engraver, & the performance of woodblocks* (Charing, 2021)

Willis and Sotheran, *A catalogue of upwards of fifty thousand volumes, of ancient and modern books* (1862)

Wilson, Adrian, *The making of the Nuremberg chronicle* (Amsterdam, 1976)

Wilson, Lea, *Bibles, Testaments, Psalms and other books of the Holy Scriptures in English, in the collection of Lea Wilson* (1845)

Windle, John and Karma Pippin, *Thomas Frognall Dibdin, 1776–1847: a bibliography* (New Castle, DE, 1999)

Winlock, William Crawford, 'The international exchange system', in George Brown Goode (ed.), *The Smithsonian Institution, 1846–1896* (Washington, DC, 1897), pp. 397–418

Winstanley, D.A., 'Halliwell Phillipps and Trinity College library', with an additional note by R.W. Hunt, *The Library* 5th ser. 2 (1948), pp. 250–82

Winston, Charles, *Memoirs illustrative of the art of glass painting* (1865)

Wise, Thomas J., *A bibliography of the writings of Alfred, Lord Tennyson*, 2 vols. (1908)

 Catalogue of the Ashley library, 11 vols. (1922–36)

Woerth, Eric, *Le duc d'Aumale: l'étonnant destin d'un prince collectionneur* (Paris, 2006)

Wolf, Melvin H., *Catalogue and indexes to the title-pages of English printed books in the British Library's Bagford collection* (1974)

[Wood, H.H.], 'Jottings from the note-book of an undeveloped collector', *Cornhill Magazine* 16 (1867), pp. 485–500

Zedelmaier, Heinrich, *Bibliotheca universalis und bibliotheca selecta: das Problem der Ordnung des gelehrten Wissens in der frühen Neuzeit* (Cologne, 1992)

25th Report of the Science and Art Department of the Committee of Council on Education (1878), C.2098

29th Report of the Science and Art Department of the Committee of Council on Education (1882), C.3271

26th Congress, 1st session, House of Representatives, Report no. 586, 6 June 1840, 'Exchange of books'

Index

Aberdeen 286, 300
access 71–2, 313–14, 317–19
Acton, Lord (1834–1902) 62, 287–8
adversaria 316–17
Agnew, picture dealers 189, 203
agricultural depression 119
Albert, Prince Consort (1819–61) 195
Aldines 45, 47, 98, 128, 133, 219, 225, 252
Ames, Joseph (1689–1759) 21, 34, 284, 315
Angers 95
anniversaries 280–4 *See also* Gutenberg
annotation 316–17
Antwerp 285; *Conférence du Livre* 302–3
Arber, Edward (1836–1912), on collectors 121–2
    and Stationers' Company 285, 286, 312
Archaeology of reading project 316–17
Armstrong, Sir William (1810–1900) 146
Art Union of London 145
Arundel Society 145, 201
Ashbee, C.R. (1863–1942) 296
Ashburnham, Earl of (1840–1913) 97,
    99–100, 103, 123, 184, 341 n.45
Asher, Adolphus 84–5
Ashton, John 244
Atkyns, Richard (1615–77) 48
Aubry, Auguste 262
auctions 31
    behaviour at 122–3
Aumale, duc d' (1822–97) 3, 31, 201, 264
Aumale, Ernest 202
autograph collecting 233–44
    meaning of 156
Autun 109
Axon, William (1846–1913) 266–7, 274–5

Baber, Henry 88
Bachelin-Deflorenne, booksellers 158, 264
Bachelin, Antoine 31, 126, 201
Baedeker, Karl (1801–59) 18, 64
Bagford, John (d.1716) 244, 247, 248
ballads, broadside 237–8
Barat, Nicolas (d.1706) 32
Barnard, F.A. 82

Barnum, T.P. (1810–91) 282
Barrois, Joseph (1784–1855) 103
Barrois, Théophile 135
Barry, Sir Redmond (1813–80) 274–5
Barthès and Lowell 99
Baskerville, John (d.1775) 252
Bastard, comte de 187–8
Bath Abbey 265
Baughan, Rosa (1829–1911) 243–4
Bauzonnet, Antoine, bookbinder 98
Baxter, John, printer 21–2
Beckford, Wiliam (1760–1844) 121, 265
Bedford, Francis, bookbinder (1799–1883)
    165, 183, 184
beer cellar 115
Beijers, booksellers 206
Bellaert, Jacob 64
Bellot, facsimilist 241
Benson, Arthur (1862–1925) 95
Bent, William (1747–1813) 38
Béraldi, Henri (1849–1931) 139
Berjeau, Jean-Philibert (1809–91) 210, 263
Berlin 37, 74
Bernard, Auguste 30, 60, 263
Bernard, Edward (1638–97) 6, 109
Betbeder, facsimilist 241
Bethnal Green 294
Bewick, Thomas (1753–1828) 221–3
Biber, George Edward (1801–74) 84
Bibles in 1877 exhibition 296
    and Fry 296–7
Bibliographer, The 265–6
Bibliographical Society 260, 267, 277, 293, 299,
    300, 301, 305, 311
bibliography, definitions of 4, 267, 275, 276–7,
    353 n.35
bibliomania 31–5, 175
Bicknell, Elhanan (1788–1861) 146, 258–9
Bigmore, E.C. 303
Birmingham, Shakespeare Memorial Library 294
black-letter books 131, 252
Blackburne, Edward Lushington (1803–88)
    144

419

Blades, William (1824–90) 4–6, 46, 50, fig.1
    and bookbinding 177
    on Bradshaw 295–6
    and British Museum 84
    and Caxton 4, 59, 315–16
    and Caxton exhibition 195, 211–12, 298
    death 303
    Enemies of books 291, 293
    on formats 276
    on Humphreys 191
    and invention of printing 65, 66
    his library 303–4
    and printers' habits 278, 316
    and T.B. Reed 20–1
    and Wheatley 265
Bliss, Philip (1787–1857) 177
block-books 58, 194, 199, 200–1, 206, 263
Blomfield, Charles (1786–1857) 157
Blor, Albert 77
blurbs 133
Bodleian Library 108
    catalogues 82
    cataloguing rules 307
    and minor publications 306–7
    and music 215
    and photography 193
    reforms in 293
Bodoni, Giambattista 47
Bohn, Henry George, bookseller (1796–1884)
    34, 129, 133–4, 135, 137, 188, 254, 267
    and Nuremberg Chronicle 182–3
Bolland, Sir William (1772–1840) 73, 183
Bologna, Pietro 286
Bond, E.A. (1815–98) 191, 267
book fairs 13
Book Prices Current 261, 301
book trades, employees in 15
book-breaking 128
bookbinders in Paris 96, 98, 99, 100
bookbindings, 161–84
    blind-stamped 163, 171–4, 183–4, 199, 260
    conservation of 174–84
    description of 149, 183
    at exhibitions 162, 197, 198–9, 206, 213
    facsimiles of 161–2, 169
    fine 158
    fragments 174–8
    from Little Gidding 160, 164, 198
    materials 252
    reproductions 172–4
    structures 170
    treasure 171, 200
    values of 181–4
bookcases 144
Booksellers Association 305
booksellers, directories of 137–8, 256, 301
bookstalls 129–31, 156, 260
Boone, booksellers 135
Borchier, Henri-Léonard (1817–88) 100, 104–5
Bordeaux 96, 113
Bossange, Hector (1795–1884) 99
Boston, John 6
Boston, Lincs, parish library 111
Botfield, Beriah (1807–63) 11, 149–50, 224
    and cathedral libraries 11, 110–11
    and Caxton 50
    and Nuremberg Chronicle 183
Bouchot, Henri (1849–1906) 167
Boulard, Antoine-Marie-Henri (1724–1825)
    33
Bovet, Alfred 236
Bowtell, John (1753–1813) 177
Bradshaw, Henry (1831–86) 6, 46
    and ballads 248
    and Berjeau 263
    biography 20, 296
    and Blades 9, 54
    and bookbindings 165–6, 178–9
    and British Museum 78–9, 276
    and Campbell 60
    and codicology 278–9
    collected papers 296
    and collational formulae 231
    and Conway 55–6
    and Coster 179
    and De Meyer sale 51–5
    death and obituaries 295–6
    and Hessels 56, 60, 63
    and Holtrop 9, 52, 54–5
    and inter-library loans 114
    and Library Association 270, 275–6
    and music 215
    and palaeotypographical society 267, 316
    and photography 189
    and Power 256
    and printers' habits 278, 316
    and reference books 9
    and Sandars 278–9
    and Stevens 113
    on study of early books 277–8
    and Van der Linde 61
    and Wheatley 264, 265
    and woodcuts 55
Bragge, William (1823–84) 294
Brandes, Carl Heinrich (1811–59) 99
Breslau 268

Bright, Benjamin Heywood (1787–1843) 125, 248
Brighton 143
Brinkman, booksellers 39
Brinley, George (d.1875) 121
Briquet, C.M. (1839–1918) 42
Bristol 270
British Association 240
British Museum
  arrangements for readers 75
  Ashburnham papers 193
  catalogues 7–8, 75, 76–8, 81–3, 302, 307–8, 313
  cataloguing arrears 307
  cataloguing rules 307–8
  Commission (1847) 80–7
  and copyright deposit 36 n.29, 83–4
  and exchanges 114
  exhibitions 140, 194, 205
  Grenville library 36, 50–1
  guides 251
  Huth bequest 150–1
  incunables 84, 279, 316
  King's Library 82
  pamphlets 84, 249
  Parthenon marbles 251
  and photography 192–3
  reading rooms 140, fig.10
  sales 73
  total of books in 36
  uncatalogued books 379 n.55
Brockhaus, publishers 162
Brooke, Stopford (1832–1916) 231, 282
Brown, Horatio (1824–1926) 286–7
Brown, John Carter (d.1874) 121
Bruges 171
Brunet, Gustav (1805–96) 34, 73, 167
Brunet, Jacques-Charles (1780–1867) 13, 129, 133, 136, 158, 171, 219, 236
Brussels Bibliothèque Royale 28, 104
Brydges, Sir Egerton (1762–1837) 22
Bullen, George (1816–94) 78–9, 165, 192, 211–12, 275, 312
Bulletin du Bibliophile Belge 27–8, 262
Bulletin du Bibliophile founded 27
Burger, Konrad (1856–1912) 110, 268
Burlington Fine Arts Club 147, 170, 209
Burns, Robert (1759–96) 238, 280, 282, 283
Burton, John Hill (1809–81) 254–5, 259, 289, 291
Byron, Lord (1788–1824) 237, 281

Caen 95

Cambridge, college libraries 111–12
  public library 294
  Trinity College 55, 82, 93–4, 115, 281
  union catalogue 108–9
Cambridge University Library
  adversaria in 157
  ballads 248
  bindings in 165, 174, 177
  catalogue 8
  and loans 114–15
  and minor publications 306–7
  and Sandars 260, 278–9
  and Wheatley 264
Campbell, M.F.A.G. (1819–90) 46, 56, 110, 114
Cape Town 10
Cardiff public library 294
Carlyle, Thomas (1785–1881) 84, 233, 306
Carnegie, Andrew (1835–1919) 294
Carpentras 97–8
Carter, John (1905–75) 225
Caslon, type founders 42, 298
Castellani, Carlo 287
catalogues *See also* Lincoln
  access to 74
  card 8
  computer-based 8–9
  criticised 73–4, 85
  details in 85–6
  guard-book 8
  and photography 77
  printed 84–5, 112, 248–9
  private libraries 148–9, 150–1
cathedral libraries in England 110, 111
  and readers 111
Catnach Press 222, 245
Caumont, Arcisse de (1801–73) 251
Caxton exhibition (1877) 178–9, 195, 204–6, 211–12, 297–8
  printed catalogue 211–12
Caxton, William (d.1491)
  and Blades 4, 59, 315–16
  and Christianity 40
  memorials 25
  monument proposed 47, 50
  celebrated 48, 50–1
  his dates 48, 50–1, 201, 331 n.11
  memorial window 50
  portrait 149
  reputed house 25, fig.2
  his types 54, 211–12
Caxton, William
  books printed by, bindings on 176

Caxton, William (cont.)
    fragments 177–9
    stolen 97
Cercle de la Librairie 206–7
Chambers, William (1800–83) 25
Champion, publisher 293
changes recognised 1, 4–9, 12, 16, 17, 19, 27, 39, 121–2, 126–32, 139, 289, 311
    and Dibdin 33
    and Johnson 23
chap-books 244
Charavay, Étienne (1848–99) 235, 236, 240
Chartier, Roger 11
Chasles, Michel (1793–1880) 241
Chassant, Alphonse (1808–1907) 99
Chatelain, Emile (1851–1933) 276
Chatsworth 149, 151
Chatto and Windus, publishers 256, 261
Chatto, W.A. (1799–1864) 28
Chéron, Paul (1819–81) 35
Chesterfield, Lord (1694–1773) 32
Chetham Society 150
Chiswick Press 43
Christie-Miller, William (1789–1848) 247
Christie, Richard Copley (1830–1901) 260
Chromolithography 187–8
Churton, Edward, bookseller 254
Clark, J.W. (1833–1910) 29
Clarke, Frederick 160
Clarke, William 110
Claudin, Anatole (1833–1906) 46, 124, 126, 167, 201, 206, 293, fig.8
    as scholar 268, 305–6
Claye, Jules, printer (1806–86) 25, 43–4
Clegg, James 138, 301
Coalbrookdale Iron Company 50
Cochran, John, bookseller 232
Cochrane, J.G. (1781–1852) 82
codex, invention of 11
codicology 278–9
Coislin, marquis de 124
Colburn, Henry, bookseller (1784–1855) 220
Cole, Sir Henry (1808–82) 162, 196–7, 202–3, 205
Collier, John Payne (1789–1883) 150, 156–7, 242, 284–5
    and cataloguing 85–6
Cologne chronicle 57–8
Colón, Hernando (1488–1539) 105–6
colour-plate books 204
commercial crisis 30–1
composing machines 299
consortia, library 7

Constantin, L.A. *see* Hesse
Conway, William (1856–1937) 55–6, 265
Copenhagen 74
Copinger, W.A. (1847–1910) 260, 267, 311, 314, 318–19
    and incunables 110
Copyright Act (1842) 36
copyright, deposit copies 36, 83–4, 336, 29
    reform of 39
Corsellis, Frederick 48, 51
Corser, Thomas (1793–1876) 148–51
Coster, Laurens, 27, 29
    Bradshaw and 179
    celebrated 47
    statue 47, fig.3
    controversy over 57–67
    and Loftie 210
Cotton, Henry 149
Courtois, Edme Bonaventure (1754–1816) 234
Cousin, Jules (1830–99) 276
Coverdale Bible 210, 212, 318
Covid-19 xiii
Coxe, H.O. (1811–81) 274, 293, 296, 307
Craig, James Gibson (1799–1886) 167
Craven, Frederick 146
Crawford, Lord 247, 248, 270, 300
Croker, J.W. (1780–1857) 78, 83, 84, 247
Croly, George (1780–1860) 40–1
Crossley, James (1800–83) 150
Cruikshank, George (1792–1878) 223–4, fig.9
Cuijpers, Pierre (1827–1921) 251
Cundall, Joseph (1818–95) 162–3, 172
Cutter, Charles (1837–1903) 7, 274, 307

D'Angers, David (1788–1856) 47–8, fig.4
Dampier, Thomas (1748–1812) 149
Daniel, George 150
Danner, John 144
Dante commemorated 281
Daru, comte 39
Daudet, Alphonse (1840–97) 241
De Backer, Augustin (1809–73) 285
De Meyer, Jean (d.1869) 51–5
De Morgan, Augustus (1806–71) 30
    and British Museum catalogue 86
    career 87
    on catalogues 73, 75, 82, 85
    on Panizzi 75
    and retrospective bibliography 87–92
De Ricci, Seymour (1881–1942) 19
De Vinne, T.L. (1828–1914) 303
De Vries, Abraham 27

Debure, Guillaume-François (1731–82) 39, 46
Debure family 126
Dee, John (1527–1608) 317
Delepierre, Octave (1802–79) 263
Delisle, Léopold (1826–1910) 46, 232
    and bindings 178
    and catalogue of printed books 76
    and codicology 277
    and the comte de Bastard 188
    and 1878 exhibition 200
    incunables catalogue 109–10, 279
    and library collaboration 112–13
    and Libri 100, 103, 106
    and Morrison collection 239
Derby 213
Desbarreaux-Bernard, Tibulle (1798–1880) 42
Descuret, Jean-Baptiste Félix (1795–1871) 32
destruction of libraries 10, 294
Dewey, Melvil (1851–1931) 7, 274
Dibdin, Thomas Frognall (1776–1847) 27, 256, 304
    and bibliomania 32–3
    books 22, 34, 252–3
    and Cologne chronicle 58
    and Dawson Turner 238
    illness and death 32–3
    and Lincoln Cathedral 73
    and Nuremberg Chronicle 182, 183
    obituaries 33–4
    and Shakespeare 253–4
    and Spencer library 148, 158
    on type 43
Dickens, Charles (1812–70) 224, 225, 228–9, fig.9
digitisation 7, 317–19
Dijon 109, 279
Dilke, Charles Wentworth (1789–1864) 77, 78
Dillon, John 237
Dinaux, Arthur (1795–1864) 155
Dingelstedt, Franz von (1814–81) 59
disposals, library 12, 73, 306, 372 n.63
Dobree, Peter Paul (1782–1825) 157
Dobson, Austin (1840–1921) 224, 225, 290
documentation 284–8
Double, Léonard 264
Dresden 213, 273
Du Rieu, Willem (1829–96) 115–16
Duff, Edward Gordon (1861–1924) 20, 169–71, 174, 278, 296, 300
Dugast-Matifeux, Charles (1812–97) 201
Dulau, booksellers 136–7
Duncan, Johan (c.1690–1753) 246
Dundee 143
Dunn, George (1864–1912) 173–4, 316

Dupont, Paul (1796–1879) 30
Duprat, François Antoine (b.1795) 125–6
Durham university library 143
Duru, bookbinder 98
Duverger, Eugène (1801–63) 29
Dyce, Alexander (1798–1869) 148–9
Dziatzko, Karl (1842–1903) 7, 66, 110

Early English Text Society 45, 151, 191, 264
Eastlake, Sir Charles (1793–1865) 144, 145–6
Ebert, F.A (1791–1834) 268, 277
École des Chartes 284
Edinburgh 143, 247, 294
Edinburgh Bibliographical Society 293, 301
Edmond, J.P. (1850–1906) 286, 300
Edwards, Edward (1812–86)
    on annotation 156
    on auctions 122
    and bookbindings 162, 172, 178
    and British Museum 76
    career 273
    death 295
    and librarianship 273
    and size of libraries 37
    and Sunday opening 140
Edwards, Francis, bookseller 135
Edwards, John Passmore (1823–1911) 303–4
Egerton, Lord (1806–83) 150
electronic publishing xiii–xiv, 4
Eliot, George (1819–80) 233–4
Ellesmere, Earl of (1800–57) 81, 220
Elliot Stock, publishers 264, 265, 291, 292, 293, 298
Ellis, F.S. (1830–1901) 124, 135, 151, 184, 209
Ellis, Sir Henry (1777–1869) 81
Enschedé, printers and typefounders 136, 206, 298
ephemera 244–50
Essling, prince d' (1799–1863) 124
Estienne, Henri (d.1598) 29
Euing, William (1788–1874) 183, 248
Ewart, William (1798–1869) 268
exchanges of books 113–16
exhibitions 194–203; visitor numbers 202
exhibitions, international See also Great Exhibition (1851)
    London (1862) 162, 196, 197–9
    (1871) 202
    (1874) 199, 202
    (1885) 213
    Paris (1867) 196, 197, 199
    (1874) 199–203, 206

extra-illustration 128
Eyton, J.W.K. (d.1872) 123

Fabian, Bernhard 10
facsimiles 45, 104, 169, 173, 192, 240, 263, 283, 315–16
Fallersleben, Hoffmann von (1798–1874) 268
Fenton, James 298
Fenton, Roger (1819–69) 189, 193
Fine Art Society 222
Fineschi, Vincenzio (1727–1823) 286, 287
Firmin-Didot, Ambroise (1790–1876) 28–9, 164, 201, 206, 264
first editions, modern 224–32
Fitzgerald, Percy (1824–1935) 229, 289–90
Fleischmann, J.M. (1707–68) 298
Folger, Henry Clay (1857–1930) 316
Folkard, H.T. (1850–1916) 271–2
Fonderie Deberny 44
Fonderie Générale 44
Fontaine, Pierre-Jules (1801–82) 234
forgeries 314
    of autographs 239–44
    of bindings 164, 167
    and Libri 100
Forman, Harry Buxton (1842–1917) 230–1
formats, descriptions of 90, 276
Forshall, Josiah (1795–1863) 83
Forster, John (d.1876) 143, 146, 148, 149, 227, 249
Fortescue, G.K. (1847–1912) 78, 83
Fossi, Ferdinando (1720–1800) 286
Fourdrinier, Henri (d.1854) 41
Fournier, Édouard (1819–80) 163–4, 178, 179
Fournier, Henri 24–5
Fournier, Pierre-Simon (1712–68) 29, 299
France, Anatole (1844–1924) 43
France, poor state of libraries in 94–104
Fry, Francis (1803–86) 296–7
Fulia, Rinaldo 287
Furnivall, F.J. (1825–1910) 45

Gage, Sir Thomas (1810–66) 198
Ganay, marquis de (1803–81) 200
Garnett, Richard (1835–1906) 77, 78, 192–3, 274, 293–4
Garrick, David (1717–79) 249
Gesamtkatalog der Wiegendrucke 110
Gesner, Conrad (1516–65) 13
Ghent university library 246
Gillott, Joseph (1799–1872) 146
Gladstone, William (1809–98) 130–1, 294
Glasgow 270, 284, 294

Glover, J.H. 82
Goblet, René (1828–1905) 109
Goebel, Theodor (1829–1916) 303
Goldschmidt, E.Ph. (1887–1954) 172, 174, 312
Gosford, Earl of 121
Göttingen 74
Grand-Carteret, John (1850–1927) 245–6
Gray, Thomas (1716–71) 156, 238
Great Exhibition (1851) 139, 189, 197
Greenaway, Kate (1846–1901) 256
Greenwood, Thomas (1851–1908) 140, 142, 269
Grégoire, abbé (1750–1831) 125
Grenville, Thomas (1755–1846) 36, 143, 148–9, 150–1
Gresswell, William Parr (1765–1854) 27
Griffiths, Acton Frederick (1759–1815) 150
Grolier Club 10
Groningen university library 246
Grosvenor Gallery 204
Gruel, Léon (1841–1923) 169
guidance for collectors
    manuals 251–62
    periodicals 262–6
Guild and School of Handicraft 296
Guizot, François (1787–1874) 31, 97, 99, 105, 274, 284
Günther, Johann 234–5
Gutenberg Bible 66, 64, 136, 150, 206, 219
    binding of 361 n.70
    exhibited 212, 213
    reproduced 192
Gutenberg, Johann (d.1468)
    commemorations 27, 47, 66, 125–6, 195
    and early printing 28–9, 56–8, 63–4
    exhibition (1840) 195
    exhibition (1878) 206
    press 361 n.69
    statue 47–8, fig.4
Gyles, Arthur 138

Haarlem *See also* Coster, Laurens and Hessels, J.H
    guidebook 64
    library 58
    Van der Linde 61–2
Hachette, publishers 15
Haenel, Gustav (1792–1878) 6, 109, 111
Hagué, Louis (1823–91) 164, 167, 168
Hain, Ludwig (1781–1836) 27, 55, 88, 110, 219, 314
Hale, Edward Everett (1822–1909) 75

Halliwell-Phillipps, J. (1820–89) 93–4, 143, 247–8, 317
Hamburger, G.C. (1726–73) 220
Hamilton Palace 121, 265, 370 n.30
Hamilton, Sir William (1730–1803) 251
Hannett, John (1803–93) 168, 172, 175–6
Hansard, Thomas (1776–1833) 20, 24, 42
Harleian miscellany 246
Harris, John, facsimilist (1791–1873) 316
Harrisse, Henry (1829–1910) 106
Hartshorne, C.H. (1802–65) 111
Harvard University Law School 174
Harvey, Gabriel (d.1631) 316–17
Harwood, Edward (1729–94) 256
Hazlitt, W.C. (1834–1913) 160, 301
Heber, Richard (1773–1833) 33, 34, 119, 124, 135, 247
Hébrard, Jules-Joseph, bookseller 123
Heinsius, Wilhelm (1768–1817) 38
Henry Bradshaw Society 296
Hereford 172
Herring, Richard (1829–86) 40–2
Hesse, Léopold ('L.A. Constantin') (1779–1844) 34, 274
Hessels, J.H. (1836–1926)
    and Bradshaw 56, 60, 63, 295
    early career 60, 304
    in *Encyclopaedia Britannica* 66–7
    and photography 191–2
    and Van der Linde 60–6, 210
Hindley, Charles (d.1893) 163, 222, 245–6, 248
Hinrichs, Johann Conrad (1763–1813) 38
Hoe, Richard (1812–86) 303
Holiday, Henry (1839–1927) 50
Holmes, John (1758–1841) 74, 85
Holmes, Richard 209
Holtrop, J.W. (1806–70) 4, 6, 46–7, 263, 276; and photography 189
Horne, T.H. (d.1862) 111
Hugo, Thomas (1820–76) 222
Humphreys, Henry Noel (1810–79) 43, 59, 190–1
Huth, Alfred (1850–1910) 150–1
Huth, Henry (1815–78) 150–1

Illustrated London News 2, 221, 223
illustration, attractions of 128, 204, 221–4
incunables, catalogues of 78–9, 109–10, 159, 279, 302
Index Society 264
Inglis, J.B. (1780–1870) 263, 292
Inspecteur Général des Bibliothèques 11

inter-library loans 114–16
Ionides, Constantine (1833–1900) 146
Ireland, Alexander (1810–94) 290–1
Ireland, W.H. (1775–1835) 155, 242
Ironmongers' Hall 195–6

Jackson, John (1801–48) 28
Jacquemart, Jules (1837–80) 161
James, Sir Henry (1803–77) 190, 192
Jannet, Pierre 44
Jenkinson, Francis (1853–1923) 65, 215, 296
Jenson, Nicolas (d.1480) 43
Jesuit order 39
Jewett, Charles Coffin (1816–68) 108, 274
Joanne, Adolphe (1813–81) 18
Johnson, Charles Plumptre 229–30
Johnson, John, printer (1777–1848) 20, 22–4
Jones, John (d.1882) 146
Jones, John Winter (1805–81) 209, 210
Junius, Hadrianus (1511–75) 58
Jupp, Edward Basil (1812–77) 222

Kayser, Christian Gottlob (1782–1857) 38
Kegan Paul, publishers 293
Kelmscott Press 43, 163
Kerney, Michael 159, 167
Kerr, Robert (1823–1904) 144
King's College London xiii
Klemm, Heinrich (1819–86) 213
Kloss, Georg (1787–1854) 155
Knight, Charles (1791–1873)
    and Caxton 25, 50, 125
    and cheap books 15, 25, 221
    and Coster 59
    on history of printing 30
    and periodicals 38
Knuttel, W.P.C. (1854–1921) 246, 249

Lacroix, Paul (1806–84) 96, 128, 137, 164, 188, 240, 263
Lalanne, Ludovic (1815–98) 100, 104–5
Lamartine, Alphonse de (1790–1869) 59
Lambeth Palace library 48, 78, 82–3
Lang, Andrew (1844–1912) 224, 225, 289–90
Laon 95, 97
Laurent, Eugénie-Marie, bookseller 126, 128
Lavater, Johann Kaspar (1741–1801) 233
Laverdet, Auguste-Nicolas (1805–65) 236
Lawler, John 158
Le Roux de Lincy, Antoine (1806–69) 164
leisure 139, 142
Lemerre, Alphonse (1838–1912) 43–4, 293
Lempertz, Heinrich, auctioneer 161

Lenormand, Sébastien (1757–1837) 176
Lenox, James (1800–80) 121, 297
Lescure, M.F.A. de 240–1
Leslie, John (1766–1832) 88
Leuven university library 10, 104
Leypoldt, Frederick (1835–84) 274
librarianship 94–5, 268
Library Association 111, 292
    bibliography and 267
    Blades at 66
    Bradshaw and 20, 270, 275–6, 277
    Edmond and 300
    founded 301, 305
    Garnett at 192–3, 293–4
    Stevens at 77
    at Wigan 272
Libri, Count Guglielmo (1802–69) 88, 96–103
    auctions 98–9, 101, 103, 123–4, 125, fig.6
    and bookbindings 161–2
    and Panizzi 97
    and catalogues of manuscripts 97
    and puffing books 101, 104
Lilly, Joseph, bookseller (1804–70) 135
Lincoln Cathedral 73, 110–11
Lincoln's Inn 73
Lingard, John (1771–1851) 233
Little Gidding bindings 160, 164, 198
Liverpool 146–7, 203–4, 213, 233, 269–70, 295
Lodge, John (1793–1850) 177
Loftie, W.J. (1839–1911) 256, 258–60, 290
    biography 208–9
    and exhibition of books 210
London Institution 248, 298
London Library 82
London Topographical Society 264
Longman, publishers and booksellers 15, 292
Longpérier, Adrien de (18176–82) 200
Lottin, A.M. (1726–93) 299
Louis-Philippe, King (1773–1850) 3, 17, 31
Lovenjoul, Charles de (1836–1907) 239
Lowndes, William Thomas (d.1843) 22, 129, 136, 219, 221, 254, 267, 301
Luard, H.R. (1825–91) 157
Lubbock, Sir John (1834–1913) 291
Lucas, Vrain-Denis (1818–82) 241–2
Luchtmans, booksellers 126
Luckombe, Philip 43
Lyon 109, 279

Mabillon, Jean (1632–1707) 200, 242
MacAlister, J.Y.W. (1826–1925) 267, 291–2
Macaulay, Lord (1800–59) 130–1, 237
Mackey, George, dealer 243

Macleod, Dianne Sachko 146
Macmillan, publishers 15, 224, 258, 290, 292
Madden, J.P.A. (1808–89) 159
Madden, Sir Frederic (1801–73) 81, 87, 93–4, 188
    and ballads 248
    and Libri 97
made-up copies 162, 297
magazines, illustrated 221
Maggs, Uriah, bookseller (d.1913) 135
Mahon, Lord (1805–75) 147
Mainz, early printing in 57–8, 63–4, 66
Maire, Albert (1856–1931) 276
Maitland, J.A. Fuller (1856–1936) 214
Maitland, S.R. (1792–1866) 78, 83, 85
Maltby, Edward (1770–1859) 143
Manchester 5, 204
    Art Treasures Exhibition 145, 195
    Chetham's Library 143, 247
    public library 249, 294–5
Mangeart, Jacques (1805–74) 105
manuals for collectors 251–62
manufacture, changes in 16, 19, 39–45
Marchand, Prosper (1678–1756) 21
Marius-Michel, bookbinders 166, 167
Marseille 113
Marsh, John Fitchet (d.1880) 143
Marthens, John (1830–1902) 303
Martin, Gabriel 39
Martin, Louis-Aimé (1782–1847) 124, 155
Maskell, Alfred 213
Matthew, James E. 215
Matthews, Brander (1852–1939) 290
Matton, Auguste (1819–1905) 42
Maxwell, James Clerk (1831–79) 294
Mayer, Joseph (d.1886) 295
Mayhew, Henry (1812–287) 131
Mayor, J.E.B. (1825–1910) 113
McCulloch, J.R. (1789–1864) 38
McKerrow, R.B. (1872–1940) 315, 318
McKie, James (1816–91) 283
McLean, Ruari (1917–2006) 15–16
mechanics' institutes 142
Meerman, Gerard (1722–71) 21
Meisenbach, Georg (1841–1912) 189
Melanchthon, Philip (1497–1560) 155
memorials 280–4
Mentelin, Johann (d.1478) 29, 47, 125
Metz 113
Meulman, Isaac (1807–68) 246
Meusel, Johann Georg (1743–1820) 220
Meyer, Paul (1840–1917) 44–5
Michelet, Jules (1798–1874) 96

microforms 317–18
middle classes 143–4, 146
Middleton-Wake, Charles (1828–1915) 65–6
Middleton, Conyers (1683–1850) 50
Midoux, Étienne 42
Milan 74
Miller & Richard, type founders 42
Milnes, Richard Monckton (1809–85) 83, 232, 240, 241
Milton, John (1608–74) 282
minor publications, importance of 91
Mohr, Louis 303
Molbech, Christian (1783–1857) 273
Molière, Jean-Baptiste (1622–73) 241, 281
Molini, bookseller 98
Mommsen, Theodore (1817–1903) 115–16
Monk, James (1784–1856) 157
Montfaucon, Bernard de (1655–1741) 6
Moore, Sir John (1761–1809) 284
Moreau, Georges 245–6
Morel, Charles 44–5
Moretto, Antonio 287
Morison, Stanley (1889–1967) 3, 4, 18
Morris, Richard (1833–94) 45
Morris, William (1834–96) 43, 163, 184, 258
Morrison, Alfred (1821–97) 239
Moxon, Joseph (1627–91) 299
Mudie's Library 269
Muller, Frederik (1817–81)
    bookseller 46, 60, 135, 246, 303
Munby, Arthur (1828–1910) 260
Munich 37, 38, 74, 85, 113
Munsell, Joel (1808–80) 302
Murray, James (1837–1915) 17
Murray, John, publisher (1808–92) 18, 237
Museums Association 305
museums, visiting 139–40, 142
Musgrave, Sir William 249
music, exhibition of 171, 213–16

Nancy 109
Nantes 113
Napoleon (1769–1821) 74, 284
Napoleon III (1808–73) 3
National Gallery 142, 145, 146
National Trust 10
Natural History Museum 139
Netherclift, Frederick (1817–92) 156, 240
New York State Library 303
New York, Astor Library 255
    Columbia College 113
Newcastle-upon-Tyne 147
Newsham, Richard (d.1883) 146

newspapers 84
Nichols, John 284
Nicholson, E.W.B. (1849–1912) 293, 307
Nicholson, James B. (1820–1901) 175–6, 181
Nicolai, Friedrich (1733–1811) 220
Nijhoff, booksellers 206
Nimmo, J.C., publisher (d.1899) 287
Nisard, Charles (1808–90) 30, 163
Nodier, Charles (1780–1844) 27, 175
Norwich 10, 147

Offor, George (1787–1864) 195, 196, 296
offprints 250
old masters 203–4
Olivier, F.J. 262
Osborne, Thomas (d.1767) 182, 246
Osmont, Jean-Baptiste (1703–73) 39
Osterley Park 121, 248
Otago university library 132
Ottley, William Young (1771–1836) 57, 59
Oxford, college libraries 112 See also Bodleian Library
    early printing in 51

Palaeographical Society 191, 267
Palaeotypographical society, rumoured 267, 316
pamphlets 83, 84, 246–50
Panizzi, Antonio (1797–1879) 36, 81
    and copyright deposit 83–4
    and catalogues 7, 75, 86, 307–8
    and incunables 78, 82
    publications 304–5
    and Royal Society 88
paper 40–1, 43, 252
    description of 90–1
    waste 131–2
parchment, books on 83
Paris, Archives Nationales 105
Paris, auctions 122–3
    bookbinders 164, 174
    newspapers in 2
Paris, Bibliothèque de l'Arsenal 99, 112
Paris, Bibliothèque de la Ville 10, 113
Paris, Bibliothèque Mazarine 99, 112
Paris, Bibliothèque Royale/Impériale/Nationale 37, 83, 99, 103, 104–5, 106
    cataloguing arrears 307
    collaboration 112–13
    in disorder 74
    exhibitions 206
    new catalogue of printed books 76
    readers in 75

Paris, Eiffel Tower 17
Paris, Gaston (1839–1903) 45
Paris, Paulin (1800–81) 76
parish libraries 11, 111
Parr, Samuel (1747–1825) 148
Parthenon marbles 251
patrimoine 108
Payne and Foss, booksellers 98, 103, 104, 126, 135, 183, 224, 253
Pearson, Edwin, bookseller 222
Pearson, Emily 59
Pearson, Karl (1857–1936) 279
Peignot, Gabriel (1767–1849) 233–4, 235
Pelechet, Marie (1840–1900) 109, 159, 279, 302
Penny Magazine 25, 50, 221, 223
Penzance 143
Pepys, Samuel (1633–1703) 244, 247, 264
Perkins, Henry (d.1855) 150, 181, 183
Perrin, Louis (1795–1865) 43–4
Petzholdt, Julius (1812–91) 273
Phillipps, Sir Thomas (1792–1872) 34
Philobiblon Society 31, 135, 219, 237
photography 169, 173–4, 188–93, 236, 243, 316, 317–18
    and catalogues 77–8
Pichon, baron (1812–96) 106
Pickering, publishers 99, 209, 226–7
Pickering, William (1796–1854) 135
Picton, Sir James (1805–89) 295
Pilinski, Adam (1810–87) 164, 241
Pixérécourt, Guilbert de (1773–1844) 247
Plantin, Christophe (d.1589) 284–6, 288, 302
playing cards 177
Pollard, Graham (1903–76) 225
Poole, W.F. (1821–94) 274
Porson, Richard (1759–1808) 157
postal charges 129
Pouchin, H. 306
Power, John 137, 145, 255–6, fig.11
Preston 146
price guides 19, 261, 301
Prideaux, Sarah T. (1853–1933) 170
printers', manuals 22–5
    waste 166
printing, bibliography of 303
    heroes of 40, 47, 125
Proctor, Robert (1868–1903) 174, 177, 300, 302, 316
profit and book collecting 14, 244, 258–9
Prothero, G.W. (1848–1922) 296
Prout, Samuel (1753–1852) fig.2
provenance 155–60
Public Libraries Act (1850) 142, 249

public libraries, in England 268–73, 269, 294
    gifts and bequests 143
    in USA 274
publishers' catalogues 13
Pugin, A.W.N. (1812–52) 251
Pushkin, Alexander (1799–1837) 281

Quaritch, Bernard (1819–99) 46, 232
    career 135–6
    catalogues 121, 134, 136, 179, 183–4, 305
    and bookbindings 165–9, 183–4
    Dictionary of book collectors 159–60
    and exhibitions 209, 210
    and Gutenberg Bible 136
    and Libri 101
    and new collectors 305
    as publisher 190, 214, 215, 222, 303
Quérard, Joseph-Marie (1797–1865) 129, 219

Racine, Jean (1639–99) 235
Rathbone, Philip (d.1895) 146–7, 203
Ravaisson, Félix (1813–1900) 95, 97, 112
Raveneau, Jacques (b.1635) 242
readers 12–13, 15, 19, 73, 313
    and time saving 8, 88
Reading University Library 247
Reed, Sir Charles (1819–81) 211
Reed, T.B. (1852–93) 20–1, 46, 297–300
    death 304
    his library 304
Reichensperger, August (1808–95) 251
Reiffenberg, Frédéric de (1795–1850) 28, 104
relics 168
Renouard, A.-A. (1765–1853) 27, 46, 133, 219
reproductions, 187–8 *See also* Facsimiles, Photography
retrospective bibliography 45, 87–92, 129
Reuss, Jeremias David (1750–1837) 220
Reynolds, Herbert E. 111
rings, auction 160, 370 n.30
Ripoli Press 286, 287
Ris, Louis Clément de (1820–82) 196
Rivington, publishers 99
Roberts, William 131, 145
Robinson, J.C. 198
Rockstro, W.S. (1823–95) 214
Rodd, Thomas, bookseller (1796–1849) 93–4, 97, 99, 126, 183, 292
Roediger, Francesco 286
Rooses, Max (1839–1914) 285, 302
Roscoe, William (1753–1831) 175, 203, 269–70

Rosenthal, Ludwig, bookseller (1840–1928) 215
Rouen 200
Rousseau, Jean-Jacques (1712–78) 281
Routh, Martin (1755–1854) 143
Routledge, publishers 292
Rouveyre, Édouard (1849–1930) 44, 134, 293
Rowlandson, Thomas (1756–1827) 223–4
Roxburghe Club 17, 22–4, 50, 73, 135, 220–1, 254
Royal Archaeological Institute 208–11
Royal Institution 248–9
Royal Society 73, 88, 160, 265, 266, 338 n.27
Royer, Louis (1793–1868) 47
Ruble, baron Alphonse de (1834–98) 200
Ruelens, Charles (1820–90) 115, 285
Ruskin, John (1819–1900) 35, 203, 261
Russell, John Fuller (1813–84) 121, 195, 209, 210–11, 213

Sadleir, Michael (1888–1957) 224
sales of library books 73, 372 n.63
Sampson Low, publishers 38, 292
Sandars, Samuel (1837–94) 65, 260
    and Bradshaw 278–9
    lectures 65
Schedel, Hartmann (1440–1514) 181–4
Schiller, Friedrich (1759–1805) 280
Schulz, Otto-August (1803–60) 234–5
Schwenke, Paul (1853–1921) 66
science, bibliography and 62, 318
Scott, Henry T. 243–4
Scott, Sir Gilbert (1811–78) 251
Scott, Sir Walter (1771–1832)
    manuscripts 237–8, 365 n.74
    statues 281, 283–4
Seillière, baron (1813–73) 201
Seiz, Johann, editor 62
Seizinger, J.G., librarian 273
Selden, John (1584–1654) 247
Sélestat 47
Seré, Ferdinand (1818–55) 164
Settled Lands Acts 119
Seville, Biblioteca Colombina 105–7
Shakespeare, William (1564–1616)
    commemorated 280–2
    first folio 45, 181–2, 208, 219, 282
    forgeries 155, 367, 242
    Hamlet 253–4
    prices of 181–2
    second folio 156–7
Shaw, Henry (1800–73) 137
Sheepshanks, John (d.1863) 146

Shelley Society 230–1
Shelley, Percy Bysshe (1792–1822) 230–1
Shepherd, Richard Herne (1842–95) 226–8
Shepherd, Thomas Hosmer (1793–1864) fig.10
Shoberl, Frederic (1775–1853) 220
Shoults, William (1839–87) 132
Silvestre, Joseph-Balthazar (1791–1861) 188
Silvestre, L.-C., bookseller 30
Simier, René (1772–1843), bookbinder 354 n.59
Simonides, Constantine (1820–90) 242
Simpkin Marshall, publishers 292
Singer, S.W. (1783–1858) 48, 50
Sinker, Robert (1838–1913) 55
size of books 36–7
size-notation 276
Skeat, W.W. (1835–1912) 45
Slade, Felix (1788–1868) 194, 196, 198
Slater, J.H. 145, 224, 225–6, 259, 260–2, 290
Smith, Alexander Howland (1859–1913) 243
Smith, John Russell, bookseller (1810–94) 248, 263
Smith, John, printer 23
Smith, Lucy Toulmin (1838–1911) 265
Smith, W.H., libraries 269
Smithsonian Institution 114, 267
Société des Bibliophiles François 17
societies, antiquarian 25, 27, 147
societies, bibliographical 266–8
societies, bibliophile 305 *See also* Roxburghe Club, Philobiblon Society, Société des Bibliophiles François
societies, publishing 255
Society of Antiquaries 147, 207–8, 209, 266, 272
Society of Arts 165
Sommerard, Alexandre du (1779–1842) 188
Sotheby, Samuel Leigh (1805–61) 30, 42, 59, 155–6, 157
South Kensington Museum 142, 143, 146, 148, 249
    bookbindings in 171–3
    and buying 196
    exhibitions 162–71, 198
    and photography 193
Spalding Gentlemen's Society 147
Spencer, Earl 22–3, 104, 148, 182
St Albans 177
St Bride Printing Library 303–4
St Gallen 215
St Petersburg 37, 328 n.11
Standidge, C.W. (1834–77) 209, 211

Stationers' Company 284–6, 288
Stationers' Hall 36
Stephen, Sir Leslie (1832–1904) 17
Stephens, George (1813–95) 189–90
stereotyping 23, 25, 221–2, 223, 363 n.16
Stevens, Henry (1819–86) 121
    and British Museum 36
    and Cambridge 113
    and Caxton exhibition 212, 296–7
    death 295
    and library catalogues 77–8
Stewart, C.J., bookseller 197, 266
Stirling university library xiii
Stower, Caleb (d.1816) 22
Strasbourg, and early printing 47–8, 50
    Bibliothèque Municipale 10
Strickland, Hugh Edwin (1811–53) 108
Sunday opening 140, 142
Sunderland library 119–21, 158–9, 265, 370 n.30, fig.7
Sussex, Duke of 148, 183
Swaffham 111
Swansea 294
Sweet, Henry (1845–1912) 191
Swift, Jonathan (1667–1745) 131
Symonds, J.A. (1840–93) 287
Syston Park 121

Talbot, Henry Fox (1800–77) 188
Taschereau, Jules (1801–74) 76
Taylor, Archer (1890–1973) 149
Taylor, Thomas (d.1892) 271
Techener, Jacques-Joseph (1802–73) 46, 96, 98–9, 104, 123, 124, 125, 126, 161, 206, 232
Techener, Léon (1832–88) 202
Tenison Library 73
Tennyson, Lord (1809–92) 226–8
Texier, Edmond (1815–87) 34–5
Thane, John, printseller (1748–1818) 240
The Hague, Royal Library 246, 249 See also Campbell, Holtrop
    and inter-library loans 114
thefts 74, 93–107
Thibaudeau, Alphonse (d.1892) 239
Thierry-Poux, Olgar (1838–94) 56, 268
Thomas-Stanford, Charles (1858–1932) 174
Thomas, Ernest, librarian and lawyer 262, 265, 275, 277, 292
Thomason, George, bookseller 78, 83, 84
Thompson, Charles Thurston (1816–68) 193
Thompson, Edward Maunde (1840–1929) 65, 191, 267

Thomson, Richard, librarian 23
Thorpe, Thomas, bookseller (1791–1851) 134, 135, 234
Thorvaldsen, Bertel (1770–1844) 47, 281
Timbuktu 10
Timperley, C.H. (1794–1869) 20, 28, 43
Tite, Sir William (1798–1873) 181, 195, 207–10, 211, 237
Tomlinson, Charles (108–97) 59
Toulouse 109, 279
tourism 18
Tours 95, 97
Towneley family 121
Townshend, Chauncy Hare (1798–1868) 143
transport 17
Trautz, bookbinder 98
Trémont, baron de (1779–1852) 236
Tross, Edwin (1822–75) 31, 124
Troyes 97, 200
Trübner, Nicolas (1817–84) 263, 266, 274, 291, 292
    imports bookcases 144
Tuer, Andrew (1838–1900) 248, 298
Tupper, G.I.F. (d.1911) 54, 315–16
Turner, Dawson (1775–1858) 147, 232, 238–9, 240, 245
Turner, Fr John 247
Type Facsimile Society 316
type, imitations and copies 42–3, 44, 231, 283, 364 n.48
    modern faces 252
    specimens 298
typecasting machines 299

uncatalogued books 249, 307, 379 n.55
union catalogues
    early 6–8
    incunables 109–10
    manuscripts 8, 97, 105, 109, 111
    printed books 77, 79, 108
Upcott Gill, publishers 243, 261
Upcott, William (1779–1845) 48, 232–3, 252–3
Uppsala 84
Utrecht 64–5
Uzanne, Octave (1851–1931) 35, 293

Valenciennes 95, 105
Van der Linde, A. (1833–97) 60–4, 210
Van Praet, Joseph (1754–1837) 83
Vander Haeghen, Ferdinand (1830–1913) 51–2, 245, 315
Vatican Library 205

Vattemare, Alexandre (1796–1864) 113–14
vellum *see* parchment
Venice 286–7, 288
Vernon, Robert (d.1849) 146
Versailles 17, 109, 159, 279
Viardot, Jean 1
Victoria and Albert Museum *see* South Kensington Museum
Victoria, Queen (1819–1901) 2–3, 17
    and exhibitions 195, 196, 197, 207, 209, 211, 212, 215
Vidal, Léon (1833–1906) 189
Villemain, Abel-François (1790–1870) 97
Villenave, Mathieu de (1762–1846) 235
Viollet-Le-Duc, Eugène (1814–79) 251
Vitet, Ludovic (1802–73) 95

Walford, Cornelius (1827–85) 77
Walker Art Gallery 203–4
Warren, F.E. 295
Warren, J. Leicester (1835–95) 226
Warrington 143
waste paper 131–2
Waterhouse, Alfred (1830–1905) 271
Watkins, John 220
Watt, Robert (1774–1819) 220–1
Wattenbach, Wilhelm (1819–97) 192
Weale, W.H.J. (1832–1917) 265, 304
    and bindings 163, 165, 169–73, 179–80
    career 171–2
    and music 215–16
Werdet, Edmond (1793–1870) 40, 59
Westmacott, Sir Richard (1775–1856) 81
Westminster Abbey 50
Westwood, J.O. (1805–93) 136–7

Weyer, Sylvain van de (1802–74) 34
wheat, price of 119
Wheatley, Henry B. (1838–1917) 163, 165, 169, 264–6
    on changes 289
    and Elliot Stock 291
Whitaker, Joseph, publisher 13
Whitehead, Thomas Miller 222
Whittaker, John, bookbinder 176
Wigan public library 270–2, 294–5, fig.12
    disposals 372 n.63
Wighton, Andrew (1804–66) 146
Willis and Sotheran, booksellers 283
Willis, George 183
Wilson, Lea 296
Wimborne 343 n.17
Winnard, J.T. (d.1873) 270–1
Winsor, Justin (1831–97) 274
Wisbech 143
Wise, Thomas James (1839–1937) 231, 238, 261–2
Wodhull, Michael (1740–1816) 121
wood-engraving 221–3
Woodward, Bernard 209
Woolley photographs 316
Wordsworth, William (1770–1850) 83, 282
Wyman, C.W.H. (1832–1909) 303

Yale University 113
yellow-backs 228
Yemeniz, Nicolas (1783–1871) 98, 125, 157–8, 236, 346 n.22

Zaehnsdorf, Joseph (1853–1930) 165, 167
Zotenberg, Hermann (1836–94) 44–5